A PRETTY COPY

changed his headgear, but the change was immed occasion of a second print showing him in his nev a small man, and when he preached it is recorded t two hassocks. His political views were strong, and up in his phrase 'that he would be happy to see Pitt dug up again and hanged.'

Of his enthusiasm for books there is ample contemporary evidence. Dibdin, who portrays him as Lepidus in the *Bibliomania,* records how on a sick bed he was miraculously restored to health by the mere sight of one volume of the Pinelli copy of the Complutensian Polyglot on vellum. Though happily married, he was a tireless advocate of the bachelor state for collectors – 'Never think of marriage' he would say to a young man, 'and if the thought should occur, take down a book and begin to read until it vanishes'. On theological and classical books he was widely learned and his own library, sold immediately after his death, was rich in these two fields. If it did not contain a great deal of interest to the modern collector, one may certainly covet the 300 bound volumes of book sale catalogues which the collection included.

Sale Catalogues of Libraries of Eminent Persons

Sale Catalogues of Libraries of Eminent Persons

General Editor: A. N. L. Munby, *Litt.D.*

Volume 10

Antiquaries

Edited, with introductions, by

STUART PIGGOTT, *F.B.A.*

Abercromby Professor of Prehistoric Archaeology

University of Edinburgh

Mansell

with Sotheby Parke Bernet Publications

ISBN: 0 7201 0378 9

Mansell Information/Publishing Ltd, 3 Bloomsbury Place, London WC1A 2QA

Sotheby Publications Ltd, 34 & 35 New Bond Street, London W1A 2AA

Printed in Great Britain
by the Scolar Press Ltd

Contents

Ralph Thoresby

A local historian, working at the end of the seventeenth and the beginning of the eighteenth centuries in the intervals of running a family business in Leeds as a cloth and wool merchant, Ralph Thoresby is an early example of the merchant-antiquary, but unfortunately does not come down to us over the centuries as an endearing character. Born in 1658 of a Parliamentarian and Presbyterian father, he was a dutiful son, and when at the age of nineteen his father recommended him to keep a journal because 'I have thought this a good method for one to keep a good tolerable decorum in actions', he at once began a diary which he continued throughout his life. A selection of what are presumably the less depressing entries was published as *The Diary of Ralph Thoresby* by Joseph Hunter in 1830, and we see how he followed his father's further instruction to keep a record of the sermons he had attended, for he collected nonconformist preachers as assiduously as he did coins and books, in the intervals of noting the business at the mill, his devotional reading, his topographical and antiquarian tours, and his periodic mortifying self-examinations, usually ending with comments such as 'was mightily ashamed of myself'. His travels on business took him as far afield as Rotterdam, and the firm prospered: one cannot escape the suspicion that his public act of conformity with the Church of England in 1699 was primarily a move thought to be good for trade. His one major antiquarian work was his local history, *Ducatus Leodiensis*, begun in 1691 and published in 1715; Gibson enlisted him as one of the revisers of Camden, he corresponded with Hearne and others, and Hickes thought well of him. He was a Fellow of the Royal Society, and died in 1725.

He formed a considerable library and a collection of antiquities, coins, manuscripts and curiosities famous in his day as the *Musæum Thoresbyanum*, leaving both collections to his son Ralph, on whose death in 1764 they were sold. The books were amalgamated with 'several other LIBRARIES lately purchased', to a total of 20,000 volumes in 6,561 lots, so that the distinction of Thoresby's own library could only be made by guesswork from among those titles published before 1725; apart from the obvious antiquarian and historical works of the period he is likely to have owned, identification can hardly go further. Something more however can be said of the Musæum.

Apart from the 1764 sale catalogue, there is another list of the collection published as an appendix to the *Ducatus* in 1715 and again in the enlarged edition of 1816. From this we see that it was originally far larger and more miscellaneous than the 1764 catalogue suggests, and had included a considerable number of natural history and ethnographical specimens that doubtless decayed over the years, like the stuffed dodo in 'Tradescant's Ark', the comparable collection which formed the nucleus of the Ashmolean Museum in Oxford, as Sir Hans Sloane's did of the British Museum. The good coin collection survived, the nucleus of which was Lord Fairfax's collection that had been bought by Thoresby's father. He was zealous in building up his series of autograph letters — 'I have been a long time procuring both antient and modern Autographs of noted persons in Church and State' he wrote to John Strype in 1707. 'My honoured friends have supplied me with many of the modern worthies.' But, he goes on, is there any chance of Strype providing him with something of Cranmer, or Fox the martyrologist? If he did get them they may lurk under lot 74, 'Letters and Autographs of Bishops, and eminent Divines'.

The 'Curiosities' in the sale were very miscellaneous and do not seem to include the Late Bronze Age swords from Ireland and the Isle of Man, or the fine Early Bronze Age grave-group from Broughton-in-Craven identifiable in the 1715 catalogue. Nor is there the famous Roman shield of which Thoresby was so proud, but which from the original description and sketch was almost certainly a Scottish Highlander's targe of recent date, unfamiliar to Englishmen before 1715, but perhaps after the events of the intervening years recognizable by 1764 for what it was.

Of the sale catalogues of the library one of the two copies in the British Library is reproduced (S.C.–S.491): no others have been located. The Bodleian copy (MUS. BIBL. III 8° 614²) of *Musæum Thoresbyanum* has been used, since it contains more prices and buyers than the two other copies noted, one of which is in the Department of Manuscripts, the British Library, and the other in the collection of Dr A. N. L. Munby. Grateful acknowledgement is made to the authorities of both libraries.

A

CATALOGUE

OF

TWENTY THOUSAND VOLUMES,

Including the LIBRARY of the late Eminent

Mr. *RALPH THORESBY*, Gent. F. R. S.

Late of LEEDS,

And of ſeveral other LIBRARIES, lately purchaſed;

In which are great Numbers of the beſt Books, in all Branches of Learning, and in elegant Condition.

Amongſt great Numbers equally valuable are the following:

FOLIO.

Rapin and Tindal's Continuat. 5 vol.
Hollinſhed's Chronicle. 4 vol.
Carte's Hiſt. 4 vol. Tyrrel, 5 vol. Brady, 3 vol.
Ruſhworth, 8 vol.
Rymer's Fœdera, 20 vol.
Clarendon's Hiſt. and Continuation, 4 vol. *both large and ſmall pap.*
Heads and Lives of the Illuſt. Men of the Britiſh Nation, *large paper, in ruſſia leather*
Gibſon's Camden, 2 vol.
Stukeley's Itinerary, Stone-Henge and Abury
Borlaſe's Cornwall, 2 vol.
Dugdale's Warwickſhire, 2 vol. *large and ſmall paper*
Horſley's Britannia Romana, *large paper, in ruſſia leather*
The ſame, *ſmall paper*
Dugdale's Monaſticon, 3 tom.
——— by Stevens and Continuation in Engliſh, 3 vol.
——— Warwickſhire, 2 vol. *l. pap.*
The ſame, *ſmall paper*, 2 vol
Plot's Oxfordſhire and Staffordſhire
Chauncy's Hertfordſhire
Peck's Deſiderata Curioſa, 2 vol.
Tanner's Notitia Monaſtica
Thoreſby's Leeds, *large paper*
Morton's Northamptonſhire, *in ruſſia leather*
State Tryals, 8 vol.
Stuart's Antiq. of Athens
Wood's Ruins of Palmyra
Blair's Chronolog. Tables
Religious Ceremonies and Cuſtoms of all Nations, *with cuts, l. pap. bound in ruſſia*

FOLIO.

Mariana's Hiſtory of Spain, by Stevens, *l. pap.*
Harris's Voyages, by Campbell, 2 vol.
Churchill's Voyages and Supplem. 8 vol.
Le Brun's Voyages to the Levant
Voyages de Norden, 2 tom.
——— de Le Brun en Levant, Moſcovie, Perſe, &c. &c. 3 tom.
Dictionaires, viz. Bayle, 5 vol. General, 10 vol. Johnſon, 2 vol. Chambers and Supplem. 4 vol. Chambers, 2 vol. Supplem. to Chambers, 2 vol. Collier, 4 vol. Ainſworth, 2 vol. James, 3 vol. Miller, Calmet, 3 vol. Somner's Saxon, Davies's Welch and Lat. &c. &c.
H. Stephani Theſaurus Ling. Gr. 5 tom.
Du Freſne Gloſſarium, 6 tom.
Hoffmanni Lexicon, 4 tom.
Dictionaire & Oeuvres de Bayle, 8 tom.
——— de Moreri, 8 tom.
——— d'Herbelot
——— de Trevoux, 5 tom.
——— de Menage, 2 tom.
Aſſemanni Biblioth. Orient. 4 tom.
Golii Lexic. Arab.
Vocabol. della Cruſca, 6 tom.
Muſæum Florentinum, 10 tom. *corio ruſſ.*
Bible, *l. paper, by* Buck *and* Daniel
——— *l. paper, in turkey leather Edinb. by* Watſon
Davila, Ital. *bound in turkey leather Par. Stamp. Real*
Montfaucon, *grande papier*, 15 tom.
Campbell's Vitruvius Britan. *1ſt impreſſ.* 3 vol.

Which will be ſold (for Ready Money only) the Prices printed in the Catalogue, on *February* 27. 1764, and continue on Sale till all are ſold.

At THOMAS PAYNE's, Bookſeller,

Next the *Mews-Gate*, in *Caſtle-Street*, *St. Martin's*.

Catalogues to be had (Price 6d) at the following Bookſellers, *viz.* Mr. BROTHERTON's *Cornhill*; H. PAYNE, *Pater-noſter Row*; LEWIS, in *Ruſſel-ſtreet*, *Covent Garden*; OWEN, *Temple-Bar*; ROBSON, *New Bond-ſtreet*; RIDLEY, *St. James's-ſtreet*; WALTER, *Charing Croſs*; Meſſ. MERRIL and MATTHEWS, at *Cambridge*; at CHILD's Coffee-Houſe, *St. Paul's Church-yard*; and at the Place of SALE.

Where is given the full Value for any Library, or Parcel of Books.

BRITISH MUSEUM

INDEX CAPITUM.

FOLIO.

QUARTO.

OCTAVO.

DUODECIMO.

TRACTS.

PAMPHLETS.

APPENDIX.

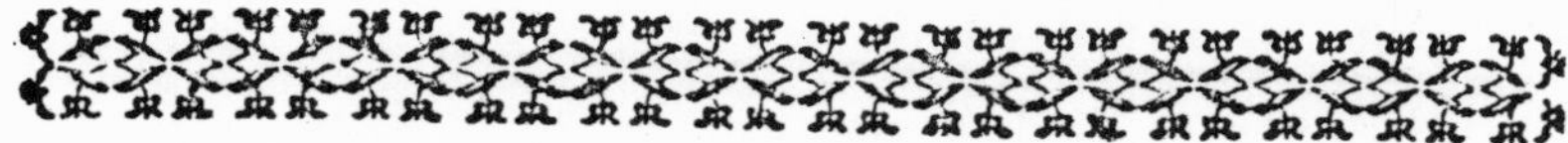

History and Antiquities of Great Britain *and* Ireland.
F O L I O.

1 RAPIN's History of England, with Notes by Tindal, 2 vol. *new and very neat,* 1l 10s — — 1732
2 The same, *with heads and monuments,* 2 vol. 1l 16s — 1732
3 The same, *with heads and monuments,* 2 vol. 2l — 1732
4 The same, with Tindal's Continuation and Medalic History, *with heads, monuments and plans,* 5 vol. *new and very neat,* 7l 7s 1732
5 Compleat History of England, from the earliest Account to the Death of King William, by Bp. Kennet, *with cuts,* 3 vol. *best edition,* 1l 11s 6d — — 1719
6 Guthrie's Hist. of England, *with cuts,* 3 vol. *in boards,* 1l 11s 6d 1744
7 Castrations to Hollingshead's Chronicle, *in boards,* 7s 6d
8 Lewis's History of Great Britain, with Lhuyd's Breviary of Bretayne, 7s 6d — — — 1729
9 Strype's Life of Archbishop Parker, 4s — 1711
10 ——— of Archbishop Grindal, 3s — 1710
11 ——— of Archbishop Cranmer, 5s — 1694
12 ——— of Archbishop Whitgift, *in boards,* 4s — 1718
13 ——— Annals of the Reformation, 4 vol. 1l 7s 1725, &c.
14 ——— Memorials of the Reformation, 3 vol. 1l 1s 1721
15 Barnes's History of Edward III. and his Son Edward the Black Prince, *with cuts, fair,* 7s 6d — — 1688
16 Oldmixon's History of the Stuarts, 7s 6d — 1730
17 Bp. Burnet's History of his own Times, 2 vol. *neat,* 1l 1s 1724, &c.
18 Jeake's Charters of the Cinque Ports, *in boards,* 4s — 1728
19 Bp. Nicolson's English, Scotch and Irish Historical Libraries, *best edition, very fair,* 1l — — 1736
20 Sandford's Genealogical History of the Kings of England, *with cuts, very fair,* 9s — — 1677
21 Speed's History of Great Britain, *with seals and coins, and effigies of the author,* 6s — — 1632
22 Lediard's General Naval History of England, from the Conquest, 2 vol. in one, 14s — — 1735
23 The same, 2 vol. *very fair,* 18s — 1735
24 Sir H. Spelman's English Works, relating to the Laws and Antiquities of England, with his Life by Bp. Gibson, 10s 6d — 1727
25 Fortescue de Laudib. Legum Angliæ, with Selden's Notes, *very fair,* 10s 6d — — — 1737
26 Bacon's Historical and Political Discourses of the Laws and Government of England, 9s — — 1739
27 The same, *a fair copy,* 10s 6d — — 1739
28 The same, *large paper, fair,* 18s — 1739
29 Brady's Complete History of England, from J. Cæsar to the End of Henry III. 5s — 1685
30 ——— Historical Treatise of Cities and Burghs, 2s 6d 1704

B 31 Acher-

31 Acherley's Britannic Conſtitution, or Fundamental Form of Government in Britain, wherein the Privileges of both Houſes of Parliament are exhibited, 7s 6d —— —— 1726

32 Dr. Johnſton's Excellency of Engliſh Monarchy, wherein is treated the Benefits of Kingly Government, the Badges of Sovereignty, the Duty of Subjects, and the Miſchiefs of Faction, *very fair and neat,* 5s —— —— —— 1686

33 Bedford on Hereditary Right of the Crown of England, 2s 6d

34 Life, Reign and Death of Edward II. by E. F. 2s —— 1680

35 Life of Archbp. Williams, by Bp. Hacket, 3s —— 1693

36 Life of Archbp. Uſher, with a Collection of 300 Letters, 5s 1686

37 Lloyd's Lives of eminent Perſons who ſuffered in the Civil Wars, from 1637 to 1666, with the Life of King Charles I. 4s 1668

38 The ſame, *very fair,* 5s —— —— 1668

39 Salmon's Critical Review and Abridgment of State Trials, 7s 6d 1738

40 State Trials at Large, 6 vol. *a bad copy,* 4l 4s —— 1719

41 Grafton's Chronicle, *very fair, wants the title,* 15s 1569

42 The ſame, *exceeding fair and neat, and marble leaves,* 1l 5s 1569

43 Lord Bacon's Hiſtory of Henry VII. *very fair,* 2s —— 1622

44 Martyn's Hiſtory of the Kings of England, *very fair,* 2s 6d 1615

45 Herbert's Life of Henry VIII. 3s —— 1649

46 Habington's Hiſtory of Edward IV. 2s —— 1640

47 Buck's Hiſtory of Richard III. 2s 6d —— 1647

48 Prynne's Breviate of the Life of Archbp. Laud, 2s 6d 1644

49 Report of the Secret Committee relating to the Earl of Orford, *in boards,* 2s —— —— —— 1742

50 Walpole's Report of the Secret Committee, 2s 6d —— 1715

51 Carkeſſe's Book of Rates, with Supplement, 2 vol. *very fair and neat,* 10s 6d —— —— —— 1728

52 Daniel's Preſent State of the Britiſh Cuſtoms, 6s —— 1752

53 *Crouch's Complete Guide to the Officers of his Majeſty's Cuſtoms in the Out Ports* —— —— —— 1732

54 Journals of the Houſe of Commons, 28 vol. *in boards,* 20l

55 Carew's Hiſtorical Account of the Rights of Elections of the ſeveral Counties, &c. of Great Britain, taken from the Journals, *new and very neat,* 1l 11s 6d —— —— 1755

56 D'Ewe's Journal of the Parliaments in the Reign of Queen Elizabeth, *very fair,* 12s —— —— 1693

57 Ryley's Pleadings in Parliament, *large paper, gilt leaves,* 9s 1661

58 Collins's Baronies by Writ, *very fair,* 1l 1s —— 1734

59 *Thurloe's (Secretary to Oliver Cromwell) State Papers, containing very curious and authentic Memorials of the Engliſh Affairs, from* 1638 *to the Reſtoration, with his Life and a general Index,* 7 vol. *new and elegantly bound,* 3l 10s —— —— 1742

60 The ſame, 7 vol. *new and neatly bound in ruſſia,* 5l 5s 1742

61 The ſame, 7 vol. *large paper, in boards,* 4l —— 1742

62 Lord Burghley's State Papers in the Reign of Q. Elizabeth, publiſhed by Haynes and Murden, 2 vol. *neat,* 1l 15s 1740, &c.

63 —— State Papers, publiſhed by Murden, *fair and very neatly bound,* 18s —— —— 1759

64 The ſame, *elegantly bound, marble leaves,* 1l 1s —— 1759

65 Rymer's Fœdera, 20 tom. *neatly bound in* 10 vol. 10l 10s *Hagæ Com.* 1739

66 Ruſh-

66 Rushworth's Historical Collections during the Rebellion, *with MSS. additions in the margin*, 8 vol. 5l 5s —— 1659, &c.
67 The same Book, 8 vol. *good copy*, 4l 4s —— 1659, &c.
68 Clarendon's History of the Rebellion, 3 vol. *very fair*, 2l 5s 1704
69 The same, with his Life and Continuation, 4 vol. 3l 15s 1707, &c.
70 The same, 4 vol. *elegantly bound in russia leather, marble leaves*, 5l 15s 6d 1702, &c.
71 The same, 4 vol. *large paper, in russia leather*, 8l 8s
72 Clarendon's Life and Continuation, *in sheets*, 1l 5s — 1759
73 The same, *in boards*, 1l 6s 6d —— 1759
74 Memoirs and Letters of the Marquis of Clanricarde, *new and neat*, 1l 1s —— —— —— 1757
75 Whitlocke's Memorials of the English Affairs, 10s 6d 1682
76 Ludlow's Memoirs, *best edition, new and neat*, 14s — 1751
77 King Charles's Works, *finely printed*, 2 vol. *gilt leaves*, 15s 1662
78 Life and Letters of the Duke of Ormonde, published by Carte, 3 vol. *elegantly bound, gilt leaves*, 3l 3s —— 1735
79 Martin Folkes on English Coins, *imperial paper*, 1l 1s 1745
80 Plates to Folkes's Coins, *large paper, in boards*, 1l 10s
81 Wood's Athenæ Oxonienses, 2 vol. *best edition, in rough calf*, 18s 1721
82 The same, 2 vol. *very fair*, 1l 1s —— 1721
83 The same, 2 vol. *elegantly bound in one, large paper, new*, 1l 4s 1721
84 *Heads of Illustrious Persons of Great Britain and Ireland, engraved by Houbraken, with their Lives by Birch, 2 vol. in one, new and neatly bound*, 2l 5s —— —— 1747
85 The same, *fair and neat*, 2l 2s —— 1747
86 The same, *first and best impressions, large paper, elegantly bound in russia*, 6l 6s —— —— —— 1743
87 Sandford's History of the Coronation of King James II. *with cuts, the best impressions*, 1l 1s —— 1687
88 Earl of Castlemaine's Embassy to Rome, *with cuts, large paper, and very fair*, 6s —— —— 1688
89 Madox's Formulare Ang. *large paper*, 15s —— 1702
90 —— Firma Burgi, or Historical Essay concerning Cities, Towns and Buroughs of England, 10s 6d —— 1726
91 —— The same, *very fair*, 12s —— 1726
92 —— Baronia Anglica, with the Index to the History of the Exchequer, *very fair*, 15s —— —— 1736
93 —— History of the Exchequer
94 Life of Sir Leoline Jenkins, containing a Compleat Series of Letters relating to the Treaties of Cologn and Nimeguen, 2 vol. 15s —— —— 1724
95 Cleaveland's Genealogical History of the Family of Courtenay, 10s 6d —— —— 1735
96 Lives of the Professors of Gresham College, with the Life of Sir Tho. Gresham the Founder, also an Appendix of Orations, Lectures and other Papers in no other Collection, by J. Ward, *with a fine print of the founder and of the college, new, in boards*, 9s 1740
97 The same, *new and neatly bound*, 12s —— 1740
98 Archbishop Laud's Remains, by Wharton, vol. 2. 5s
99 Collection of State Tracts, published in the Reign of King William III. 3 vol. *fair and neat*, 2l 12s 6d —— 1705
100 Le Neve's Fasti Ecclesiæ Anglicanæ, or Essay towards a regular Succession of Dignitaries in the Cathedrals of Engl. and Wales, 4s 1716

101 Selden's Tracts on the Laws of England. 2s 6d ——— 1683

102 Selden on the Dominion of the Sea. 2s 6d ——— 1652

103 Maitland's Hiſtory of Edinburgh and the Town of Leith, *with a great many cuts, neat,* 14s ——— *Edinb.* 1753

104 The ſame, *new and elegantly bound, marble leaves,* 18s 1753

106 Gordon's Journey through Scotland, *with a great many cuts,* 10s 6d 1726

107 Maitland's Hiſtory and Antiquities of Scotland, 2 vol. *new and very neatly bound,* 2l 2s ——— ——— 1757

108 Burnet's Lives of the Dukes of Hamilton, *very fair,* 5s 1676

109 Memoirs of Sir James Melvil, by Scot, 3s 6d ——— 1683

110 Monro's Expedition with the Scotch Regiment, *very fair,* 3s 6d 1637

111 Keating's General Hiſtory of Ireland, *with the arms and genealogies of the ancient families of Ireland,* 18s ——— 1723

112 Ware's Antiquities and Hiſtory of Ireland, *very fair,* 14s 1705

113 Coxe's Hiſtory of Ireland, 2 vol. 14s ——— 1689

114 Speed's Maps of England, Scotland and Ireland, 1l 1s 1676

115 The ſame, *firſt impreſſion, very neatly bound,* 1l 5s ——— 1611

116 Adams's Index Villaris, or Alphabetical Table of all the Cities, &c. in England and Wales, 7s 6d ——— 1680

117 The ſame, *very fair and neat,* 10s 6d ——— 1680

118 Camden's Britannia, with Improvements and Additions by Bp. Gibſon, *very fair and neat copy,* 18s ——— 1695

119 The ſame, 2 vol. *laſt edition, new and elegantly bound in ruſſia, with a gold border, marble leaves,* 3l 13s 6d ——— 1753

120 Morton's Natural Hiſtory of Northamptonſhire, *with cuts, elegantly bound in ruſſia,* 1l 15s ——— ——— 1712

121 Sammes's Antiquities of Ancient Britain, *with cuts,* 5s 1676

122 Moll's Deſcription of England and Wales, *with maps, coloured,* 7s 6d ——— ——— ——— 1724

123 Maitland's Hiſtory of London, *with a great number of cuts of the moſt remarkable buildings,* 2 vol. *in boards,* 2l 2s ——— 1756

124 The ſame, 2 vol. *fair and neat,* 2l 5s ——— 1756

125 Peck's Antiq. Annals of Stanford, *with cuts,* 12s 1727

126 Stow's Survey of London and Weſtminſter, *with a great number of cuts, very fair, neatly bound in* 3 vol. 1l 1s ——— 1720

127 Dart's Hiſtory and Antiquities of Canterbury Cathedral, *with cuts,* 10s 6d ——— ——— 1727

128 Stow's Survey of London, enlarged by Munday, 6s 1633

129 *Stukeley's Itinerarium Curioſum, or Account of Antiquities of Great Britain, with a great number of cuts* ——— 1724

130 Stukeley's Abury, a Temple of the Druids, *with cuts, in boards,* 15s ——— ——— ——— 1743

131 ——— Stonehenge and Abury, 2 vol. *neatly bound,* 2l 2s 1740 & 1743

132 N. Salmon's Hiſtory of Hertfordſhire, with an Account of the Ancient Monuments, and the Character of thoſe that have been the chief Poſſeſſors of the Lands, 9s ——— ——— 1728

133 The ſame, *very fair and elegantly bound,* 12s 6d ——— 1728

134 Harris's Hiſtory of Kent, with Views of the Principal Seats of the Nobility and Gentry, *very fair,* 1l 15s ——— 1719

135 Accurate Deſcription and Hiſtory of the Cathedrals of Canterbury and York, *with 170 cuts, very fair and neat,* 16s ——— 1755

136 Drake's Hiſtory and Antiquities of York, *with a great number of cuts, very fair,* 1l 11s 6d ——— ——— 1736

137 Wright's

137 Wright's History and Atiquities of Rutland, *with cuts, very fair,* 7s 6d — — — 1684
138 Thoresby's Antiquities of Leeds, *with cuts, large paper, very fair and neat,* 1l 16s — — — 1715
139 The same, *small paper, new and very neat,* 1l 1s — 1715
140 The same, *new, small paper, elegantly bound in russia, marble leaves,* 1l 11s 6d — — 1715
141 Gunter's History of the Church of Peterburgh, *with cuts, large paper, very fair and elegantly bound,* 18s — 1686
142 Plot's Natural History of Oxfordshire, *with cuts, very fair,* 7s 6d — — 1676
143 —— Oxfordshire, *best edit.* 15s — 1705
144 —— Natural History of Staffordshire, *with cuts,* 1l 4s 1686
145 —— The same, *with cuts, large paper and very fair,* 1l 11s 6d 1686
146 —— The same, *large paper, very fair and elegantly bound,* 1l 16s
147 Chauncey's Historical Antiquities of Hertfordshire, *with cuts, fair,* 2l 5s — — — 1700
148 Morant's History and Antiquities of Colchester, *with cuts, in boards,* 17s — — — 1748
149 Dugdale's Monasticon, and Stevens's Continuation, 3 vol. *with cuts, very fair and neat* — 1718, &c.
150 ——— *Origines Juridicales, with cuts, very fair,* 14s 1666
151 ——— Antiquities of Warwickshire, *very fair, with cuts, by Hollar, first impressions,* 2l 2s — — 1656
152 ——— The same, with great Additions by Thomas, 2 vol. *with cuts, large Paper, new and elegantly bound,* 5l 5s — 1730
153 ——— Summons to Parliament, *very fair,* 1l 4s 1685
154 Peck's Desiderata Curiosa, 2 vol. *with cuts very neat,* 2l 2s 1732, &c.
155 Bourne's History of Newcastle upon Tyne, *very fair,* 10s 6d 1736
156 Coker's Survey of Dorsetshire, *with cuts, new and neat,* 9s 1732
157 Leycester's Historic. Antiquities of Great Britain and Ireland, *stained, elegantly bound,* 7s 6d — — 1673
158 Jones's Antiquity of Stone-Heng, 3s — 1655
159 Burton's Description of Leicestershire, *with a great number of manuscript additions,* 1l 5s — — 1622
160 Weever's Ancient Funeral Monuments of England and Ireland, *very fair,* 10s 6d — — 1631
161 Burton's Comment. on Antoninus's Itinerary through Britain, *with the map and author's effigies,* 5s — — 1658

History and Antiquities of various Nations, Voyages, and Travels. FOLIO.

162 COmplete System of Geography of the whole World, *with 70 maps, by Bowen, neatly engraved,* 2 vol. *new and very neat,* 3l 3s — — — 1747
163 Montfaucon's Antiquities of France, *with a great number of cuts,* 2 vol. *very neat,* 1l 16s — — 1750
164 *Montfaucon's Antiquities Explained and Represented in Sculptures,* by Humphreys, *with the Supplement, in boards,* 15 vol. *bound in* 7. *very fair,* 4l 4s — — — 1721
165 Montfaucon's Antiquities of Italy, *with cuts,* 6s — 1725
166 The Antiquities of Athens, measured and delineated by James Stuart and Nic. Revet, *with cuts, in boards,* — 1763

167 Ruin

167 Ruins of Palmyra, by Wood, *with cuts, neat,* 3l 5s 1753
168 Ruins of Athens, by Le Roy, *translated into English, with fine cuts, very neat,* 1l 10s —— —— 1759
169 Blair's Chronology and History of the World from the Creation, *illustrated in 56 tables, neatly engraved, very fair and neatly bound,* 2l 8s —— —— —— 1756
170 Tallent's Chronological Tables, *in boards,* 3s
171 Horrebow's Natural History of Iceland, *with cuts, large paper, sewed,* 4s —— —— —— 1758
172 The same, *small paper, neatly bound,* 7s 6d —— 1758
173 Ceremonies and Religious Customs of all Nations in the World, *with a great number of cuts, with the original French plates by Picart,* 6 vol. *very fair, in boards,* 4l 4s —— —— 1731
174 The same, 6 vol. *with a great number of cuts, large paper, in boards, new,* 3l 10s —— —— 1731
175 Rycaut's History of the Turks, from 1679 to 1699, *with cuts, fair,* 9s —— —— —— 1700
176 Mariana's General History of Spain, translated by Stevens, *large paper,* 2l •s —— —— —— 1692
177 Thuanus's History of his own Times, translated by Wilson, 2 vol. 1l 4s —— —— —— 1729
178 Howell's General History of the World, 4 vol. *bound in* 3, *very fair,* 1l 5s —— —— —— 1680
179 The same, 3 vols, *very fair, and very elegantly bound,* 2l 2s 1680
180 Sir W. Raleigh's History of the World, *very fair and neat,* 6s 1652
181 The same, *fair,* 6s —— —— 1665
182 The same, with his Life and Tryal, 7s 6d —— 1677
183 The same, with his Life, by Oldys, 2 vol. in 1. 1l 11s 6d 1736
184 The same Edition, *new and elegantly bound,* 2l —— 1736
185 Ancient Universal History, *with maps, notes, cuts, &c. together with the Supplement,* 10 vol, *in boards, not cut,* 8l 8s 1736, &c.
186 The same, with Supplement, 8 vol. *fair and neat,* 8l 8s 1740, &c.
187 *The same, with Supplement,* 8 *vol. new and elegantly bound, marble leaves,* 10l 10s —— —— 1736, &c.
188 Tacitus's Works, with Political Discourses, by Gordon, *very fair,* 1l 1s —— —— —— 1728
189 The same, 2 vol. *very fair and neat,* 1l 4s —— 1728
190 Cæsar's Commentaries, by Duncan, *with fine cuts, fair and neat,* 2l 2s —— —— —— 1753
191 Thucydides, by Hobbes, *with cuts, very fair,* 6s 1676
192 The same, 5s —— —— 1648
193 The same, 4s —— —— —— 1634
194 Diodorus Siculus, by Booth, *neat,* 1l —— 1700
195 Gordon's Life of Pope Alexander VI. and his Son Cæsar Borgia, *very fair and neat,* 7s 6d —— —— 1729
196 Castelneau's Memoirs of Francis II. and Charles IX. of France, translated from the French, *bound in morocco, gilt leaves,* 7s 6d 1724
197 Davila's History of the Civil Wars of France, *large print,* 6s 1647
198 The same, *last edition, with an index, very fair and neat,* 12s 1678
199 History of the Life of the Duke of Espernon, being a Continuation of Davila to 1642, englished by Cotton, *fair,* 5s —— 1659
200 Mezeray's General History of France, *very fair,* 18s 1683
201 The same, *very fair and neat, marble leaves,* 1l 1s —— 1683

202 Guic-

202 Guicciardin's History of the Warres of Italie, englished by Fenton, 5s —— —— —— 1618
203 The same, 5s —— —— 1599
204 Memoirs of the Sieur de Pontis, by Cotton, 3s —— 1694
205 Commentaries of Montluc, Marefchal of France, *very fair*, 4s 1674
206 Spon's History of the City and State of Geneva, *with cuts, very fair*, 2s —— —— —— 1687
207 Sir Hans Sloane's Natural History of Jamaica, *with a great number of cuts, very fair and neatly bound in red calf*, 2 vol. 3l 13s 6d
208 Browne's Civil and Natural History of Jamaica, *with 50 copper-plates, neat*, 1l 5s —— —— 1756
209 Hughes's Natural History of Barbadoes, *with cuts, new and very neat*, 18s —— —— —— 1750
210 Ligon's History of Barbadoes, *with cuts*, 3s —— 1657
211 The same Book, 3s 6d —— —— 1673
212 Royal Commentaries of Peru, translated by Rycaut, *with cuts, very fair*, 1l 4s —— —— 1688
213 Ludolphus's History of Ethiopia, *with cuts*, 5s —— 1682
214 The same, *very fair*, 6s —— —— 1682
215 The same, *very fair and neat*, 7s 6d —— 1682
216 Polybius's History, translated by Grimstone, 2s 6d 1635
217 Vertot's History of the Knights of Malta, *with a great number of cuts*, 2 vol. 1l 1s 6d —— —— 1728
218 The same, 2 vol. *new and elegantly bound, marble leaves*, 2l 2s 1729
219 Another Copy, 2 vol. *stained*, 18s
220 Desolis's History of the Conquest of Mexico, by Townsend, *with cuts, fair*, 9s —— —— —— 1724
221 Prince Cantemir's History of the Growth and Decay of the Othman Empire, by Tindal, *with cuts, new and neatly bound*, 14s 1756
222 Platina's Lives of the Popes, by Sir P. Rycaut, and continued to the Present Time, *fair*, 5s —— —— 1688
223 The same, *very fair*, 6s —— —— 1688
224 Knolles's General History of the Turks, with the Lives and Conquest of the Othman Kings, *2d edit.* 6s 1610
225 Livy's Roman History, with the Supplements of Frensheim and Dujatius, *translated into English, very fair*, 9s —— 1686
226 Machiavel's Works, *very fair*, 9s —— 1680
227 The same, *fair and neat*, 9s —— —— 1694
228 The same, *very fair, and bound in morocco, gilt leaves*, 15s 1675
229 The same, *last edition*, 10s 6d —— 1720
230 Philostratus's Life of Apollonius Tyaneus, with Notes, by Blount, 3s —— —— — 1680
231 Annals of C. Tacitus, englished by Greenwey 1640—Malvezzi's Discourses on Tacitus 1642, 2s 6d
232 Am. Marcellinus's Roman History, translated into English, 3s 1609
233 Strada's History of the Low Country Warres, *with cuts*, 2s 6d 1650
234 Harris's Collection of Voyages continued and greatly enlarged by Campbell, *with cuts and maps*, 2 vol. *new and elegantly bound*, 5l 5s —— —— 1744
235 Churchill's Collection of Voyages, with additional ones from the Harleian Collection, *with a great number of cuts*, 8 vol. *neat*, 6l 6s —— 1732
236 Breval's Travels through Europe, *with a great number of cuts*, 4 vol. *neat*, 1l 10s —— 1726, &c.

237 Norden's

237 Norden's Travels in Egypt and Nubia, *with a great number of cuts, large paper, elegantly bound in russia, with a gold border, gilt leaves,* 2 vol. 5l 5s — 1725
238 The same, in French, *with cuts, in boards,* 2 vol. 4l 4s *Copen.* 1755
239 Pococke's Description of the East, and some other Countries, *with cuts, neatly bound in* 3 vol. 2l 10s — 1743
240 The same, *elegantly bound in russia leather,* 2 vol. 3l 10s 1743
241 Chishull's Travels to Turkey, *new and neat,* 10s 6d 1747
242 The same 1747 — *Chishull's Antiquitates Asiaticæ, fair and neat* 1728, 16s
243 Dr. Brown's Travels through Germany, &c. *with cuts, fair,* 4s 1685
244 The same, *very fair and neat,* 6s — 1685
245 The same, *large paper, very fair,* 10s 6d 1685
246 Chardin's Travels into Persia and East Indies, *with cuts, very fair,* 9s — — 1686
247 Smith's Travels in Europe, Asia, Africa and America, from 1593 to 1629, *with cuts,* 6s — — 1630
248 Knox's Relation of the Island Ceylon, *with cuts, very fair,* 7s 1681
249 Herbert's Travels into Asia and Africa, *with cuts, best edition, very fair,* 5s — — 1677
250 Hackluyt's Collection of Voyages and Travels, 3 vol. *bound in one,* 1l 15s — — 1599
251 Tavernier's Voyages to Persia and East Indies, with his Voyage to Tonquins, *with cuts,* 14s — — 1678
252 Lenschoton's Voyage to the East and West Indies, *black letter,* 5s — — — 1598
253 Voyages de M. Le Brun en Perse, & aux Indes Orientales, *avec d'un grand nombre des figures en taille douce,* 2 tom. 1l 11s 6d *Amst.* 1718
254 ——— de M. Le Brun en Levant, Perse & aux Indes Orientales, *avec d'un grand nombre des figure en taille douce,* 3 tom. 4l *Dest & Amst.*
255 Voyage du Chev. Chardin en Perse & aux Indes Orientales, *avec fig.* 4s — — — *Lond* 1686
256 Leven en Bedryf Vanden Heere Michiel de Ruiter Admiraal van Hollandt. door Ger. Brandt, *met figuren,* 10s 6d — *Amst.* 1700

Miscellaneous Books. FOLIO.

257 Compleat Collection of Milton's Hist. and Polit. Works, with his Life, by Dr. Birch, 2 vol. 1l 5s — 1738
258 The same, 2 vol. *large paper, very fair and neat,* 2l 2s 1738
259 Grotius on the Rights of Peace and War, with Barbeyrac's Notes, *new and elegantly bound in russia, with a gold border, marble leaves,* 1l 14s — — 1738
260 Puffendorf's Law of Nature and Nations, with Barbeyrac's Notes, 7s 6d — — — 1717
261 Test and Contest, from Nov. 1756 to July 1757, *sewed,* 5s
262 Sir William Temple's Works, 2 vol. *fair,* 1l 1s — 1720
263 The same, 2 vol. 18s — — 1720
264 The same, 2 vol. *fair and neat,* 1l 4s — 1740
265 The same, 2 vol. *new and very neatly bound,* 1l 10s — 1750
266 Lord Bacon's Works, with his Life, by Mallet, 3 vol. *new, and elegantly bound in russia, marble leaves,* 4l 10s — 1753

267 Life

267 Life of Lord Bacon, by Mallet, *with many other pieces to complete the edition of his Works in* 1730, *boards*, 5s ——— 1760
268 Locke's Works, 3 vol. *fair*, 1l 11s 6d ——— 1722
269 The same, *fine paper*, *fair*, 3 vol. 2l 7s —— 1740
270 The same, *fine paper*, *neat*, 3 vol. 2l 10s ——— 1740
271 The same, *fine paper*, *elegantly bound in morocco*, *gilt leaves*, 4l 4s 1740
272 The same, with his Life and Posthumous Pieces, published by Desmaizeaux, *neat*, 2l 10s ——— ——— 1751
273 The same, 3 vol. *new and elegantly bound*, 3l — 1759
274 The Moral and Philosophical Works of T. Hobbes, now first collected, with his Life, Critical and Historical Notes, *new and very neat*, 18s ——— ——— — 1750
275 Letters of Mr. Pope and his Friends, *large paper*, 2 vol. *very fair and neat*, 12s ——— ——— 1737
276 Bishop Hooper's Works, with a Preface, by Dr. Hunt, *new and very neat*, 18s ——— ——— 1757
277 Earl of Clarendon's Collection of Tracts, 10s 6d — 1727
278 Roberts's Merchants Map of Commerce, *best edition*, 5s 1700
279 Alg. Sidney on Government, *very neat*, *gilt leaves*, 6s 1698
280 The same, with his Life and Apology, *very fair*, 10s 6d 1751
281 Boccalini's Advertisement from Parnassus, englished by Hughes, *best edition*, *neat*, 4s ——— ——— 1706
282 Harrington's Political Works, with his Life, by Toland, 14s 1737
283 The same, *best edition*, *very fair*, 16s ——— 1747
284 Hobbes's Leviathan, *fair*, 4s ——— — 1651
285 The same, 3s ——— ——— 1651
286 The same, *fine paper*, *elegantly bound in morocco*, *gilt leaves*, 7s 6d 1651
287 Cudworth's Intellectual System of the Universe, *very fair*, 10s 6d 1678
288 Æsop's Fables, English, by L'Estrange, 2 vol. in one, *very fair*, 5s ——— ——— — 1699
289 Prophecies of Michael Nostradamus, *very fair*, 3s 6d 1672
290 Bishop Taylor's Cases of Conscience, 2 vol. *very fair*, 5s 1660
291 The Adventurer, by Mr. Hawksworth and others, 2 vol. *neatly bound in one*, 14s ——— ——— 1753
292 The same, in 2 vol. *neat*, 14s ——— — 1753
293 The Works of Sir Thomas More, Kt. *black letter*, *very fair*, 5s 1557
294 Bapt. Porta's Natural Magick, *fair*, 3s ——— 1658
295 Sir T. Brown's Enquiries into Vulgar Errors, 2s ——— 1646
296 ——— Works, *very fair*, 10s ——— 1686

Poetry, Romances, &c. FOLIO.

297 OVID's Metamorphoses, Lat. and Engl. with Historical Explications, by Banier, *with fine cuts by Picart*, *new and elegantly bound*, *marble leaves*, 3l 3s ——— ——— 1732
298 Pope's Works, 2 vol. *large paper*, *with neat head and tail pieces*, *elegantly bound in morocco*, *with a gold border*, *and gilt leaves*, 1l 16s ——— ——— ——— 1717
299 Homer's Iliad, by Pope, 6 vol. in 3. *large paper*, *with Hollar's cuts*, *fine impressions*, *elegantly bound in morocco*, *gilt leaves*, 4l 4s 1715
300 Homer's Iliad and Odyssey, by Pope, 11 vol. *small paper*, *very fair and neat*, 3l 3s ——— ——— 1715
301 ——— Iliad, by Pope, *bound in* 6 vol. *gilt leaves*, 1l 10s

302 Shakespear's Works, *4th edition, bound in morocco, gilt leaves,* 18s — — — 1685
303 Chaucer's Works, *very fair,* 5s — — 1687
304 The same, by Urry, *fair,* 18s — — 1721
305 The same, *new and very neatly bound,* 1l 1s — 1721
306 Ben Johnson's Works, *fair,* 10s 6d — 1692
307 Juvenal and Persius, by Dryden, *large paper, very fair,* 6s 1693
308 The same, by Holyday, *with notes and cuts, very fair,* 6s 1673
309 Milton's Paradise Lost, *with cuts, large paper,* 7s 6d 1688
310 Virgil's Æneis, in Scottish Verse, by Gawin Douglas, *very fair,* 6s *Edinb.* 1710
311 Dryden's Fables, Ancient and Modern, *very fair,* 5s 1700
312 Spenser's Works, 5s — — 1611
313 The same, *wants the title,* 4s
314 The same, with his Life, *beautifully printed, best edition,* 10s 6d 1679
315 The same, *very fair and neat,* 12s 6d — 1679
316 Andr. Marvel's Miscellaneous Poems, 2s — 1681
317 Orlando Furioso, by Harrington, *very fair and neatly bound, marble leaves,* 15s — — 1634
318 Sandy's Paraphrase on the Divine Poems, 2s — 1638
319 Drayton's Polyolbion, both parts, *with the maps,* 6s 1613
320 The same, *very fair,* 10s 6d
321 Lord Brookes's Poems, 2s 6d — 1633
322 Astrea, a Romance, 9s — — 1657

Dictionaries and Lexicons, in various Languages. FOLIO.

323 BAYLE's Dictionary, revised and corrected by Des Maizeaux, with his Life of Bayle, 5 vol. *new and very neat,* 4l 14s 6d 1734
324 The same, 5 vol. *large paper, new and very neatly bound,* 7l 7s 1734
325 The same, 5 vol. *large paper, bound in morocco, with a gold border and gilt leaves,* 9l 9s — — 1734
326 Johnson's English Dictionary, 2 vol. *new and very neat,* 4l 4s
327 The same, 2 vol. *2d hand,* 3l 10s — 1755
328 Chambers's Dictionary of Arts and Sciences, *with cuts,* 2 vol. 3l 3s — — — 1741
329 The same, 2 vol. 3l 7s — — 1741
330 The same, 2 vol. *neat,* 3l 7s — 1740
331 The same, with Supplement, 4 vol. *new and very neat,* 8l 8s
332 Supplement to Chambers's Dictionary, 2 vol. *new and very neat,* 4l 4s — — — 1753
333 Ainsworth's Dictionary of the Latin and English, 2 vol. *very fair and neat,* 2l 15s — — 1752
334 The same, 2 vol. *new and neatly bound,* 3l 3s — 1752
335 The same, 2 vol. *new and very elegantly bound, marble leaves,* 3l 10s
336 Collier's Great Historical, Geographical, Genealogical and Poetical Dictionary, containing a curious Miscellany of Sacred and Prophane History, 4 vol. *very fair,* 2l 10s — 1701, &c.
337 The same, 4 vol. *exceeding fair and neat,* 2l 15s 1701, &c.
338 Appendix to Collier's Dictionary, *fair,* 1l 5s — 1721
339 Bailey's English Dictionary, improved by Dr. Scott, *with cuts, fair and neat,* 1l 11s 6d — — 1755

340 General

340 General Dictionary, Historical and Critical, in which Bayle's Dictionary is included, with Observations by Bernard, Birch and Lockman, 10 vol. 9l 9s —— —— 1734
341 The same, *very fair and very neatly bound, marble leaves, &c.* 12l 12s
342 Dr. James's Medicinal Dictionary, 3 vol. *with cuts, in boards,* 4l 4s —— —— 1743
343 Minsheu's Dictionary of eleven Languages, 4s —— 1617
344 ——— Dictionary, Spanish and English, 2s 6d — 1623
345 Delpino's Dictionary, Spanish and English, and English and Spanish, *new and very neatly bound,* 1l 10s —— 1763
346 Pineda's Spanish and English Dictionary, *very fair,* 1l 1s 1740
347 Torriano's Italian and English Dictionary, 9s —— 1688
348 Lhuyd's Archæologiæ Britannica, or Account of the Languages of Great Britain, *very fair,* 7s 6d —— 1707
349 The same, *new and neatly bound,* 9s —— 1707
350 The same, *large paper, very fair and neat,* 12s — 1727
351 Miller's Gardener's Dictionary, *with cuts,* 2 vol. *very fair,* 1l 5s 1737
352 The same, in 1 vol. *last edition, new and neatly bound,* 3l 3s 1759
353 Rider's Universal English Dictionary, 12s —— 1759
354 Calmet's Dictionary of the Bible, *with a great number of cuts,* 3 vol. 2l 15s —— —— 1732
355 *Somneri Dictionarium Saxonico-Latino-Anglicum, cum Glossario,* 0s *Oxon.* 1659
356 *Davis's Welch and Latin Dictionary,* 1l 1s — 1632
357 Catalogus Impressorum Librorum Bibliothecæ Bodleianæ, *nit. comp. & novus,* 2 tom. 1l 8s —— *Oxon.* 1738
358 Idem, *ch. max.* 2 tom. 1l 17s —— *ib.* 1738
359 Montfaucon Bibliotheca Bibliothecarum Manuscriptorum, 2 tom. *exemp. pulch. & nit. comp.* 1l 5s —— *Par.* 1739
360 Rob. Stephani Thesaurus Linguæ Latinæ, 4 tom. *compact. in* 2 vol. 2l 10s —— —— *Lond.* 1734
361 Idem, *nitid. compact. in* 4 vol. 3l 3s —— *ib.* 1734
362 Idem, 4 tom. *elegant. comp. in corio russico & novus,* 5l 5s *ib.* 1734
363 Idem, 5 tom. *ch. max. nov. & elegant. compact.* *ib.* 1734
364 Hen. Stephani Thesaurus Græc. Linguæ, 4 tom. *maculat.* 3l 3s *ap. ips. Steph.* 1572
365 Idem, cum Glossario, 5 tom. *exemp. nitidiss. & elegant. compact. foliis marmor.* 7l —— —— *ib.* 1572
366 Fabri Thesaurus Eruditionis Scholasticæ, 2 tom. *nit. compact.* 1l 7s *Lips.* 1735
367 Idem, *edit. opt.* 2 tom. 1l 15s —— *ibid.* 1749
368 Du Fresne Glossarium ad Scriptores Mediæ & Infimiæ Græcitatis, 2 tom. *ch. max. elegant. compact. in* 1 vol. 1l 1s *Lugd.* 1688
369 Du Fresne Glossarium ad Scriptores Mediæ & Infimiæ Latinitatis, *edit. nova & auctior. opera & studio Monachor. S. Benedicti,* 6 tom. *nov. & elegant. comp.* 6l —— *Paris.* 1733
370 Martinii Lexicon Philologicum, access. Jo. Clerici Dissertat. Etymologica, 2 tom. *nit. comp. in memb.* 12s —— *Ultraject.* 1697
371 Hoffmanni Lexicon Universale, 4 tom. *edit. opt. compact. in memb.* 4l *L. Bat.* 1698
372 Pitisci Lexicon Antiq. Romanarum, *cum fig.* 3 tom. *semi-comp.* 1l 16s *Hag. Com.* 1737
373 Idem, 2 tom. *nit. compact.* 2l 2s —— *Leov.* 1713

C 2 374 Suidæ

374 Suidæ Lexicon, Gr. & Lat. a Kustero, 3 tom. *ch. max. elegant. comp.* 2l 10s ——— ——— *Cantab.* 1705
375 Calepinus VII. Linguarum, hoc est, Lexicon Latinum, *edit. opt. nov & nitid. compact.* 14s ——— *Patav.* 1758
376 Scapulæ Lexicon, Græco-Latinum, 6s *Amst. ap. Westen.* 1687
377 Idem, *exemp. pulch. edit. opt.* 1l 1s *Amst. apud Elz.* 1652
378 Constantini Lexicon, Gr. & Lat. *edit. opt.* 1l 11s 6d *Genev.* 1592
379 Idem, *pulch. exemp. compact. in membrana,* 2l 5s ——— 1592
380 Phavorini Dictionarium Græce, *exemp. pulch.* 9s *Bas.* 1538
381 Idem, 7s ——— ——— *ib.* 1538
382 Junii Etymologicum Anglicanum, edidit T. Lye, *pulch.* 18s *Ox.* 1743
383 Idem, *exemp. pulcher.* 1l
384 Budæi Comment. Linguæ Græcæ, 7s 6d *Par. ap. R. Steph.* 1548
385 Phil. Aquinatis Dictionarium Hebraicum, *exemp. pulch.* 10s 6d *Par.* 1629
386 Assemani Bibliotheca Orientalis Clement. Vaticana, 4 tom. *exempl. pulch. nit. comp. in membr.* 5l 5s ——— *Romæ* 1719
387 Golii Lexicon Arabico-Latinum, *exemp. pulch. comp. in membran.* *L. Bat.* 1653
388 Gussetii Comment. Ling. Ebraicæ, *exemp. pulch. nit. comp. in membr.* 1l 1s ——— ——— *Amst.* 1702
389 Skinneri Etymologicon Linguæ Anglicanæ, *exemp. pulch.* 9s *Lond.* 1671
390 Hesychii Lexicon, cum Notis Doct. Virorum, integris & Animadvers. Jo. Alberti, tom. 1. *semi-comp.* 1l 11s 6d *L. Bat.* 1746
391 Tanneri Bibliotheca Britannica-Hibernica, *splendiss. compact. foliis deaur.* 1l 4s ——— ——— *Lond.* 1748
392 Baudrand Dictionaire Geographique & Historique, 2 tom. en 1 vol. 9s ——— ——— *Par.* 1705
393 Dictionnaire Universel de la France, Ancienne & Moderne, & de Nouvelle France, 3 tom. 2l 2s ——— *ib.* 1726
394 Dictionnaire Historiq. & Critiq. par M. Bayle, corrigee & augmentee par l'Auteur, 3 tom. *grande papier, bien relie,* 1l 11s 6d *Rott.* 1702
395 Le Grand Dictionnaire Historiq. ou le Melange Curieux de l'Histoire Sacrée & Profane, par Moreri, 8 tom. *bien relie,* 6l 6s *Amst.* 1740
396 Le meme, 8 tom. *nouv. & bien relie,* 7l 7s — *ib.* 1740
397 *Le meme Livre, avec le Supplement,* 8 tom. *bien relie,* 5l 5s *Par.* 1732
398 Dictionnaire de la Langue Francoise, Ancienne & Moderne, par Richelet, 3 tom. *mellieure edit. nouv. & fort bien relie,* 2l 15s *Lyon* 1759
399 *Dictionnaire Fr. & Lat. de Trevoux,* 5 tom. *fort bien relie,* 3l 13s 6d *Par.* 1732
400 Dictionnaire Etymologique de la Langue Francoise, par Menage, 2 tom. *nouv. & fort bien relie,* 2l 8s ——— *ib.* 1750
401 Le meme, 2 tom. *nouv. & proprement relie en russiq.* 3l *ib.* 1750
402 Dictionnaire Oeconomique, par Chomel, *avec fig.* 4 tom. *nouv. & fort bien relie,* 4l ——— ——— *ib.* 1740
403 Bibliotheque Orientale, ou Dictionnaire Universel, par M. Herbelot, 2l 2s ——— ——— *ib.* 1697
404 Vocabulario della Crusca, 4 tom. *carta grandu,* 1l 11s 6d *Firen.* 1691
405 Il medessimo, 6 tom. *in boards, wants a leaf, the best edition,* 4l 4s *Firenz.* 1729
406 Il medessimo, 6 tom. 5l 5s ——— *Napoli* 1746

Libri

Libri Classici, Gr. & Lat. FOLIO.

407 Ciceronis Opera omnia, a Grutero, *exemp. pulch. elegant. comp. in corio turcico, foliis deaurat.* 2 tom. 1l 1s *Hamb.* 1618

408 Ciceronis Opera, 2 tom. *typis elegant. exemp. pulch. & elegant. compact.* 1l 16s ——— *Paris. apud Car. Steph.* 1555

409 Horatius, *exemp. pulch. corio turcico, foliis deaur.* 1l 5s *Par. typis Regiæ* 1642

410 Virgilius, *typis elegant.* 1l 5s ——— *ib. apud ib.* 1641

411 Terentius, *nit. compact.* 12s ——— *ib. apud ib.* 1642

412 Idem, *exemp. pulch.* 15s ——— *ib. apud ib.* 1642

413 Virgilius, a Pontano, *exempl. pulch. eleg. comp. fol. marmor.* 15s *Lugd.* 1604

414 Virgilius, Comment. Guellii, *exemp. pulch. eleg. comp. in corio russic. fol. marmor.* 1l 1s ——— ——— *Antv.* 1575

415 Virgilius, Comment. Servii, *exemp. pulch. nit. comp.* 18s *Paris apud R. Steph.* 1532

416 Plinii Hist. Naturalis, a Galenio & aliis, *exemp. pulch. eleg. comp. in corio maurit. fol. deaur.* 15s ——— *Genev.* 1582

417 ——————— a Harduino, *ch. max. & splendiss. compact. in corio moroc.* 3 tom. 8l 8s ——— *Par.* 1723

418 Senecæ Opera omnia, Notis & Scholiis Lipsii, 5s *Antv.* 1615

419 Ammianus Marcellinus, a Gronovio, *exemp. pulch. nit. comp. in membr.* 1l 4s ——— ——— *L. Bat.* 1693

420 Quintiliani Orat. & Declamat. Annotat. Mosellani & alior. *nit. comp.* 9s ——— ——— *Par. ap. Vascos.* 1542

421 Idem, Notis Capperonii, *exemp. pulch. nitidiss. comp.* 1l 1s *Par.* 1725

422 J. Cæsaris Comment. a Rosseto, *exemp. pulch. eleg. comp. in corio maurit. fol. deaur.* 7s 6d ——— *Lausan* 1571

423 Livius, a Grynæo & aliis, *exemp. pulch.* 7s 6d *Par. ap. Vascos.* 1552

424 Libanii Sophistæ Epistolæ, Gr. & Lat. a Wolfio, *exemp. pulch. nitid. comp.* 12s ——— ——— *Amst.* 1738

425 Plutarchi Opera omnia, Gr. & Lat. a Cruserio & Xylandro, Notis Maussaci, 2 tom. *macul.* 2l 10s *Par. typis Reg.* 1624

426 Juliani (Imp.) Opera & Cyrilli contra eundem, Libri x. Gr. & Lat. Notis Spanhemii & alior. 2 tom. *nitid. compact. in* 1 vol. 15s *Lips.* 1696

427 Demosthenis & Æschinis Opera, Gr. & Lat. a Wolfio, 7s 6d *Aur. Allob.* 1607

428 Idem, Græcé, *exemp. pulch. & elegant. compact. in corio moroc.* 1l 4s *Par. apud Benenat.* 1573

429 Idem, a Wolfio, cum Scholiis Ulpiani, 2 tom. *exemp. pulch. nit. comp.* 1l 1s ——— ——— *Bas.* 1572

430 Idem, a Wolfio & Scholiis Ulpiani, *exemp. eleg. & nit. comp. in membr.* 2l 12s 6d ——— ——— *Franc.* 1604

431 Dion. Cassius, Gr. & Lat. a Leunclavio, *exempl. pulch.* 12s 6d *Hanov.* 1606

432 Dion. Cassius, Gr. & Lat. a Fabricio, 2 tom. *edit. opt. nov. & nitid. comp.* 3l 10s ——— ——— *Hamb.* 1750

433 Idem, 2 tom. *nov. & eleg. comp. in corio russico,* 4l 4s *ib.* 1750

434 Josephus, Gr. & Lat. a Hudsono, 2 tom. *ch. max. eleg. comp.* 1l 10s *Oxon.* 1720

435 Aris-

435 Ariſtophanes, Gr. & Lat. a Kuſtero, *nov. & eleg. comp. in corio turcico, fol. deaur. & marmor.* 3l 3s ——— *Amſt.* 1710
436 Themiſtii Orationes, Gr. & Lat. Notis Petavii & Harduini, *exempl. pulch.* 9s ——— ——— *Par. typ. Reg.* 1684
437 Homeri Ilias & Odyſſea, Græce, *typis elegant. ch. max. nitid. compact.* 2 tom. 3l 3s ——— ——— *Glaſg.* 1756
438 Idem, 2 tom. *ch. min. elegant. comp.* 2l 2s ——— *ib.* 1756
439 Polybius, Gr. & Lat. a Caſaubono, *exemp. pulch. elegant. comp. in corio ruſſico,* 3l ——— ——— *Par.* 1609
440 Thucydides, Gr. & Lat. a H. Stephano, 7s 6d *ap. ipſum Steph.* 1564
441 Idem, Gr. & Lat. *edit. 2da,* 12s ——— *ap. eund.* 1588
442 Idem, Gr. & Lat. a H. Stephano & Laur. Valla, 10s 6d *Francof. ap. Wechel.* 1594
443 Idem, *exemp. pulch.* 12s ——— *ib. apud ib.* 1594
444 Idem, Gr. & Lat. a Hudſono, *exemp. pulch. nit. comp. in memb.* 1l 4s *Oxon.* 1696
445 Idem, Hudſono, *pulch.* 1l 1s ——— *ib.*
446 Herodotus, Gr. & Lat. ex Interpretat. Laur. Vallæ, cum Adnotationib. T. Galei & Ja. Gronovii & Notis Valckenarii & Weſſelingii, *ſutus,* 2l 5s ——— ——— *Amſt.* 1763
447 Herodotus, Gr. & Lat. a H. Stephano, 14s *Excud. H. Steph.* 1570
448 ——— Gr. & Lat. a Laur. Valla & H. Stephano, *exempl. pulch.* 10s 6d ——— ——— *Francoſ.* 1608
449 Diodorus Siculus, Græce, *nit. comp.* 12s *ap. H. Steph.* 1559
450 Stobæi Sententiæ ex Theſauris Græcorum Delectæ, Gr. & Lat. *edit. opt.* 15s ——— ——— *Aur. Allob.* 1609
451 Idem, *paulul. maculat.* 9s ——— ——— *ib.* 1609
452 Platonis Opera, Gr. & Lat. a Ficino, 18s ——— *Lugd.* 1590
453 Idem, Græce, *exemp. pulch. nit. comp.* 10s 6d *Baſ.* 1556
454 Idem, cum Comment. Procli, Græce, 2 tom. *nitid. compact.* 1l 1s *ibid.* 1534
455 Plotini Opera omnia, Gr. & Lat. a Ficino, *ch. max.* 8s *ib.* 1580
456 Brodæi & H. Stephani Epigrammata, cum Annot. Brodæi, 10s 6d *Francſ.* 1600
457 Luciani, Philoſtrati & Calleſtrati Opera, Græce, 15s *Ven. ap. Ald.* 1503
458 Lucianus, Græce, cum Notis plurimis MSS. Joan. Doneti & T. Pellet, M. D. 1l 1s ——— *Venet. apud Ald.* 1503
459 Proclus in Platonis Theologiam, Gr. & Lat. a Æm. & Fr. Portii, 5s *Hamb.* 1618
460 Thucydides & alior. cum Scholiis Græce, 9s *Baſ.* 1540
461 Jo. Grammaticus in Ariſtotelem de Generatione, Græce, 9s *Ven. apud Ald.* 1527
462 Orationes Rhetorum Græcorum, Græce, 15s *ib. apud ib.* 1513
463 Olympeodorus in Meteora Ariſtotelis, Græce, 5s *Ven.* 1551
464 Demoſthenis Orationes, cum Vita ſuo, per Libanum & Plutarch. Græce, *exemp. pulch.* 12s ——— *Ven. apud Ald.* 1504
465 Jo. Grammaticus in Poſteriora Reſolutor. Ariſtotelis, Græce, 7s 6d *ib. apud ib.* 1503

Divinity

Divinity and Ecclesiastical History. FOLIO.

466 BIBLE and Apocrypha, *fine paper*, 2 vol. *new and very neatly bound*, 3l 3s — — *Camb.* 1762
467 Bible and Apocrypha, *fine prints, very fair, bound in rough calf*, *Cambridge, by Hayes* 1674
468 Bible, Common Prayer and Apocrypha, *gilt leaves*, 2l 12s 6d *Cambridge, by Buck and Daniel* 1638
469 Common Prayer, with the Form of Consecrating Bishops, Priests and Deacons, *large paper, very fair*, 12s — 1754
470 Stackhouse's History of the Bible, *with a great number of cuts*, 2 vol. 1l 15s — — — 1750
471 Patrick, Lowth and Whitby on the Old and New Testament, 6 vol. 4l 14s 6d — — — 1727, &c.
472 Patrick, Lowth and Whitby, 6 vol. *very fair*, 5l 5s 1738, &c.
473 Patrick, Lowth and Whitby, with Arnold on the Apocrypha, 7 vol. *new and neat*, 6l — — 1738, &c.
474 Patrick's Comment. on the Historical Books of the Old Testament, 2 vol. *very fair*, 1l 1s — — 1727
475 Lowth's Comment. on the Prophets, 1l 5s — 1739
476 Arnold's Comment. of the Apocrypha, &c. 3 Parts, *elegantly bound*, 18s — — — 1752
477 Whitby on the New Test. 2 vol. *very fair*, 1l 5s 1727
478 The same, *very neat, last edition*, 2 vol. 1l 16s — 1760
479 Hammond's Paraphrase and Annotations on the New Testament, 7s — — — 1671
480 The same, *very fair*, 9s — — 1689
481 The learned Dr. Pocock's Theological Works, published by Twells, 2 vol. with his Life and Writings, 14s — 1740
482 Bishop Gibson's Codex Juris Ecclesiastici Anglicani, 2d Edition, with Improvements and great Additions by the Author, 2 vol. *new and neatly bound*, 3l 15s — — 1761
483 Bishop Fleetwood's Works, *new and very neat*, 18s — 1737
484 The Works of the Author of the Whole Duty of Man, *large print*, 8s — — — 1703
485 Hooker's Ecclesiastical Politie, and his other Works, with his Life, by Walton, 5s — — 1682
486 Dr. Fiddes's Sermons, *very fair*, 6s — 1720
487 Warner's Ecclesiastical History of England, 2 vol. *new, in boards*, 1l 8s — — — 1759
488 Bishop Blackall's Sermons, with his Life, by Archbishop Dawes, 2 vol. *in boards*, 9s — — 1723
489 The same, 2 vol. *fair and neat*, 14s — 1723
490 Tillotson's Sermons, 3 vol. *fair*, 1l 7s — 1720
491 The same, with his Life, by Dr. Birch, 3 vol. *neat*, 2l 5s 1752
492 The same, with his Life, by Birch, 3 vol. *very neat*, 2l 7s 1752
493 Stackhouse's Compleat Body of Divinity, *very fair, and elegantly bound and gilt leaves*, 1l 10s — — 1755
494 Critical and Practical Exposition of the Pentateuch, with Notes Theological, Moral, Philosophical, Critical and Historical, *very fair*, 8s — — — 1748

495 New-

495 Newcourt's Ecclesiastical History of the Diocese of London, *with cuts, large paper, very neat,* 1l 5s —— 1708
496 The same, *very neat,* 2 vol. *small paper,* 15s —— 1708
497 Jos. Mede's Works, *fair,* 10s 6d —— 1672
498 History of the Reformation and other Ecclesiastical Transactions in and about the Low Countries, from the viiith Century to the Synod of Dort, in which all the Revolutions that happened in Church and State, on Account of the Divisions between the Protestants and Papists, the Arminians and Calvinists, are fairly and fully represented, by Ger. Brandt, translated from the Low Dutch, 4 vol. *very fair,* 1l 4s —— —— 1720
499 Cave's Lives of the Fathers, *with cuts, best edit. very fair,* 10s 6d 1716
500 Prideaux's Connection, 2 vol. 12s —— 1717
501 St. Cyprian's Works, with Notes, by Marshal, 7s 6d 1717
502 Tillemont's Ecclesiastical Memoirs, 2 vol. *very fair,* 15s 1731
503 Chillingworth's Works, *best edition,* 10s 6d —— 1742
504 The same, *new and very neatly bound,* 14s — 1742
505 Causin's Holy Court, *with cuts, best edit.* 9s —— 1664
506 Daubuz's Comment. on the Revelations, *very fair,* 9s 1720
507 Cowel's Account of the Greek Church, *very fair,* 5s 1722
508 Echard's Ecclesiast. Hist. of the three first Centuries of Christianity, *very fair,* 5s —— —— 1719
509 Millar's History of the Church under the Old Testament, from the Creation of the World, *very fair,* 10s 6d —— 1730
510 Scot's Christian Life, with useful Index, *very fair and neat,* 12s 1729
511 Book of Homilies, appointed to be read in Churches, *fair,* 5s 1713
512 Father Paul's Hist. of the Council of Trent, by Brent, *in morocco, gilt leaves,* 7s 6d —— —— 1640
513 The same, with the History of the Inquisition, and Life of Father Paul, *best edition,* 7s 6d —— —— 1676
514 Bishop Burnet's Hist. of the Reformation, 3 vol. *very fair,* 2l 7s 1715
515 The same, 3 vol. *very fair, elegantly bound in russia, marble leaves,* 3l 15s —— —— —— 1679, &c.
516 Bishop Beveridge's Works, 2 vol. *new and neat,* 1l 15s 1729
517 Barrow's Works, 3 vol. in 2. *very fair,* 18s —— 1700
518 Bishop Hall's Works, *fair,* 6s —— 1647
519 —— Explication of hard Texts of the Old and New Testament, 5s —— —— 1633
520 Jackson's Works, with his Life, 3 vol. *very fair,* 18s 1673
521 Bishop Stillingfleet's Works, with his Life, 6 vol. *with MSS. notes on the margin, fairly wrote,* 5l —— 1710
522 —— Sermons, *very fair,* 7s 6d
523 —— Antiquities of the British Churches, 3s — 1685
524 Bishop Pearson on the Creed, *with the indexes, very fair,* 6s 1723
525 The same, *best edition, new and very neat,* 10s 6d — 1741
526 Knox's History of the Reformation of the Church of Scotland, *large paper, very fair,* 6s —— —— 1644
527 St. Augustine of the Citie of God, *fair,* 3s 6d —— 1620
528 The same, 3s —— —— 1620
529 Pilkington's Evangelical History and Harmony, *in boards,* 5s 1747
530 Du Pin's History of Ecclesiastical Writers 16 Centuries, in 7 vol. 1l 1s —— —— —— 1696, &c.
531 The same, 17 Centuries, *compleat and very neat,* 8 vol. 1l 16s 1696, &c.

532 Du

532 Du Pin's History of the Canon of the Old and New Testament, 2 vol. 6s — — — 1699
533 The Byble in Englyshe, *black letter,* 10s 6d — 1540
534 Bishop Burnet's Exposition of the XXXIX Articles, 4s 1700
535 The same, 6s — — — 1737
536 The same, *new and elegantly bound,* 10s 6d — 1737
537 Supplycacion of Soulys, made by Sir Thomas More 1531—Confutacyon of Tindale's Answere, made by Sir Thomas More, *black letter, very fair* 1532, 7s 6d
538 Elwood's Sacred History of the New Testament, *very fair,* 6s 1709
539 Langbaine's Review of the Councel of Trent, 2s — 1638

Statute, Civil, Common and Ecclesiastical Law. FOLIO.

540 STatutes at large from Magna Charta to the 14th Geo. II. by Hawkins, 7 vol. *very fair and neat,* 4l 4s — 1735, &c.
541 Statutes at large, by Cay, 6 vol. to 1757, *very neatly bound, gilt, &c.* 9l 9s — — 1758
542 Statutes at large, 3 Geo. III. *fine paper, sewed,* 12s
543 Cay's Abridgment of the Statutes, 2 vol. 12s — 1739
544 The same, *best edition, new,* 2 vol. 2l 12s 6d — 1762
545 Nelson's Abridgment of the Common Law, 3 vol. 1l 1s 1725
546 Bacon's New Abridgment of the Law, 4 vol. *neat,* 5l 5s 1762
547 Comyn's Digests of the Laws of England, *new, in boards,* 1l 5s 1762
548 Wood's Institute of the Laws of England, 10s 6d — 1745
549 The same, *8th edition, very neat,* 14s — 1754
550 The same, *last edition, new and neat,* 1l 4s — 1763
551 Cowell's Law Dictionary, *interleaved with fine writing paper,* 5s 1708
552 Watson's Clergymans Law, *best edition,* 14s — 1747
553 The same, *fair and neat,* 15s — 1747
554 Barlow's Justice of Peace, *very fair,* 10s 6d — 1745
555 General Abridgment of Cases in Equity, 5s — 1732
556 The same, *2d edition, fair,* 7s 6d — — 1734
557 The same, *2d edition,* 6s — — 1734
558 The same, *3d edition, stained,* 5s — 1739
559 Cases in Equity in the Time of Lord Talbot, *very fair,* 9s 1741
560 Malory's Quare Impedit, 6s — — 1737
561 The same, *fair,* 7s 6d — — 1737
562 The same, *new,* 9s — — 1737
563 Sir Matthew Hale's History of the Pleas of the Crown, 2 vol. 1l 4s — — — 1736
564 The same, vol. 2. 6s — — 1736
565 Bridgman's Conveyances, 2 vol. 12s — 1710
566 The same, 2 vol. in one, *fair,* 14s — 1725
567 Bird's Modern Conveyancer, *fair,* 15s — 1729
568 Lilly's Practical Conveyancer, 7s 6d — — 1742
569 Cases in Chancery, 7s 6d — — 1707
570 Mills's Rules, Orders and Notices in the Courts of King's Bench and Common Pleas, 6s — — 1742
571 Francis's Maxims of Equity, 5s — — 1728
572 The same, *fair,* 6s — — 1728
573 Fortescue de Laudibus Legum Angliæ, *very fair,* 10s 6d 1741

D 574 Pro-

574 Proceedings on the Quo Warranto, touching the Charter of London, 2s 6d — — — 1690
575 Laws concerning Bankrupts, by Davies, 6s — 1744
576 Nelson's Lex Maneriorum, 4s — — 1726
577 Duke's Law of Charitable Uses, 3s — — 1676
578 Coke upon Littleton, *2d edition*, 6s — 1629
579 The same, *9th edition, very fair*, 8s — — 1684
580 The same, *10th edition, very fair*, 2l 2s — 1719
581 The same, *best edition, with several hundred manuscript references wrote in a very fair hand* — — 1738
582 Coke's Institutes, part 2, 3, 4. in 3 vol. *fair*, 15s 1671
583 Jacob's Common Law Common Placed, *very fair*, 6s 1733
584 Prynne on the 4th Part of Coke's Institute, 4s — 1669
585 Modern Cases in Law and Equity, 15s — 1730
586 Thesaurus Brevium, 3s — — 1687
587 Wingate's Maximes of the Common Law, 3s 6d 1658
588 Shephard's Epitome of the Common and Statute Law, 3s 6d 1656
589 Registrum omnium Brevium Judic. 3s — 1531
590 Reports, by Dyer, *best edition, large paper*, 18s — 1688
591 ——— Dyer, 4s — — 1672
592 ——— Plowden, 10s 6d — — 1684
593 ——— Croke, 3 vol. 1l 11s 6d — 1669
594 ——— Sir Thomas Raymond, 3s — 1696
595 ——— The same, *very fair and neat*, 12s — 1743
596 ——— Peere Williams, 3 vol. *very fair*, 3l 3s — 1740
597 ——— The same, 3 vol. *best edit. neat*, 4l 4s — 1746
598 ——— Modern, 7 vol. 1l 11s 6d — 1720, &c.
599 ——— The same, 7 vol. 1l 1s — — 1682
600 ——— The same, 7 vol. *very fair*, 2l 2s — 1720, &c.
601 ——— The same, 7 vol. *best edition*, by Pickering, *new*
602 ——— Vernon, 2 vol. 1l 7s — 1726
603 ——— The same, *very fair*, 2 vol. 1l 10s — 1726
604 ——— Ventres, 5s — — 1701
605 ——— Comyns, *very fair*, 1l — 1744
606 ——— Saunders, 2 vol. in one, 3s 6d — 1686
607 ——— The same, 2 vol. in one, *best edition*, 1l 1s 1722
608 ——— Holt, published by Farresley, 9s — 1738
609 ——— Carthew, 6s — — 1728
610 ——— Lutwych, 2 vol. 1l 1s — 1704
611 ——— The same, *very fair*, 2 vol. 1l 4s — 1704
612 ——— The same, by Nelson, 4s — 1718
613 ——— Sir W. Jones, 9s — 1675
614 ——— The same, *with manuscript references*, 12s — 1675
615 ——— Sir T. Jones, *fair*, 10s 6d — 1729
616 ——— Rolle, 2 vol. 5s — — 1675
617 ——— The same, 2 vol. *very fair*, 8s — 1675
618 ——— Leonard, 4 vol. in 2. 15s — 1658
620 ——— The same, *best edition, very fair*, 1l 15s 1687
621 ——— Shower, 2 vol. *very fair*, 1l 15s — 1708
622 ——— Pollexfen, *fair*, 1l 1s — — 1702
623 ——— Benloe and Dallison, 2s — — 1689
624 ——— Palmer, 4s — — 1688
625 ——— Keilway, 5s — — 1688
626 ——— in Chancery, by Barnardiston, 10s 6d — 1742

627 Salkeld,

627 Reports, by Salkeld, 2 vol. in one, *beſt edition, neat,* 1l 5s 1742

628 ——— Levinz, 2 vol. 5s ——— 1702

629 ——— Hobart, 2s 6d ——— 1671

630 ——— The ſame, *beſt edition,* 10s ——— 1724

631 ——— Yelverton, *beſt edition, new,* 7s 6d ——— 1735

632 ——— Vaughan, *beſt edition, fair,* 1l 1s ——— 1706

633 ——— The ſame, *1ſt edition,* 12s ——— 1677

634 ——— Carter, 4s ——— 1688

635 ——— Littleton, 2s 6d ——— 1683

636 ——— Style, 10s 6d ——— 1658

637 ——— The ſame, *very fair,* 12s ——— 1658

638 ——— Anderſon, 2 vol. 7s ——— 1664

639 ——— The ſame, 2 vol. in one, *fair,* 9s ——— 1664

640 ——— Saviſe, 2s 6d ——— 1675

641 ——— The ſame, *large paper,* 3s ——— 1675

642 ——— Popham, 2s 6d ——— 1656

643 ——— The ſame, *beſt edition, fair,* 5s ——— 1682

644 ——— Hutton, 2s ——— 1656

645 ——— The ſame, *beſt edition,* 4s ——— 1682

646 ——— Davis, 3s 6d ——— 1674

647 ——— Kelyng, 3s 6d ——— 1708

648 ——— Aleyne, 4s ——— 1688

649 ——— Hetley, 3s ——— 1657

650 ——— Ley, 3s ——— 1659

651 ——— Bridgman, 5s ——— 1659

652 ——— Noy, 4s ——— 1656

653 ——— Owen, 3s ——— 1656

654 ——— Winch, 5s ——— 1657

655 ——— Lane, 5s ——— 1657

656 ——— Latch, 2s 6d ——— 1661

657 ——— in the King's Bench and Common Pleas, during the Reigns of King James and King Charles I. *MSS. fairly wrote,* 7s 6d

658 General Index to the Books of Reports, 4s ——— 1726

659 Precedents in Chancery, 12s ——— 1733

660 Shower's Caſes in Parliament on Writs of Error, 2s 1698

661 Sheppard's Law of Common Aſſurances, 4s ——— 1669

662 Index Vectigalium, or an Abbreviated Collection of Laws of Tonnage and Poundage, 2s ——— 1670

663 Laws of Bermuda, *very neat,* 4s ——— 1719

664 Murray's Laws of Scotland, 5s ——— 1681

665 The ſame, *very fair,* 7s ——— 1681

666 Macdowell's Inſtitute of the Laws of Scotland, *large paper, neatly bound, marble leaves,* 3 vol. 4l 14s 6d ——— 1751

667 Stair's Inſtitute of the Laws of Scotland, *large paper, new and neat,* 2l 15s ——— 1759

668 The ſame, *ſmall paper,* 1l 16s ——— 1759

669 Deciſions of the Engliſh Judges during the Uſurpations, from 1655 to the Reſtoration, *new,* 9s ——— 1762

670 Deciſions of the Court of Seſſions, from 1752 to 1756 incluſive, *new,* 9s ——— 1760

671 Dalrymple's Deciſions of the Court of Seſſions, from 1698 to 1718, *new,* 9s ——— 1758

672 Wilkins Leges Anglo-Saxonicæ Eccleſiaſt. & Civiles, 15s *Lond.* 1731

673 Ærodii Pandectæ, recognitæ a Oldenburgero, 5s *Genev.* 1677

D 2 674 Cragii

674 Cragii Jus Feudale, *nov. & nit. comp.* 18s — *Edinb.* 1732
675 Idem, *nov. & elegant. comp.* 1l — *ib.* 1732
676 Bracton de Legibus 1569—Finch's Law, *both elegant copies, and neatly bound in one vol.* — — 1613

Livres Francois, Italien & Espagnole. FOLIO.

677 HISTOIRE de France, par le P. Daniel, 3 tom. 1l 5s *Par.* 1713
678 Le meme, 3 tom. *bien relie,* 1l 10s — *ib.* 1713
679 Les Hommes Illustres qui ont paru en France, par Perrault, *avec leurs effigies,* 2 tom. in 1 vol. 1l 11s 6d
680 L'Etat Militaire de l'Empire Ottoman, par le Comte de Marsigli, Fr. & Ital. *avec fig.* 12s — — *Haye* 1732
681 Histoire de Polybe, trad. par Du Ryer, *exemp. elegant. grand papier, fort bien relie en maroq. dore sur les tranches,* 15s *Par.* 1655
682 Appian Alexandr. des Guerres des Romaines, trad. par Odet, *grand papier, fort bien relie en maroq. dore sur les tranches,* 15s *ib.* 1660
683 Histoire des Traitez de Paix & autres Negociations du xvii Siecle, 2 tom. *bien relie,* 1l 5s — *Amst.* 1725
684 ——— d'Angleterre, d'Ecosse & d'Irelande, par M. Larrey, *avec des portraits des Rois, bel. exemp.* 4 tom. 1l 7s *Roterd.* 1697
685 L'Etat de la France, par le Comte de Boulainvilliers, avec l'Histoire des Anciens Parlemens de France, par le meme, 3 tom. *demi relie,* 1l 7s — — *Lond.* 1727
686 Le meme, 3 tom. *bien relie,* 1l 16s — *ib.* 1727
687 Memoires Oeconomique de Henri le Grand, par le Duc de Sully, 2 tom. *bel. exemp.* 14s — *Amst. & Par.* 1664
688 Le meme, en 4 vol. *fort bien relie en maroq. dore sur les tranches. The second Volume is damaged at the beginning,* 1l 16s *Amst. & Par.* 1644
689 Ambassade du Comte de Bethune, Vers l'Empereur Ferdinandii, 6s *Par.* 1667
690 Histoire des Troubles de la Grand Bretagne, par M. Salmonet, 6s *ib.* 1661
691 Negociations de le President Jeannin, *avec le portrait de l'auteur,* 6s — — — *ib.* 1656
692 Histoire de la Navigation aux Indes Orientales, par les Hollandois, *avec fig.* 5s — — *Amst.* 1609
693 Histoire Militaire de Flandre, depuis 1690 jusq; 1694, par le Chev. de Beauvain, *avec un grand nombre des fig.* 2 tom. *demi relie,* 2l 12s 6d — — *Par.* 1755
694 L'Art de la Guerre, par Principes & par Regles, de M. Puysegur, *avec un grand nombre des fig. le meilleure edit.* 2 tom. en 1 vol. 2l 10s *Par.* 1748
695 Le meme, 2 tom. *bel. exemplaire,* 3l — *ib.* 1748
696 Metamorphoses d'Ovide, en Lat. & en Francois, par Banier, *avec un grand nombre des fig. par Picart, fort bien relie,* 2 tom. en 1 vol. 2l 12s 6d — — *Amst.* 1732
697 Ecole de Cavalerie, par M. De la Guerinier, *avec fig. nouv. & fort bien relie, grand papier,* 1l 16s — *ib.* 1751
698 Description du Menage Moderne, par le Baron d'Eisenberg, *avec fig. par Picart, bel. exemp. fort bien relie,* 12s *Par.* 1727

699 Les

699 Les Forces de l'Europe, l'Asie, l'Afrique & l'Amerique, par M. De la Force, 12 tom. *relie en 1 vol. avec un grand nombre des fig.* 3l 3s *Amst. chez P. Mortier*

700 Description des Arts & Metiers, par l'Acad. Roy. des Sciences, *avec fig.* 4 tom. *cousu,* 1l 1s —— *Par.* 1761

701 Histoire de la Vie du Connestable de Lisdiguieres, 3s *ib.* 1638

702 Medailles de Louis XIV. par Menestrier, 5s — *ib.* 1691

703 Vie de Mich. de Ruiter, par Ger. Brandt, *avec grand nomb. des fig. bien relie,* 12s —— —— *Amst.* 1698

704 Les Vies de Plutarque, trad. par M. Amyot, 2 tom. *bel. exemp. fort bien relie en marcq. dore sur les tranches,* 1l 10s *Par.* 1655

705 Memoires de Philip de Comines, *fort bien relie en marôq. dore sur les tranches,* 1l 16s —— —— *Par.* 1649

706 Histoire d'Herodote, trad. par Du Ryer, *bel. exemp. fort bien relie en marcq. dore sur les tranches,* 10s 6d —— *ib.* 1658

707 La Sainte Bible, avec l'Apocryphe, *fort bien relie,* 10s 6d *Amst.* 1702

708 Ambassade de la Comp. Orient. des Provinces Unies, Vers l'Empereur de la Chine, par M. Nieuhof, *avec un grand nombre des fig.* 7s 6d *Leide* 1665

709 Histoire du Concile de Trente, par Le P. Paolo, trad. par Le Courayer, avec Notes, 2 tom. *fort bien relie,* 1l 1s — *Lond.* 1736

710 Histoire des Eglises Evangeliq. de Vallees de Piemont, par M. Leger, *avec fig.* 6s —— —— *Leide* 1669

711 Oeuvres de Fr. de la Mothe le Vayer, 2 tom. *bel. exemp. fort bien relie en maroq. dore sur les tranches,* 1l 11s 6d —— *Par.* 1662

712 Comment. du Droit Civil au Pays de Normandie, par Tarrien, *bel. exemp. dore sur les tranches,* 7s 6d —— *Rouen* 1654

713 Lettres du Card. D'Ossat, *fort bien relie en maroq. dore sur les tranches,* 9s —— —— —— *Par.* 1624

714 *Le Parnasse Francois, par M. Tillet, avec portraits, fort bien relie,* 18s *ib.* 1732

715 Chroniques d'Enguerran de Monstrelet, 2 tom. en 1 vol. 12s *Par.* 1572

716 Histoire du Mareschal de Guebriant, par M. Laboureur, 5s *ib.* 1657

717 —— des Juifs, par Joseph, trad. par Dandilly, *avec fig.* 6s *Amst.* 1681

718 —— Universelle du Sieur D'Aubigne, 6s —— *Maille* 1616

719 Le meme, 3 tom. *bel. exemp. fort bien relie,* 15s *ib.* 1616

720 Discours de la Religion & Castramentations des anciens Romains, par M. du Choul, *avec d'un grand nombre des medailles, grand papier, fort bien relie en marcq. dore sur les tranches,* 12s 6d *Lyon* 1556

721 Hist. des Anciens Parlements de France, par Boulainvilliers, *demi relie,* 5s —— —— *Londr.* 1737

722 Chronique de Jean Frossart, 3 tom. *demi relie,* 12s 6d *Par.* 1530

723 Davilla Historia della Guerra Civili di Francia, *belliss. essemp.* 2 vol. 2l 5s —— —— *Venet.* 1733

724 Il medessimo, 2 tom. *bene ligato,* 2l 10s — *ib.* 1733

725 *Il medessimo, carta granda, 2 tom. in 1 vol. bound in morocco and gilt leaves,* 4l 14s 6d — *Parigi nella Stampa Reale*

726 Il medessimo, *belliss. essemp.* 14s —— 1646

727 Catalogo de gli Antichi Monumenti Dissotterrati della Discoperta Citta di Ercolano, da M. Ott. Ant. Bayarde, *carta granda, new, very neatly bound, marble leaves,* 2l 2s *Napoli nella Reg. Stamperia* 1755

728 Anti-

728 Antichita Siciliane Spiegate del Padr. Giuf. Mar. Pancrazi, *con fig. carta granda,* 2 tom. in one vol. *elegantly bound in ruſſia leather, marble leaves,* 3l 3s ——— *Napoli* 1751
729 Opere del Card. Bembo, 4 vol. *carta granda,* 2l 2s *Venez.* 1729
730 Orlando Furioſo di Arioſto, *con fig. curioſ. & annotaz. de piu celebri autori,* 1l 1s —— ——— *ib.* 1730
731 Opere del Cardinale Bentivoglio, 15s —— *Parig.* 1648
732 Dante, con l'Eſpoſitione di C. Landeno & di Al. Velutello, *bene ligato,* 1l 1s ——— ——— *Venez.* 1564
733 L'Antichita d'Aquileia Profane e Sacra, da Bertoli, *con fig.* 6s *Venez.* 1739
734 L'Antiche Siracuſe, da Bonanni e Colonna, con le Dichiarazioni della Pianta dell'Antiche da Vinc. Mirabella, *con fig.* 2 tom. 10s *Palerm.* 1717
735 La Gieruſalemme di Taſſo, Figurata da Bern. Caſtello, con le Annotat. Scipio Gentili e di Giul. Guſtavini, *belliſſ. eſſemp.* 12s 6d *Gen.* 1617
736 Il medeſſimo, *in turkey leather, gilt leaves,* 18s *Genoua* 1617
737 Biblia in Lingua Italiana, da Mat. D'Erberg, *very fair and gilt leaves,* 15s ——— ——— *Colog.* 1712
738 Ola-Magno Hiſtoria Gotho, *wants the title,* 5s *Ven.* 1565

Books of Prints and Medals. FOLIO.

739 BONNANNI Numiſmata Pontificum Romanor. & Hiſt. Templi Vaticani, *cum multis figuris, chart. max.* 3 tom. *nit. comp. in memb.* 3l 3s ——— ——— *Roma*
740 Grand Cabinet Romain, avec les Explications de M. De la Chauſe, *avec fig.* 7s 6d ——— —— *Amſt.* 1706
741 Antiquitates Sacræ & Civiles Romanor. Explicatæ, cum Tab. Æneis, Lat. & Fr. *nit. comp.* 9s ——— *H. Com.* 1726
742 Liebe Gotha Numaria, ſiſtens Theſauri Fridericiani Numiſmata Antiq. *cum fig. nov. & nit. comp.* 1l 1s —— *Amſt.* 1730
743 Vaillant Numiſmata Ærea Imperat. *cum fig. ch. max. exemp. pulch. & nit. comp.* 1l 5s ——— —— *Par.* 1688
744 Cauſei Romanorum Muſeum, *cum multis fig.* 2 tom. *edit. opt. ſemi-comp.* 1l 7s ——— —— *Rom.* 1746
745 Idem, 2 tom. *nit. compact.* 1l 15s ——— *ibid.* 1746
746 Muſelli Numiſmata Antiqua, 3 tom. *exemp. pulch. nit. comp. in membr.* 3l 3s ——— ——— *Veronæ* 1751
747 Idem, 3 tom. *nit. compact.* 3l 3s ——— *ib.* 1751
748 Patini Numiſmata Imperat. Romanor. *cum fig.* 12s *Par.* 1697
749 Vita, Paſſio & Reſurrectio J. Chriſti, expreſſa variis Iconibus a Collart, 6s
750 Imagines Vett. Illuſtr. Philoſophor. Poetar. Rhetorum & Oratorum, a Petr. Bellorio, *ſemi-comp.* 18s ——— *Romæ* 1685
751 Muſeum Odeſcalcum, a Bartollo, 2 tom. *cum fig. ſutus,* 15s *Rom.* 1747
752 Vaillant Numiſmata Græca, *exemp. pulch.* 10s 6d *Amſt.* 1700
753 Vaillant Hiſt. Ptolemæorum Regum Ægypti, *cum medaillis,* 10s 6d *Amſt.* 1701
754 Agoſtino Dialoghi interno alle Medaglie, *ligat. in cor. turc. fogl. inornato,* 10s 6d —— — *Rom.* 1592

755 Eve-

755 Evelyn's Numismata, or Discourse on Medals, *with cuts, very neat and gilt leaves,* 10s 6d ——— — 1697
756 *Museum Florentinum,* 10 tom. *exemp. elegant. & elegant. comp. in corio russico,* 40l ——— — *Florent.* 1731, &c.
757 Cabinet de Bibliotheque de S. Genevieve, par Molinet, *avec des grand nombre des fig.* 1l 4s ——— *Par.* 1692
758 *Antiquite Expliquee, par Montfaucon, avec le Supplement, grand papier,* 15 tom. 15l 15s ——— ——— *ib.* 1722
759 Le meme, *le premiere impression,* 15 tom. *grand papier, fort bien relie,* 20l ——— ——— *Par.* 1719
760 *Medailles sur les Principaux Evenements du Regne de Louis le Grand, avec des Explications Historiq. le premier impression, grand papier, eleg. relie en maroq. doree sur les tranches,* 3l 3s ——— *Par.* 1702
761 Ninety-four Prints and Maps of the History of the Old and New Testament, *neatly engraved,* 1l 1s
762 Loggan's Cantabrigia Illustrata, *in boards,* 10s 6d *Cantab.*
763 Les Proportions du Corps Humain, Mesurees sur les plus belles Figures de l'Antiquite, par Audran, 9s ——— *Par.* 1693
764 Histoire Metallique de Pays Bas, par Van Loon, *avec grand nombre des fig.* 5 tom. *tres elegant. relie,* 3l 3s ——— *Haye* 1732
765 Principes du Dessein, par Lairesse, *avec grand nombre des fig. bien relie,* 18s ——— ——— *Amst.* 1729
766 Histoire Metalliq. de Guillaume III. Roy d'Angleterre, par Chevalier, *avec fig.* 6s ——— ——— *ib.* 1692
767 Vestigi dell'Antichita di Roma, da Stef. du Perac, *con fig.* 10s 6d *Rom.* 1621
768 Perrier's Statues, 18s ——— *Romæ* 1653
769 Jos. Martinii Theatrum Basilicæ Pisanæ, *cum fig.* 9s *Romæ* 1705
770 Fabrettus de Columna Trajana Syntagma, *cum fig.* 4s *ib.* 1683
771 Panvinii Marliani, &c. Antiquitat. Romæ, *cum multis figuris par* De Bry, 4 tom. *pulch.* 1l 7s ——— *Franc.* 1607
772 Idem Liber, 4 tom. 1l 4s ——— *ib.* 1607
773 Jac. Biaei Numismat. Imperat. Roman. Aur. Argent. & Ærea, *cum fig.* 6s ——— ——— *Ant.* 1617
774 Goltzii Opera omnia, *cum multis fig. edit. opt.* 5 tom. *elegant. compact.* 4l 14s 6d ——— — *Brug.* 1557, &c.

Libri Theologici & Historici Ecclesiast. Gr. & Lat. FOLIO.

775 BIBLIA Hebraica & Novum Test. Gr. cum Lat. Interpretatione Interlineari Ariæ Montani, 1l 1s ——— *Antv.* 1571
776 Idem, *exemp. pulch. nit. comp.* 1l 5s *Antv. ap. Plant.* 1584
777 Idem, *exemp. elegant. lineis rubr. fol. deaur. absq; titulis,* 15s *Antv. ap. Plant.*
778 Vetus Test. juxta LXX Interpretes, cura J. Grabe, 2 tom. *exemp. pulch.* 1l 7s ——— ——— *Oxon.* 1707
779 Idem, *exemp. pulch. & elegant. comp. in cor. ruff.* 2l *ib.* 1707
780 Biblia Sacra, Lat. Vulg. Sexti v. cum Sacra Chronolog. *exemp. pulch.* 9s ——— ——— *Par.* 1662
781 Biblia Sacro-Sancta, juxta Vulg. Edit. cum Scholiis a Isidoro Clario, *exemp. pulch. nit. comp. in corio turc. fol. deaur. libr. rariss.* 1l 16s *Venet. ap. Junt.* 1557

782 N.

782 N. Test. Gr. ex edit. R. Stephani, *pulch. exemp.* 10s 6d · *Franc.* 1601
783 Idem, Gr. cum Scholiis J. Gregorii, *ch. max. exemp. pulch.* 7s 6d *Oxon.* 1703
784 Idem, Gr. a Millio & Kustero, *exemp. pulch.* 14s *Lips.* 1723
785 Idem, Gr. a Millio & Kustero, *nit. comp.* 15s *ibid.* 1723
786 Calasii Concordantiæ Sacror. Biblicor. Hebraicor. 4 tom. 5l 5s *Rom.* 1621
787 Schmidii Concordantiæ Nov. Test. Gr. *exemp. pulch.* 14s *Goth.* 1717
788 Tossani Lexicon Concordantiæ Biblicum Vet. & Nov. Test. *exemp. pulch.* 5s —— ——— *Francf.* 1687
789 Vitringa in Jesaiam, 2 tom. *exemp. pulch. nit. comp. in membr.* 4l *Leovard.* 1714
790 Idem, *exemp. pulch. eleg. comp. in membr.* 2 tom. 4l 4s *ib.* 1714
791 Hier. Pradi & Jo. Bapt. Villalpandi Explanationes in Ezechielem, *cum fig. exemp. elegans, lineis rubris, nit. comp. in corio maurit. foliis deaur.* 3 tom. 3l 13s 6d —— — *Rom.* 1596
792 Hieron. Natalis Adnotat. & Meditationes in Evangelia, *cum fig. multis, sculp. a* Hier. Wierx, 1l 1s ——— *Antv.* 1607
793 Jo. Clerici Comment. in Pentateuch. & Libri Hist. Vet. Test. 2 tom. 15s ——— ——— *Amst.* 1696
794 ——— Harmonia Evangelica, *nov. & nit. comp.* 12s *ib.* 1699
795 Alcorani Textus Univers. a Marracio, 2 tom. in 1 vol. *exemp. pulch. nit. comp. in membr.* 1l 10s ——— *Patav.* 1698
796 Critici Sacri, sive Doctiss. Viror. in SS. Biblia Annotat. 9 tom. *Lond.* 1660—Thesaurus Theolog. sive Sylloge Dissertat. Vet. & Nov. Test. 2 tom. 1701—Idem, a Museo Ikenii, 2 tom. *nit. & uniform. comp. in* 13 vol. 7l 7s
797 Cotelerii Patres Apostolici, Gr. & Lat. Notis Clerici, *edit. opt.* 2 tom. 1l 7s ——— ——— *Amst.* 1724
798 *S. Chrysostomi Opera omnia, Gr. & Lat. edit. Benedictini,* 13 tom. *nov. & splendiss. comp.* 10l 10s —— *Par.* 1718
799 Idem, Græce, a H. Savillo, *exemp. pulch.* 8 tom. 1l 10s *Eton.* 1612
800 Spondani Continuatio Annalium Ecclesiast. Baronii, 2 tom. *exemp. pulch. nit. comp.* 12s ——— — *Lugd.* 1678
801 Bedæ Hist. Ecclesiastica, cui access. Leges Anglo-Sax. cura Wheloci, 4s ——— ——— *Cantab.* 1643
802 ——— Eccles. & Opera, cura J. Smith, *exemp. pulch.* 10s 6d *ibid.* 1722
803 Idem, *exemp. pulch. nit. comp.* 12s —— *ibid.* 1722
804 Idem, *nov. & elegant. comp. in corio russic. fol. marmorat.* 1l 1s *ibid.* 1722
805 Eusebii Hist. Ecclesiast. item Preparat. & Demonstrat. Evang. Græce, 2 tom. *exemp. pulch. nit. comp.* 15s *Par. ap. R. Steph.* 1544
806 Forbesii Opera omnia, 2 tom. 8s —— *Amst.* 1703

Medicine, Surgery, Natural History, Husbandry, Gr. Lat. French and English. FOLIO.

807 COWPER's Anatomy of Human Bodies, *with a great number of fine plates, revised by* Albinus, 2l 12s 6d ——— 1737
808 Wiseman's Surgery, 4s ——— —— 1676
809 Snape's Anatomy of a Horse, *with cuts, very fair,* 7s 6d 1683
810 Hope's Compleat Horseman, *with cuts, very fair and neat,* 10s 6d 1717

811 Glau-

811 Glauber's Chymical and Medic. Works, *with cuts*, 9s 1689
812 The fame, *very fair*, 12s ——— ——— 1689
813 The fame, *very fair and neat*, 14s ——— 1689
814 Swammerdam's Book of Nature, or the Hiftory of Infects reduced to diftinct Claffes, confirmed by particular Inftances, *illuftrated with a great number of copper plates, with his Life by Boerhaave, and Notes by Hill, in boards*, 1l 5s ——— ——— 1758
815 The fame, *new and very neat*, 1l 11s 6d ——— 1758
816 Willughby on Birds, *with cuts, very fair*, 1l 11s 6d *Lond.* 1678
817 Gefner's Hiftory of four-footed Beafts, with the Hiftory of Serpents, by Topfell, *neatly bound*, 9s ——— ——— 1607
818 Pliny's Natural Hiftorie of the World, englifhed by Dr. Holland, 10s 6d ——— ——— 1634
819 Pitfield's Natural Hiftory of Animals, *with cuts, very fair*, 5s 1688
820 Grew's Defcription of the Rarities at Grefham College, *with cuts*, 5s ——— ——— ——— 1686
821 The fame, *very fair and neat*, 6s ——— — 1686
822 Grew's Anatomy of Plants, *with cuts*, 6s ——— 1682
823 The fame, *very fair*, 7s 6d ——— — 1682
824 Pettus on Knowing, Judging, Affaying, Fining, Refining and Inlarging the Bodies of Metals, *with cuts, bound in morocco, gilt leaves*, 15s ——— ——— ——— 1683
825 Pettus Fodinæ Regales, or Hiftory, Laws and Places of the chief Mines and Mineral Works in England, 3s 6d ——— 1670
826 Hill's Natural Hiftory of Plants, *with cuts*, 1l 1s — 1751
827 —— Nat. Hift. of Foffils and Plants, *with a great number of cuts*, 2 vol. *very fair and neat*, 2l 12s 6d ——— 1748, &c.
828 —— Britifh Herbal, *with a great number of cuts, very neat*, 1l 5s 1756
829 The fame Book, *neat*, 1l 2s 6d
830 Salmon's Englifh Herbal, *with a great number of cuts*, 15s 1710
831 Parkinfon's Flower-Garden, *with cuts*, 6s ——— 1656
832 —— Herbal, *with cuts, exceeding fair and neat*, 2 vol. 1l 7s 1640
833 The fame, *very fair and very neatly bound in one* vol. 1l 4s 1640
834 Gerarde's Herbal, enlarged by Johnfon, *with cuts, very fair*, 1l 1s ——— ——— 1636
835 Laurence's Syftem of Agriculture and Gardening, *with cuts, very fair*, 12s ——— ——— 1726
836 Quintinye's Complete Gardener, by Evelyn, *with cuts*, 5s 1693
837 Evelyn's Sylva, or Difcourfe on Foreft Trees, with his Pomona, or Appendix on Fruit Trees 1699—Rea's Flora, Ceres and Pomona 1665, 3s
838 Evelyn on Foreft Trees, and his Pomona, *with cuts, very fair*, 15s ——— ——— 1706
839 Mangeti Theatrum Anatom. acceffit Euftachii Tabulæ Anat. *cum fig. multis*, 2 tom. 1l 1s ——— *Genev.* 1717
840 Euftachii Tabulæ Anat. Notis Lancifii, 15s — *Rom.* 1728
841 Boneti Sepulch. Anat. 3 tom. *edit. opt. femi-comp.* 1l 5s *Genev.* 1700
842 Medicæ Artis Principes poft Hippocratem & Galenum, 2 tom. in one vol. ——— ——— *ap. H. Steph.* 1567
843 Freind Opera omnia Medica, *exemp. pulch.* 10s 6d *Lond.* 1733
844 Idem, *exemp. pulch. nit. comp.* 12s ——— *ib.* 1733
845 Vieuffens Neurographia Univerfalis, *cum fig.* 4s *Lugd.* 1685
846 Idem, *exemp. pulch. nit. comp.* 6s ——— *ib.* 1716

E 847 Hoff-

847 Hoffmanni Opera omnia Physico-Medica, 6 tom. *semi-comp. in* 7 vol. 3l 15s — — — *Genev.* 1740
848 Idem, cum Supplementis, 12 tom. *compact. in* 6 vol. 3l 15s *ibid.* 1740
849 Hippocratis Opera cum Œconomia, Gr. & Lat. *edit. opt. macul.* 1l 1s *ibid.* 1657
850 Malphigii Opera omnia, *cum fig.* 14s — *Lond.* 1686
851 Ætii Opera Medica, 7s 6d — — *Bas.* 1542
852 Jo. Raii Hist. Plantarum, 3 tom. 2l 5s — *Lond.* 1686
853 Sennerti Opera omnia Medica, 3 tom. 7s 6d — *Lugd.* 1650
854 Dioscoridis Opera omnia, Gr. & Lat. a Saraceno, 5s 1598
855 Tralliani & Rhazæ Opera Græce, *semi-comp.* 18s *exemp. pulch. ap. R. Steph.*
856 Pauli Æginetæ Opera Græce, 1l 1s — *Bas.* 1538
857 Aretæi Opera, Gr. & Lat. Notis Boerhaave, *semi-comp. macul.* 7s 6d *L. Bat.* 1731
858 Aretæi Opera, Gr. & Lat. Notis Wigan, *semi-comp.* 1l 1s *Oxon.* 1723
859 Idem, a Boerhaave, *ch. max. nov. & eleg. comp.* 1l 1s *L. Bat.* 1735
860 Gualtieri Index Testarum Conchyliorum, *cum tabulis* 110. *nov. & nit. compact.* 3l 3s — — *Florent.* 1742
861 Idem, *semi-comp.* 2l 12s 6d — — *ibid.* 1742
862 Sendelii Historia Succinorum Corpora Aliena involventium, *cum fig. semi-comp.* 18s — — *Lips.* 1742
863 Idem, *nit. comp.* 1l 4s — — *ibid.* 1742
864 Ruysch Theatrum Animalium omnium, *cum 260 tabulis ornatum, exemp. pulch. nit. comp.* 2 tom. 2l 2s — *Amst.* 1718
865 Johnstoni Hist. Natur. Quadruped. Avium & Insector. 3 tom. *nit. comp.* in 1 vol. *cum multis fig.* 1l 4s — *ibid.* 1674
866 Idem, 2 tom. *nit. comp.* 1l 6s — *ib.* 1657
867 Idem, 2 tom. *elegant. comp. fol. marmorat.* 1l 10s *ibid.* 1657
868 Aldrovandi Opera, *cum fig. multis,* 12 tom. *exemp. pulch. nit. & uniform. comp.* 6l 6s — — *Bonon.* 1642, &c.
869 Histoire des Oyseaux, *avec leurs Portraicts,* par Belon, 7s 6d *Par.* 1555

Libri Latini Historici & Miscellanei. FOLIO.

870 CAR. a Sancto Paulo Geographia, Notis Holstenii, *cum mappis chart. max.* 9s — — *Amst.* 1704
871 Chronicon Paschale a Mundo condito ad Heraclii Imper. Annum xx. Gr. & Lat. a Car. Du Fresne, *ch. max. & eleg. comp.* 1l 5s *Par. typ. Reg.* 1688
872 Fr. Godwinus de Præsulibus Angliæ, edid. Gul. Richardson, *ch. max.* 2 tom. 1l 1s — — *Cantab.* 1743
873 Gul. Cavei Hist. Litteraria, 2 tom. *charta max. edit. opt.* 1l 16s *Oxon.* 1740
874 Salengre Thesaurus Antiq. Romanor. *cum fig. ch. max. elegant. comp.* 3 tom. 2l 2s — — *H. Com.* 1716
875 Gruteri Corpus Inscript. *cum multis fig. ch. max.* 4 tom. *splendiss. comp.* 4l 4s — — *Amst.* 1707
876 Lud. Muratori Nov. Thesaurus Vett. Inscriptionum, 4 tom. *cum fig.* 4l 4s — — *Mediol.* 1739, &c.
877 Chorographia Sacra Brabantiæ, a Sandero, *cum fig. multis, nit. comp.* 3 tom. 2l 2s — — *H. Com.* 1727

878 Jo

878 Jo. Bapt. Donii Inscriptiones antiquæ nunc primum Editæ Notis Illustr. & 26 Indicibus, Auctæ ab Ant. Fr. Gorio, *ch. max. exemp. pulch.* 18s ——— ——— *Florent.* 1731
879 Wood Hist. & Antiquit. Univ. Oxoniensis, 9s — *Oxon.* 1674
880 Pocock Inscriptiones Antiq. Gr. & Lat. *nit. comp.* 9s 1752
881 Maittaire Marmora Oxon. cum Appendice & Notis, *exemp. pulch.* 1l 10s ——— ——— *Lond.* 1732
882 Prideaux Marmora Oxon. *cum fig. pulch. exemp.* 7s *Oxon.* 1676
883 *Thuani Hist. sui Temporis, cura T. Carte,* 7 *tom. exemp. elegant. nit. comp.* 6l 6s ——— *Lond. ap. Buckleium* 1733
884 Thesaurus Historiæ Helveticæ, *nov. & nit. comp.* 12s *Tigur.* 1735
885 Bochartus de Animalibus Scripturæ Sacræ, 2 tom. 9s *Lond.* 1663
886 Idem, *exemp. pulch.* 2 tom. 10s 6d ——— *ibid* 1663
887 Bocharti Opera omnia, *cum chart. geogr.* a Leusdeno & Villimandio, 3 tom. in 2 vol. 1l 16s ——— *L. Bat.* 1682
888 Ja. Sponii Miscellanea Eruditæ Antiquit. *cum fig.* 12s *Lugd.* 1685
889 Lazius de Migrationibus Gentium, 5s ——— *Bas.* 1572
890 Dugdale Monasticon Anglicanum, *cum fig. per Hollar,* tom. 1. & 2. 3l 3s ——— ——— *Lond.* 1682
891 Henriq. Hortensi Menologium Regula, Constitut. & Privilegia Ordini. Cistertiensis, 5s ——— ——— *Antw.* 1630
892 Mauroceni Hist. Venet ab 1571 ad 1615, *exemp. elegans.* 7s 6d *Venet.* 1623
893 *Bellendenus de Tribus Luminibus Romanorum, Lib. raris.* 1l 11s 6d *Par.* 1633
894 Chishull Antiquitates Asiaticæ, *nit. comp.* 9s *Lond.* 1728
895 Ludolphi Hist. Æthiopica, *cum comment. & fig. multis,* 2 tom. *exemp. pulch.* 18s ——— ——— *Francf.* 1691
896 Corpus Francicæ Historiæ Veteris & Sinceræ, *nit. comp. fol. deaurat.* 6s *Hanov.* 1613
897 Duglossi Historia Polonica, 2 tom. *pulch. exemp. nit. comp. in membr.* 15s ——— ——— — *Lips.* 1711
898 Sibbaldi Scotia Illustrata, sive Prodromus Hist. Naturalis, *cum fig. ch. max. elegant. comp.* 10s 6d ——— *Edinb.* 1684
899 Scriptores Historiæ Anglicanæ, a Sparke, 6s ——— *Lond.* 1724
900 Camdeni Anglica, Normanica, Hibernica, Cambrica, 7s 6d *Francf.* 1603
901 Hist. Brit. & Anglic. Scriptores xx. a Galeo, 3 tom. *exemp. pulch.* 2l 2s *Oxon.* 1691
902 Balleus de Scriptorib. Britanniæ, 9s ——— *Bas.* 1557
903 Whartoni Anglia Sacra, sive Hist. Archiepisc. & Episcopor. Angliæ, 2 tom. 9s ——— ——— *Lond.* 1691
904 Mat. Parisiensis Vitæ duorum Offarum, 3s ——— *ibid.* 1639
905 Spelmannus de Vita Ælfredi Mag. Anglor. Regis, cum Supplement. 2s 6d ——— ——— *Oxon.* 1678
906 Hollandi Herologia Anglica, *cum effigieb. prim. impress.* 12s 6d *Arnh.* 1620
907 Idem 1620—Verheiden Effigies & Elogia Præstant. aliquot Theologor. *qui oppugnarun Rom. Antichrist. H. Com.* 1602, 15s
908 Verheiden Effigies & Elogia Theologorum, 4s ——— *ibid.* 1602
909 Beringii Florus Danicus, *exemp. pulch.* 7s 6d *Othing* 1698
910 Historiæ Anglicanæ Decem Scriptores, a Twysden, *elegant. comp. in corio russ.* 2 tom. in 1 vol. 2l 2s ——— *Lond.* 1652

E 2 911 Paul.

911 Paul. Jovii Hist. sui Temporis, 2 tom. *elegantiss. compact. fol. marmorat.* 1l 1s — — *Lutet.* 1598
912 Idem, 2 tom. in 1 vol. *exemp. pulch. lineis rubr.* 12s *ib. ap. Vascosan* 1553
913 Torfæi rerum Orcadensium Historia, 5s — *Hauniæ* 1697
914 Jul. Pollucis Onomasticon, Gr. & Lat. Comment. Jungermanni & alior. *edit. opt.* 2 tom. *nit. comp.* 1l 1s — *Amst.* 1706
915 Harduini Opera varia, *cum fig. chart. max. & nit. comp.* 15s *ib.* 1733
916 Rogeri Baconi Opus Major, *edidit.* S. Jebb, 12s *Lond.* 1733
917 Idem, *ch. max. exemp. pulch.* 15s — *ibid.* 1733
918 Petit Leges Atticæ, *nit. comp.* 9s — *Par.* 1635
919 Idem, cum Notis Wesselingii & alior. *exemp. pulch. nit. comp. in membr.* 1l 8s — — *L. Bat.* 1742
920 Junius de Pictura Veterum, 6s — *Roterd.* 1694
921 Idem, *exemp. pulch. nit. comp.* 8s — *ibid.* 1694
922 Sanchez de Sancto Matrimonii Sacramento, 15s *Lugd.* 1620
923 Grotius de Jure Belli ac Pacis, cum Comment. Vander Meulin & Notis Gronovii, 3 tom. 18s — *Ultraj.* 1696
924 Boissardus de Divinatione & Magicis Præstigiis, *cum fig. per De Bry, exemp. pulch.* 6s — — *Oppenh.*
925 Seldeni Mare Clausum, 2s — — *Lond.* 1635
926 Crussi Germano Græcia, *exemp. pulch.* 7s 6d — *Bas.* 1583
927 Paul. Benii Eugubini Comment. in Aristotelis Poeticam *Venet.* 1624 —Ejusdem Comment. in Virgilii Æneidem *ib.* 1622, 7s 6d
928 Milles Nobilitas Politica, vel Civilis, *ch. max.* 2s *Lond.* 1608
929 Buchanani Opera omnia, cura Ruddimanni, 2 tom. *nit. comp. in* 1 vol. 9s — — *Edinb.* 1715
930 Idem, 2 tom. *nit. comp.* 12s — *ibid.* 1715
931 Corpus Poetarum Latinorum, a Mattaire, 2 tom. 2l 2s *Lond* 1713
932 Idem, 2 tom. *nov. & elegant. compact.* 2l 8s — *ib.* 1713
933 Spencer de Legibus Hebræorum, ed. Chappelow, 2 tom. *pulc. exemp.* 18s — — — *Cant.* 1727
934 Epithalamia Oxoniensia in Nuptias Reg. Geo. III. *sutus,* 5s *Oxon.* 1762
935 Gratulatio Acad. Oxon. in Nuptias Frederici Princip. Walliæ, *sutus,* 2s 6d — — — *ibid.* 1736
936 Gratulatio Acad. Cantabrig. de Pace 1713, *elegant. comp. in corio maurit. fol. deaur.* 2s 6d — — *Cant.* 1713
937 Gratulatio Univ. Oxon. ob Natum Geo. Princ. Walliæ, *sutus,* 5s *ibid.* 1762
938 Pietas Acad. Oxoniens. in Obitum Reg. Carolinæ, *sutus,* 3s 6d *Oxon.* 1738
939 Pietas Acad. Oxon. in Obitum Reg. Geo. I. & Gratulat. in Inaugurat. Reg. Geo. II. *sutus,* 3s 6d — *ibid.* 1727

Books of Maps, Architecture and Mathematics, Greek, Latin, French and English. FOLIO.

940 PTolemæi Geographia, Gr. & Lat. â Bertio, *edit. opt. exemp. pulch.* 2l 12s 6d — — *L. Bat.* 1618
941 A Collection of sixty-six Maps, chiefly French and Italian, 1l 5s
942 Compleat Atlas *containing* 73 *maps, by* Bowen, *neatly coloured, bound in rough calf,* 18s

943 Moll's

943 Moll's large Atlas, *containing 30 maps, very fair and neat,* 1l 11s 6d
944 Twenty-five large Maps of several Parts of Europe, Asia, Africa and America, by Bowen, Price and others, *coloured, in boards,* 15s
945 Atlas Russicus, curâ & Opera Acad. Imper. Scientiar. Petropolitanæ, *in boards,* 1l 4s ——— ——— *Petropol.* 1745
946 Sea Charts, by Michelot and Bremond, for the Mediterranean, 10s 6d *Par.*
947 Nouvel Atlas de la Chine, Tartaire, & du Thibet, par D'Anville, *peintees,* 10s 6d ——— ——— *Haye* 1737
948 Tables Chronologique & d'Histoire Universelle, par M. Du Fresnoy, 6s ——— ——— ——— *Par.* 1733
949 L'Ecole des Armes, avec l'Explication Generale des Principales Attitudes & Positions concernant l'Escrime, par M. Angelo, *avec fig. demi relie,* 1l 11s 6d ——— ——— *Lond.* 1763
950 Lairesse's Principles of Drawing, *with copper-plates from Alb. Durer, Le Clerc, Hollar, and other eminent Masters, sewed,* 6s 1752
951 Kirby's Perspective of Architecture, *with a great number of cuts,* 2 vol. *new and half bound,* 3l 3s ——— ——— 1761
952 Alberti's Architecture, Ital. and Engl. by Leoni, *with a great number of cuts,* 3 vol. *in one, boards,* 1l 1s ——— 1739
953 The same, *very fair and neatly bound,* 1l 5s ——— 1739
954 The same, *first impressions,* 3 vol. *in boards,* 1l 4s ——— 1726
955 Campbell's Vitruvius Britannicus, *with above two hundred large cuts, first impression, very fair,* 3 vol. *large paper,* 7l 7s — 1715
956 The same, 3 vol. *small paper, neatly bound in red calf, 1st edition,* 5l 5s ——— ——— ——— 1715
957 The same, 3 vol. *elegantly bound in 1 vol. russia leather,* 5l 10s
958 Ware's Compleat Body of Architecture, *with a great number of cuts, fair and neat,* 1l 10s ——— ——— 1756
959 Architecture de Palladio, avec des Notes d'Inigo Jones, traduit par Leoni, *avec grand nombre de fig.* 2 tom. *bel. exemp.* 1l 10s *Haye* 1726
960 Evelyn's Parallel of Ancient and Modern Architecture, *with cuts, very fair,* 6s ——— ——— ——— 1707
961 The same, with Wotton's Elements of Architect. 6s 1723
962 Halfpenny's Art of Sound Building, *with cuts,* 5s — 1725
963 Garret's Designs of Farm Houses, *with cuts, sewed,* 2s 6d 1747
964 Studio d'Architectura Civile, da Domenic Rossi, *with a great number of cuts, first impression, a fine copy,* 1l 11s 6d ——— *Rom.* 1702
965 Desseins de Decorations de Pavillons, par Le Brun, 10s 6d *Par.*
966 Vignola Regola d'Architettura, *con fig.* 5s
967 Les Cinque Ordres d'Architecture de Scammozzi, *avec le planches originales,* par Davilar, 6s ——— — 1685
968 Architettura Universale di Vinc. Scammozzi, 2 tom. *le vera ediz. buon ligat.* 18s ——— ——— *Venet.* 1616
969 Architettura di Palladio, 18s ——— *ibid.* 1601
970 Putei Perspectiva Pictorum, & Architectorum, *cum multis elegant. fig. exemp. pulch.* 2 tom. *edit. opt.* 2l 2s ——— *Rom.* 1702
971 Holmes's Academy of Armory, or Display of Heraldry, containing a Storehouse of Arms and Armory, 10s 6d 1688
972 Dodson's Anti-Logarithmic Canon, being a Table of Numbers consisting of eleven Places of Figures, corresponding to all the Logarithms under 10,000, *very neat,* 12s ——— 1742

973 Shel-

973 Shelvocke's Great Art of Artillery, *with a great number of cuts* 7s 6d —— —— 1729

974 Kersey's Elements of Algebra, 2 vol. *bound in* 1. *very fair*, 14s 1673

975 Burnet's Theory of the Earth, 2 vol. *large print, and very fair*, 5s —— —— —— 1684

976 Leybourn's Surveying, with Cunn's Appendix, 5s —— 1722

977 Wallis's Algebra, *with cuts*, 5s —— 1685

978 Hooke's Posthumous Works, containing his Cutlerian Lectures on Earthquakes, and Improvement of Navigation, with a large Account of his Life, by Waller, *with cuts, very fair*, 7s 1705

979 Euclid's first Six Elements of Geometry, with Annotations and useful Supplements, by Scarborough, *large paper, very fair and neatly bound*, 10s 6d —— —— 1705

980 Flamsteedii Historia Cœlestes Britannicæ, *cum fig.* 3 tom. *nov. & elegant. comp.* 3l 3s —— —— *Lond.* 1725

981 Hevelii Cometographia, *cum fig.* 10s 6d —— *Gedani* 1668

Miscellaneous Books in English. QUARTO.

982 MILTON's Paradise Lost, by Bentley, with Notes, 7s 6d 1732

983 The same, with Notes, by Bishop Newton, *with cuts*, 2 vol. *new and neatly bound*, 2l 5s —— —— 1754

984 Milton's Poetical Works, by Bishop Newton, and his Prose Works, with his Life, by Dr. Birch, 5 vol. *new and very elegantly bonnd, by Johnson*, 6l 16s 6d —— —— 1761

985 The same, 5 vol. *elegantly bound in russia leather*, 6l 16s 6d 1745

986 Thomson's Works, with his Life, 2 vol. *new and elegantly bound*, 2l 10s —— —— —— 1762

987 The same, 2 vol. *new and elegantly bound, by Johnson*, 2l 15s 1762

988 Horace, Lat. and Engl. with Notes, by Francis, 2 vol. 1l 10s 1749

989 The same, 2 vol. *new and elegantly bound, by Johnson*, 2l 5s 1749

990 Sophocles, translated by Francklin, with a Dissertation on Tragedy, 2 vol. *in boards*, 17s —— —— 1759

991 The same, 2 vol. in 1. *new, and neatly bound*, 1l 1s 1759

992 The same, *elegantly bound in russia leather*, 1l 5s

993 Waller's Poems, by Fenton, *with head and tail pieces, new, and elegantly bound, marble leaves*, 1l 4s —— 1729

994 Virgil's Bucolics and Georgics, Lat. and Engl. with Notes, by Martin, *cuts coloured*, 2 vol. *in* 1. *new and elegantly bound*, 1l 16s 1749

995 The same, *neat, in* 2 vol. 1l 15s —— 1749

996 Gay's Poems, *large print*, 2 vol. *elegantly bound in one*, 1l 1s 1720

997 Homer's Iliad, by Pope, *with head and tail pieces, large paper, neatly bound in morocco, gilt leaves*, 6 vol. 5l 5s —— 1715

998 Homer's Iliad and Odyssey, by Pope, *with head and tail pieces*, 11 vol. *very fair and neat*, 5l 15s 6d —— 1715, &c.

999 Lord Lansdowne's Works, 8s —— —— 1732

1000 Thomson's Seasons, *with cuts, very fair*, 6s —— 1730

1001 Fingal

1001 Fingal and Temora, Epic Poems, *neatly bound in one vol. new,* 1l —— —— —— 1762, &c.
1002 Fingal, an Epic Poem, *in boards,* 8s —— 1762
1003 Virgil's Æneid, by Pitt, 2 vol. *sewed,* 6s —— 1744
1004 The same, 2 vol. *large paper, very fair and neat,* 16s 1740
1005 Blacklock's Poems, with his Life, by Spence, *in boards,* 3s 1756
1006 Spenser's Fairie Queen, *with fine cuts from Mr. Kent's designs,* 3 vol. *neat,* 1l 7s —— —— 1751
1007 Lloyd's Poems, *in boards,* 5s —— —— 1762
1008 Leonidas, a Poem, by Glover, *in boards,* 3s —— 1737
1009 The same, *very fair and neat,* 5s —— 1737
1010 Caractacus, a Dramatic Poem, by Mason, *very fair and elegantly bound,* 3s —— —— 1759
1011 Callimachus's Hymns, with Notes, by Dod, *new and elegantly bound, by Johnson,* 10s 6d —— —— 1755
1012 Manners of the Age, in 13 Moral Satyrs, *large paper, neatly bound, gilt leaves,* 7s 6d —— —— 1733
1013 Orlando Furioso, Ital. and Eng. by Huggins, 2 vol. *new and very neat,* 1l 11s 6d —— —— 1757
1014 The same, 2 vol. *elegantly bound in morocco, gilt leaves,* 2l 2s 1755
1015 Akinside's Pleasures of Imagination 1744—Pleasure, a Poem, Lat. and Eng. — New Dunciad 1742 — Institute of the Order of the Garter, a Dramatic Poem 1742, 4s
1016 Ramsay's Poems, 6s —— —— *Edinb.* 1721
1017 Persius's Satyrs, translated into English Verse, *neat,* 4s 1741
1018 Pope's Dunciad, by Warburton 1743—Akinside's Pleasures of Imagination—Armstrong on Health, 5s
1019 Amyntor and Theodore, or the Hermit, a Poem, *neat,* 2s 6d 1747
1020 Pindar, with Notes, and a Dissertation on the Olympic Games, by West, 9s —— —— 1749
1021 The same, *very fair and elegantly bound, with a gold border,* 12s —— —— 1749
1022 Hesiod's Works, with Notes, by Cook, 2 vol. 5s —— 1728
1023 Harding's Chronicle of Englande, *black letter,* 10s 6d *printed by Grafton* 1543
1024 The Picture, a Tragecomedie, by Massinger, 1s —— 1630
1025 Pope Blount's Remarks upon Poetry, Ancient and Modern, 2s —— —— —— 1695
1026 Dr. Brown's Dissertat. on Poetry and Music, with the Cure of Saul, a Sacred Ode, *in boards,* 6s —— —— 1763
1027 Brumoy's Greek Theatre, containing the best Greek Plays, with Critical Observations, translated into English by Mrs. Lennox, 3 vol. *in boards,* 1l 5s —— —— 1759
1028 The same, *new and very neatly bound,* 1l 11s 6d —— 1759
1029 *The same, new and elegantly bound, by Johnson,* 3 vol. 2l 1759
1030 Don Quixote, by Smollet, with Cuts designed by Hayman, and engraved by Grignion, 2 vol. 1l 10s —— 1755
1031 The same, 2 vol. *new and elegantly bound,* 1l 16s —— 1755
1032 Don Quixote, by Jarvis, with Cuts by Vandergucht, 2 vol. *elegantly bound, best edition,* 2l 7s —— —— 1742
1033 Addison's Works, 4 vol. *large paper, very fair and neat,* 3l 3s 1721
1034 The same, 4 vol. *large paper, elegantly bound by Robiquet,* 4l 1721
1035 The same, 4 vol. *small paper,* 1l 5s —— —— 1721

1036 Ad-

1036 Addison's Works, with the Drummer, 4 vol. *fine paper, printed by Baskerville, new, half bound, very neat,* 4l 4s *Birmingh.* 1761
1037 Swift's Works, with his Life and Notes, by Hawkesworth, *with cuts,* 6 vol. *new and neatly bound,* 3l 15s —— 1755
1038 The same, 6 vol. *elegantly bound in russia,* 5l —— 1755
1039 Dr. Middleton's Works, 4 vol. *neat,* 1l 16s —— 1752
1040 The same, 4 vol. 1l 10s —— 1752
1041 The same, with his Life of Cicero, 6 vol. *new and elegantly bound, marble leaves,* 3l 13s 6d —— —— 1752, &c.
1042 The same, with his Life of Cicero, 6 vol. *large paper, very fair,* 4l 14s 6d —— —— —— 1752, &c.
1043 Middleton's Miscellaneous Tracts, *in boards,* 4s —— 1752
1044 The same, *fair and neat,* 6s —— —— 1752
1045 Morgan's Phœnix Britannicus, or Collection of scarce and curious Tracts, 5s —— —— —— 1732
1046 Sir T. Brown's Enquiries into Vulgar Errors, with his Garden of Cyrus, 2s 6d —— —— 1669
1047 Bibliotheca Literaria, or Collection of Inscriptions, Medals, &c. *in 10 numbers, which are all that were published,* 5s —— 1722
1048 Harleian Miscellany, or Collection of scarce Pamphlets and Tracts found in Lord Oxford's Library, 8 vol. *in boards,* 3l 13s 6d 1744
1049 Lord Somers's Collection of Tracts, the four first vol. *in boards,* 1l 5s —— —— —— 1748
1050 Scapin Triumphant, or Journey to Petersfield and Portsmouth, by William Rover 1757—Hanway's eight Days Journey from Portsmouth to Kingston upon Thames, with his Essay on Tea, *very neat* 1756, 8s
1051 Nath. Bacon on the Laws of Government of England, with Selden's Notes, *new and elegantly bound,* 15s —— 1760
1052 Hogarth's Analysis of Beauty, *with the cuts, sewed,* 10s 6d 1753
1053 Real Story of John Carteret Pilkington, *sewed,* 2s 1760
1054 Sheridan's Lectures on Elocution, *sewed,* 7s —— 1762
1055 Rog. Ascham's English Works, with his Life, and Notes by Bennet, *very fair,* 12s —— —— 1761
1056 Demosthenes Orations against Philip of Macedon, Engl. with Notes, by Leland, 7s 6d —— —— 1756
1057 Cumberland's Law of Nature, translated, with an Introduction, and an Appendix, and Notes, by Maxwell, 5s —— 1727
1058 The same, *very neat,* 6s —— —— 1727
1059 The same, *large paper, very neat,* 9s —— 1727
1060 Hutcheson's System of Moral Philosophy, 2 vol. *new and elegantly bound,* 1l 8s —— —— 1755
1061 Ramsay's Philosophic Principles of Natural and Revealed Religion, 2 vol. 16s —— —— 1751
1062 Burgh's Dignity of Human Nature, *very fair,* 10s 6d 1754
1063 *Dr. Is. Watts's Works,* 6 *vol. new and elegantly bound,* 3l 10s
1064 Locke's Letters on Toleration, *very scarce,* 7s 6d —— 1689
1065 Religion of Nature delineated, by Wollaston, 1s 6d 1726
*1065 The same, *elegantly bound in green morocco, with a gold border, gilt leaves,* 6s —— —— —— 1726
1066 The same, *with the head of the author,* 2s —— 1731
1067 Pliny's Letters, by Lord Orrery, with Notes and Observat. 2 vol. *very neatly bound,* 1l 1s —— —— 1751
1068 Aglionby's Lives of Eminent Painters, *in boards,* 3s —— 1719

1069 Fresnoy

1069 Fresnoy's Art of Painting, with Remarks, by Dryden, *large paper, very fair and neat, gilt leaves,* 10s 6d —— 1695
1070 Catalogue of the Collection of Pictures, &c. belonging to King James II. and of Queen Caroline, at the Palace of Kensington, *sewed,* 9s —— —— —— 1758
1071 Ripa Iconologia, or Moral Emblems, illustrated with 326 Figures, with their Explanations, *very fair and neat,* 4s —— 1709
1072 Bulwer's Man Transformed, or the Artificial Changling, *with a great number of cuts,* 5s
1073 Wilson's Arte of Rhetorique, *black letter,* 2s —— 1555
1074 Parkyn's Inn Play, or Cornish Hugg Wrestler, 1s 6d 1727
1075 Lisle's divers Ancient Monuments in the Saxon Tongue, 2s 1638
1076 Hume's History of England, from Julius Cæsar to the End of the Stuarts, 6 vol. *compleat,* 3l 15s —— 1759
1077 The same, 6 vol. *new and elegantly bound,* 4l 10s — 1762
1078 The same, 6 vol. *large paper, new and elegantly bound,* 6l 6s 1762
1079 Hume's History of the Stuarts, 2 vol. *sewed,* 1l 1s 1754
1080 Hume's History of the Stuarts, 2 vol. *large paper, sewed,* 1l 10s 1755
1081 Antiquities of the County of Louth in Ireland, *in upwards of ninety views and plans, representing with explanations the principal ruins, curiosities and ancient dwellings in the county of Louth, 2d edit. with additions, by T. Wright, Esq;* *in boards,* 15s 1758
1082 The same, *new and neat,* 18s —— 1758
1083 The same, *elegantly bound in russia leather, with a gold border, marble leaves,* 1l 4s —— —— —— 1758
1084 Dale's Antiquities of Harwich and Dovercourt, with Notes and Observations on Natural History, *large paper, with cuts, elegantly bound, marble leaves,* 12s 6d —— —— 1730
1085 The same, *small paper,* 5s —— —— 1730
1086 Thomas's Survey of Worcester Cathedral, *with an appendix and cuts, large paper, neat,* 14s —— —— 1736
1087 Masters's History of Corpus Christi College, Cambridge, 2 vol. *sewed,* 6s —— —— —— 1753
1088 The same, *large paper, neatly bound in russia,* 1l 1s — 1753
1089 Willis's History of Cathedrals, *with cuts,* 3 vol. *neat,* 1l 4s 1727
1090 Ballard's Memoirs of the most celebrated learned Ladies of Great Britain, *very neatly bound, and marble leaves,* 12s — 1752
1091 Lewis's History and Antiquities of the Abbey and Church of Faversham, *with cuts, very fair,* 7s —— 1727
1092 Widmore's Enquiry into the Foundation of Westminster Abbey 1734 —His History of Westminster-Abbey, *sewed* 1751, 3s
1093 ——— History of Westminster-Abbey, *in boards,* 4s 1751
1094 ——— The same, *very neatly bound in russia,* 9s — 1751
1095 Rowland's Mona Antiqua Restaurata, or Antiquities of the Isle of Anglesey, *with cuts, very fair,* 1l 1s 6d —— 1723
1096 History and Antiquities of Windsor Castle, the Royal College and Chapel of St. George, *large paper, with cuts, neat,* 12s 6d 1749
1097 Stukeley's Medallic History of Carausius, Book I. *with cuts, elegantly bound, marble leaves,* 8s —— —— 1757
1098 The same, 2 vol. *elegantly bound in one, marble leaves* 14s 1757
1099 Ornaments of Churches considered, with an Account of the Altar Piece and Stained Glass in St. Margaret's Church, Westminster, *elegantly bound, marble leaves,* 7s 6d —— 1761

F 1100 Lewis's

1100 Lewis's History and Antiquities of the Isle of Tenet, *with cuts, very fair, best edit.* 14s — — 1736
1101 The same, *large paper, new and neat,* 1l 1s — 1736
1102 Willis's History and Antiquities of the Town, Hundred and Deanry of Buckingham, 10s 6d — — 1755
1103 The same, *new, in boards,* 10s 6d — 1755
1104 The same, *new and elegantly bound,* 14s
1105 Wise's Further Observat. on the White Horse and other Antiquit. of Berkshire 1742 — Amyntor and Theodora, a Poem by Mallet, 3s 6d — — 1747
1106 Wise's Letter concerning the White Horse Vale, *cuts* 1738 — Impertinence and Imposture of modern Antiquarians display'd — Wise's Further Observat. on the White Horse, *with cuts, very neat,* 9s — — — 1738
1107 Norden's Speculum Britanniæ, or Description of Middlesex and Hertfordshire, *with Maps, elegantly bound in yellow morocco, gilt leaves,* 6s — — 1723
1108 Carew's Survey of Cornwall, with his Life, 3s 6d 1723
1109 England Illustrated; or a Compendium of the Natural History, Geography, Topography, and Antiquities of England and Wales, *with Maps of the several Counties, and with a great number of Cuts,* 2 vol. *half bound,* 2l 12s 6d — 1764
1110 Somner's Antiquities of Canterbury, 3s — 1640
1111 Kilburne's Survey of Kent, *very fair and elegantly bound,* 6s 1659
1112 Lambarde's Perambulation of Kent, 3s 6d — 1596
1113 Britannia Depicta, or Survey of the Roads in England and Wales, by Owen, 2 vol. 5s — — 1720
1114 Ames's Account of Printing in England, *new and neat,* 1l 1s 1749
1115 Colley Cibber's Life 1740 — His Character and Conduct of Cicero, *very neat,* 9s — — 1747
1116 Life of Sir Dudley North, and of Dr. John North, by Rog. North, 3s — — — 1744
1117 The same, *very fair,* 4s — — 1744
1118 Seacome's Genealogical and Historical Account of the House of Stanley, with a full Description of the Isle of Man, *with the Arms of the Families, neat,* 10s 6d — 1735
1119 Ancient Dialogue concerning the Exchequer, published by Madox, *very neat,* 7s — — — 1751
1120 Ecton's Thesaurus Rerum Ecclesiast or Account of the Valuations of all the Ecclesiastical Benefices in England and Wales, *neat,* 12s — — 1754
1121 The same, *best edit. new and very neatly bound,* 16s 1763
1122 Sprat's History of the Royal Society, *large paper,* 4s 1667
1123 Boate's Natural History of Ireland, with Additions by Molyneux, *with cuts, new and neat,* 14s — — 1755
1124 Brewster's Collect. Ecclesiast. or Collection of Treatises relating to the Rights of the Clergy, 6s 1752
1125 Letters and Remains of Lord Bacon, publish'd by Stephens, 3s 1734
N. B. *These are not in the Edition of Bacon's Works, published* 1730
1126 Goodall's Historical Account of the College of Physicians in London, 3s — — 1684
1127 Bp. Sprat's Relation of the Conspiracy of Blackhead and Young, *both parts,* 1s 6d — — 1693

1128 Buchanan

1128 Buchanan on the Government of Scotland, 1s —— 1619
1129 Godwin's Catalogue of English Bishops, with their Lives and Actions, 1s 6d —— —— 1615
1130 Journal of the Proceedings of Parliament from Nov. 3. 1640, to Nov. 8. 1641, 1s 6d —— —— 1656
1131 Taylor's History of Gavelkind, 1s —— 1663
1132 Of Navigation and Commerce, with some Remarks on the Royal Hospital at Greenwich, by Gander, *turkey leather and gilt leaves*, 2s
1133 Causes of the Decline of the Foreign Trade, by Sir Mat. Decker, 1s 6d —— —— 1744
1134 Yarranton's England's Improvement by Sea and Land, *with cuts*, part 2d, 1s 6d —— —— 1681
1135 Houghton's Letters on Husbandry and Trade, 1s 6d 1681
1136 Salmasius's Confutation of Milton, in Defence of K. Charles I. 1s 6d —— —— 1660
1137 Folkes's Tables of English Gold and Silver Coins, *neatly bound*, 12s
1138 The same, *in boards*, 10s —— —— 1745
1139 Warner's History of Ireland, Vol. I. *in boards, new*, 18s 1763
1140 Birch's History of the Royal Society, containing great Numbers of Papers never before publish'd, *with cuts*, 4 vol. *very fair*, 1l 16s
1141 Sprat's History of the Royal Society, *with cuts, large paper*, 4s 1667
1142 The same, *last Edition, very fair*, 4s —— 1734
1143 Palmer's History of Printing, *with many MS. Observations, wrote in a fair Hand, very fair*, 12s 6d —— 1733
1144 Middleton's Life of Cicero, 2 vol. *very neat*, 1l 4s 1757
1145 The same, 2 vol. *new and elegantly bound*, 1l 8s — 1757
1146 The same, 2 vol. *large paper, new and neat*, 2l —— 1757
1147 The same, 2 vol. *large paper, neatly bound in russia*, 2l 5s 1741
1148 Life of Erasmus, by Jortin, Vol. I. *very neat*, 10s 6d 1758
1149 Memoirs of the Duke of Sully, 3 vol. translated into English, *new and elegantly bound by* Robiquet, 2l 5s —— 1761
1150 Life and Reign of Philip King of Macedon, by Leland, *in boards*, 15s —— —— 1761
1151 Stanley's History of Philosophy, and Lives, &c. of the Philosophers, *with Notes, very fair*, 14s — —— 1743
1152 The same, *very fair, and elegantly bound in 2 vol.* 1l 1743
1153 Hooke's Roman History, 3 vol. *new and neatly bound*, 3l 3s 1763
1154 The same, Vol. 3d, *in boards, new*, 19s —— 1763
1155 Hooke's Observations on the Roman Senate, 5s —— 1758
1156 Dionysius Halicarnassensis, translated with Notes by Spelman, 4 vol. *new, and elegantly bound by* Johnson, 2l 15s —— 1758
1157 The same, 4 vol. *new, and elegantly bound in russia, marble leaves*, 3l 3s —— —— —— 1758
1158 Busching's System of Geography, *with maps*, 6 vol. *new and very neat*, 5l 5s —— —— 1762
1159 Machiavel's Works, translated with Notes by Farnworth, 2 vol. *new, in boards*, 1l 10s —— —— 1762
1160 The same, 2 vol. *new and very neat*, 1l 15s —— 1762
1161 Davila's History of the Civil Wars of France, 2 vol. *new and very neat*, 1l 11s 6d —— —— 1758
1162 The same, 2 vol. *new, neatly bound by* Robiquet, 1l 16s 1758
1163 Description of the Royal Palace and Monastery of St. Laurence, called the Escurial in Spain, by Thompson, *cuts, sewed*, 18s 1760

F 2 1164 Sir

1164 Sir Isaac Newton's Chronology of Ancient Kingdoms, *new, and neatly bound,* 7s 6d —— —— 1728
1165 The same, *new and elegantly bound by* Johnson, 10s 1728
1166 Kennedy's Complete System of Astronomical Chronology, *new and very neat,* 14s —— —— 1762
1167 Cambridge's Account of the War in India between the English and French, *in boards,* 12s —— —— 1761
1168 Rimius's Memoirs of the House of Brunswick, *very fair,* 5s 1750
1169 Templeman's Survey of the Globe, *in boards,* 6s
1170 Atlas Minor, 62 Maps by Moll, *neatly coloured,* 5s
1171 Maps of Pomponius Mela, by Reynolds and Moll, *sewed,* 2s 1719
1172 Geographia Classica, with Maps by Moll, 1s 6d — 1717
1173 French Coasting Pilot, being a Description of Bays, Roads, Rocks, &c. on the Coast of France, *with a great number of Charts, sewed,* 8s —— —— —— 1761
1174 Collection of Voyages and Travels by Green, publish'd by Astley, *with a great number of Cuts and Maps,* 4 vol. *very fair and neat,* 2l 2s —— —— 1745
1175 The same, 4 vol. *new and very elegantly bound in russia with a gold border, gilt and marble leaves.* 3l 10s —— 1745
1176 Anson's Voyage round the World, *with cuts, new and very neatly bound,* 18s —— —— 1756
1177 The same, *large paper, elegantly bound in russia leather, 1st impression,* 1l 16s 1748
1178 Muller's Voyages from Asia to America, to discover the North West Coast of America, *with maps coloured* 1761 — Bp. Clayton's Journal from Cairo to Mount Sinai, *very neat,* 10s 6d 1753
1179 Hanway's Travels thro' Russia into Persia, *with cuts,* 2 vol. *new and very neat,* 1l 7s —— —— 1754
1180 The same, 2 vol. *new and elegantly bound by* Johnson, 1l 11s 6d 1761
1181 The same, 4 vol. *the first and best edition, new and very neat,* 2l 10s —— —— —— 1753
1182 Keysler's Travels through Germany, Bohemia, Hungary, Switzerland, Italy and Lorraine; being the most authentic Account hitherto published, *neat,* 1l 16s —— 1756
1183 The same, 4 vol. *new and neatly bound,* 2l 5s —— 1756
1184 The same, 4 vol. *large paper, elegantly bound in morocco, gilt leaves,* 4l 4s —— —— —— 1756
1185 Wright's Travels through France and Italy, *with a great number of cuts,* 2 vol. in one, *very fair,* 1l 5s —— 1730
1186 Another Copy, 1l 1s
1187 Blainville's Travels through Holland, Germany, Switzerland, and other Parts of Europe, *with Maps,* 3 vol. 18s — 1743
1188 Tournefort's Voyage to the Levant, *with a great number of cuts,* 2 vol. *very fair and neat,* 14s —— 1718
1189 Bell's Travels from Petersbourg to divers Parts of Asia, 2 vol. *finely printed, new and elegantly bound,* 1l 10s —— 1763
1190 Strahlenberg's Description of Russia, Siberia, and Great Tartary, *with cuts, and the large map, very fair,* 7s —— 1738
1191 Bucaniers of America, *with cuts, very fair,* 5s —— 1684

Libri

Libri Classici & Authores Antiqui, Gr. & Lat. QUARTO.

1192 PLutarchi Vitæ, Gr. & Lat. cum Lectionib. Var. & Notis Bryani, 5 tom. *nit. comp.* 2l 12s 6d ——— *Lond.* 1729
1193 Idem, 5 tom. *nov. & elegant. comp.* 3l 10s — *ib.* 1729
1194 Idem, 5 tom. *splendidiss. comp. in cor. maurit. flav. & fol. deaurat.* 5l 15s 6d ——— ——— *ib.* 1729
1195 Idem, 5 tom. *elegantiss. comp. in corio russ. fol. marmorat.* 5l 5s *ib.* 1729
1196 Ciceronis Opera, Notis Oliveti, 9 tom. *nov. & elegantiss. comp.* 5l 15s 6d ——— ——— *Genev.* 1758
1197 Idem, 9 tom. *nov. & elegantiss. comp. in corio russico, fol. marmorat.* 7l 7s ——— ——— ——— *ib.* 1758
1198 Ciceronis Opera, Notis Var. & Gronovii, *nit. comp.* in 4 tom. 16s ——— ——— *L. Bat.* 1692
1199 ——— Opera, Notis Var. accurante Schrevelio, *comp. in membr.* 7s ——— ——— ——— *Amst.* 1661
1200 ——— Orationes, Notis in usum Delph. 3 tom. 1l 11s 6d *Par.* 1624
1201 ——— Opera ad Artem Oratoria, Notis in usum Delph. 2 tom. *nit. compact.* 1l 10s ——— ——— *ib.* 1687
1202 ——— Epist. ad Familiares, Notis Delph. 9s *ib.* 1685
1203 Val. Flaccus, cura P. Burmanno, *ch. max. pulch. exemp.* 1l 7s *Leide* 1724
1204 Livius, cum Notis Varior. & Drakenborchii, 7 tom. *exemp. pulch. nitid. comp. in membr.* 5l 5s ——— *L. Bat.* 1738
1205 Idem Liber, 7 tom. *nov. & eleg. compact. in membrana,* 5l 15s 6d
1206 Idem, in usum Delphini, 6 tom. 2l 12s 6d — *Par.* 1679
1207 Lactantii Opera omnia, Notis Le Brun & Du Fresnoy, 2 tom. *nov. & nit. comp.* 1l 7s ——— — *ib.* 1748
1208 Sallustius, Notis Delph. *exemp. pulch.* 9s ——— *ib.* 1676
1209 Suetonius, Notis Delph. *exemp. pulch.* 9s ——— *ib.* 1684
1210 Suetonius, Notis varior. Grævii, *pulch.* 5s *Traject.* 1691
1211 Suetonius, cum Comment. Petr. Almeidæ, *pulch.* 8s *H. Com.* 1727
1212 Lucani Pharsalia, cum Comment. P. Burmanno, 13s *Leide* 1740
1213 Aur. Victor, Notis Delph. 5s ——— *Par.* 1680
1214 Idem, *exemp. pulch. & nit. comp.* 7s 6d ——— *ib.* 1726
1215 Val. Maximus, Notis Delph. 15s ——— *ib,* 1679
1216 Idem, Notis varior. & Ab. Torrenii, *exemp. eleg.* 1l *Leidæ* 1726
1217 Scriptores Rei Rustica, curante Gesnero, 2 tom. *pulch.* 1l 5s 1735
1218 Tacitus, a Gronovio, 2 tom. *nov. & elegant. compact. per* Johnson, 2l 5s ——— — ——— *Traject.*
1219 Poetæ Latini minores, Notis varior. cura P. Burmanno, 2 tom. *nit. exemp.* 18s ——— ——— *Leidæ.* 1731
1220 Quintilianus de Instit. Oratoria, a Gibsono, 2s *Oxon.* 1693
1221 Silius Italicus, cura Drakenborch. *pulch. exemp.* 18s *Traj.* 1717
1222 Idem, *nov. & elegant. compact. per* Johnson, 1l 4s
1223 Quintus Curtius, Notis Delph. 9s ——— *Par.* 1678
1224 Quintiliani Opera, ex recens: Obrecht, 2 tom. 6s *Argent.* 1698
1225 Idem, Notis varior. & Burmanni, 2 tom. *nit. compact.* 1l 5s *L. Bat.* 1720

1226 Terentius,

1226 Terentius, Notis varior. & Westerhovii, 2 tom. *nit. comp.* 1l 4s *H. Com.* 1726

1227 Idem, *nit. compact in membrana,* 2 tom. 1l 4s — *ibid.*

1228 Idem, 2 tom. *nov. & nit. comp.* 1l 8s —— *ibid.*

1229 Plinii Epistolæ, Notis varior. & Longolii, 18s *Amst.* 1734

1230 Manilii Astronomicon, cum Notis Bentleii, *nov. & nit. comp.* 10s *Lond.* 1739

1231 Idem, *nov. & elegantiss. comp. per* Johnson, 12s *ibid.*

1232 Virgilius, Notis varior. & Masvicii, 2 tom. *nit. comp.* 1l 5s *Leov.* 1717

1233 Virgilius, Notis Delph. *pulch.* 14s —— *Par.* 1682

1234 Virgilius, Notis Taubmanni, *exemp. pulch.* 7s — 1618

1235 Virgilius, *literis majusculis, ch. max.* 18s — *Florent.* 1741

1236 Horatius, Notis R. Bentleii, *& notis manuscriptis, J. Tunstall,* 2 tom. 12s —— *Cant.* 1711

1237 Ovidii Metamorphoses, Notis Delph. *nov. & nit. comp.* 10s 6d *Dubl. ap. Grierson* 1729

1238 —— Idem, *nov. & elegant. comp.* 12s 6d —— *ibid.* 1729

1239 —— Opera omnia, a Burmanno, 4 tom. *pulch. ex mp.* 2l 15s *Amst.* 1727

1240 Lucretius, Notis varior. & Havercampii, 2 tom. *exemp. pulch. & nit. comp.* 2l 10s —— —— *L. Bat.* 1725

1241 Pet. Arbitri, Notis Burmanni, 2 tom. *nov. & elegant. compact. per Johnson,* 1l 10s —— —— *Amst.* 1743

1242 Anthologia Veterum Latinorum Epigrammat. & Poemat. Notis var. & Burmanni, tom. 1. *nov. & elegant. comp.* 15s

1243 Idem, Lib. *semi-comp.* 12s —— *Amst.* 1759

1244 Claudianus, Notis Delph. *exemp. pulch.* 1l 5s — *Par.* 1677

1245 Juvenalis & Persius, Notis Delph. *nit. comp. fol. deaurat.* 12s 6d *ibid.* 1684

1246 Idem & Persius, Notis varior. & Casauboni, 2 tom. *exemp. pulch.* 1l 1s —— —— —— *L. Bat.* 1696

1247 Phædrus, Notis in usum Delph. *exemp. pulch.* 5s *Par.* 1675

1248 Propertius, cum Notis & Indicib. 5s —— *Amst.* 1702

1249 Idem, *ch. max. nit. comp.* 7s 6d —— *ibid.* 1702

1250 Idem, cura Broukhusii, 7s —— —— *ibid.* 1727

1251 Tibullus, Notis & varia Lectionib. *cum figuris,* 8s *ib.* 1708

1252 Ennii Fragmenta, a Merule, 2s 6d —— *L. Bat.* 1595

1253 Antiqui Rhetores Latini, *exemp. pulch.* 4s —— *Par.* 1599

1254 Homeri Opera, Gr. & Lat. a Clarke, 2 tom. *nov. & elegant. comp. per* Johnson, 2l 8s —— —— *Lond.* 1654

1255 Homeri Odyssea, Gr. & Lat, a Clarke, *exemp. pulch. nit. compact. in corio turcico,* 1l 7s —— —— *ibid.* 1740

1256 Homeri Ilias & Odyssea, Græce, *edit. rariss.* 2 tom. 10s 6d *Lovan.* 1523

1257 Homeri Odyssea, Gr. & Lat. a Didymo, *exemp. pulch.* 7s 6d *Amst.* 1653

1258 Sapphus Fragmenta & Elogia, Gr. & Lat. a Wolfio, 5s *Hamb.* 1733

1259 *Sapphus & Octo Poetriæ, Gr. & Lat. a Wolfio, ch. max. nit. comp.* 15s —— *ibid.* 1733

1260 Anacreon, Gr. & Lat. a Maittaire, *exemp. pulch.* 3s *Lond.* 1740

1261 Idem, Gr. & Lat. Notis & Indice, a Maittaire, *nitidiss. comp.* 12s *ibid.* 1740

1262 Idem, *interfol. charta alba,* 15s —— *ibid.* 1740

1263 Ælianus

1263 Ælianus de Natura Animalium, Gr. & Lat. a Gronovii, 2 tom. *semi-comp.* 14s ——— ——— *Lond.* 1744
1264 Idem, 2 tom. *ch. max. nov. & nit. comp.* 1l 5s *ibid.* 1744
1265 Lysiæ Orationes & Fragmenta, Gr. & Lat. a Taylor, *ch. max. nit. comp.* 1l 11s 6d ——— ——— *ibid.* 1739
1266 Idem, *ch. max. elegant. comp. in corio russ. fol. deaurat.* 2l 2s *ib.* 1739
1267 Idem, *chart. mag. exemp. pulch.* ——— ——— *ibid.*
1268 Demosthenes & Æschinus, Gr. & Lat. a Taylor, tom. 3. *semi-comp.* 15s ——— ——— *Cantab.* 1747
1269 Maximus Tyrius, Gr. & Lat. a Davisio & Marklando, *nit. comp.* 12s ——— ——— *Lond.* 1740
1270 Anthologia, veterum Græcor. Poetar. Epigrammata, Gr. & Lat. a Lubina, 4s ——— ——— *Genev.* 1604
1271 Longinus, Gr. & Lat. a Tollio, 5s ——— *Traject.* 1694
1272 Opus Aureum & Scholasticum, pars 2da. Gr. & Lat. a Mich. Neandro, 4s ——— ——— *Lips.* 1579
1273 Sophoclis, Gr. cum Scholiis Græcis, necnon Annotat. H. Steph. 8s ——— ——— — *ap. Steph.* 1603
1274 Idem *exemp. pulch. nit. comp. in membr.* 12s ——— *ibid.* 1603
1275 Sophocles, Græce, *nit. comp.* 12s — *Par. ap. Turneb.* 1552
1276 Hesiod, Gr. & Lat. a Robinsono, *pulch. exemp.* 12s *Lond.* 1737
1277 Euripidis Hippolytus, Græce, Notis Marklandi, *sewed,* 1s *Ox.* 1756
1278 Juliani (Imper.) Opera omnia, Gr. & Lat. 5s *Paris.*
1279 Auctores Musicæ Antiquæ, Gr. & Lat. Notis Meibomii, *exemp. pulch.* 10s 6d ——— ——— *Amst.* 1652
1280 Nonni Dionysiaca, Græce, *nit. comp.* 7s 6d *Antv. ap. Plant.* 1569
1281 Lucianus de Morte Peregrini, Gr. & Lat. Notis T. Fabri, *exemp. pulch. nit. comp. fol. deaur.* 2s 6d ——— *Par.* 1653
1282 Epictetus, Gr. & Lat. Notis Uptoni, 2 tom. 12s *Lond.* 1741
1283 Euripides, Gr. & Lat. a Cantero, 2 tom. *pulch.* 15s *apud P. Steph.* 1602
1284 Excerpta ex Collect. Polybii, Diodor. Siculi, &c. Gr. & Lat. Notis Valesii, 5s ——— ——— *Par.* 1634
1285 Horapollinis Hieroglyphica, Gr. Lat. cum Notis varior. cura Pauw, *pulch. exemp.* 6s ——— ——— *Traj.* 1727
1286 Anacreon, Gr. & Lat. Notis Pauw, *elegant. comp. per* Johnson, 8s *ibid.* 1732
1287 Idem, Gr. & Lat. Notis Pauw, 5s ——— 1732
1288 Budæi Epistolæ Græce, 1s 6d — *Par. ap. Benenat.* 1567
1289 Procli Sphæra, Gr. & Lat. a Jo. Bainbridge, 1s *Lond.* 1620

Livres Francois. QUARTO.

1290 HIstoire de France, par le P. Daniel, *avec des fig. medailles,* 6 tom. *bien relie,* 1l 16s ——— ——— *Amst.* 1725
1291 Le meme, avec le Continuation, 7 tom. *bien relie,* 2l 2s *ib.* 1725
1293 Le meme, 17 tom. *edition mellieure nov. & fort bien relie,* 12l 12s *Par.* 1757
1293 Abrege Chronologiq. de l'Histoire de France, par le Sr. Mezeray, *avec fig.* 3 tom. 15s ——— — *ib.* 1717
1294 Le meme, 3 tom. *fort bien relie,* 18s ——— *ib.* 1717
1295 Le meme, 3 tom. *le mellieur edit. fort bien relie,* 1l 7s *ibid.* 1668
1296 Histoire de Francois I. par Varillas, 2 tom. 8s *ibid.* 1685

1297 Histoire

1297 Histoire de Francois I. 2 tom. en 1 vol. 5s —— *Par.* 1665
1298 Histoire des Revolut. de France, avec des Remarq Critiq. par De la Hode, *nov. & fort bien relie,* 8s —— *Haye* 1738
1299 Traite Historiq. des Monnoyes de France, par Le Blanc, *avec des fig.* 10s 6d —— —— *Amst.* 1692
1300 *Histoire Militaire, de Louis le Grand, Roy de France, par le Marq. de Quincy, avec grand nombre des fig.* 7 tom. *grand papier, fort bien relie,* 7l 7s —— —— *Par.* 1726
1301 Le Siecle de Louis XIV. par Voltaire, *grand papier,* 9s *Lond.* 1752
1302 Le meme, *grand papier, fort bien relie,* 10s —— *ibid.* 1752
1303 Memoires de la Ligue, 6 tom. *nov. & fort bien relie,* 3l 3s *Amst.* 1758
1304 Le meme, 6 tom. *bien relie,* 2l 12s 6d —— *ibid.* 1758
1305 Recherches & Considerat. sur les Finances de France, 2 tom. *nov. & bien relie,* 1l 1s —— —— *Basle.* 1758
1306 Histoire de Charles le Mauvais Roi de Navarre, 2 tom. *nov. & fort bien relie,* 1l 1s —— —— *Par.* 1758
1307 Histoire de Charles IX. par Varillas, 2 tom. 5s *ibid.* 1683
1308 Memoirs du Duc de Sully, 3 tom. *fort bien relie,* 1l 10s *Lond.* 1747
1309 Memoires Militaires sur les Grecs & les Romains, par Guischardt, *avec fig. bien relie,* 12s —— —— *Haye* 1758
1310 Antiquitez & Histoires Gauloises & Francoises, par Fauchet, 2s 6d *Genev.* 1611
1311 Vie de Philippe de Mornay, *bien relie,* 2s —— *Leyde* 1647
1312 Lettres du Cardinal d'Ossat, avec les Notes de M. Amelot, 2 tom. *bien relie,* 8s —— —— *Par.* 1698
1313 Histoire du Duc de Bouillon, par Marsollier, 4s *Par.* 1719
1314 La Coustume Reformee du Pays & Duche de Normandie, avec les Comment. par Berault, 5s —— —— *Rouen.* 1612
1315 Histoire de Philippe de Valois, & du Roi Jean, 2s 6d *Par.* 1588
1316 Explication des Tableaux de la Galiere de Versailles, 3s *Vers.* 1687
1317 Labyrinthe de Versailles, *cum fig.* 2s —— *Amst.*
1318 Funerailles des Romains, Grecs & autres Nations, par Guicard, *relie en maroq. dore sur les tranches,* 5s —— *Lyon* 1581
1319 Histoire Universelle de Thou, avec la Suite, par Rigault, *fort bien relie, en* 11 tom. *feuilles marbre,* 6l 6s —— *Haye* 1740
1320 Histoire d'Angleterre, par Rapin, avec le Continuation, *fig.* 13 tom. *fort bien relie,* 3l 3s —— —— *Haye* 1727
1321 Memoires de Fred. Henri Prince d'Orange, *avec fig.* 6s *Amst.* 1733
1322 Histoire Generale d'Allemagne, par le P. Barre, 11 tom. *bien relie,* 6l 6s —— —— —— *Par.* 1748
1323 —— d'Italie, par Guichardin, 3 tom. *grand papier, fort bien relie,* 1l 16s —— —— —— *Lond.* 1738
1324 —— de Christine Reine de Suede, 4 tom. *bien relie, marbre sur les tranches,* 1l 11s 6d —— —— *Amst.* 1751
1325 —— Generale du Portugal, par M. de la Clede, 2 tom. 12s *Par.* 1735
1326 —— de Paraguay, par Charlevoix, *avec fig.* 3 tom. *fort bien relie & nouv.* 1l 11s 6d —— —— *ibid.* 1756
1327 —— Generale des Huns, des Turcs, des Mogols, par Deguignes, 5 tom. *nouv. & fort bien relie,* 3l —— *ibid.* 1756
1328 Reflex. Critiq. sur les Hist. des Anciens Peuples, par Fourmont, 2 tom. *bien relie,* 15s —— —— *ibid.* 1735

1329 Histoire

1329 Histoire Naturelle des Isles Antilles de l'Amerique, *avec fig.* 3s *Rot.* 1658
1330 ——— des Indes Orient. & Occid. par Maffee, 2s 6d *Par.* 1665
1331 La Terre Sainte ou Terre de Promission, par Roger, *avec fig.* 3s *ibid.* 1664
1332 Histoire de la Laponie, par Scheffer, *avec fig.* 3s 6d *ibid.* 1678
1333 Nouvelle Relation de l'Interieur du Serrail, par Tavernier, 2s *ibid.* 1675
1334 Histoire du Serrail, par Baudier, 2s ——— *ibid.* 1631
1335 ——— de Ciceron, avec des Remarq. Historiq. par Morabin, 2 tom. *nouv. & fort bien relie, par Robiquet,* 15s ——— *Rot.* 1745
1336 Geographe moderne, Nat. Historiq. & Politiq. par Du Bois, *avec chartes,* 4 tom. *relie, en* 2 vol. 10s 6d — *Leide* 1729
1337 Polybe, avec un Comment. par M. de Folard, *avec fig.* 6 tom. *le meilleure edit. bien relie,* 4l 4s ——— — *Par.* 1726
1338 Les Cæsars de l'Empereur Julien, *avec des remarq. & medailles,* par Spanheim, 5s ——— ——— *ibid.* 1696
1339 Recherches d'Antiquite, par Spon, *avec d'un grand nombre des fig.* 5s ——— ——— ——— *Lyon.* 1683
1340 Histoire generale de la Marine, 2 tom. *tres elegant. relie en maroq. dore sur les tranches,* 1l 16s ——— ——— *Par.* 1744
1341 Comparisons des Grands Hommes de l'Antiquite, 2 tom. par Rapin, *grand papier,* 4s ——— ——— *Par.* 1684
1342 Negociations du Card. de Ferrare, 2s 6d ——— *ibid.* 1658
1343 Relation de la Chine, par Magaillans, 2s 6d — *Par.* 1688
1344 Histoire de Carausius Empereur de la Gr. Bretagne, *avec de medailles, bel exemp. elegant. relie en maroq. dore sur les tranches,* 12s *ib.* 1740
1345 Descript. des les Guerres entre le Roy d'Anglet. Provinces Unies, *avec fig.* 2s ——— ——— *Amst.* 1668
1346 Theatre de la Guerre en Allemagne, par le Rouge, 5s *Par.* 1741
1347 Voyage de Cyrus, par le Chev. Ramsay, 7s 6d *Lond.* 1730
1348 Le meme, *bien relie,* 9s ——— ——— *Lond.* 1730
1349 Voyage du Levant, par Tournefort, *avec d'un grand nombre des fig. beau exemp. eleg. relie,* 1l 10s — *Par. l'Imprim. Royale*
1350 Voyages de Tavernier, *avec fig.* 3 tom. 15s ——— *Par.* 1676
1351 ——— de Jean Struys en Moscovie, en Tartarie & Indies, *avec fig.* 6s ——— ——— ——— *Amst.* 1681
1352 Voyage de Siam, par Tachard, *avec fig. bel exemp.* 7s 6d *Par.* 1686
1353 Relations de l'Isle de Madagascar & du Brasil, par Flacourt, 2s 6d *ibid.* 1651
1354 Voyages de Pietro della Valle, 4 tom. 1l 1s — *ibid.* 1670
1355 ——— de Vinc. le Blanc, 2s ——— *ibid.* 1649
1356 Voyage de Constantinop. de Grelot, *avec fig.* 4s *ibid.* 1680
1357 Voyages de Mendez Pinto, 3 tom. 4s ——— *ibid.* 1628
1358 Voyage de Levant fait en 1621, *avec fig.* 5s — *ibid.* 1629
1359 Voyage de Levant, par le Baron de Beauvau, *avec fig.* 3s 6d *Nancy* 1619
1360 Voyage de Levant, par Du Loir, 2s 6d ——— *Par.* 1654
1361 Voyage du Sr. de Stochove faites es Annes 1630, 31, 32 & 33. 3s 6d ——— ——— ——— *Brux.* 1643
1362 Navigat. Peregrinat. & Voyages faicts en la Turquie, par Nicolay, *avec d'un grand nombre de fig. bien relie,* 5s *Anvers.* 1576
1363 Les Vies de Plutarque, trad. avec Remarq. Historiq. par Dacier, *fort bien relie,* 8 tom. 3l 10s ——— *Par.* 1721

G 1364 Abrege

1364 Abrege de la Vie de plus Fameux Peintures, 3 tom. *avec les Portraits par D'Argenville, fort bien relie,* 2l 10s — *Par.* 1741
1365 Entretiens sur les Vies & sur les Oeuvrages de plus excellens Peintures, par Felibien, 4 tom. in 2 vol. *fort bien relie,* 15s *Par.* 1696
1366 Le meme, Tom. 3, 4. *relie in* 1 vol. 5s — *ib.* 1684
1367 Le meme, Tom. 3, 4. en 2 vol. 6s —— *ib.* 1684
1368 Conferences de l'Acad. Roy. de Peinture & de Sculpture, par Felibien, 2s 6d —— —— *ib.* 1669
1369 Discours prononces dans les Conferences de l'Acad. Roy. de Peinture & de Sculpture, par Coypel, 5s —— *ib.* 1721
1370 Principes de l'Architecture de la Sculpture & de la Peinture, par Felibien, 7s 6d —— —— *ib.* 1690
1371 Recueil Historiq. de la Vie des Architectes, par Felibien, 3s *ib.* 1687
1372 Histoire Ancienne, avec la Maniere d'Etudier les Belles Lettres, par Rollin, 8 tom. *bien relie,* 4l 4s ——. *ib.* 1740
1373 Hist. Ancienne, Romaine, & Belles Lettres, par Rollin, 16 tom. *grand papier, fort bien relie,* 14l 14s —— *ib.* 1740
1374 Hist. Romaine, par Rollin & Crevier, 8 tom. *grand papier, nouv. & elegant. relie.* 7l 7s —— —— *ib.* 1752
1375 Maniere de Etudier les Belles Lettres, par Rollin, 2 tom. 1l 1s *ib.* 1744
1376 Histoire Romaine, par Catrou & Rouille, *avec fig.* 20 tom. *elegant. relie par* Robiquet, 5l 5s —— *ib.* 1725
1377 —— des Empereurs, avec Notes par Tillemont, 5 tom. *fort bien relie,* 2l —— —— *ib.* 1720
1378 Analyse Geographique de l'Italie, par le Sr. D'Anville, *demi relie,* 5s —— —— *ib.* 1744
1379 Histoire des Papes, 5 tom. 1l 10s —— *Haye* 1732
1380 Philostrate de la Vie d'Apollonius, trad. par De Viginere, 4s *Par.* 1611
1381 Histoire generale d'Espagne de Mariana, trad. avec des Notes par Charenton, 5 tom. *fort bien relie, elegam essemp.* 2l 5s *ib.* 1725
1382 Notice de l'Ancienne Gaule, par D'Anville, *demi relie,* 7s 6d *Par.* 1760
1383 Histoire des Grands Chemins de l'Empire Romaine, par Bergier, *bien relie en maroq. dore sur les tranches,* 6s —— *ib.* 1622
1384 Methode pour Etudier l'Histoire, par Du Fresnoy, *avec de cartes Geographique,* 4 tom. *grand papier, bellisss. essemp. fort bien relie,* *ib.* 1729
1385 Histoire du Pontificate de St. Leon le Grand, par Maimbourg, 2s 6d —— —— *ib.* 1687
1386 *Recueil d'Antiquites Egyptiennes, Etrusques, Grecques & Romaines, avec a'un grand nomb. des fig.* 5 tom. *nouv. & bien relie,* 6l 6s *ib.* 1752
1387 Essais de Montaigne, avec des Remarques, par Colle, 3 tom. *nouv. & fort bien relie,* 1l 4s —— *Lond.* 1724
1388 Le meme, *tres elegant. relie en maroq. flave, dore sur les tranches,* 2l 5s —— — *ib.* 1724
1389 Jugemens des Savans, par Andr. Baillet, 7 tom. *grand papier, beau essemp. fort bien relie,* 2l 5s *Par.* 1722
1390 L'Esprit des Loix, par Montesquieu, 10s 6d *Genev.* 1749
1391 De l'Esprit, par Helvetius, *fort bien relie,* 12s *Par.* 1758

1392 Droit

1392 Droit de la Nature & des Gens, par Pufendorf, avec des Notes par Barbeyrac, 2 tom. 9s ——— *Amst.* 1734
1393 Droit des Gens, ou Principes de la Loix Naturelle, per Vattel, 2 tom. *nouv. & fort bien relie,* 18s ——— *Lond.* 1758
1394 Droit de la Guerre & de la Paix, par Grotius, avec les Notes par Barbeyrac, 2 tom. 8s ——— *Amst.* 1724
1395 Principes du Droit Politique, *cousu,* 4s ——— 1754
1396 Combinaison generale des Changes des Principales Places de l'Europe par Rapport a la France, par Le Sr. Darius, 3 tom. *fort bien relie,* 15s ——— *Par.* 1728
1397 L'Education des Princes, par Varillas, 2s 6d *ib.* 1684
1398 Les Entretiens d'Ariste & Eugene, 2s 6d ——— *ib.* 1681
1399 Discours sur l'Heautontimorumenos de Terence, 2s *ib.* 1656
1400 Explication Nouvelle de l'Apotheose d'Homere, par M. Scott, 1s 6d *Amst.* 1714
1401 L'Ambassadeur & ses Fonctions, par Wicquefort, 2 tom. 8s *Colegn.* 1715
1402 Essai sur l'Entend. Humain, par Locke, trad. avec Remarq. par Coste, *relie en maroq. dore sur les tranches,* 5s *Amst.* 1729
1403 Philippiques de Demosthene, avec des Remarq. & Preface, par Tourreil, 5s ——— *Par.* 1701
1404 Le meme, *bien relie,* 6s ——— *Haye* 1701
1405 Livres de Hieron. Cardanus, trad. de Lat. par Le Blanc, 2s *Par.* 1556
1406 Ornithologie, ou Methode contenant la Division des Oiseaux en Ordres Sections, &c. avec une Description de Chaque Espece, par M. Brisson, *enriche de plusieurs figures,* 6 tom. *tres eleg. relie par* Johnson, 7l 7s ——— *Paris* 1760
1407 Le meme, 6 tom. *nouv. & bien relie,* 6l 10s *Par.*
1408 Ruses Innocentes dans Lequelles se voit Comment, ou prend les Oyseux Passagers, &c. *avec fig.* 2s 6d ——— *ib.* 1660
1409 Reflexions Critiq sur la Poesie & sur la Peinture, par Du Bos, 3 tom. *nouv. & fort bien relie,* 1l 7s ——— *ib.* 1755
1410 La Henriade de Voltaire, *avec fig. elegament. relie,* 7s 6d *Lond.* 1728
1411 Oeuvres de St. Evremond, 3 tom. *fort bien relie,* 1l 1s *ib.* 1709
1412 ——— diverses de Rousseau, 2 tom. *fort bien relie, marbre sur les tranches,* 1l 1s ——— *ib.* 1723
1413 ——— Le meme, 3 tom. *grand papier, nouv. & fort bien relie en russie marbre sur les tranches,* 3l 3s ——— *Brux.* 1743
1414 ——— de Nic. Boileau, 2 tom. *avec fig. bien relie,* 14s *Amst.* 1718
1415 ——— Le meme, 2 tom. *fort bien relie,* 15s ——— *ib.* 1718
1416 ——— *de Moliere, 6 tom. avec fig. eleg. & elegamente relie, le veritable Edition,* 7l 7s ——— *Paris* 1734
1417 Brumoy Theatre des Grecs, 3 tom. *fort bien relie,* 1l 11s 6d *ib.* 1730
1418 Oeuvres d'Horace avec des Remarq. par Dacier, Sanadon & autres, 2 tom. *fort bien relie,* 1l 1s ——— *Hamb.* 1733
1419 Poesies d'Horace, trad. avec Remarq. par Sanadon, 2 tom. 1l 16s *Par.* 1728
1420 Le meme, 2 tom. *grand papier, fort bien relie,* 2l 10s *ib.* 1728
1421 Metamorphoses d'Ovide, trad. avec Remarq. & Explicat. Histories, par Banier, *avec plusieurs fig.* 2 tom. *grand papier, eleg. relie,* 1l 10s ——— *ib.* 1738

1422 Bibliotheque Poetique depuis Marot jusq. aux Poetes de nous Jours, 4 tom. *bien relie marb. sur les tranches* —— *Paris* 1745
1423 Le meme, 4 tom. *eleg. relie en maroq. & dore sur les tranches*, 3l *ib.* 1745
1424 Fables Nouvelles, par La Motte, *avec grand nomb. des fig. bien relie*, 16s —— —— *ib.* 1719
1425 Le meme Livre, *grande papier*, 1l 5s —— *ib.* 1719
1426 Oeuvres Poetique de Joachim du Bellay Angevin, 1s 6d *ib.* 1565
1427 Bibliotheque des Auteurs Ecclesiastiq. avec les Prolegomenes sur la Bible & Bibliotheque des Historiens, par Du Pin, 18 tom. 1l 11s 6d —— —— *Amst.*
1428 Theatre Nouveau des Guerres Presentes aux Pais Bas Autrichiens Francois & Hollandois, *en* 38 *belles Cartes Geograph. peintée*, 3s —— —— —— 1745
1429 Histoire des Revolutions dans l'Europe en Matiere de Relig. par M. Varillas, 4 tom. 12s —— *Par.* 1686
1430 Nouv. Testament, trad. avec Notes, par L'Enfant, 2 tom. 8s *Amst.* 1731
1431 Hist. du Concile de Pise, par l'Enfant, *avec fig. bien relie*, 3s *Utrecht.* 1731
1432 — du Concile de Constance, par L'Enfant, *avec fig.* 5s *Amst.* 1714

Libri Italiana & Hispan. QUARTO.

1433 DAvila Hist. della Guerre Civile di Francia, *very beautifully and correctly printed*, 2 tom *neatly bound*, 1l 11s 6d *Lond.* 1755
1434 The same; 2 tom. *new and elegantly bound*, 1l 16s *ib.* 1755
1435 The same, 2 tom. *new and elegantly bound in russia leather*, 2l 2s *ib.* 1755
1436 Giannone Istoria Civile del Regno di Napoli, 4 vol. *neatly bound and new*, 2l 2s — —— — *Haia* 1723
1437 Ficoroni Piombi Antici, *con fig. half bound*, 7s 6d *Rom.* 1743
1438 Il medessimo, *ligat. in pergam.* 9s —— *ib.* 1740
1439 Annali di Corn. Tacito, trad da Gior. Dati, 3s 6d *Venet.* 1582
1440 Corn. Tacito Opere, trad. di G. Can. d'Anghiari, 2s 6d *ib.* 1620
1441 Il medessimo, 4s —— —— *ib.* 1644
1442 Loschi Comment. di Roma, *bene ligat.* 2s 6d *Vicenz.* 1668
1443 Giosesso delle Antichita & Guerre Guidaiche, *con fig.* 4s *Venet.* 1608
1444 Il medessimo, 2s —— —— *ib.* 1604
1445 *Hecatommithi, overo Cento Novelle di Gio. Bat. Giraldi*, 1l 1s *ib.* 1608
1446 Plinio Historia Naturale, trad. par Chr. Landino, *bene ligat. fogl. marmor.* 7s 6d —— —— *ib.* 1543
1447 Il medessimo, trad. par Domenichi, 9s —— *ib.* 1589
1449 Plinio Lettere, trad. Gio. Ant. Tedeschi, *bene ligat. in pergam.* 8s *Rom.* 1717
1450 Oratione Militari di Autori Antichi Raccolte, par Remegio, 5s *Vineg.* 1557
1451 Scelta Curiosa & Ricca Officina di Istorie, da Astolsi, 5s *Venet.* 1602
1452 Vescovi di Fiesole di Voltevia, & d'Arezzo di Ammirato, *ligat. in turc.* 2s 6d —— —— *Firenz.* 1637

1453 Pa.

1453 Pa. Giovio Istorie del suo Tempo, 2 tom. 6s — *Vineg.* 1581
1454 Onosandro dell'Ottimo Capitano Generale & del suo Ufficio, trad. par Cotta, *bene legat.* 4s — *ib.* 1546
1455 Ant. Mongitore Sicilia Ricercata nella Cose piu Memorabili, *con fig.* 2 tom. 6s — *Palerm.* 1742
1456 Machiavelli Opere, 6s — *Vinc.* 1550
1457 Il medessimo Libro, Ediz. di Martinelli, 2 tom. 1l 16s *Haya*
1458 Statue, di Gio. Andr. Borboni, *con fig. bene ligato,* 7s 6d — *Roma* 1661
1459 Buonaroti Osservaz. Istoriche sopra alcuni Medagli antichi, *con fig.* 6s — *ib.* 1698
1460 Saggi Dissertaz. Accad. pubblic. Lettre nella Accad. Etrusca, *con fig.* 4 tom. *bene ligat.* in 2 vol. 18s — *ib.* 1742
1461 Haym Tesoro Britannico overo il Museo Nummaria, *con fig.* 2 tom. 14s — *Lond.* 1719
1462 Scelta Medaglione piu rara nella Biblioth. delle Card. Gasp. Carpegna, *bene ligat.* 3s — *Rom.* 1679
1463 Descrizione de Cartoni da Carlo Cignani e de Quadri dipinti, da Seb. Ricci, *bene ligat.* 5s — *Venez.* 1749
1464 Baglione Vite de Pittori, Scultori, Architetti, ed Intagliatori, 5s — *Napoli* 1733
1465 Bellori Vite Pittori, Scultori & Architettti moderni, 5s *Rom.* 1672
1466 Il medessimo, *bene ligat.* 6s — *ib.* 1672
1467 Pascoli Vite de Pittori, Scultori, ed Architetti Perugini, 5s — *Rom.* 1732
1468 Raccolta di Lettere sulla Pittura, Scultura ed Architettura, 3 tom. *bene ligat.* 1l 1s — *ib.* 1754
1469 Scannelli Microcosma della Pittura, 3s — *Cesen* 1657
1470 Enea Vico sopra le Medaglie de gli Antichi, 2s 6d *Vineg.* 1555
1471 Vinc. Vittoria Osservaz. sopra la Felsina Pittrice, 2s *Rom.* 1703
1472 Dante Opere, con varie Annotazioni e Copiosi Rami adornata, *carta granda,* 5 tom. *sewed,* 4l 10s — *Venez.* 1757
1473 Il medessimo, 5 tom. in 4 vol. *carta granda, eleganze legat. per* Johnson, 6l — *ib.* 1757
1474 La Gerusalemme Liberata di Tasso, *con le Fig. di Bern. Castelli,* 2 tom. *nuevo & eleganze ligat. per* Johnson, 1l 11s 6d — *Lond.* 1724
1475 Il medessimo, 2 tom. *new and elegantly bound in russia leather,* 2l 2s — *ib.* 1724
1476 Il medessimo, 5s — *Vineg.* 1593
1477 *Torq. Tasso Opere, con le Annotaz. di vari Autori,* 12 tom. *new and elegantly bound,* 7l 7s — *Venez.* 1735
1478 Petrarcha brevemente Esposti, per Lod. Castelvetro, 2 tom. *nuevo & bene ligat.* 1l 10s — *ib.* 1754
1479 The same Edit. 2 tom. *large paper and neatly bound,* 2l 2s
1480 Il medessimo, colla Spositione, di Andr. Gesualdo, *bene ligat. fogl. dornat.* 7s 6d — *Vineg.* 1533
1481 Averani Lezioni sopra Petrarca, 1s 6d — *Raven* 1707
1482 Ariosto Orlando Furioso, *con fig.* da G. Porro, *bene ligat.* 1l 1s — *Venet.* 1584
1483 Il medessimo, *con fig.* 7s 6d — *Vineg.* 1564
1484 Il medessimo, *con fig.* da G. Porro, 15s — *Venet.* 1584
1485 Eneide di Virgilio, con Osservaz. d'Erc. Udine, *bene ligat.* 6s — *Venet.* 1607
1486 Maffei Teatri antichi e moderni, *bene ligat.* 3s — *Veron.* 1753

1487 Pro-

1487 Prometeo Legato Tragedia d'Eschilo, Gr. & Ital. con Annotaz. *nuevo & bene ligat.* 4s ——— *Roma* 1754
1488 Pastor Fido, *con Annotaz. & fig.* 3s 6d —— *Venet.* 1602
1489 Il medessimo, per Rolli, *con fig. bene ligat.* 6s *Lond.* 1718
1490 Rime e Prose di Gio. della Casa, *bene ligat.* 4s *Vineg.* 1558
1491 L'Opere d'Oratio, Commentate da Gio. Fabrini, *belliss. essempl. bene ligat.* 6s ——— —— *Venet.* 1669
1492 Eneide di Virgilio, da Annib. Caro, 2s —— *ib.* 1581
1493 La Semiramis Tragedia — Semiramis Bosca Beccia di Manfredi, 2s *Berg.* 1594
1494 Sonetti del S. Bern. Rotà in Morte della S. Portia Capece sua Moglie, 3s ——— ——— *Nap.* 1560
1495 Raccolte di Tutti gli Antichi Poeti Latini, cola Loro Versione nella Italiana Favella, 32 tom. *nuevo & bene ligat.* 1l 10s *Milan* 1731
1496 Boccaccio Decamerone, di Salviati, 6s — *Firenz.* 1582
1497 Il medessimo, *belliss. essemp. bene ligat. in pergam.* 1l 5s *This Edition is an exact Imitation of that printed by Giunta* ——— 1527
1498 Il medessimo, per Rolli, *belliss. essemp. bene ligat.* 1l 1527
1499 Il medessimo, Ediz. di Martinelli, *finely printed, new, in boards,* 18s *Lond.* 1762
1500 Novelle del Bandello, 3 tom. 1l 16s —— *ib.* 1740
1501 Il medessimo, *carta granda,* 3 tom. *new and elegantly bound,* 3l 3s *ib.* 1740
1502 *Fra. Saviero Quadrio della Storia e della Ragione d'Ogni Poesia,* 7 *tom. nuevo & eleganz. ligat.* 3l 13s 6d — *Bolog.* 1739
1503 Minturino Arte Poetica, *bene ligat.* 7s 6d *Napol.* 1725
1504 Le Orazioni di Cicerone, trad. da Dolce, 3 tom. *bene ligat.* 1l 1s *Venez.* 1735
1505 Cicerone della Partitione Oratoria, trad. di Luca, 4s *Vineg.* 1567
1506 Lettere di Principi, 3 tom. 10s 6d —— *Venet.* 1570
1507 Spaccio de la Bestia Trionfante, di Jordano Brunoa, *MSS. Copy of the printed Book, wrote in a fair Hand, neatly bound,* 15s
1508 Marmi del Doni Acad. Peregrino, *belliss. ligat. foglio dornat.* 6s *Vineg.* 1552
1509 Discorso di Faust. Summo, contre le Tragecomedie, & contre il Pastor Fido, 2s ——— —— *Vicenz.* 1601
1510 L'Arte a Scriver ogni sorte Lettera, antica & moderna, di Giov. Bapt. Palatino, con xv Tavole belliss. 2s 6d *Rom.* 1561
1511 La Biblia, cioe i Libri del Vecchio e del Nuovo Test. par Diodati, 7s 6d ——— ——— 1607
1512 Autos Sacramentales, Alegoricos, y Histor. di Calderon, 2s *Carago.* 1717
1513 Explication de unas Monedas de Oro de Emperadores Rom. por Juan de Quinonas, 4s ——— *Madr.* 1620
1514 Guerres Civiles de Inglaterra Tragica Muerta de su Roy Carlos, *very neat* ——— ——— 1659
1515 Poesia del Conde Villamediana, 2s 6d — *Carag.* 1629
1516 Declaracion Magistral sobre las Satiras de Juvenal & Persio, por Diego Lopez, 2s 6d — — *Carag.* 1642
1517 La Biblia en Espanol, 4s ——— 1569
1518 El Pelegrino en su Patria, por Felix de Vega Carpio, *sewed,* *Madr.* 1733

Dict-

Dictionaries, Lexicons, &c. in various Languages.
QUARTO.

1519 ALtieri's Ital. and Engl. Dictionary, 2 vol. *elegantly bound with a large gold border, and ornamented on the leaves,* 1l 16s 1726
1520 Ainsworth's Dictionary of the Latin Tongue, with Additions, by Patrick, *last edition, new,* 1l 4s ——— 1761
1521 The same, *very fair,* 16s ——— ——— 1746
1522 Boyer's French and English Dictionary, 13s ——— 1729
1523 Lambarde's Alphabetical Description of England and Wales, *stained, neatly bound,* 5s ——— ——— 1730
1524 Baretti's Italian and English Dictionary, 2 vol. *new and very neat,* 1l 16s ——— ——— 1760
1525 Danet's Dictionary of Roman and Greek Antiquities, *with maps,* 5s ——— ——— 1700
1526 Dictionaire Francoise & Hollandoise, par Marin, 2 tom. *demi-relie,* 9s *Amst.* 1748
1527 Hederici Lexicon Græcum, a Patrick, 9s ——— *Lond.* 1739
1528 Hederici Lexicon Græcum, *edit. opt. nit.* 15s *ibid.* 1755
1529 Diction. Ital. Lat. & Franc. par Antonini, 2 tom. *nit. relie en velin,* 15s ——— ——— *Venise* 1754
1530 Le meme, 2 tom. 1l 5s ——— ——— *Par.* 1743
1531 Le meme, 2 tom. *le meilleure edit. nouv. & fort bien relie,* 1l 10s *Lyon* 1760
1532 Littleton's Lat. and Engl. Dictionary, 5s ——— 1715
1533 Minterti Lexicon in Nov. Test. Gr. & Lat. *nitid. compact.* 12s *Franc.* 1728
1534 Morell Thesaurus Græcæ Poeseos, sive Lexicon Græco-Prosodiarum, 2 tom. 1l 1s ——— ——— *Etonæ* 1762
1535 Harpocrationis, Lib. de Vocibus, Gr. Notis Gronovii, *nit. comp. in membr.* 4s ——— ——— *L. Bat.* 1696
1536 Ammonius de Adfinium Vocabulorum Differentia, Græce, Notis Valckenaer, *sutus,* 4s ——— *ibid.* 1739
1537 Phrynichi Eclogæ Nominum & Verborum Atticorum, cum Verf. Lat. & Notis Nunnesii & Hoeschelii, *sutus,* 3s 6d *Traj.* 1739
1538 H. Stephanus de bene Instituendis, Græcæ Linguæ, 6s *Excud. H. Steph.* 1587
1539 Placentinii Comment. Græcæ Pronun. *sutus,* 3l *Rom.* 1751
1540 ——— Epitome Græcæ Palæogri. & de Recta, Græci Sermonis Pronunciat. *sutus,* 3s ——— ——— *ibid.* 1735
1541 Herodotus de Vita & Patria Homeri, Græce, & item Hist. Græcar. & Latinar. Literarum, J. Reinoldii, *nit. comp.* 5s *Lond.* 1752
1542 Rudimentum Linguæ Hebrææ, MSS. *very neatly wrote,* 1s 6d
1543 Funccius de Imminenti, Lat. Ling. Senectute, 4s *Marp.* 1736
1544 ——— de Virile Ætate, Ling. Lat. 4s ——— *ibid.* 1727
1545 ——— de Adolescentia, Ling. Lat. 3s ——— *ibid.* 1723
1546 Casley's Catalogue of Manuscripts in the King's Library, *with cuts, very neat,* 15s ——— ——— 1734
1547 The same, *large paper, elegantly bound, marble leaves,* 1l 1s 1734
1548 Bibliotheca Smithiana, seu Catalogus Librorum. J. Smithii, *nov. & elegant. comp.* 15s ——— ——— *Venet.* 1755
1549 Fabricii Bibliographia Antiquaria, 4s ——— *Hamb.* 1713

Mathematics,

Mathematics, Experimental Philosophy, Architecture, &c. Engl. French. Ital. Lat. &c. QUARTO.

1550 PHilosophical Transactions from 1720 to 1736, in 18 vol. 9l 9s
1551 Hooke's Philosophic. Tracts, *cuts*, 7s 6d —— 1674
1552 ——— Philosophic. Lectures and Tracts, 5s —— 1674
1553 Pemberton's View of Sir J. Newton's Philosophy, *with cuts, in boards*, 4s ——— ——— ——— 1728
1554 The same, *fair and neat*, 8s ——— ——— 1728
1555 Lord Bacon's Philosophic. Works abridged, by Shaw, with Notes, 3 vol. 2l 2s ——— ——— 1733
1556 De Moivres's Doctrine of Chances, *in boards*, 4s 1718
1557 The same, *2d edition, corrected by the author*, 10s 6d 1738
1558 The same, *last edition, new and neat*, 15s —— 1756
1559 Desagulier's Experimental Philosophy, *with cuts*, 2 vol. *damaged*, 1l 1s ——— ——— ——— 1734
1560 The same, 2 vol. *very fair*, 1l 10s —— 1745
1561 The same, 2 vol. *new and neat*, 1l 16s —— 1763
1562 The same, with Gravesende's Philosophy, 4 vol. *new and very neat*, 3l 3s
1563 Smith's Optics, *with cuts*, 2 vol. *new and very neatly bound in* 1 vol. 1l 6s ——— ——— 1738
1564 The same, in 2 vol. *new and very neatly bound*, 1l 10s 1738
1565 The same, *large paper, new and very neatly bound in one vol.* 1l 11s 6d ——— ——— ——— 1738
1566 The same, 2 vol. *large paper, new and very neatly bound*, 1l 16s 1738
1567 Turpin's Art of War, translated by Otway, *large paper*, 2 vol. *in boards*, 1l 16s ——— ——— 1761
1568 Smart's Tables of Interest, Discount, Annuities, &c. *very neat*, 7s ——— ——— 1726
1569 The same, *elegantly bound in morocco, gilt leaves*, 10s 6d 1726
1570 Maseres on the Negative Sign in Algebra, *in boards*, 13s 1758
1571 The same, *new and neat*, 15s 1758
1572 Rutherforth's System of Natural Philosophy, *with cuts*, 2 vol. *fair and neat*, 1l 10s ——— ——— 1748
1573 Sir Isaac Newton on the Quadrature of Curves, Engl. with a Comment. by Stewart, *very neat*, 9s ——— ——— 1745
1574 Yearly Bills of Mortality from 1657 to 1758, with Observations, by Graunt, Petty and Morris, *new and neat*, 12s —— 1759
1575 Switzer's Hydrostatics and Hydraulics, Philosophic and Practical, *with cuts*, 2 vol. *very fair*, 15s ——— 1729
1576 Langley's Young Builder's Rudiments, *with cuts, in boards*, 2s 6d 1730
1577 Wright's Description of Rowley's Quadrant, *very neat*, 4s 1756
1578 Sir Isaac Newton's Optics, with his Tract. de Quadratura Curvarum, 3s ——— ——— ——— 1704
1579 Haye on Annuities upon Lives, 2s —— 1727
1580 The same, *new*, 2s 6d ——— ——— 1727
1581 Lewis's Philosophic. Commerce of Arts, *with cuts, sewed*, 5s 1763
1582 Brunetti's Book of Ornaments, with 60 Designs, *very neat*, 5s 1736
1583 Salmon's Palladio Londinensis, *with cuts*, 5s 1752
1584 Aglionby on Painting, with the Lives of Painters, *very fair*, 4s 1684

1585 Junius

1585 Junius on the Painting of the Ancients, 2s ——— 1638
1586 Waring de Æquationib. Algebraicis, & Curvarum Proprietatib. *sutus*, 7s 6d ——— ——— *Cantab.* 1762
1587 Gregorii Astronomiæ, *fig.* 2 tom. 7s ——— *Genev.* 1726
1588 Trevigar Ele. Section. Conicarum, 3s — *Cantab.* 1731
1589 Cotesii Harmonia Mensurarum & ejusd. Opuscula Mathemat. *nov.* & *nit. comp.* 10s 6d ——— ——— *ibid.* 1722
1590 Newtoni Principia, cum Comment. Perpetuo, a Le Seur & Jacquier, 3 tom. *exemp. pulch.* 1l 11s 6d ——— *Genev.* 1739
1591 Vauban de l'Attaque & de Defense des Places, *avec fig. demi-relie*, 5s *Haye* 1737
1592 Le meme, tom. 2. *demi-relie*, 4s ——— *ibid.* 1742
1593 Rivard Elemens de Mathemat. *avec fig. cousu*, 4s *Par.* 1744
1594 La Science du Calcul, ou les Elemens des Mathemat. *cousu*, 2s *ibid.* 1714
1595 Essai sur la Tactique de l'Infanterie, *avec fig.* 2 tom. *fort bien relie en* 1. *vol.* 12s ——— ——— *Genev.* 1761
1596 Bouguier Traite de Navigation, *avec fig. fort bien relie*, 12s *Par.* 1753
1597 Memoires d'Artillerie, Recueillis, par M. Suivry, de St. Remy, *avec fig.*, 3 tom. *tres eleg. relie, marbre sur les tranches*, 1l 16s *ibid.* 1745
1598 *Perspective Pratique, par un Jesuite, avec d'un grand nombre des fig.* 3 tom. *exemplaire elegant.* 1l 15s ——— *ibid.* 1679
1599 L'Architecture de Vignole, avec les Comment. de Daviler & Dictionnaire de l'Architect. *avec fig. beau exempl. fort bien relie*, 10s 6d *Par.* 1710
1600 Bion sur les Instrumens Mathematiques, *avec fig.* 4s *Haye* 1723

Libri Historici, Geogr. Antiq. & Numismata. QUARTO.

1601 CORradini Vetus Latium Profanum & Sacrum, *cum fig.* 5 tom. *nit. comp.* 15s ——— — *Rom.* 1724
1602 Cellarii Geographia Antiqua, 2 tom. *exemp. pulch.* 12s *Lips.* 1701
1603 Moses Chorenensis Hist. Armeniacæ, Armenie & Lat. a Whistone, *sutus*, 3s 6d ——— ——— *Lond.* 1736
1604 Orosius adversus Paganos, cum Annotat. Havercampi, *cum fig. semi-comp.* 10s ——— ——— *L. Bat.* 1728
1605 Biretii Parallela Georg. Vetus & Novæ, 3 tom. 10s 6d *Par.* 1648
1606 Blasii Caryophili Opusc. de Marmorib. Antiq. & Paschales Caryophilis de Thermis Herculanis, *nit. comp.* 6s — *Traject.* 1743
1607 Mascovius de Rebus Imperii Romana Germanici, *semi-comp.* 6s *Lips.* 1741
1608 Marianæ de Rebus Hispaniæ, 6s ——— *Mogunt.* 1605
1609 Cotovici Itinerarium Hierosolymitanum & Syriacum, *cum fig.* 6s *Antv.* 1619
1610 Card. Bembi Hist. Rerum Venetarum, *exemp. pulch. nit. comp.* 2s 6d *Par.* 1551
1611 Rudbeckii Laponica Illustrata, Lat. & Suecice, *exemp. pulch. elegant. compact.* 7s 6d ——— ——— *Upsalæ* 1701
1612 Fontaninus de Antiquitatib. Hortæ Coloniæ Etruscor. *cum fig. nit. comp. in membr.* 5s ——— ——— *Romæ* 1723

H 1613 Scheu-

1613 Scheuchzeri Itinera & Alpina, *cum fig.* 3s —— *Lond.* 1708
1614 Van Dale de Oraculis Vet. Ethnicorum, *exemp. pulch.* 6s *Amst.* 1700
1615 Marshami Canon Chronicus Ægypt. Ebraic & Græcus, 2s 6d *Lipf.* 1676
1616 Sigonius de Republica Hebræor. *exemp. pulch.* 2s 6d *L. Bat.* 1701
1617 ——— de Antiquo Jure Provinciar. *eleg. comp. fol. marm.* 4s *Venet.* 1568
1618 Relandi Palæstina, *cum fig. nit. comp.* 2 tom. 12s *L. Bat.* 1714
1619 Pfeiffei Antiq. Græcarum Gentilium, 4s — *Regiom.* 1689
1620 Monumenta Paderbornensia ex Hist. Rom. Franc. Saxon. *cum multis fig.* 4s ——— ——— *Francof.* 1713
1621 Cuperi Harpocrates & Monumenta Antiqua, *cum fig.* 2s *Traj.* 1694
1622 Boxhornii Origines Ga licæ, *exemp. pulch. nit. comp.* 2s *Amst.* 1654
1623 Battelii Antiq. Rutupinæ & St. Edmundi Burgi, *nov. & nit. comp.* 10s ——— ——— —— *Oxon.* 1745
1624 Idem, *ch. max. nov. & nit. comp. in corio russ. fol. marmor.* 18s *ibid.* 1745
1625 Taylor Comment. ad L. Decemviralem de Inope Debitore in Partis dissecando *Cantab.* 1742—Marmor Sandvicense, cum Comment. J. Taylor, *cum fig. nov. & nit. comp. fol. marmor. ib.* 1743, 9s
1626 Majoris Historia de Gestis Scotorum, *ch. max. nit. comp. fol. deaurat.* 7s ——— ——— — *Edinb.* 1740
1627 Gibsoni Chronicon Saxonicum, 5s ——— *Oxon.* 1692
1628 Antonini Iter Britan. Comment. Gale, 2s 6d *Lond.* 1709
1629 Leslæus de Origine Morib. & Rebus Gestis Scotorum, 2s *Rom.* 1675
1630 Florent. Wigornensis Chronicon, *nit. comp.* 2s *Lond.* 1592
1631 Norisii Annales & Epocheæ Syromacedonum, *addit.* Fasti Consulares, *ch. max.* 5s ——— ——— *Florent.* 1691
1632 *Numismata Antiqua Pembrochiana, ch. max. exemp. pulch.* 3l 3s 1746
1633 Vaillant Hist. Regum Parthorum, *cum fig.* 2 tom. *semi-comp.* 8s *Par.* 1725
1634 ——— Idem, *comp. in membr.* 10s 6d ——— *ibid.* 1725
1635 ——— Hist. Regum Syriæ, *cum fig.* 6s ——— *ibid.* 1681
1636 ——— Idem, *nit. comp.* 7s ——— — *ibid.* 1681
1637 ——— Selectiora Numis. in Ære Max. Moduli, *fig.* 4s *ibid.* 1695
1638 Seguini Selecta Numis. Antiq. *cum fig.* 4s ——— *ibid.* 1684
1639 ——— Idem, 2s 6d ——— ——— *ibid.* 1666
1640 Augustini Gemmæ, & Sculpturæ, cum Ennaratione, a Gronovio, *cum fig. ch. max. nit. comp. in membr.* 10s 6d — *Franq.* 1695
1641 Harduinus de Nummis Antiquis, *cum fig.* 3s *Par.* 1689
1642 Jac. de Wilde Selecta Numis. Antiq. *cum fig.* 4s *Amst.* 1692
1643 Spanhemius de Præstantia & usu Numism. Antiquor. *cum fig. ch. max.* 5s ——— ——— *ibid.* 1671
1644 Chr. Wren Sylloge Numismat. Antiquor. *cum fig. sutus,* 2s *Lond.* 1708
1645 Hamelarii Numis. Aurea Imp. Rom. 2s 6d *Antv.* 1627
1646 Stradæ Thesaurus Antiq. Numism. 1s 6d ——— *Lugd.* 1553
1647 Patarol Opera omnia, *cum fig.* 2 tom. *exemp. pulch.* 6s *Venet.* 1743
1648 Occonis Numismata Imp. Romanor. 2s 6d *Aug. Vind.* 1601
1649 Imagines Illustr. ex Antiq. Marmorib. Numismat. & Gemmis expressæ, per Fulv. Ursinum, *exemp. pulch.* 9s — *Antv.* 1606
1650 Seldenus de Nummis, 1s ——— — *Lond.* 1675
1651 Kedderi Nummi diversi ex Argento Sueci, 2s 6d *Lipf.* 1706

1652 Schoon-

1652 Schoonhovii Emblemata, *cum fig.* 1s 6d — *L. Bat.* 1625
1653 Metamorph. Ovidianarum, Lib. xv. Æneis formis ab Ant. Tempesta incisi & in Pictor. editi. a P. de Jode, *nit. comp.* 10s 6d *Antv.* 1606

Libri Miscellanei & Poetici. QUARTO.

1654 HEATH Notæ, sive Lectiones ad Tragic. Græc. Vet. *sutus*, 15s ——— ——— *Oxon.* 1762
1655 Idem, *nov. & nit. comp.* 17s 6d ——— *ib.* 1762
1656 *Hyde Hist. Religionis Vet. Persarum & Parthorum & Mediorum, semi-comp.* 11s 6d ——— ——— *ibid.* 1760
1657 *Idem, nov. & nit. comp.* 14s ——— *ibid.* 1760
1658 Baringii Clavis Diplomatica, cum Tabulis Æneis, *nov. & nit. comp.* 15s ——— ——— *Hanover.* 1754
1659 Palmerii Exercitat. in optimos Auctores Græcos, *pulch. exemp. ch. max.* 5s ——— ——— *L. Bat.* 1668
1660 Origenis de Oratione, Gr. & Lat. a Reading, *exemp. pulch.* 3s *Lond.* 1728
1661 Riccii Differtat. Homericæ, 3 tom. *comp. in* 1 vol. 8s *Flor.* 1740
1662 Philoponus de Mundi Creatione, 2s 6d ——— *Viennæ* 1630
1663 Bergeri Comment. de Personis, vulgo Larvis Mascheris, *nit. comp.* 7s 6d ——— ——— *Franc.* 1723
1664 Spinozæ Opera Posthuma, *exemp. pulch.* 5s ——— 1677
1665 Arnobius contra Gentes, cum Comment. *exemp. pulch.* 5s *L.B.* 1651
1666 Hagemeieri Epist. de Jure Publico Europæi *Franc.* 1686—Freheri Origines Palatinæ, 2s ——— *Heidelb.* 1686
1667 Regin. Polus de Concilio, *exemp. pulch.* 2s ——— *Rom.* 1562
1668 Angeriani Erotopægnion, 2s ——— *sine loco & anno*
1669 Possevini Cicero Collatus cum Ethnicis & Sacris Script. *exemp. pulch.* 2s 6d ——— *Patav.* 1593
1670 Conringius de Bibliotheca Augusta, *exemp. pulch.* 2s *Helmst.* 1684
1671 Fracastorii Syphilis, sive Morbus Gallicus, *sutus*, 1s *Lond.* 1720
1672 Rhodomani Poesis Chrestianæ, Gr. & Lat. 3s *Franc.* 1586
1673 Petr. Ang. Bargæi Poemata omnia, *exemp. pulch. nit. comp. in corio maurit. fol. deaur.* 6s ——— ——— *Par.* 1587
1674 Gregorii Nazianzeni Carmina, Gr. & Lat. 4s *Venet.*
1675 Poemata quædam Joan. Marchio. Normanbiæ, *nitid. comp.* 1s *Lond.* 1695
1676 Tho. Mori Epigrammata, 2s 6d ——— *Basil.* 1520
1677 Burmanni Orationes, *nov. & nit. comp.* 8s *H. Com.* 1750

Divinity and Ecclesiastical History, English, Greek and Latin. QUARTO.

1678 HOLY Bible, translated by Miles Coverdale, dedicated to K. Edwarde the Syxte, *black letter*, 7s 6d *wants the title*
1679 Holy Bible, with Apocrypha, *fine paper*, 2 vol. *new and neatly bound in russia leather*, 2l 15s ——— *Cambr.* 1762
1680 Benson's Paraphrase and Notes on St. Paul's Epistles, vol. 1. *in boards*, 10s ——— ——— 1752
1681 Bp. Ellis's Tracts on the Liberty Spiritual and Temporal of the Protestants in England, *in boards*, 6s ——— ——— 1763

H 2 1682 Chap-

1682 Chappelow's Comment. on the Book of Job, 2 vol. *half bound*, 10s — — — 1752
1683 The same, 2 vol. *bound*, 12s — — 1752
1684 Cruden's Concordance to the Old and New Testament, *new and very neatly bound*, 1l 1s — — 1761
1685 Macknight's Harmony of the Gospels, *very fair*, 10s 1756
1686 The same, *in boards*, 7s — — 1756
1687 The same, *new edition*, *new and very neat*, — 1763
1688 Sykes's Paraphrase on the Epistles to the Hebrews, *new and neat*, 7s 6d — — — 1755
1689 Taylor on the Epistle to the Romans, 9s — 1754
1690 Lancaster's Comment. on the Revelations, *very neat*, 6s 1730
1691 Foster's Discourses on Natural Religion and Social Virtue, 2 vol. *neatly bound in one*, 15s — — 1749
1692 The same, in 2 vol. *neat*, 16s — 1749
1693 The same, 2 vol. *new and neatly bound*, 1l 1s — 1749
1694 The same, 2 vol. *new and elegantly bound*, *marble leaves*, 1l 4s 1749
1695 Locke's Paraphrase and Notes on St. Paul's Epistles, 7s 1742
1696 The same, 6s — — 1709
1697 The same, *last edition*, *new and neat*, 10s — 1763
1698 Pierce and Hallet on St. Paul's Epistles, 10s 6d — 1733
1699 Clarke's Annotat. of the New Test. 2s 6d — 1683
1700 —— Survey of the Bible, 2s 6d — 1693
1701 Parker on the Law of Nature and Christian Religion, *large paper*, 2s — — — 1681
1702 Middleton's Free Inquiry into Miraculous Powers, with the Introduction, 4s — — — 1749
1703 Three Sermons for propagating the Gospel, by the Bishops of Oxford, Landaff, and Chichester—Sermon before the Governors of the London Hospital, by the Bishop of Peterborough, *very neat*, 2s
1704 Whiston's Chronology of the Old Testament, and Harmony of the Evangelists, 2s — — 1705
1705 Bp. Burnet's Collect. of Tracts and Discourses, 3 vol. 15s 1704
1706 Newe Testament in Englyshe and in Latin, *black letter*, *very fair*, 10s 6d — — — 1538
1707 *Layton's Tracts in Defence of the Mortality of the Soul*, 2 *vol. very fair and scarce*, 12s
1708 Allix's Ancient Churches of Piedmont & Albigenses, 2s 6d 1690
1709 A full and plaine Declaration of Ecclesiastical Discipline owt off the Word off God, and off the Decliningе off the Churche off England from the same, *black letter*, *very fair and elegantly bound in blue turky*, *gilt leaves*, 15s — — 1574
1710 Bp. Bonner's Book of Homelies, *black letter*, *very fair*, 3s 1555
1711 Letter concerning Origen and his Opinions, 1s — 1661
1712 Dialogue on the Mahometan Religion, translated from the Arabic, 1s — — — 1615
1713 Vetus Testament. ex Vers. lxx. Interpret. a Breitingero, 4 tom. *exemp. pulch. & nit. comp.* 2l — *Tigur.* 1730
1714 —— Idem, 4 tom. *nov. & eleg. comp. fol. marmor.* 2l 10s *ib.* 1730
1715 Biblia Hebraica, *cum punctis*, 4s
1716 Idem, *sine punctis*, a Fostero, *ch. opt. semi-comp.* 15s *Oxon.* 1750
1717 Idem, a Fostero, 2 tom. *ch. opt. comp.* 18s — *ibid.* 1750
1718 Idem, a Fostero, *ch. opt. nov. & elegant. comp. in* 1 *vol.* 1l *ib.* 1750
1719 Nov. Test. Græce. & Græc. Vulg. 2 tom. 12s *Genev.*

1720 Nov.

1720 Nov. Test. Syriacum & Lat. a Luesdeno, *exemp. pulch.* 7s 6d *L. Bat.* 1708

1721 Sacrorum Evangelior. Versio Gothica, cum Interpr. Lat. & Notis Benzelii, cum Observat. Ed. Lye, *nit. comp.* 15s *Oxon.* 1750

1722 Idem, *nov. & nit. compact* 18s

1723 Psalmi Davidis Interp. & Notis Johnstoni, *ch. max. nit. comp. fol. marmor.* 7s 6d —— —— *Lond.* 1741

1724 Clerici Historia Ecclesiastica duorum primorum a Christo nato Sæculorum, *exemp. pulch.* 12s —— *Amst.* 1716

1725 Idem, *ch. max. exemp. pulch. nit. comp.* 18s — *ibid.* 1743

1726 Turettini Nubes Testium pro Moderatio inter Protestantes, *ch. max.* 3s 6d —— —— *Genev.* 1719

1727 Glassii Philologiæ Sacræ, *exemp. pulch. nit. comp. in membr.* 12s *Amst.* 1711

1728 Huetii Demonstratio Evangelica, *exemp. pulch. nitidiss. comp.* 5s *Franc.* 1722

1729 Limborch de Veritate Relig. Christ. Amica Collatio cum Erudito Judæo, 2s 6d —— —— *Goudæ* 1687

1730 Wolfii Curæ Philolog. & Critic. in Evang. & Actas Apostolor. 5 tom. *exemp. pulch.* 1l 10s —— *Basil.* 1741

1731 Idem, 5 tom. *nit. comp.* 1l 11s 6d —— *Hamb.* 1739

1732 Idem, 5 tom. *nit. comp. fol. marmor.* 2l —— *Basil.* 1741

1733 Kircheri Concordantiæ V. Test. Gr. Ebræis Vocib. Respondentes, 2 tom. *nit. comp.* 8s —— *Franc.* 1607

1734 Evangelie, Gothice, Islandice, Suecice & Lat. *exemp. pulch. nit. comp.* 10s 6d —— —— *Stockh.* 1671

1735 Reinoldii Census habitus Nascente Christo, *sutus,* 1s 6d *Oxon.* 1738

1736 Fabricius de Veritate Relig. Christ. *nov. & nitid. compact.* 7s *Hamb.* 1725

1737 Psalterium Davidis, Lat. & Saxon, a Spelmanno, 5s *Lond.* 1640

1738 Wagensellii Sota, seu de Uxore Adulterii Suspecta, *exemp. pulch.* 6s *Altdorf.* 1674

1739 Idem, *exemp. pulch. nit. comp. in membr.* 7s *ibid.* 1674

1740 Vitringa de Synagoga Vetere, 4s —— *Francq.* 1696

1741 Van Dale de Origine ac Progressu Idolatriæ, *exemp. pulch.* 4s *Amst.* 1696

1742 Quatuor Evangelia, Gothice & Anglo-Saxonice, a Junio, 5s *Dordr.* 1665

1743 Idem, *exemp. pulch.* 6s —— —— *ibid.* 1665

Physick, Natural History, &c. Chemistry, Husbandry, &c. English, Latin and French. QUARTO.

1744 BERENGER's New System of Horsemanship, *new and very neat,* 9s —— —— 1754

1745 Bradley's Account of the Works of Nature, *with a great number of cuts,* 6s —— —— —— 1721

1746 Astruc on the Venereal Disease, 9s —— 1754

1747 Neumann's Chemistry, Engl. with Addit. by Lewis, *new and very neat,* 18s —— —— — 1759

1748 The same, *very fair,* 15s —— —— 1759

1749 Dr. Mead's Medical Works, in Engl. *neat,* 16s —— 1762

1750 Owen's Natural Hist. of Serpents, *with cuts, sewed,* 3s 1742

1751 Da

1751 Da Costa's Natural Hist. of Fossils, vol. 1. *sewed,* 4s 1757
1752 Greenhil's Art of Embalming, *with cuts,* 6s
1753 Quincy's Lectures of Pharmacy, *in boards,* 2s 6d — 1723
1754 The same, *neat,* 3s ——— ——— 1723
1755 Pomet's History of Druggs, *with a great number of cuts,* 2 vol. 9s ——— ——— ——— 1712
1756 The same, *bound in* 1 *vol.* 9s ——— 1725
1757 Godartius of Insects, English, with Notes, by Lister, *with cuts,* 2s 6d ——— ——— ——— 1682
1758 Webster's History of Metals, 3s 6d ——— 1671
1759 The same, *very fair,* 4s ——— ——— 1671
1760 Evonymus's Book of Destillatyon of Waters, *black letter, very fair,* 2s ——— ——— — 1559
1761 Schoole of Salernes Regiment of Health, 1s ——— 1649
1762 Lisle's Observat. in Husbandry, *neat,* 15s ——— 1757
1763 The same, *very neatly bound, marble leaves,* 16s — 1757
1764 Agricola on Husbandry and Gardening, by Bradley, *with cuts,* 5s ——— ——— ——— 1721
1765 Miller's Gardeners Dictionary abridged, *with cuts, neat,* 1l 1s 1763
1766 Columella's Husbandry, by Gibson, *new and very neatly bound,* 15s ——— ——— ——— 1745
1767 Du Hamel's Pratic. Treatise of Husbandry, *with cuts, new and neat,* 15s ——— ——— ——— 1762
1768 Langley's Principles of Gardening, *with cuts,* 6s 1728
1769 James's Theory and Practice of Gardening, *with cuts, very fair,* 5s ——— ——— ——— 1728
1770 Meager's English Gardener, *with cuts,* 1s ——— 1699
1771 Blith's Survey of Husbandry, 1s 6d ——— 1652
1772 Hartlib's Legacy of Husbandry, 2s 1655
1773 Markham's Art of Planting, Graffing and Gardening, 1s 1640
1774 Riegeri Introd. ad Notitiam Rerum Natural. & Arte Factar. 4 tom. *nov. & nit. comp.* 1l 7s ——— *H. Com.* 1742
1775 Boerhaave Elementa Chemiæ, 2 tom. *cum fig. edit. opt. elegant. comp. fol. marmor.* 18s ——— ——— *L. Bat.* 1732
1776 Van Swieten Comment. in Aphorismos Boerhaave, 3 tom. *exemp. pulch.* 1l 11s 6d ——— ——— *ibid.* 1742
1777 Idem, *exemp. pulch. nit. comp.* 3 tom. 1l 11s 6d *Par.* 1755
1778 Ramazzini Opera omnia Medica, *nit. comp. in membr.* 6s *Lond.* 1718
1779 Astruc de Morbis Venereis, 2 tom. *nit. comp.* 18s *Par.* 1740
1780 Morgagni Adversaria Anatomica omnia, *cum fig. nitid. comp.* 6s *L. Bat.* 1723
1781 Santorini Observat. Anat. *fig. semi-comp.* 2s *Venet.* 1724
1782 Petiti Comment. in Libros Aretæi, 2s ——— *Lond.* 1726
1783 Papæ Consulti Medici, *semi-comp.* 2s ——— *Venez.* 1734
1784 Pharmacopœia Londinens. 2s 6d ——— *Lond.* 1746
1785 Hippocratis de Morbis Popularib. Gr. & Lat. a Freind, *semi-comp.* 1s ——— ——— ——— *ibid.* 1707
1786 Pisonis de Cognoscend. & Curandis Corporis Morbis, cum Præfat. Boerhaave, 2 tom. *nit. comp.* 7s ——— *L. Bat.* 1736
1787 Ruyschii Opera omnia, *cum multis fig.* 2 tom. *nitid. comp.* 1l 4s *Amst.* 1710
1788 Idem, *elegant. comp. in membr.* 4 tom. 1l 7s — *ibid.* 1721
1789 Boerhaave Methodus Studii Medici, a Haller, 2 tom. *nov. & semi-comp.* 16s ——— ——— *ibid.* 1751

1790 Leeuwen-

1790 Leeuwenhoeck Epist. Physiologicæ, *fig.* 3s — *Delph.* 1719
1791 Alpinus de Præsag. Vita & Morte Ægrotant. cum Præfat. Boerhaave, *semi-comp.* 3s — — *L. Bat.* 1733
1792 Idem, *nit. comp.* 4s — — 1733
1793 Idem, *nit. comp.* 4s — — 1733
1794 Stahlii Fundam. Chemiæ, 2 tom. *nit. comp.* 8s *Hamb.* 1734
1795 Severinus de Recondita Abscessuum Natura, *cum fig. semi-comp.* 3s *Norimb.* 1746
1796 Daventeri Ars Obstetricandi, *cum fig. semi-comp.* 2s 6d *L. Bat.* 1724
1797 Poterii Opera Chemiæ, Notis Hoffmanni, 6s *ibid.* 1733
1798 Vander Linden de Scriptis Medicis, *edit. opt.* 6s *Francof.* 1698
1799 Bellini Opuscula Medica, *cum fig.* 2s 6d — *Norib.* 1686
1800 Anonymi Introd. Anatomica, Gr. & Lat. a Laurenbergio, 2s *L. Bat.* 1696
1801 Phile de Proprietate Animalium, Gr. & Lat. a Corn. de Pauw, 2s 6d — — — *ibid.* 1618
1802 Boetii de Boot Icones Florum, Herbar. ac Fruct. Select. 2s *Traject.* 1730
1803 Histoire de la Medicine, par Le Clerc, *avec fig. demi relie,* 6s *Brug.* 1640
1804 Le meme, *relie en velin,* 7s — *Amst.* 1723
1805 Le meme, 2s — — *ibid.* 1723
1806 Pomet Hist. Generale des Drogues, *avec fig.* 2 tom. *fort bien relie,* 16s — — *ibid.* 1702
1807 Winslow Exposition Anatomiq. *avec fig. bien relie,* 9s *Par.* 1735
1808 Le meme, *fort bien relie,* 10s 6d — *ibid.* 1732
1809 Traite des Maladies de l'Oeil, par Maitrejan, 3s *ibid.* 1732
1810 L'Art de la Verrerie de Neri, Merret & Kunckel, *avec fig. nouv. & tres eleg. relie,* 14s — — *Rouen* 1707 *Par.* 1752

Civil and Common Law. QUARTO.

1811 DOctrina Placitandi, 2s — 1677
1812 Lord Somers's Argument in the Banker's Case, *large paper,* 2s — — —
1813 Godolphin's Orphan's Legacy, 2s — 1733
1814 The same, 1s 6d — — 1685
1815 Godolphin's Repertorium Canonicum, 2s — 1674
1816 Brownlow's Writs Judicial, 1s — — 1680
1817 Moyle's Book of Entries, 1s — — 1653
1818 Brownlow's and Goldesborough's Reports, 2s — 1685
1819 Hughes's Grand Abridgment of the Law, 3 vol. 4s 1651
1820 Sheppard's Touchstone of Common Assurances, 7s 1660
1821 West's Presidents, 2s — — 1651
1822 Callis's Reading on the Sewers, 1s 6d — 1622
1823 Burne's Ecclesiastical Law, 2 vol. *new, in boards,* 2l — 1647
1824 Swinbourne on Spousals, 2s — 1763
1825 Pigott on Common Recoveries, *in boards,* 6s — 1686
1826 Doderige's English Lawyer, 1s — — 1739
1827 Special and Selected Law Cases, 1s — 1631
1828 Eden Elementa Juris Civilis, *elegant. comp. in corio maurit. fol. deaur.* 10s 6d — — *Oxon.* 1744 1641

1829 Grotius

1829 Grotius de Jure Belli ac Pacis, cum Notis Barberacii & Comment. Coccеii, 5 tom. *exemp. pulch. & nit. comp.* 2l 2s *Lausani* 1751
1830 Heineccii, Notæ ad Vinnii Comment. in Institut. Imper. *sutus,* 1s 6d ——— ——— 1747
1831 Vinnii Comment. in Institut. Imperial. 2s 6d *L. Bat.* 1709
1832 Gravinæ Originis Juris Civilis, *nov. & nit. comp.* 7s *Lipſ.* 1737
1833 Vinnii Tractatus V. de Pactis, Jurisdictione, &c. 2s 6d *Ultraj.* 1697
1834 Bynkershoeck Opera, 6 tom. *sutus,* 1l 10s — *Lugd.* 1752, &c.

History and Antiquities of Great Britain and Ireland. OCTAVO.

1835 RAPIN's History of England, and Continuation by Tindal, to 1757, 21 vol. *new and very neatly bound,* 6l 6s
1836 Tindal's Continuation of Rapin's History, to the Death of George II. 13 vol. *best edition, very neat,* 2l 15s —— 1744
1837 Hume's Hist. of England, from Julius Cæsar to the Revolution, 8 vol. *in boards, new,* 2l ——— 1763
1838 ——— The same, 8 vol. *new and neatly bound,* 2l 8s 1763
1839 Political State of Great Britain from 1709 to 1739 inclusive, *elegantly and uniformly bound,* 55 vol. 18l 18s
1840 Clarendon's History of the Rebellion, 6 vol. 18s 1707
1841 ——— The same, 6 vol. *very fair,* 1l 1s — 1717
1842 ——— The same, 6 vol. *with the heads,* 1l 4s 1721
1843 ——— The same, with the Life and Continuation, 9 vol. *very fair and neatly bound,* 2l 2s ——— 1721, &c.
1844 ——— The same, 10 vol. *large paper, very fair and neat, with the heads,* 3l 3s ——— ——— 1717, &c.
1845 ——— Life and Continuation of his History, 3 vol. *sewed, new,* 15s ——— ——— — 1760
1846 ——— The same, 3 vol. *new and neat,* 18s — 1760
1847 ——— The same, 2 vol. *large paper, sewed, new,* 15s
1848 ——— The same, 2 vol. *new and neatly bound,* 18s
1849 Clarendon and Whitlock compared by Oldmixon, 1s 6d 1727
1850 The same, *very fair,* 2s —— ——— 1727
1851 Howell's Medulla Hist. Anglicanæ, *with cuts,* 4s 1750
1852 Critical History of England, by Oldmixon, 2 vol. 3s 1724
1853 Jeffery of Monmouth's British Hist. with a Preface, by Thompson, *very fair,* 4s ——— —— ——— 1718
1854 Echard's History of the Revolution, 1s 6d —— 1725
1855 D'Orlean's History of the Revolution in England, 2s 1711
1856 Patten's History of the Rebellion in 1715, 1s 6d — 1717
1857 Bishop Parker's History of his own Time, 2s —— 1727
1858 Salmon's Chronological History of England, 2 vol. *with heads, best edition,* 7s ——— ——— 1747
1859 Coke's Detection of the Court and State of England, 3 vol. *best edition,* 6s. ——— —— ——— 1719
1859 Lord Walpole's Answer to Bolingbroke's Letters on History, *very neat,* 3s 6d —— ——— —— 1763

1860 Lord

1860 Lord Bolingbroke's Remarks on the History of England, *in boards,* 2s 6d — — — 1745
1861 — The same, *neat, in vellum,* 3s 6d — 1747
1862 — Dissertation on Parties, 2s — 1735
1863 — The same, *large print,* 3s — 1749
1864 — Letter to Windham, *in boards,* 3s — 1753
1865 — The same, *bound, very fair,* 3s 6d — 1753
1866 — The same, *very fair and neat,* 4s — 1753
1867 — Political Tracts, *neat, in vellum,* 3s 6d — 1748
1868 Higgons's Remarks on Bishop Burnet's History, 2s 1725
1869 — The same, 2s — — 1727
1870 — Short View of the English History, *large paper,* 3s 1723
1871 Historical Account of Taxes of England from the Conquest to 1725, by Stevens, 2s 6d — — 1725
1872 Report of the Lords relating to the Publick Records, *neat,* 1s 1719
1873 Fleetwood's Chronicon Preciosum, 2s — 1707
1874 Leake's Historic. Account of English Money, *with cuts, fair,* 5s 1744
1875 Edmonds and Carew's Negotiations between England and France, 3s — — — 1749
1876 Conduct of the Dutchess of Marlborough, 1s 6d — 1742
1877 Annals of Q. Anne, 11 vol. *very fair,* 1l 5s — 1703
1878 Hornby's Specimen of the Mistakes in Dugdale's Baronage, *neat,* 2s — — — 1730
1879 Parliamentary Hist. of England from the earliest Times to the Restoration, 24 vol. *new and very neat,* 7l 7s — 1762
1880 Arch. Grey's Debates of the H. of Commons from 1667 to 1694, 10 vol. *in boards,* 2l 10s — — 1763
1881 Chandler's Hist. Proceedings and Debates of the Lords and Commons from the Restoration to 1742, in 22 vol. *neat,* 5l 5s 1742
1882 British Parliamentary Register, 3s — 1753
1883 Willis Noticia Parliamentaria, Vol. 3. *fair and neat* 1750
1884 The same, Vol. 1. 1s — — 1715
1885 Discourse on Supreme Power and Common Right, 1s 1680
1886 Petyt's ancient Rights of the Com. of England, 1s 6d 1680
1887 Pettus's Constitution of Parliaments, 1s — 1680
1888 Journal of the House of Commons on the Popish Plot, 1s 1680
1889 Transaction of the Parliament relating to the Popish Plot, 1s 1680
1890 Regicides no Saints nor Martyrs, 1s — 1700
1891 Trial of Admiral Byng, with his Defence, *very fair and neat,* 2s 6d — — — 1757
1892 State Trials abridged, 9 vol. *fair and neat,* 1l 7s — 1720
1893 Life of the Duke of Marlborough, by Lediard, *with cuts,* 3 vol. 9s — — — 1730
1894 The same, *with cuts, another edition,* 2 vol. *fair,* 7s 1743
1895 The same, *new and very neat,* 2 vol. 9s — 1743
1896 Life of Wicliffe, by Lewis, *fair and neat,* 2s 6d — 1723
1897 — of Bernard Gilpin and Bishop Latimer, by Gilpin, *fair,* 4s — — — 1753
1898 — of the Earl of Orrery, and Mem. of the Family of Boyle, by Budgel, 1s 6d — — 1732
1899 — The same, *very fair,* 2s — — 1732
1900 — of Archbishop Whitgift, by Paule, 1s 6d — 1699
1901 — of Bishop Aylmer, by Strype, 1s — 1701

I 1902 Life

1902 Life of Baxter abridged, with a Continuation, by Calamy, 4 vol. *very fair,* 12s —— —— 1713
1903 —— of Dr Swift, by the Earl of Orrery, *in boards,* 1s 6d 1752
1904 —— The same, *bound,* 2s —— —— 1752
1905 The same, *new and very neatly bound, marble leaves,* 3s. 1752
1906 —— of Dr. Swift, by Delaney, 2s —— 1754
1907 —— of Archbishop Tillotson, by Dean Young, 1s 1717
1908 —— of Archbishop Tillotson, by Birch, 2s 6d — 1752
1909 —— of King James I. by Harris 1753 —— Life of King Charles I. by Harris 1755 —— Life of Oliver Cromwell, by Harris, 3 vol. *new and neatly bound* 1753, &c. 15s
1912 —— of Edward the Black Prince, by Collins, *large paper, very fair and neat,* 3s 6d —— —— 1740
1913 —— of Sir John Perrot, Lord Lieutenant of Ireland, *large paper, neat,* 2s —— —— — 1728
1914 —— of Oliver Cromwell, by Kimber, 1s 6d —— 1724
1915 —— of Betterton, by Gildon, with the Amorous Widow, 1s 6d —— —— —— 1710
1916 —— The same, *very fair,* 2s —— —— 1710
1917 —— of Archbishop Williams, by Hacket, 1s —— 1715
1918 —— of Shower, by Tong, 1s —— 1710
1919 —— of Archbishop Chichele, by Duck, 1s — 1699
1920 —— of Bishop Ken, by Hawkins, 1s —— 1713
1921 —— of Mrs. Elizabeth Walker of Fyfield in Essex, 1s 1690
1922 —— of General Monck, by Gumble, 1s — 1671
1923 —— of Bishop Sanderson, by Walton, 1s —— 1678
1924 —— of the Earl of Rochester, by Burnet, 1s — 1680
1925 —— of King Richard II. 1s —— 1681
1926 —— of Robert Earl of Leicester, 1s 6d —— 1727
1927 —— of the Admirals, by Campbell, 4 vol. *new and neatly bound, with cuts,* 1l 4s —— —— 1761
1928 Lives of Dr. Donne, Sir H. Wotton, Mr. Hooker and Herbert, by Walton, 1s —— 1670
1929 —— of English Poets, by Winstanley, 1s —— 1687
1930 English Worthies in Church and State, by Fuller, 2s 1684
1931 Lloyd's State Worthies, 4s —— —— 1670
1932 —— The same, 4s —— —— 1665
1933 —— The same, *very fair,* 5s —— 1679
1934 Ludlow's Memoirs, 3 vol. 6s —— 1698
1935 The same, 3 vol. 6s —— —— 1722
1936 Memoirs of Sir John Reresby, Governor of York, 2s 1735
1937 —— The same, *neat,* 2s 6d —— 1735
1938 —— of the Earl of Danby, 1s —— 1710
1939 Welwood's Memoirs, *very fair,* 2s 6d —— 1700
1940 Smith's Memoirs of Secret Service, 1s —— 1699
1941 Memoirs of R. Dudley E. of Leicester, 1s — 1706
1942 —— of a Cavalier, or Military Journal of the Wars in England and Germany, from 1632 to 1648, 3s 6d
1943 —— of Sir John Berkley, 2s —— — 1699
1944 —— The same, *bad copy,* 1s —— 1699
1945 —— of Sir Philip Warwick, 2s —— 1702
1946 —— of Major Ramkins, *neatly bound,* 1s 6d 1719
1947 —— of Denzil Lord Holles, from 1641 to 1648, 3s 1699

1948 Me-

1948 Memoirs of the Order of the Garter, by Dawson, 1s 6d 1714
1949 Memorable Actions of Sir Thomas Grantham, 1s 1714
1950 Naval Chronicle, or Voyages, &c. of the most Celebrated English Navigators and Sea Commanders, *with cuts*, 3 vol. *neat*, 9s 1760
1951 Foster's Examination of the Scheme of Church Power in Gibson's Codex, 1s 6d — — 1735
1952 Ames's Catalogue of English Heads, *sewed*, 1s 6d 1748
1953 Catalogue of the Graduates in the University of Oxford, from 1659 to 1726, 1s — — — 1717
1954 Historical Register of Affairs at Home and Abroad, from 1714 to 1737, 24 vol. *neat and uniform*, 2l 5s
1955 The same, from 1714 to 1738, 25 vol. *compleat, neat and uniform*, 2l 12s 6d
1956 Squire on the Anglo-Saxon Government in England, 2s 6d 1745
1957 Pepy's State of the Royal Navy of England, 1s — 1690
1958 Wharton's Defects in Burnet's History of Reformation, 1s 1693
1959 Petty's Review of the Kings of England, 1s — 1698
1960 Lloyd's Historical Account of Church Government in Great Britain, 1s — — 1684
1961 Milton's Defence of the People of England, 1s — 1692
1962 History of the great Storm, Nov. 27. 1703. 1s — 1704
1963 Collins's Peerage of England, with the Arms of all the Nobility, 6 vol. *in boards, best edition*, 1l 7s — 1756
1964 Laws of Honour, or Ancient Derivation of all Titles, Dignities, &c. 2s — — — 1714
1965 Segar's Titles of Honour, 1s — — 1712
1966 History of the Family of Carteret, by Collins, *fine paper, sewed*, 3s — — — 1756
1967 Hollar's Maps of England, 4s
1968 Leland's Itinerary, published by Hearne, 9 vol. *very fair and neat*, 1l 15s — — 1710
1969 The same, *second edition*, 9 vol. *neatly bound in* 5, *large paper*, 2l 12s 6d — — 1745
1970 Powell's History of Wales, improved by Wynne, 5s 1697
1971 Aubrey's Natural History of Surrey, *with cuts, large paper*, 5 vol. *fair*, 1l 7s — — 1719
1972 Salmon's Antiquities of Surrey, *very fair*, 2s 6d — 1736
1973 Ashmole's Antiquities of Berkshire, 3 vol. *large paper*, 15s 1719
1974 London and its Environs described, *with a great number of cuts, new and very neat*, 6 vol. 1l 10s — — 1761
1975 Willis's Welch Cathedrals, *with cuts*, 4 vol. *fair and neat*, 12s 1717
1976 Herne's Account of the Charter House, *neat, and gilt leaves*, 2s — — — 1677
1977 Bearcroft's Account of the Charter House, *large paper, neat*, 4s — — — 1737
1978 Tanner's Notitia Monastica, *cuts, fair*, 2s 6d — 1695
1979 Thoresby's History of the Church of Leeds, *with cuts*, 1s 6d 1724
1980 The same, *new and neatly bound*, 3s — 1724
1981 Abingdon's Antiquities of Worcester Cathedral, *sewed*, 2s 6d 1717
1982 Izacke's Antiquities of the City of Exeter, 1s 6d 1681
1983 The same, *very fair*, 2s 6d — 1741
1984 Torr's Antiquities of York City, 2s — 1719
1985 Spelman's Villare Anglicum, 2s — — 1638

I 2 1986 Ro-

1986 Robertson's History of Scotland, 2 vol. *new and elegantly bound, by Johnson,* 14s —— —— 1761
1987 The same, 2 vol. *fair and neat,* 10s 6d —— 1761
1988 Innes's Essay on the Antient Inhabitants of Scotland, 2 vol. *fair,* 6s —— —— —— 1729
1989 Malcome's Tracts relating to the Antiquities of Great Britain and Ireland, 2s 6d —— —— 1744
1990 Interest of Scotland considered, 1s 6d —— 1736
1991 Trial of Captain Porteous in Scotland, 1s —— 1736
1992 Nicolson's Scottish Historical Library, 2s —— 1702
1993 Royal Line of Scotland, by Sir G. Mackenzie, 1s —— 1685
1994 Scotland's Soveraignty asserted, by Sir T. Craig, 1s 6d 1695
1995 Dalrymple's Collection concerning the Scottish History, 3s 1705
1996 Balcarras's Account of the Affairs in Scotland, 1s 6d 1705
1997 Drummond's History of Scotland, *with cuts,* 1s 6d 1681
1998 Proceedings of the Assembly of the Church of Scotland, 1s 1751
1999 Bishop Guthry's Memoirs of the great Rebellion, 1s 6d 1702
2000 Faithful Register of the late Rebellion, 2s —— 1718
2001 Original Letters and Papers relating to the Rebellion, 2s 1730
2002 Martin's Voyage to St. Kilda, *with cuts,* 1s 6d — 1698
2003 Nicolson's Irish Historical Library, 2s —— 1724
2004 Precedency of the Peers of Ireland in England, 1s — 1739
2005 Reflections and Resolutions proper for the Gentlemen of Ireland, 1s 6d —— —— 1738
2006 The same, *bound in morocco,* 2s 6d —— 1738
2007 Present State of Affairs in Ireland, 1s 6d —— 1730
2008 King's State of the Protestants in Ireland, with the Appendix, *very fair,* 3s —— —— *Dubl.* 1730
2009 Clarendon's History of the Rebellion in Ireland, 1s 6d 1719
2010 Monastical History of Ireland, *with cuts,* 3s — 1722
2011 Parker's Military Transactions in Ireland and Flanders, 2s 1747
2012 Borlase's Reduction of Ireland, 1s —— 1675
2013 Memoirs of Ireland from the Restoration, 1s —— 1716
2014 Petty's Political Anatomy of Ireland, 1s —— 1691

History and Antiquities of various Nations, Voyages and Travels. OCTAVO.

2015 ANcient Universal History of the World, 21 vol. *very fair, in boards,* 5l 5s —— —— 1747, &c.
2016 The same, 20 vol. *sewed,* 3l 15s —— *Dubl.* 1763
2017 *The same, with the Modern History,* 61 *vol. new, and uniformly and neatly bound,* 17l 17s —— — *Lond.*
2018 Modern Universal History, 8 first vol. *in boards,* 1l 12s 1759
2019 —— —— —— vol 12. *in boards,* 4s — 1759
2020 —— —— —— vol. 13. *in boards,* 4s —— 1759
2021 History of the Arabians, under the Government of the Caliphs, by the Abbe de Marigny, containing the Space of six hundred and thirty-six Years, translated and improved, with Notes, &c. 4 vol. 12s —— —— — 1758
2022 The same, 4 vol. *new and neatly bound,* 16s —— 1758
2023 The same, 4 vol. *new and elegantly bound, by Johnson,* 1l 1758

2024 History

2024 History of the Arabs, by the Authors of the Universal Hist. 3 vol. *very neat,* 15s —— —— *Dubl.* 1761
2025 Ockley's History of the Saracens, 2 vol. *fair,* 4s 1708
2026 The same, 2 vol. *large paper, very fair,* 6s —— 1718
2027 The same, 2 vol. *last edition, new and neatly bound,* 7s 6d 1757
2028 Josephus, by Whiston, 4 vol. *fair and neat,* 18s — 1755
2029 Du Fresnoy's Chronological Tables of Universal History, 2 vol. *new and very neatly bound,* 12s —— 1762
2030 Sanchoniatho's Phœnician History, by Bishop Cumberland, *fair,* 4s —— —— —— 1720
2031 Bishop Cumberland's Origines Gentium Antiquiss. *very fair,* 4s —— —— —— 1724
2032 Salmon's General History of the World, *very neat,* 3s 1751
2033 Montague on the Rise and Fall of the Antient Republicks, *sewed,* 3s 6d —— 1759
2034 The same, *new and neatly bound,* 5s —— 1760
2035 The same, *new and elegantly bound, by Johnson,* 6s 1760
2036 Lewis's Antiquities of the Hebrew Republick, 4 vol. *very fair,* 10s —— —— 1724
2037 Gordon's Geographical Grammar, *with the maps,* 3s 1749
2038 The same, *neatly bound in morocco,* 4s —— 1725
2039 Salmon's Geographical Grammar, *with maps,* 4s 6d 1760
2040 Wells of Antient and Present Geography, 1s 6d 1717
2041 The same, *very fair,* 2s —— —— 1738
2042 Stanyan's Grecian History, 2 vol. *fair,* 7s — 1739
2043 The same, 2 vol. *fair and neat,* 8s —— 1751
2044 The same, 2 vol. *large paper, very fair and neat,* 10s 6d 1739
2045 The same, vol. 2. *very fair,* 3s —— —— 1739
2046 Arrian's History of Alexander's Expedition, by Rooke, 2 vol. 4s —— —— 1729
2047 The same, 2 vol. *very fair,* 6s —— —— 1729
2048 Dion. Cassius, translated by Manning, 2 vol. *fair,* 5s 1704
2049 Xenophon's Expedition of Cyrus, by Spelman, 2 vol. 7s 1742
2050 —— History of Greece, by Newman, 2s — 1685
2051 —— Banquet, by Welwood, 1s —— 1710
2052 Littlebury's Herodotus, 2 vol. *with cuts,* 5s —— 1720
2053 The same, 2 vol. *new and neatly bound,* 8s — 1737
2054 The same, 2 vol. *new and elegantly bound, by Johnson,* 10s 1737
2055 Thucydides, by Hobbes, 2 vol. *with maps, fair and neat,* 8s 1723
2056 Polybius's History of the World, by Sir H. Sheers, 2 vol. 4s 1698
2057 The same, translated by Hampton, 2 vol. *new and elegantly bound, by Johnson,* 12s —— 1761
2058 Potter's Antiquities of Greece, 2 vol. *with cuts,* 4s 1728
2059 Cæsar's Comment. by Bladen, *with cuts, fair,* 3s — 1705
2060 Livy's Roman History, by Hay, with Geographical and Chronological Notes, 6 vol. *very neat,* 1l 7s —— 1758
2061 Rollin's Roman History revised and compleated by Crevier, 16 vol. *with cuts, very fair,* 2l 16s —— — 1739
2062 Gordon's Tacitus, 4 vol. *very fair,* 16s — 1737
2063 Annals and History of Tacitus, by Sir Hen. Saville, 3 vol. *large paper,* 6s —— —— 1698
2064 Kennet's Antiquities of Rome, *with cuts,* 2s — 1699
2065 The same, 2s —— —— 1721
2066 The same, 2s —— —— 1717

2067 Treatise

2067 Treatise of the Revenue and false Money of the Romans, *very neat,* 2s 6d — — — 1741
2068 Chapman's Essay on the Roman Senate, 2s — 1750
2069 Echard's Roman History, 5 vol. *very fair and neat, gilt leaves,* 18s — — — 1707
2070 Valerius Maximus, translated by Speed, 2s 6d — 1678
2071 Suetonius's History of the 12 Cæsars, 1s 6d — 1677
2072 Vertot's Revolutions of Rome, 2 vol. 6s — 1724
2073 —— History of the Bretons amongst the Gauls, 2 vol. in one, 2s — — — 1722
2074 —— The same, 2 vol. 2s 6d — 1722
2075 —— Revolutions of Portugal, *fair and neat,* 2s 6d 1754
2076 —— Revolutions in Sweden, 2s — 1723
2077 —— Revolutions in Spain, 5 vol. *fair,* 10s — 1724
2078 Guicciardin's History of Italy, by Goddard, 10 vol. *fair,* 1l 16s 1753
2079 The same, 10 vol. *new and very neat,* 2l 5s
2080 Buonamici's Comment. of the late War in Italy, by Wishart, *very fair,* 3s 6d — — 1753
2081 The same, *elegantly bound,* 4s — — 1753
2082 The same, *elegantly bound, by Johnson,* 5s — 1753
2083 Campbell's Present State of Europe, *new and neatly bound, by Johnson,* 7s — — 1761
2084 Annual Register for 1758, 59, 60, 61 and 62, in 5 vol. 1l 10s 1762
2085 —— for 1761, *in boards, new,* 5s — 1762
2086 —— The same, 1761, *new and neatly bound,* 6s 1762
2087 —— for 1760, *new and neatly bound,* 6s — 1762
2088 Heiss's History of the Empire, 2 vol. *fair,* 5s — 1727
2089 Daniel's History of France, 5 vol. *very fair,* 18s — 1726
2090 History of Lewis XI. King of France, by Du Clos, 2 vol. *very neat,* 6s — — — 1746
2091 Age of Lewis XIV, by Voltaire, 2 vol. *fair,* 7s — 1752
2092 Greaves's Works, containing an Account of the Pyramids in Egypt, the Roman Foot and Denarius, and the Grand Signior's Seraglio, &c. *with cuts,* 2 vol. 6s — — 1737
2093 The same, 2 vol. *new and very neat,* 8s — 1737
2094 Bishop Hooper's State of the Ancient Measures, &c. 3s 1721
2095 Literæ de Re Nummaria, being Remarks on the Denarii Romani, 2s — — — 1729
2096 Cumberland on the Jewish Measures and Weights, 1s 1686
2097 History of the Rise and Fall of Masaniello, Fisherman of Naples, 1s 6d — — — 1729
2098 History of the Sevarambians, from the Memoirs of Captain Siden, 3s — — — — 1738
2099 Bigges's Military History of Europe, 3s — 1755
2100 Papers relating to the Rupture with Spain, France and England, *sewed,* 2s — — — 1762
2101 ———— Campaigns in Germany and Flanders, 1s 1751
2102 Byng's Expedition to Sicily, *fair,* 2s — 1739
2103 Voltaire's History of the War, of 1741, *sewed,* 1s 6d 1756
2104 —— History of Charles XII. 2s — 1732
2105 —— The same, *very fair,* 2s 6d — 1732
2106 Brockwell's Natural History of Portugal, *with cuts, fair,* 2s 1726
2107 Sousa's General History of Portugal, by Stevens, *neat,* 2s 6d 1698
2108 Du Pin's Universal Library of Historians, 2 vol. *fair,* 4s 1709

2109 Du

2109 Du Halde's General History of China, 4 vol. *with cuts, fair and neat,* 12s ——— ——— ——— 1741
2110 Boswell's Method of Study, 2 vol. *very fair,* 6s ——— 1738
2111 Compleat History of Europe, from 1600 to 1712, 17 vol. 1l 1s ——— ——— 1705
2112 Webb's Antiquity of China, and the Chinese Language, 1s 1678
2113 Enquiry into the Management of the War in Spain, 2s 1712
2114 Bishop Hare's Management of the War, 1s 6d ——— 1711
2115 Mack Gregory's Account of the Sepulchres of the Antients, 1s 6d ——— ——— ——— 1712
2116 Merault's Siege of Rochel, 1s ——— ——— 1680
2117 Addison's first State of Mahumedism, 1s ——— 1679
2118 ——— State of the Jews in Barbary, 1s ——— 1675
2119 Cardinal Richlieu's Political Testament, 1s 6d ——— 1695
2120 Secret History of the House of Medicis, 1s ——— 1686
2121 Onf. Burrish's View of the Policy and Commerce of the United Provinces, *in boards,* 2s ——— ——— 1728
2122 The same, *bound,* 3s ——— ——— 1728
2123 The same, *very fair and neat,* 3s 6d ——— 1731
2124 De Witt's Interest and Political Maxims of Holland, *new and neatly bound,* 5s ——— ——— ——— 1746
2125 The same, *new and elegantly bound, by Johnson,* 6s 1746
2126 Lord Molesworth's Account of Denmark, 1s 6d 1694
2127 *The same, with Bishop Robinson's Account of Sweden, and the History of Count Patkul, neatly bound,* 4s ——— 1737
2129 The same, *new and very neatly bound,* 5s
2130 The same, *new and elegantly bound by* Johnson, 6s 1746
2131 Perry's State of Russia, *fair,* 3s 6d ——— 1716
2132 Present State of Russia from the High Dutch, 2 vol. 4s 1723
2133 Genuine Hist. of Nadir-Scha 1741—Journey through Russia into Persia 1742, 2s
2134 L'Abbe Lambert's Observations upon Asia, Africa and America, 2 vol. *neat,* 5s
2135 History of California, 2 vol. *with cuts, in boards,* 4s 1759
2136 The same, 2 vol. *bound,* 5s ——— 1759
2137 Neal's History of New England, 2 vol. *new and neatly bound,* 8s ——— ——— ——— 1747
2138 Douglas's Summary of the Brit. Settlements in N. America, 2 vol. *in boards,* 8s ——— ——— 1760
2139 Account of the European Settlements in America, 2 vol. 5s 1757
2140 The same, 2 vol. *neat,* 6s ——— ——— 1760
2141 The same, 2 vol. *new and elegantly bound by* Johnson, 10s 6d 1760
2142 Compleat Hist. of Spanish America, *in boards,* 2s 1742
2143 British Empire in America, 2 vol. *best Edit. with maps,* 7s 1741
2144 Description of South Carolina, 1s 6d ——— 1761
2145 Brickell's Natural Hist. of North Carolina, *with cuts,* 6s 1737
2146 Cox's Descript. of Carolina, *with a map,* 2s 6d — 1722
2147 Robson's Account of Hudson's Bay, *with cuts,* 2s 6d 1752
2148 The same, *very fair,* 3s ——— 1752
2149 New History of the East Indies, 2 vol. *neat,* 8s 1758
2150 Colden's Hist. of the Five Indian Nations of Canada, 3s 6d 1747
2151 Renaudot's Ancient Accounts of India and China, 2s 1733
2152 Le Comte's Account of China, *with cuts,* 2s ——— 1699

2153 Bar-

2153 Bartram's Travels from Penſylvania to Canada, 2s 1751

2154 Drury's Account of Madagaſcar, *with cuts, very fair,* 3s 1729

2155 The ſame, *new and neatly bound,* 4s —— 1729

2156 Dummer's Defence of the N. England Charters, 1s 6d 1721

2157 Enquiry into the Object. againſt Pſalmanaazaar's Deſcript. of Formoſa, 1s

2158 Jones's preſent State of Virginia, 1s 6d —— 1724

2159 The ſame, *fair,* 2s —— —— 1724

2160 View of the Coaſts, Countries, &c. of the South Sea Company, 1s 6d —— —— 1711

2161 Blome's preſent State of the American Iſles, &c. *with maps,* 1s 6d —— —— 1687

2162 Gage's New Survey of the Weſt Indies, 2s —— 1677

2163 The ſame, 2s —— —— 1699

2164 Narrative of the Mutiny in the Cheſterfield Man of War off the Coaſt of Guinea, 1s

2165 State of Health in Jamaica, 1s 6d —— 1679

2166 Travels of the Jeſuits into various Parts, particularly China and the Eaſt Indies, tranſlated from the French by Lockman, 2 vol. *neat,* 7s —— —— —— 1762

2167 Van Egmont's Travels through Europe, Aſia, Minor, &c. *with cuts,* 2 vol. *in boards,* 5s —— —— 1759

2168 Ulloa's Voyage to South America, *with cuts,* 2 vol. *new and neatly bound,* 12s —— —— 1758

2169 Voyage to the Eaſt Indies in 1747 and 1748, *with cuts, in boards,* 2s 6d —— —— 1762

2170 Capt. Uring's Voyages and Travels, *with maps, very fair,* 3s 6d 1727

2171 Shelvock's Voyage round the World, *with cuts,* 3s 1726

2172 Capt. Roberts's Voyage to the Canaries and Guinea, *with cuts,* 2s —— —— 1726

2173 The ſame, *fair,* 2s 6d —— —— 1726

2174 Capt. Wood's Rogers's Voyage round the World, *with maps, fair,* 3s 6d —— —— 1718

2175 Coxe's Collection of Voyages and Travels, 3 Parts, *with cuts,* 3s 6d —— —— 1741

2176 James's Voyage to the N. Weſt Paſſage 1741—Coxe's Deſcript. of Carolina 1741, *with maps, very fair and neat,* 4s

2177 Dampier's Voyage to New Holland in 1699, *with cuts,* 2s 1703

2178 Tournefort's Voyage to the Levant, 3 vol. *with cuts, new and neatly bound,* 12s —— —— 1741

2179 The ſame, *new and elegantly bound by* Johnſon, 3 vol. 15s

2180 Ellis's Voyage to Hudſon's Bay, *with cuts, fair,* 6s 1748

2181 La Hontan's Voyage to North America, 2 vol. *with cuts, very fair,* 7s —— —— —— 1703

2182 Voyages and Diſcoveries in South America, *with cuts,* 2s

2183 Narborough's Voyages and Diſcoveries to the South and North, *with cuts,* 3s —— —— 1694

2184 Monſ. de la Sale's laſt Voyage to N. America, *very neat,* 2s 1714

2185 Sharp's Voyages and Advent. in the S. Sea, 1s — 1684

2186 Daniel's Journal of his Expedition to India, 1s — 1702

2187 Bp. Clayton's Journal from Grand Cairo to Mount Sinai, *in boards,* 1s 6d —— —— 1759

2188 Campbell's Sequel to Bulkeley's and Cummins's Voyage, 1s 6d 1747

2189 Mor-

2189 Morris's Narrat. of the Distresses that besel the Crew of the Wager Store-Ship, 2s

2190 De Pontis's Account of the taking of Carthagena, *bound, with a map,* 1s

2191 The same, *bound,* 1s 6d — — 1740

2192 Maundrell's Journey from Aleppo to Jerusalem, *cuts,* 2s 6d 1714

2193 Green's Journey from Aleppo to Damascus, 2s — 1746

2194 Dr. Lister's Journey to Paris, *cuts,* 1s 6d — 1699

2195 Cockburne's Journey over Land from the Gulph of Honduras to the South Sea, 2s 6d — — 1735

2196 Bromley's Grand Tour of France and Italy, 1s 6d 1705

2197 Several Years Travels through Portugal, Spain, &c. &c. 1s 6d 1702

2198 Dobbs's Reply to Middleton's Answer, in Defence of his Voyage, 1s — — 1745

Lives, Letters and Memoirs. OCTAVO.

2199 NEW and General Biographical Dictionary, containing an Historical and Critical Account of the Lives and Writings of the most eminent Persons in every Nation, particularly the British and Irish, from the earliest Accounts of Time to the present Period, 11 vol. *new and neatly bound,* 3l 6s — 1761

2200 The same, 11 vol. *new and elegantly bound by* Johnson, 3l 16s 1761

2201 De Pile's Art of Painting and Lives of the Painters, with an Essay towards an English School, *last edit. new and neat,* 5s 1753

2202 The same, with the Supplement of Lives omitted by De Piles, *new, and neat,* 7s — — 1753

2203 Lives of the most eminent Modern Painters who have lived since or were omitted by De Piles, *sewed,* 2s — 1754

2204 The same, *bound, very neat,* 3s — 1754

2205 Blackwell's Enquiry into the Life and Writings of Homer, *in boards,* 3s — — — 1735

2206 The same, *bound,* 3s 6d — — 1735

2207 The same, *very fair and neat,* 4s — 1735

2208 The same, *large paper,* 4s — — 1735

2209 Proofs of the Enquiry into Homer's Life, *sewed,* 1s 1747

2210 Knight's Life of Erasmus, *with cuts,* 4s — 1726

2211 The same, *large paper, neatly bound, with a border of gold,* 6s 1726

2212 Middleton's Life of Cicero, 3 vol. 9s — 1742

2213 The same, 3 vol. *very fair,* 10s — 1755

2214 Life of Ernestus the Pious, Duke of Saxe-Gotha, 1s 6d 1740

2215 —— K. David, by Delaney, 3 vol. 7s 6d — 1740

2216 —— Bernard Gilpin, and Hugh Latimer, *very fair,* 4s 1753

2217 —— Hugo Grotius, by Burigny, *neat,* 2s 6d — 1754

2218 —— Mahomet, by Prideaux, 1s 6d — 1718

2219 —— The same, *neatly bound, gilt leaves,* 2s 6d — 1708

2220 Lives of the ancient Philosophers, *with cuts,* 3s 1702

2221 Pascal's Letters relating to the Jesuits, with his Life, 2 vol. *half bound,* 7s — — 1744

2222 The same, 2 vol. *new and neatly bound,* 9s — 1744

2223 Pliny's Letters, with Notes by Lord Orrery, 2 vol. *very neat,* 9s — — 1752

2224 The same, 2 vol. *new and neatly bound,* 10s — 1752

K 2225 Pliny

2225 Pliny's Letters, with Notes by Lord Orrery, 2 vol. *new and elegantly bound, by Johnson,* 12s —— —— 1759
2226 The same, by Melmoth, 2 vol. *new and neatly bound,* 8s 1763
2227 The same, 2 vol. *large paper, very neat,* 10s —— 1757
2228 Cicero's Letters, by Melmoth, 3 vol. *new and neatly bound,* 15s —— —— —— 1753
2229 —— The same, 3 vol. *new and elegantly bound, by Johnson,* 18s —— —— —— 1753
2230 —— Epistles to Atticus, by Guthrie, 2 vol. 8s 1752
2231 Fitz-Osborne's Letters, by Melmoth, *new and elegantly bound, by Johnson,* 6s —— —— —— 1758
2232 Howell's Familiar Letters, 2s 6d —— —— 1737
2233 The same, *new and neatly bound,* 5s —— —— 1754
2234 The same, *new and elegantly bound, by Johnson,* 6s 1754
2235 Mrs. Rowe's Letters, *very fair,* 3s 6d —— 1750
2236 Voiture's Familiar Letters, 2 vol. 2s —— 1701
2237 Bolingbroke's Letters on the Study of History, *neat,* 3s 6d 1752
2238 —— The same, 2 vol. *large paper, sewed,* 3s 6d 1752
2239 —— —— on Patriotism, *in boards,* 1s 6d —— 1749
2240 Cardinal Bentivoglio's Letters, from the Italian, *sewed,* 1s 6d 1753
2241 Father Paul's Letters, by Brown, *very fair,* 2s —— 1693
2242 Letters and Negociations of Sir R. Sadler, *very fair,* 2s 6d 1720
2243 D'Estrade's Letters and Negociations, 3 vol. *very neat,* 9s 1711
2244 Letters from a young Painter in Italy, 2 vol. *with cuts,* 6s 1750
2245 The same, 2 vol. *very neat,* 7s —— 1750
2246 Memoirs of the Marq. de Torcy, concerning the War which began in 1702, to the Conclusion of the Treaty of Utrecht, translated into English, 2 vol. *neat,* 8s —— 1757
2247 The same, 2 vol. *new and neatly bound,* 10s —— 1757
2248 The same, 2 vol. *new and elegantly bound, by Johnson,* 12s 1757
2249 Memoirs of the Marq. de Feuquieres of all the Wars in Europe, from 1672 to 1710, 2 vol. *new and neatly bound,* 7s 1737
2250 —— The same, 2 vol. *new and elegantly bound, by Johnson,* 9s —— —— —— 1737
2251 —— of the Baron de Pollnitz, 4 vol. *damaged,* 8s 1739
2252 —— of the Duke de Ripperda, *in boards,* 2s
2253 —— The same, *bound, very fair,* 2s 6d —— 1740
2254 —— of a Cavalier, or Military Journal of the Wars in Germany and England, from 1632 to 1648, 4s
2255 —— The same, *in boards,* 3s
2256 —— of Philip de Comines, by Uvedale, 2 vol. *very fair,* 5s —— —— —— 1712
2257 —— of the Portuguese Inquisition, *in boards,* 2s 6d 1761
2258 —— of the Marq. de Langallerie, *neat,* 1s 6d —— 1708

Miscellaneous Books. OCTAVO.

2259 SWIFT's Works, 8 vol. *elegantly bound in morocco, gilt leaves, and gold border,* 2l —— —— *Dubl.* 1735
2260 The same, 14 vol. with Notes, by Hawkesworth, 3l 7s 1755
2261 Bishop Hare's Works, 4 vol. *very fair,* 12s —— 1746
2262 Walt. Moyle's Works, 3 vol. *neat,* 7s 6d —— 1726

2263 St.

2263 St. Evremond's Works, with his Life, by Des Maizeaux, 3 vol. 6s —— —— —— 1714
2264 Sir Walter Raleigh's Works, with his Life, by Birch, 2 vol. *neat,* 9s —— —— 1751
2265 Baxter on the Nature of the Human Soul, 2 vol. 5s 1737
2266 The same, 2 vol. *very neat,* 7s —— 1745
2267 The same, 2 vol. *in boards,* 4s —— 1737
2268 Grove's System of Moral Philosophy, 2 vol. *fair and neat,* 6s 1749
2269 The same, 2 vol. *new and neatly bound,* 7s —— 1749
2270 Burnet's State of the Dead, English, with Notes by Earbery, 2 vol. 4s —— —— —— 1728
2271 The same, *new and neatly bound in* 1 vol. 4s —— 1728
2272 Burnet's Inquiry into the Doctrine of all the Philosophers of all Nations, concerning the Origin of the World, English, by Mead and Foxton, *in boards,* 4s —— —— 1736
2273 The same, *new and neatly bound in* 2 vol. 6s —— 1736
2274 Bruyere's Characters, or Manners of the Age, 1s 6d — 1699
2275 The same, with the Manner of living with Great Men, 2s 1709
2276 Sir F. Bodley's Remains, with his Life, 1s 6d —— 1703
2277 Hutchinson on Witchcraft, 1s 6d —— 1720
2278 Hutcheson on the Conduct of the Passions, *fair and neat,* 2s 6d 1728
2279 History of the Ridiculous Extravagancies of M. Oufle, 1s 1711
2280 Castiglione's Courtier, 1s 6d —— —— 1724
2281 Father Paul on the Rights of Sovereigns and Subjects, with his Life, 1s 6d —— —— —— 1722
2282 Bishop Burnet's Vindication of his Sermon at Tillotson's Funeral, 1s —— —— —— 1696
2283 Port Royal's Moral Essays, 2 vol. *very fair,* 5s — 1696
2284 Epictetus's Morals, by Stanhope, 2s —— 1700
2285 The same, 2s —— —— 1721
2286 Wollaston's Religion of Nature delineated, *new and neatly bound,* 5s —— —— —— 1759
2287 Antoninus's Commentaries, by Thomson, 1s 6d — 1747
2288 Watts's Philosophical Essays, *very fair,* 2s 6d —— 1724
2289 Carlencas's History of the Belles Lettres, 2s —— 1740
2290 Plutarch's Morals, 5 vol. 9s —— —— 1694
2291 The same, 5 vol. *exceeding fair and neat,* 15s —— 1694
2292 Ward's System of Oratory, 2 vol. *new and neatly bound,* 8s 1759
2293 Occasional Papers for the Years 1716, 17 and 18, 3 vol. 6s 1716
2294 Letters, Speeches, &c. of Lord Bacon, published by Birch, *new and neatly bound,* 4s —— —— 1763
2295 Introduction to the Public Law of Europe, 2s —— 1758
2296 The Dreamer, by Dr. King, 2s 6d —— 1754
2297 Gentleman Instructed, by Hickes, *neat,* 3s —— 1738
2298 Essay on the True Rise of Nobility, Political and Civil, 2s 1718
2299 Preceptor, containing a General Course of Education, *with maps and cuts,* 2 vol. *new and neat,* 12s —— 1758
2300 Burlamaqui's Principles of Natural and Politic Law, 2 vol. *neat,* 8s —— —— —— 1748, &c.
2301 Hobbe's Art of Rhetoric—His Dialogue on the Common Laws of England—His Considerations upon his Reputation and Religion—Vita Tho. Hobbes 1681, 2s
2302 Spectators, 8 vol. *very fair,* 1l 4s —— *Dubl.* 1728

K 2

2303 Specta-

2303 Spectators, with English Motto's and Frontispieces, 8 vol. *fair and neat,* 1l 11s 6d ——— ——— 1747
2304 Spectators, *large paper,* 8 vol. *very fair and neat,* 2l 1712
2305 The same, with Tatler and Guardian, *with frontispieces and English motto's,* 14 vol. *new and neat,* 3l 10s —— 1757, &c.
2306 Tatlers, 4 vol. *very neat,* 14s ——— 1713
2307 The same, *with frontispieces and English motto's,* 4 vol. *neat,* 18s 1759
2308 The same, *large paper,* 4 vol. *elegantly bound, marble leaves,* 1l 5s —— —— —— 1713
2309 Guardian, 2 vol. *fair,* 5s —— —— 1714
2310 The same, *with frontispieces and English motto's,* 2 vol. *neat,* 8s —— —— —— 1747
2311 The same, *very fair, marble leaves,* 2 vol. 10s —— 1747
2312 The same, *in boards,* 2 vol. 7s ——— —— 1747
2313 Montaigne's Essays, translated by Cotton, 3 vol. 5s 1700
2314 The same, 3 vol. *very fair and neat,* 9s ——— 1711
2315 The same, 3 vol. *best edition, fair and neat,* 12s 1759
2316 The same, 3 vol. *new and neat,* 15s ——— 1759
2317 Sir William Temple's Works, with his Life, 4 vol. *new and very neatly bound,* 1l 1s ——— ——— 1757
2318 The same, 4 vol. *new and elegantly bound, by Johnson,* 1l 5s 1757
2319 The same, *neatly bound in* 8 vol. 1l —— 1757
2320 Temple's Miscellanea, 3 parts in 2 vol. 3s —— 1705
*2316 Lucian's Works, translated by Dryden, 4 vol. 12s — 1711
*2317 The same, 4 vol. *half bound,* 10s ——— 1711
*2318 The same, 4 vol. *large paper, elegantly bound, by Johnson,* 1l 11s 6d
*2319 Montesquieu's Spirit of Laws, 2 vol. *new and neatly bound,* 12s ——— ——— 1758
*2320 The same, 2 vol. *new and elegantly bound, by Johnson,* 14s 1758
2321 The same, 2 vol. *neat,* 10s ——— 1758
2322 Hanway's Reflections and Meditations on Life and Religion, 2 vol. *in boards,* 5s ——— ——— — 1761
2323 Enquiry after Philosophy and Theology, *in boards,* 2s 6d 1755
2324 Hay's Religio Philosophi, or Principles of Morality and Christianity, *new and neatly bound,* 3s 6d —— —— 1760
2325 The same, *new and elegantly bound, by Johnson,* 4s 6d 1760
2326 Shaftesbury's Characteristicks, with the Letter on Design, *large paper, with cuts, best impressions,* 3 vol. *elegantly bound, by Johnson* 1714
2327 The same, 3 vol. *small paper, with cuts, neatly bound,* 10s 6d 1732
2328 Bolingbroke's Philosophic Works, 5 vol. *very fair,* 15s 1754
2329 The same, 5 vol. *new and very neat,* 1l 1s —— 1754
2330 The same, 5 vol. *new and elegantly bound, by Johnson,* 1l 7s 1754
2331 Bolingbroke's Historical and Philosophical Works, *compleat,* 11 vol. 1l 11s 6d ——— ——— —— 1754
2332 Cicero's Orations, English, with Notes, by Guthrie, 3 vol. 9s ——— ——— —— 1745
2333 ——— The same, 3 vol. 9s ——— 1741
2334 ——— The same, 3 vol. *very fair,* 10s 6d —— 1741
2335 ——— Morals, by Guthrie, 3s 6d —— 1744
2336 ——— Offices, by Guthrie, 3s 6d —— 1755
2337 ——— de Oratore, translated into English 1757—Carmina Quadragesimalia, *in boards* Oxon. 1723 2s
2338 Apuleius's Golden Ass, 2 vol. *with cuts, very fair,* 6s 1708

2339 De-

2339 Demosthenes Orations, by Leland, 2 vol. *new and neatly bound*, 10s ——— ——— ———
2340 Phalaris's Epistles, by Francklin, *large paper, neat*, 3s ——— 1757
2341 Rollin's Belles Lettres, 4 vol. 16s ——— 1759
2342 Hume's Treatise of Human Nature, 3 vol. *fair*, 7s 6d 1737
2343 The same, 3 vol. *very fair and neat*, 9s ——— 1739
2344 Reflector, representing Human Affairs as they are, 2s 1739
2345 The same, *very fair*, 2s 6d ——— ——— 1750
2346 Smith's Theory of Moral Sentiments, *very fair, bound by Robiquet*, 5s ——— ——— ——— 1750
2347 Greville's Maxims, Characters and Reflections, 2s 6d 1759
2348 Free-Thinker, 3 vol. *large paper, in boards*, 6s ——— 1756
2349 The Plebeians, 1s ——— ——— 1722
2350 Du Bos's Reflections on Poetry, Painting and Musick, translated by Nugent, 3 vol. *new and neatly bound*, 12s ——— 1719
2351 Home's Elements of Criticism, 3 vol. *neat*, 12s ——— 1748
2352 The same, 3 vol. *new and neatly bound*, 15s ——— 1762
2353 Pearce's Review of Milton's Paradise Lost, *boards*, 2s 1763
2354 *Grey's Critical, Historical and Explanatory Notes on Shakespear*, 2 *vol. very neat*, 6s ——— ——— 1732
2355 The same, 2 vol. *new and neatly bound*, 7s 6d 1754
2356 The same, 2 vol. *new and elegantly bound, by Johnson*, 10s
2357 Warton's Observations on Spenser's Fairy Queen, *neat*, 2s 6d 1754
2358 The same, 2 vol. *large paper, best edition, new and neatly bound*, 10s ——— ——— ———
2359 The same, 2 vol. *new and elegantly bound, by Johnson*, 12s 1762
2360 Warton on the Writings and Genius of Pope, 3s 6d 1762
2361 Bohours's Art of Criticism, from the French, 2s 1762
2362 ——— Arts of Logick and Rhetorick, 2s ——— 1705
2363 Aristotle's Art of Poetry, with Dacier's Notes, 3s 6d 1728
2364 Burke on the Sublime aad Beautiful, 2s 6d ——— 1705
2365 Markland's Remarks on the Epistles to Brutus, and of Brutus to Cicero, with farther Dissertations and Observations, 2s 6d 1759
2366 Dr. Tunstall's Observations on the Epistles of Cicero and Brutus, *neat*, 2s ——— ——— 1745
2367 Richardson's (Sen. and Jun.) explanatory Notes and Remarks on Paradise Lost, with the Life of Milton, 2s 6d ——— 1744
2368 Letters concerning Poetical Translations, and Virgil's and Milton's Arts of Verse, &c. 1s 6d ——— ——— 1734
2369 Boyle and Bentley's Controversy, 2 vol. *very fair*, 12s 1739
2370 Boyle against Bentley, 2s ——— ——— 1699
2371 The same, *new and neat*, 3s 6d ——— 1699
2372 Collins on Free-thinking, 1s ——— ——— 1699
2373 Dr. Bentley's Remarks upon Collins on Free-thinking, *both parts new and neatly bound*, 3s ——— *Camb.* 1744
2374 Art of Speaking, *very neat*, 3s 6d ——— ——— 1713
2375 Wotton's Reflections on Learning, 2s ——— 1743
2376 Baker's Reflections upon Learning, 2s ——— 1761
2377 Hierocles on the Golden Verses of the Pythagoreans, 1s 1697
2378 Locke's Posthumous Works, *very fair*, 4s ——— 1708
2379 ——— on Human Understanding, *very fair, and neatly bound in blue turkey*, 2 vol. 10s 6d ——— ——— 1682
2380 Bp. Wynne's Abridgment of Locke on Understanding, *neat*, 2s 1706

2381 Bp.

2381 Bp. Berkeley's Minute Philosopher, *last edit. neat,* 3s 6d 1752
2382 Bp. Hoadly on Civil Government, 2s —— 1710
2383 Fable of the Bees, by Mandeville, 2 vol. *fair,* 8s — 1724
2384 Collection of Toland's Pieces, with his Life, 2 vol. *very fair,* 6s —— —— —— 1726
2385 Toland's Letters to Serena, *very fair,* 4s —— 1704
2386 —— Vindicius Liberius, or Defence of himself, 1s 1702
2387 Brown's Estimate of the Manners and Principles of the Times, 2 vol. *very fair,* 3s —— —— 1757
2388 —— Essays on the Characteristicks, *neat,* 3s —— 1751
2389 Sidney on Government, with his Life, 2 vol. 7s 1750
2390 Monthly Review from the Beginning 1749 to 1762, with the Index compleat, in 26 vol. *in boards, not cut,* 4l 10s
2391 Hooker's Weekly Miscellany, 2 vol. *very fair,* 3s 1738
2392 Echard's Works and Contempt of the Clergy, 1s 6d 1672
2393 —— Works, 2s —— —— 1705
2394 The World Unmask'd, or the Philosopher the greatest Cheat, from the French, 2s —— —— 1736
2395 Mrs. Harrison's Miscellanies in Prose and Verse, *in boards,* 1s 6d 1756
2396 Norris's Miscellanies in Prose and Verse, *very neat,* 1s 6d 1706
2397 Virgin Unmasked, by Mandeville, 1s 6d —— 1709
2398 Transcript of Governmenr according to Religion, 1s 1681
2399 Discourse of Friendship, from the French, *bound in blue turkey, gilt leaves,* 1s —— —— 1707
2400 Wharton's Defence of Pluralities, 1s —— 1703
2401 Duke of Wharton's True Briton, 2 vol. *large paper, fair,* 8s 1723
2402 Bayle's Miscell. Reflections on the Comet, 2 vol. 3s — 1708
2403 Telliamed, or Discourses on the Diminution of the Sea, &c. *fair and neat,* 2s 6d —— —— 1750

Poetry, Plays, Novels, &c. OCTAVO.

2404 HOMER's Iliad and Odyssey, by Pope, *new edition, beautifully printed, with head and tail pieces,* 11 vol. *new and neatly bound,* 3l 3s —— —— —— 1760
2405 Pope's Works, with the same Edition of Homer's Iliad and Odyssey, 20 vol. *new and neatly bound,* 5l 15s —— 1752—60
2406 The same, 20 vol. *new and elegantly bound, marble leaves,* 6l 6s
2407 The same, 20 vol. *new and elegantly bound, by Johnson,* 7l
2408 Virgil's Georgicks, with Notes, by Martyn, *with cuts, very fair,* 4s —— —— —— 1755
2409 —— Bucolics and Georgics, by Martyn, 2 vol. *with cuts, very neat,* 9s —— —— —— 1749
2410 —— Æneis, translated into Blank Verse by A. Strahan, Esq; 3s —— —— —— 1753
2411 —— Works, by Lauderdale, *neat,* 2s
2412 —— Husbandry, by Benson, 2 parts, Latin and English, *very fair and neat,* 3s —— —— 1725
2413 Horace, Lat. and Engl. by Davidson, 2 vol. 6s —— 1741
2414 —— in English Verse, with Notes, by Duncombe, 2 vol. *new and neatly bound,* 8s —— — 1757
2415 Tibullus's Works, Engl. by Dart, 1s 6d —— 1720

2416 Lu-

2416 Lucretius, Book I. Lat. and Engl. by Evelyn, 1s — 1656

2417 Juvenal and Persius, English, by Dryden, *with cuts, very fair,* 2s 6d — — — 1711

2418 Another Copy, 2s — — — 1711

2419 Ovid's Art of Love paraphrased, with Notes, *very fair and neat,* 2s — — — 1747

2420 Theocritus's Idylliums, by Creech, 1s 6d — 1684

2421 Milton's Paradise Lost, 3d Edit. 1s 6d — 1678

2422 Milton's Paradise Lost and Regained, *finely printed by Baskerville,* 2 vol. *very elegantly bound, by Johnson, in morocco, gilt leaves* 1758

2423 ——— Poetical Works, by Bishop Newton, 4 vol. *new and very neat,* 1l 2s

2424 Spenser's Fairy Queen, with a Glossary, 2 vol. *neat,* 8s 1758

2425 The same, 2 vol. *new and very neat,* 10s — 1758

2426 Villiers Duke of Buckingham's Works, 2 vol. 5s — 1715

2427 Sheffield Duke of Buckingham's Works, 2 vol. 5s — 1729

2428 Suckling's Works, 2s — 1696

2429 Boileau's Works, with his Life, by Des Maizeaux, *with cuts,* 3 vol. 6s — — — 1712

2430 Cowley's Works, vol. 3. containing the Dramatic Works, and Nature of Plants, *with cuts,* 3s — — 1708

2431 Young's Poetical Works, 2 vol. *fair and neat,* 6s 1741

2432 ——— Love of Fame, *fair and neat,* 2s 6d — 1741

2433 Dryden's Poetical Works, containing his Poems, Tales and Translations, 4 vol. *neat,* 1l — — 1760

2434 ——— The same, 4 vol. *new and neatly bound,* 1l 4s 1760

2435 ——— Miscellany Poems, 6 vol. *large print,* 12s — 1702

2436 ——— Fables, *large print,* 3s — — 1713

2437 Hudibras, with large Annotations and Preface, by Grey, *with cuts,* 2 vol. *very fair,* 1l 1s — — 1744

2438 Butler's Genuine Remains, with Notes, by Thyer, 2 vol. *neat,* 7s 6d — — — 1759

2439 Gay's Fables, *with cuts,* 2 vol. in 1, *very neat,* 4s 1757

2440 Dennis's Select Fables, *neat,* 3s — 1754

2441 Denham's Poems, with the Sophy, 2s — 1703

2442 Fawke's Poems and Translations, *large paper, very neat,* 4s 1761

2443 Chaucer's Canterbury Tales, *very fair,* 3s 6d — 1740

2444 Fontaine's Fables and Tales, in Fr. and Engl. 2s — 1734

2445 Cooper's Historical and Poetical Medley, or Collection of old English Poetry, 3s — — — 1738

2446 Rooke's Select Translations from Sannazarius, Vida, and others, 2s — — — 1726

2447 Tate's Elegies on Q. Mary, Archbishop Tillotson, and other eminent Persons, *in blue turkey, gilt leaves,* 1s 6d — 1699

2448 Fenton's Poems, 1s — — 1717

2449 Hinchliffe's Poems, Amorous, Moral and Divine, 1s 1718

2450 Blackmore on the Creation, *large print,* 2s — 1712

2451 Rapin on Gardens, by Gardiner, *with cuts, fair,* 2s 1728

2452 Callipædiæ & Pædotrophiæ, or Art of Getting and Nursing Children, *large print,* 1s 6d — — 1710

2453 Miscellany Poems by the Earl of Dorset and others, 1s 1701

2454 Donne's Poems, *fair,* 1s — — 1669

2455 Lord Brooke's Poems, 1s — — 1670

2456 Poole

2456 Poole's English Parnassus, or Help to English Poesie, 1s 1677
2457 Beaumont and Fletcher's Works, 10 vol. *new and elegantly bound,* 2l 10s —— —— — 1750
2458 The same, 10 vol. *very neat,* 2l 2s —— 1750
2459 Shakespeare's Works, by Theobald, 7 vol. *very fair and neat,* 2l 2s —— —— —— 1733
2460 The same, by Rowe, *with cuts,* 7 vol. *very fair and neat,* 1l 1s 1709
2461 Massinger's Dramatic Works, with Notes, by Coxeter, &c. 4 vol. *very neatly bound,* 15s —— —— 1761
2462 Ben Johnson's Works, with Notes, by Whalley, 7 vol. *neatly bound,* 1l 10s —— —— —— 1756
2463 The same, *new and very neat,* 7 vol. 1l 15s — 1756
2464 Lord Orrery's Dramatic Works, 2 vol. *fair and neat,* 5s 1739
2465 Lee's Plays, 2 vol. *large print,* 6s —— 1713
2466 Congreve's Works, 3 vol. *fine print, exceeding fair and neat,* 14s 1710
2467 Wycherley's Works, *very fair,* 3s —— 1713
2468 Pamela, and the Father of a Family, two Comedies by Goldoni, Italian and English, *new and very neatly bound,* 5s — 1756
2469 The same, in 2 vol. *new and elegantly bound, by Johnson,* 8s 1756
2470 Seneca's Tragedies, by Sherburne, *with cuts,* 3s 1702
2471 The same, *very fair,* 3s 6d —— —— 1702
2472 Sophocles's Tragedies, by Adams, 2 vol. *very fair,* 4s 1729
2473 Plautus's Comedies, by Echard, *fair and neat, gilt leaves,* 2s 6d 1694
2474 Eugenia, a Tragedy—The Gamester, a Tragedy, 1s
2475 Plutus, a Comedy—Distress'd Wife, a Comedy—Alfred, a Masque, 1s 6d
2476 Medæa, a Tragedy—Themistocles, a Tragedy—Timoleon, a Tragedy—Spartan Dame, a Tragedy—Philotas, a Tragedy, 1s 6d
2477 Modish Couple, a Comedy—Modern Husband, a Comedy—Lover, a Comedy—Humours of Oxford, a Comedy, 1s 6d
2478 Earl of Essex, a Tragedy—Boadicia, a Tragedy—Foundling, a Comedy—Coriolanus, a Tragedy—Tancred and Sigismunda, a Tragedy—Suspicious Husband, a Comedy, and more, 2s
2479 Gordobuc, a Tragedy — Agamemnon, a Tragedy — Edward and Eleonora—Philotas, a Tragedy—Projector, a Comedy, &c. &c. 2s
2480 Scornful Lady, a Comedy—Edward and Eleonora—Euridici—Elmerick, 1s 6d
2481 Scanderbeg, a Tragedy—List of all the English Dramatick Poets and Plays, *neat,* 2s 6d
2482 Cibber's two Dissertations on the Theatres, with an Appendix, *boards,* 1s 6d
2483 Riccoboni's general History of the Stage, 2s —— 1754
2484 Sir Charles Grandison, 6 vol. *neat,* 18s —— 1754
2485 Tooke's Pantheon of the Heathen Gods, *with cuts,* 1s 6d 1709
2486 The same, by Tooke, *very fair, with cuts,* 2s 6d 1732
2487 Æsop's Fables, Lat. and Engl. *interlineary with cuts,* 1s 6d 1703
2488 The Spanish Decameron, 1s 6d —— 1687

Arts

Arts, Sciences, Mathematicks, Painting, &c. Engl. Lat. Fr. and Ital. OCTAVO.

2489 DE Piles's Art of Painting, with the Lives and Characters of above three hundred of the most eminent Painters; containing a compleat Treatise on Painting, Designing, and the Use of Prints, with Reflections on the Works of the most celebrated Masters, and the several Schools of Europe, and the Life of Sir Godfrey Kneller, by Buckeridge, *new,* 5s —— —— 1753

2490 The same, with the Lives of the most eminent Modern Painters who have lived since, or were omitted by De Piles, *new and neat,* 7s —— —— —— 1753

2491 The same, *new and elegantly bound, by Johnson,* 8s 1753

2492 De Pile's Art of Painting, and Lives of the Painters, 2s 1706

2493 The same, 2s 6d —— —— 1744

2494 Fresnoy's Art of Painting, by Dryden, *new and elegantly bound,* 5s —— —— —— 1750

2495 Van Gool's Lives of the Painters, in Dutch, *with a great number of prints, very elegantly engraved,* 2 vol. *new and neatly bound,* 1l 1s *Scravenhag.* 1750

2496 Webb's Inquiry into the Beauties of Painting, 2s —— 1760

2497 The same, *neat,* 2s 6d —— —— 1760

2498 Painter's Voyage of Italy, by Lodge, *with cuts,* 2s 1679

2499 Elsum on Painting, after the Italian Manner, 2s —— 1704

2500 Caylus on Encaustic Painting, by Muntz, *neat,* 2s 6d 1760

2501 Richardson's two Discourses on Painting, *very fair,* 3s 6d 1719

2502 Leon. da Vinci on Painting, *with cuts, new and neatly bound,* 5s 1721

2503 The same, *new and elegantly bound, by Johnson,* 6s 1721

2504 Salmon's Polygraphice, or the Arts of Drawing, Limning, Painting, &c. *with cuts,* 3s —— —— 1685

2505 Hales's Statical Essays, 2 vol. *with cuts, fair and neat,* 12s 1737

2506 De la Fond's New System of Music, *with plates,* 2s 1725

2507 Abridgement of the Philosophical Transactions, and the Latin Papers, translated by Baddam, *with cuts,* 10 vol. *new and neatly bound,* 2l 10s —— —— 1745

2508 All the Philosophical Papers of the Royal Academy of Sciences, abridged by Martyn, 5 vol. *with cuts, very fair and neat,* 18s 1742

2509 The same, 5 vol. *new and elegantly bound, marble leaves,* 1l 5s 1742

2510 Robins's Mathematical Tracts and Life, by Dr. Wilson, 2 vol. *with cuts, new and neat,* 10s —— —— 1761

2511 Gregory's Astronomy, by Stone, 2 vol. *with cuts,* 6s 1726

2512 Harris's Description of the Globes and Orrery, *with cuts,* 2s 1732

2513 Keill's Astronomical Lectures, *with cuts,* 3s —— 1721

2514 —— Introduction to Natural Philosophy, *new and neat,* 4s 1758

2515 Le Caille's Elements of Astronomy, by Robertson, *with cuts, new and neat,* 5s —— —— 1750

2516 The Ladies Astronomy and Chronology, by Charlton, *with cuts,* 1s 6d —— —— —— 1735

2517 Simpson's Elements of Plane Geometry, 2s —— 1747

2518 The same, *fair and neat,* 3s —— 1747

L 2519 Euclid's

2519 Euclid's Elements of Geometry, with Notes and Additions, by Stone, *with cuts, very neat,* 4s —— —— 1752
2520 —— The same, by Barrow, revised by Haselden, 1s 6d 1732
2521 —— The same, by Keill, revised by Cunn, 2s — 1733
2522 —— The same, by De Chales, 1s —— 1688
2523 —— Another Edition, *very fair,* 1s 6d —— 1745
2524 *Masere's Elements of Plane Trigonometry, with cuts, new,* 7s 1760
2525 L'Hospital's Method of Fluxions, by Stone, *cuts, neat,* 4s 1730
2526 Saunderson's Method of Fluxions, *cuts, neat,* 4s 1756
2527 Cunn's Use of the Sector revised, by Stone, 2s —— 1729
2528 Starrat's Doctrine of Projectiles, *cuts,* 2s —— 1746
2529 Cotes's Hydrostatical and Pneumatical Lectures, with Notes, by Smith, *cuts,* 3s 6d —— —— 1738
2530 Hauksbee's Physico-Mechanical Experiments, *with cuts, in boards,* 1s 6d —— —— —— 1719
2531 The same, *bound,* 2s —— —— 1719
2532 Baker on the Microscope, 2 vol. *with cuts, fair,* 6s — 1742
2533 Motte of Mechanical Powers, *cuts,* 1s 6d —— 1733
2534 Maupertuis's Figure of the Earth, *cuts, neat,* 3s — 1738
2535 Wilson's Practical Surveyor, *with cuts,* 2s —— 1725
2536 The same, with Hume's Appendix, *and cuts,* 3s 6d 1741
2537 Voltaire's Elements of Sir Isaac Newton's Philosophy, by Hanna, *with cuts, neat,* 2s 6d —— —— 1738
2538 Sir I. Newton's System of the World, *neat,* 2s 6d 1731
2539 —— Optick, *with cuts, fair,* 3s 6d —— 1721
2540 —— The same, 2s 6d —— 1718
2541 —— Optical Lectures, *with cuts,* 2s 6d —— 1728
2542 —— Universal Arithmetick, revised by Cunn, *with cuts,* 2s —— —— —— 1740
2543 Martyn's System of Opticks, *cuts, neat,* 4s —— 1740
2544 —— Philosophia Britannica, or System of the Newtonian Philosophy, 2 vol. *with cuts,* 9s —— 1747
2545 —— The same, 3 vol. *with the cuts separate,* 9s 1747
2546 Gravesande's Elements of Natural Philosophy, by Desaguliers, 2 vol. *with cuts,* 5s —— —— 1721
2547 Rohault's Natural Phhilosophy, with Dr. Clarke's Notes, 2 vol. *with cuts, fair,* 4s —— —— —— 1723
2548 The same, 2 vol. 4s —— —— 1729
2549 Rowning's System of Natural Philosophy, 2 vol. *with cuts,* 9s 1744
2550 Wingate's Arithmetic, by Dodson, *neat,* 3s —— 1751
2551 Ward's Introduction to the Mathematicks, *very fair,* 3s 6d 1740
2552 —— Posthumous Works, by Gordon, *neat,* 2s 6d 1730
2553 —— Compendium of Algebra, *very fair,* 2s —— 1730
2554 Hammond's Elements of Algebra, *fair and neat,* 3s — 1742
2555 Alexander's Algebra and Appendix, by Ditton, 1s 6d 1709
2556 Jones's Synopsis Palmariorum, *very fair,* 7s —— 1706
2557 Hardy's Elements of Arithmetic, 3s —— 1760
2558 —— System of Interest and Annuities, *sewed,* 1s 6d 1753
2559 De Moivre's Annuities upon Lives, *large paper, elegantly bound, marble leaves,* 2s 6d —— —— 1725
2560 Ray and Willughby's Philosophical Letters, published by Derham, 3s 6d —— —— —— 1718
2561 Miscellanea Curiosa, by Derham, 3 vol. *with cuts,* 7s 6d 1726
2562 Patoun's Navigation, with Tables, *neat,* 5s —— 1762

2563 Smith's

2563 Smith's Harmonics, or Philosophy of Musical Sounds, *with cuts, new and neatly bound,* 6s — — 1759
2564 Lee on the Value of Leases and Annuities for Years and Lives, 2s 6d — — — 1738
2565 Holder on Time, 1s — — — 1694
2566 Cocker's Decimal Arithmetick, 1s 6d — 1720
2567 Builder's Dictionary, 2 vol. *with a great number of cuts, fair,* 9s — — — 1734
2568 Le Clerc's Architecture, 2 vol. *with cuts, by Sturt, very fair,* 6s — — 1724
2569 Morris's Modern Designs in Architecture, 50 *plates, neatly engraved, in boards,* 4s — — — 1755
2570 Bishop Wilkins's Mathematical Magick, 1s — 1691
2571 Muller's Field-Engineer, from the French of Clairac, *with cuts, new and neatly bound,* 6s — — 1760
2572 Bland's Military Discipline, *with cuts, fair,* 4s — 1759
2573 The same, *neat,* 5s — — 1762
2574 Faucitt's Regulations for the Prussian Infantry, *with cuts,* 3s 6d 1754
2575 Goulon on the Attack and Defence of a Place, *cuts,* 2s 1745
2576 Philidor on Chess, *new, in boards,* 2s 6d — 1762
2577 The same, *bound, new,* 3s — — 1762
2578 Jefferies on Diamonds and Pearls, *sewed, without the cuts,* 2s 6d 1751
2579 The same, *bound, with cuts,* 7s 6d — 1751
2580 Blancourt's Art of Glass, *with cuts, very fair,* 5s — 1699
2581 Cramer's Art of Assaying Metals, *with cuts, fair,* 6s 1741
2582 Burnet's Theory of the Earth, 2 vol. *very fair,* 5s 1726
2583 Keill Introduct. ad Veram Physicam, *nit. comp.* 2s 6d *Cantab.* 1741
2584 ——— ad Veram Astronomiam, 1s 6d *Lond.* 1721
2585 Euclidis Element. a Clavio, *exemp. pulch. nit comp.* 3s *Amst.* 1738
2586 Idem, a Commandino, 1s — — *Oxon.* 1715
2587 Elementa Architectura, *cum fig. semi-comp.* 2s 6d
2588 Musschenbroek Institut. Physicæ, 2 tom. *fig. semi-comp.* 3s 6d *L. Bat.* 1748
2589 Taswell Physica Aristotelica, 1s 6d — *Lond.* 1718
2590 Construction & Usages des Instrumens de Mathematiq. par Bion, *avec fig.* 2s 6d — — *Par.* 1716

Trade, Husbandry, Gardening, &c. OCTAVO.

2591 KING's British Merchant, 3 vol. *neat,* 6s — 1721
2592 Complete English Tradesman, 2 vol. *very fair,* 4s 1727
2593 Crouche's Compleat View of the British Customs, 2 vol. *neat,* 4s — — — 1738
2594 The same, *last edit.* 2 vol. *neat,* 7s — 1755
2595 Smith's Memoirs of Wool, 2 vol. *sewed,* 6s — 1747
2596 Davenant on the East India Trade, *neatly bound in morocco, gilt leaves,* 2s — — — 1696
2597 Davenant on Ways and Means, 1s 6d — 1695
2598 ——— on the Ballance of Power, &c. 2s 6d 1701
2599 ——— on Grants and Resumptions, 2s — 1700
2600 ——— on Peace at Home and War Abroad, 1s 6d 1704
2601 ——— on the Publick Revenues, 2 vol. 8s — 1698

L 2 2602 Da-

2602 Davenant's Report of the Commissioners for Stating the publick Accounts, 2s — — 1712
2603 Baston's Thoughts on Trade, *neatly bound in blue turkey, gilt leaves,* 2s — — — 1716
2604 Letter to the Commissioners of Trade, 1s 6d — 1747
2605 Reflections upon the Finances and Commerce of France, *in boards,* 1s 6d — — 1739
2606 The same, *bound, very fair,* 2s 6d — 1739
2607 French Book of Rates, *very neat,* 2s — 1714
2608 State of the Island of Jamaica, and more Tracts, 2s 1726
2609 Vauban's Essay for a General Tax, 1s 6d — 1710
2610 Necessity of lowering Interest and continuing of Taxes, 1s 1750
2611 Lownds on regulating Silver Coin, 1s — 1696
2612 Essay for the Amendment of the Silver Coins, 1s 1695
2613 Huet on the Commerce and Navigation of the Ancients, 1s 1717
2614 Evelyn on Navigation and Commerce, 1s — 1674
2615 Norris's Descript. of the English Plantation in South Carolina, 2s
2616 Nicholls on the Trade of France and Great Britain, 2s 1754
2617 Child on Trade, 1s 6d — — 1698
2618 Brewster on Trade and Navigation, 1s — 1695
2619 Royal Institut. relating to the Mines, by Houghton, 1s 1694
2620 Langham's Nett Duties and Drawbacks, 1s 6d — 1734
2621 The same, 2s — — 1758
2622 Mortimer's Husbandry, 2 vol. 3s — 1712
2623 The same, 2 vol. *5th Edit.* 5s — 1721
2624 The same, 2 vol. *best edit.* 6s — — 1761
2625 The same, 2 vol. *new and neatly bound,* 10s — 1761
2626 Ellis's modern Husbandry, 8 vol. *very fair,* 1l 4s 1744
2627 Houghton's Collections relating to Husbandry and Trade, revised by Bradley, 4 vol. *very fair,* 18s — 1727
2628 Practical Husbandman and Planter, 2 vol. 5s — 1733
2629 *Stillingfleet's Miscellaneous Tracts relating to Natural History, Husbandry, and Physick; to which is added, the Calendar of Flora, with Notes and cuts, new and neatly bound,* 6s — 1762
2630 Du Hamel's Elements of Agriculture, translated by Miller, 2 vol. *with cuts, new, and neatly bound,* 10s — 1764
2631 Cook's Manner of Improving Forest Trees, *sewed,* 1s 1724
2632 Manner of Fallowing of Ground, raising of Grass Seeds, and Training of Lint and Hemp, *with cuts,* 2s — 1724
2633 Ways and Means for Inclosing, Planting, &c. Scotland, in Sixteen Years, 2s — — 1729
2634 Laird and Farmer, a Dialogue upon Scotch Farming, &c. 1s 1750
2635 Lawrence's Duty and Office of a Land Steward, *very fair,* 5s — — 1731
2636 Select Essays on Commerce, Agriculture, Mines, Fisheries, &c. *from the French, neat,* 3s 6d — — 1744
2637 Essay on Trade, &c. by the Dublin Society, *with cuts, fair,* 3s — — — 1740
2638 Miller's Gardener's Kalendar, *new and neat,* 5s 1762
2639 ——— Dictionary, 3 vol. *fair and neat,* 15s 1754
2640 Wheeler's Botanist's and Gardener's New Dictionary, *very fair,* 5s — — — 1763
2641 Switzer's Gardening, *with cuts,* 3 vol. 6s — 1718
2642 The same, 3 vol. 6s — — 1742

2643 Swit-

2643 Switzer's Practical Fruit Gardener, *with cuts*, 2s 6d 1724
2644 ——— Practical Kitchen Gardener, *with cuts*, *very fair*, 3s 6d 1724
2645 Hale's compleat Body of Husbandry. 4 vol. *with cuts*, *neat*, 18s ——— 1758
2646 Bradley's Husbandry and Gardening, *with cuts*, 2s 6d
2647 ——— compleat Body of Husbandry, *with cuts*, 2s 1727
2648 ——— Gentleman and Farmer's Guide, *with cuts*, 2s 1729
2649 ——— General Treatise of Agriculture, *with cuts*, *neat*, 5s 1757
2650 Thorley's History of Bees, *with cuts*, *very neat*, 2s 6d 1744
2651 Barham on the Silk Worm, 1s ——— 1719

Libri Classici & Authores Antiqui, Gr. & Lat. OCTAVO.

Notis Variorum.

2652 PLinii Hist. Naturalis, a Gronovio, 3 tom. 1l 10s *L. Bat.* 1669
2653 —— Epistolæ, a Veenhusio, *exemp. pulch.* *ib.* 1669
2654 —— Panegyricus, 3s ——— *ib.* 1675
2655 Ciceronis Opera ex recens. Gronovii, 11 tom. 3l 3s *Amst.* 1689
2656 ——— Epist. ad Familiares a Gronovio, 2 tom. 9s *ib.* 1677
2657 Ovidii Opera, 3 tom. *exemp. pulch.* 18s *L. Bat.* 1670
2658 Idem, *edit. opt.* 3 tom. 18s ——— *Amst.* 1702
2659 Catullus, Tibullus & Propertius, a Scaligero, *exemp. pulch.* *Traject.* 1680
2660 Senecæ Opera, a Gronovio, 3 tom. *maculat.* 15s *Amst.* 1672
2661 Idem, 3 tom. *exemp. pulch.* 1l 10s — *ib.* 1672
2662 Apollonius Rhodius Argonaut. Gr. & Lat. ab Hoelzlino *L. Bat.* 1641
2663 Juvenalis & Persius, *edit. opt.* 5s — *Amst.* 1684
2664 Idem, 4s ——— *ib.* 1684
2665 Idem, *exemp. pulch.* 6s ——— *ib.* 1684
2666 Tacitus, a Gronovio, 2 tom. *exemp. pulch. comp. in memb.* 18s *ib.* 1673
2667 Polybius, a Gronovio, Gr. & Lat. *exemp. pulch. eleg. comp. in corio maurit. fol. marmor.* 2l 2s ——— *ib.* 1670
2668 Appian, Gr. & Lat. a Tollio, 2 tom. *nitid.* 8s *Amst.* 1670
2669 Statius, a Veenhusio, 8s ——— *L. Bat.* 1671
2670 Idem, *exemp. pulch.* 10s 6d ——— *ib.* 1671
2671 Idem, *exemp. pulch. elegant. comp. in corio turcico*, 15s *ib.* 1671
2672 Suetonius, ex recens. Oudendorpii, 2 tom. *cum fig. exemp. pulch. nit. comp.* 10s ——— *ib.* 1651
2673 L. Florus, a Grævio, 2 tom. *exemp. pulch.* 5s *Amst.* 1702
2674 Idem, a Salmasio, 2s ——— *ib.* 1660
2675 Phœdri Fabulæ, a Burmanno, 3s 6d *H. Com.* 1718
2676 Idem, *pulch.* 4s ——— *ib.* 1718
2677 Idem, a Laurentio, *cum fig. exemp. elegant. corio maurit. fol. deaur.* 10s 6d ——— *Amst.* 1667
2678 Sallustius, 4s ——— *ib.* 1690
2679 Idem, *exemp. pulch.* 6s ——— *ib.* 1690
2680 Horatius, a Bond, 3s ——— *L. Bat.* 1658
2681 Idem, 4s ——— *ib.* 1663
2682 Idem, *edit. opt.* 5s ——— *ib.* 1670
2683 Livius, a Gronovio, 6 tom. *exemp. pulch.* 1l 4s *Basil.* 1740
2684 Plautius, a Gronovio, 2 tom. 12s — *Amst.* 1684

2685 Au-

Notis Variorum.

2685 Ausonius, a Tollio, *exemp. pulch. nit. comp. in memb.* 7s *Amst.* 1671
2686 Justinus, a Gronovius, *nitid.* 6s — *L. Bat.* 1719
2687 Corn. Nepos, a Van Haveren, *exemp. pulch.* 7s *ib.* 1734
2688 Quintus Curtius, a Pitisco, 2 tom. *cum fig. exemp. pulch.* 8s *H. Com.* 1708
2689 J. Cæsar, a Vossio, *cum fig.* 4s —— *Amst.* 1697
2690 Idem, *edit. opt. cum fig. exemp. pulch.* 7s *L. Bat.* 1713
2691 Idem, in 2 vol. *exemp. pulch.* 8s —— *ib.* 1713
2692 Lucianus, Gr. & Lat. a Benedicto, 2 tom. 14s *Amst.* 1687
2693 Idem, Gr. Lat. Benedicti, 2 tom. 6s *Salmurii* 1619
2694 Virgilius, a Schrevelio, 4s —— *L. Bat.* 1657
2695 Terentius, *edit. opt.* 6s —— *Amst.* 1686
2696 Idem, *exemp. pulch. elegant.* 7s 6d —— *ib.* 1686
2697 Erasmi Colloquia, 3s —— *L. Bat.* 1729
2698 Idem, a Schrevelio, *nitid.* 3s 6d —— *Amst.* 1693
2699 Boetius de Consolat. Philosophiæ, 4s *L. Bat.* 1679
2700 Pervigilium Veneris, 2s 6d —— *H. Com.* 1712
2701 Aulus Gellius, *nitid.* 6s —— *L. Bat.* 1666
2702 Val. Maximus, a Thysio, 5s —— *ib.* 1679
2703 Idem, *nitid.* 6s — —— *ib.* 1670
2704 Senecæ & Syri Mimi, a Grutero, *nitid.* 2s 6d *ib.* 1727
2705 Menandri & Philemonis Reliquiæ, Gr. & Lat. a Clerico, *sutus,* 3s —— —— *Amst.* 1709
2706 Lactantius, a Gallæo, 4s —— *L. Bat.* 1660
2707 Barclaii Argenis, *nitid.* 2s 6d —— *ib.* 1664
2708 Auctores de Re Militari, a Vegetio & alior. *cum fig. exemp. pulch.* 7s 6d —— —— *Vesal.* 1670

Notis in usum Delph.

2709 Ciceronis Opera curavit Ernestii, 6 tom. *nov. & nit. comp.* 1l 16s *Lips.* 1703
2710 Epictetus Enchirid. cum Cebetis Tabulis, a Wolfio, *nitid.* 2s 6d —— —— *Lond.* 1670
2711 Ciceronis Opera omnia, a Verburgio & Variis, 16 tom. in 12 vol. 1l 11s 6d —— —— *Amst.* 1724
2712 Cicero de Officiis, Notis Toley, 2s — *Oxon.* 1719
2713 —— Idem, a Pearce, *nit. comp.* 4s —— *Lond.* 1745
2714 —— de Legibus, a Davisio, *exemp. pulch.* 2s 6d *Cant.* 1727
2715 —— de Natura Deorum, a Davisio, *exemp. pulch.* 3s 6d *ib.* 1733
*2715 —— de Finibus, a Davisio, 3s 6d — *ib.* 1741
2716 —— Idem, *exemp. pulch. nit. comp.* 4s — *ib.* 1741
2717 —— Libri qui ad Artem Orator. 3 tom. 7s 6d *Oxon.* 1714
2718 —— Idem, 3 tom. in 1 vol. 5s —— *ib.* 1718
2719 —— Idem, 3 tom. *ch. max. nov. & nit. comp.* 15s *ib.* 1718
2720 —— Idem, 3 tom. *ch. max. nov. & elegant. comp. par* Johnson, 1l 1s —— —— *ib.* 1718
2721 —— de Oratore, 2s —— *ib.* 1714
2722 —— de Claris Oratoribus, 2s 6d — *ib.* 1716
2723 Horatius, 3s —— —— *Lond.* 1740
2724 Idem, *exemp. pulch.* 4s —— *ib.* 1762
2725 Virgilius, 3s —— —— *ib.* 1722
2726 Idem, *cum fig. exemp. pulch.* 4s —— *ib.* 1759
2727 Martialis, 2s 6d — —— *ib.* 1701

2728 Jug

2728 Juvenalis & Persius, 2s —— *Lond.* 1691 } Ut. Delph.
2729 Idem, 2s —— —— *ib.* 1722
2730 Idem, 2s —— —— *ib.* 1736
2731 J. Cæsar, 2s —— —— *ib.* 1693
2732 Ciceronis Orationes, 1s 6d —— *ib.* 1706
2733 Ovidii Metamorph. Lat. & Angl. a Davidson, 3s *ib.* 1748
2734 Idem, *exemp. pulch.* 3s 6d —— *ib.* 1759
2735 Eutropius, Lat. & Ang. a Clarke, 1s 6d —— *ib.* 1744
2736 Ovidii Epistolæ, Lat. & Ang. cum Notis, 2s 6d *ib.* 1746
2737 Virgilius, a Stirling, 2 tom. *cum Clavis Virgiliana, and a large Index, exemp. pulch.* 6s —— —— *ib.* 1741
2738 Corn. Nepos, Lat. & Ang. a R. Arrol. 1s *Edinb.* 1744
2739 Livius, 2 tom. 5s —— —— *Cant.* 1679
2740 —— a Hearnio, 6 tom. in 3 vol. 15s —— *Oxon.* 1708
2741 —— in 6 tom. 18s —— *ib.* 1708
2742 —— Idem, 6 tom. *ch. max exemp. pulch.* 1l 11s 6d *ib.* 1708
2743 Callimachus, Notis Ernesti, 2 tom. *eleg. comp. per* Johnson, 1l 5s *L. Bat.* 1761
2744 Terentius, access. Var. Lectiones, 2 tom. *cum fig. nitid.* 7s *Lond. ap. Sandby* 1751
2745 Horatius, 2 tom. *cum fig. nitid.* 8s —— *ib. ap. ib.* 1749
2746 Idem, 2 tom. *nit. comp.* 10s —— *ib. ap. ib.* 1749
2747 Terentius, *ch. max. nit. comp. fol. marmorat.* 6s *Dubl.* 1745
2748 Horatius, *ch. max. nit. comp. fol. marmorat.* 6s *ib.* 1745
2749 Sallustius, *ch. max. nit. comp. fol. marmorat.* 5s *ib.* 1747
2750 Juvenalis & Persius, *ch. max. nit. comp. fol. marmorat.* 5s *ib.* 1746
2751 Virgilius, *nit. comp. fol. marmor.* 4s —— *ib.* 1745
2752 Val. Flaccus Argonaut. recens. N. Heinsii & Burmanni, *nov. & nit. comp.* 4s —— —— *Patav.* 1720
2753 Quintiliani Institut. Oratoriar. Notis Car. Rollin, *nit. comp.* 4s *Lond.* 1738
2754 Lucretius, Notis S. Creech, 1s 6d —— *ib.* 1717
2755 Eutropius, a Hearnio, *ch. max.* 4s —— *Oxon.* 1703
2756 L. Florus, 2s 6d —— *Lond.* 1715 } Maittaire, *ch. max. nit. comp.*
2757 Corn. Nepos, 2s —— —— *ib.* 1715
2758 Q. Curtius, 2s —— —— *ib.* 1716
2759 Juvenalis & Persius, 2s —— *ib.* 1716
2760 Horatius, 3s 6d —— —— *ib.* 1715
2761 Horatius, Notis J. Bentleii, 1s —— *Cant.* 1713
2762 Idem, Cuninghamii, 2 tom. 3s —— *Lond.* 1721
2763 Idem, *typis & fig. eleg.* a Pine, 2 tom. *nit. comp. fol. marmor.* 1l 5s *ib.* 1733
2764 Lucretius, a Gifanio, *edit. opt nit.* 2s *Antv. ap. Plant.* 1566
2765 Cæsaris, Notis S. Clarke, *semicomp.* 2s 6d —— *Lond.* 1739
2766 Persius, Comment. Casauboni, 1s —— *Par.* 1615
2767 Lactantii Opera omnia, Cellarii, 2s —— *Lips.* 1698
2768 Ovidii Metamorph. *cum fig. par De Bry,* 2s 6d *Franc.* 1619
2769 Apulei Opera omnia, recens. Elmenhorstio, 9s *ib.* 1621
2770 Boetius Consol. Philosoph. a Bernartio, 1s —— *Ant.* 1607
2771 Xenophontis Orationes, Gr. & Lat. a Wells, 1s 6d *ib.*
2772 —— Cyropœdia, Gr. 1s 6d —— *ib.*
2773 —— de Cyri Expedit. Gr. & Lat. a Wells, *ch. max.* 9s —— —— *ib.*

2774 Xe:

774 Xenophontis de Cyri Institut. Gr. & Lat. a Hutchinsono, 3s *Lond.* 1747

2775 —— Idem, 3s —— —— *ib.* 1738

2776 —— Idem, *exemp. pulch.* 3s 6d — — *ib.* 1747

2777 ———— Memorab. Gr. & Lat. a Simsono, *semicomp.* 2s 6d *Oxon.* 1749

2778 —— Idem, *nov. & nit. comp.* 5s —— *ib.* 1759

2779 —— Idem, *nov. & eleg. comp. per* Johnson, 6s *ib.* 1759

2780 ———— Apologia pro Socrate, Gr. & Lat. a Gilman, 2s *Lond.* 1720

2781 Homeri Ilias, Gr. *ch. max. exemp. pulch.* 6s *Oxon.*

2782 ——— Ilias, Gr. & Lat. a Clarke, 2 tom. 7s 6d *Lond.* 1740

2783 ——— Batrachomy. Graece, a Maittaire, 3s — *ib.* 1721

2784 Aristotelis de Rhetorica, Gr. *ch. max. elegant. comp.* 7s 6d *Oxon.* 1759

2785 —— Idem, Gr. & Lat. 3s 6d —— *Cant.* 1728

2786 ———— Ethica, Gr. & Lat. Notis Wilkinson, *ch. max. exemp. pulch.* 6s —— —— *ib.* 1716

2787 —— Idem, *ch. min. exemp. pulch.* 3s 6d —— *ib.* 1716

2788 ———— de Politica, Gr. & Lat. a Heinsio, *nitid.* 2s *L. Bat.* 1621

2789 Aristophanes, Gr. *nit. comp.* 3s 6d —— *Bas.* 1522

2790 Platonis Dialogi v. Gr. & Lat. Notis Forster, 3s *Oxon.* 1752

2791 —— Idem, *exemp. pulch.* 3s 6d ——— *ib.* 1752

2792 ——— Parmenides, Gr. & Lat. a Thomsono, *semi comp.* 2s *ib.* 1727

2793 ——— Symposia, Græce, 6s ——— *ib.*

2794 ——— de Rebus Divinis, Gr. & Lat. 1s — *Cant.* 1683

2795 Longinus, Gr. & Lat. 1s ——— *Oxon.* 1710

2796 —— Idem, Gr. & Lat. a Pearce, 2s 6d — *Lond.* 1752

2797 —— Idem, Pearce, *pulch.* 3s —— *ib.* 1752

2798 —— Idem, Pearce, 2s 6d —— *Amst.* 1733

2799 Callimachi Hymni & Epigram. Gr. & Lat. 2s 6d *Lond.* 1741

2800 —— Idem, *exemp. pulch.* 3s —— — *ib.* 1741

2801 —— Idem, *nov. & elegant. comp. per* Johnson, 5s *ib.* 1741

2802 —— Idem, *nov. & elegant. comp. in corio turcico,* 6s *ib.* 1741

2803 Musæi Grammat. de Herone & Leandro, cum Schol. Græc. recens. Mat. Rover, Gr. & Lat. *nov. & nit. comp.* 2s 6d *L. Bat.* 1737

2804 Sophocles, Græce, 4s ——— *Par. ap. S. Colineum* 1508

2805 —— Idem, Gr. & Lat. 2 tom. a Johnsono, 3s *Oxon.* 1705

2806 Tyrtæi & alii Elegia Græce, cum Notis, *nit. comp.* 2s 6d *ib.* 1760

2807 —— Idem, *nov. & nit. comp.* 3s —— *ib.* 1760

2808 Platonis, Lysiæ Orat. Funebres, Gr. & Lat. cum Notis Angl. *nitid. comp.* 2s 6d ——— —— *ib.*

2809 Demosthenes Orat. Gr. & Lat. Notis Lucchesinii, edid. G. Allen, 2 tom. *nov. & nit. comp.* 10s ——— *Lond.* 1755

2810 Plutarchi Vitæ Paral. Demosth. & Ciceronis, Gr. & Lat. Notis Bartoni, *nit. comp.* 3s —— —— *Ox.* 1744

2811 Zosimi Hist. Gr. & Lat. Notis illust. 1s 6d — *ib.* 1679

2812 Herodian, Gr. & Lat. recogn. & Notis illust. 2s *ib.* 1678

2813 Theocritus, cum Scholiis Græc. 2s ——— *ib.* 1699

2814 Phalaridis Epistolæ, Gr. & Lat. a Boyle, 2s — *ib.* 1718

2815 Æschinis Socratici Dial. Gr. & Lat. a Horreo, 1s 6d *Leov.* 1718

2816 Luciani Dialogi, Gr. & Lat. a Kent, 2s 6d *Cant.* 1713

2817 Iso-

2817 Iſocratis, Gr. & Lat. a Battie, 2 tom. *nit. compact.* 8s *Cant.* 1729, &c.
2818 Epictetus Theophraſtus, Gr. & Lat. a Aldrich, *ſutus*, 1s 6d *Ox.* 1707
2819 Ariſtæ Hiſt. LXXII Interp. Gr. & Lat. 1s —— *ib.* 1692
2820 Hierocles, Gr. & Lat. a Needham, 1s 6d *Cant.* 1709
2821 Idem, Gr. & Lat. cum Notis, *nit. comp.* 2s 6d *Lond.* 1742
2822 Idem, *nov. & nit. comp.* 4s —— *ib.* 1742
2823 Theophraſti Charact. Gr. & Lat. cum Notis Angl. a Newtono, *nit.* 2s —— —— *Oxon.* 1754
2824 —————— Gr. & Lat. a Needham, *extemp. pulch.* 5s *Cant.* 1712
2825 Fabulæ Æſopicæ, Gr. & Lat. *pulch.* 1s 6d *Oxon.* 1718
2826 Halicarnaſſei de Structura Orat. Gr. & Lat. a Uptono, 1s 6d *Lond.* 1702
2827 Dionyſius de Situ Orbis, Gr. & Lat. a Hill, cum Tab. Geogr. *exemp. pulch.* 3s 6d —— —— *Lond.* 1658
2828 Idem, Gr. & Lat. cum Tab. Geog. a Wells, 1s 6d *ib.* 1738
2829 Idem, Gr. & Lat. a And Papio, 1s *Antv. ap. Plant.* 1575
2830 Ariſtophanis, Plutus & Nubes, Gr. & Lat. cum Schol. Græc. 1s 6d *Lond.* 1732
2831 Poetæ Minores Græci, Gr. & Lat. 1s 6d *Cant. ap. Buck* 1735
2832 Ariſteneti Epiſtolæ, Gr. & Lat. 1s —— *Par.* 1639
2834 Rhetores Selecti, a Galeo, Gr. & Lat. 1s 6d *Oxon.* 1676
2835 Euripidis Tragœdiæ, Gr. 2 tom. cum Schol. 5s *Baſil.* 1537

Libri Hiſtorici. OCTAVO

2836 GUIL. Neubrigenſis Hiſt. Angliæ, 3 tom. *ch. max.* 12s *Oxon.* 1719
2837 Idem, *ch. minor. exemp. pulch.* 9s — *ib.* 1719
2838 Acta Apoſtolor. Gr. & Lat. Literis Majuſcul. *ch. max. ſemicomp.* 10s 6d —— —— *ib.* 1715
2839 Idem, *nit. comp.* 12s 6d —— *ib.* 1715
2840 Rob. de Aveſbury Hiſt. de Geſtis Edwardi III. *ch. max.* 7s 6d *ib.* 1720
2841 Idem, *ch. min. ſemicomp.* 4s —— *ib.* 1720
2842 Benedict. Abbas Petroburgenſ. de Vitæ Henrici II. & Richardi II. 2 tom. *ch. max. ſutus*, 7s —— *ib.* 1735
2843 Idem, 2 tom. *ch. min. nit. comp.* 8s — *ib.* 1735
2844 Roſſi Hiſt. Regum Angliæ, 3s —— *ib.* 1745
2845 Idem, *nit. comp.* 4s — —— *ib.* 1745
2846 Idem, *ch. max. nit. comp.* 5s —— *ib.* 1745
2847 Caii Vindiciæ Antiquit. Oxonienſes, 2 tom. *nit. comp.* 10s *ib.* 1730
2848 Hemingi Chartular. Eccleſ. Wigornienſes, 2 tom. *ſemicomp.* 7s *ib.* 1723
2849 Idem, 2 tom. *nit. comp.* 8s —— *ib.* 1723
2850 Idem, [illegible]n. *nov. & eleg. comp.* 12s — *ib.* 1723
2851 T. Livii Vita Henrici V. *nit.* 5s —— *ib.* 1716
2852 Camdeni Annales Reg. Eliz. 3 tom. 9s *ib.* 1717
2853 Joh. de Trokelowe Annales Edwardi II. *ſemicomp.* 4s *ib.* 1729
2854 Tho. Sprotii Chronica, *nit. comp.* 3s 6d *ib.* 1719

Edidit. Tho. Hearne.

2855 Antiquit. Prioratus Majoris Malverne, a G. Thomas, *ch. max. nit. comp.* 4s —— —— *Lond.* 1725

M 2856 Aq-

2856 Aſſeri Annales Rer. Geſtar. Ælfredi Magni recenſ. Fr. Wiſe, 1s 6d *Oxon.* 1722
2857 Idem, *nit. comp.* 2s ——— ——— *ib.* 1722
2858 Fleetwood Inſcriptiones Antiquæ. 1s 6d ——— *Lond.* 1691
2859 Lelandus de Scriptorib. Britan. a Hall, 2 tom. en 1 vol. 2s *Ox.* 1709
2860 Idem, *ch. max.* 2 tom. 3s ——— *ib.* 1709
2861 Symeonis Hiſt. Eccleſ. Dunhelmenſis, a Bedford, 2s *Lond.* 1732
2862 Muſgrave Geta Britannicus, *fig.* 2s ——— *ib.* 1715
2863 ——— Antiquitates Britannicæ, 4 tom. *cum multis fig.* 8s *ib.* 1719
*2863 Epitaphium Jul. Vitalis, cum Notis Dodwelli & Comment. Muſgrave, *cum fig.* 1s 6d ——— *Iſcæ Dunm.* 1711
2864 Somneri Portus Iccius, a Gibſono, *ch. max. nit. comp.* 2s 6d *Ox.* 1694
2865 Buchanani Hiſt. Rerum Scotica, 2s ——— *Ultraj.* 1698
2866 Seiz Hiſtoria de Inventione Artis Typographicæ, *ch. max. exemp. pulch. elegant. comp. in memb. fol. deaur.* 5s *Harlem.* 1741
2867 Melalæ Hiſt. Chronica, Gr. & Lat. a Hodio, 2s 6d *Oxon* 1691
2868 Petavii Rationar. Temporum, 2 tom. in 1 vol. *ſemicomp. cum fig.* 4s *L. Bat.* 1724
2869 Gotf. Lengnick Jus Public. Regni Poloni, 2 tom. *ſemicomp.* 2s *Gedan.* 1742
2870 Palladii Antiquit. Urbis Romæ, Ital. & Lat. a Hearnio, *nit. comp.* 2s 6d ——— ——— *Oxon.* 1709
2871 Almeloveen Faſti Conſulares, *nov. & eleg. comp. per* Johnſon, 5s *Amſt.* 1740
2872 Relandi Faſti Conſulares, cum Appendice Andr. Relandi, *nit. comp.* 2s 6d ——— ——— *Traj.* 1715
2873 Bernardi de Menſuris & Ponderib. Antiq. *cum fig.* 2s 6d *Oxon.* 1688
2874 Dodwelli Exercitat. duæ de Ætat. Phalaridis & Pythagoræ, 1s *Lond.* 1704
2875 Hen. Kippingii Antiquit. Romanæ, *cum fig. exemp. pulch.* 2s 6d *L. Bat.* 1713
2876 Emmii Vetus Græciæ Illuſtrata, 3 tom. *nit. comp. fol. marmorat.* 6s ——— ——— *ib.* 1626
2877 Bellorii Selecti Nummi duo Antoniani, 1s *Romæ* 1676
2878 Alciati Hiſt. Mediolani, *nit. comp.* 2s — *Mediol.* 1625
2879 *Grotii Hiſt. Gothorum, Vandal. & Langobardorum* *Amſt.* 1655

Libri Miſcellanei & Poetici. OCTAVO.

2880 P. Alyonii de Exilio, *elegant. exemp. lib. rariſſ.* *ap. Aldum*
2881 P. Gruteri Lampas, ſive Fax Artium Liberalium, 6 tom. *exemp. pulch.* 18s ——— ——— *Francof.* 1602
2882 Hugo de Prima Scribendi Origine, Notis Trotzii, *nit. comp.* 4s *Traj.* 1738
2883 Bentleii Emendat. in Menandri & Philem. 1s 6d *Cant.* 1713
2884 Horrei Miſcellanei Critici, 2s 6d ——— *Leov.* 1738
2885 ——— Obſervat. Criticæ, *nit. comp.* 3s 6d — *ib.* 1736
2886 Moſchopuli Scholia ad Homeri Iliados, Gr. & Lat. *nit.* 3s *Traject.* 1719
2887 Tunſtalli Epiſt. ad Middletono Vitæ Ciceronis Scriptorem, 1s 6d *Cant.* 1741

2888 Vir-

2888 Virgilius Collatione Scriptor. Græcor. Illustrat. a Fulv. Ursino, *nit. comp.* 5s —— —— *Leov.* 1747
2889 Pauw Notæ in Pindaro, *sutus,* 1s —— *Lond.* 1747
2890 Buxtorfii Synagoga Judaica, 1s 6d —— *Basil.* 1680
2891 Dawes Miscellanea Critica, 3s —— *Cant.* 1745
2892 Grotius de Jure Belli ac Pacis, Notis Barbeyrac, 2 tom. 7s *Amst.* 1735
2893 Cumberlandus de Legibus Naturæ, 1s 6d — *Dubl.* 1720
2894 Puffendorfius de Officio Hominis & Civis, Notis T. Johnson, *nov. & nit. comp. per* Johnson, 6s —— *Lond.* 1758
2895 Lipsii Opera omnia, 8 tom. *cum fig. nit. comp.* 10s *Vesal.* 1675
2896 D'Orville Critica Vannus, *exemp. pulch.* 5s *Amst.* 1737
2897 Burnetius de Fide & Officiis Christ. 1s 6d — *Lond.* 1727
2898 Almanni Principia Ethica, 2 tom. 3s —— *Turic.* 1753
*2898 Trapp Prælectiones Poeticæ, *nit. comp.* 1s 6d *Oxon.* 1711
2899 Idem, 2 tom. 2s —— —— *ib.* 1711
2900 Psalmi Davidis Gr. & Lat. a Du Port, 2s 6d *Lond.* 1742
2901 Miltoni Paradisum Amissum & Recuperatum, a Hogæo, 1s 6d *Lond.* 1690
2902 Perpiniani Orationes, 1s —— *Veron.* 1732

Divinity and Ecclesiastical History, Engl. Latin, &c. OCTAVO.

2903 SERMONS by Abernethy, 4 vol. 10s —— 1748
2904 —— The same, 4 vol. *very neat,* 14s —— 1762
2905 —— by Abernethy on the Attributes, 2 vol. *very neat,* 8s 1757
2906 —— The same, 2 vol. *elegantly bound in blue turkey, gilt leaves,* 12s —— —— 1746
2907 —— by Bp. Atterbury, published by Himself, 2 vol. 4s 1723
2908 —— The same, 2 vol. *neat,* 5s —— 1726
2909 —— The same, 2 vol. *in boards,* 4s —— 1751
2910 —— by Butler, at Boyle's Lectures, 2s 6d — 711
2911 —— by Bp. Butler at the Rolls, 2s 6d —— 726
2912 —— by Bp. Blackall, 1s 6d —— 1706
2913 —— by W. Berriman at Boyle's Lectures, 2 vol. *very neat,* 5s 1733
2914 —— by Bisse on the Common Prayer 1717—Bp. Mangey on the Common Prayer, 2s —— —— 1717
2915 —— by Bisse on the Common Prayer, 1s —— 1716
2916 —— by Burnet, 2 vol. *in boards,* 5s —— 1747
2917 —— by T. Burnet at Boyle's Lectures, 2 vol. 3s 6d 1726
2918 —— The same, 2 vol. *very fair,* 4s —— 1726
2919 —— Burnet's Abridgment of the Sermons at Boyle's Lectures, 4 vol. 10s —— —— 1737
2920 —— by Blair, 5 vol. 10s 6d —— 1722
2921 —— by Boyse, 2 vol. 4s —— — 1708
2922 —— by Dr. S. Clarke, 10 vol. 1l 10s —— 1730
2923 —— The same, in 8 vol. *very fair and neat,* 1l 10s 1756
2924 —— (XVII) by Dr. S. Clarke, *neatly bound in blue turkey,* 3s 6d —— —— 1724
2925 —— by Cotes, 2s —— —— 1721
2926 —— by Coneybeare, 2 vol. *large paper, elegantly bound, marble leaves,* 10s 6d —— —— 1757
2927 —— The same, 2 vol. *small paper, very fair and neat,* 8s 1757

M 2 2928 Ser-

2929 SERMONS by Cockburn, 1s 6d — — 1697
2930 ——— by Collier, 1s 6d ——— 1726
2931 ——— The same, *neat*, 2s — — 1726
2932 ——— by Creyghton, 2s — — 1720
2933 ——— by B. Calamy, 2s — — 1729
2934 ——— by Clagget, 1s 6d — — 1689
2935 ——— by Doddridge on Regeneration, 3s — 1742
2936 ——— by Duchal, Vol. 1. *neat*, 3s 6d — 1762
2937 ——— by Dorman, 2s — — 1745
2938 ——— by Duke, 2s — — 1714
2939 ——— by Dod on the Miracles, 2 vol. *neat*, 6s 1757
2940 ——— by Bp. Fleetwood on relative Duties, 2s 1732
2941 ——— The same, 2s — — 1716
2942 ——— by Foster, Vol. 3. and 4. *sewed*, 5s — 1744
2943 ——— by Gastrell at Boyle's Lectures, 1s 6d — 1702
2944 ——— by Gurdon at Boyle's Lectures, 2s — 1723
2945 ——— by Gough, *neat*, 2s 6d — 1751
2946 ——— by Gardiner on the Beatitudes, 2 vol. 3s 1712
2947 ——— by Hickman, 2 vol. 5s — 1700
2948 ——— The same, 2 vol. *fair*, 6s — 1718
2949 ——— (XVI) by Bp. Hoadly, 3s 6d — 1754
2950 ——— (XX) by Bp. Hoadly, 3s — 1755
2951 ——— (XXXVI) by Bp. Hoadly, 2 vol. *neat*, 8s 1754
2952 ——— by How on the Prodigal Son, 2s — 1761
2953 ——— by Hancock at Boyle's Lecture, 1s 6d — 1707
2954 ——— by Hunt on the Attributes, 4 vol. *neat*, 12s 1748
2956 ——— by Ibbott at Boyle's Lecture, 3s — 1727
2957 ——— by Ibbot, 2 vol. *neat*, 14s — 1726
2958 ——— by Bp. Kidder, 1s 6d — 1697
2959 ——— by Bas. Kennet, *sewed*, 1s 6d — 1749
2960 ——— The same, *fair*, 2s — — 1727
2961 ——— The same, *neat*, 2s 6d — 1749
2962 ——— by Archbishop Leighton, *new and neat*, 4s 6d 1758
2963 ——— by Bp. Leng at Boyle's Lecture, 2s — 1730
2964 ——— The same, 2s — 1719
2965 ——— by Littleton, 2 vol. *large paper*, *neat*, 4s 1735
2966 ——— by Mudge, 1s 6d — 1729
2967 ——— by Moss, 8 vol. 1l 5s — 1736
2968 ——— by Maynard, 1s 6d — 1722
2969 ——— by Outram, 2s 6d — — 1696
2970 ——— by Bp. Patrick on Contentment, 2s — 1719
2971 ——— The same, *very fair*, 2s 6d — 1719
2972 ——— The same, *very fair and neat*, 3s — 1719
2973 ——— by Reading, 4 vol. for all Sundays in the Year, *in boards*, 10s 6d — — 1755
2974 ——— The same, 4 vol. *new and neatly bound*, 16s 1755
2975 ——— by Reading on Mortification, &c. 2s 6d 1724
2976 ——— by Rogers, 2 vol. *fair and neat*, 6s — 1749
2977 ——— The same, 4 vol. 12s — 1749
2978 ——— by Archbishop Sharp, 7 vol. *neat*, 1l 1s 1717
2979 ——— The same, 7 vol. *neat*, 1l 1s — 1729
2980 ——— The same, 7 vol. *neat*, 1l 1s — 1722
2981 ——— The same, 7 vol. *new and neatly bound*, 1l 10s 1748
2982 ——— by Archbishop Secker, *neat*, 3s — 1758

2983 Ser-

2983 SERMONS by Dean Sherlock, 2s

2984 —— The same, 2 vol. *compleat and neat,* 5s 1700

2985 ——— by Stevens, 2 vol. *neat,* 5s 1719

2986 ——— by Straight, 2 vol. 5s 1737

2987 ——— by Scott, 2 vol. 4s 1741

2988 —— The same, 3 vol. *fair and neat,* 7s 6d 1697

2989 ——— by Bp. Smalridge, 2s 1700

2990 ——— by Shorey, 1s 6d 1717

2991 ——— by Stradling, 2s 1725

2992 ——— by Terry, *in boards,* 1s 6d 1692

2993 ——— by Trapp against Popery, 1s 6d 1746

2994 ——— by Bp. Weston, 2 vol. *neat,* 5s 1726

2995 ——— by Warren, 2 vol. *in boards,* 3s 6d 1747

2996 —— The same, 2 vol. *neat,* 5s 1739

2997 ——— by Wharton, 2 vol. *very fair,* 5s 1739

2998 ——— by Archbishop Wake, 2 vol. *very neatly bound, gilt leaves,* 7s 1728

2999 ——— by Whichcote, 4 vol. *very neat,* 16s 1737

3000 ——— by Bp. Wilkins, 1s 6d 1702

3001 —— The same, *neat,* 2s 1682

3002 ——— by Whitby, 2s 1682

3003 ——— by Whitby on the Attributes, 2 vol. in 1. 3s 1720

3004 ——— by Young, 2 vol. *very fair,* 5s 1710

3005 *Practical Preacher, consisting of select Discourses from the Works of the most eminent Writers,* 4 *vol. new and neat,* 1l 1s 1720

3006 Protestant System, containing Discourses of the most eminent Dissenters, 2 vol. *neat,* 7s 1762

3007 Prideaux's Connection of the Old and New Testament, 3 vol. in 2. *compleat,* 5s 1761

3008 The same, 3 vol. 6s 1720

3009 The same, 4 vol. *with cuts,* 10s 1718

3010 The same, 4 vol. *with cuts, neat,* 12s 1725

3011 The same, 4 vol. *with cuts, very neat,* 14s 1725

3012 Shuckford's Connection, 3 vol. *with cuts, neat,* 10s 6d 1749

3013 Shuckford on the Creation and Fall, *neat,* 3s 6d 1743

3014 Kennicott's State of the Hebrew Text, 2 vol. *in boards,* 10s 1753

3015 The same, 2 vol. *new and neatly bound,* 12s 1753

3016 Stanhope on the Epistles, &c. *very fair,* 4 vol. 14s 1753

3017 *New Testament, with References in Words at Length and Notes,* 2 *vol. by Fox, neat,* 6s 1726

3018 The same, 2 vol. *new and neatly bound,* 8s 1748

3019 Howell's Hist. of the Bible, 3 vol. *with cuts, new and neatly bound,* 15s 1746

3020 Collyer's Sacred Interpreter of the Bible, 2 vol. *very neat,* 6s 1752

3021 Patrick's Paraphrase on the Psalms, 1s 6d 1746

3022 ——————— on Proverbs, 1s 1700

3023 ——————— on Job, 1s 1683

3024 Clarke's Paraphrase, 2 vol. *very fair,* 7s 1697

3025 Green's Translation of the Psalms, with Notes, *large paper, neatly bound,* 4s 1741

3026 Le Pluche's Truth of the Gospel, 2 vol. *neat,* 5s 1762

3027 Campbell's Authenticity of the Gospel History, 2 vol. *in boards,* 4s 1751 1759

3028 Trapp's

3028 Trapp's Explanatory Notes on the Gospels, *sewed*, 2s 6d 1748
3029 Essay for a new Translation of the Bible, 1s 6d 1727
3030 Welchman on the 39 Articles—Lyttleton on St. Paul, *in boards* 1747, 2s
3031 Grotius on the Christian Religion, with Le Clerc's Notes, *new and neatly bound*, 4s —— —— 1761
3032 Collins on the 39 Articles, 1s 6d —— 1724
3033 Berriman's Dissertation on 1 Tim. iii. 16. 2s —— 1741
3034 Costard's Observations on Job, *elegantly bound, marble leaves*, 2s 6d —— —— —— 1747
3035 Patrick on Proverbs, 1s 6d —— —— 1683
3036 —— on the Psalms, Proverbs, Ecclesiastes and Job, vol. 5s —— —— —— 1680
3037 Bishop Stillingfleet's Ecclesiastical Cases, 2 vol. *very fair*, 5s 1702
3038 Bennet's Memorial of the Reformation, 4s —— 1721
3039 King on the Primitive Church, 1s 6d
3040 The same, 1s 6d —— —— 1737
3041 Revelation examined with Candour, vol. 3. *in boards*, 3s 6d 1763
3042 West on the Resurrection, *neat*, 3s 6d —— 1747
3043 The same, *elegantly bound in morocco, with a gold border, and gilt leaves*, 6s —— —— —— 1747
3044 The same, *neat*, 3s 6d —— —— 1754
3045 Another Copy 1747 — Littleton on the Conversion, &c. of St. Paul, *very fair and neat*, 5s —— 1748
3046 Bishop Gibson's Directions to his Clergy, 1s —— 1744
3047 Clarke and Leibnitz's Letters, 1s 6d —— 1717
3048 Wake's genuine Epistles of the Apostolick Fathers, 2s 1719
3049 Playfere's Tracts on Predestination and Providence, 2s 1719
3050 Sennertus's Meditations, 1s 6d —— —— 1704
3051 Jortin's Remarks on Ecclesiastical History, 3 vol. *very fair*, 15s 1752
3052 —— on the Christian Religion, 2s 6d —— 1746
3053 —— The same, *very neat, marble leaves*, 3s 6d 1752
3054 —— Six Dissertations, *very fair*, 3s —— 1755
3055 Bennet's Christian Oratory, 2 vol. 5s —— 1728
3056 Whitby on Original Sin, *very fair*, 3s —— 1739
3057 —— on the Five Points, 2s —— —— 1710
3058 Lucas on Happiness, 2 vol. 4s —— 1704
3059 The same, 2 vol. 4s —— —— 1697
3060 Watts on the World to come, 2 vol. *in boards*, 4s 1739
3061 —— Evangelical Discourses, *in boards*, 2s —— 1747
3062 Waterland's Doctrine of the Eucharist, *neat*, 2s —— 1737
3063 —— on the Athanasian Creed, *fair*, 2s —— 1728
3064 Chandler's Defence and Vindication of Christianity, 3 vol. *fair*, 5s —— —— —— 1725, &c.
3065 Reeves's Apologies of Justin Martyr, Tertullian and Minucius Felix, 2 vol. 4s —— —— 1709
3066 Min. Felix and Tertullian's Apology, 1s —— 1708
3067 Jenkins's Reasonableness of the Christian Religion, 2 vol. 4s 1715
3068 The same, *large paper, very fair, and gilt leaves*, 2 vol. 8s 1708
3069 Bishop Beveridge's Necessity and Advantage of Publick Prayer, 1s —— —— —— 1708
3070 Barclay's Apology for the Quakers, 2s 6d —— 1736
3071 Marshall's Penitential Discipline of the Primitive Church, 2s 1714
3072 Horneck's great Law of Consideration, 2s —— 1704

3073 Tho.

3073 Tho. a Kempis, by Stanhope, 2s —— 1704
3074 The ſame, 2s —— —— 1721
3075 Archbiſhop Leighton's Expoſitory Works, &c. 2 vol. *fair*, 7s 1748
3076 *Lord Barrington's Miſcellanea Sacra*, 2 vol. 9s —— 1725
3077 The ſame, 2 vol. *very fair, and elegantly bound*, 12s 1725
3078 Biſhop Warburton's Divine Legation of Moſes, 4 vol. *very neat*, 18s —— —— —— 1755
3079 Ray on the Creation, 2s 6d —— —— 1704
3080 —— Three Phyſico Theolog. Diſcourſes. *cuts*, 3s 1713
3081 Derham's Aſtro-Theology, 2s —— —— 1715
3082 —— Phyſico-Theology, 2s 6d —— —— 1732
3083 Reading's Life of Chriſt and the Virgin Mary, *with cuts*, 2s 6d 1740
3084 Scott's Chriſtian Life, 5 vol. 8s —— 1700
3085 Biſhop Squire on Indifference for Religion, *large paper, elegantly bound, marble leaves*, 5s —— —— 1758
3086 The ſame, *ſmall paper, neat*, 2s —— 1758
3087 Parſon's Chriſtian Directory, by Stanhope, *very fair*, 3s 1754
3088 Benſon on the Chriſtian Religion, 2 vol. *very fair*, 5s 1759
3089 Rogers's Review of the Church of Chriſt, 1s 6d — 1721
3090 Biſhop Hoadley on the Nature, &c. of the Sacrament, 2s 1735
3091 —— —— Tracts, 3s —— —— 1715
3092 Biſhop Burnet's Paſtoral Care, 1s —— — 1692
3093 Steele's Chriſtian Hero, *very neat*, 1s —— 1710
3094 Sharp's ſecond Argument, in Defence of Chriſtianity, *new*, 3s 6d —— —— —— 1762
3095 The ſame, both parts, in 2 vol. *fair*, 5s — 1755, &c.
3096 Rubric and Canons of the Church, conſidered by Dr. T. Sharp, *elegantly bound*, 4s —— —— 1753
3097 St. Athanaſius's Orations againſt the Arrians, 2 vol. 3s 1713
3098 Swinden on the Nature and Place of Hell, with a Supplement, *neat*, 2s 6d —— —— —— 1727
3099 Archbiſhop Potter's Theolog. Works, 3 vol. *in boards*, 7s 6d 1753
3100 The ſame, 3 vol. *large paper, new*, 15s —— 1753
3101 Potter on Church Government, *large paper, new*, 5s — 1753
3102 Sherlock on a Future State, *neat*, 2s —— 1726
3103 —— (Bp.) on Prophecy, *neat*, 3s 6d —— 1735
3104 Abridgment of Hooker's Works, with his Life, 1s 6d 1705
3105 Revelation examined with Candour, by Delaney, 2 vol. in 1. *neat*, 3s 6d —— —— —— 1732
3106 Berington on the Moſaical Creation, Deluge, &c. 2s 1750
3107 Paſſeran on Religion and Government, *ſewed*, 1s — 1734
3108 Lowman on the Civil Government of the Hebrews, *in boards*, 2s —— —— —— 1740
3109 The ſame, *neat*, 3s —— —— 1745
3110 David's Pſalms, by Johnſon, 2s 6d —— 1706
3111 Burnet's State of the Dead, *very neat*, 4s —— 1728
3112 Lord Herbert's Religion of the Gentiles, 2s —— 1705
3113 Howard's Hiſtory of Religion, 1s —— 1704
3114 Hunt's Eſſays on the Diſpenſations of God to Mankind, 2s 1728
3115 The ſame, *in boards*, 1s 6d —— —— 1728
3116 Hales (of Eton) Tracts, 1s —— — 1677
3117 Wharton's Defence of Pluralities, 1s —— — 1692
3118 Sacred Exerciſes for Weſtminſter School, 1s 6d —— 1755
3119 Pluralities Indefenſible, by Newton, *in boards*, 1s 6d 1743

3120 Ham-

3121 Hammond's Practical Catechism, *neat, gilt leaves,* 1s 6d 1662
3122 Dodwell on Jepthah's Vow, 1s — — 1745
3123 White's three Letters to a Dissenter, *boards,* 1s 6d 1743
3124 Sykes's Examination of Warburton's Account of antient Legislators, 1s 6d — — — 1744
3125 Colliber's Thoughts concerning Souls — Colliber on the Known God—Enquiry into the Demoniacks, *very neat,* 2s
3126 Clarke's Reply to Nelson, 1s 6d — 1714
3128 —— Modest Plea for the Scripture Notion of the Trinity, 1s 6d — — — 1719
3129 Middleton's Letter from Rome, 2s — — 1741
3130 Barclay's Letter to the Scotch on the Common Prayer, 2s 1713
3131 Collins on Freethinking 1713 — Collins's Grounds of the Christian Religion, *neat* 1724,
3132 Collins's Scheme of literal Prophecy 1727 — Letter to Dr. Rogers, *very neat* 1727, 3s
3133 Collins, Bentley, and others on Free-Thinking, 2s 1713
3134 Collins on Free-Thinking 1713 — Bentley's Remarks on Free-Thinking, 1s 6d — — 1725
3135 Bentley's Remarks on Free-Thinking, *very neatly bound,* 2s 6d 1743
3136 Christianity not mysterious, by Toland, 1s 6d — 1702
3137 Power of the Magistrate in Matters of Religion, by Tindal, 1s 6d — — — 1697
3138 Christianity as old as the Creation, by Tindal, 3s 6d 1731
3139 Conybeare's Defence of Revealed Religion, 2s 6d — 1732
3140 The same 1732 — Robinson on Revelation 1733 — and more Tracts, 3s
3141 Foster against Tindal, 1s — — 1731
3142 The same, *fair and neat,* 2s — — 1731
3143 Bible and New Testament, *ruled with red lines, bound in morocco, gilt leaves, very fair,* 6s — *by Daniel* 1657
3144 Bible and New Testament, *ruled with red lines, blue turkey, gilt leaves,* 10s 6d — — *printed by Hills* 1660
3145 New Testament, in Greek and English, 2 vol. *bad copy,* 4s 1729
3146 Tate and Brady's Psalms, *neat and gilt leaves,* 1s 6d 1760
3147 The same, *bound in blue turkey, gilt leaves,* 2s — 1759
3148 Real Principles of Catholicks, *neat,* 2s — 1749
3149 *Patrum Apostolic. Opera Genuina, Gr. & Lat. Notis Russelii,* 2 *tom. semi-comp.* 5s — — *Lond.* 1746
3150 Idem, 2 tom. *ch. max. exemp. pulch.* 10s 6d *ibid.* 1746
3151 Liber Psalmorum, Heb. & Lat. a Hare, 2 tom. 6s *ibid.* 1736
3152 Palairet Observat. in Nov. Test. *exemp. pulch. eleg. comp. in corio turcico fol. deaur.* 6s — — *L. Bat.* 1752
3153 Liber Jobi in Versiculos Metrice, cum Vers. Lat. a Grey, 2s 6d *Lond.* 1742
3154 Psalmi Davidici, a Johnstono, 3s — *ibid.* 1741
3155 Burnetius de Statu Mortuorum, 2s — *ibid.* 1733
3156 S. Irenæi Fragmenta Anecdota, Gr. & Lat. a Grabio, 2s *H. Com.* 1715
3157 Alberti Observat. in Nov. Test. *L. Bat.* 1725—Idem Periculum Criticum, *nit. comp. ibid.* 1727, 4s
3158 Alberti Glossar. Græc. in Nov. Test. *nit. comp.* 3s *ibid.* 1735
3159 Novatiani Opera, a Jacksono, *exemp pulch.* 1s 6d *Lond.* 1728

3160 Historia

3160 Historia Jeschuæ Nazareni, a Huldrico, Gr. & Lat. 1s *Lugd. Bat.* 1705
3161 Tertulliani Apologeticus, a Havercampo, *cum fig. pulch.* 3s *ib.* 1718
3162 Fogg Theologia Speculativa, 1s 6d ——— *Lond.* 1712
3163 Turrettini Historia Ecclesiastica, 2s ——— *Genev.* 1734
3164 Erasmi Ecclesiastes sive Concionator Evangel. 2s *Lond.* 1730
3165 Missale Romanum, *MSS. on vellum, finely illuminated and emboss'd with gold, the figures neatly coloured, very ancient,* 1l 1s
3166 Biblia Hebraica, Notis Leusdeni, 2 tom. *nitid.* 18s *Amst.* 1667
3167 Vetus & Nov. Test. Græc LXX. Interpretes, cum Schol. *exemp. pulch. eleg. comp. in corio turcico, fol. deaur.* 7s 6d *Lond. ap. Daniel* 1653
3168 Bibliorum Pars Græca & Nov. Test. interlin. cum Interpretat. Latina, *exemp. pulch. nit. comp. in corio russico,* 6s *Officina Plant.* 1612
3169 Nov. Test. Græce, *caret titulo,* 2s *Cant. ap. Buck*
3170 ——— Gr. & Lat. a Beza, 2s *ap. H. Steph.* 1567
3171 ——— Gr. & Lat. Theologis Lovaniensib. 2s *Colon.* 1592
3172 ——— Gr. a Maittaire, *ch. max. exemp. pulch. nit. comp. in corio turcico fol. deaur.* 4s ——— *Lond.* 1714

History and Antiquities in English. DUODECIMO.

3173 ENgland's Gazetteer, or Description of all the Towns, &c. in England, 3 vol. *very fair,* 6s ——— 1751
3174 The same, 3 vol. *neatly bound,* 7s 6d ——— 1751
3175 Salmon's Modern Gazetteer, *with maps, new,* 3s ——— 1762
3176 Description of the Great Roads and principal Cross Roads of England and Wales, *neat,* 2s 6d ——— 1756
3177 Geographia Mag. Britann. or Maps of all the Counties in England and Wales, *in boards,* 2s 6d ——— ——— 1748
3178 British Curiosities in Art and Nature, 1s ——— 1721
3179 The same, 1s ——— ——— 1728
3180 Reeves's History of London, *with cuts,* 2s ——— 1764
3181 Description of the Town and University of Cambridge, *with cuts, neat,* 2s ——— ——— 1763
3182 The same, *sewed,* 1s 6d
3183 Verstegan's Antiquities of the English Nation, *cuts,* 1s 6d 1655
3184 English and Scots Compendium, with the Arms, 3 vol. *last edition, neat,* 12s ——— ——— — 1760
3185 Salmon's Peerage of England, 1s 6d ——— 1758
3186 Welwood's Memoirs of England, 1s 6d ——— 1718
3187 The same, 1s 6d ——— ——— 1710
3188 The same, 1s 6d ——— ——— 1736
3189 Heylin's Help to English History, *gilt leaves,* 1s ——— 1671
3190 Lords Protests from 1641 to 1745, 2s ——— 1745
3191 Chamberlayne's State of England, 1s ——— 1669
3192 Rapin's Hist. of Engl. Question and Answer, 1s ——— 1735
3193 Dalrymple's Feudal Property in Great Britain, *very neat,* 2s 6d 1759
3194 Life of King William, *neat,* 2s ——— 1744
3195 —— of Thomas Firmin, 6d ——— — 1698
3196 —— of King Richard II. by Howard, 1s ——— 1681
3197 —— of Henrietta Maria, Queen to K. Charles I. 6d 1671
3193 Lives of Henry III. and IV. by Cotton and Heywood, 1s 1679

N 3199 Life

3199 Life of James Duke of York, 6d ——— 1683
3200 —— of King Edward II. by Faulkland, 1s —— 1680
3201 Lives of Edward and Richard II. by Howard, 1s 1690
3202 Essay on Q. Mary, by Bp. Burnet, 1s ——— 1695
3203 Johnston's Assurance of Abby Lands in England, 1s 1687
3204 Proceedings against the Earl of Clarendon, 1s —— 1700
3205 Holles on the Judicature of the House of Peers, 1s 1669
3206 Memorials of Thomas Lord Fairfax, 1s ——— 1699
3207 Historical Collections in K. James's Reign, 1s —— 1683
3208 Hales on the just Interest of the Kings of England, 1s 1703
3209 Treatise of the Nobilitie of the Realme, 1s —— 1642
3210 Passages relating to the Long Parliament, 1s —— 1670
3211 Antiquity, &c. of the High Court of Parliament, 1s 1658
3212 *The Puritan's Admonitions to the Parliament, part* 1. *and* 2, *black letter, elegantly bound in morocco, gilt, and gilt leaves, very fair, and very scarce,* 15s
3213 Account of the Man whose Hands and Legs rotted off, at Kings Swinford, 1s ——— ——— —— 1678
3214 Harrington's State of the Church of England, 2s —— 1653
3215 Sacheverell's Account of the Isle of Man, 1s —— 1702
3216 Sprat on Sorbiere's Voyage to England, 1s — 1665
3217 The same, 1s ——— ——— 1668
3218 Hume's History of the House of Douglas and Angus, 2 vol. 3s ——— ——— ——— 1748
3219 The same, 2 vol. 3s ——— —— 1743
3220 The same, 2 vol. *large paper, very elegantly bound in morocco, finished with small tools, and gilt leaves,* 12s ——— 1743
3221 Davies's true Causes why Ireland was never subdued, 2s 1747
3222 *Rollin's Roman History,* 16 *vol. very neatly bound,* 2l — 1740
3223 Grandeur and Declension of the Romans, 1s —— 1734
3224 Montesquieu's Causes of the Rise and Fall of the Roman Empire, 2s ——— — ——— —— 1752
3225 Roman History, Question and Answer, 2s —— 1737
3226 Mably's Observations on the Romans, *neat,* 2s — 1751
3227 Rowe's Translation of Sallust, 1s ——— 1715
3228 The same, *neat,* 1s 6d ——— —— 1726
3229 Crusius's Lives of the Roman Poets, 2 vol. 3s —— 1733
3230 Life of Pomponius Atticus, *fair,* 1s ——— 1667
3231 Lives and Maxims of the Antient Philosophers, 1s 1726
3232 Life of the Archbishop of Cambray, 1s ——— 1723
3233 Memoirs of the House of Brandenburg, with Supplement, 2s 6d 1751
3234 Voltaire's Works, by Smollet, 9 vol. *very fair,* 1l 1s 1761
3235 ——— Age of Lewis XIV. 2 vol. *neat,* 4s —— 1753
3236 Prospect of Government and Civil Policy in Europe, 1s 1681
3237 Young's Chronologia Enucleata, or Pocket Library, 1s 1739
3238 View of Paris, 2 vol. Fr. and Engl. *sewed,* 3s 6d 1763
3239 Description of the City House of Amsterdam, *cuts,* 1s 1751
3240 Salmon's Foreigner's Guide through the two Universities, 1s 1748
3241 Discourse touching Tangier, *blue turkey, gilt leaves,* 1s 1680
3242 Candidates for the Crown of Spain discuss'd, 1s —— 1699
3243 Colden's History of the five Indian Nations of Canada, 2 vol. *fair and neat,* 4s ——— ——— 1755
3244 Keate's History of Geneva, *new and neatly bound,* 3s 1761
3245 The same, *new and elegantly bound, by Johnson,* 4s 1761

3246 L.

3246 L. Addison's Revolution of Fez and Morocco, 1s — 1671
3247 Greaves's Description of the Pyramids, *sewed*, 1s 1646
3248 ——— on the English Weights and Measures, 1s 1745
3249 Newes from Spayne and Holland, 1s — 1593
3250 Addison's Present State of the Jews, 1s — 1676
3251 Ronquillo's Idea of the Court of France, 1s — 1704
3252 Morden's Atlas Terrestris, 1s 6d
3253 Grand Tour of Europe, by Nugent, 4 vol. *fair*, 6s 1749
3254 The same, *last edition*, *neat*, 10s — 1756
3255 Condamine's Tour of Italy, *sewed*, 2s — 1763
3256 Compendium of Modern Travels, *with cuts*, 4 vol. *neat*, 6s *Dubl.* 1757
3257 Bishop Burnet's Travels through Switzerland, Italy, &c. &c. &c. *new*, 2s — — — 1750
3258 Addison's Travels through Italy, *neat*, 2s — 1701
3259 Travels and Adventures of James Massey, 1s 6d — 1743
3260 Gulliver's Travels, 2s — — 1747
*3260 Patin's Travels through Germany, Switzerland, &c. 1s 1697
3261 Lassell's Voyage to Italy, 1s — — 1670
3262 Blount's Voyage to the Levant, 1s — — 1669

Poetry, Plays and Novels. DUODECIMO.

3263 POPE's Works, 9 vol. *his own edition, large paper*, 1l 15s 1736
3264 —— The same, 9 vol. *small paper, very neatly bound*, 1l 7s 1743
3265 —— The same, with Bishop Warburton's Notes, 9 vol. *new and neatly bound*, 1l 7s — — 1757
3266 —— The same, 9 vol. *new and elegantly bound, by Johnson*, 1l 16s 1757
3267 —— The same, 9 vol. *small edit. very neat*, 1l 1s *Glasg.* 1756
3268 —— The same, 9 vol. *fine paper, elegantly bound*, 1l 11s 6d *Glasg.* 1756
3269 —— Homer's Iliad, 6 vol. *with cuts, fair*, 10s 6d 1720
3270 —— The same, 6 vol. *with cuts, very fair*, 12s — 1750
3271 —— Dunciad, with Warburton's Notes, *sewed*, 1s 1749
3272 —— The same, *in boards*, 1s — 1736
3273 —— The same, *bound*, 1s
3274 —— The same, *very neatly bound*, 2s — 1749
3275 Waller's Poems, *small edition, fair*, 2s — 1712
3276 Another Copy, *fine paper, neat*, 3s 6d — 1712
3277 Prior's Poems, *neat*, 3s — — 1754
3278 The same, 2 vol. 3s — — 1741
3279 Hamilton's Poems, 2s — — 1760
3280 Cooke's Poems and Translations, 1s 6d — 1742
3281 Glover's Leonidas, *very fair*, 3s — 1739
3282 Dryden's Poems, 2 vol. *neat*, 4s — 1743
3283 ——— Poems and Fables, 2 vol. *new and neatly bound*, 5s 1752
3284 ——— Fables, *neat*, 2s 6d — — 1755
3285 Addison's Works, 3 vol. *neat*, 6s — — 1753
3286 The same, with his Travels, 4 vol. 7s — 1726
3287 Dodsley's Collection of Poems, 6 vol. *new and elegantly bound, by Johnson*, 1l 7s — 1758
3288 Young's Works, 4 vol. *new and neatly bound*, 12s — 1762
3289 The same, 4 vol. *new and elegantly bound, by Johnson*, 16s 1762

N 2 3290 Young's

3290 Young's Night Thoughts, *neat,* 2s 6d —— 1760
3291 The same, *neat,* 2s 6d —— —— 1755
3292 Gay's Poems, 2 vol. *neat,* 5s —— —— 1762
3293 The same, 2 vol. *new and neatly bound,* 6s —— 1762
3294 The same, 2 vol. *very fair,* 4s —— —— 1745
3295 Gay's Fables, *with cuts, neat,* 2s 6d —— —— 1762
3296 The same, *with cuts, very neat,* 3s —— 1762
3297 Hudibras, *with Hogarth's cuts, neat,* 2s 6d —— 1761
3298 The same, *new and neatly bound,* 3s —— 1761
3299 The same, *small edition, with cuts,* 2s —— 1720
3300 Butler's Posthumous Works, *with cuts, neat,* 2s — 1754
3301 Oldham's Works and Remains, 2 vol. *with cuts,* 3s 1722
3302 Thomson's Seasons, 1s 6d —— —— 1744
3303 The same, *fair,* 2s —— —— 1744
3304 The same, *new and neatly bound,* 3s —— 1762
3305 The same, *new and elegantly bound, by Johnson,* 4s 1762
*3305 Rochester's Works, with the Tragedy of Valentinian, *neat,* 2s 6d —— —— 1732
3306 Cowley's Works, *compleat,* 3 vol. 7s 6d —— — 1721
3307 Philips's Poems, *neat,* 2s —— —— 1762
3308 Denham's Poems, with the Sophy, *small sort,* 2s 1719
3309 Hervey's Contemplation on a Flower Garden, in blank Verse, by Newcomb, *neat,* 2s —— —— 1757
3310 Blackmore's Creation, a Philosophical Poem, *small sort,* 2s 1715
3311 Love and Honour, a Dramatick Poem, *bound in morocco, gilt leaves,* 2s —— —— — 1742
3312 Fair Circassian—Young's Poem on the last Day—Garth's Dispensary, 1s 6d
3313 Pomfret's Poems, 1s —— —— 1720
3314 Ramsay's Poems, 2 vol. *fair,* 3s —— — 1724
3315 Loveling's Latin and English Poems, 2s —— 1741
3316 Milton's Paradise Lost, *with cuts, 9th edition, elegantly bound in morocco, by Johnson,* 7s 6d —— —— 1711
3317 The same, *small edition,* 1s 6d —— —— 1753
3318 Milton's Paradise Lost and Regained, 2 vol. *with cuts, neat,* 5s —— —— —— 1760
3319 —— The same, 2 vol. *new and neatly bound,* 6s — 1760
3320 —— Paradise Regained, *with cuts, neat,* 2s — 1760
3321 Hughes's Poems and Plays, 2 vol. *new and neatly bound,* 5s 1735
3322 The same, 2 vol. *new and elegantly bound, by Johnson,* 7s 1735
3323 The same, 2 vol. *second hand,* 3s —— 1735
3324 Works of celebrated Authors, 2 vol. 3s 6d —— 1750
3325 Steele's Poetical Miscellanies, 2s —— 1714
3326 Donne's Poems, 1s —— —— 1639
3327 Randolph's Poems and Plays, 1s —— 1668
3328 The same, 1s —— —— 1643
3329 Bishop Hall's Satires, in six Books, 1s 6d —— 1753
3330 Barnaby's Journal, *with cuts,* 1s 6d —— 1723
3331 Abuses Stript and Whipt by Wither, 1s — 1617
3332 Hayward's British Muse, 3 vol. *fair,* 4s 6d — 1738
3333 Poetical Dictionary, or Beauties of the English Poets, 4 vol. *very neatly bound,* 10s 6d —— —— 1761
3334 Gildon's Art of Poetry, 2 vol. *neatly bound in morocco, gilt leaves,* 3s —— —— —— 1718

3335 Horace's

3335 Horace's Works, Latin and English, by Francis, 4 vol. 8s 1750
3336 The same, 4 vol. *very fair and neat,* 9s —— 1750
3337 The same, 4 vol. *new and neatly bound,* 12s —— 1756
3338 The same, 4 vol. *new and elegantly bound, by Johnson,* 15s 1756
3339 Horace, in Latin and English, with Bentley's Notes, and Notes upon Notes, 2 vol. *half bound,* 2s 6d
3340 Horace, Lat. with Engl. Comment. and Notes, by Hurd, 2 vol. *new and elegantly bound, by Johnson,* 10s —— 1757
3341 Horace, Lat. with Engl. Prose, by Towers, with Notes, *new and neat,* 2 vol. 5s —— —— *Dubl.* 1742
3342 Horace, translated by Creech, 1s 6d —— 1720
3343 —— Latin and English, by Creech, 2 vol. 3s 1718
3344 Horace's Odes, Epodes, &c. by Oldisworth—Virgile Travestie, 2s
3345 Odes of Horace, 1s —— —— 1719
3346 Pindar's Odes, by West, 2 vol. *fair and neat,* 5s 1753
3347 Virgil's Works, Lat. and Engl. with Notes, by Warton, &c. 4 vol. *new and elegantly bound,* 13s —— —— 1763
3348 —— Æneid, in blank Verse, by Trapp, *with cuts and notes,* 3 vol. 5s —— —— —— 1755
3349 —— The same, 3 vol. *fair and neat,* 6s —— 1755
3350 —— by Lauderdale, 2 vol. Lat. and Engl. 3s
3351 Juvenal and Persius, by Dryden, *fair,* 2s —— 1754
3352 The same, *very neat,* 2s 6d —— —— 1754
3353 The same, *small edition, morocco, gilt leaves,* 2s 6d 1713
3354 Garth's Ovid, 2 vol. *with cuts, neat print,* 4s —— 1720
3355 The same, 2 vol. *with cuts, neat,* 5s —— 1751
3356 Another Copy, 2 vol. *new and neatly bound,* 6s 1751
3357 Ovid's Art of Love, *with cuts, very neat,* 2s 6d 1757
3358 —— The same, *elegantly bound, marble leaves,* 3s 1757
3359 —— The same, *new and neat,* 3s —— 1757
3360 —— Epistles and Amours, *neat,* 2s 6d —— 1748
3361 —— The same, *neat,* 2s 6d —— 1761
3362 The same, *new and very neat,* 3s —— 1761
3363 Lucan's Pharsalia, by Rowe, 2 vol. *neat,* 5s —— 1753
3364 The same, 2 vol. *new and elegantly bound, by Johnson,* 8s 1733
3365 Tibullus, Latin and English, with Notes, by Grainger, 2 vol. *neat,* 4s —— —— —— 1759
3366 Persius's Satyrs, translated by Sheridan, 1s 6d —— 1739
3367 Plautus's Comedies, by Echard, 2s —— 1716
3368 Theocritus, englished by Creech, 2s —— 1721
3369 Vida's Art of Poetry, by Pitt, 1s —— 1725
3370 Satires of Ariosto, translated into English, 1s 6d —— 1759
3371 Shakespear, 9 vol. *best small edition, new and elegantly bound, by Johnson,* 1l 11s 6d —— 1751
3372 —— by Theobald, 8 vol. *with cuts, new and neatly bound,* 1l 4s —— —— 1762
3373 —— The same, 8 vol. *new and elegantly bound, by Johnson,* 1l 12s —— —— —— 1762
3374 —— Another Edition, 8 vol. *neatly bound,* 1l 4s 1740
3375 Collection of old Plays, published by Dodsley, 12 vol. 1l 10s 1744
3376 Moliere's Plays, Fr. and Engl. 10 vol. *new,* 1l 1s —— 1754
3377 Farquhar's Plays and Poems, &c. 2 vol. *new and neatly bound,* 6s —— —— 1725
3378 Congreve's Plays and Poems, 3 vol. 5s —— 1725

3379 Con-

3379 Congreve's Plays and Poems, 3 vol. *with cuts, very neat,* 7s 6d 1753
3380 ——— Plays, *neat,* 2s — ——— 1735
3381 Centlivre's Plays, 3 vol. *new and neatly bound,* 9s 1761
3382 Cibber's Plays, 4 vol. *new and neatly bound, marble leaves,* 14s 1760
3383 The same, *new and neat,* 4 vol. 12s ——— 1760
3384 Vanbrugh's Plays, 2 vol. *neat,* 5s ——— 1759
3385 Otway's Plays, 2 vol. *very fair and neat, with cuts,* 4s
3386 Lee's Plays, 3 vol. *with cuts, fair and neat,* 7s 6d 1734
3387 Southerne's Plays, 2 vol. 6s ——— 1713
3388 Gay's Plays, *neat,* 3s ——— ——— 1760
3389 Steele's Plays, *neat,* 2s 6d — ——— 1761
3390 The same, *neat,* 2s ——— ——— 1747
3391 Ben Johnson's Plays, 1s 6d
3392 Collection of Tragedies and Comedies by the best Authors, 4 vol. *in boards,* 6s ——— ——— 1735
3393 ——— of 16 Comedies by the most eminent Authors, *neatly bound in* 4 vol. 7s
3394 Plays. Lottery — Oedipus — Indian Emperor — Ignoramus — Busy Body —— Spanish Fryar — Confederacy — Humorous Lieutenant, 2 vol. *neat,* 3s
3395 —— Silent Woman — Funeral — Chances — Refusal — Inconstant —Man of Mode, *neat,* 2s
3396 —— Stratagem —Double Gallant—Hamlet—Orphan —Bold Stroke for a Wife—Tunbridge Walks, 1s 6d
3397 Victor's History of the Theatres of London and Dublin, 2 vol. 3s ——— ——— 1761
3398 Gil Blas, *small edit.* 4 vol. *with cuts,* 6s ——— 1749
3399 Continuation of Don Quixote, translated by Baker, 2 vol. *with cuts,* 3s 6d ——— ——— 1745
3400 Rabelais's Works, 4 vol. 8s ——— *Dubl.* 1738
3401 Atalantis, 4 vol. *with the Key, very neat,* 7s — 1736
3402 Joseph Andrews, 2 vol. *with cuts, elegantly bound by* Johnson, 7s ——— ——— 1762
3403 The same, 2 vol. *new and elegantly bound by* Johnson, 8s 1762
3404 History of Lady Charlotte Villars, 1s ——— 1756
3405 Lydia, 2 vol. *sewed,* 2s ——— ——— 1755
3406 Memoirs of the Marquis of Feux, 2 vol. *very fair,* 3s 1745
3407 ——— of the Chevalier Pierpoint, 2 vol. *sewed,* 2s 1763
3408 ——— of the Life of Count Grammont, *fair,* 2s 1760
3409 ——— of Fanny Hill, 2s 6d
3410 Life of Lazarillo de Tormes, 1s
3411 Scarron's Comical Works, 2 vol. *with cuts,* 3s — 1727
3412 Oriental Tales, 2 vol. 3s ——— 1759
3413 Tales of the Faries, by the Countess d'Aulnoi, *neat,* 2s 1753
3414 Arabian Nights Entertainment, 6 vol. *new and neatly bound,* 15s
3415 The same, 6 vol. *new and elegantly bound by* Johnson, 1l 1s

Miscellaneous

Miscellaneous Books. DUODECIMO.

3416 TAtler, 4 vol. *fair*, 6s
3417 Guardian, 2 vol. with English Mottos, 3s 6d 1754
3418 The same, 2 vol. *very neatly bound*, 5s 1756
3419 World, 4 vol. *neatly bound*, 10s 6d 1756
3420 The same, 4 vol. *new and neatly bound*, 12s 1761
3421 Adventurer, 4 vol. *new and neatly bound*, 12s 1761
3422 Connoisseur, 4 vol. *new and neatly bound*, 12s 1762
3423 The same, 4 vol. *2d hand*, 8s 1761
3424 Inspector, by Dr. Hill, 2 vol. 3s 1755
3425 Craftsman, 7 vol. *fine paper, very fair, marble leaves*, 10s 6d 1753
3426 Another Copy, *compleat*, 14 vol. *small paper, fair and neat*, 1l 15s 1731
3427 Independent Whig, 4 vol. *very fair*, 6s 1731
3428 Freeholder, by Addison, 1s 6d 1732
3429 Trenchard and Gordon's Tracts, 2 vol. *fair*, 4s 1723
3430 Pillars of Priestcraft and Orthodoxy shaken, 2 vol. *fair*, 3s 1751
3431 Swift's Works, 13 vol. *fair and neat*, 1l 7s 1752
3432 The same, with Notes by Hawkesworth, 14 vol. *new and elegantly bound by* Johnson, 2l 15s 1742
3433 Tom Brown's Works, 4 vol. *neat, marble leaves*, 7s 1760
3434 The same, 4 vol. *very fair*, 6s 1730
3435 Francis Osborne's Works, 2 vol. *very fair*, 3s 6d 1715
3436 Rollin's Belles Lettres, 4 vol. *fair*, 8s 1722
3437 Apothegms of the Ancients from Erasmus, &c. 2 vol. 3s 1742
3438 Reflexions upon Ridicule, 2 vol. 3s 1753
3439 Eloisa, by Rousseau, 4 vol. 8s 1739
3440 Maintenon's Letters, *very fair*, 2s 1761
3441 Le Blanc's Letters on the English and French Nations, 2 vol. *very fair*, 4s 1754
3442 Cato's Letters, 4 vol. 5s 1747
3443 Voiture's Works, 2 vol. *fair and neat*, 4s 1724
3444 New Art of Letter-Writing, *neat*, 1s 6d 1740
3445 Miscellany Letters from Mist's Weekly Journal, 4 vol. *very fair*, 10s 1762
3446 Jennings on the Nature and Origin of Evil, *neat, in boards*, 1s 6d 1722
3447 ——— Works, 2 vol. *new, and elegantly bound by* Johnson, 8s 1757
3448 Emilius, or System of Education by Rousseau, 2 vol. *in boards*, 3s 1761
*3448 Fordyce on Education, 2 vol. *very fair*, 4s 1762
3449 Locke on Education, *very fair*, 2s 1755
3450 Clarke on Education, 1s 1732
3451 —— Essay on Study, 1s 6d 1730
3452 —— The same, 1s 6d 1737
3453 Barclay on Education, 1s 6d 1731
3454 Hickes's Education of a Daughter, 1s 1743
3455 Bowles on the Roman Classics, *new*, 1s 6d 1707
3456 Felton on the Classics, 1s 1760
3457 Actor, a Treatise on the Art of Playing, 1s 1718
1750

3458 School

3458 School of Man, with the Key, *sewed*, 1s — 1753
3459 The same, *bound*, 1s 6d — — 1753
3460 The same 1753 — Manners, translated from the French, *in boards*, 2s — — 1752
3461 Fugitive Pieces on various Subjects, 2 vol. *new and elegantly bound by* Johnson, 8s — — 1761
3462 Gentleman's Library, containing Rules for Conduct, *neat*, 2s 1754
3463 Strength and Weakness of Human Reason, 1s — 1737
3464 Duncan's Elements of Logick, *very neat*, 2s 6d 1759
3465 Seneca's Morals, by Bennet, *fair*, 1s 6d — 1745
3466 Military Memoirs of Marshal Turenne, by Williamson, 1s 1740
3467 Memorable Things of Socrates, *neat*, 2s — *Glasg*. 1757
3468 Cicero's Thoughts, *very neat*, 2s — 1751
3469 ——— Tusculan Disputations, 1s 6d — 1715
3470 ——— on Old Age and Friendship, 1s — 1704
3471 ——— Nature of the Gods, 1s — 1683
3472 Bohours's Ingenious Thoughts of the Fathers, 1s 6d 1727
3473 Casaubon on Enthusiasm, 1s — 1656
3474 C. Blount's Miscellaneous Works, 2s — 1695
3475 Pope's Blount's Essays, 1s — — 1697
3476 Watts's Doctrine of the Passions, 1s 6d — 1732
3477 Edinburgh Entertainer, 2s — — 1750
3478 Trapp's Lectures on Poetry, *neat*, 2s — 1742
3479 Voltaire's Critical Essays on Dramatick Poetry, *very neat*, 1s 6d 1761
3480 Babouc, or the World as it goes, by Voltaire — Humorous Lieutenant, *neat*, 1s 6d — — 1753
3481 Micromegas, a Comic Romance by Voltaire, 1s 6d 1753
3482 Hutchinson's Introduction to Moral Philosophy, *neatly bound*, 3s 6d — — 1747
3483 Hume on Principles of Morals, *sewed*, 1s — 1751
3484 —— Four Dissertations, 2s — 1757
3485 Hutcheson of the Passions, 1s 6d — 1728
3486 Bp. Wilkins on the Beauty of Providence, Epictetus's Maxims, &c. 1s — — 1670
3487 Swift's Tale of a Tub, *with cuts*, 1s — 1724
3488 —— Intelligencer, *neat*, 1s — — 1730
3489 Abdeker, or Art of preserving Beauty, *neat*, 1s 6d 1754
3490 Pancirollus's Memorable Things lost, 2 vol. in 1. 3s 6d 1715
3491 Orations of Demosthenes, with Tourreill's Preface, 1s 6d 1744
3492 Paterson's Commentary on Milton's Paradise Lost, *neat*, 2s 1744
3493 Bolingbroke's Letters on Patriotism, *sewed*, 1s — 1750
3494 Temple of the Muses, 1s — 1728
3495 Parent's Directory and Youth's Guide, by Collyer, *neat*, 2s 1761
3496 Webb on the Beauties of Poetry, *sewed*, 1s — 1762
3497 Sir W. Raleigh's Select Essays, 1s — 1667
3498 Marvel's Rehearsal transpros'd, vol. 2s 6d — 1673
3499 Transpros'd Rehearsed, 1s — — 1673
3500 Sir T. Brown's Christian Morals, 1s — 1716
3501 Alarm, or Gentleman's Monitor, 1s — 1719
3502 Boyce's Vindication of his Remarks on King's Invent. of Men, 1s — — 1695
3503 Enquiry into the Causes of Prodigies and Miracles, *very scarce*, 4s — — 1727

3504 Rey-

3504 Reyner's Consid. concerning Marriage, 1s — 1675
3505 Case of Catherine Vizzani, by Bianchi, 1s — 1751
3506 The Moralists, *very neat,* 1s 6d — 1709
3507 Epictetus's Manual, by Stanhope, 6d — *Glasg.* 1753
3508 Selden's Table Talk, *neat,* 1s 6d — *Glasg.* 1755
3509 Governour, by Sir Tho. Elyot, *black letter,* 1s 6d 1557
3510 General Rules to know all Things past, present, and to come, by Heydon, 1s — — 1660
3511 Reflexions and Maxims on the Conduct of Human Life, 1s 1756
3512 *Marquis of Worcester's Century of Inventions, scarce,* 2s 6d 1663
3513 Le Brun on Painting and Sculpture, *cuts,* 1s 6d — 1701
3514 History and Art of Engraving, *with cuts, in boards,* 3s 6d 1747
3515 Grey's Memoria Technica, 1s 6d — 1732
3516 The same, 1s 6d — — 1737
3517 The same, *in boards,* 1s — — 1732
3518 Science of Military Posts for the Use of Regimental Officers, with the Manner of attacking and defending Posts, *with cuts,* translated from the French of M. de Cointe, with Notes by the Translator, *sewed,* 2s 6d — — 1761
3519 The same, *bound, new,* 3s — — 1761
3520 Cautions and Advices to the Officers in the Army, particularly Subalterns, *new,* 2s 6d — — 1760
3521 The same, *2d hand,* 1s 6d — — 1760
3522 Seymour's Compleat Gamester, *neat,* 1s 6d — 1754
3523 Hoyle on Piquet, *morocco, gilt leaves,* 1s 6d — 1754
3524 Graunt on the Bills of Mortality, 1s — 1665
3525 Bekker's World bewitched, 1s — — 1695
3526 Gentleman Angler, 1s — — 1725
3527 Saunders's compleat Fisherman, 1s — 1724
3528 Knowledge of Medals, from the French, 1s — 1715
3529 Every Man his own Broker, *sewed,* 1s — 1761
3530 King's British Merchant, 3 vol. *fair and neat,* 5s 1743
3531 Locke's Papers on Money, Interest and Trade, 3s 1696
3532 Vaughan on Coin and Coinage, 1s — 1675
3533 Webster's Mathematicks, 3 vol. *very fair,* 6s — 1751
3534 Interest at one View, by Hayes, 1s — 1744
3535 Castaing's Interest Book, 1s — 1733
3536 The same, 1s — — 17 2
3537 Harris's Short Treatise of Algebra, 1s — 1714

Livres Francois. OCTAVO & DUODECIMO.

3538 Histoire Generale, par Voltaire, 7 tom. *cousu,* 12s 1758
3539 —— Le meme, 7 tom. *fort bien relie,* 18s 1758
3540 —— Le meme, 7 tom. *tres bien relie per* Johnson, 1l 5s 1758
3541 —— des Empires par Guyon, 12 tom. *bien relie,* 18s *Par.* 1736
3542 —— des Empereurs Romains, par Crevier, 12 tom. *demi relie,* 1l 7s — — *Par.* 1749
3543 —— Le meme, 12 tom. *bien relie,* 1l 16s — *ib.* 1749
3544 —— Chronologique des Empereurs, par Richier, 2 tom. *nouv. & elegam. relie,* 8s — — *ib.* 1754
3545 Tablettès Chronologiques, par Du Fresnoy, 2 tom. *nouv. & fort bien relie,* 10s — — *ib.* 1763

O 3547 Hist.

3546 Histoire Ancienne, par Rollin, 14 tom. *beau exemp. fort bien relie,* 1l 11s 6d —— —— *Paris* 1730

3547 ——— Le meme, 13 tom. *beau exemp. tres bien relie,* 1l 15s *ib.* 1733

3548 ——— du Bas-Empire, par Le Beau, 6 tom. *bien relie,* 15s *ib.* 1757

3549 ——— du Siecle d'Alexandre, *cousu,* 1s — *Amst.* 1762

3550 ——— de Theodose le Grand, par Flechier, 1s *Par.* 1699

3551 ——— des Grecs, *cousu,* 1s ——— *Lond.* 1758

3552 ——— de Boece Senateur Romain, *bien relie,* 2s *Par.* 1715

3553 ——— de l'Exil de Ciceron, par Morabin, 1s 6d *ib.* 1725

3554 ——— de Apollone de Tyane, 1s —— *ib.* 1705

3555 Ceremonies & Coust. de Juifs, par Simonville, 1s *Haye* 1682

3556 Mœurs des Israelites, par Fleury, 1s 6d — *Par.* 1712

3557 Histoire de Constantinople, par Cousin, 8 tom. 12s *ib.* 1685

3558 Idée du Gouvernement de l'Egypte, par Mascrier, *avec fig. tres bien relie,* 2s 6d —— —— *ib.* 1743

3559 Descript. des Plains d'Heliopolis & de Memphis, *bien relie,* 2s *Par.* 1755

3560 Histoire Romaine, par Rollin, 16 tom. *beau exemp. bien relie,* 2l 5s *ib.* 1748

3561 Causes de la Grandeur des Romains, par Montesquieu, *fort bien relie,* 3s —— —— *Edinb.* 1751

3562 Observat. sur les Romains, par Mably, 2s *Genev.* 1751

3563 Incertitude des Cinq Premiers Siecles de l'Hist. Romaine, 1s *Utrec.* 1738

3564 Abrege Chronolog. de l'Histoire d'Italie, *fort bien relie,* 4s *Par.* 1761

3565 Hist. de la Conjurat. de Naples, 1s —— *ib.* 1706

3566 —— des Revolutions Romaine, par Vertot, 3 tom. 4s 6d *Haye* 1720

3567 —— Le meme, 3 tom. 4s —— *Par.* 1720

3568 —— Le meme, 3 tom. *bien relie,* 5s —— *ib.* 1732

3569 —— des Revolut. de Suede, par Vertot, 2 tom. 2s 6d *ib.* 1722

3570 —— Le meme, 2 tom. *bien relie,* 3s — *Par.* 1722

3571 —— Le meme, 2 tom. in 1 vol. 1s 6d — *Haye* 1729

3572 —— des Revolut. de Portugal, par Vertot, 1s *Amst.* 1722

3573 —— de la dern. Revolut. de Perse, 2 tom. 2s *Haye* 1728

3574 —— de la derniere Revolut. de Genes, 2 tom. en 1 vol. *bien relie,* 2s 6d —— —— *Genev.* 1750

*3574 —— des Revolut. d'Angleterre, par d'Orleans, 3 tom. 4s 6d *Par.* 1695

3575 Memoires de la derniere Revolut. d'Angleterre, 2 tom. 2s *Haye* 1722

3576 Descript. des Isles Britanniques, par Epilly, *avec des cartes, cousu,* 1s 6d —— —— — *Par.* 1759

3577 Hist. du Divorce de Henry VIII. par Le Grand, 3 tom. 3s *ib.* 1688

3578 Revolut. d'Ecosse & d'Irlande en 1707, 1708 & 1709, par Hooke, *bien relie,* 2s —— —— *Haye* 1758

3579 Delices de la Grand Bretagne & de Irlande, *avec un grand nomb. des fig.* 8 tom. *bien relie,* 16s —— *Leide* 1727

3580 —— Le meme, 8 tom. en 6 vol. *bien relie,* 14s *ib.* 1727

3581 ——— de la Suisse, *avec fig.* 4 tom. 8s — *ib.* 1714

3582 ——— de l'Italie, *avec fig.* 4 tom. 7s — *Par.* 1707

3583 —— Le meme, 4 tom. *fort bien relie,* 10s — *ib.* 1707

3584 De-

3584 Descript. du Gouvernment du Corps Germanique, 1s 6d 1741
3585 Annales de l'Empire depuis Charlemagne, par Voltaire, 2 tom. 3s *Basle* 1754
3586 Hist. Politique du Siecle, 2 tom. *bien relie*, 2s 6d *Lond.* 1754
3587 De l'Hist. Dannemarc, par Mallet, *cousu*, 1s *Cop.* 1760
3588 Memoires de la Paix de Munster, 4 tom. 4s *Amst.* 1710
3589 L'Hist. Critique des Personnes les plus Remarquables de tous les Siecles, 2 tom. 2s 6d —— *Par.* 1699
3590 —— sur l'Etat present de Moscovie, 2 tom. 2s 6d *ib.* 1725
3591 Hist. de la Floride, par Richelet, 2 tom. 2s 6d *ib.* 1670
3592 Anecdotes de Pologne, 2 tom. 2s —— *Amst.* 1699
3593 —— de la Maison Ottomane, 2 tom. 2s *ib.* 1722
3594 Relation de l'Etat de Genes, par Le Noble, 1s *Par.* 1685
3595 Oeuvres de Machiavel, 6 tom. *bien relie*, 12s *Haye* 1743
3596 Education Complete, ou Abrege de l'Hist. Universelle, par Beaumont, 3 tom. *bien relie*, 6s —— — *Lond.* 1753
3597 Hist. du Siecle de Louis XIV. par Voltaire, 2 tom. *demi relie*, 3s *Haye* 1752
3598 —— Le meme, 2 tom. *demi relie*, 3s — *Lond.* 1752
3599 —— Le meme, 2 tom. *relie*, 3s 6d —— *Edinb.* 1752
3600 —— Le meme, 2 tom. *fort bien relie*, 4s — *Haye* 1752
3601 —— Le meme, 3 tom. *bien relie*, 4s — *Lond.* 1752
3602 —— de la Empire de Russie sous Pierre Le Grand, 2 tom. par Voltaire, *cousu*, 6s — —— 1759, &c.
3603 —— de Charles XII. par Voltaire, 2 tom. 2s 6d *Basle* 1731
3604 —— de Guerre de MDCCXLI. par Voltaire, *cousu*, 1s *Lond.* 1757
3605 —— Le meme, *bien relie*, 1s 6d —— *ib.* 1736
3606 —— de Gustave Adolphe, par De Prade, 1s *Par.* 1686
3607 —— des Princes d'Orange, 1s —— *Amst.* 1593
3608 —— de Dom Inigo de Giupuscoa, par Rafiel de Selva, 2 tom. 2s 6d —— —— *Haye* 1736
3609 —— de Christine de Suede, par Lacombe, *cousu*, 1s *Stock.* 1762
3610 —— de Duc de Mercoeur, 1s —— *Colog.* 1698
3611 —— de l'Empereur Jovien & Julien, 2 tom. *fort bien demi relie*, 3s *Par.* 1748
3612 —— du Card. Ximenes, par Marsolier, 2 tom. *bien relie*, 3s 6d *ib.* 1739
3613 Anecdotes du Duc d'Olivares, 1s —— *ib.* 1722
3614 Politique de Ferdinand, par Varillas, 1s — *Amst.* 1688
3615 Memoires de Suede, par Linage, 3 tom. 1s 6d *Colog.* 1677
3616 Hist. de France, abrege par Mezeray, 7 tom. *avec fig.* 9s *Amst.* 1692
3617 —— Le meme, 7 tom 9s —— *ib.* 1715
3618 —— Le meme, 9 tom. *fort bien relie*, 16s — *ib.* 1723
3619 —— Le meme, 14 tom. *meilleur edit. nouv.* & *fort bien relie*, 2l 12s 6d *ib.* 1755
3620 —— de France, abrege par Daniel, *avec fig.* 9 tom. 12s *Par.* 1724
3621 —— de la Monarchie Francois, par l'Abbe Du Fresnoy, 3 tom. *bien relie*, 5s —— —— *ib.* 1753
3622 —— de France, abrege par Henault, 2 tom. *fort bien relie*, 8s *ib.* 1751
3623 —— des Guerres & des Negociat. de Westphalie, par Bougeant, 6 tom. *fort bien relie*, 18s —— —— *ib.* 1751
3624 Annales Politiques de l'Abbe de St. Pierre, 2 tom. *bien relie*, 4s *Lond.* 1758
3625 —— Le meme, 8vo. 2 tom. *fort bien relie en* 1 *vol.* 5s *ib.* 1757

O 2 3626 An-

3626 Annales Politiques de l'Abbe de St. Pierre, 2 tom. *bien relie,* 6s *Lond.* 1757
3627 L'Hist. Oeconom. des Mers Occident. de France, par Tiphaigne, *cousu,* 1s 6d ——— — *Par.* 1760
3628 Origine de la Ville de Caen, 1s —— *Rouen* 1702
3629 L'Heritiere de Guyenne, par Larrey, 1s — *Rot.* 1691
3630 Histoire Militaire du Regne de Louis XIV. 2 tom. *demi relie,* 3s 6d *Haye* 1760
3631 Descript. de la Louisiana, par Hennepin, 1s 6d *Par.* 1683
3632 Charlevoix Hist. de la Nouv. France, 6 tom. *demi relie,* 18s *ib.* 1744
3633 Campagne de Duc de Noailles en Allemagne, 2 tom. *cousu,* 2s 6d *Amst.* 1760
3634 Memoires du Commis. de sa Majeste tres Chret. & de sa Maj. Britan. 3 tom. *cousu,* 4s 6d ——— — *ib.* 1755
3635 L'Hist. du Card. Mazarin, par Aubery, 3 tom. 3s *ib.* 1718
3636 Anecdotes du Card. Richelieu, 2 tom. 3s — *ib.* 1717
3637 Negociations de Monf. Jeannin, 2 tom. 3s — *Par.* 1659
3638 Le meme, en 4 tom. 6s ——— *Amst.* 1695
3639 Commentaires de Blaize de Montluc, 2 tom. 3s *Par.* 1661
3640 Parallele des Romains & des Francois, 2 tom. *nouv. & fort bien relie,* 6s ——— ——— *Par.* 1740
3641 Memorial de Paris, 2 tom. *bien relie,* 6s —— *ib.* 1749
3642 Curiositez de Paris, de Versailles & des Environs, *avec fig.* 3 tom. *bien relie,* 6s ——— ——— *ib.* 1742
3643 Memorables Journées des Francois, 2 tom. 3s *ib.* 1682
3644 Hist. de Henry Duc de Bouillon, par Marsolier, 3 tom. 4s 6d *ib.* 1719
3645 —— Militaire de Louis XIII. par Ray, 2 tom. *fort bien relie,* 4s *ib.* 1755
3646 —— de Louis XI. par Du Clos, 3 tom. *bien relie,* 4s 6d *Amst.* 1746
3647 —— des Campagnes de Duc de Vendosme de Bellerive, 1s *Par.* 1715
3648 —— des Camisards, 2 tom. 3s — *Lond.* 1744
3649 —— de Henry III. Roy de France & de Pologne, 2 tom. 2s *Colog.* 1699
3650 Explicat. Historiq. de Versailles, par Combes, 1s *Par.* 1681
3651 Hist. de la Paix entre France & d'Espagne, 1s *Colog.* 1667
3652 Testam. Politiq du Card. Alberoni, 1s 6d *Laus.* 1753
3653 ——— du Marq. de Louvois, 1s — *Colog.* 1695
3654 ——— de M. Colbert, 1s ——— *Haye* 1693
3655 ——— du Card. de Richlieu, 1s — *Amst.* 1688
3656 Recherches & Considerat. sur les Finances de France, 6 tom. *cousu,* 8s ——— ——— *Lond.* 1755
3656 Hist. & Commerce des Colonies Angloises dans l'Amerique Septent. *cousu,* 1s ——— ——— *Lond.* 1755
3657 Reflex. Politiq. sur les Finances & le Commerce, par Dutot, 2 tom. *bien relie,* 3s ——— ——— *Haye* 1738
3658 Le meme, 2 tom. *nouv. & fort bien relie,* 5s *ib.* 1754
3659 L'Hist. generale des Finances, par Beaumont, 2 tom. *bien relie,* 3s *Amst.* 1760
3660 Essai Politique sur le Commerce, 1s —— *ib.* 1735
3661 Theorie de l'Impot, *cousu,* 2s ——— *Avig.* 1761

3663 Let-

3663 Lettres, Memoires & Negociat. d'Estrades, 5 tom. 5s *Brux.* 1709
3664 Ambassades de Monf. de la Boderie en Angleterre, 5 tom. *beau exemp. tres elegamen. relie, dore sur les tranches,* 1l —— *Par.* 1750
3665 Memoires du Comte de Forbin, 2 tom. 3s —— *Amst.* 1730
3666 ——— de Monf. de Bordeaux, 4 tom. *bien relie,* 9s *ib.* 1758
3667 ——— de Duc de Villars, 3 tom. *cousu,* 3s — *Haye* 1736
3668 ——— de M. Arnaud d'Andilly, 2 tom. 2s 6d *Hamb.* 1734
3669 ——— de Mareschal de Grammont, 2 tom. 3s *Par.* 1716
3670 ——— de M. de Gourville, 2 tom. 3s —— *ib.* 1724
3671 ——— du Marq. Maffei, 2 tom. 2s 6d —— *Haye* 1740
3672 ——— de Duc de Sully, 8 tom. *bien relie,* 18s *Par.* 1747
3673 ——— de l'Abbe de Montgon, 8 tom. *bien relie,* 16s *ib.* 1750
3674 ——— de Marq. de Feuquierre, 4 tom. *bien relie,* 6s *Lond.* 1740
3675 ——— Historiq. & Militaire, par le Marq. de Feuquieres, 2 tom. 3s *Amst.* 1735
3676 ——— & la Vie de Baron de Sirot, 2 tom. 3s *Par.* 1683
3677 ——— de Comte de Chavagnac, 1s —— *Amst.* 1701
3678 ——— Le meme, *fort bien relie,* 1s 6d —— *ib.* 1701
3680 ——— de d'Ablancourt, 1s —— *Par.* 1701
3681 ——— de Duc de Mont-Morency, 1s —— *ib.* 1666
3682 ——— de Duc de Bouillon, 1s —— *ib.* 1666
3683 ——— de Monf. de Torcy, 3 tom. *bien relie,* 6s *Lond.* 1757
3684 ——— de M. d'Artagnan, 3 tom. 3s —— *Colog.* 1700
3685 ——— a l'Hist. de Louis XIV. par Choisy, 3 tom. 3s *Utr.* 1727
3686 ——— d'Espagne sous le Regne de Philippe V. 4 tom. *demi relie,* 6s —— *Amst.* 1756
3687 ——— de Monf. L*** contenant l'Hist. des Guerres Civiles des Annes 1649, 2 tom. *bien relie,* 3s —— 1729
3688 ——— Supp. aux Memoires de Comines, 1s 6d *Bruss.* 1713
3689 ——— de France sous la Regence de Marie de Medicis, 2 tom. 2s 6d —— *Haye* 1720
3690 ——— a l'Hist. de la Maison de Brandebourg, 1s *ib.* 1751
3691 ——— Hist. Critiq. de M. Bruys, 2 tom. *fort bien relie,* 3s *Par.* 1751
3692 ——— & Reflex. du Regne de Louis XIV. 1s *Rott.* 1716
3693 ——— du Sieur de Pontis, 2 tom. 2s —— *Amst.* 1678
3694 ——— de Puysequr, 1s —— —— *ibid.* 1690
3695 { ——— & Negociat. de la Cour de Savoye —— *Basle* 1705
{ Apologie du Card. de Bouillon, &c. 1s —— *Colog.* 1706
3696 Vie des plus Fameux Peintures, *avec leur portraits,* 4 tom. *nouv. & fort bien relie,* 2l 2s —— *Par.* 1762
3697 —— Le meme, 4 tom. *bien relie,* 1l 16s —— *ib.* 1762
3698 —— des Peintures, par Felibien, 6 tom. 10s 6d *Amst.* 1706
3699 —— du Card. d'Amboise, par Le Gendre, 2 tom. 2s 6d *Rouen.* 1724
3700 —— de Gasp. de Coligny, 1s —— *Colog.* 1686
3701 —— de Mahomed, par Boulainvilliers, *bien relie,* 2s *Lond.* 1730
3702 —— Le meme, par Gagnier, 2 tom. 3s — *Amst.* 1732
3703 —— de Charles V. Duc de Lorraine, 1s —— *ib.* 1691
3704 —— de Jacques II. Roi de la Gr. Bret. par Bretonneau, 1s *Par.* 1703
3705 —— du Card. de Richelieu, 2 tom. par Le Clerc, 2s *Col.* 1695
3706 —— du Card. Commendon, par Flechier, 1s *Par.* 1694
3707 —— de Pythagore, par Dacier, 2 tom. 2s 6d *ibid.* 1706

3708 Vie

3708 Vie & les Choses memorable de Socrate, par Charpentier, 1s 6d *Amst.* 1699
3709 —— des Poetes Grecs, par le Fevre, 1s —— *ib.* 1700
3710 —— d'Emeric Comte de Tekeli, 1s —— *Colog.* 1693
3711 —— du Tasse, 1s —— —— *Par.* 1695
3712 Lettres & Negociat. de Comte d'Estrades, 6 tom. 7s 6d *Brux.* 1709
3713 —————— d'Estrades Colbert Marq. de Croissy, &c. 3 tom. 3s —— —— — *Haye* 1710
3714 Ambas. & Negociat. d'Estrades, 2 tom. 1s 6d *Amst.* 1718
3715 Lettres & Negociat. du Chev. Carleton, 3 tom. *cousu,* 4s 6d *Haye* 1759
3716 ——— & Memoires de Mad. de Maintenon, 15 tom. *beau exemp. & fort bien relie,* 1l 11s 6d ——— *Amst.* 1756
3717 ——— de Maintenon, *cousu,* 1s ——— *Par.* 1753
3718 ——— d'une Peruvienne, *cousu,* 1s ——— *Peine*
3719 ——— sur les Anglois, par Voltaire, 1s 6d *Basle* 1734
3720 ——— de le Blanc, 3 tom. *bien relie,* 4s 6d — *Haye* 1745
3721 ——— de Rabelais, 1s 6d —— — *Par.* 1710
3722 ——— de Loredano, Fr. & Ital. 1s —— *Brux.* 1712
3723 ——— Choisies, de Bayle, 3 tom. 3s —— *Rotterd.* 1714
3724 ——— Choisies, de Guy Patin, 3 tom. 3s *Haye* 1707
3725 ——— & Memoires du Baron de Pollnitz, 5 tom. 7s 6d *Amst.* 1737
3726 ——— de Louis XIV. avec Remarq. par Morelly, 2 tom. *cousu,* 1s 6d ——— —— *Lond.* 1755
3727 ——— du Louis XII. & du Card. d'Amboise, 4 tom. 5s *Bruss.* 1712
3728 ——— de Richelet, 2 tom. 2s 6d —— *Haye* 1708
3729 ——— de Filtz-Moritz, *cousu,* 1s —— *Amst.* 1718
3730 ——— Provinciales, par Montalte, Notes de Wendrock, 4 tom. *elegam. relie, par Johnson,* 12s —— *ibid.* 1753
3731 ——— de Bellegarde, 1s ——— *ibid.* 1707
3732 ——— de Rousseau, 5 tom. *bien relie,* 7s 6d *Genev.* 1750
3733 Voyages de Monconys, *avec fig.* 4 tom. 8s *Par.* 1695
3734 ——— Le meme, en 5 tom. *eleg. relie, par Johnson,* 15s *ibid.* 1695
3735 ——— de Biervillas Portugais en Indes Orient. 2s *ibid.* 1736
3736 ——— de Dellon, 3 tom. 4s 6d —— *Colog.* 1711
3737 ——— du Lucas, 3 tom. *avec fig. fort bien relie,* 6s *Rouen.* 1719
3738 ——— de Frezier, 2 tom. *avec fig.* 3s —— *Amst.* 1717
3739 ——— de Chardin en Perse, 10 tom. *bien relie,* 1l 1s *ib.* 1711
3740 ——— & Avant. de Franc. Leguat, *avec fig.* 2s *Lond.* 1708
3741 ——— de la Campag. des Indes Orientales, *avec fig.* 12 tom. *bien relie,* 1l 11s 6d —— —— *Rouen.* 1725
3742 ——— des Indes Occident. par Durret, *avec fig. bien relie,* 2s 6d *Par.* 1720
3743 ——— du Nord, *avec fig.* 3 tom. 4s —— *Amst.* 1715
3744 ——— du Nord, par Outhier, *avec fig. demi relie,* 2s *ib.* 1746
3745 ——— (Nouveau) du Nort, *avec fig.* 1s — *ibid.*
3746 ——— du Levant, par Tollot, *bien relie,* 2s *Par.* 1742
3747 ——— dans la Palestine, par la Roque, *avec fig.* 2s *Amst.* 1718
3748 ——— de Greece, d'Egypte, des Pais Bais, &c. 1s 6d *Haye* 1724
3749 ——— de Perse, par Sanson, *avec fig.* 1s —— *Par.* 1695
3750 ——— de Siam, par Tachard, *avec fig.* 3 tom. 4s *Amst.* 1688
3751 ——— de Siam, par Choisy, *bien relie,* 2s *Trevoux.* 1741

3752 Voyages

3752 Voyages Royaume de Siam, par Loubere, *avec fig.* 2 tom. *beau exemp. relie en maroq. dore sur les tranches,* 7s —— *Par.* 1691
3753 —— de France, par la Force, 2 tom. *avec fig. bien relie,* 4s *ibid.* 1755
3754 —— Pittoresque de Paris, *avec fig. bien relie,* 3s *ibid.* 1752
3755 —— de Seigneur Franc. Drach. *Par.* 1641—Rivii Hist. Navalis Mediæ *Lond.* 1640 —— Grasseri Itinerarium *Bas.* 1624 2s 6d
3756
3757 Memoires pour un Voyageur, *avec fig.* 2s *Amst.* 1738
3758 Relat. de divers Voyages, par de Grand-Pierre, 1s 6d *Par.* 1718
3759 Entretiens des Voyageurs, sur la Mer, *avec fig.* 4 tom. en 2 vol. 3s —— —— *Colog.* 1715
3760 L'Utilite des Voyages, par Baudelot, *avec fig.* 2s *Par.* 1693
3761 Le meme, en 2 tom. *bien relie,* 4s —— *Rouen.* 1727
3762 Voyage Litteraire de France, Hol. & Angl. 1s 6d *Haye* 1735
3763 —— en Allemagne, &c. par Patin, *avec fig.* 1s *Lyon* 1674
3764 —— du Marq. de Ville au Levant, 2 tom. 1s *Amst.* 1671
3765 Campagne des Isles de l'Amerique, 1s 6d — *Troyes* 1719
3766 Hist. Naturelle des Isles Antilles, par Rochefort, 2 tom. *avec fig.* 4s —— —— —— *Lyon* 1677
3767 —— de l'Expedit. de Trois Vaisseaux, 1s 6d *Haye* 1739
3768 —— des Boucaniers dans les Indes, *avec fig.* 2 tom. 3s *Par.* 1686
3769 —— Le meme, 2 tom. *bien relie,* 5s —— *ib.* 1699
3770 Oeuvres de Voltaire, *avec fig.* 17 tom. en 12mo. *bien relie,* 2l *Dresden* 1752
3771 —— Le meme, 18 tom. en 8vo. *fort bien relie,* 3l 3s 1757
3772 L'Esprit de M. de Voltaire, *bien relie,* 3s 6d —— *Amst.* 1760
3773 Micromegas, par Voltaire, 1s 6d —— *Lond.* 1752
3774 Candide, par Voltaire, *bien relie,* 2s —— 1759
3775 L'Esprit par Helvetius, 2 tom. 5s —— —— *Par.* 1758
3776 Exposition des Loix, *fort bien relie,* 2s —— *ib.* 1701
3777 Reveries Serieuses & Comiques, 1s 6d —— *ib.* 1728
3778 L'Espion Turc dans les Cours des Princes Chretiens, *avec fig.* 7 tom. 12s —— —— *Lond.* 1742
3779 Traite de l'Opinion, ou Memoirs de l'Esprit Humain, par Le Gendre, 6 tom. *bien relie,* 12s —— *Par.* 1735
3780 Essais de Montaigne, par Coste, 5 tom. 10s 6d *Haye* 1727
3781 Oeuvres de St. Pierre, 18 tom. 1l 10s —— *Rotterd.* 1738
3782 —— de St. Evremond, *avec fig. gravees par Picart,* 7 tom. *bien relie,* 15s —— —— *Amst.* 1739
3783 —— Le meme, par Des Maizeaux, 12 tom. *fort bien relie,* 1l 1s —— 1753
3784 —— de Marq. de Argens, 33 tom. *nouv. & tres bien relie,* 4l 4s
3785 —— de Voiture, 2 tom. 3s —— *Haye* 1754
3786 —— de Rabelais, 2 tom. 3s —— *Par.* 1693
3787 —— Le meme, 8 tom. *fort bien relie,* 14s 1679
3788 —— de Scarron, 6 tom. 7s 6d —— *Amst.* 1752
3789 —— de Montesquieu, 6 tom. *fort bien relie,* 15s *ib.* 1712
3790 Les Belles Lettres, par Rollin, avec le Supplement, 5 tom. 7s *ib.* 1739
3791 —— Le meme, 4 tom. *bien relie,* 7s —— *Par.* 1726
3792 —— Le meme, 4 tom. *fort bien relie,* 8s —— *ib.* 1732
3793 —— Le meme, 4 tom. *fort bien relie,* 9s —— *ib.* 1732
ib. 1755

3794 L'Hist.

3794 L'Hist. d'Hercule le Thebain, *bien relie,* 2s 6d *Par.* 1758
3795 Causes de la Corrupt. de Goust, par Dacier, 1s *ib.* 1714
3796 Le meme, *bien relie,* 1s 6d ——— *Haye* 1734
3797 Nouv. Litteraires, par Clement, 4 tom. *bien relie,* 5s *ib.* 1754
3798 Des Beaux Arts, par Lacombe, *bien relie,* 2s *Par.* 1761
3799 L'Etat des Arts en Angleterre, par Rouquet, *tres eleg. relie en maroq. & dore sur les tranches,* 5s ——— *ib.* 1755
3800 L'Esprit des Beaux Arts, 2 tom. *bien relie,* 3s 6d *ib.* 1753
3801 Melanges de Poesies d'Eloquence & d'Erudit, 1s *ib.* 1700
3802 ——— de Litterature, d'Histoire & de Philosophe, 4 tom. *bien relie,* 12s ——— ——— *Amst.* 1759
3803 Reponse a l'Hist. des Oracles de Fontenelle, 1s *Strasb.* 1707
3804 Bibliotheque Critique, par Simon, 4 tom. 5s *Par.* 1708
3805 Apologie des Lettres Provinciales, 2 tom. 2s *Rouen* 1697
3806 Recherches Historiques & Curieuses, 1s 6d — *Par.* 1723
3807 Recreations Litteraires, de Poesies & Lat. 1s 6d *ib.* 1723
3808 Memoires de Histoire de Critique, &c. par Artigny, Tom. 3, 4, 5, 6, 7. *cousu,* 5s ——— ——— *Par.* 1750
3809 Reflexions Critiq. sur la Poesie & sur la Peinture, 2 tom. 2s 6d *Utrecht* 1732
3810 Du Poeme Epique, par Bossu, *cousu,* 1s ——— *Haye* 1714
3811 Theorie des Sentimens agreables, *bien relie,* 1s 6d *Lond.* 1750
3812 Relation du Parnasse, 1s ——— *Amst.* 1739
3813 L'Esprit du Guy Patin, 1s ——— *ib.* 1710
3814 Bibliotheque Francois, 16 tom. *bien relie,* 16s *ib.* 1723
3815 Remarq. Critiq. Morales, Historiques, 1s ——— *ib.* 1692
3816 Bibliotheque Choisie, par Le Clerc, 28 tom. 1l 11s 6d *ib.* 1703
3817 L'Chef d'Oeuvres d'un Inconu Poeme de Matanasius, 2 tom. *demi relie,* 2s 6d ——— ——— *Haye* 1732
3818 Critique des Avant. de Telemaque, 2 tom. 1s 6d *Cologn.* 1700
3819 Dissertat. Critiq. sur l'Iliade d'Homere, par Terrasson, 2 tom. 2s 6d ——— ——— *Par.* 1715
3820 Remarq. sur Virgile & sur Homere, 1s 6d — *ib.* 1715
3821 Education des Enfans, par Crousaz, 2 tom. 2s *Haye* 1722
3822 Magazin des Enfans, par Beaumont, 2 tom. 5s *Lond.* 1758
3823 Etudes Convenables aux Demoiselles, 2 tom. *nouv. & fort bien relie,* 6s ——— ——— *Par.* 1762
3824 Le Guerre Seraphique, 1s ——— *Haye* 1740
3825 Droit Natural, par Burlamaqui, *cousu,* 1s 6d *Gen.* 1748
3826 Origine des Loix des Arts & des Sciences, par Gouguet, *avec fig.* 6 tom. *bien relie,* 15s — ——— *Par.* 1758
3827 Droit des Souverains, par F. Paolo, 2 tom. 3s *Haye* 1721
3828 Maniere de Negocier avec les Souverains, par Callieres, 2 tom. *bien relie,* 3s ——— ——— *Lond.* 1750
3829 Secretaire de la Cour, 2 tom. *fort bien relie,* 5s *Par.* 1758
3830 L'Hist. de l'Esprit & du Coeur, par d'Argens, 1s 6d *Haye* 1744
3831 Reflexions de Rochesoucault, par Bossuet, *bien relie,* 2s *Laus.* 1747
3832 Caracteres de Theophraste, par Coste, 2 tom. *cousu,* 2s 6d *Dresde* 1755
3833 Pensées Ingenieuses, 1s ——— *Par.* 1692
3834 Pensées Ingenieuses des Peres de l'Eglise, 1s 6d *ib.* 1715
3835 ——— Le meme, 1s ——— — *ib.* 1700
3836 ——— Le meme, *bien relie,* 1s 6d ——— *Amst.* 1700
3837 ——— de Pascal sur la Religion, 1s 6d — *Haye* 1743

3838 Pen-

3839 Pensées diverses, par Goudar, *bien relie*, 1s 6d *Lond.* 1750
3840 Dialogues des Morts, par Fontenelle, 1s — *Haye* 1724
3841 Le meme, 2 tom. 1s 6d ——— *Par.* 1700
3842 Le meme, 2 tom. 1s 6d — —— *ib.* 1716
3843 Dialogues des Morts d'un tour Nouv. 1s — *Haye* 1709
3844 Theologie Payenne, par Burigny, 2 tom. *bien relie*, 4s *Par.* 1754
3845 Essais Politique & Morale, *tres bien relie*, 2s —— 1760
3846 Philosophe de Rotterdam accuse & convaincu, 1s *Amst.* 1706
3847 Diversitez Curieuses servir de Recreation a l'Esprit, 7 tom. 7s *ib.* 1696
3848 Dissertat. sur la Subordinat. avec Reflex. sur l'Art Militaire, 1s 6d *Avignon.* 1753
3849 Principes du Droit Politique, par Rousseau, *cousu*, 1s 6d *Amst.* 1762
3850 Ocellus Lucanus en Grec & Franc. avec Dissertat. par le Marq. d'Argens, *cousu*, 1s 6d ——— *Utrecht.* 1762
3851 Bibliotheque des Auteurs anciens & mod. 1s *Haye* 1702
3852 Compar. de l'Eloq. de Demost. & Ciceron, 1s *Par.* 1670
3853 Discours Philos. sur la Creat. par Vallade, 1s *Amst.* 1700
3854 Ordonnance du Roi sur la Infanterie, 1s 6d *Par.* 1753
3855 L'Esprit du Siecle, 1s —— —— *ib.* 1707
3856 L'Homme plus que Machine, 1s 6d — *Lond.* 1748
3857 Etat de l'Homme dans le Peche Originel, 1s —— 1714
3858 Maniere de Negocier, par Callieres, 1s — *Amst.* 1716
3859 Memoires d'un Honnete Homme, 1s —— *Lond.* 1749
3860 L'Art de Connoitre les Hommes, par Bellegarde, 1s *Amst.* 1709
3861 Caracteres d'Epictete & du Cebes, par Bellegarde, 1s *Haye* 1734
3862 Reflex. sur le Ridicule, par Bellegarde, 1s — *Amst.* 1707
3863 Le meme, 2 tom. 1s 6d ——— *Par.* 1697
3864 Mots a la Mode, 1s —— —— *Haye* 1692
3865 Physique Occulte, par Vallemont, *avec fig.* 2 tom. 1s *Par.* 1696
3866 Cinq Dialog. faits a l'Imitat. des Anciens, par Tubero, 1s *Mons.* 1671
3867 Dialogues de la Sante, 1s — — *Amst.* 1684
3868 L'Art de Vivre Heureux, 1s ——— *Par.* 1692
3869 Modeles de Conversat. par Bellegarde, 1s — *ib.* 1697
3870 Miroir pour les Personnes Coleres, 1s —— *Leige* 1686
3871 De la Sagesse, par Charron, 1s —— *Leide* 1646
3872 Scaligeriana 1695 — Recueil des Chansons Choisies, 2s *Par.* 1694
3873 Valesiana, *cousu*, 1s —— —— *ib.* 1695
3874 Le meme, *relie*, 1s 6d —— —— *ib.* 1625
3875 Sorberiana, 1s —— —— *ib.* 1694
3876 Cesar, par d'Ablancourt, 2 tom. *bien relie*, 3s *ib.* 1731
3877 Q. Curce, par Vaugelas, 2 tom. *bien relie*, 3s *ib.* 1716
3878 Tite-Live, par Du Ryer, 8 tom. 8s —— *Lyon* 1695
3879 Thucydide, par d'Ablancourt, 3 tom. 3s — *Par.* 1671
3880 Cyropœdie de Xenophon, par Charpentier, 2 tom. 3s *Haye* 1732
3881 Quintilien de l'Institut. de l'Orateur, trad. par Gedoyn, 4 tom. *bien relie*, 10s —— —— *Par.* 1752
3882 Oeuvres de Platon, par Dacier, 2 tom. 4s — *ib.* 1699
3883 Rhetorique d'Aristote, par Cassandre, 1s 6d *Amst.* 1698
3884 Le meme, 2s —— —— *ib.* 1733
3885 Poetique d'Aristote, par Dacier, *bien relie*, 2s 6d *ib.* 1733
3886 Ciceron sur les Nat. des Dieux, par Olivet, 2 tom. 4s *Par.* 1732

P 3887 Ci-

3887 Ciceron Lettres a Atticus, 2 tom. 2s —— *Par.* 1691
3888 —— Le meme, avec Remarq. 1s —— *ib.* 1701
3889 —— Le meme, par Mongault, Lat. & Fr. 6 tom. 15s *ib.* 1738
3890 —— de la Divination, par Regnier, 1s 6d *ib.* 1710
3891 Lettres de Pline le Jeune, 3 tom. 2s —— *ib.* 1699
3892 Le meme, trad. par Sacy, 2 tom. 1s — *Rotterd.* 1703
3893 Philippiques de Demosthene & Catilinaires de Ciceron, par D'Olivet, 2s —— —— *Par.* 1736
3894 Epistres de Seneque, 2 tom. 2s —— *ib.* 1681
3895 L'Eneide de Virgile, Lat. & Fr. par Marolles, 3 tom. 4s *ib.* 1662
3896 Le meme, 3 tom. *bien relie,* 6s —— *ib.* 1662
3897 Lucrece, Lat. & Fr. par Marolles, 2s —— *ib.* 1659
3898 Oeuvres de Lucrece, Lat. & Fr. par le Baron Coutures, 2 tom. 2s 6d —— —— *ib* 1692
3899 L'Iliade & l'Odyssee d'Homere, trad. par Dacier, *avec fig.* 6 tom. *bien relie,* 10s 6d —— — *Amst.* 1712
3900 Le meme, 6 tom. *bien relie,* 12s —— *Par.* 1711
3901 Premier Livre d'Iliade en Vers Fran. par Regnier, 1s *ib.* 1700
3902 Oeuvres d'Horace, par Dacier & Sanadon, 8 tom. *bien relie,* 1l 7s *Amst.* 1736
3903 *Poesies d'Horace, trad. avec Remarq. par Sanadon, 8 tom. grand papier, eleg. relie,* 2l 2s —— —— *ib.* 1750
3904 Oeuvres d'Horace, Lat. & Fr. par Dacier, 8 tom. *fort bien relie,* 12s —— —— *Par.* 1709
3905 Pharsale de Lucain, par Brebeuf, 1s —— *Haye* 1682
3906 Le meme, 1s — —— *Par.* 1681
3907 Satyre de Petrone, avec Remarq. & Fig. Lat. & Fran. 2s *Cologn.* 1694
3908 Le meme, 2 tom. Lat. & Fran. *avec fig. stained,* 1s *ib* 1694
3909 Terence, trad. par Dacier, *fig. bien relie,* 3 tom. 5s *Hamb.* 1732
3910 Plaute, par Dacier, 3 tom. 4s —— *Par.* 1691
3911 Le meme, 3 tom. 3s 6d —— *ib.* 1683
3912 Le meme, 3 tom. *bien relie,* 4s 6d —— *ib.* 1683
3913 Le meme, avec Notes par Guedeville, 10 tom. *avec fig. fort bien relie,* 1l —— —— *Leide* 1719
3914 Tragedies de Sophocle, par Dacier, 2s — *Par.* 1693
3915 L'Oepide & l'Electre de Sophocle, 1s 6d —— *ib.* 1692
3916 Satires de Perse, trad. par Le Noble, 1s — *Amst.* 1706
3917 Idylles de Bion & de Moschus, avec Remarq. 1s *ib.* 1688
3918 Anacreon & Sapho, Gr. Lat. Fr. par Longepierre, 1s *Par.* 1692
3919 Anacreon & Sapho, Gr. Lat Fr. par Dacier, 1s 6d *ib.* 1681
3920 Le meme, *relie en marcq. dore sur les tranches,* 2s 6d *ib.* 1681
3921 Le meme, 1s 6d —— —— *Amst.* 1716
3922 Odes de Anacreon & de Sapho, Gr. Lat. & Fr. par le Poete sans Fard, 1s 6d —— —— *Rotterd.* 1712
3923 Chef d'Oeuvres de P. Corneille, *bien relie,* 2s 6d *Oxon.* 1716
3924 Theatre de la Foire, 4 tom. 8vo. *nouv. & fort bien relie,* 14s *Par.* 1755
3925 Theatre de Corneille, 10 tom. *avec fig. cousu,* 15s *ib.* 1723
3926 —— Le meme, 10 tom. *avec fig. fort bien relie,* 16s *Amst.* 1723
3927 —— de P. Corneille, 5 tom. *bien relie,* 10s *Par.* 1723
3928 Oeuvres de Corneille, 19 tom. *nouv. & fort bien relie,* 2l 5s *ib.* 1758

3929 Oeuvres

3929 Oeuvres de Corneille, 19 tom. *nouv. & elegant. relie par* Johnson, 3l 3s —— —— *Par.* 1758
3930 —— de Moliere, 4 tom. 5s —— *Amst.* 1725
3931 Theatre des Grecs, par Brumoy, 6 tom. *bien relie,* 14s *ib.* 1732
3932 —— de Pradon, 1s — —— *Par.* 1695
3933 —— de la Fontaine, 1s —— *Haye* 1702
3934 —— de Riviere, *bien relie,* 1s 6d — *Paris* 1716
3935 Recueil de Pieces de Theatre, 2 tom. *bien relie,* 3s *Dubl.* 1749
3936 —— de Pieces Theatre Italien, 1s — *Par.* 1750
3937 Pieces de Theatre Franc. *bien relie,* 1s 6d —— *ib.*
3938 Cenie Comedie, par Grafigny, *elegant relie, dore sur les tranches,* 2s *ib.* 1751
3939 Oeuvres de la Grange Chancel, 3 tom. 4s 6d *ib.* 1735
3940 —— Le meme, 6 tom. *fort bien relie,* 6s — *ib.* 1735
3941 —— de M. de la Fosse, 2 tom. *nouv. & fort bien relie,* 5s *ib.* 1747
3942 —— de Regnard, 2 tom. 2s 6d —— *ib.* 1714
3943 —— de D'Ancourt, 8 tom. 10s 6d — *ib.* 1711
3944 —— de Pradon, 2 tom. *fort bien relie,* 5s *Par.* 1744
3945 —— de Campistron, *avec fig. bien relie,* 2s — *ib.* 1715
3946 —— Le meme, 2 tom. 2s 6d —— *Amst.* 1722
3947 —— de Le Grand, *bien relie,* 1s 6d — *Par.* 1716
3948 —— de Barbier, *bien relie,* 1s 6d —— *ib.* 1707
3949 —— de Pradon, *bien relie,* 1s 6d —— *ib.* 1700
3950 —— de Crebillon, *bien relie,* 1s 6d — *ib.* 1716
3951 —— de la Fosse, *bien relie,* 1s 6d —— *ib.* 1718
3952 —— de la Grange, *bien relie,* 1s 6d —— *ib.* 1718
3953 —— diverses de Rousseau, avec Supplement, 4 tom. 5s *Amst.* 1726
3954 —— Le meme, 2 tom. *bien relie,* 3s — *Lond.* 1731
3955 —— Le meme, 4 tom. revue par Seguy, *grand papier, nouv. & elegant. relie, par* Johnson, 1l 4s —— *Par.* 1743
3956 —— de Boileau, 3 tom. *fort bien relie,* 6s — *ib.* 1757
3957 —— de Fontaine, 4 tom. *fort bien relie,* 8s *ib.* 1744
*3957 —— Le meme, 4 tom. *fort bien relie,* 8s — *ib.* 1744
3958 —— de Gresset, 2 tom. *fort bien relie,* 4s — *ib.* 1758
3959 —— de Clement Marot, 6 tom. 6s —— *Haye* 1731
3960 —— de Santeuil, 1s —— —— *Par.* 1698
3961 Anti Rousseau, par Gacon, 1s 6d —— *ib.* 1716
3962 Madrigaux, de M. D. L. S. 1s —— *Leige* 1687
3963 Contes & Nouvelles, par Fontaine, 1s 6d —— *Amst.* 1699
3964 Le meme, *bien relie,* 2s —— —— *ib.* 1731
3965 Le meme, 1s —— —— *ib.* 1696
3966 Fables par Fontaine, *avec fig. bien relie,* 5 tom. 6s *Par.* 1709
3967 Poesies Choisies en Prose & en Vers, 2 tom. *demi relie,* 1s 6d *Haye* 1714
3968 L'Iliade par M. de la Motte, *avec fig.* 1s 6d *Par.* 1714
3969 Poesies de la Constitut. Unigenitus, 2 tom. *demi relie,* 2s *Villefran.* 1724
3970 Regles de la Poesie Francois, par Chalons, 1s *Par.* 1716
3971 Poeme de S. Prosper contre les Ingrats, Lat. & Franc. *elegant. relie en maroq.* 2s 6d —— —— *ib.* 1655
3972 Bibliotheque Poetique depuis Marot jusq. aux Poete de nos jours, 4 tom. *fort bien relie,* 10s —— *Par.* 1745
3973 Poetique Francois, par Marmontel, 2 tom. *cousu,* 6s *ib.* 1763

P 2 3974 Contes

3974 Contes Moraux, par Marmontel, 2 tom. *fort bien relie,* 5s *Par.* 1761
3975 ——— Nouv. ou la Fees Alamode, 4 tom. 5s *ib.* 1715
3976 ——— Chinois, par Guellette, *avec fig.* 2 tom. 2s 6d *Haye* 1725
3977 Telemaque, 2 tom. *avec fig. elegant. bien relie,* 9s *Lond. Chez Dodsley* 1738
3978 Don Quixote, 2 tom. *demi relie,* 4s — *Brux.* 1706
3979 Avant. de Pomponius Chevalier Romain, 1s *Rome* 1724
3980 Nouvelle Heloise. par Rousseau, 6 tom. *nouv. & elegant. relie en* 3 vol. *par* Johnson, 10s 6d ——— 1761
3981 Memoires de Lenclos, *bien relie,* 2s —— *Amst.* 1754
3982 Berger Extravagant, 2 tom. *bien relie,* 3s *Rouen* 1640
3983 Persile & Sigismonde, 4 tom. *bien relie,* 5s *Par.* 1738
3984 Histoire du Chevalier Caissant, 1s —— *ib.* 1714
3985 ——— du Prince Titi, 1s ——— *ib.* 1736
3986 Anecdotes de la Cour de Dom Jean Roi de Navarre, 2 tom. 2s *Amst.* 1744
3987 Lettres d'une Pereuvienne, *demi relie,* 1s 6d *Peine*
3988 Hypolite Comte de Douglas, 1s —— *Amst.* 1706
3989 Le Masque de Fer, *demi relie,* 1s —— *Haye* 1759
3990 Hist. de Manon Lescaut, 2 tom. *elegant. relie par* Johnson, 5s *Amst.* 1756
3991 Le Geomyler, 1s —— —— *ib.* 1739
3992 Romant Comique, par Scarron, *cousu,* 6d — *ib.* 1717
3993 Decameron de Boccace, *bien relie,* 2s 6d — *Lyon* 1558
3994 Le Romant de la Rose, 2s —— *Par.* 1543
3995 *Memoires de l'Academie Royale des Sciences en 67 tom. compleat, avec fig. fort bien relie,* 12l 12s —— — *Amst.* 1723
3996 Histoire de l'Academie Royale des Inscriptions & Belles Lettres, *avec fig.* 16 tom. *bien relie,* 1l —— —— *ib.* 1731
3997 Traite de la Peinture & de la Sculpture, par Richardson, 3 tom. 6s *ib.* 1728
3998 Vies des Peintres, par Felibien, 5 tom. 7s 6d *Lond.* 1705
3999 Cours de Peinture, par De Piles, 2s —— *Par.* 1708
4000 Conference de M. Le Brun sur l'Expression, *avec* 43 *fig.* 2s *Lond.* 1701
4001 Descript. des Tableaux du Palais Royal, 3s — *Par.* 1737
4002 Plans & Descript. des Maisons de Pline, 1s *Amst.* 1706
4003 Sentimens sur la Maniere de Peinture, par Bosse, 2s *Par.* 1649
4004 Newtonianisme pour les Dames, par Algarotti, 2 tom. 2s *ib.* 1738
4005 Maniere de la Perspective de M. Desargues, par Bosse, *avec fig.* 2 tom. 4s — —— *Par.* 1647
4006 L'Art de Peinture & Dialogue sur le Coloris de Fresnoy, Lat. & Fr. 2s 6d ——— ——— *ib.* 1673
4007 Memoire Artificielle, par Buffier, 1s —— *ib.* 1711
4008 Recreations Mathematiq. & Physiq. par Ozanam, 4 tom. *avec fig. fort bien relie,* 12s —— —— *ib.* 1735
4009 Cabinet d'Architecture, &c. par Le Compte, 3 tom. *bien relie,* 15s *ib.* 1699
4010 Regles des 5 Ordres d'Architecture de Vignole, 1s 6d *ib.* 1604
4011 Histoire du Ciel, 2 tom. *avec fig. bien relie,* 5s *ib.* 1740
4012 Recueil touchant quelques nouv. Machine, par Papin, *avec fig.* 1s *Cassel.* 1695
4013 Curiositez de la Nature & de l'Art, *avec fig.* 1s 6d *Par.* 1703

4014 Science

4014 Science des Emblemes Devises, &c. par C. Ripa, *avec fig.* 2 tom. 3s —— —— *Amst.* 1698
4015 Principes de Musique. par Lovlie, 1s —— *ib.*
4016 Explicat. d'une Medaille d'Or du Cab. du Roy, 1s 6d *Par.* 1699
4017 Histoire des Medailles, par Patin, *avec fig.* 1s — *ib.* 1695
4018 Le meme, 1s —— —— *ib.* 1665
4019 Science des Medailles, 1s ———— *ib.* 1693
4020 Jeu des Eschets de Gioach. Græco, 1s 6d —— *ib.* 1713
4021 Foucher sur les Hygometres, 1s —— *ib.* 1686
4022 Physiques des Corps Animees, *bien relie,* 2s — *ib.* 1755
4023 Principe de l'Harmonie, par Romeau, *avec fig.* 2s *ib.* 1750
4024 Reglemens & Statuts concern. le Commerce, 1s 6d *Lyon* 1720
4025 Petite Guerre par Grand Maison, *demi relie,* 1s 1756
4026 L'Art de la Guerre, par Ray, 2 tom. 4s — *Par.* 1754
4027 Science de la Guerre, *avec fig.* 2s —— *Turin* 1744
4028 Essay sur les Feux d'Artifice, *avec fig. bien relie,* 2s 6d *Par.* 1745
4029 Maniere de Fortifier, par Vauban, *avec fig.* 1s 6d *Amst.* 1718
4030 Fortificat Nouvelle, par Pfesinger, *avec fig.* 2s 6d *Haye* 1740
4031 *Hist. Ecclesiastiq. & Bibliotheq. Ecclesie, par Du Pin,* 19 *tom. beau exemp.* 1l 1s —— —— *Par.* 1713
4032 Abrege de l'Hist. Ecclesiastique, 13 tom. *fort bien relie,* 2l 2s

4033 Nouv. Test. 1s 6d — —— *Par.* 1752
4034 Le meme, avec Reflexions Morales, par Quesnel, 4 tom. 6s *Lond.* 1735

4035 Le meme, en Lat. & en Franc. 2 tom. 2s *Brux.* 1702
4036 Le meme, avec Notes, 1s —— *Mons.* 1684
4037 Le meme, par Martin, 1s —— *ib.* 1710
4038 L'Apocalypse de S. Jean. trad par De Sacy, 1s *Lond.* 1750
4039 Motifs de la Conversion, *relie en maroq.* 1s *Brux.* 1703
4040 Le Clerc sur l'Incredulite, 1s —— *Par.* 1682
4041 Hist. du Christianisme d'Ethiope & d'Armenie, par La Croze, *cousu,* 1s —— —— *Amst.* 1696
4042 Fenelon sur l'Existence de Dieu, *bien relie,* 1s 6d *Haye* 1739
4043 Lettres concernant Relig. &c. par Fenelon, *bien relie,* 1s 6d *Par.* 1718

4044 Apologie Catholiq. contre les Libelles Declarat. Escrites, 1s *ib.* 1718
4045 Sermons par Bourdaloue, 15 tom. 1l 11s 6d 1585
4046 ——— de Claude, 2s —— —— *Lyon* 1756
Genev. 1724

Italian and Spanish. OCTAVO and TWELVES.

4047 TRagedie di Euripide, Gr. & Ital. con l'Annotaz. del P. Carmeli, 10 tom. *nouv. & bene ligat.* 2l 10s *Padova* 1743
4048 Il medessimo, 10 tom. *nuev. & eleganz. ligat. per* Johnson, 3l *ib.* 1743

4049 *Epistole Eroiche, di Ovidio, tradotte da Remegio, con fig. eleganz. ligat. in maurit. nuev.* 12s —— *Par.* 1762
4050 Il medessimo, *eleganz. ligat. per* Johnson, 10s 6d *ib.* 1762
4051 Lucreze delle Nature delle Cose, trad. par Marchetti, *con fig. curios.* 2 tom. *bene ligat.* 1l 1s —— *Amst.* 1754
4052 Il medessimo, *eleganz. ligat.* 2 tom. 1l 4s — *ib.* 1754

4053 Iliade

053 Iliade & Odyssea d'Omero, trad. da Salvini, 2 tom. *bene ligat.* 8s *Padoua* 1742

4054 Gieuvenale e Persio con Annotaz. dal Rovigo, 2 tom. *bene ligat.* 7s *Venez.* 1758

4055 Farsaglia di Lucano, trad. da Abriani, *bene ligat.* 5s *ib.* 1668

4056 Opere del Metastasio, *nuev.* & *bene ligat.* 9 tom. 2l *Par.* 1755

4057 Il medessimo, 9 tom. *nuev.* & *eleganz. ligat. per* Johnson, 2l 10s *ib.* 1755

4058 Il medessimo, 8 tom. 1l 4s ——— *Rom.* 1751

4059 Poesie Drammat. di Apostolo Zeno, 10 tom. 1l 5s *Veneg.* 1744

4060 Rime de gli Arcadi, 9 tom. 18s ——— *Roma* 1716

4061 Poesie del Berardino Rota con le Annotaz. di Scip. Ammirato, Tom. 1. 2s 6d — ——— *Napol.* 1726

4062 Rime di vari Autori Brescani Raccolti da Roncalli, *nuev.* & *bene ligat.* 3s 6d ——— ——— *Bresce* 1761

4063 Filli di Sciro del Conte Guidub. Bonarelli, 1s 6d *Lond.* 1728

4064 Sonetti del Burchiello, di Burchielli, *bene ligat.* 5s *ib.* 1751

4065 Canzoni Anacreont. di Buraffaldi, *bene ligat.* 2s *Veneg.* 1743

4066 L'Italiana Liberata di Trissino, per Antonini, *bene ligat.* 3 vol. 7s 6d ——— ——— *Par.* 1729

4067 Raccolta di Rime Italiana, 2 tom. 3s ——— *ib.* 1744

4068 Rime di Antonini, 2 tom. 2s 6d ——— *ib.* 1739

4069 Verita Essaminata a favor del Popolo di Genoua, 1s 1628

4070 Teatro Italiano, 4 tom. *bene ligat. fogl. inorn.* 8s *Veron.* 1723

4071 Il medessimo, 3 tom. *nuev.* & *bene ligat.* 9s *Veneg.* 1746

4072 Opere di Moliere, 8 tom. 10s ——— *Lips.* 1697

4073 Il medessimo, 4 tom *nuev.* & *bene ligat.* 12s *Venez.* 1756

4074 Comedie di Ang. Nelli, 5 tom. *nuev.* & *eleganz. ligat. per* Johnson, 1l 5s ——— ——— *Milan.* 1762

4075 Nuovo Teatro Comico, di Car. Goldoni, 8 tom. *nuev.* & *bene ligat.* 1l 4s ——— ——— *Venez.* 1757

4076 Comedie di Carlo Goldoni, 10 tom. *nuev.* & *bene ligat.* 1l 5s *Pesaro* 1753

4077 Opere di Lod. Ariosto, 4 tom. *cicuto,* 7s — *Venez.* 1760

4078 Il medessimo, 4 tom. *nuev.* & *bene ligat.* 10s 6d *ib.* 1760

4079 Orlando Innamorato, di Berni, 2 tom. *nuev.* & *bene ligat.* 7s *ib.* 1760

4080 Morgante Maggiore di Luig. Pulci, 2 tom. *nuev.* & *bene ligat.* 6s *Torin.* 1754

4081 Obras de Camoens, *con fig.* 3 tom. *nuev.* & *bene ligat.* 9s *Par.* 1759

4082 Ricciardetto di Nic. Carteromaco, 2 tom. *nuev.* & *bene ligat.* 5s *ib.* 1735

4083 Girone il Cortese, di Luig. Alamanni, 2 tom. *nuev.* & *bene ligat.* 5s ——— ——— *Bergamo* 1757

4084 Opere Volgari, di Jac. Sanazzaro, 2 tom. *nuev.* & *bene ligat.* 7s ——— ——— *Venez.* 1741

4085 Arcadia, di Sannazaro, 1s ——— *ib.* 1620

4086 Satire e Rime, di Ariosto, 1s 6d ——— *Lond.* 1716

4087 L'Aminte da Tasse, Fr. & Lat. *con fig. cicuto,* 1s *Haye* 1681

4088 Aminta di Tasso, con illustrat. da Fontanini, 2s *Rom.* 1700

4089 Il medessimo, *eleganz. ligat. per* Johnson, 4s *Venez.* 1730

4090 Il medessimo, con le Annotaz. di Menagio, *bene ligat.* 3s *ib.* 1736

4091 Il

4091 Il Fedele Comedia di Pasqualigo, *bene lig. in maurit. fogl. inor.* 2s *Venet.* 1579
4092 Rosmunda Tragedia, di Ruccellai, *cicuto,* 6d *Lond.* 1737
4093 Alceo Favola Pescat. di Ongaro, *cicuto.* 6d —— *ib.* 1727
4094 Due Commedie e una Novella del Segretario Fiorentino, *cicuto,* 1s —— —— *Traject.* 1733
4095 Amor per Vendetta — Amor Bisbetico — La Gran Costante nelle fede il Girello, 1s
4096 Pastor Fido, di Guarini, *cicuto,* 6d —— *Veneg.* 1750
4097 Il medessimo, con le Rim. di Guarini, 6d *Venet.* 1627
4098 Gierusalemme Liberata, di Tasso, 1s 6d — *ib.* 1642
4099 Eneide di Virgilio, di Annib. Caro, 1s — *Rom.* 1604
4100 Rime di Fenarvolo, 1s — —— *Venet.* 1574
4101 Petrarca, 1s —— —— *ib* 1585
4102 Il medessimo, *cicuto,* 1s 6d —— *Venez.* 1739
4103 Rime di Balducci, 2 tom. 2s —— *Rom.* 1645
4104 —— del Cav. Paoli, 1s —— *ib.* 1637
4105 Epistole Eroiche del Bruni, 1s —— *Bolog.* 1663
4106 Cicceide Legitima, *bene ligato,* 2s 6d
4107 Poesie Liriche di Virg Casarini, 1s —— *Veneg.* 1669
4108 Novelliero Italiano, 4 tom. *bene ligat.* 16s — *ib.* 1754
4109 Decamerone, di Boccacci, 2 tom. *nuev.* & *bene ligato,* 10s *Amst.* 1761
4110 Don Chisciotte della Mancha, 2 tom. *bene ligat.* 9s *Venez.* 1738
4111 Auvenimenti di Telemaco, 2s 6d —— *Leiden* 1704
4112 Chronologia de gli Antichi Ebrei, Eglizi da Lampeiano, *bene ligat.* 2s 6d —— —— *Dresde* 1737
4113 Difeso del Petrarca per Casaregi Canevari Tommasi, 2s *Lucca* 1709
4114 Dissertatione contro i Fatalisti di J. Vincenzo, 2 tom. *bene ligat.* 4s —— —— *ib.* 1744
4115 Osservaz. sopra Felsina Pittrice da Vittoria, 1s *Rom.* 1703
4116 Storia della Favola confrontata colla Storia Santa, 1s *Venez.* 1753
4117 Giro del Mondo di Gem. Careri, *con fig. bene ligat.* 9 tom. in 5 vol. 11s —— —— *ib.* 1749
4118 Rime & Prose di Giov. della Casa, 2s — *Firenz.* 1564
4119 Antichita di Pozzuolo, da Capaccio, *con fig.* 2s *Rom.* 1652
4120 Se l'Huomo diventa Buono o Cattivo Volontar. per Portio, 1s *Fiorenz.* 1551
4121 Hist. Fiorentine di Machiavegli, 1s 6d — *Venet.* 1540
4122 Il medessimo, 1s 6d —— —— *Piacenz.* 1587
4123 Vita di Pietro Aretino, *cicuto,* 1s —— *Padoua* 1741
4124 Dissertazione contro i Materialisti, di T. Vincenzo, 2 tom. *cicuto,* 4s —— —— *ib.* 1750
4125 Hist. di Vinegia, di Domenichi, 1s 6d — *Vineg.* 1545
4126 Gravina della Ragion Poetica, 4s —— *Napol.* 1716
4127 —— Tragedie Cinque, 4s —— *ib.* 1712
4128 —— della Tragedia, *eleganz. ligat.* 4s —— *ib.* 1731
4129 Modo di Comporre in Versi di Ruscelli, 1s *Venet.* 1605
4130 Lettres du Card. Bentivoglio, Ital. & Fr. 1s 6d *Brux.* 1713
4131 —— di Pietro Bembo, 2 tom. 3s —— *Vineg.* 1752
4132 Prose di P. Bembo, 1s —— *Venet.* 1606
4133 Discorso sopra le Vicende della Litteratura, 1s 6d *Torin.* 1760
4134 Pinaroli Antiche di Roma, *con fig.* 3 tom. 3s *Rom.* 1725
4135 Tirannia d'Imeneo, da Gio. Rossii, 1s — *Venet.* 1663

4136 Ro.

4136 Rettorica della Puttane composta conforme le precetti di Cipriano, 1s 6d —— —— *Cambria* 1642
4137 Dianea di Loredano, 1s —— *Venet.* 1647
4138 Favole Heroiche per Audin, 1s —— *Bolog.* 1681
4139 Opere Scelta, di Pallavicino, 1s — *Villa Fr.* 1666
4140 Pitture di Bologna, 1s —— *Bolog.* 1706
4141 Cleopatra, 7 tom. en 6 vol. 6s —— *Venet.* 1672
4142 Vita & Lettre di Marq. Aurelio Imperator. 1s *ib.* 1574
4143 Saggio di Proverbi o detti-Sent. da Lena, 1s *Lucca* 1674
4144 Cortegiano di Castiglione, 1s —— *Vineg.* 1587
4145 Cardinalismo di Santa Chiesa, 3 tom. *bene ligat.* 2s 1668
4146 Vero Ritratto d'un Principe Christiano, 1s *Colog. nello Anno presente*
4147 Libro delle Preghiere Publiche, 1s —— *Lond* 1685
4148 Xenophon della Vita di Ciro — Fatti de Greci di Xenophon—Xenophon della Impressa di Ciro—Opere Morali, di Xenophon, 7s 6d *Vineg.* 1548
4149 Thucydide delle Guerre della Morea, 10s 6d *Vinet.* 1550
4150 Polybio, tradotto per Domenichi, 7s 6d — *Vineg.* 1545
4151 Comment. di Giulio Cesare, trad. par Ortica, 3s *Venet.* 1517
4152 Valerio Massimo, trad. di Dati, 2s 6d —— *ib.* 1586
4153 Epistole Famigliari, di Cicerone, 2s 6d *Ven. ap. Ald.* 1551
4154 Seneca de Beneficii, trad. par Varchi, 1s 6d *Fiorenz.* 1574
4155 Eclogas y Georgicas de Virgilio, 2s — *Madr.* 1618
4156 Novo Test. en Portug. trad. pelo P. Ferreiza, 2s *Amst.* 1712
4157 Introduccion del Symolo de la Fe, por Granda, 5 tom. 5s *Madr.* 1654
4158 Novelas de Cervantes, *con fig.* 2 tom. *buon ligato,* 5s *Haye* 1739
4159 Don Quixote de la Mancha, 2 tom. *con fig.* 9s *Amberes* 1719
4160 Las Obras y Relaciones de Ant. Perez, 1s *Genev.* 1644

Libri Classici & Authores Antiqui. DUODECIMO.

4161 HOratius, Juvenal & Persius, Terentius, Virgilius, Catullus, Tibullus, & Propertius, Lucanus, Phœdrus, Lucretius, Ovidius, Q. Curtius, Corn. Nepos, Sallustius, J. Cæsar
N. B. *The above set of Classics, neatly printed by Brindley,* 20 *vol. ruled with red lines, elegantly bound in yellow morocco, marble leaves,* 2l 15s *Lond.* 1748, &c.
4162 Ovidii Opera, a Maittaire, 3 tom. 4s —— *Lond.* 1715
4163 Idem, 3 tom. *ch. max. exemp. pulch.* 10s 6d — *ib.* 1715
4164 Idem, cum Notis Heinsii, 6 tom. *nit. comp.* 6s *Amst.* 1661
4165 Idem, accurante N. Heinsii, 3 tom. 2s 6d — *ib.* 1717
4166 Idem, D. Heinsius recens. 1s —— *ib.* 1663
4167 Idem, 5 tom. *lin. rubr. nit. comp. corio maurit. fol. deaur.* 10s *Lond. typis Brindley* 1745
4168 Ovidii Epistolæ & Amores D. Heinsius, 1s *L. Bat. ap. Elz.* 1629
4169 Virgilius, a Maittaire, 2s —— *Lond.* 1715
4170 Idem, 2s —— —— *Dubl.* 1745
4171 Idem, *exemp. eleg. & nitid. comp. fol. deaur.* 5s *Ven. ap. Ald.* 1555
4172 Idem, cura Steph. Andr. Philippe, *cum fig. elegant.* 3 tom. *nit. comp.* 12s —— —— *Par.* 1745

4173 Vir-

4174 Virgilius, *cum multis fig.* 2 tom. *nov. & eleg. comp. per Johnson,* 10s ——— ——— *Lond. ap. Sandby* 1750
4175 Idem, *maculat.* 2s 6d ——— *L. Bat. ap. Elz.* 1636
4176 Plautus, a Capperonier, *typis elegant. nov. & eleg. comp. per Johnson,* 3 tom. 18s ——— ——— *Par.* 1759
4177 Terentius, *cum fig. multis,* 2 tom. *nit. comp.* 4s *Lond. ap. Sanby* 1751
4178 Idem, 2 tom. in 1 vol. *nov. & eleg. comp. per Johnson,* 5s *ib. ap. ib.* 1751
4179 Idem, a Philippe, 2 tom. *cum fig. elegant. comp. fol. deaur.* 10s *Par.* 1753
4180 Idem, accessf. variæ Lectiones, 1s ——— *Cantab.* 1723
4181 Idem, ex recens. Heinsiana, 1s 6d *L. Bat. ap. Elz.* 1635
4182 Idem, *vera edit. nit. comp. in corio maurit. fol. deaur.* 5s *ib. ap. ib.* 1635
4183 Horatius, *cum fig. multis,* 2 tom. 5s *Lond. ap. Sandby* 1749
4184 ——— 2 tom. in 1 vol. 3s ——— *ib. ap. ib.* 1749
4185 ——— a Maittaire, 1s 6d ——— ——— *ib.* 1715
4186 ——— cum Lect. Venus. Rutgersii, *sutus,* 1s 6d *Traject.* 1699
4187 ——— *nit. comp.* 6s ——— ——— *Ven. ap. Ald.* 1501
4188 ——— ex recens. D. Heinsii, 1s ——— *Amst.* 1718
4189 ——— Idem, 6d ——— ——— *ib.* 1690
4190 ——— accessf. variæ Lectiones, 1s ——— *Cantab.* 1701
4191 ——— Idem, 1s ——— *Lond. typ. Brindley* 1744
4192 ——— Idem, *nit. comp.* 1s 6d ——— *ib. ap. ib.* 1744
4193 ——— curante Philippe, *eleg. comp. fol. deaur.* 6s *Par.* 1754
4194 Val. Flacci Argonaut. a N. Heinsio & Burmanno, *nit. comp.* 3s *Patav.* 1720
4195 ——— *nov. & eleg. comp.* 4s ——— ——— *ib.* 1720
4196 ——— *nov. & eleg. comp. per Johnson,* 5s ——— *ib.* 1720
4197 ——— Idem, a N. Heinsio, 1s 6d ——— *L. Bat.* 1724
4198 Statius, *exemp. pulch. & eleg. comp. in corio turc. fol. deaur.* 5s *Ven. ap. Ald.* 1502
4199 Juvenalis & Persius cura Rigaltii, *exemp. pulch. nit. comp.* 2s 6d *Lutet. ex offic. R. Steph.* 1616
4200 Idem, 1s ——— ——— *Lond. typ. Brindley* 1744
4201 Catullus Tibul. & Propert. a Maittaire, 2s 6d ——— *ib.* 1715
4202 ——— cum Fragment. Galli, 1s ——— *Amst.* 1686
4203 Lucretius a Maittaire, 1s 6d ——— *Lond.* 1713
4204 Martialis Epigrammat. a Maittaire, 1s ——— *ib.* 1716
4205 Silius Italicus cum Argu Buschii, 1s 6d — *Par. ap Colin.* 1531
4206 Ciceronis Opera, a Gronovio, 11 tom. *exemp. pulch.* 1l 5s *Lugd. Bat.* 1692
4207 ——— de Officiis, a Grævio, *exemp. pulch.* 1s 6d *Amst.* 1691
4208 ——— Epist. ad Atticum cum Schol. Manutii, *nit. comp. in corio turc. fol. deaur.* 2s ——— *Par. ap. R. Steph.* 1543
4209 Livius ex recens. Gronovii, 2s ——— *Amst. ap. Elz.* 1678
4210 ——— 3 tom. *comp. in cor. turc. fol. deaur. maculat,* 4s 6d *L. Bat. ap. Elz.* 1654
4211 ——— *comp. in memb.,* 3 tom. 6s ——— *ib. ap. ib.* 1654
4212 ——— Notis Clerici, 10 tom. 1l ——— *Amst.* 1710
4213 Sallustius, *cum fig. typis eleg. nit. comp. fol. deaur.* 4s *Par.* 1744
4214 Idem, *ch. max. nit. comp. fol. deaur.* 4s ——— *Edinb.* 1755
4215 Idem, *nit. comp.* 3s ——— ——— *ib.* 1755

Q 4216 J.

4216 J. Cæsaris, a Maittaire, 1s 6d —— Lond. 1736
4217 ——— ex Scaligero, *exemp. pulch.* 4s L. Bat. ap. Elz. 1635
4218 Corn. Nepos, a Maittaire, 1s —— Lond. 1715
4219 Quintiliani Institut. Oratoria, Notis Rollin, 2 tom. *sutus*, 3s 6d Par. 1754
4220 Tacitus recens. Lallemand, 2 tom. *typis eleg. nitid. comp.* 12s ibid. 1760
4221 ——— a Gronovio, 4 tom. *typis eleg. nit. comp.* 8s Glasw. 1752
4222 ——— Notis Grotii, 2 tom. *macul.* 3s — ap. Elz. 1640
4223 Quintus Curtius, 2 tom. *nit. comp.* 2s 6d Lond. typ. Brindley 1746
4224 Plinii Epist. & Panegyricus, a Boxhornio, 1s L. Bat. 1653
4225 —— *exemp. pulch.* 4s —— ib. ap. Elz. 1640
4226 —— a Maittaire, 1s 6d —— Lond. 1741
4227 —— a Cellario, 1s 6d —— Lips. 1693
4228 Senecæ Opera, a Gronovio, 3 tom. 9s L. Bat. ap. Elz. 1649
4229 Idem, cum Notis, a Gronovii, 4 tom. *exemp. pulch. nit. comp. in memb.* 12s —— —— ib. ap. ib. 1640
4230 Notis Gronovii ad Senecas, 1s 6d —— ib. ap. ib. 1649
4231 L. Florus, a Salmasio, 1s 6d —— ib. ap. ib. 1638
4232 Sulpitius Severus, 1s —— ib. ap ib. 1635
4233 Aulus Gellius, 1s —— —— Amst. 1666
4234 ——— *exemp. pulch.* 1s 6d —— —— ib. 1665
4235 ——— *nit. comp. in cor. turc. fol. deaur.* 2s —— Par. 1560
4236 Boetii Consolat. Philosophiæ, 1s —— L. Bat. 1656
4237 Homeri Opera, Gr. & Lat. a Lederlino & Berglero, 2 tom. *nov. & nit. comp.* 8s —— —— Patav. 1762
4238 ——— Idem, Gr. & Lat. 2 tom. 4s —— Amst. 1650
4239 ——— Odyssea, Gr. & Lat. a Berglero, 1s 6d — ib. 1707
4240 Pindarus, Gr. & Lat. 2s 6d —— —— Lond. 1755
4241 ——— Gr. & Lat. *nit. comp.* 3s —— ib. 1755
4242 ——— Gr. & Lat. *chart. opt. nit. comp.* 4s Glasg. 1744
4243 ——— Gr. & Lat. *eleg. comp. in corio turc. fol. deaur.* 6s Lond. 1755
4244 ——— Gr. & Lat. a Porto, 1s —— apud Commel. 1598
4245 ——— & Carmina VIII. Lyrico, Gr. & Lat. a H. Stephano, 2 tom. 2s —— —— —— 1600
4246 ——— 2 tom. *nit comp. in turc. fol. deau.* 4s 1600
4247 ——— Gr. & Lat. 2 tom. in 1 vol. 1s — H. Steph. 1566
4248 Anacreon, Græce & Lat. cum Observat. H. Stephani Par. apud Morel. 1556—Anacreon, Lat. a Hel. Andrea Lutet. ap. R. Steph. 1556—Les Odes d'Anacreon, trad. par Belleau Par. chez. Wechel 1556, 5s
4249 Anacreon, Græce & Lat. cum Observat. H. Steph. *exemp. pulch.* Par. apud Morel. 1556
4250 Anacreontis Carmina, Gr. & Lat. 1s — Lond. 1733
4251 Poetæ Minores Græci, Gr. & Lat. 1s — ap. Buck
4252 Juliani Imp. Opera, Gr. & Lat. a Martinio, 2s Par. 1583
4253 Aristotelis de Mundo, Gr. & Lat. 1s 6d —— L. Bat. 1591
4254 ——— de Poetica, Gr. & Lat. a Goulstono, 2s Cantab. 1696
4255 ——— Idem, Gr. & Lat. *nit. comp. in memb.* 2s Glasg. 1745
4256 ——— Idem, Gr. & Lat. 1s —— Edinb. 1731
4257 ——— Idem, Græce, *nit.* 1s 6d —— Oxon. 1760
4258 ——— Idem, Græce, *nov. & nit. comp.* 2s —— ib. 1760
4259 Cebetis Tabulæ, Gr. & Lat. a Johnsono, 1s —— Lond. 1720
4260 Idem, Gr. & Lat. *nit.* 1s —— Glasg. 1747

4261 Epictetus,

4261 Epictetus, Gr. & Lat. cum Schol. Græcis, 1s *Dresd.* 1756
4262 Epictetus & Cebetis Tab. Gr. & Lat. 1s —— *Glasg.* 1744
4263 Longinus de Sublimitate, Gr. & Lat. 1s —— *ib.* 1751
4264 Idem, Gr. & Lat. *nit. comp.* 1s 6d —— *ib.* 1751
4265 Theocritus, Gr. & Lat. *semi-comp.* 1s —— *ib.* 1746
4266 Xenophontis de Agesilao Rege Orat. Gr. & Lat. *nit.* 1s *ib.* 1748
4267 Sophocles, Gr. & Lat. a Johnsono, 2 tom. *nit. comp.* 5s *ib.* 1745
4268 ——— Gr. & Lat. a Cantero, 1s 6d *Heidelb.* 1697
4269 ——— Græce, a Cantero, 2s *Antv. ap. Plant.* 1579
4270 ——— Græce, a Cantero *L. Bat.* 1593 — Aristophanes Græce *ibid.* 1597, 2s
4271 Æschylus, Gr. & Lat. 2 tom. *nov. & nit. comp.* 6s *Glasg.* 1746
4272 Phile de Animalium, Gr. & Lat. 1s 6d —— *Genev.* 1596
4273 Aristophanes, Lat. a Divo, 1s —— *Venet.* 1538
4274 Idem, Gr. & Lat. a Scaligero, 2s —— *Amst.* 1670

Historici & Antiquitates, Miscellanei & Poetici, Lat. DUODECIMO.

4275 ANtiquitat. Albionens. a Langhornio, 1s *Lond.* 1673
4276 Portus Iccius Illustrat. Somneri, 1s 6d —— *Oxon.* 1694
4277 Leonis Africani Descript. Africa, 1s —— *Antv.* 1556
4278 Nicolaus de Synedrio Ægyptiorum, 1s — *L. Bat.* 1706
4279 Gryphius de Scriptorib. Hist. Seculi XVII. 1s *Lips.* 1710
4280 Benjamini Itinerar. Lat. a Montano *Antv.* 1575—Ortelii Itinerar. *ib.* 1584—Divæus de Antiquit. Galliæ Belgicæ *ib.* 1584—Wimmanni Navigat. Morris Aretori *Bas.* 1753, 2s
4281 Hist. de Rebus Marchionis Montisrosarum, 1s —— 1647
4282 Poyetus de Magistratib. Atheniens. *nit. comp.* 2s *Bas.* 1583
4283 Bertellii Theatrum Urbium, Ital. *nit. comp.* 2s *Patav.*
4284 Ruperti Historia Universalis, 2s —— *Franeq.* 1698
4285 Tragicum Theatrum Actorum Londini Celebrat. *cum effigieb.* 2s 6d *Amst.* 1649
4286 Olai Magni Septentrional. Hist. Brevier, 1s *L. Bat.* 1652
4287 Respublica Achæor. & Veientium, a Schoockio, *corio turc. fol. deaur.* 4s —— —— —— *Traject.* 1664
4288 Idem, *eleg. comp. in corio turc. fol. deaur.* 5s —— *ib.* 1664
4289 Simleri Descriptio Vallesiæ & Alpium, *corio turc. fol. deaur.* 2s *L. Bat.* 1633
4290 Brietii Annales Mundi, 7 tom. 7s —— *Par.* 1662
4291 Rob. Stephani Responsio ad Censuras Theolog. Parisiens. 1s *Oliv. R. Steph.* 1552
4292 Selectæ e Profanis Scriptorib. Historicæ, 1s —— *Par.* 1734
4293 Sambuchus Imitatione Ciceroniana, *exemp. pulch. & nit. comp. in corio turc. fol. marm.* 5s —— —— *ib.* 1561
4294 Selectæ Historiæ e Profan. & Sacris Scriptorib. 1s 6d *Lond.* 1746
4295 Schefferi Suecia Literata *Hamb.* 1698 — Sannazarii Opera omnia *Francf.* 1709—Dekeni Observ. Poeticæ *Kilon.* 1691, 1s 6d
4296 Cuperi Harpocratis *Amst.* 1676—Catechismus Judæorum, Heb. & Lat. *Franeq.* 1690, 1s 6d
4297 Hutchesoni Philos. Moralis, 2 tom. *semi-comp.* 1s 6d *Glasg.* 1742
4298 Idem, *sutus in* 1 *vol.* 2s —— —— *ibid.* 1745

Q 2 4299 Hutchesoni

4299 Hutchesoni Philos. Moralis, *comp. in 1 vol.* 2s 6d *Glasg.* 1742
4300 Starkii Sapientia Indorum, Gr. & Lat. 2s —— *Berol.* 1697
4301 Ursatus de Notis Romanorum, *nit. comp.* 1s 6d *Par.* 1723
4302 Voluseni de Animi Tranquillitate, *exemp. pulch. nit. comp.* 2s 6d *Edinb.* 1751
4303 Meursius de Gloria *L. Bat.* 1601—Ejusd. Græcia Ludibunda item Souterius de Tab. Lusoria *ib.* 1625, 1s 6d
4304 Clerici Opera Philosoph. 4 tom. *nit. comp.* 4s *Amst.* 1704
4305 H. Stephano Pseudo Cicero, *exemp. pulch. nit. comp.* 2s 6d *Excud. H. Steph.* 1577
4306 Compend. Artis Logicæ, 1s —— —— *Oxon.* 1723
4307 Columella de Re Rustica, 1s —— *Dubl.* 1732
4308 Gronovii Observationes in Libri III. 1s — *L. Bat.* 1662
4309 ——— Observat. Libri novus *Daven.* 1652—Idem, Observat. Monobiblos *ib.* 1651, 1s 6d
4310 ——— Observat. Liber novus, 1s —— *ib.* 1652
4311 Ammani Dissertat. de Loquella, 1s —— *Amst.* 1600
4312 Rhau de Musica Practica, 1s —— —— 1536
4313 Cromwellii Literæ, a Miltono, 1s —— 1676
4314 Historiæ Sacræ, a Nicholsio, 1s —— *Lond.* 17 0
4315 De Juvenilibus Theod. Bezæ Poematis, 1s — *Amst.* 1683
4316 Pugna Porcorum, par Porcium, 1s —— 1644
4317 Erasmi Moriæ Encomium, Comment. Listrii, 1s Oxon. 1633
4318 Busbequii Epistolæ, 1s —— —— *Amst.* 1660
4319 Idem, 1s —— —— *L. Bat.* 1633
4320 Neri de Arte Vitraria, *cum fig.* 1s 6d —— *Amst.* 1686
4321 Heinsii Exercitat. ad Nonni in Johan. Metaphras. Gr. & Lat. 1s 6d *L. Bat.* 1627
4322 Polignac Anti-Lucretius, 2 tom. *exemp. pulch.* 3s *Lond.* 1748
4323 Musæ Anglicanæ, 3 tom. 3s —— *ib.* 1721
4324 Selecta Poemata Italorum, cura A. Pope, 2 tom. *nit. comp.* 4s *ib.* 1740
4325 Lusus Westmonasteriensis, 1s 6d —— *ib.* 1740
4326 Bourne Poemata, Lat. & Engl. 2s —— *ib.* 1750
4327 Idem, 1s —— —— *ib.* 1735
4328 Hilarii Cortæsii Volantillæ, *nit. comp. in corio turc.* 2s *Par. apud Colin.* 1533
4329 Joviani Pontani Dialogus, 1s —— *Aldus*
4330 Pontani Opera, 2 tom. *exemp. pulch. nit. comp. fol. deaur.* 4s *ib.* 1518
4331 Boconii Opera omnia, Lat. & Fr. *nit. comp.* 1s 6d *Amst.* 1727
4332 Bezæ Poemata, 1s —— —— *Lond.* 1713
4333 Sibyllina Oracula, Gr. & Lat. 1s —— *Basil.* 1555
4334 Menagii Poemata, 1s —— —— *Amst.* 1687
4335 Vanierii Prædium Rusticum, *nit. comp.* 2s — *Tolos.* 1730
4336 Idem, *nit. comp.* 2s 6d —— *Par.* 1746
4337 Taubmanni Melodæsia sive Epulum Musæum, 1s *Lips* 1563
4338 Rebelles Macropedii Fabulæ, 1s 6d — *Buscducis* 1539
4339 Johannis Secundi Opera, 1s —— *L. Bat.* 1651
4340 Jac. Zevecotii Poemata, 1s —— —— *ib.* 1725
4341 Marcelli Palingenii Stellati Poeta, 1s —— *Basil.* 1552
4342 Tho. Mori Epigrammata, 1s —— —— *Lond.* 1638
4343 Buchanani Poemata, 1s —— —— *Amst.* 1687

Dictionaries,

Dictionaries, Grammars, &c. English, Latin, French, Italian, &c. OCTAVO *& Infra.*

4344 JOHNSON's English Dictionary, 2 vol. *new and neatly bound*, 10s

4345 The same, *new and neatly bound in* 1 *vol.* 9s

4346 Bailey's English Dictionary, *new and neatly bound*, 6s 1763

4347 Fenning's English Dictionary, *new and neatly bound*, 6s 1741

4348 Defoe's Compleat English Dictionary, 2s —— 1735

4349 Dictionary of the Bible, 3 vol. *neat*, 9s —— 1759

4350 The same, 3 vol. *new and neatly bound*, 12s — 1759

4351 Young's Latin and English Dictionary, 2 vol. *new and elegantly bound, by Johnson*, 8s —— —— 1757

4352 Boyer's French and English Dictionary, *very fair*, 5s 1738

4353 Wheeler's Botanists and Gardeners Dictionary, *neat*, 5s 1763

4354 Neve's Builder's Dictionary, *neat*, 2s —— 1736

4355 Buchanan's Compleat English Scholar, *neat*, 4s 1753

4356 White on the English Verb, *large paper, neatly bound*, 3s 1761

4357 Brightland's English Grammar, 1s —— 1728

4358 Weston's Short Hand, *best edition, neatly bound, marble leaves*, 12s —— —— 1743

4359 Macaulay's Short Hand, *neat*, 3s 6d —— 1747

4361 Lyle's Short Hand, *in boards*, 5s —— 1762

4362 The same, *very neatly bound, marble leaves*, 6s —— 1762

4363 Port Royal's Primitives of the Greek Toague, by Nugent, *fair and neat*, 4s —— —— 1748

4364 Milner's Greek Grammar, *neat*, 2s 6d

4365 Massey's Origin and Progress of Letters, *with plates, very neat*, 5s —— —— —— 1763

4366 Foster on the different Natures of Accent and Quality, *neat*, 3s 1762

4367 The same Book, *second edition, with great additions, new and neat*, 6s —— —— 1763

4368 Græcæ Linguæ Dialecti, a Maittaire, *nov. & nit. comp.* 5s *Hag. Com.* 1738

4369 Clavis Homerica, 2s —— —— *Lond.* 1727

4370 Vigerius de Præcipuis Græcæ Idiotismis, 1s —— *ib.* 1695

4371 Idem, 1s —— —— *ib.* 1678

4372 Idem, 1s 6d —— —— *ib.* 1729

4373 Idem, 1s 6d —— —— *Argent.* 1708

4374 Idem, Notis Hoogeveen, *exemp. pulch.* 3s 6d *L. Bat.* 1742

4375 Moeris Atticista de Vocibus Atticis & Hellenicis-Martinus de Græcar. Literar. Pronunciat. 1s —— *Oxon.* 1712

4376 Bos Ellipses Græcæ, 2s —— —— *L. Bat.* 1750

4377 Wolluis de Verbis Grecor. Mediis, *nit.* 1s 6d *Lips.* 1723

4378 Funus Linguæ Hellenisticæ, a C. Salmasio, 1s *L. Bat.* 1643

4379 Milner's Latin Grammar, 2s 6d —— 1742

4380 Clarke's Introduction to making of Latin, 1s —— 1752

4381 Bowles's Aristarchus, or Institution of the Latin Tongue, *sewed*, 1s 6d —— —— —— 1748

4382 The same, *bound neat*, 2s —— —— 1748

4383 Wallis Grammatica Ling. Anglicanæ, 1s 6d — *Oxon.* 1674

4384 Rudimanni Institut. Gram. Lat. 2 tom. 2s 6d *Edinb.* 1725

4385 Holme

4385 Holmes Clavis Grammaticalis, 1s — *Lond.* 1739
4386 Ver. Flaccus & Pomp. Festus, 1s — *Genev.* 1593
4387 Terentii Varonis Opera, Notis Scaligeri, &c. 2s *Par.* 1585
4388 Theod. Gazæ Institut. Grammat. Gr. & Lat. 2s *ib. apud Wechel.* 1529
4389 Traite des Langues, par Tremblay, 1s 6d — *Amst.* 1709
4390 Laur. Vallæ de Ling. Lat. Elegantia, 1s — *Cantab.* 1688
4391 Grammaire Generale & Raisonne, *semi-comp.* 1s *Par.* 1754
4392 Wallis Institut. Logica, 1s 6d — *Oxon.* 1729
4393 Turneri Clavis Eloquent. Ciceronianæ, 1s 6d — *Lond.* 1737
4394 Baxteri Glossarium Antiq. Rom. *nit. comp.* 2s 6d *ib.* 1726
4395 Schrevelii Lexicon, Gr. & Lat. *nit. comp.* 2s 6d *Dresd.* 1724
4396 Timæi Sophistæ Lexicon Vocum Platonicar. Animadvers. Ruhnkenii, *sutus,* 2s — — *L. Bat.* 1754
4397 Moeridis Atticistæ, Notis Hudsoni—Timæi Sophistæ Lexicon recens. Ruhnkenii, *sutus Lips.* 1756, 1s 6d
4398 Parei Lexicon Criticum, Ling. Lat. *exemp. pulch.* 5s *Norimb.* 1645
4399 Pasoris Lexicon in Nov. Test. Gr. & Lat. 1s 6d *Lond.* 1650
4400 Dawsoni Lexi. Nov. Test. Gr. & Lat. *pulch.* 2s 6d *ib.* 1754
4401 Idem, *exemp. pulch. nit. comp.* 3s 6d — *ib.* 1755
4402 *H. Stephani Ciceronian Lexicon, Gr. & Lat. exemp. eleg. & nit. comp. in corio maurit.* 6d — — *ap. ips. Steph.* 1557
4403 Casaubonus de Ling. Heb. & de Ling. Saxon, 1s *Lond.* 1650
4404 Othonis Lexicon Rabbinico Philolog. 2s — *Genev.* 1675
4405 Bennet Grammat. Hebræa, 1s — *Lond.* 1731
4406 Altingi Fundam. Punctat. Ling. Sanctæ, 1s 6d *Franc.* 1717
4407 Bythneri Institut. Ling. Sanct. 1s — *Lond.* 1675
4408 Schickardi Horologium Ebræum, 1s — *ib.* 1722
4409 Musæum Meadianum, *sutus,* 1s 6d — *ib.* 1755
4410 Bibliotheca Meadiana, *with the prices affixed,* 10s 6d *ib.* 1755
4411 Idem, *without the prices,* 1s — *ib.* 1755
4412 Catalogus Biblioth. Harleianæ, 2 tom. 2s 6d — *ib.* 1743
4413 Bibliotheca Sacra, par Le Long, 2 tom. 3s *Antv.* 1709
4414 ——— Aprosiana, Notis Wolfii, *nit. comp. fol. marm.* 2s *Hamb.* 1734
4415 ——— Colbertina, 3 tom. *eleg. comp. in* 2 vol. *fol. marm.* 5s *Par.* 1728
4416 ——— Latina, a Fabricio, 3 tom. 5s — *Hamb.* 1712
4417 ——— Septentrionis Eruditi, 1s — *Lips.* 1699
4418 King's compleat Guide for High-Germans, English and Dutch, 1s *Lond.* 1706
4419 Vocabularium Anglo Saxonicum, a Bensono, *nitid. comp.* 3s *ibid.* 1701
4420 Idem, *semi-compact.* 2s
4421 Boyer's French Grammar, 1s — 1717
4422 The same, *very fair,* 2s — — 1756
4423 The same, 1s — — — 1733
4424 The same, 1s — — — 1741
4425 Rogissard's French Grammar, 1s — — 1734
4426 The same, 1s — — — 1745
4427 Pineda's Spanish Grammar, 1s — — 1726
4428 Principes de la Langue Latine, 1s — *Saumur.* 1675
4429 Grammaire Espagnolle & Francoise, par Sobrino, 1s *Bruss.* 1717

4430 Dictionaire

4430 Dictionaire Comiq. Satyriq. &c. par Le Roux, 2 tom. en 1 vol. 2s *Amst.* 1718
4431 Le meme, *fort bien relie,* 3s 6d —— *ibid.* 1750
4432 Diction. Portatif de Sante, 2 tom. *nouv. & bien relie,* 6s *Par.* 1760
4433 Dictionaire Neologique avec l'Eloge Historiq. de Pentalon Phœbus, *bien relie,* 3s —— —— *Amst.* 1748
4434 Diction. Ital & Fr. par Duez, 2 tom. 2s 6d — *Leide* 1660
4435 Methode de la Langue Greque, par Port Royal, 2s 6d *Par.* 1673
4436 Le meme, 4s —— —— —— *ib.* 1682
4437 Le meme, 4s —— —— —— *ib.* 1696
4438 Methode de la Langue Lat. par Port Royal, 1s 6d *ib.* 1681
4439 Le meme, *bien relie,* 2s 6d —— —— *ib.* 1696
4440 Tribbechovi Græcæ Vulg. Elementa, Gr. & Lat. 1s *Jenæ* 1705
4441 Synonymes Francois, par Girard, *bien relie,* 2s *Amst.* 1742
4442 Barretti's Italian Library, containing an Account of the Lives and Works of the most valuable Italian Authors, *very fair,* 4s 1757
4443 Port Royal's Method of Learning the Italian Tongue, *neat,* 3s 6d —— —— —— 1750
4444 Veneroni's Italian and English Grammar, 2s 6d — 1729
4445 Altieri's Italian and English Grammar, 1s 6d — *Venez* 1736
4446 Grammaire Italienne, par Antonini, 1s —— *Par.* 1746

Divinity and Ecclesiastical History. English, Greek and Latin. DUODECIMO.

4447 CLARKE's Sermons, 11 vol. *small edit. very fair,* 18s 1749
4448 The same, 11 vol. *new and very neat,* 1l 1s 1749
4449 Tillotson's Sermons, 12 vol. *small edit.* 15s —— 1748
4450 Du Pin's History of the Church from the Beginning of the World, 4 vol. *very fair,* 6s —— —— 1724
4451 Enthusiasm of Methodists and Papists compared, by Bp. Lavington, 2 vol. *neat,* 3s 6d —— —— 1754
4452 Bp. Warburton's Doctrine of Grace, 2 vol. *new and neat,* 3s 6d —— —— —— 1763
4453 Bp. Hoadly on the Sacrament, *very fair and neat,* 2s 1761
4454 Nelson's Christian Sacrifice, 1s —— 1708
4455 Derham's Physico Theology, 2s —— *Glasg.* 1752
4456 Watts's Miscellaneous Thoughts in Prose and Verse, 2s 1734
4457 ——— on the Love of God, 1s 6d —— 1734
4458 ——— on Self-Murther, 1s ——— 1716
4459 ——— Guide to Prayer, 1s ——— 1743
4460 ——— on the Holiness of Times, Places and People, 1s 1738
4461 ——— Psalms of David, *new and very neat,* 2s 6d 1758
4462 Stanhope's Thomas a Kempis, 1s —— 1702
4463 Clarke on the Church Catechism, 1s —— 1731
4464 Gastrell's Christian Institutes, 1s —— 1717
4465 Cambray's private Thoughts on Religion, 1s 6d 1719
4466 Addison's Evidences of the Christian Religion, *neat,* 2s 1753
4467 The same, 1s 6d —— —— 1730
4468 Green on Gospel Justification, *new,* 2s —— 1758
4469 Coyte's Sermons, 2 vol. *sewed,* 3s —— 1761
4470 Bp. of Sodar and Man's Instructions for the Indians, *very neat,* 2s —— —— — 1741

4470 Bp.

4471 New Manual of Devotions, 2s ——— 1742
*4471 Bp. Patrick's devout Christian, 1s 6d ——— 1746
4472 Inett's Guide to the Devout Christian, 1s 6d — 1754
4473 New Weeks Preparation, 2 parts in 1 vol. *neatly bound in black calf,* 2s
4474 Appeal to the Common Sense of all Christian People, *very neat,* 1s ——— ——— ——— 1754
4475 Christianity not Mysterious, by Toland, 1s ——— 1696
4476 Directions to the Missionaries in China for Preaching Christianity, *MSS.* —— Plethonis Libellus de Fato, una cum Camariotæ Orationib. in Plethonem de Fato, Gr. & Lat. *nit. comp.* 2s 6d *L. Bat.* 1722
4477 Pettus Volatiles from the Hist. of Adam and Eve, 1s 1674
4478 Last Hours of Dr. Rivett, 1s ——— 1682
4479 Moral Essay on the Soul of Man, by Port Royal, 1s 6d 1690
4480 Bates's Funeral Sermon on Baxter, 6d ——— 1692
4481 Grounds of the Old Religion by a Cath. Convert, 1s 1751
4482 Bp. Bates's Declaration of Bonner's Articles, concerning the Clergy of London Dyocese, *black letter,* 2s 6d — 1561
4483 Tyndale's Obedience of a Christen Man, *black letter* —Tyndale's Parable of the wicked Mammon, *black letter,* 2s 6d 1549
4484 Consolat. for the Sufferers of Persecution for Righteousness 1544—Lamentation of the Church by Bp. Ridley—Letters of the Constant wytres of Christ John Carcles 1566 —Viret's Epistle to the Faithful, *all black letter,* 2s ——— — 1582
4484 The Augustan Confession of Fayth, *black letter,* 2s *no date*
4485 Lambert on the Will of Man, *black letter,* 2s — 1548
4486 Erudition for any Chrysten Man, by King Henry VIII. *very fair, black letter, eleganely bound in morocco, gilt leaves,* 10s 6d 1543
4487 Common Prayer Book, *neat, gilt leaves,* 2s 6d — 1760
4488 The same, English and Low Dutch, 1s 6d — 1728
4489 Fabricii Codex Pseudepigraph. Vet. & Nov. Test. 4 tom. 8s *Hamb.* 1713
4490 Catechesis Racoviens, Notis Oederi, 2 tom. 5s *Francf.* 1739
4491 Reinho Rus Harmonia Evang. 2 tom. 4s *Jenæ* 1727
4492 Wolfii Anecdota Græc. Sacra & Prof. 4 tom. in 2 vol. 5s *Hamb.* 1722
4493 Grotius de Veritate Relig. Christ. Notis Clerici. 1s *Lond.* 1718
4494 Idem, 1s ——— ——— *H Com.* 1724
4495 D'Outrein de Clangore Evangelii, 1s 6d ——— *Amst.* 1714
4496 Buxtorfii Synagoge Judaica, 1s ——— *Bas.* 1661
4497 Leusdeni Compend. Græc. Nov. Test. 1s — *Lond.* 1750
4498 Idem, 1s ——— ——— *L. Bat.* 1688
*4498 Pfaffius de Genuin. Lect. Nov. Test. 1s 6d *Amst.* 1709
4499 Pritii Introduct. in Lect. Nov. Test. 1s 6d — *Lips.* 1704
4500 Clerici Quest. Hieronymianæ, 2s ——— *Amst.* 1700
4501 Elis Defensio Articul. Ecclef. Anglicanæ, 6d — *ib.* 1700
4502 Idem, 6d ——— ——— *ib.* 1709
4503 Andrews Preces Privatæ, Gr. & Lat. *nit. comp.* 1s *Oxon.* 1675
4504 Biblia Lat. exemplar. Castigata, 5 tom. *nit. comp. fol. deaur. minore. form.* 10s — ——— *Antv. ap. Plant.* 1577
4505 —— Hollandice, *nit. comp. fol. deaur.* 2s — *Dord.* 1739
4506 —— Hebraica, 2 tom. 8s ——— *Antv. ap. Plant.*

4507 Biblia

4507 Biblia LXX. Interpret. Gr. 2 tom. 4s *Cantab. ap. Field* 1665
4508 Idem, in 1 vol. 4s ——— ——— *ib.* 1665
4509 Idem, *exemp. pulch. nit. comp.* 4s ——— *Amst.* 1683
4510 Nov. Test. Gr. a Maittaire, 2 tom. *ch. max. exemp. pulch. nit. comp. fol. deaur.* 8s ——— ——— ——— *Lond.* 1714
4511 Idem, Gr. a Bowyer, 2 tom. *nov.* 6s ——— *ib.* 1763
4512 Idem, Gr. a Curcellæo, 1s 6d ——— *Amst.* 1699
4513 Idem, Gr. Var. Lect. 2s ——— ——— *ib.* 1711
4514 Idem, Gr. & Lat. a Leusdeno, 2 tom. *nit. comp. fol. deaur.* 3s 6d *ib.* 1741
4515 Idem, Gr. 1s ——— *L. Bat. ap. Elz.* 1633
4516 Idem, Gr. *exemp. pulch, eleg. comp. in corio turc. fol. deaur.* 4s *Cantab. apud Jefferies*
4517 Idem, Gr. a Leusdeno, *nit. comp.* 2s ——— *Amst.* 1741
4518 Idem, Gr. *exemp. pulch. lin. rubris,* 2s 6d *Antv. ap. Plant.* 1574
4519 Idem, Gr. *bound in shagreen, with silver clasps,* 5s *Amst. apud Bleau* 1633
4520 Idem, cum Apocrypha & Liturgia Anglic. Gr. *corio turc. fol. deaur.* 3s ——— ——— *Cantab.* 1665
4521 Idem, Lat. Interprete Beza, 1s ——— *Lond.* 1746
4522 Liturgia Eccles. Anglic. Græce, *ch. max.* 3s *Cantab.*
4523 Idem, *ch. min.* 1s 6d ——— ——— *ibid.*
4524 Johnstoni Psalmi Davidici, 1s 6d ——— *Lond.* 1741
4525 Hebrew Text of the Psalmes and Lamentations, by Robertson, 1s *ib.* 1656
4526 Liber Psalmorum, a Leusdeno, Heb. & Lat. 1s 6d *ib.* 1726

Law. OCTAVO & *Infra.*

4527 BRitish Acts from the Union 1707, to the 18th of George II. in 16 vol. 2l 12s 6d ——— *Edinb.* 1718, &c.
4528 Stewart's Index to the Scotch Statutes, 1s 6d ——— *ib.* 1707
4529 Laws and Acts of Scotland, 3 vol. *very scarce* *ib.* 1683
4530 Wood's Institute of the Law of England, 2 vol. 4s 1720
4531 ——— Institute of the Civil Law, 2s ——— 1721
4532 Irish Statutes abridged, 1s ——— ——— *Dubl.* 1724
4533 Readings on the Statute Law, 5 vol. 1l 5s ——— 1723
4534 The same, *very fair,* 5 vol. 1l 10s ——— 1723
4535 Burn's Justice of Peace, 3 vol. *best edition, elegantly bound, marble leaves,* 1l 1s ——— ——— 1762
4536 Coke's Reports, in English, 7 vol. *very fair,* 2l 5s 1727
4537 Grey's System of Ecclesiastical Law, *large paper, very fair,* 6s 1730
4538 Watson's Clergyman's Law, 2 vol. 3s ——— 1712
4539 Consett's Practice of Ecclesiastical Courts, 1s ——— 1708
4540 Lord Ward's Justice of Peace, 2 vol. *new,* 12s 1762
4541 Dalrymple's History of Feudal Property, *new and very neat,* 4s ——— ——— ——— 1758
4542 Hawkins's Pleas of the Crown abridged, 2 vol. 4s ——— 1728
4543 Wiseman's Excellency of the Civil Law, 1s ——— 1686
4544 Hale's History and Analysis of the Law, 2 vol. 2s ——— 1713
4545 The same, in one vol. 3s ——— ——— 1739
4546 Finch's Description of the Law of England, 4s ——— 1759

R 4547 Yorke's

4547 Yorke's Law of Forfeiture for High Treaſon, *large paper, beſt edition, very neat,* 3s 6d —— —— 1748
4548 Bohun's Privilegia Londini, 3s —— 1723
4549 The ſame, 2d Edition, 1s 6d —— 1716
4550 Common Law epitomized, by Gliſſon and Gulſton, 1s 1679
4551 Penal Laws relating to the Cuſtoms and Exciſe, 1s 1726
4552 Forſter's Digeſt of all the Laws relating to the Cuſtoms, 2s 1717
4553 Laws of the Stannaries of Cornwall, *very fair,* 2s
4554 Laws of Sewers, 2s —— —— 1726
4555 Baron and Feme, 1s —— —— 1700
4556 Goodinge's Law againſt Bankrupts, 1s —— 1719
4557 The ſame, 1s 6d —— —— 1726
4558 General Syſtem of the Laws concerning Bankrupts, *very fair,* 4s —— —— —— 1761
4559 Statutes at large concerning Bankrupts, 1s —— 1733
4560 Law of Corporations, 3s —— —— 1702
4561 Law concerning Eſtates Taile, by Curſon, 2s 6d 1703
4562 Gilbert's Law of Evidence, 2s 6d —— 1756
4563 The ſame, *very fair,* 3s —— —— 1760
4564 Gilbert's Law of Deviſes and Revocations, 1s —— 1739
4565 —— on Tenures, 2s —— —— 1730
4566 —— Hiſtorical View of the Court of Exchequer, 2s 1731
4567 Modern Practice of the Court of Exchequer, 2s —— 1731
4568 Gilbert's Hiſtory of the Court of Common Pleas, 2s 1737
4569 Barnes's Notes of Caſes in the Common Pleas, 1s 6d 1740
4570 Seſſions Caſes relating to Settlements, 2 vol. 5s — 1750
4571 Attorney's Practice in the K. Bench, 2 vol. 4s — 1743
4572 —— The ſame, 2 vol. 5s —— 1750
4573 —— Practice in the Com. Pleas, 2 vol. 4s — 1746
4574 Mills's Rules and Orders of the King's Bench, Common Pleas and Chancery, 2s —— —— 1729
4575 Inſtructor Clericalis, with the Doctrine of Demurrers, 7 vol. 1l 1s —— —— —— 1721
4576 Crown Circuit Companion, 2 vol. in 1. 2s 6d — 1749
4577 The ſame, with a MSS. Index of Statutes relating to Felony, &c. *ſewed,* 1s 6d —— —— 1749
4578 Reports in the Court of Chancery, 4 vol. 5s — 1715
4579 Practice of the Court of Chancery, 2s —— 1706
4580 Legal Judicature in Chancery, 1s —— 1726
4581 Judicial Authority of the Maſter of the Rolls, 1s 6d 1728
4582 Trials per Pais, by Duncomb, 1s 6d —— 1702
4583 The ſame, *6th edition,* 3s —— —— 1725
4584 The ſame, *the beſt edition,* with the Law concerning Trials, 2 vol. 9s —— —— —— 1739
4585 Wentworth's Office and Duty of Executors, 1s 6d 1720
4586 The ſame, 2s —— —— 1728
4587 Termes de la Ley, 2s —— —— 1708
4588 Conveyancer's Aſſiſtant and Director, 2s —— 1702
4589 Brown of Fines and Recoveries, 2 vol. 4s —— 1718
4590 Compleat Sheriff, 1s 6d —— —— 1710
4591 Scroggs on Courts Leet and Courts Baron, 1s 6d — 1714
4592 The ſame, *beſt edition, very fair,* 3s —— 1728
4593 Towneſend's Preparative to Pleading, 2s —— 1721
4594 Tenant's Law, 2s —— —— 1760

4595 Laws

4595 Laws concerning Gameing, by Nelson, 1s —— 1751
4596 The same, 1s 6d —— —— 1753
4597 Law concerning Non compos Mentis, 1s —— 1700
4598 Philipps's Grandeur of the Law, 6d —— 1685
4599 Noye's Maximes of Law, 1s —— 1651
4600 Whyte's Sacred Law of the Land, 1s —— 1652
4601 Mackenzie's Institution of the Laws of Scotland, 1s 1694
4602 Petyt's Miscellanea Parliamentaria, 1s —— 1681
4603 —— Lex Parliamentaria, 1s 6d —— 1690
4604 Davies on Impositions, Tonnage and Poundage, 1s 1656
4605 Index to the Records, 1s —— —— 1739
4606 Hawkins's Abridgment of Coke upon Littleton, 2s 1736
4607 The same, 2 vol. *fair and neat*, 3s —— 1751
4608 Holbourne's Reading on the Statute of Treasons, 1s 1681
4609 Williams's Jus Appellandi, 1s —— —— 1683
4610 Perkins's Profitable Book of the Law, 1s —— 1642
4611 Magna Charta, with Observations, by Cooke, 1s 1680
4612 Coke's Compleat Copyholder, 1s —— —— 1673
4613 Wingate's Britton, 1s 6d —— —— 1640
4614 Plowden's Commentaries Abridgment, 1s —— 1659
4615 Page's Law of Brethren, 6d —— —— 1658
4616 Smith's Commonwealth of England, 1s —— 1633
4617 Brydall's Jus Sigilli, 6d —— —— 1673
4618 Phillipps's Principles of the Law, 6d —— 1660
4619 Corpus Juris Civilis, *interfoliat. cum chart. alba*, 4 tom. *nit. comp.* 1l 1s —— —— *Amst.* 1664
4620 Heineccii Syntagma Antiq. Rom. Jurisprudent. *semi-comp.* 3s *Argent.* 1734
4621 —— Idem, 2 tom. *semi-comp.* 4s —— *ibid.* 1730
4622 —— Elementa Juris Civilis, *semi-comp.* 1s 6d *Amst.* 1733
4623 Duck de Jure Civili Romanorum, 1s —— *Lond.* 1679
4624 Menagii Amœnit. Juris Civilis, 1s 6d —— *Francof.* 1680
4625 Theophili Institut. Lat. a Curtio, 2 tom. 2s —— *Par.* 1681
4626 Regnerus de Jurejurando Vet. Rom. *sutus*, 1s *Traj.* 1728
4627 Zouchæi Quæstiones Juris Civilis, 1s —— *Lond.* 1682
4628 —— Elementa Jurisprudentiæ, 1s —— *Amst.*
4629 Justiniani (Imp.) Institut. Typis Rubr. 1s *Amst.* 1664
4630 Clarkei Praxis Curiæ Admiralit. *nit. comp.* 1s *Lond.* 1743

Physick, Surgery, Natural History, &c. English, French and Latin. OCTAVO *& Infra.*

4631 WOodward's Natural History of the Earth, *fine paper, elegantly bound, gilt leaves*, 4s —— 1723
4632 Mead's Med. Precepts and Cautions, *very fair*, 3s 1751
4633 —— The same, in 12mo. *very fair*, 1s 6d *Dubl.* 1751
4634 —— on Poisons, *large paper, half bound*, 3s —— 1745
4635 —— The same, *large paper, very neat*, 5s —— 1745
4636 —— Monita & Præcepta Med. *sutus*, 1s 6d *Lond.* 1751
4637 —— on the Small Pox, *very neat*, 2s —— 1748
4638 —— on the Plague, *large paper, very neat*, 4s 1744
4639 —— de Imperio Solis ac Lunæ in Hum. Corp. *ch. max. nit. comp.* 3s —— —— *Lond.* 1746

R 2 4640 Mead's

4640 Mead's de Variolis & Morbilis, *nit. comp.* 2s 6d *Lond.* 1747
4641 ——— Medica Sacra, *ch. max. nit. comp.* 3s — *ib.* 1749
4642 ——— Idem, *ch. min.* 2s ——— ——— *ib.* 1749
4643 Medical Essays and Observations, 6 vol. 18s *Edinb.* 1733
4644 Cheselden's Anatomy of the Human Body, *very fair, with cuts, 6th edition,* .. 4s
4645 Dionis's Chirurgical Operations, 2s ——— 1733
4646 Atkins's Navy Surgeon, 2s 6d ——— 1751
4647 Gooche's Cases in Surgery, *with cuts,* 3s ——— 1758
4648 Pringle's Observations on the Diseases of the Army, *new and very neatly bound,* 5s ——— ——— — 1761
4649 Cleghorn on the Diseases in Minorca, *fair and neat,* 2s 6d 1751
4650 Robinson's Observations on Medicines, 2s 6d ——— 1752
4651 Lobb on the Small Pox, 2s ——— — 1741
4652 Nihell's Art of Midwifry, 2s 6d ——— 1760
4653 Parson's Description of the Human Bladder, *cuts, very neat,* 3s ——— ——— ——— 1742
4654 Robinson's Animal Oeconomy, 2s 6d ——— 1734
4655 ——— on Consumptions, *very neat,* 2s ——— 1728
4656 Bennet on Consumptions, 2s ——— — 1720
4657 Morton on Consumptions, 1s 6d ——— 1694
4658 Lind on the Scurvy, *sewed,* 2s 6d ——— *Edinb.* 1753
4659 ——— on Preserving the Health of Seamen in the Navy, 1s 1757
4660 Profilly on the Venereal Disease, 2s 6d ——— 1748
4661 Floyer and Baynard on Cold Baths, 2s 6d ——— 1706
4662 The same, *very fair,* 4s ——— ——— 1732
4663 Mandevile on Hypochondriac Diseases, 3s ——— 1730
4664 History of Long Livers, 1s 6d ——— — 1722
4665 The same, *neat,* 2s ——— ——— 1722
4666 Bellinger on the Nutrition of the Fœtus in the Womb, 1s 1717
4667 Keil on Animal Secretion, 1s ——— ——— 1708
4668 Jones's Mysteries of Opium, 3s ——— — 1701
4669 Arbuthnot on the Effects of Air, *very fair,* 2s — 1733
4670 Baker's Natural History of the Polype, 2s ——— 1743
4671 Cave's Medicinal Epistles, Engl. by Quincy, 1s 1714
4672 Woodward's State of Physick, 1s 6d ——— 1718
4673 Fuller on the Power of Exercise, 1s 6d ——— 1705
4674 Tournefort's History of Plants round Paris, 2 vol. 4s 1732
4675 Blair's Botanic Essays, 2s 6d ——— ——— 1720
4676 Guidott on Bathe Waters, 1s ——— 1676
4677 ———. Collection of Treatises on the City and Waters of Bath, *neat,* 2s 6d ——— 1725
4678 Baylies on the Use and Abuse of Bath Waters, 2s 6d 1757
4679 Shaw's Practice of Physic, 2 vol. *new and very neatly bound,* 8s ——— ——— ——— 1753
4680 Pierce's History and Memoirs of Bath, 1s ——— 1713
4681 Taverner on Witham Spa, 1s ——— — 1737
4682 Wood's Treatise on Farriery, *in boards,* 3s ——— 1757
4683 Bracken's Farriery improved, 2 vol. *fair,* 4s 1739
4684 The same, vol. 1. 2s ——— ——— 1739
4685 Bracken's Pocket Farrier, *half bound,* 1s ——— 1737
4686 Keil's Anatomy of the Human Body, *fair,* 1s 6d 1746
4687 Monro's Anatomy of the Bones, 1s 6d — 1726
4688 The same, *very fair,* 2s ——— ——— 1741

4689. Monro's

4689 Monro's Anatomy of the Bones, 2s —— 1750
4690 Douglas's Description of the Muscles, 1s 6d —— 1750
4691 Whytt's Physiological Essays, *new*, 2s 6d —— 1761
4692 Helvetius's Golden Calf, 1s —— —— 1670
4693 Cooper's Philosophical Epitaph, *neatly bound in turkey, gilt leaves*, 2s —— —— —— 1673
4694 Pemberton's College Dispensatory, 2s 6d —— 1748
4695 Quincy's Dispensatory, 3s 6d —— —— 1749
4696 The same, *new and very neat*, 6s —— —— 1761
4697 Lewis's Edinburgh Dispensatory, *fair*, 2s —— 1748
4698 New Dispensatory, by Lewis, *new*, 6s —— 1754
4699 Glass's Art of Cookery, *new*, 5s —— 1763
4700 Gelleroy's London Cook, or Art of Cookery made easy, *new*, 5s —— —— —— 1762
4701 Chapelle's Modern Cook, *with cuts*, 3s 6d —— 1744
4702 The same, *large print*, 3 vol. *with cuts, very fair*, 7s 6d 1736
4703 Geoffroy de Materia Medica, 3 tom. 15s —— *Par.* 1741
4704 Hoffmanni Dissertat. Physico-Medicæ, 4 tom. *semi-comp.* 3s *L. Bat.* 1713
4705 Martinii Comment. in Eustachii Tab. Anat. 2s 6d *Edinb.* 1755
4706 ——— de Similibus Animalib. & Animal. Calore, 2s *Lond.* 1740
4707 Russel de Usu Aquæ Marinæ in Morb. Gland. 3s *Oxon.* 1750
4708 Hovius de Motu Circul. Humor. in Oculis, *fig.* 1s 6d *Lugd. Bat.* 1674
4709 Caius de Canibus Britannicis & ejusd. Opuscula, a Jebb, *ch. max.* 2s 6d —— —— —— *Lond.* 1729
4710 Heisteri Compend. Anatom. *cum fig.* 2s —— *Amst.* 1748
4711 Palladius de Febribus, Gr. & Lat. Notis Bernardi, *semi-comp.* 1s 6d *L. Bat.* 1745
4712 Idem, *nit. comp.* 2s —— —— *ib.* 1745
4713 Harris de Morbis Infantum, 1s 6d —— *Lond.* 1705
4714 Blancardi Lexicon Medicum, 2s —— *L. Bat.* 1735
4715 Alstoni Index Medicament. Simplic. *interfol. cum additionib. MSS.* 2 tom. *semi-comp.* 3s —— —— *Edinb.* 1752
4716 Raii Synopsis Stirpium Britannic. 3s —— *Lond.* 1696
4717 Linnæi Fauna Suecica, *cum fig. nit. comp.* 4s *L. Bat.* 1746
4718 ——— Genera Plantarum, 2s —— *Par.* 1743
4719 ——— Orat. de Telluris Habitab. Incremento, *nit. comp.* 1s 6d *ib.* 1744
4720 ——— Species Plantarum, 2 tom. 10s —— *Holm.* 1753
4721 Geodartius de Insectis, Notis Listeri, *fig.* 2s —— *Lond.* 1685
4722 Comment. in Boerhaave Aphorismos, 6 tom. *nitid. comp.* 7s *ibid.* 1738
4723 Boerhaave Prælect. in proprias Institut. Notis Halleri, 7 tom. *nit. comp.* 12s —— —— *Gotting.* 1739
4724 Idem, 7 tom. *nit. comp.* 12s —— —— *ib.* 1740
4725 Wepferi Observat. Anatomicæ, 1s —— *Amst.* 1681
4726 Dales Pharmacologia, 2 tom. 2s —— *Lond.* 1710
4727 Laurentius de Sanandi Strumas Galliæ Regib. concessæ, 3s *Par.* 1609
4728 Ramazzinus de Morbis Artificium, 1s 6d *Ultraj.* 1703
4729 De Graaf de Natura Succi Pancreat. *fig.* *L. Bat.* 1671—Ejusd. de Viror. Organis Generat. *cum fig.* *ibid.* 1668, 1s 6d

4730 De

4730 De Graaf de Organis Generat. Viror. & Mulierum, *cum fig.* 1s 6d *L. Bat.* 1668 & 1672

4731 Oribasii Collect. Medicinales, a Rasario, 2s —— *Par.* 1555

4732 P. Æginetæ Opera, a Guinterio, 1s 6d —— *Lugd.* 1567

4733 Idem, 2s —— —— *ibid.* 1589

4734 Prædium Rusticum, *exemp. pulch.* 1s 6d *Lutet. ap. C. Steph.* 1554

4735 Nomina, Lat. & Gr. Arborum, Fruct. Herbar. Piscium & Avium *Lutet. ap. C. Steph.* 1554—Seminarium & Plantar. Fructiferarum Arbor. *ibid. ap. R. Steph.* 1548 — Libellus de Re Hortensi *ibid. ap. R. Steph.* 1545—Clusii Antidotarium *Antv.* 1561, 2s 6d

4736 Crameri Ars Docimastica, 2 tom. 3s 6d —— *L. Bat.* 1730

4737 Raii Catalogus Plantar. Angliæ, 1s —— *Lond.* 1677

4738 Redus de Insectis, *fig.* 1s —— —— *Amst.* 1671

4739 Neri Ars Vitriaria, *fig.* 1s 6d —— *Argent.* 1668

4740 Schola Salernitana, a Jo. de Mediolano, 1s 6d *Rotterd.* 1657

4741 Bibliotheque Choise de Medicine, par Planque, *avec fig.* 12 tom. *cousu,* 15s —— —— *Par.* 1748

4742 ———— de Physique & d'Hist. Nat. 5 tom. *fort bien relie,* 7s 6d *Par.* 1758

4743 Conrs de Chirurgie, par Dionis, *avec fig.* 2s 6d *ib.* 1740

4744 Traite de Venerie, *avec fig. fort bien relie,* 3s —— *ib.* 1750

4745 Oeuvres d'Hippocrate, avec des Remarques, 2 tom. *bien relie,* 4s *ibid.* 1697

4746 Observations sur la Physique, 1s —— *ibid.* 1719

4747 Maniere d'Amoler les Os, par Papin, *avec fig.* 1s *Amst.* 1688

4748 Spectacle de la Nature, *avec un grand nombr. des fig.* 7 tom. *demi-relie,* 17s 6d —— —— *Par.* 1732

4749 Hist. des Insectes, par Goedart, *avec fig.* 3 tom. *bien relie,* 6s *Haye* 1700

4750 Hist. Naturelle du Cacao & du Sucre, *avec fig.* 1s *Amst.* 1720

4751 Elemens de Chymie Pratiq. par Macquer, 3 tom. *bien relie,* 7s *Par.* 1751

4752 Cuisinier Royal & Bourgeois, par Massialot, *avec fig.* 3 tom. *bien relie,* 6s —— —— 1748

Tracts. QUARTO.

4753 LORD Digby's Apology for himself 1642—Milton's Character of the Long Parliament 1641—Treatise on the East India Company and Trade, & 9 more Tracts, 2s

4754 Extremities urging the Lord General Sir Fra. Veare to offer the Anti parle with the Archduke Albertus 1602—Declaration of the Army at Sea made by the United Provinces 1600—Coppie of such Newes as came from Holland, relating to Grave Maurice's Camp 1602—Prayer and Thankesgiving for the Safetie of her Majestie 1694—Vita & Obitus Ric. Cosin *Lond.* 1598—Le Institutioni dell Imperio contenute nella Bolla Dora *Venet.* 1559 — La Corona del Principe di Ciro Spontone *Verena* 1590—Occurrences in the Queen of France's Voyages from Florence to Marsailles 1601—Sir Anth. Sherley's Travels to Persia 1601, 5s

4755 Hak

4755 Hakluyt's History of the West Indies—New England's Prospect—Whitbourn's Discovery of Newfound-Land—Sir Thomas More's Utopia, 2s 6d

4756 Tracts, viz. Bp. Laud's Speech against Prynne, &c.—Rebels Catechism 1643—Vox Populi, or Peoples Claim 1681—Prince Ruport's Declaration 1642—Pym's Speech at a Conference with the Lords. 1642——Life of Stephen Marshal 1680——Winstanley's New Year's Gift for the Parliament and Army 1650—Last Will of Sir John Presbyter 1647—Baxter's Search for the English Schismatic 1681—A most learned, conscientious and devout Exercise, or Sermon by Oliver Cromwell in the Year 1649, and 12 more Tracts, 1l 1s

4757 Practices of the Commissioners for Sick and Wounded, 6d 1695

4758 Bacon's Elements of Com. Law 1635—Bacon's Use of the Law 1635—Priviledges of the Parliament of England 1641—Readings on the Stat. of Wills, Jointures and Forceable Entry—City Law 1647, 1s 6d

4759 Chroniq. Bourdeloise, par De Lurbe 1594—Lope's Report of the Kingdom of Congo, *with cuts* 1591 — History of Tamerlane 1597, 2s

4760 Collection of State Papers 1688—Account of Irish Parliament—Killing no Murder—Account of the supposed Murder of Mr. Harrison, 1s 6d

4761 Collection of Original Letters—Account of Battles, Sieges and Military Transactions during the Great Rebellion, in 34 different Tracts, from 1642 to 1651, with the following Heads, beautifully engraved, viz. Earl of Manchester—Oliver Cromwell and Colonel Lambert—Robert Earl of Essex—Col. Masse—Sir Thomas Fairfax —Another of the same — Honourable General Lambert—Oliver Cromwell—King Charles II. 6s

4762 List of the Army, and Names of the Officers under Lord Essex, with his Effigy 1642—Sir J. Hotham's Letter on the Plot at Hull 1642 —Proceed. of the Marq. of Hertford and the rest of the Cavelleers in Wels 1642—Relation of the Plot against the City of Bristol 1642—Relation of the Marchings of Red Trained Bands of Westminster, the Green Auxiliaries of London, and the Yellow Auxiliaries of the Tower Hamlets, under Sir William Waller, with a great many more Tracts on the same Subject, 4s

4763 Charge of the Scottish Commissioners against Canterbury, and the Lieutenant of Ireland 1641—Decree of the Star-Chamber concerning Printing in 1687—Relation of the Death and Sufferings of Archbishop Laud 1644—and many more Tracts relating to those Times, 2s

Tracts. OCTAVO.

4764 POWER and Harmony of Prosaic Numbers 1749—Bayley on Languages 1756—Cooper on Warburton's Edition of Pope 1751—Middleton on the Rom. Senate, and other Tracts 1749 2s 6d

4765 Three Discourses on Private Judgment, on the Authority of Magistrates, and the reuniting of Protestants 1718—Enquiry concerning Superstition 1730——Seagrave on the 39 Articles, and more Tracts 1738 1s 6d

4766 Ro-

4766 Rotherham's Sketch of One Great Argument 1754—Essays, Letters, &c. of Sir Harry Beaumont 1753—Warburton's View of Bolingbroke 1754—Miscellaneous Observations on Bolingbroke's Works 1755, 1s 6d

4767 Bishop Berkeley on Tar Water 1744—Hales on Tar Water 1747—Prior on Tar Water 1746—Bp. Berkeley's two Letters on the Benefit of Tar Water, and other Tracts, 2s

4768 Græcæ Grammat. Compend. 1742—Edwards's Tryal of the Letter Y 1753—Dyson's Letter to Warburton in Defence of the Pleasures of Imagination 1744—Johnson's Noctes Nottingham. 1718 and more Tracts, 2s

4769 Godfrey's Experiments on Various Subjects 1737—Smith of Common Water 1723—Willis's Method for the Plague 1691—Hancocke on Common Water, and more Tracts 1722, 2s

4770 Norris's Dialogue between Dean Sherlock and Dr. Sherlock 1718—Discourse on Witchcraft 1736—Plea for Human Reason 1730—Jackson on Civil and Ecclesiastical Government 1710, 2s

4771 Leland on Bolingbroke's History 1753—Literal Sense of Demoniacks in the New Test. 1737—Christianity not founded on Argument 1743—Littleton on St. Paul, and more Tracts, 3s

4772 Bishop of Bangor's Answer to Hare's Sermon 1720—Argument of the Divine Legation fairly stated 1751—Remarks on the Jesuit-Cabal, and more Tracts, 1s 6d

4773 Becket on the King's Evil 1722—Fouquier's Ways and Means to support the War 1756—Bp. Berkley's Querist 1750—Oxford Honesty, or a Case of Conscience—Ascanius, or the Young Adventure, and more Tracts, 2s 6d

4774 Massey's Collection of Barbarous Words and Phrases 1755—Manwaring of Harmony and Numbers 1744—Power of Numbers and Principles of Harmony 1749—Gronovii Notæ in Terentium 1701, and more Tracts, 3s

4775 Lyttleton's Observations on Cicero's Life 1741—Spence's Dialogue on Beauty 1752—Hay on Deformity 1754—Blacow's Letter to Dr. King on the Riot at Oxon. and other Tracts, 3s

4776 Politicks on both Sides, and Sequel 1734—Considerations on the Publick Funds, Revenues, &c. 1735—Case of the Sinking Fund 1735, and more Tracts, 1s 6d

4777 Earthquake and Fire at Lisbon 1755—Ranby's Narrative of Lord Orford's Illness 1745—Cause of Consumption in Young Men 1753—Watson on Electricity 1746, and other Tracts, 2s

4778 Original Letters to an Honest Sailor—Remarks on Dr. King's Speech 1750—Bolingbroke's Spirit of Patriotism 1749, and other Tracts, 2s

4779 Ralph's Review of the Publick Buildings of London and Westminster 1734—Clarke on Moral Good and Evil 1725—Ainsworth on Domestic Education 1736—Compendious Way of teaching the Languages 1721, and more Tracts, 2s 6d

4780 Letters from Mr. Hutcheson to Lord Sunderland 1722—English Inquisition, or Money raised without Act of Parliament, 1718, 1s

4781 Essay on Nursing and Management of Children 1748—Tolver on the Teeth 1752—Observations on the Venereal Disease 1754, and more Tracts, 2s

4782. Elfrida,

4782 Elfrida, by Mason 1757——Merope, par Voltaire *Par.* 1744—Vind. of Nat. Society 1757—Report of General Officers relating to the Expedition to France 1758—Candid Reflexions on the Report of General Officers 1758, 3s

4783 Wood's Thoughts on the Study of the Laws 1726—Advocate of the Jesuites against the Protestants of Thorn 1725——Natural History of Superstition 1709—Exercise on the Creation 1717—History of Providence 1723, and more Tracts, 2s

4784 Patten's History of the Rebellion 1715——Faction detected, with the Answer 1743—Plan for a National Militia, 3s 1745

4785 Cheyne's own Account of his Life and Writings 1731——Enquiry into the Legal Constitution of the College of Physicians 1753——Proceedings of the College of Physicians relating to Dr. Schomberg 1754, and two more Tracts, 2s

4786 Journal of the Plague of Marseilles 1721——Bradley on the Plague at Marseilles 1721, 1s 6d

4787 Original Letters to an Honest Sailor—Byng's Expedition to Sicily 1739—Letters between Matthews and Lestock 1744—Mem. of the House of Hesse Cassel——Henry and Rosamond, a Tragedy, and three more, 2s

4788 Scripture Vindicated, by Waterland, 3 parts—Waterland on Regeneration 1740——Seed's Sermon on the Death of Dr. Waterland 1742, 2s

4789 Present for an Apprentice 1740——Haye's Book-Keeping 1739—Letter from Barbadoes relating to Governor Byng 1740——Lottery Dreams——Moore's Natural History of Pigeons 1735—Mrs. Chandler's Poems 1736, 3s

4790 Letter to the Inhabitants at Lisbon on the Earthquake—Middleton on Bishop Sherlock's Discourses——The Moravians comp. and detected, by Lavington, and more Tracts, 1s 6d

4791 Pearce, Middleton and Waterland on Scripture——Syke's Letter on Sincerity 1734—Jackson on Matter and Spirit, and more Tracts, 1s 6d

4792 Hervey's Letter to Hanmer, with Reply——Lucina sine Concubitu——Letters between the Royal Family on the Birth of the Princess Augusta 1737, and more Tracts, 3s

4793 Bliss on Prescience—Pearce on Miracles——Evidence of Christ's Resurrection cleared 1744——Lyttleton on St. Paul, 2s

4794 Milton on Education —— English Presbyter. Eloquence — Hay on Deformity—Journey to Scarborough, and more Tracts, 2s

4795 Conduct of the Allies and late Ministry 1711——Allies and late Ministry defended, 4 parts 1711, 2s 6d

4796 Management of the War, in four Letters to a Tory Member 1710——Faults on both Sides 1710—Kennet's Letter to Bishop Nicolson 1713—Inquiry into the Miscarriages of the four last Years of Queen Anne 1714——Memoires of the Duke of Melfort 1714, and more Tracts, 2s

4797 Bradly on the Plague of Marſ. 1721——Ill State of the Pract. of Physick 1702, and more Tracts, 1s

4798 Argu. for Self Defence 1710——Fleetwood's Serm. against such Delight in War—Groans of Europe, with 16 more Tracts, 1s 6d

4799 Review of the Excise Scheme 1733—Excise Scheme dissected 1734—Letter against the Extens. of Excise Laws, and more Tracts, 1s 6d

S 4800 Letter

4800 Letter from Gen. B—th to W. P—tt, Esq;——Adm. Byng's Defence—Expedit. against Rochefort stated 1758——Narrat. to the Expedit. to the Coast of France 1758—Letter to two Great Men on the Peace, and more Tracts, 2s 6d

4801 Modest Apology for my own Conduct——Observat. on the Convent. with Spain—Case of the Hanover Forces, and more Tracts, 2s

4802 Enq. into the Cond. of G. Brit.—Cond. of Domest. Affairs from 1721 to the Present Time—Thoughts on the Present Post. of Affairs 1742——Modest Enq. into the State of Foreign Affairs, and more Tracts, 2s 6d

4803 Value of Ch. and Col. Leases 1719——Case of the Forf. Estates in Scot. 1718, and more Tracts, 1s 6d

4804 XIX Sermons by Cradock, Newcome, Waugh, Sherlock, and others, 1s 6d

4805 Sermons by Hoadly, Ibbot, and others, 1s 6d

4806 Reasons for and against secl. Sir G. C. from being L. Mayor of Lond. and 4 more Tracts on the same Subject, 2s —— 1737

4807 Bracken's Pock. Farrier 1735—Advice to a Son in the University 1708—Newton of College Leases 1700—Hales on Heredit. Descents 1735——Guide for Brewing, 2s

4808 Sermons, by Trimnel, Hoadly, Bently, Wake, with the Will of Archbp. Tennison, 1s

4809 L'Orphelin de la Chine, par Voltaire —— Slare's Use of Pyrmont Waters, and more Tracts, 1s 6d

4810 Sir Tho. Double at Court, 2 parts, 1s 6d —— 1710, &c.

4811 Lett. &c. betw. the Royal Fam. on the Birth of the Pr. Augusta ——Whitfield's Journal from Gib. to Georgia —— Life and Death of Capt. Porteous—Thoughts on the Tillage of Ireland, and more Tract, 2s

4812 Narrative of the Elect, of Ld Mayor 1739——Proceed. of the Com. Hall at the Elect. of Ld Mayor 1739—K. of Spain's Manifesto—— Observ. on the Declarat. of War——Observat. on the Convent. and more Tracts, 1s 6d

4813 Consid. on the High Duties, by Decker 1744—Horsley's Exam. of Consid. on High Duties 1744—Account of the Num. of Men able to bear Arms in France 1744——Nat. Hist. of the Hanover Rat.—Duchess of Marlborough's Will, and more Tracts, 2s

4814 Further Report relating to the E. of Orford—State of Briti. Influ. in Holl.——Thoughts on the present Posture of Affairs, and more Tracts, 2s

4815 Expedit. to Carthag.——Jour. of the Exped. to Carth.—Tryal of Sir C. Ogle— Case of the Hanov. Forces, and more Tracts, 2s

4816 Desc. of the Slavery among the Moors——Houston's Coast of Guinea 1725 —— Import. of Gibral. 1725——Voyages of Sir W. Raleigh, 2s

4817 Mauclerc on the Power of Imag. in Preg. Wom. 6d 1747

4818 Account of the Welch Charity Schools, and the Rise of Methodism in Wales, 6d —— —— 1752

4819 Athanasian Creed, a Preservative against Heresies 1735 — Trougheat's Defence of the Athan. Creed, 1s —— 1760

4820 Treaty of Seville 1729—Observ. on the same 1729—Treaty, &c. Impart. considered—Observ. on the Treaty exam.—Sedition and Defamat. displayed, and more Tracts, 1s 6d

4821 White-

4821 Whitefield's Seven Journals from Dec. 28. 1737, to June 1740—His Account of the Orph. H. at Georgia 1741——Account of God's Dealings with Whitefield, 1s 6d

4822 Remarks on Clarissa, 1s ——— ——— 1749

4823 Swift on Precedence betw. Physi. and Civilians——His Letter to a Gent. in H. Orders 1720, 1s

4824 Proceed. relat. to the Build. West. Bridge, 1s ——— 1738

4825 Serious Address to Lay Methodists 1745 ——Enthus. of Methodists compared 1749, 1s

4826 Pilloniere's Answ. to Snape——Snape's Vindicat.—Pillonniere's Reply, and more Tracts, 1s

4827 Spicileg. Shuckfordia, or Nosegay for the Critics 1754——Essent. Arti. of the Hutchins. Creed 1750——Dissertat. upon 2 Kings x. 22, 1s 6d

4828 Original Letters to an Honest Sailor, 1s

4829 Letter on Redu. the Land-Tax to 1s in the Pound 1732—Letters and Instruct. concern. the Excise, with more Tracts relat. to the same Subject, 2s

4830 Letters and Memori. betw. Gr. Br. Fra. and Spain 1727——Mons. Palm's Memor. and more Tracts, 1s 6d

4831 Remarq. de Motraye sur l'Hist. de Cha. XII.—Achilles, an Opera ——Art of Politicks, 1s

4832 Art and Pleasures of Hare Hunting, 1s ——— 1750

4833 Enq. into Domest. Affairs 1734—Grand Accuser the greatest of all Crim.——Life of Sir R. Cochran——Moral Reflex. on the Ministr. of C. Alberoni, and more Tracts, 1s 6d

4834 Life and Char. of Rob. Hush. 1713—Dr. Tripe's Lett. to Nestor Ironside——Oliver's Pocket Looking Glass, and more Tracts, 1s

4835 Remarks on the Craftsf. Vind. of his two Hon. Patrons, with Answ. by Mr. Pultney and Lord Bolingbroke, and Replies, 1s 6d

4836 Crit. Remarks on Sir C. Gran. Claris. and Pam. 1s 1754

4837 Old Stories, which were Fore-run. of the Revol. 1688, 1s

4838 Let. to the Tories 1747—Let. on Carte's Hist. of Engl.—Case of M. de la Bourdonais 1748——and more Tracts, 1s 6d

4839 Adm. Matthews's Answ. and Defence——Sent. on Adm. Lestock—Resolut. of the Court-Mart. against Adm. Matthews—Proceed. of the N. Engl. Forces against Cape Breton, 1s

4840 Priestcraft in Perfection——Vindic. of the Ch. of Engl. by Bedford 1710, 1s

4841 Resurrect. Reconsidered—Resurrect. Defenders stript of all Defence ——Supernaturals examined, all by Anett, 3s

4842 Collins, Jackson and Gretton on Lib. and Necessity, 1s 1729

4843 Guy's Will 1725——Journal of the Polish Camp of Radewitz, and more Tracts, 1s

4844 Belhaven's Speech on the Un. 1706——Mackworth's Free Parl. and more Tracts, 1s

4845 Pretender's Decla. transposed by Asgil——Compl. Hist. of the Rebel. 1716—Trien. Act stated——Life of St. Veronica, by Geddes, and more Tracts, 2s

4846 Neces. of lower. Int. and contin. Taxes 1750——Winter Even. Conversat. in a Club of Jews, &c. 1s

4847 Joe Miller's Jests, 1s ——— ——— 1745

4848 Perronet's Plain Account of the Methodists——His Let. to Bp. Lavington, 1s

4849 Bibliotheq. Volante *Amst.* 1700 —— Good's Measuring, and more Tracts, 1s
4850 Le Caffé – L'Orpheline de la Chine —— Candide, par Voltaire, 2s
4851 Paral. de la Conduite du Roi avex celle du Roi d'Angl. *Amst.* 1758 —— Hist. du Marq. de Fratteaux *Par.* 1753 —— Burman's Orat. against the Study of Humanity, 2s
4852 Hale to the Drinkers of Spiritu. Liq. 6d —— 1751

Pamphlets. FOLIO.

4853 MORRIS's Observations on the past Growth and present State of London, 1s 6d —— —— 1751
4854 Marshall's Chronologic Tables of Sacred History, 2s 1713
4855 Bowick's Antiquities of Middlesex, part 1. 2s 6d —— 1705
4856 Act for Draining, &c. the Fens lying on the River Witham in Lincolnshire, 1s —— —— 1762
4857 Decree in the Exchequer, relating to Hatfield Chase, 6d 1757
4858 Papers relating to Indian Trade at New York, 1s 1724
4859 Morris on Arranging and Ballancing the Accounts of Landed Estates, 3s —— —— —— 1759
4860 Hutcheson's Abstract of Publick Debts, 2s 6d —— 1723
4861 Crookshanks on Hutcheson, relating to Publick Debts and Funds, 1s —— —— —— 1718
4862 Hutcheson's Answer to Crookshank's Remarks, 1s 1719
4863 Nicolls on the Tobacco Trade to Great Britain, 6d 1727
4864 Observations on Trade and Taxes, 1s —— 175
4865 Report of the Committee relating to the Lottery 1753, 6d 1755
4866 Report of the Secret Committee, by Mr. Walpole, 1s 1715
4867 Further Report of the Secret Committee against the Earl of Orford, 1s —— —— —— 1742
4868 Tryal of Admiral Byng, 2s —— —— 1757
4869 The same, with some additional Papers, 2s 6d —— 1757
4870 Trial of the Earl Ferrers, 1s —— —— 1760
4871 —— of Lord Lovat, 2s 6d —— —— 1747
4872 —— of Miss Blandy, 1s —— —— 1752
4873 Gascoyne's Account of Canning and M. Squires, 1s 1754
4874 Tryal of Col. Bayard of New York for High Treason, 1s 1702
4875 Lairess's Principles of Drawing, *cuts,* 3s —— 1739
4876 Douglas's Description of the Guernsey Lilly and Coffee Berry, *cuts,* 1s 6d —— —— 1725
4877 Tull's Horse-hoeing Husbandry, 3s —— 1733
4878 Pope's Essay on Man, 4 parts —— The Fourth Satire of Horace imitated 1733 — and more Poetic Tracts, 1s 6d
4879 Trade of Great Britain considered — and more Tracts, 1s
4880 Account of the Murders, &c. committed by J. Palmer and others in Worcestershire 1708 — Tit for Tat, with Lord Hervey's Letter 1734 — and more Tracts, 1s 6d
4881 Proceedings of the Peers relating to the Publick Accounts of the Kingdom 1702 — and more Tracts, 1s 6d

Pamphlets

Pamphlets. QUARTO.

4882 DEcline of Foreign Trade, by Decker, 1s 6d —— 1744
4883 Clear Account of the Revenues of France, 2s 1760
4884 Remarks on the Trade of England and Ireland, 1s 1691
4885 Scheme to secure the Strength of the British Nation by Fornication, 1s 6d —— —— —— 1747
4886 Burgher of Amsterdam on the Indian Trade, 6d —— 1724
4887 Naked Truth, in an Essay on Trade, 1s —— 1696
4888 England's Safety in Trade's Encrease, by Robinson, 1s 1641
4889 Coke on Trade, 1s —— —— 1670
4890 Motives for enlarging the Woollen Trade, 1s —— 1645
4891 Bellers's College of Industry, 6d —— 1696
4892 True Way of Taxing, 6d —— 1693
4893 Reasons for a Registry, 6d —— —— 1678
4894 Cheshire Weaver's fatal Consequence of Smuggling Wool, 1s 1727
4895 Observations on British Wool, 6d —— 1738
4896 Address to the People of England on the Excise of Wine and Tobacco, 6d —— —— 1733
4897 Letter concerning the Trade to Africa, 6d —— 1750
4898 Increase of Wealth by Subscrip. of Money, 6d —— 1675
4899 Layton's Observation on Money and Coin, 1s —— 1697
4900 Arckin's Mysteries of Counterfeiting the Coin, 6d 1696
4901 Treatise of Taxes and Contributions, 1s —— 1662
4902 Swift's Propos. for giving Badges to Beggars, 6d —— 1737
4903 Charges issuing out of the Crown Revenue of England, 6d 1647
4904 Proceedings of the Committee of Customes, 1s —— 1655
4905 Importance of the African Company considered, 6d 1745
4906 Case of the African Company, with the Supplement, 1s 1730
4907 Apology for the Builder, 1s —— 1685
4908 Evans's Geographical, Historical, Political, Philosophical and Mechanical Essays, 1s —— —— 1755
4909 Present State of North America, 1s —— 1755
4910 Randolph's State of the Islands in the Archipelago, 1s 1687
4911 Last East Indian Voyage, 6d —— 1606
4912 Proceedings of the English Army in the West Indies, 6d 1655
4913 Discovery of New Britain, 6d —— —— 1652
4914 Description of New York, 6d —— 1670
4915 Description of Carolina, 6d —— 1666
4916 Sarate's History of the Conquest of Peru, *cuts, black letter*, 1s 1581
4917 Description of Fez and Morocco, 6d —— 1670
4918 Crown's Journey to Germany, *wants the title*, 6d
4919 Norden's Colossal Statues at Thebes in Egypt, 1s 6d 1741
4920 Hist. and Antiquity of Wheatfield in Suffolk, 1s —— 1758
4921 Wise on some Antiquities in Berkshire, *cuts*, 1s 6d —— 1738
4922 Stukely's Antiquities near Graham's Dike, *cuts*, 1s
4923 Cunningham's Essay on Macduff's Cross, 1s —— 1678
4924 Soligne's Essay on Old Rome, 6d —— 1701
4925 Certificate from Northamptonshire relating to Pluralities, 6d 1641
4926 Langbaine's Foundation of the University of Oxford and Cambridge, 1s —— —— 1651
4927 Mackenzie's Siege of Londonderry, 6d —— 1690

4928 Ha-

4928 Hamilton's Actions of the Inniskilling Men 1690—History of the Northern Affairs of Ireland, 1s —— 1690
4929 Copies of Colston's Settlements at Bristol, 1s
4930 Convention between Great Britain and Spain 1739—Tryal of Peter Zenger, Printer at New York 1738—Bishop Gibson's Observations on the Methodists 1744—Observations upon the Vagrant Laws 1742—Catalogue of the Harleian Pictures and Coins 1741, 2s
4931 Middleton's Letter from Rome, 1s —— 1729
4932 London Fishery laid open, 1s —— —— 1759
4933 Army's Plea for their present Practice 1659—Narration of the Treatment of the Episcopal Ministers at Edinburgh 1708—and more Tracts, 1s
4934 *Report concerning the ruinous Condition of the River Witham,* 1s
4935 Full Vindication of his Prussian Majesty's Conduct, 6d 1756
4936 Duke of Newcastle's Letter to Mr. Michel, 6d —— 1753
4937 The same, *fine paper,* 1s —— —— 1753
4938 Memorial of the East India Company against the Complaints of the Dutch East India Company, 2s 6d —— 1762
4939 Account of the Proceedings of the States of Holland, concerning the Hostilities at Bengal, 1s —— —— 1762
4940 Dispute between the Govr. and Com. House of Assembly in South Carolina, 1s —— —— —— 1763
4941 Documents of Fr. Administration in Germany, 6d 1758
4942 Treaty between Great Britain and the Emperor of Russia, 1s 1755
4943 Memorial of the Negotiation of France and England, 1s 1761
4944 Treaty between Great Britain, Hungary and Sardinia, 6d 1743
4945 Treaty of Aix la Chapelle 1748, 6d —— 1749
4946 Papers relating to the Rupture with Spain, 1s —— 1762
4947 Treaty of Madrid, 6d —— —— 1750
4948 Report of the Commiss. sent to Spain on Gibraltar, 1s 1728
4949 Cond. of Gr. B. in respect to Neut. Nations, 1s 6d 1758
4950 Review of the Milit. Operat. in N. America, 1s 6d —— 1757
4951 Clarke's Cond. of the French in N. Amer. 1s *Bost.* 1755
4952 Dignities and Revenues of the Kings of Engl. 1s —— 1737
4953 Anstis upon the Knighthood of Bath, 1s —— 1725
4954 Transact. of the 6th Sess. of the 1st Parl. of K. Geo. II. 6d 1733
4955 Account of Scotland's Grievances, 6d
4956 Boyse's Vindic. of the Rev. Mr. Osborn, relating to the Affairs of Ireland, 6d —— —— —— 1690
4957 Smith's Commonwealth of England, 1s —— 1679
4958 Creshald's Legacy to his four Sons, 6d —— 1658
4959 Sir J. Cheeke's True Subject, 6d —— 1641
4960 Epitome of Aspersions cast at the Civilians, 6d —— 1631
4961 Ludlow's Letter to Sir E. S. relating to K. Cha. I. and K. Ja. II. 1s —— —— —— 1691
4962 Petition to the Parl. against Imprison. for Debt, 6d 1622
4963 Power of the Peers and Com. in Point of Judic. 6d — 1640
4964 Second Narrative of the late Parliament, 6d —— 1658
4965 Journal of the Commons from Jan. 7. to Feb. 24. 1673, 6d
4966 Kingdome's Case, 6d —— —— 1643
4967 Milton's Tenure of Kings and Magistrates, 1s —— 1649
4968 Jus Regium, or King's Right to grant Forfeit. 6d 1701
4969 Treatise of Monarchie, 6d —— —— 1643
4970 Vindication of K. Charles I. 6d —— —— 1711

4971 Pour-

4971 Pourtraiture of Truths most sacred Majesty, 6d

4972 Life of Sir Tho. Bodley, 6d 1649

4973 Life of Sir Fr. Drake, by Clarke, 6d 1647

4974 Characture of K. Charles II. 6d 1671

4975 Treasons of Rob. E. of Essex against Q. Eliz. 1s 1660

4976 Proceed. of the Eccles. Commiss. against Bp. Compton, 1s 1601

4977 Tryal of Mr. Ja. Annesley for Murder, 6d 1688

4978 Tryal of Ja. Naylor the Quaker, 1s 1742

4979 Tryal of P. Zenger, Printer at N. York, 6d 1657

4980 Tryals of Witches in N. England, 1s 1738

4981 Case of the King against Broadfoot, by Foster, 6d 1693

4982 Case of Col. Alured, 6d 1758

4983 Hogarth's Analysis of Beauty, *wants the prints*, 4s 1659

4984 Bellers's Delineat. of Univers. Law, 1s 6d 1753

4985 Plan for establish. the Magdelen Charity, 1s 1754

4986 Hendley's Defence of Charity Schools, 6d 1758

4987 Plan for an Academy of Arts in general, 6d 1725

4988 Arnoux's Parallels of the Eng. and Fr. Lang. 1s 1755

4989 Art of Modern Gaming, 6d 1731

4990 Jesuit Cabal farther opened, 6d 1726

4991 Letter to Dr. Bentley on his Gr. Test. 6d 1747

4992 Middleton's Remarks on Bentley's Propos. 1s 1721

4993 Letter to Maxwell on the Engl. Language, 6d 1721

4994 Huddesforth's Reply to the Defence of the Rect. of Exeter Coll. 6d 1755

4995 Dr. Packe's Reply to Gray on Worger's Case, 6d 1755

4996 Letters to Dr. Reynolds on Eccles. Courts, 6d 1727

4997 Kinnersley's Letter to the E. of Sund. 6d 1724

4998 Richardson's Thoughts upon Thinking, 6d 1719

4999 Emmerton's Marriage with Mrs Hyde consid. 6d 1755

5000 Vindicat. of the Surrey Demoniack, 6d 1682

5001 Prophecies of Mart. Luther 1664 — Lilly's Collect. of Prophecies 1645, 1s 1698

5002 Second Book of Virgil's Æneid, Notes by Theobald, 1s

5003 Fourth Book of the Dunciad, 1s

5004 Dunciad, by Pope, complete, 2s 1750

5005 Pope's Ethic Epistles, *Warburton's Notes*, 1s 1743

5006 Scale, or Woman weighed with Man, 6d 1748

5007 West's Poem on Education, 6d 1752

5008 Thomson's Castle of Indolence, 1s 1751

5009 Morris's Hermitage, a Poem, 6d 1748

5010 Power of Harmony, a Poem, 6d 1743

5011 Somerville's Rural Games, 1s 1745

5012 Causidicade, a Poem, 6d 1740

5013 Patriotism, a Mock Heroick Poem, 1s 1743

5014 Traveller, *an Arabic Poem*, English, with Notes by Chappelow, 1s 1763

5015 Publick Virtue, a Poem, by Dodsley, 1s 1758

5016 Lively Picture of Adoll Worship, a Poem, 6d 1753

5017 Christianity the Light of the Moral World, a Poem, 6d 1748

5018 Latin and English Poems, by a Gentleman of Trinity College, Oxford, 2s 1745

5019 Castara, a Collect. of Poems, 1s 1731

5020 Medea, a Tragedy, by Glover, 1s 1634

1761

5021 Solon,

5021 Solon, a Trag. Comedy, by Bladen, 1s —— 1705
5022 All Mistaken, a Comedy, by Howard, 1s —— 1710
5023 Love's a Jest, a Comedy, by Motteux, 1s —— 1696
5024 Tartuffe, a Comedy, by Melbourne, 6d —— 1707
5025 Henry VI. part 2. by Crown, 1s —— 1681
5026 Revolution of Sweden, a Tragedy, by Mrs. Trotter, 1s 1706
5027 Caligula, a Tragedy, by Crowne, 1s —— 1698
5028 Conspiracy, a Tragedy, by Killigrew, 1s —— 1638
5029 Cataline's Conspiracy, by B. Jonson, 1s —— 1635
5030 City Politiques, a Comedy, by Crown, 6d —— 1688
5031 Salmacida Spolia, a Masque, 1s —— 1639
5032 Mall, or Modish Lovers, a Comedy, 1s —— 1674
5033 Strange Discovery, a Trag-Comedy, by J. G. 1s 6d 1640
5034 Phænix in Flames, a Tragedy, by Lower, 1s 6d —— 1639
5035 White Devil, a Tragedy, by Webster, 1s —— 1612
5036 The same, 1s —— —— 1672
5037 A Mad World my Masters, 1s 6d —— 1640
5038 Jealous Lovers, a Comedy, by Randolph, 1s —— 1634
5039 Aristippus, or the Jovial Philosopher, 1s 6d —— 1630
5040 Volpone, or the Foxe, by B. Johnson, *the Original Edition, with the Dedicat. to both Univers.* 1s 6d —— 1607
5041 Cœlum Britannicum, a Masque, by Carew, 1s —— 1634
5042 Arcădia, a Pastoral, by Shirley, 1s 6d —— 1640
5043 Cupid's Revenge, by Beaumont and Fletcher, 1s —— 1630
5044 Fuimus Troes, the True Troianes, 1s —— 1633
5045 Philaster, or Love lies a Bleeding, by Beaumont and Fletcher, 6d —— —— 1634
5046 Cruel Brother, a Tragedy, by Davenant, 1s —— 1630
5047 Nero, a Tragedy, 1s 6d —— —— 1624
5048 Just Italian, 1s —— —— 1630
5049 Love's Labours lost, a Comedy, by Shakespeare, 1s 1631
5050 Merchants Publ. Counting-house, by Postlethwayt, 1s 1750
5051 Langwith's Observat. on Arbuthnot on Coins, 1s —— 1747
5052 Salmon's Proposal to perform Music in Mathemat. Proport. 1s 1688
5053 Gadbury's Cardines Cœli, 6d —— 1685
5054 Hunt's Demonstrat. of Astrology, 6d —— 1696
5055 Philpot on the Flux and Reflux of the Sea 1673—Propos. for the full Peopl. the City of London 1672, and two more, 1s
5056 Wallis on Gravity and Gravitation, 6d —— 1675
5057 Wallis's Defence of the R. Society against Dr. Holder, 1s 1678
5058 Papin's New Digester, and Air Pump, *with cuts*, 2 parts, 2s 1681, &c.
5059 Clerke's Spot Dial, 1s —— —— 1687
5060 Whiston and Haukesbee's Course of Experim. Philos. *cuts*, 1s 6d
5061 Description of a New Astron. Instrum. for tak. Altitude of the Sun at Sea, without an Horizon, 6d —— —— 1735
5062 Smith's New Instrum. for tak. Altitudes at Sea, 6d
5063 Knight on Attraction and Repulsion, 1s 6d —— 1754
5064 Ellicot on the Influence of Pendulum Clocks, 6d
5065 Boyle on the Degradation of Gold, 6d —— 1739
5066 Platte's Subterranean Treasure, 6d —— 1679
5067 The same, 6d —— —— 1639
5068 Burgh's Method to determine Areas, 6d —— 1724
5069 Hoadly and Wilson's Electric. Experiments, *1st edit.* 6d 1756
5070 Hoadly on Respiration, *with cuts*, 1s 6d —— 1740

5071 Bat-

5071 Battie's Treatise on Madness, 1s ——— 1758
5072 Oliver on Warm Bathing in Gouty Cases, 1s ——— 1751
5073 Boerhaave's Elem. of Chemistry, No 1. 6d
5074 Rutty on the Urinary Passages, 1s ——— 1726
5075 Certain Method to know the Disease, 1s ——— 1742
5076 Gardiner on the Circulat. of the Blood, 1s ——— 1702
5077 Douglas's Method of cutting for the Stone, *with cuts,* 1s 1723
5078 Tyson's Anat. of a Porpess, 1s ——— 1680
5079 Index Materiæ Medicæ, 1s ——— ——— 1724
5080 Robinson's Medical Lectures, 6d
5081 Causes of the Discontents relating to the Plague, 6d 1721
5082 Evelyn on the smoaky Air of London, 1s ——— 1661
5083 Chovet's Anat. Syllabus, 6d ——— ——— 1732
5084 Letter to Dr. Pitt at Oxford, by a Lady, 6d
5085 Account of the strange Abstinence of Martha Taylor, 6d 1669
5086 Constant Residence of the Clergy on their Liv. necessary, 1s 1760
5087 Considerat. on the Residence of the Clergy, 1s ——— 1756
5088 Leechman on the Temper, &c. of a Minister of the Gospel, 1s ——— ——— ——— 1749
5089 Nature of Ration. and Irrational Souls, 6d ——— 1696
5090 Turner on the Soul's seperate Existence, 6d ——— 1703
5091 Pilkington's Index to the Bible, 1s ——— 1749
5092 Articles of Religion, by Q. Eliz. 1597—Articles of Enquiry by Archbp. Matthews 1622—Hasnet 1628—Neale 1636—Laud 1634—Williams 1641, and two more, 2s 6d
5093 Articles of Religion, published by Q. Eliz. 1s 6d *printed by Jugge and Cawood* 1571
5094 Kennicott's Serm. on Christ. Fortitude, 6d ——— 1757
5095 Hunt's Dissertat. on Proverbs vii. 22, 23. 6d ——— 1743
5096 Merrick's Dissertat. on Prov. ix. 1—6, 1s ——— 1744
5097 Hardy's Sermon on Libertie and Tyrannie, 6d ——— 1647
5098 Parson's Serm. on the E. of Rochester, 1s ——— 1680
5099 Heathcote's two Serm. at Boyle's Lect. 1s ——— 1763
5100 Swinton Metilia, *cum fig.* 6d ——— *Oxon.* 1750
5101 Twenty-four Designs of Vases, by Marot, 1s
5102 Seldenus de Nummis, 6d ——— *Lond.* 1675
5103 Kederi Catalogus Numm. in Museo Grainger, 1s *ibid.* 1728
5104 Hunt de Usu Dilect. Oriental. 1s ——— *Oxon.* 1748
5105 Hanbury Horologia Scroterica Prælibata, 1s ——— *Lond.* 1683
5106 Hooper de Valentinianor. Hæresi, 1s ——— *ibid.* 1711
5107 Powney Templum Harmoniæ, 6d ——— *ibid.* 1745
5108 Solomon de Mundo Vanitate, Lat. & Angl. 1s *Oxon.* 1735
5109 Barford in Prun. Pythium Pindari, 1s ——— *Cantab.* 1751
5110 Fracastorii Syphilis, 1s ——— ——— *Lond.* 1720
5111 Statuta Provinc. & Synod. *Traject.* 1684—Synod. Dioceff. Cameracensis *Brux.* 1567, 1s
5112 Barford Oratio in Funere Gu. Georga, S. T. P. 6d *Cantab.* 1756
5113 Heathcote Fidei Fundam. Ratio, 6d ——— *ibid.* 1759
5114 Swedenborg de Cultu & Amore Dei, pars 2. 6d *Lond.* 1745
5115 Stuart de Struct. & Motu Musculari, *cum fig.* 1s *ibid.* 1738
5116 Jessop Proposit. Hydrostaticæ, 6d ——— *ibid.* 1687
5117 Appendix ad Hist. Animal. Angl. Tractat. 1s *Eborac.* 1681
5118 Battie Oratio Harvæiana, 6d ——— *Lond.* 1746
5119 Hoadly Oratio Harvæiana, 6d ——— *ibid.* 1742

T 5120 Fasci-

5120 Fasciculis Observat. Medicinalium, 6d ——— *Oxon.*
5121 Hollings Status Humanæ Naturæ, 1s ——— *Lond.* 1734
5122 Manning de Aquis Mineralibus, 1s ——— *ibid.* 1746
5123 Middleton Append. de Servili Medicor. Condit. 2s *ibid.* 1761
5124 Lettre du Duc de Newcastle, a M. Michel, 1s ——— *Lond.* 1753
5125 *Roma Tutrice delle Arti Pittura, Scultura e Architt.* 1s *Rom.* 1710
5126 Traite de la Poudre de Projection, 6d ——— *Brux.* 1707
5127 Lezioni sopra il Tremoto, 1s ——— *Rom.* 1748

Pamphlets. OCTAVO.

5128 WAYS, &c. to enlarge Trade and Commerce, by Lucas, 6d
5129 Trade and Navigat. of Gr. Brit. considered, 1s 1730
5130 Considerat. on the Gin Trade, 6d ——— 1736
5131 Appeal to Landholders on Excise, on Wine, &c. 6d — 1733
5132 Conduct of the City of London relating to the Excise Bill, 6d ——— ——— ——— 1733
5133 Thoughts of a Merchant on the Excise, 6d ——— 1733
5134 Case of the Traders of London and the Wharfingers, 6d
5135 City Corruption displayed, 6d ——— 1739
5136 Sir J. Barnard's Proposal for raising 3 Millions, 6d 1746
5137 Letter to Sir J. Barnard on his Proposal, 6d ——— 1746
5138 Cries of the Public, 6d ——— ——— 1758
5139 Essay to make Money plentiful, 1s ——— 1734
5140 Statutes relating to the Game, 6d ——— 1726
5141 Machiavell's Scheme to raise 50,000 Men, 6d ——— 1747
5142 Burn's Digest of the Militia Laws, 6d ——— 1760
5143 Question relating to a Scots Militia, 6d ——— 1760
5144 Whiston on the Militia, 6d ——— ——— 1757
5145 Method of speedy Manning a Fleet, 6d ——— 1754
5146 Treatise on Maritime Affairs, 6d
5147 Fauquirer's Ways and Means for raising Money, 6d 1756
5148 Fielding's Provision for the Poor, 1s ——— 1753
5149 Robe's Criterion, relat. to Spirit. Liq. and the Poor, 6d 1746
5150 Unreasonableness of Imprisonment for Debt, 6d — 1729
5151 Essay on Credit and the Bankrupt Act, 6d ——— 1707
5152 Report from the Committee of Secrecy, by Mr. Walpole, 6d 1714
5153 Second Report on the Publick Accounts, 6d ——— 1712
5154 Stanhope's Answ. to the Commiss. sent into Spain, 6d 1714
5155 Elking's View of the Greenland Trade, 6d ——— 1722
5156 England's Path to Wealth and Honour, 6d ——— 1750
5157 British Golden Mines discovered, 6d ——— 1720
5158 Case of the Revival of the Salt Duty, 6d ——— 1732
5159 Smith's Review of the Manufact. compl. against the Wool-Grower, 3 parts, 1s 6d ——— ——— 1753
5160 Woollen Labourers Advocate, by Peard, 2s ——— 1733
5161 Consequences of Trade to the Wealth of a Nation, 6d 1740
5162 Supplement to the State of the Woollen Manufact. 6d 1744
5163 Method to pay the Nation. Debt without a New Tax, 6d 1744
5164 Proposals for prevent. the Running of Wool, 6d — 1731
5165 Thoughts on the Woollen Manufactories, 6d ——— 1735
5166 Golden Fleece of Gr. Britain, 6d ——— 1737
5167 Case of the Clothiers and Weavers, 6d ——— 1739

5168 Hard

5168 Hard Case of the Retail. Traders of London, 6d
5169 Interest of England with respect to Callicoes, 6d — 1720
5170 Letter on the Brit. and Irish Manufact. of Linnen, 6d 1738
5171 National Merchant, 1s — — 1736
5172 Spanish Merchants Address to all Englishmen, 6d — 1739
5173 Advant. and Disadvant. of the prohib. Merch. of Spain, 6d
5174 Perrin's State of the Br. and Fr. Sugar Colonies, 6d 1740
5175 Bennet on the Sugar Colonies and Trade, 6d — 1738
5176 Considerat. on the Americ. Trade, 6d — 1740
5177 Detection of the Directors of the African Company, 6d 1749
5178 National Advant. of the African Trade, 1s — 1746
5179 Advantages of the E. India Trade considered, 6d 1720
5180 Importance of the Ostend Company considered, 6d 1726
5181 Expediency of a Trade to Turkey, 6d — 1753
5182 Holland Merchants Companion, 6d — 1715
5183 Turky Merchants vindicated, 6d — 1720
5184 Reasons of the Decay of Trade, 6d — 1707
5185 Walker's Propos. for a Land Credit, 6d — 1721
5186 Improvement of enclosed Commons, 6d — 1732
5187 Allen's Ways and Means to raise the Value of Land, 6d 1736
5188 Richard's Gent. Steward instructed, 1s — 1730
5189 Nature, &c. of the Laws for the Reduction of Interest, 6d 1751
5190 Tract on the National Interest, 6d — 1757
5191 Governing Causes of Natur. Rate of Interest, 6d 1750
5192 Thoughts on the Interest of Money, 6d
5193 Considerat. on the Publick Funds, 6d — 1735
5194 Essay on the Sinking Fund, 6d — 1737
5195 Animadvers. on Hutcheson on Funds, 6d — 1718
5196 Considerat. on the Improv. of Publ. Revenues, 6d 1733
5197 Observations on Trade, 6d — — 1734
5198 Essay on the Inequality of Taxes, 6d — 1746
5199 Proposal for a Tax upon Houses laid open, 6d — 1756
5200 Hooke on the National Debt and Capital, 6d — 1750
5201 Hist. of the National Debt, 6d — 1761
5202 Essay on the Public Debts of this Kingdom, 6d — 1726
5203 Loggin on the Management of the Customs, 6d — 1720
5204 Hottoman's Free State of France, 6d — 1711
5205 Present State of the Fr. Revenues and Trade, 1s — 1720
5206 Progress of the Fr. Trade and Navigation, 1s — 1756
5207 Memorials of the Counc. of Trade in France, 1s — 1701
5208 The same, in Fr. and Engl. 1s 6d — 1744
5209 Advantages of the Trade of Fr. and Gr. Br. 6d — 1749
5210 French Way of paying National Debts, 6d
5211 Remarks on the Inq. into the Reven. &c. of France, 6d 1749
5212 Danger of Brit. and Irel. becom. Provin. to France, 6d 1746
5213 Mun's Engl. Treasure by Foreign Trade, 1s — 1713
5214 Harris's Essay on Money and Coins, 2 parts, 3s — 1757
5215 The same, part 2. 1s 6d — — 1758
5216 Univers. Remedy for all Diseases of the Coin, 6d 1696
5217 Considerat. about Raising of Coin, 6d — 1696
5218 Essay on the Ballance of Civil Power in Engl. 6d 1748
5219 Palladium of Gr. Brit. and Ireland, 1s — 1762
5220 Letter from a By-Stander on the Land Forces, 6d 1742
5221 Proper Answ. to the By-Stander, 6d — 1742

T 3 5222 Lett.

5222 Letter to Carte, Author of the Full Anſwer to the By-Stander, 6d 1742
5223 Full Anſw. to the By-Stander, 1s 1742
5224 King of Pruſſia's Motives for ſiezing the Effects of Engliſh Merchants, 1s 1752
5225 Galba, a Dialogue on the Navy, 6d 1748
5226 Abbé de la Ville's Mem. to the States Gen. 6d 1747
5227 Gibraltar a Bulwark to Gr. Brit. 6d 1725
5228 Select Tracts relat. to the Colonies, 6d
5229 Proceed. of the Hudſon's Bay Committee, 6d 1749
5230 Deſcript. of the Coaſts, &c. of the Span. W. Indies, 6d 1740
5231 Account of South Carolina and Georgia, 6d 1733
5232 Treaty with the Indians of the ſix Nations, 6d 1742
5233 Repreſent. of his Maj. Right to Nova Scotia, 6d 1756
5234 State of Penſylvania, 6d 1755
5235 Anſwer to the State of Penſylvania, 6d 1755
5236 State of Minorca, 6d
5237 State of the Brit. and Fr. Colonies in N. Am. 1s 6d 1755
5238 Conſiderat. on the German War, 1s 1760
5239 Anſw. to the Conſid. on the Germ. War, 6d 1761
5240 Candid Anſw. to the Conſid. on the Germ. War, 6d 1760
5241 Occaſional Thought on the Germ. War, 6d 1761
5242 German Politicks, 6d 1744
5243 Operations of the Brit. and Allied Armies, 6d
5244 Caſe of the Brit. Troops in Germany, 6d 1761
5245 Caſe of the Heſſian Forces, 6d 1731
5246 Caſe of the Hanover Forces, 6d 1743
5247 Caſe of the Dutch Ships conſidered, 6d 1759
5248 Profit and Loſs of Gr. Brit. in the War with Spain, 6d 1741
5249 Obſervat. on the Papers relat. to Rupt. with Spain, 6d 1762
5250 Propoſals for carrying on the War with Vigour, 6d 1757
5251 Politic. Analyſis of the War, 6d 1762
5252 View of the Politicks of Europe, 6d
5253 Narrat. of the Campaigns in Germ. and Flanders, 6d 1751
5254 Account of ſome Tranſact. in the E. Indies, 6d 1753
5255 Journal of the Campaign on the C. of Fr. 1s 1758
5256 Memoirs of the Revolut. in Bengal, 1s 1760
5257 Account of the late Enterpr. on the C. of France, 6d 1758
5258 Account of the Grand Expedit. to the C. of France, 6d 1757
5259 Narrat. of the Enterpr. againſt St. Maloes, 6d 1758
5260 Expedition againſt Rochefort conſidered, 6d 1758
5261 Braddock's Expedit. to Virginia, 6d 1755
5262 Sir G. Byng's Expedit. to Sicilly, 6d 1739
5263 Particulars relating to Adm. Byng, 6d 1756
5264 Adm. Byng's Defence, 6d 1757
5265 Appeal to the People relat. to Adm. Byng, 6d 1756
5266 Trial of Sir J. Mordaunt at a Court Martial, 6d 1758
5267 Conſid. on the Trial of Sir J. Mordaunt, 6d 1758
5268 Trial of Lord George Sackville, 1s 6d 1760
5269 Anſw. to a Letter to a Command. of the Br. Forces, 6d 1759
5270 Conduct of Gen. Shirley in North Am. 1s. 1745
5271 Enq. into the Conduct of Capt. Moſtyn, 6d 1745
5272 Conduct of Capt. Crookſhanks in 1747, 1s 1759
5273 Minutes of C. Mart. on the Cond. of Capt. Moſtyn, 6d 1745

5274 Caſe

5274 Case of Col. Burston. 6d — —— 1756
5275 Report of the Gen. Off. on the Cond. of Gen. Stuart, 6d 1757
5276 —— of Gen. Off. relat. to the Expedit. to France. 6d 1758
5277 Thoughts on the Use and Abuse of great Officers, 6d 1754
5278 Military Arguments fully considered, 6d —— 1758
5279 Reply to Military Argum. considered, 6d — 1758
5280 Enq. into Mr. Wooley's Conduct in the S. Sea, 6d 1755
5281 Articles of Impeach. against L. Oxford, and his Ans. 1s 1717
5282 Tryal of Capt. Porteous, 1s —— 1736
5283 Tryal of B. Greenwood for Robb. Wheatley, 6d 1740
5284 Tryal of the Czarewitz, 6d —— — 1725
5285 Case of Eliz. Canning, 6d — —— 1753
5286 Clear Case of Eliz. Canning, by Fielding, 6d — 1753
5287 Refutat. of Gascoyne's Account of his Conduct, 6d 1754
5288 Miss Blandy's own Account of Mr. Cranston, 6d 1752
5289 Kane's Campaigns of K. W. and Q. Anne, 1s — 1745
5290 Cox's Appeal in behalf of Eliz. Canning, 6d — 1753
5291 State Anatomy of Gr. Britain, 2 parts, 1s
5292 Conduct of the two Brothers vindicated, 6d — 1749
5293 Enquiry into the Conduct of the two Brothers, 6d 1749
5294 Tracts to prove the Abilit. of the T. Brothers, 6d 1749
5295 Conduct of the Ministry examined, 6d —— 1756
5296 Cond. of the late and present Minist. compared, 6d 1742
5297 Remarks on the Cond. of Gr Brit. and Holland, 6d
5298 Conduct of a right Hon. Gentle. justified, 6d — 1761
5299 Apology for a late Resignation, 6d —— 1748
5300 Resignation discussed, 6d —— —— 1748
5301 Key to the Business of the present Session, 6d —— 1742
5302 Morrice's Essay on Insur. Enemies Ships, 6d — 1758
5303 Defence of the Estimate of the Times, 6d — 1758
5304 Dialogue between Pasq. and Marfino, 2 *parts*, 1s 1737
5305 Sir Tho. Double at Court, 6d
5306 Things as they are, 2 *parts*, 1s —— 1758
5307 Further Report of the Cond. of the E. of Orford, 1s 1742
5308 Review of the Report of the Secr. Committ. 6d — 1715
5309 Enquiry into the true Interest of Engl. 6d —— 1746
5310 Lord Grey's Hist. of the Rye House Plot, 1s —— 1754
5311 Secret Hist. of the white Staff, 6d —— 1714
5312 Hist. of the Mitre and Purse, 6d —— 1714
5313 Supplem. to the Hist. of the Crown Inn, 6d
5314 Dispute betw. the King and Senate of Swed. 6d 1756
5315 Happ. of a People under a Philosoph. King, 6d 1750
5316 Letter to the People of England, 6d —— 1760
5317 Burnet's Essay on Government, 1s —— 1713
5318 Thoughts concern. Government, 6d —— 1713
5319 Memorials of Affairs of State, 6d —— 1740
5320 Case of the Surrender of Mr. Knight consid. 6d 1721
5321 Naked Truth, 6d —— —— 1735
5322 Faction detected by the Evidence of Facts, 1s — 1743
5323 True State of England, 1s —— 1726
5324 Project for securing the Church and State, 6d — 1723
5325 Collect. of Cases, &c. in Parliament, 1s —— 1757
5326 Hist. of that Parliam. that sent Sir R. Walpole to the Tower, 6d —— —— 1763

5327 Pro-

5327 Propos. for Remed. the Charge of Suits at Law. 6d 1730
5328 Eight Speeches in Parl. on Import. Occasions, 1s 1733
5329 Asgill's Jure Divino, 6d —— 1710
5330 Short View of the unfortunate Reigns, 6d —— 1736
5331 Connak's Account of Princes of Wales, 6d — 1751
5332 Comber's Vind. of the Revolut. in 1688, 1s — 1758
5333 Causes of the late Rebellion, 6d —— 1746
5334 Reflexions on the Law and Lawyers, 6d — 1759
5335 Ollyffe's Essay to prevent Capit. Crimes, 6d — 1731
5336 Fielding on the Increase of Robbers, 1s —— 1751
5337 West on Treasons and Bills of Attainder, 6d —— 1716
5338 —— Inquiry into the Manner of making Peers, 2s 1719
5339 Animadv. on West's Inquiry, 1s 6d —— 1724
5340 Cond. of the Ministers of the P. Bill, 6d —— 1719
5341 Asgill on the Peerage Bill, 6d —— 1719
5342 Rom. Catholicks, &c, who refused the Oaths, 6d 1745
5343 Review of the Reign of George II. 2s —— 1762
5344 Hallifax's Character of K. Charles II. 1s 6d — 1750
5345 Enquiry into the Merit. of Assassinat. 6d —— 1738
5346 Middleton on the Roman Senate, 1s —— 1747
5347 Intrigues at the Conclave at chusing a Pope, 6d 1724
5348 Proceed. against Protest. in the Inquisit. 6d —— 1734
5349 Review of the propos'd Nat. of the Jews, 1s —— 1753
5350 Algern. Sydney's Letters to Mr. Saville, 1s —— 1742
5351 Letter on the Prospect of a Peace, 6d —— 1763
5352 Remarks on the Letter on Peace, 6d —— 1760
5353 Letter to the Duke of Newcastle, 6d —— 1757
5354 —— on Settling 100,000 l. per Ann. on the Prince, 6d
5355 —— upon the News of the Town, 6d — 1755
5356 —— on Affairs at Home and Abroad, 6d — 1740
5357 —— on K. of Prussia's Motives, 6d —— 1756
5358 —— to Mr. Pitt on his Resignation, 6d —— 1761
5359 Second and Third Letter to the Whigs, 6d —— 1748
5360 Letter from the Dss. of Marlb. in the Shades, 6d 1759
5361 Cathcart's Letter to Admiral Vernon, 6d —— 1744
5362 Letter to a late Noble Com. of the Br. Forces, 6d 1759
5363 —— to Lord Blakeney on his Def. of Minor, 6d 1757
5364 Third Letter to the People of Engl. 6d —— 1756
5365 Fifth Letter to the People of Engl. 1s —— 1757
5366 Blacow's Letter on the Oxford Riot 1747, 6d — 1755
5367 Letter of Cl. Tolomei on Princes punish. Magistr. and Ministers, 1s —— —— —— 1739
5368 Letter to Dr. Codex on his Instruct. to the Crown, 6d 1734
5369 Life and Conduct of Dr. Codex, 6d —— 1735
5370 View of the polite Writers in Gr. Brit. 6d —— 1740
5371 Account of the Suffer. of Serres for the Prot. Rel. 6d 1745
5372 Narrat. of the Deaths of the Engl. Gent. at Bengal, 6d 1759
5373 Lives of the Princes of Orange, 6d —— 1734
5374 Life of James Duke of Hamilton, 6d —— 1742
5375 —— the Marefchal Bellisle, 6d —— 1745
5376 —— of Judge Price, 6d —— 1734
5377 —— Barton Booth, Esq; 6d —— 1733
5378 Memoirs of Barton Booth, Esq; 1s —— 1733
5379 Life of Lord Lovat, 6d — —— 1746

5380 Lives

5380 Lives of the most eminent mod. Painters since De Piles wrote, 2s
5381 Life of Sr. Wenefrede, by Bp. Fleetwood, 6d 1754
5382 Memoirs of Dr. George Leyburn, 1s 1713
5383 ——— of Mr. Geo. Whitefield, 6d 1722
5384 Life of Dr. Tho. Bray, 6d 1742
5385 Hist. of the Heresie of Jo. Wicliffe, &c. 6d 1746
5386 Hist. of Thamas Kouli Kan, 6d 1717
5387 Life of Count Patkul, 6d 1741
5388 ——— Uriel Acosta a learned Jew, 6d 1717
5389 Adventures of Capt. De la Fontaine, 6d 1740
5390 Character of John Duke of Buckingham, 6d 1741
5391 Memoirs of the Q. Dowag. of Spain, 6d 1729
5392 Life of the Marchioness Urbino, 1s 1746
5393 Egerton's Life of Mrs. Oldfield, 2s 1735
5394 Life of Polly Haycock, 6d 1731
5395 Ans. to Frauds and Abuses at St. Paul's, 6d 1713
5396 Inquiry into the late Proceed. of the Univ. of Oxford, 6d 1751
5397 Account of the Differ. betw. the Mr. and Fellows Trin. Col. Camb. 6d
5398 Defence of the Rector, &c. of Exeter Col. Oxf. 6d 1711
5399 Conybeare's Answ. to Dr. Newton in relat. to Hart Hall, 1s 6d 1754
5400 Management of Card. Alberoni, 6d 1735
5401 Rules and Orders for suppress. the Rage of Fires, 6d 1718
5402 Standing Orders of the House of Lords, 1s 1715
5403 Depositions concern. the Riot at Oxford, 6d 1744
5404 Fiction unmasked, by Harris, 1s 1716
5405 List of the Abscenters of Ireland, 6d 1752
5406 Observat. on the pres. State of Ireland, 6d 1730
5407 Thoughts on the Tillage of Ireland, 6d 1731
5408 Schemes from Ireland Eccles. and Politic. 6d 1737
5409 Ill Situation of the Affairs of Ireland, 6d 1732
5410 Pres. State of Ireland considered, 6d 1732
5411 Tracts concern. the pres. State of Ireland, 6d 1730
5412 Hist. of the Dublin Election 1749, 6d 1729
5413 Tour through Ireland, 1s 6d 1753
5414 Conclusion of Burnet's Hist. of his Own Times, 6d 1746
5415 Reflect. on Burnet's Posthum. History, 1s 1734
5416 Rymer's 1st Letter to Bp. Nicholson, 6d 1724
5417 ——— 2d Letter to Bp. Nicholson, 6d 1702
5418 Cockburn's Remarks relat. to Scotland, 1s 1702
5419 Causes of Miscarriage at Darien, 6d
5420 Defence of the Scots abdicat. Darien, 6d 1700
5421 ——— of the Scots Settlem. at Darien answ. 6d 1700
5422 Rose, or Detect. of Old Engl. Journal and Thistle, 6d
5423 Scot Gent. Letter on the Depend. of Scotland, 6d
5424 Propos. for public Works at Edinburgh, 6d 1746
5425 Martin's Voyage to St. Kilda, 6d
5426 Rise and pres. State of the Magdalen Charity, 1s 1749
5427 Regulations of the Foundling Hospital, 6d 1761
5428 State of the Navigat. of Lyn, Wisbeach and Boston, 1s 1756
5429 Cat. of the Duke of Powis's Estate at Hendon, 1s 1751
5430 Wood's Descript. of the Exchange at Bristol, 2s 1745

5431 Cow-

5431 Cowley's Descript. of Wilton House, 1s —— 1752
5432 Summary of Religious Houses in Engl. and Wales, 1s 1717
5433 Woodward's Account of Rom. Urns near Bishopsgate, 6d 1713
5434 The same, 3*d edit.* 1s —— —— 1723
5435 Burrington on the Numb. of Inhabit. in London, 6d 1757
5436 Account of New Forest and Richmond Park, 6d 1751
5437 Collection of Welch Travels, 6d — —— 1738
5438 Skurrey's Descript. of the City of Heraclea, 1s — 1750
5439 Webb's Catalog. of Seeds and hardy Plants, 6d 1760
5440 Switzer's Method of rais. Brocoli, 6d —— 1729
5441 Tremblay's Art of Hatching Fowls, 6d —— - 1750
5442 Tusser's 500 Points of Husbandry, 2s —— 1745
5443 Six Letters from A——d B——r to Fath. Shelden, 6d 1756
5444 Bower's Answer to the Six Letters, 6d —— 1741
5445 The same, 2 parts, 1s —— —— 1757
5446 Final Detection of A——d B——r, 1s — 1758
5447 Bower's Answer to a New Charge, 6d —— 1757
5448 ——— Reply to the full Confutation, 6d —— 1757
5449 ——— Affidavit, 6d —— —— 1756
5450 Conduct of the Jesuits relat. to Mr. Bower, 6d — 1758
5451 Examinat. of the Laws of Nature, 6d — 1750
5452 Thoughts concern. Happiness, 6d — —— 1738
5453 Temple's Sketches, 6d —— —— 1758
5454 Place on Space a necessary Being, 6d —— 1728
5455 Lyon on the Infallib. of Hum Judgment, 6d — 1723
5456 Polite Philosopher, 6d —— —— 1758
5457 Hay's Essay on Deformity, 6d ——— 1754
5458 Essay on Lying, 6d —— —— 1720
5459 Cheyne's Account of himself and Writings, 6d — 1744
5460 Zouch on the Punishm. of Ambassadors, 6d —— 1757
5461 Ranby's Narrative of Lord Orford's Illness, 6d — 1745
5462 Vices of London and Westminster, 6d
5463 Archer on social Bliss, 6d — — 1749
5464 Picture of Love unveiled, by Norris, 6d —— 1744
5465 Proceed. betw. Mrs. Weld and her Husband, 1s — 1732
5466 Asgil on Divorce, 6d —— —— 1717
5467 Modest Defence of the Stews, 1s —— 1740
5468 Self Murder and Duelling the Effects of Cowardice, 6d 1728
5469 Killing no Murder, 6d —— —— 1745
5470 Mr. Foote's Letter in Defence of the Minor, 6d — 1760
5471 Four Letters betw. a Noble Lord and a young Lady, 6d 1762
5472 Eight Letters on the Custom of Vails Giving, 6d 1760
5474 Letter on the Right of Appeal from the Chanc. of the Univ. in Matters of Discipline, 6d —— —— 1752
5475 Letters on the Gen. Reading of the Gr. Test. 1 Tim. iii. 16. 1s —— —— 1758
5476 Hervey's Letter to Sir Tho. Hanmer, 1s
5477 Proper Reply to Hervey's Letter to Hanmer, 1s — 1742
5478 Measure for Measure, in Ans. to the prop. Reply, 1s 1742
5479 Letter to Lady Vane on her Memoirs in Pereg. Pickle, 6d 1751
5480 ——— a Bencher of the Inner Temple, 6d —— 1729
5481 Card. Bentivoglio's Letters, 1s —— 1753
5482 Unfortunate Mother's Advice to her absent Daughter, 6d 1761
5483 Dissertat. upon Horace, 6d — —— 1708

5484 Squire

5484 Squire on the Gr. Chronology and Language, 1s 6d 1741
5485 Avison's Defence of his Music. Expression, 6d — 1753
5486 Essay on the Liberty of the Press, 6d
5487 Proceed. at Cambridge against the W—r Club, 6d 1750
5488 Shower's Reflexions on Earthquakes, 6d — 1750
5489 Bp. Berkley's Querist, 1s — — 1750
5490 Theology and Philosophy in Cicero's Somn. Scipio. explained, 6d — — 1751
5491 Disputat. on the State of the Univ. of Cambridge, 6d 1750
5492 Remarks on Sir Ch. Grandison, Clarissa and Pamela, 6d 1754
5493 Formey's Discourse on the Death of Marsh. Keith, 1s *Edinb.* 1764
5494 Expediency of securing our Americ. Colonies, 6d *ib.* 1763
5495 Egotist, or Colley upon Cibber, 6d — 1743
5496 Modest Apology for my own Conduct, 6d — 1753
5497 Curliad, a Hypercritic on the Dunciad, 6d — 1729
5498 Essay on Tragedy, 6d — — 1749
5499 Edwards's Canons of Criticism, 1s — 1750
5500 Letter to Mr. Warburton on Shakespear, 6d — 1750
5501 Oldmixon's Essay on Criticism, 6d — 1728
5502 Jortin's Remarks on Spenser's Poems, 1s 6d — 1734
5503 Common Sense a common Delusion, 6d — 1752
5504 Perronet's Vindicat. of Mr. Locke, part 1. 6d — 1736
5505 The same, 2 parts, 1s — — 1736
5506 Terracon on anc. and mod. Learning, 6d — 1716
5507 Essay on the Useful. of Mathemat. Learning, 6d 1701
5508 Useful Transact. in Philosophy, 6d — 1709
5509 Apology for Mr. Toland, 6d — — 1697
5510 Toland's Pantheisticon, 1s — — 1757
5511 Reflect. on Toland's Amyntor, 6d — 1699
5512 Bentley's Remarks on Freethinking, 1s — 1737
5513 Dialogue in the Shades below, 6d
5514 Hobbs on Liberty and Necessity, 6d — 1684
5515 De la Faye on Virgil's Gates of Sleep, 1s — 1743
5516 Gwyn's Essay on Design, 6d — 1749
5517 Reply to Dr. Golding and Mr. Lowth, 6d — 1759
5518 Dr. King's Oration at Oxford, 6d — 1750
5519 Apology for the Monthly Review, 6d — 1763
5520 Occasional Critic, 6d — — 1757
5521 True State of the People called Unitas Fratrum, 1s 1755
5522 Behaviour of gr. Churchmen since the Reformat. 6d 1748
5523 Examinat. on the Scheme of Ch. Power in Gibson's Codex, 1s — — 1735
5524 Turner on Ecclesiast. Authority, 6d — 1716
5525 Treatise on St. Matthias's Day, 6d — 1719
5526 Ancient and modern Idolatry compared, 6d — 1716
5527 Rudd's Observat. on the Engl. Letters, 6d — 1755
5528 Holmes's French Grammar, 6d — 1741
5529 Albion, a Poem by Theobald, 6d — 1720
5530 Westminster Verses on the Coronat of K. Geo. II. and Q. Caroline, 6d — — 1761
5531 Naval Lyric in Imitat of Pindar, 6d — 1730
5532 Jones's Poems on several Occasions, 1s — 1749
5533 War with Priestcraft, a Poem, 6d — 1732
5534 Armstrong's Art of preserv. Health, 1s — 1745

U 5535 Por-

5535 Portraiture of Socrates, 6d —— —— 1717
5536 Coriolanus, a Tragedy by Thomson, 6d —— 1749
5537 Boadicia, a Tragedy by Glover, 6d —— 1753
5538 Alfred, a Masque by Mallet, 6d —— 1751
5539 Comus, a Masque by Milton, 6d —— 1738
5540 Gil Blas, a Comedy, by Moore, 6d —— 1751
5541 Man of Taste, a Comedy by Millar, 6d —— 1735
5542 Distressed Wife, a Comedy by Gay, 6d —— 1743
5543 Englishman in Bourdeaux, a Comedy, 6d —— 1764
5544 Amorous War, a Trag. Comedy, 1s —— 1659
5545 Smith's Compend. Division, 6d —— 1751
5546 Simpson's Trigonometry, 1s — —— 1748
5547 Smith's Treatise of Fluxions, 6d —— 1737
5548 Martin on Visual Glasses, 6d —— 1758
5549 Ferguson on the Harvest Moon, 6d —— 1747
5550 Jackson's Harmony of Sounds, 1s —— 1726
5551 Ham's Laws of Chance, 1s —— —— 1738
5552 Hugenius's Value of Chances, 6d —— 1714
5553 Mathematician, No. 1. 6d — —— 1745
5554 Turner's Mathematic. Exercises, 6d —— 1750
5555 Jurin upon distinct and indistinct Vision, 6d — 1739
5556 Davenport's Table Air Pump, 6d —— 1737
5557 Steele's Account of the Fish Poole, 6d —— 1718
5558 Account of Earthquakes, 6d —— 1750
5559 Dissertat. on Metaphys. Nat. Philos. and Theology, 6d 1747
5560 Leekey on the Use of the Pen, 6d —— 1744
5561 Cole's Short Hand, 6d —— —— 1707
5562 Webster's Book keeping, 6d —— 1749
5563 Shaw's Grammat. Dict. of the Lat. Tongue, 6d 1726
5564 Wintringham on Elixity of the Hum. Body, 6d 1743
5565 Reflect. on Bleeding, Vomit. and Purg. in Fevers, 6d 1728
5566 Willan on the King's Evil, 6d —— 1746
5567 Reflexions Physical and Moral on the Air and Water, 6d 1756
5568 Haller on the sensible Part of Animals, 6d — 1755
5569 Knight on Catholicons, 6d — —— 1749
5570 Douglas on the Effects of Bark in Mortificat. 6d 1732
5571 Bennet on the Gout, 6d — —— 1734
5572 Gataker on the Use of Knight Shade, 6d — 1757
5573 Ayscough on the Use of Spectacles, 6d —— 1752
5574 Cheseiden's Append. to his Anatomy, 6d — 1730
5575 Mead on Poisons, 6d —— —— 1702
5576 Discourse on Convulsions in Children, 6d — 1721
5577 Observat. on Epidemic. Fevers, 6d —— 1741
5578 Ingram on the Plague, 1s 6d —— 1755
5579 Colbatch on the Plague, 6d — —— 172
5580 Midriff's Observat. on the Spleen and Vapours, 6d 1721
5581 Essay on the Skin of Human Bodies, 6d —— 1724
5582 Hermippus Redivivus, 1s — —— 1744
5583 Burges on Inoculation, 6d — —— 1754
5584 Monro's Remarks on Battie's Treat. of Madness, 6d 1758
5585 Dissertat. on the Lues Venerea, 6d —— 1731
5586 Hauksbee on the Venereal Disease, 6d —— 1743
5587 Boerhaave's Experim. on Mercury, 6d
5588 Harris on crude Mercury, 6d —— 1734

5589 Trea-

5589 Treatife of the Ufe and Properties of Quickfilver, 6d
5590 Seehl on the Volat. Salt. of Sulphur, 6d —
5591 Method of Curing the Plague among the Cattle, 6d 1744
5592 Brocklefby on the Mortality among the Cattle, 6d 1747
5593 Davies on the Peftilent. Contag. among the Cattle, 6d 1746
5594 Layard on the Contag. Diftemp. among the Cattle, 6d 1757
5595 Proceed. of Chelfea Hofpit. againft Mr. Lee, Surgeon, 6d 1757
5596 Ranby's Account of the Tranfact. againft Mr. Lee, 6d 1753
5597 Glafs's Cafe of Geo. Griffin relat. to a Fracture in the Head, 6d —— —— 1754
5598 Maffey on the Diftemp. of Mr. Hurdman, 6d — 1739
5599 Thomfon's Cafe of Mr. Winnington, 6d —— 1730
5600 Douglas's Anfw. to Thompfon's Cafe, 6d — 1746
5601 Campbell's Anfw. to Thompfon's Cafe, 6d —— 1746
5602 Quincy's Exam. of Woodward's State of Phyfic, 6d 1746
5603 Account of Medic. Controverfy in the City of Cork, 6d 1719
5604 Douglas's Letter to Dr. Smelle, 6d —— 1749
5605 Defence of the Letter to Dr. Lobb on his Writings, 6d 1748
5606 Grounds of Phyfick examined, 6d 1753
5607 Tennet's Phyfical Enquiries, 6d —— 1703
5608 Dover's Legacy to his Country, 1s —— 1742
5609 Arnaud's Alarm touching Health, 6d —— 1732
5610 Abufes in the Practice of Phyfic, 6d —— 1740
5611 Modern Quacks, or Phyfic. Impoftor detected, 6d 1752
5612 Apothecary detected, 6d —— 1718
5613 Two Socias, or the true Dr. Byfield, 6d —— 1748
5614 Bp. Berkley on Tar-Water, 6d —— 1719
5615 Prior on Tar Water, 1s —— —— 1744
5616 Anti Siris, or Engl. Wifdom relat. to Tar Water, 6d 1746
5617 Experiments on the Malvern Waters, 6d 1744
5618 Hoffman on Mineral Waters, with Notes by Shaw, 1s 1731
5619 Phyfical Ufe of Com. Water 1726 — Treatife of Warm Drink, 1s —— ——
5620 Hancock of Com. Water the beft Cure for Fevers, 6d 1725
5621 Smith's Curiofities of Com. Water, 6d —— 1723
5622 Watfon on Electricity, 2 parts, 1s —— 1723
5623 Lambert's Art of Confectionary, 6d 1746
5624 Perfect Practice of Gardening, 6d ——
5625 Inquiry into the Nature, &c. of Baptifm, 1s — 1759
5626 Letters betw. the Bp. of Clogher and Mr. Penn on Baptifm, 6d —— —— 1757
5627 White's 3 Letters to a Diffent. Gent. 6d —— 1756
5628 Sharp on the Heb. Words Elohim and Berith, 1s 1747
5629 Adam's Effay on Miracles, 1s —— 1751
5630 Woolfton's 1ft Difcourfe on Miracles, 1s —— 1742
5631 ——— 2d Difcourfe on Miracles, 1s —— 1728
5632 ——— 3d Difcourfe on Miracles, 1s —— 1727
5633 Owen on Scripture Miracles, 1s —— 1728
5634 Dodwell's Anfw. to Middleton on Miracles, 6d — 1755
5635 Middleton's Examin. of Sherlock on Prophecy, 1s 1749
5636 Lardner's Remarks on Ward's Differt. on Script. 1s 1750
5637 Leland's Reflect. on Bolingbroke's Letter, 1s — 1702
5638 Shaftfbury on Enthufiafm, 6d —— 1753
5639 Young's Vindicat. of Providence, 6d —— 1708
1747

U 2 5640 Pro

5640 Proceed. againſt Profeſſor Simſon, 6d —— 1727
5641 Caſe of Profeſſor Simſon, 6d —— 1727
5642 Animadv. on the Caſe of Profeſſ. Simſon, 6d — 1728
5643 Trial of Will. Whiſton, before L. C. J. Reaſon, 6d — 1734
5644 Hiſt. of Ancient Paganiſm, 6d —— 1743
5645 Defence of the Ch. of Engl. from Prieſtcraft, 6d 1711
5646 Burnet's State of the Dead, 1s —— — 1727
5647 —— Theory of the Viſible World, 1s —— 1729
5648 Jackſon on Matter and Spirit, 6d —— 1735
5649 Sufficien. and Perfect. of the Scripture, 6d —— 1719
5650 Petition to prevent the Smuggling of Souls, 6d 1752
5651 Reflect. on the Death of Freethinkers, 6d —— 1713
5652 Inquiry whether the Chr. Religion is a Benefit, 6d 1732
5653 Blow at the Root, 6d —— —— 1749
5654 Heathcote's Reply to Patten's Serm. on Reaſon, 1s 1756
5655 Rimius's Supplem. to the Narrat. of the Moravians, 1s 1755
5656 Colliber's Enquiry into the Nature of God, 6d 1718
5657 Barrow on the Pre-exiſtent Lapſe of Hum. Souls, 1s 1762
5658 Four Queries concern. Miracles, 6d —— 1747
5659 Natural Eſtate of the Hum. Body and Soul, 6d —— 1753
5660 Vindication of Mankind, 6d —— 1717
5661 Letters and Diſſertat. on Religion, 6d —— 1747
5662 Thoughts on Man's Free Agency, 6d
5663 Enquiry into the Evid. of the Chr. Religion, 6d — 1728
5664 Benſon's Evidences of Chriſt's Reſurrection, 6d — 1754
5665 Law of Truth, 6d —— —— 1733
5666 Sequel to the Eſſay on Spirit, 6d —— — 1752
5667 High Flown Epiſcop. Claims examined, 6d —— 1737
5668 Dialogue betw. a Japoneſe and Formoſan, 6d —— 1707
5669 Conference between a Myſtic. an Hutchinſon, a Calvin. &c. 6d —— —— —— 1761
5670 —— between two Popiſh Prieſts and ſome Proteſt. Divines, 6d —— —— —— 1735
5671 Remarks on the Bp. of Litchfield and Coventry's Charges, 6d 1738
5672 Waterland's Uſe of the Sacraments, 6d —— 1736
5673 Rutherforth's four Charges, 6d —— —— 1763
5674 Troughear's Defence of the Athan. Creed, 6d 1760
5675 Explanat. of 1 Cor. xi. 6d —— — 1755
5676 Faweit's Expoſit. of the 9th Chap. of Romans, 6d —— 1752
5677 Lardner on Romans xi. 11. 6d —— — 1752
5678 Diſcourſe on Governm. and Religion, calculated for the 30th of January, 1s
5679 Exception to Hoadly's Plain Account of the Sacrament, 6d 1736
5680 Wincheſter Converts, 6d —— —— 1735
5681 Whiſton's Prim. Euchariſt revived, 6d —— 1736
5682 Remarks on Hoadly's Plain Account, 6d —— 1735
5683 Second Letter to Hoadly, 6d —— 1735
5684 Caſe of Subſcrip. to the 39 Articles, 6d —— 1721
5685 Middleton's Letter to Dr. Waterland, 6d —— 1731
5686 Hare on the Study. Script. 6d —— 1735
5687 Chandler's Inſtitut. of the Sabbath, 6d —— 1761
5688 Pillars of Hell Torments ſhaken, 1s —— 1754
5689 Three Queſtions on Religion, 6d —— 1757
5690 Tryal of the Witneſſes of the Reſurrect. of Jeſus, 6d 1733

5691 Re-

5691 Resurrection of Jesus considered, by Annet, 2s —
5692 Sequel of the Resur. of Jesus considered, 1s
5693 Resurrect. of Jesus demonstrat. to have no Proof, 1s
5694 Resurrect. reconsidered, 1s 6d — —
5695 Resurrect. Defenders stript of all Defence, 1s 6d 1744
5696 Supernaturals examined, 2s 1745
5697 Evidence of the Resurrection cleared, 6d —
5698 Hist. and Charact. of St. Paul examined, 2s 1744
5699 Hist. of Joseph considered, 1s 6d —
5700 Deism fairly stated, by a Moral Philos. 1s — 1744
5701 Morgan's Vind. of the Moral Philosopher, 1s — 1746
5702 Dissert. on the Light of the Gospel and Nature, 1s 1741
5703 Epist. to the Admirers of the Bp. of Lond. Letter, 6d
5704 Short Survey of the Bible, 1s — 1750
5705 Bradbury's Sermons on Prof. Swearing, 6d — 1753
5706 Croxall's Answ. to the Bp. of Lond. Pastor. Letter, 6d 1742
5707 Sermon on the Union, 6d — 1730
5708 Lavington's Nature of a Type, 1s 6d — — 1745
5709 Smalbroke's Serm. on Propagat. the Gospel, 6d 1734
5710 Bisse's Beauty of Holiness, Com. Prayer, 6d 1733
5711 Storck de Cicuta, pars 2. 1s — — 1716
5712 Hartley de Lithontriptico, a J. Stephens, 6d — 1761
5713 Jurin Dissert. Physico-Mathematicæ, 6d — 1746
5714 Heathcote Hist. Astronomiæ, 6d — *Lond.* 1732
5715 Toupe Emendat. in Suidam, 2s 6d — — 1747
5716 Buchanani Logica, 6d — — 1760
5717 Museum Meadianum, 1s 6d — — *Lond.* 1737
5718 Welsted de Ætate Vergente, 6d — — *ibid.* 1755
5719 Synopsis Compend. Libror. Grotii, Clarkii & Lockii, 1s *ibid.* 1724
5720 Burton Versio Metrica SS. Scripturæ, 1s *Cant.* 1751
5721 Du Clos Elemens des Mathematiques, 1s — *Oxon.* 1736
5722 Arretez Princes Guerriers, 6d — *Lyon* 1737
5723 Il Riccio Rapito, di Alesf. Pope, 1s — *Haye* 1761
Firenz. 1739

Pamphlets. TWELVES.

5724 DECKER on the Decline of Foreign Trade, 1s 1750
5725 Misselden on Free Trade, 1s — 1622
5726 Locke's further Consider. on the Value of Money, 1s 1695
5727 Puckle's England's Path to Wealth, 6d 1700
5728 Decus & Tutamen, a Treat. on Money, 6d — 1696
5729 Clark's Landed Man's Assistant, 6d —
5730 Judicature of the H. of Peers in Appeals, 6d — 1675
5731 Toland's Account of Berlin and Hanover, 6d — 1705
5732 Davies's Causes why Irel. was never sub. 1s — 1747
5733 Greave's on Engl. Weights and Measures, 1s — 1745
5734 History of the Art of Engraving, *with cuts and engraved marks,* 2s — — — 1747
5735 Grey's Memoria Technica, 6d — 1730
5736 Bion on the Torments of the Fr. Protestants, 6d 1708
5737 Adventures of Mr. Judas Hawke, 1s — 1751
5738 Life and Charact. of Count Bruhl, 1s
5739 Hist. of Croesus K. of Lydia, 6d — — 1755

5740 Oeco-

5740 Oeconomy of Human Life, 6d ——— 1751
5741 School of Man, 6d ——— ——— 1753
5742 Clarke on Education, 6d —— —— 1720
5743 Jennings on the Nat. and Orig. of Evil, 1s —— 1759
5744 Hutcheson's Thoughts on Laughter, 6d ——— 1758
5745 Defence of Locke on Hum. Understand. 6d —— 1702
5746 Infallibility of Hum. Judgment, 6d ——— 1719
5747 Orrery's Remarks on the Life of Dr. Swift, 1s —— 1752
5748 Joe Miller's Jests, 6d
5749 Teagueland Jests, 6d ——— ——— 1747
5750 Tryal of Witches, before Sir M. Hale, 6d — 1682
5751 Secret Instruct. of the Jesuites, 6d ——— 1723
5752 Ferguson's Scottish Proverbs, 1s ——— 1687
5753 Nomenclature, Engl. and Ital. 1s ——— 1726
5754 Hoyle's Game of Whist, 6d —— —— 1743
5755 Armstrong's Art of Preserv. Health, 1s ——— 1757
5756 Pope's Essay on Man, by Warburton, 1s ——— 1745
5757 Scribleriad, an Heroic Poem, 6d ——— 1752
5758 Tyrtæus's Elegies, in Engl. 6d ——— 1761
5759 Clouds, a Comedy, by Aristophanes, 1s —— 1759
5760 Whole Prophecies of Scot. Engl. Fr. Irel. and Denmark, 6d 1680
5761 Cherrie on the Slac. in Scots Meeter, by Montgomery, 6d 1675
5762 K. Henry VIII. against Luther on the Sacraments, 6d 1688
5763 Elwall's Way to remove Hirelings out of the Church, 6d 1738
5764 Watts on Holiness of Times and Places, 6d —— 1738
5765 Adams on Miracles, 6d —— ——— 1754
5766 Simpson's Princip. of Nat. Bodies, 6d ——— 1677
5767 Wonderful Cure of Mary Mallard, 6d ——— 1694
5768 Primitive Physic, 6d
5769 Dover's Physicians Legacy, 1s —— — 1733
5770 James's Dissert. on Fevers, 6d —— —— 1749
5771 Hansell's Causes of Diseases, 6d ——— 1730
5772 Gould on Ants, 6d —— ——— 1747
5773 Musei Petiveriani Centuriæ X. 1s 6d —— *Lond.* 1695
5774 Burgelii Exercitat. Academicæ, 6d ——— *Lips.* 1739
5775 Welchman in XXXIX Artic. Eccles. Angl. 6d *Oxon.* 1713
5776 Compend. Artis Logicæ, 6d ——— *ibid.* 1696
5777 Vida de Arte Poetica, 6d —— — *ibid.* 1723
5778 Ignoramus Comœdia, 6d ——— *Westm.* 1731
5779 Memoires d'un Militaire, 1s —— *Wesel* 1759
5780 Hist. du Marquis de Fratteaux, 1s ——— *Par.* 1753
5781 Lettre de M. L *** a M. B ***, 6d ——— *Haye* 1751
5782 Lettres de M. Van Hoey, 6d —— *Lond.* 1743
5783 Candide, par Voltaire, partie 2. 1s ——— 1761
5784 Reflexions sur le Comique Larmoyant, 6d *Par.* 1749
5785 ——— sur les Femmes, 6d —— *Lond.* 1730
5786 Les Animaux plusque Machines, 6d —— 1750
5787 Motifs pour la Liberte du Commerce du Levant, 6d *Leyde* 1755
5788 Le Pythagore Moderne, 6d —— — 1762
5789 Discours sur la Liberte du Dannemarc, 6d — *Copen.* 1760
5790 Cabinet du Cabinet au Luxembourg, 6d —— *Par.* 1761
5791 La Farce de M. P. Pathelin, 1s —— *ib.* 1723
5792 Tragedie de Semiramis, 1s —— —— *ib.* 1749
5793 Propoz Rustiques, 1s —— —— 1732

APPEN-

APPENDIX.

FOLIO.

5794 ATLAS Maritimus & Commercialis, or General View of the World, so far as it relates to Trade and Navigation, describing all the Coasts, Ports, Harbours, and noted Rivers, *with 54 large charts, half bound,* 1l 5s —— —— 1728

5795 Dart's Hist. and Antiq. of the Cathedral Church of Canterbury, *with a great number of cuts, large paper, best impressions,* 1l 1s 1727

5796 Bible, with Com. Prayer and Apocrypha, *a beautiful copy, large paper, ruled with red lines, bound in turkey, and gilt leaves,* 4l 4s *Cambridge, printed by Buck and Daniel* 1638

5797 Bible, with Apocrypha, *adorned with* 300 *fine cuts, neatly engraved by Sturt, an exceeding fine copy, ruled with red lines, elegantly bound in blue turkey, with large silver clasps, and gilt leaves, with a russia leather case, fine paper,* 5l 5s —— *Edinb. by Watson* 1722

5798 Bible, with Apocrypha, *royal paper, bound in rough calf,* 2l 2s *Oxford* 1739

5799 Ceremonies and Religious Customs of all the Nations in the World, *with a great number of cuts, by Picart, large paper,* 6 vol. *new and elegantly bound in russia, marble leaves,* 8l 8s —— 1733

5800 Madox's Baronia Anglica, and Index to the Hist. of the Exchequer, *large paper,* 18s —— —— 1736

5801 Camden's Britannia, with Additions by Bp. Gibson, *with cuts and maps,* 2 vol. *best edition,* 2l 10s —— 1722

5802 Borlase's Nat. Hist. & Antiquit. of Cornwall, *with cuts,* 2 vol. *very neat,* 4l 4s —— —— 1754

5803 Complete History of England, with the Lives of all the Kings and Queens, collected by Bp. Kennet, 3 vol. *very fair and neat, best edition,* 1l 11s 6d —— —— 1719

5804 *Collection of Prints from Poussin and C. Lorrain, by Arth. Pond, Esq; very fair, in boards,* 3l 3s

5805 Harris's Collection of Voyages and Travels, greatly improved and brought down to the present Time, by Campbell, *with cuts and maps,* 2 vol. *very neat,* 4l 14s 6d —— 1744

5806 Clarendon's Hist. of the Rebellion, 3 vol. *very fair, bound in vellum,* 2l 5s —— —— *Oxford* 1707

5807 Clarendon's History of the Civil War, *with cuts and plans,* and his Life and Continuat. 2 vol. *neatly bound,* 2l 12s 6d *Oxford,* 1732 and 1759

5808 Dugdale's Antiquities of Warwickshire, with Additions, by Dr. Thomas, *with cuts,* 2 vol. *very fair,* 3l 15s

5809 Horsley's Britannia Romana, or Roman Antiquities of Britain, *illustrated with above* 100 *cuts, very fair,* 2l 8s — 1732

5810 The same, *large paper, elegantly bound in russia, with a gold border, gilt leaves,* 4l 10s —— —— 1732

5811 Tanner's

5811 Tanner's Notitia Monaſtica, or Account of all the Abbies, Priories, and Houſes of Friers in Engl. and Wales, *neatly bound,* 1l 15s 1744
5812 Hiſt. of the Life and Reign of K. William III. by Harris, *with plans of ſieges, and other cuts, new and neat,* 18s — *Dublin* 1749
5813 Hollingſhed's Chronicles, with the Caſtrations, *very fair and neatly bound, in* 4 vol. 4l 4s —— —— 1586
5814 Carte's General Hiſt. of England, 4 vol. *new and neat,* 4l 14s 6d 1747, &c.
5815 Tyrrel's General Hiſt. of England, 5 vol. 1l 11s 6d 1697
5816 Brady's Hiſtory of England, 3 vol. *very fair and neat,* 1l 1s 1684
5817 Complete Collection of State Tryals, 6 vol. *very fair and neat,* 6l 6s —— —— —— 1730
5818 The ſame, 8 vol. *compleat, and very fair and neat,* 13l 13s 1730
5819 Gibbs's Rules for Drawing Architecture, *with cuts, very fair and neat,* 15s —— —— —— 1753
5820 Drayton's Poetical Works, 14s —— —— 1748
5821 *Dictionary of Deciſions of the Court of Seſſion,* 2 *vol. large paper, new and neatly bound,* 3l 10s —— —— *Edinb.* 1741
5822 Spence's Polymetis, *with a great number of cuts, the firſt impreſſions, very fair and neat,* 2l 15s —— — 1747
5823 Foſter's Crown Law, *elegantly bound, marble leaves,* 1l 5s 1752
5824 Bp. Smalridge's Sermons, 10s —— — 1724
5825 Engliſh Euclide, being the firſt ſix Elements of Geometry, with Annotations, by Scarburgh, *large paper, in boards,* 5s 1705
5826 Grotius on War and Peace, with Barbeyrac's Notes, *fair and neat,* 1l 1s —— —— —— 1738
5827 Stackhouſe's Hiſt. of the Bible, *with cuts, the beſt impreſſions,* 2 vol. *very fair,* 2l 5s —— —— 1752
5828 Another Copy, *with cuts,* 2 vol. 1l 10s —— 1742
5829 Mackenzie's Lives and Characters of Eminent Writers of the Scots Nation, 3 vol. 1l 11s 6d —— —— 1722
5830 Pantoppidan's Natural Hiſtory of Norway, *with a great many cuts, new and neatly bound,* 18s
5831 Jacob's Law Dictionary, *beſt edition, new and neatly bound,* 1l 4s
5832 Drummond of Hawthornden's Works, 6s —— 1711
5833 The ſame, *very fair and neat,* 7s 6d —— 1711
5834 Bayle's Dictionary, with his Life, by Des Maizeaux, 5 vol. 4l —— —— —— 1734
5835 Biographia Britannica, or Lives of moſt eminent Perſons who have flouriſhed in Great Britain and Ireland, 6 vol. *in boards,* 7l 1747
5836 Kæmpfer's Hiſtory of Japan, *with a great number of cuts,* 2 vol. 1l 5s —— —— —— 1727
5837 Another Copy, *new and very neatly bound, in* 1 *vol.* 1l 7s 1727
5838 Scott's Chriſtian Life, *very fair,* 9s —— 1729
5839 Juvenal and Perſius, by Dryden, *large paper,* 5s 1693
5840 Gianone's Hiſtory of the Kingdom of Naples, Engl. by Ogilvie, 2 vol. 2l 2s —— —— —— 1729
5841 Holmes's Academy of Armory, or Diſplay of Heraldry, *a great number of cuts, very fair,* 10s 6d —— 1701
5842 Stebbings's Polemical Tracts, *very fair,* 5s —— 1727
5843 Archbiſhop Tillotſon's Works, 3 vol. 1l 5s —— 1720
5844 Lord Bacon's Works, with his Life, by Rawley, with the Appendix, 5 vol *very fair, neatly bound, marble leaves,* 2l 15s 1730, &c.
5845 Rea's Flora, or Complete Florilege, 2s 6d —— 1702

5846 Dixon

5846 Dixon on the Nature of the Two Testaments, *neatly bound in morocco, gilt leaves,* 6s ——— ——— 1675
5847 Evelyn of Medals, *with cuts, interleaved, in boards,* 6s 1697
5848 ——— Discourse of Forest Trees, 4s ——— 1679
5849 History of Appian of Alexandria, *very fair,* 7s 6d 1679
5850 Brown's Ars Pictoria, *with cuts, stained,* 4s ——— 1675
5851 Lomatius on Painting, Carving and Building, 4s ——— 1598
5852 Art de la Guerre par Principes & par Regles, par le Mareschal De Puysegur, *avec fig. grand papier, eleg. relie en marcq. dore & marbre sur les tranches,* 3l 3s ——— ——— *Par.* 1748
5853 Histoire de France, par M. Le Gendre, *grand papier,* 3 tom. *bien relie,* 1l 1s ——— ——— *ibid.* 1718
5854 Dictionaire, de Bayle, avec sa Vie, par Des Maizeaux, avec les Oeuvres de Bayle, 8 tom. *nouv. & elagamen. relie,* 8l 8s *Amst.* 1730, &c.
5855 Bibliotheque Historiq. de la France, avec des Notes, par M. Le Long, 12s ——— ——— *Par.* 1719
5856 *Dictionaire Geographique, Historiqu. & Critiq. par Martiniere,* 6 tom. *tres eleg. relie, dore & marbre sur les tranches,* 7l 7s *Dijon.* 1739
5857 Dictionaire de la Langue Francoise, par Richelet, 3 tom. *fort bien relie,* 1l 16s ——— ——— *Lyon.* 1718
5858 Andersoni Thesaurus Deplomat. & Numism. Scotia, *cum sigillis & chartis, exemp. pulch. nit. comp.* 3l 10s ——— *Edinb.* 1739
5859 Virgilii Bucolica, Georgica & Æneis, Italico Versu reddita ab Ant. Ambrogi, *cum fig. semi-comp. ch. max.* 1l 11s 6d *Romæ* 1763
5860 Poli Synopsis Criticorum, 5 tom. 1l 5s ——— *Lond.* 1669
5861 St. Athanasii Opera omnia, Gr. & Lat. *edit. Benedicti,* 3 tom. *semi-comp.* 2l 12s 6d ——— ——— *Par.* 1698
5862 Rumphii Herbarium Amboinense, Plurimas complectens Arbores, Fructius, Herbas, Plantas terrestres & aquaticas quæ in Amboina reperientur, *cum fig. multis,* 7 tom. *nov. & elegant. compact.* 8l 8s *Amst.* 1741, &c.
5863 Calasio Concordantiæ Bibl. Hebraicor. edidit. G. Romaine, 4 tom. *nit. comp.* 2l 12s 6d. ——— ——— *Lond.* 1747
5864 Thesaurus Brandenburgicus, sive Gemmar. Numismat. in Cimeliar. Elect. Branden. cum Comment. L. Begero, *& mult. fig.* 3 tom. *nov. & elegant. compact.* 2l 10s ——— ——— *Col.* 1696
5865 Museum Veronense, hoc est, Collectio Antiquar. Inscript. atq; Anaglyphorum, accedunt Taurinensis adjungitur & Vindobonensis, *cum fig. sutus,* 1l 7s ——— ——— *Veronæ* 1749
5866 Gratulatio Acad. Cantabrig. in Pacem, *ch. max. nov. & nitid. comp.* 4s ——— ——— *Cantab.* 1763
5867 Scapulæ Lexicon, Gr. Lat. *nov. & elegant. compact.* 1l 4s *L. B. ap. Elz.* 1652
5868 S. Skinner Etymologica Anglica, *cha. max. exemp. pulch.* 1l 1s *Lond.* 1671
5869 Strabonis Geographia, Gr. & Lat. a Casaubono, 15s *Par.* 1620
5870 Idem Lib. *edit. opt. exemplar pulch.* 2 tom. ——— *Amst.* 1707
5871 Paracelsi Opera omnia Medico-Chemico-Chirurgica, 2 tom. *nit. comp.* 6s ——— ——— ——— *Genev.* 1658
5872 Casauboni Animadvers. in Athen. Dipnosophistas, 5s *Lugd.* 1621
5873 Collection of the Gold and Silver Coins of the Kings of Scotland, from Robert to K. William and Q. Mary, 5s
5874 Am. Marcellinus, Annot. Valesii, *cum fig. exemp. pulch.* 12s *Par.* 1681

X 5875 Ger.

5875 Ger. Jo. Vossii Opera omnia, 6 tom. 3l 3s —— *Amst.* 1697
5876 Ang. Politiani Opera, 2 tom. *exemp. pulch. comp. in membr.* 18s *Venet. ap. Aldum* 1498
5877 Whartoni Anglia Sacra sive Hist. de Archiepisc. & Episcopis Angliæ, 2 tom. 9s —— —— *Lond.* 1691
5878 *Fred. Hoffmanni Opera omnia,* 6 tom. *nov. & elegant. compact.* 5l 5s
5879 Corn. Agrippa de Occulta Philosophia 1533—Jo. Reuchlin de Arte Cabalistica, 2s 6d —— —— *Hagenau* 1517
5880 Lister Historia Conchyliorum, Lib. 1 & 2. *sutus,* 5s *Lond.* 1685
5881 Cragii Jus Feudale, *edit. opt.* 16s —— *Edinb.* 1732
5882 Thesaurus Historiæ Helveticæ, *nit. comp.* 7s 6d *Tigur.* 1735
5883 Platonis Opera omnia, Græce, *cum procli comm.* 12s *Basil.* 1556
5884 Postlethwaite's Hist. of the Publ. Revenue, from 1688 to 1758, *half bound,* 1l 15s
5885 Military Hist. of the Duke of Marlborough and Pr. Eugene, *with a great number of cuts and plans,* 2 vol. *large paper, new and neat,* 2l 2s —— —— —— 1736
5886 Antiquity Explained and Represented in Sculpture, by Montfaucon, Engl. by Humphreys, with the Supplement, in 7 vol. *compleat,* 5l 5s —— —— —— 1721
5887 Swan's British Architect. *with 60 copper-plates,* 10s 6d 1745
5888 Salmon's Universal Traveller, *with a great number of cuts and maps,* 2 vol. *half bound,* 1l 8s —— —— 1752
5889 Lucan's Pharsalia, Engl. by Rowe, 7s 6d —— 1718
5890 Townsend's Hist. of the Conquest of Mexico, *with cuts,* 8s 1734
5891 Dr. J. Owen's Sermons, with his Life and Letters, 7s 6d 1721
5892 Le Bruyn's Voyage to the Levant, *with a great number of cuts, very fair,* 2l 15s —— —— —— 1702
5893 Broughton's Dictionary of all Religions, 2 vol. in one, 15s 1745
5894 Common Prayer, with the Form of consecrat. Bps. Pr. & Deacons, *very neat, and gilt leaves,* 7s 6d —— 1732
5895 Bayle's Dictionary, by Des Maizeaux, 5 vol. and the Biographia Britannica, 6 vol. in all 11 vol. *new and neatly bound,* 13l 13s
5896 Locke's Pieces, published by Des Maizeaux, 4s —— 1739
5897 —— on Hum. Understand. *best edition, in boards,* 3s 1706
5898 Castlenau's Memoirs of the Reigns of Cha. IX. and Fra. II. Kings of France, 4s —— —— 1724
5899 Du Pin's Hist. of Eccles. Writers 17 Centuries, *compleat,* in 6 vol. *very fair,* 1l 11s 6d —— —— 1696, &c.
5900 Ward's Lives of the Professors of Gresh. Coll. with the Founder's Life, *cuts,* 9s —— —— —— 1740
5901 Sir Tho. Brown's Works, 8s —— 1686
5902 Archbp. Usher's Life, and a Collection of 300 Letters, published by Parr, 5s —— —— 1686
5903 Hall's Chronycle, from the Reigne of Hen. IV. to Hen. VIII. *black letter,* 16s —— *imprynted by Grafton* 1550
5904 Camoen's Lusiad, Engl. by Fanshaw, 7s 6d —— 1655
5905 Earl of Orrery's Plays, 2s —— —— 1670
5906 Lord Brooke's Plays and Poems, 2s —— —— 1633
5907 Coke's 2d, 3d and 4th Institute, 2 vol. *best edition,* 2l 1681
5908 Siderfin's Reports, *very fair,* 4s —— —— 1683
5909 Lyndwood Provinciale, *very fair,* 5s —— *Oxon.* 1679
5910 Chishull Antiquitates Asiaticæ, *semi-comp. ch. max.* 9s *Lond.* 1728

5911 *Meermani*

5911 *Meermani Thesaurus Juris Civilis & Canonici,* 7 tom. *nov. & eleg. comp.* 6l 6s — — *Hag. Com.* 1751
5912 Vitringæ Comment. in Isaiam, 2 tom. *exemp. pulch.* 3l 16s *Leov.* 1714
5913 Arriani, Gr. & Lat. a Gronovio, *nit. comp. in membr.* 8s *Lugd. Bat.* 1704
5914 Dante con l'Espositione di Landino, *con fig.* 10s 6d *Venet.* 1564
5915 Plans & Desseins des Batimens, Cascades & Fontaines de la Moutagne d'Hiver dans Hesse Cassel, par Guerniere, 15s *Cassel* 1749

Appendix. QUARTO.

5916 MEmoires de Conde, Servant d'Eclaircissement & de Preuves a l'Histoire de Monf. De Thou, *grande papier, avec grande nomb. des portraits,* 6 tom. *tres elegam. relie en maroquin doree sur les tranches* 1743—Pieces Originales & Procedures du Proces fait, a Rob. Franc. Damiens, *grande paper, relie en maroquin, & doree sur les tranches,* 9l 9s — — — *Par.* 1757
5917 Histoire des Guerres d'Italie, par Guichardin traduit, d'Ital. *grande papier, & d'un grande nomb. des portraits tres eleg. relie en maroquin, & dorees sur les tranches,* 3 tom. 4l 4s — *ibid.* 1738
5918 Fontanini Eloquenza Italiana, *new and gilt,* 15s
5919 Oeuvres de Montesquieu, *nouveau & eleg. relie,* par Johnson, 3 tom. 2l 10s — — *Par.*
5920 Catullus, Tibullus & Propertius cura Vulpio, *elegantiss. compact.* per Johnson, *ch. max.* 4 tom. 4l 4s — *Patav.*
5921 Milton's Paradise Lost, with Notes, by Bp. Newton, *cuts, first impressions,* 2 vol. *new and very neat,* 2l 2s —
5922 Lord Bolingbroke's Works, 5 vol. *very fair,* 3l 13s 6d 1749
5923 Turpin's Art of War, by Otway, 2 vol. *in boards,* 1l 1s 1754
5925 Rimius's Memoirs of the House of Brunswick, *in boards,* 4s 1761
5926 Norden's Togograph. & Historic. Descript. of Cornwall, *with cuts, very fair,* 5s — — 1750
5927 Carew's Survey of Cornwall, 3s 6d — 1728
5928 Plans of Harbours, Bars, Bays and Roads in St. George's Channel, by Morris, *sewed,* 2s 6d — — 1723
5929 Moll's Atlas Minor, or 62 Maps of all the Empires, Kingdoms, &c. in the Known World, *neatly coloured,* 6s 1748
5930 Hooke's Rom. History, 3 vol. *new and neatly bound,* 2l 17s 1751, &c.
5931 Life of Erasmus, by Jortin, 2 vol. *neat,* 1l 5s —
5932 Castiglione's Courtier, and other Works, Ital. and Engl. *very neat, and gilt leaves,* 7s 6d — — 1758
5933 Life of Cicero, by Middleton, 2 vol. 1l 1s — 1727
5934 Sallust, Engl. with Political Discourses, by Gordon, *in boards,* 7s 6d — — — 1741
5935 Seneca's Tragedies, Engl. by Newton and others, *very fair and neat,* 2s 6d — — — 1744
5936 Arbuthnot's Tables of Ancient Coins, Weights and Measures, 10s 6d — — — 1581
5937 Ames's Historic. Account of Printing in Engl. *in boards,* 18s 1727
5938 Middleton's Introd. Discourse 1747—Hoadly on Respirat. 1740, and more Tracts, 2s 1749
5939 Garnett's Dissert. on the Book of Job, 2s 6d — 1749

X 2 5940 Cum-

5940 Cumberland's Laws of Nature, Engl. with an Introduct. on the Usefulness of Revelation, by Maxwell, 5s
5941 Lamy's Introduct. to the Holy Scriptures, by Bundy, *with cuts*, 7s 6d —— —— 1723
5942 Frezier's Voyage to the South Sea, *with cuts*, 9s 1717
5943 Historia de la Ville & Principaute d'Orange, *avec fig.* 5s *Avign.* 1741
5944 Sir T. Brown's Vulgar Errors and Relig. Medici, 2s 1672
5945 General Treatise of Monies and Exchanges, 5s — 1707
5946 Markham's Way to get Wealth, *very fair*, 2s —— 1676
5947 Ainsworth's Lat. & Eng. Dictionary, 2 vol. *very fair*, 14s 1736
5948 Hill's Review of the Royal Society, *neat*, 7s — 1751
5949 Æschyli Tragœdiæ, Gr. & Lat. curante de Pauw, 2 tom. *exemp. pulch. nit. comp.* 1l 15s —— *Hag. Com.* 1745
5950 Juvenalis & Persius, *nov. & nit. comp. fol. marmor.* 15s *Birming. ap.* Baskerville 1761
5951 Idem, *nit. compact.* 12s
5952 Virgilius, *nov. & elegant. compact. fol. deaurat.* 1l 7s *Birmingh. ap.* Baskerville 1757
5953 Suetonius Comment. Pitisci, *cum fig.* 2 tom. *exemp pulch. nitid. compact in membrana*, 1l 5s —— *Leovard.* 1714
5954 Q. Curtius, Notis Var. & Snakenburg, *exemp. pulch. nit. comp. in memb.* 1l —— —— *L. Bat.* 1724
5955 Tacitus, Notis Var. & Gronovii, 2 tom. *nov. & nit. compact.* 2l 2s *Traject. Bat.* 1721
5956 Idem, 2 tom. *nov. & elegantiss. compact. per* Johnson, 2l 6s
5957 Livius, Notis Var. & Drakenborch, 7 tom. *exemp. pulch. nit. comp.* 5l 5s —— —— *L. Bat.* 1738
5958 Buchanani Opera omnia, curante Ruddimanno, 2 tom. *semicomp.* 12s —— —— *ib.* 1725
5959 Virgilius, a Masvicio, *cum fig.* 2 tom. *nova & elegantiss. compact.* 1l 10s —— —— *Leov.* 1717
5960 Homeri Ilias, Gr. & Lat. a Clarke, 2 tom. 16s *Lond.* 1729
5961 Horatius, Notis Bentleii, 10s 6d —— *Amst.* 1713
5962 Sallustius, Notis Var. & Havercampi, *exemp. pulch. nit. comp. in memb* 1l 4s —— —— *ib.* 1742
5963 Plinii Panegyricus, Notis Var. a Arntzenio, 8s *ib.* 1738
5964 Chariton de Chaerea & Callirrhoe, Gr. & Lat. cum Observat. D'Orville, 2 tom. 18s — —— *ibid.* 1750
5965 Terentius, Notis Delph. *comp. in memb.* 14s *Par.* 1675
5966 Aristophanes, Gr. & Lat. curante Berglero, *exemp. pulch. nit. comp. in memb.* 1l 7s — —— *L. Bat.* 1760
5967 Petronius Arbiter, Notis Varior. & Burmanno, 2 tom. 16s *Traj. ad Rh.* 1709
5968 Fragmenta Mulier. Græcar. Gr. & Lat. a Wolfio, 6s *Hamb.* 1735
5969 Pietas & Gratulatio Coll. Cantabrig. apud Novanglos, *eleg. comp. fol. deaurat.* 4s —— *Bostoni Massach.* 1761
5970 Stanleii Historia Philosophiæ, *cum additamen.* 14s *Lips.* 1711
5971 Marianæ Historiæ de Rebus Hispaniæ, 6s *Mogunt.* 1605
5972 Vetus Test. Græc. ex Vers LXX Interpretum, *exemp. pulch.* 7s 6d *Lond. ap. Daniel* 1653
5973 Ovidii Metamorph. Libror. figuræ elegantiss. a C. Passæo Laminis Æneis incisæ, cum Epigram. Lat. & Germanice, a Salsmanno, 5s —— —— *Arnh.* 1607

5974 Barth.

5974 Barth. Casai de Crudelit. Hispanior. in Regionum Indicar. *cum fig.* par De Bry, 6s — Francf. 1598
5975 Cocklæus de Vita Theoderici Regis Ostrogothor. & Italiæ, *exemp. pulch.* 6s — Stockb. 1699
5976 Fabricii Bibliotheca Latina, 2 tom. *nov. & elegant. comp.* in 1 vol. 18s — Venet. 1728
5977 Novum Test. juxta exemplar Millianum, *nov. & elegant. comp.* 16s Oxon. *typis* Baskerville 1763
5978 Idem Liber, *semicompact.* 13s
5979 Vitringa Observat. Sacræ, 2 tom. 10s 6d Franeq. 1712
5980 Witsius in Symbolum Apostolorum, 4s — Amst. 1697
5981 Blount Censura Celebr. Authorum, *semicomp.* 4s Col. Allob. 1694
5982 Turretini Institutio Theologiæ Elenticæ, 4 tom. 10s Traj. ad Rh. 1734
5983 Simonis Hist. Method. Ling. Græcæ, 1s 6d Par. 1615
5984 Manethonis Apotelesmatica, Gr. & Lat. a Gronovio, 3s L. Bat. 1698
5985 Blondel de Thermis Aquisgranens. & Porcetanar, 1s 6d Aquis. 1658
5986 Xavier Hist. Christi Persice & Lat. a Lud. de Dieu, 2s 6d L. Bat. 1639
5987 Hoppius in Institut. Justinianeas, 7s — Francf. 1731
5988 Pignorii Mensa Isiaca, accesf. Ejusd. de Magna Deum Matu, nec non, Tomasini Manus Ænea, *cum fig.* 2s Amst. 1669
5989 Erpenii Grammatica Arabica, 2s 6d — L. Bat. 1656
5990 Burn's Justice of Peace, 2 vol. *new and neat*, 1l 15s 1764
5991 —— Ecclesiast. Law, 2 vol. *elegantly bound and marble leaves, new*, 2l 8s — 1763
5992 Heister's General System of Surgery, *with cuts, neat*, 18s 1763
5993 Bibliotheque Choisie de Medecine, par M. Planque, *avec fig.* 6 tom. *cousu*, 2l 12s 6d — Par. 1748
5994 Libro de Medicina Llamado Tesoro de los Probes, con un Regimiento de Sanidad, 2s — Sevilla 1543
5995 Van Swieten Comment. in Aphorismos Boerhaave, 3 tom. *semicomp.* 7s 6d — Venet. 1745
5996 Scribonius Largus, Notis Jo. Rhodii, *exemp. pulch. comp. in memb.* 12s — Patav. 1655
5997 C. Aurelianus, Notis Almeloveen, *exemp. pulch.* 4s Amst. 1709
5998 Vander Linden de Scriptis Medici, *edit. opt.* 6s Norimb. 1686
5999 Boerhaave Prælect. in Proprias Institut. Notis Halleri, 7 tom. *sutus*, 14s — Venet. 1743
6000 Koran, englished with Notes by Sale, 1l 1s — 1734
6001 Bp. Overal's Convocation Book, *with the Heads of Archbp. Sancroft and the Author*, 2s — 1690
6002 Malcolm's System of Arithmetick, *very fair*, 7s 6d 1730
6003 Plans des Ports & Rades de la Mer Mediterrannee, par les Srs. Michelot & Bremond, *cousu*, 2s 6d
6004 Discours sur l'Histoire Universelle, par Bossuet, *fort bien relie*, 10s 6d Par. 1732
6005 Morale des Peres de l'Eglise, par M. Barbeyrac, *fort bien relie*, 6s Amst 1728
6006 London Chronicle from 1757 to 1762 both inclus. 12 vol. *in boards*, 2l 12s 6d
6007 Pope's Homer's Iliad and Odyssey, 11 vol. with his Works, 4 vol. *large subscription paper, with head and tail pieces, elegantly bound in morocco, gilt leaves*, 17l 17s — 1715, &c.

6008 Cib-

6008 Cibber's Plays, 2 vol. 12s ——— 1721
6009 Croyat's Crudities, *an elegant Copy, with all the cuts* 1611
6010 Snelling's View of the Silver and Gold Coin and Coinage of England, *cuts, in boards,* 18s ——— 1762
6011 Robertson's Hist. of Scotland, 2 vol. *fair and neat,* 1l 1s 1759
6012 Maclaurin's Fluxions, 2 vol. *very fair, in boards, large paper,* 18s *Edinb.* 1742
6013 Smith's System of Opticks, *large paper,* 2 vol. 1l 5s 1738
6014 Maclaurin's Account of Newton's Philos. Discoveries, *large paper, cuts, in boards,* 8s —— —— 1748
6015 Allen Ramsay's Poems, 3s ——— *Edinb.* 1721
6016 Thucydides, engl. by Smith, *very fair and neat,* 2 vol. 1l 1753
6017 Ecton's Thesaurus Rerum Ecclesiast. *very fair, elegantly bound in russia, marble leaves,* 18s —— —— 1754
6018 Macknight's Harmony of the Gospels, *new, elegantly bound in morocco, with a gold border and gilt leaves,* 18s — 1756
6019 Hume's Hist. of England, 6 vol. *new and elegantly bound by* Johnson, 4l 14s 6d —— —— 1762
6020 Chubb's Tracts, *very fair,* 4s ——— 1730
6021 Benson's Hist. of the Plant. of the Chr. Relig. 2 vol. *sewed,* 4s —— —— 1735
6022 Walpole's Anecdotes of Painting in England, *with cuts,* 4 vol. *in turkey leather* — ——— 1762—1764
6023 Altieri's Ital. & Eng. Dictionary, by Palermo, 2 vol. 1l 5s 1749
6024 Ludwig's German & Eng. Dictionary, 2 vol. 1l 7s 1736
6025 Dictionaire Franc. & Flamand, par Halma, 2 tom. *demi relie,* 5s *Utrecht.* 1719
6026 Essais de Montaigne, avec des Remarq. par P. Coste, 3 tom. *nouv. & fort bien relie,* 1l 4s ——— *Lond.* 1724
6027 Historia della Guerre Civile di Francia, di Davila, 2 tom. 1l 4s *ib.* 1755
6028 Opere del Cav. Guarini, *con fig.* 4 vol. 1l 10s *Veron.* 1737
6029 Osservazioni Istoriche sopra alcuni Medaglioni Antichi, di Buonarrot, *con fig.* 7s 6d —— —— *Roma* 1698
6030 Usserius de Symbolo Apost. Rom. Eccles. 1647 — Potter on the Number 666 1647 — Callis on Sewers 1647 — Howell's Prehemin. of Parliament, 1s 6d — —— 1644
6031 Stanihurst de Reb. Gestis in Hibernia, 2s — *Antv.* 1584
6032 Davies's Causes why Ireland was never subdued 1612 — Government of Ireland under Sir Jo. Perrot 1626, 2s
6033 Answ. to the Irish Queries relat. to the Eng. Forces, 2s 1651
*6033 Hist. of the Lives of the Kings of Scotland, 2s *Dubl.* 1722
6034 Mac Curtin's Antiq. of Ireland, 4s —— *ib.* 1717
6035 Nicol's Hist. of Precious Stones, 2s ——— 1652
6036 Voyage de l'Ameriq par Ant. de Ulloa, *avec fig.* 2 tom. *bien relie,* 1l 15s —— —— *Amst.* 1752
6037 Hist. du Concile de Pise, par L'Enfant, *avec fig.* 2 tom. 7s *ib.* 1724
6038 —— du Concile de Constance, par L'Enfant, *avec fig.* 2 tom. 4s *ib.* 1718
6039 Nouv. Denombrement du Royaume, par Generalitez, Elections, Paroisses & Feux, 4s —— —— *Par* 1720
6040 Achitettura di Vitruvio, *con Comment. & Fig.* 2s 6d *Purug* 1533
6041 Efructi della Lingua da Dom. Cavalcha, 3s —— 1483

6042 Dict.

6042 Dict. Ital. & Franc. par Veneroni, 2 tom. *cousu*, 5s *Venise* 1737
6043 Il Malmantile Racquistato di Perl. Zipoli, colle Note di Puc. Lamoni, 2 tom. 15s ——— ——— *Firenz.* 1731
6044 Diccionario, Espan. & Fran. par Sobrino, *derniere Edit.* 12s
6045 Biblia Espanol. 6s ——— ——— *Bruss.* 1734
6046 Buonanni sopra l'Onferno, di Dante, 2s *Fiorenz.* 1569
6047 Le Tre Fontaine di Nic. Liburnio sopra la Grammatica & Eloq. di Dante, Petrarcha & Boccaccio, 2s — *Vineg.* 1526
6048 Hist. del Concilio Tridentino, di P. Polano, 2s 6d *Gen.* 1660
6049 Grammat. Franceza e Portug. por De Lima, 1s 6d *Lisb.* 1733
6050 Flegra in Betulia di Luigi Manzini, 1s 6d *Bologn.* 1695
6051 Orlando Furioso, di Ariosto, 7s 6d — *Venet.* 1575
6052 Obras de Ben. Gero. Feijo, 12 tom. 1l 16s *Madr.* 1742
6053 Memoires de l'Acad. Roy. de Chirurgie, *avec fig.* Tome 1. 10s 6d *Par.* 1743
6054 Oeuvres Philosophiques, *cousu*, 3s ——— *Lond.* 1751

APPENDIX. OCTAVO.

6055 ANderson's Genealogic. Hist. of the House of Yvery in its different Branches of Yvery, Luvel, Perceval and Gournay, 2 vol. *very scarce, a fine copy, elegantly bound* — 1742
6056 Kinderley's anc. & pres. State of the Navigat. of Lyn, Boston, Wisbeach, Spalding, &c. *sewed*, 1s 6d ——— 1751
6057 —— The same, *large paper, sewed*, 2s ——— 1754
6058 Birch's Life of Henry Pr. of Wales, *in boards*, 2s 6d 1760
6059 Life of Mr. R. Boyle, by Birch, 2s 6d ——— 1744
6060 ——— Archbp. Tillotson, by Birch, 2s 6d — 1752
6061 ——— Mr. Whiston, wrote by himself, *in boards*, 2s 6d 1749
6062 ——— Col. Cibber, 3s 6d ——— 1750
6063 ——— of Mrs. Oldfield, by Egerton, 2s — 1731
6064 Langbaine's Account of Eng. Dramatick Poets, 1s 1691
6065 Hist. of England to the Death of Q. Anne, *with cuts*, 4 vol. 10s ——— ——— 1722
6066 Davenant on Ways and Means of supplying the War, 1s 6d 1695
6067 Plan of the English Commerce, 2s 6d ——— 1728
6068 Hearne's Vindicat. of the Oath of Allegiance, 2s 6d 1731
6069 Hist of the Parliament 1700, 1s ——— 1702
6070 Izacke's Antiq. of Exeter, *very fair*, 3s ——— 1731
6071 Sir Rob. Cotton's Pieces, and Verstegnan's Antiquities of the English Nation, 2s 6d ——— ——— 1679
6072 Lodges's Peerage of Ireland, *with the Arms of the Nobility*, 4 vol. *neat*, 18s ——— 1754
6073 Lindsay's Hist. of England both Church and State, by Quest. and Answ. *neat*, 4s ——— ——— 1748
6074 Magna Charta Libertat. Civitat. Waterford, Edit. Cuningham, *very neatly bound in morocco, gilt leaves*, 3s — *Dubl.* 1752
6075 Account of the Irish Rebellion 1641, *very fair*, 1s 6d 1647
6076 Smith's ancient and present State of the County and City of Cork, *with cuts*, 2 vol. 12s ——— ——— *Dubl.* 1750
6077 Precedency of the Peers of Ireland 1739 — Segar's Titles of Honour, 1s 6d ——— ——— 1712

6078 Bor-

6078 Borlace on the Reduct of Ireland, 1s 6d —— 1675
6079 Lawrence's Interest of Ireland, 1s 6d —— 1682
6080 Toland's Succession to the Crown of England, 1s 1701
6081 King's State of the Protestants in Ireland, 1s 6d 1692
6082 Vertot's Revolut. of the Romans, 2 vol. *very fair*, 5s 1721
6083 —————— in Sweden, *very fair*, 2s —— 1723
6084 —————— of Portugal, 1s 6d —— 1723
6085 —————— in Spain, 5 vol. *very fair*, 10s — 1724
6086 Memoirs of the Viscount Turenne, 2 vol. 6s —— 1740
6087 Voltaire's Age of Lewis XIV. 2 vol. *neat*, 7s — 1752
6088 Armstrong's Hist. of Minorca, 2s 6d —— 1752
6089 Cambridge's Account of the War in India, *cuts*, 4s 1761
6090 Charlevoix's Voyage to North America, 2 vol. *new and elegantly bound by* Johnson, 12s —— 1761
6091 Campbell's present State of Europe, 3s — 1757
6092 History of Virginia, *with cuts*, *very fair*, 2s 6d — 1722
6093 Journey thro' the Netherlands, 1s 6d —— 1732
6094 Dickenson's Account of Florida, 1s 6d —— 1700
6095 Froger's Voyage to the Straits of Magellan, 1s 6d 1698
6096 Molyneux's Conjunct Expeditione, *with Plans*, 3s 1759
6097 Memorials of Trade in France, Fr. & Eng. 1s 6d 1736
6098 Cæsar's Commentaries by Bladen, *with cuts*, 2s 6d 1732
6099 The same, by Duncan, 2 vol. 8s —— 1755
6100 Voltaire's Hist. of the War 1741, 2s —— 1756
6101 Wallace's Dissertat. on the Numbers of Mankind, *in boards*, 2s *Edinb.* 1753
6102 The same, *bound*, 3s —— — *ib.* 1753
6103 Cavalliers Memoirs of the Cevennes, 2s —— 1723
6104 Life of Pope Sixtus V. by Leti, *very fair*, 4s — 1704
6105 ——— St. Ignatius Founder of the Jesuits, 2s — 1686
6106 Stanyan's Grecian Hist. 2 vol. *with cuts*, 6s —— 1707
6107 Voltaire's Hist. of the Russ. Emp. under Peter the Great, Vol. 1. *in boards*, 3s
6108 Emilius, or Essay on Education by Rousseau, *with cuts*, 2 vol. *in boards*, 6s —— —— 1763
6109 Waller's Poems, *with cuts*, *large paper*, *elegantly bound by* Johnson, 9s —— —— 1711
6110 Howel's Letters, *new and neat*, 5s —— 1754
6111 Fielding's Works, with his Life, 8 vol. *new and very neat*, 2l 8s —— —— 1762
6112 The same, *new and elegantly bound by* Johnson, 3l
6113 True Briton by the D of Wharton, 2 vol. 6s — 1723
6114 Montesquieu's Miscel. Pieces, *in boards*, 2s 6d — 1759
6115 Whichcote's Moral and Relig. Aphorisms and Letters, *very fair and neat*, *large paper*, 3s 6d —— 1753
6116 Tale of a Tub. by Swift, 1s —— 1705
6117 Aaron Hill's Works, 4 vol. *very neat*, 12s —— 1754
6118 Mrs. Cockburn's Works, 2 vol. *very neat*, 6s — 1751
6119 Hume on Human Nature, 2 vol. *fair and neat*, 4s 1739
6120 King's Origin of Evil, Engl. with Notes by Law, 2 vol. 3s —— —— 1732
6121 The same, *last edit. with Additions*, *new and very neat*, 7s 1759
6122 Fable of the Bees, by Mandeville, 2 vol. 7s 1724, &c.

6123 En-

6122 Enquiry into the Practice of Virtue, in Anf. to the Fable of the Bees, 2s —— —— —— 1725
6123 Berkley's Minute Philofopher, 2 vol. 5s —— 1732
6124 Hutchefon's Ideas of Beauty and Virtue, 1s 6d — 1729
6125 ———— Conduct of the Paffions, 2s —— 1730
6126 Swift's Works, 11 vol. *very fair*, 1l 15s *Dubl.* 1746
6127 Cicero's Orator. with Notes, by Guthrie, 3s 6d — 1742
6128 Burlamaqui's Princip. of Nat. Law, 3s 6d —— 1748
6129 Pliny's Epift. and Panegyrick, with his Life, by Henley, 2 vol. 3s —— —— —— 1724
6130 Fordyce's Dialogues on Education, 3s 6d —— 1745
6131 Feme Coverts, or Ladies Law, 1s —— 1732
6132 Venette's Myfteries of Conjugal Love, 2s 6d —— 1712
6133 Longinus on Sublime, by Smith, *in boards*, 2s — 1739
6134 Toland's Amyntor, or Defence of Milton's Life, 1s 1699
6135 Baker's Reflect. upon Learning, 1s 6d —— 1708
6136 Gentleman Inftructed, 1s 6d —— —— 1716
6137 Pearfon's Great Cafe of Tithes, 1s —— 1732
6138 Earbery's Occafional Hiftorian, 1s 6d —— —— 1730
6139 Le Clerk's Thoughts on Critical, Hiftorical, Morality and Politics, 1s 6d —— —— —— 1700
6140 Hoadly's Meafures of Submiffion, 1s —— 1706
6141 Locke's Familiar Letters, 2s —— — 1708
6142 Frefnoy's Art of Painting, by Dryden, 3s —— 1716
6143 Howard's Hift. of Religion, 1s —— — 1694
6144 Memoires of Literature, by La Roche, 8 vol. *in boards*, 8s 1722
6145 Method. of Learn. to draw in Perfpect. 1732—Critic. Review of the Publ. Buildings in Lond. and Weftm. 1734—Stukely on the Gout, and 6 more Tracts 1734, 3s
6146 Newton on the Expence of Univ. Education, 1s — 1734
6147 Pope's Rape of the Lock 1714—Gay's Trivia, and 7 more Tracts 1730, 2s
6148 Lover's Mifcell. with the Life of Mrs. Oldfield 1731—View of the Town, or Memoirs of London, and more Tracts 1731, 1s 6d
6149 Character of K. Charles I, 1738—Card. Tencin's Plea for fettling the Pretender on the Brit. Throne 1745, and more Tracts, 1s 6d
6150 Character of Rob. Hufh 1713—Dr. Tripe's Letter to Neftor Ironfide 1714—Oliver's Pocket Looking-Glafs 1712, and more Tracts, 1s
6151 Defence of the Public Stews, by Mandeville 1724—Enq. into the Conduct of Gr. Britain 1727——Life of Count Patkul 1717, 1s 6d
6152 Drummer, by Addifon 1735—Zayre de Voltaire *Par.* 1733—Voltaire on the Civ. Wars of France 1731, 1s
6153 Langley's Defcript. of Newgate 1722—Letters from a Lady in Covent Garden to an Officer abroad 1745—Arguments refpect. Infolvency—De Veil's Practice of a Juftice of Peace 1747, and more Tracts, 1s 6d
6154 Spenfer's Faerie Queen, with Notes, by Church, 4 vol. *large paper*, 1l 4s —— — 1758
6155 Pope's Works, with Homer's Iliad and Odyffey, *with cuts*, 20 vol. *very neat*, 5l 10s —— —— 1751
6156 Shakefpear's Works, by Hanmer, 6 vol. *fair*, 1l 4s 1745
6157 The fame, 6 vol. *very fair and neat*, 1l 8s —— 1745

Y 6158 Beau-

6158 Beaumont and Fletcher's Works, 7 vol. 15s —— 1711
6159 Milton's Paradise Lost, *with cuts,* 2s 6d —— 1705
6160 Regicide, or James I. of Scotland, a Tragedy, by Smollet, 1s6d 1749
6161 Muses Library, or Series of old Engl. Poetry, *new and neat,* 3s 6d 1737
6162 Parnell's Poems, *very fair,* 2s 6d —— 1737
6163 Hildeb. Jacob's Poetic. Works, *neat,* 2s —— 1735
6164 Young's two Plays, 1s —— —— 1719, &c.
6165 Congreve's Works, 3 vol. *large print,* 9s —— 1717
6166 Garth's Dispensary, 1s —— —— 1706
6167 Juvenal and Persius, Engl. by Dryden, *with cuts,* 2s 1711
6168 Virgil, *with cuts,* Engl. by Dryden, 3 vol. *very fair,* 10s 6d 1709
6169 Collect. of Ballard Operas, 3 vol. *neatly bound,* 6s
6170 D'Urfey's Operas, Comic Stories and Poems, 1s 6d 1721
6171 Gay's Plays and Opera, *neatly bound,* 2s 6d
6172 Balguy's Sermons, 2 vol. *new and neat,* 9s —— 1760
6173 Conybeare's Sermons, 2 vol. *new and neat,* 7s 6d 1757
6174 South's Sermons, 6 vol. *very fair,* 18s —— 1715
6175 Whiston's Sermons at Boyle's Lect. 1s —— 1708
6176 Rogers's Sermons on Div. Revelat. 1s 6d —— 1727
6177 Bentley's Sermon at Boyle's Lect. 2s —— 1734
6178 Young's Historical Dissertation on Idolatr. Corrupt. 2 vol. *neatly bound,* 4s —— —— —— 1734
6179 Lucas's Enq. after Happiness, 2 vol. *very fair and neat,* 7s 1753
6180 Newton on the Church Catechism, 1s —— 1717
6181 Wilkins on Nat. and Revealed Religion, 1s — 1722
6182 Payne's Evangelical Discourses, *sewed,* 3s —— 1763
6183 Kempis's Imitation of Christ, Engl. by Payne, *sewed,* 3s 1763
6184 England's Conversion and Reformat. compared, 3s *Antw.* 1725
6185 Widdrington's Annotat. on the New Testament, 2 vol. *fair and neat,* 8s —— —— 1730
6186 New Test. translat. from the Lat. Vulg. with Annot. by Nary, *large paper, very fair and neatly bound, in blue turkey, gilt leaves,* 7s 6d 1719
6187 Pilkington's Remarks on Scripture, *in boards,* 2s —— 1759
6188 Warburton's Julian, *very fair,* 2s —— 1750
6189 Henry's Method for Prayer, 1s 6d —— 1727
6190 Drelincourt on Death, 2s 6d —— —— 1732
6191 Stanhope on the Epistles and Gospels, 4 vol. 10s 1705
6192 Brandt's Hist. of the Reformation abridged, 2 vol. 3s 1725
6193 Hoadly on the Sacrament, *in boards,* 1s —— 1749
6194 Candid Disquit. relat. to the Ch. of Engl. *boards,* 1s 1749
6195 Chandler's Review of the Hist. of the Man after God's own Heart, *in boards,* 4s —— —— 1762
6196 Burnet's State of the Dead, 2s 6d —— 1730
6197 Leland's View of the Deistic Writers, 2 vol. *new and neat,* 12s 1764
6198 Bp. Clayton's Vindicat. of the O. and N. Test. 2s 6d 1759
6199 *Annett's Tracts on Subjects Natural and Supernatural,* 2 vol. 10s 1749
6200 Bentley on Freethinking 1743—Hare on the Study of Scripture, 2s —— —— 1735
6201 Rights of the Christian Church, by Tindal, 1s — 1707
6202 Christianity not Mysterious, by Toland, 1s 6d —— 1702
6203 Letter to the Author of the Grounds, &c. of the Christian Religion, 2s —— 1737
6204 *Modest Remarks upon Bp. Sherlock's Discourses upon Prophecy, by Ilisse,* 5s

6205 Account

6205 Account of the Life and Character of Chubb 1747—Horler's Mem. of Chubb 1747—Vindicat. of the Memory of Chubb 1747—Second Letter to Horler in Defence of Chubb 1747, 2s

6206 Discourse on Ridicule and Irony in Writing, 1s 6d 1729

6207 Collins's Letter to Dr. Rogers on Div. Revelat. 1s 6d 1727

6208 ——— Discourse on Freethinking, 1s ——— 1713

6209 Philosophic. Dissert. upon Death, 1s ——— 1732

6210 Collins on Liberty and Necessity, 1s ——— 1729

6211 Toland's Defence of himself, 1s ——— ——— 1702

6212 ——— Letters to Serena, 3s ——— ——— 1705

6213 Keill's Introduct. to Nat. Philosophy, *new and neat*, 4s 1758

6214 Pluche's Hist. of the Heavens, *with cuts*, 2 vol. 5s 1740

6215 Whiston's Theory of the Earth, 3s ——— — 1737

6216 Wells's Young Gent. Mathematics, *cuts*, 3 vol. *very fair*, 9s 1725

6217 Hooke's Philosophic. Experiments, 2s ——— 1726

6218 Gravesande's Algebra, 1s 6d ——— ——— 1728

6219 Dalrymple's Essay on the Art of War, 4s ——— 1761

6220 Hale's Causes of Earthquakes, and 3 more Tracts on Earthquakes, 1s ——— ——— ——— 1750

6221 Watson's Sequel to the Experim. on Electricity 1746—Martin on Electricity 1746—Manningham on the Little Fever 1746—Polite Philosopher 1736, and more Tracts, 2s

6222 Le Dran's Operat. in Surgery, *with cuts, in boards*, 3s 1749

6223 The same, with Pharmacop. Chirurgic. *with cuts, in boards*, 3s 6d ——— ——— ——— 1749

6224 The same, *large paper, in boards*, 5s ——— 1749

6225 Nelson on the Governm. of Children, *in boards*, 1s 6d 1753

6226 Carpenter's Retired Gardener, *with cuts, fair*, 2s 1717

6227 Stillingfleet's Tracts on Nat. Hist. Husbandry and Physic, *sewed*, 3s ——— ——— ——— 1762

6228 Switzer's Pract. Kitchen Gardener, *with cuts*, 2s 6d 1727

6229 Davenant on Public Revenues, 2 vol. *neat*, 9s — 1698

6230 Quincy's Dispensatory, *very fair*, 3s 6d ——— 1749

6231 Shaw's Practice of Physic, 2 vol. 5s ——— — 1753

6232 Verral's System of Cookery, *very fair*, 3s ——— 1759

6233 Pott on Ruptures, *very fair*, 3s ——— 1756

6234 Theophrastus's Characters, Gr. and Lat. with Engl. Notes, by Newton, 2s ——— ——— ——— 1754

6235 Shaw's Chemical Lectures, 3s ——— — 1734

6236 Woodward's Nat. Hist. of the Earth, 1s 6d ——— 1726

6237 ——— Essay towards Nat. Hist. of tho Earth, 1s 6d 1723

6238 Kennedy on external Remedies, 1s ——— 1715

6239 Freind's Prælect. Chymicæ, 1s ——— *Lond.* 1726

6240 Dissertat. au Sujet d'un Polype Extraord. par M. Manne, *elegant. relie en maroq. doree sur les tranches*, 1s 6d — *Avign.* 1717

6241 Observat. d'une Masse Skirreuse, par M. Manne, *eleg. relie en maroq. doree sur les tranches*, 1s 6d ——— — *ibid.* 1746

6242 ——— d'un Polype Extraord. par M. Manne, *elegant. relie en maroq. doree sur les tranches*, 1s 6d ——— *ibid.* 1746

6243 ——— d'une Maladie des Os du Crane avec carie, par M. Manne, *eleg. relie en maroq. doree sur les tranches*, 1s 6d — *ibid.* 1747

6244 ——— d'une Playe a la Tete avec Fracas, par M. Manne, *eleg. relie en maroq. doree sur les tranches*, 2s 6d ——— 1729

Y 2 6245 War-

6245 Warlizius de Morbis Biblicis, *ſutus*, 1s —— *Vitemb.* 1714
6246 Raii Methodus Plantarum, 1s —— —— *Lond.* 1682
6247 Beckeri Tripus Hermeticus Fatidibus, 1s —— *Francf.* 1689
6248 Traite de la Traille au Haut Apparcil, par Morand, 1s *Par.* 1728
6249 Nov. Teſt. Gr. & Lat. a Beza, *caret titulo*, 1s
6250 Nov. Teſt. Gr. juxta Exemplar Millianum, typis Baſkerville, *ſutus*, 5s —— —— — *Oxon. e Typogr. Clar.* 1763
6251 Idem, *nov. & nit. comp.* 6s —— — *ib. ap. ib.* 1763
6252 Ciceronis Opera omnia, Notis varior. & Verburgii, 16 tom. *eleg. compact.* a Johnſon, 3l 3s —— *Amſt.* 1724
6253 Ovidii Opera, Notis varior. & Cnippingii, 3 tom. *nit. comp.* a Johnſon, 18s —— —— *L. Bat.* 1670
6254 Ciceronis Orationes, Notis var. & Grævii, 6 tom. *exemp. pulch. nit. comp.* 1l 11s 6d —— — *Amſt.* 1699
6255 Cicero de Officiis, Notis var. & Grævii, 5s — *ibid.* 1688
6256 Eutropius, Notis var. & Havercampii, 7s *L. Bat.* 1729
6257 Corn. Nepos, Notis varior. & Van Staveren, 7s *ibid.* 1734
6258 Lucianus, Notis varior. & Benedicte, 2 tom. 15s *Amſt.* 1687
6259 Boethius de Conſolat. Philoſ. Notis varior. 3s 6d *L. Bat.* 1671
6260 Plautus, Notis variorum & Gronovii, 2 tom. *nitid. comp.* 14s *Amſt.* 1684
6261 Æliani Varia Hiſtoria, Gr. & Lat. a Perizonio, 2 tom. 9s *Lugd. Bat.* 1701
6262 Luciani Opera, Gr. & Lat. a Benedicto, 2 tom. 9s *Salm.* 1619
6263 Zoſimi Hiſtoria, Gr. & Lat. 1s 6d —— *Oxon.* 1679
6264 Herodiani Hiſtoria, Gr. & Lat. 1s 6d —— *ibid.* 1699
6265 Ovidii Metamorphoſes, Lat. & Angl. *new and neat*, 4s *Lond. ap. Davidſon* 1748
6266 Terentius, Lat. & Angl. a Patrick, 2 tom. *new and neat*, 8s *Lond.* 1750
6267 Horatius, Lat. & Angl. 2 tom. *nov. & nit. comp.* 8s *Lond. ap. Davidſon* 1746
6268 Virgilius, Lat. & Angl. 2 tom. *nov. & nit. comp.* 9s *ib. ap. ib.* 1748
6269 C. Nepos, Lat. & Angl. cum Notis Clarke, 1s 6d *Lond.* 1748
6270 Salluſtius, Lat. & Angl. a Clarke, 1s 6d —— *ib.* 1743
6271 Elegiaca Græca, *nov. & nit. comp.* 2s 6d —— *Oxon.*
6272 Stradæ Proluſiones Academicæ, 2s —— *ibid.* 1745
6273 Dion. Halicarnaſſeus de Struct. Orationis, Gr. & Lat. a Uptono, 2s *Lond.* 1728
6274 Terentii Varrones Opera omnia, *edit. opt.* 9s — *Dordr.* 1619
6275 Monumenta Vetuſtates Kempiana, *ſutus*, 1s *Lond.* 1720
6276 Bullerii Diſſertat. Sacrum Sylloge, *ſutus*, 1s *Amſt.* 1750
6277 Burton Iter Surrienſe & Suſſexienſe, *nit. comp.* 2s 6d *Lond.* 1755
6278 Triveti Annales VI. Regum Angliæ Edid. Ant. Hall, 2 tom. 4s *Oxon.* 1719
6279 Strada de Bello Belgico, *cum fig.* 2 tom. *nit. comp.* 5s *Antv.* 1649
6280 Tolandi Pantheiſticon, *exemp. pulch. nit. comp.* 7s 6d *Coſmop.* 1720
6281 Waræus de Antiq. Hiberniæ, 1s —— *Lond.* 1654
6282 Homerus Hebraicus, a Bogan, *nit. comp.* 3s *Oxon.* 1658
6283 Vita Tho. Hobbes, per Seipſum, *nit. comp.* 1s *Carolop.* 1681

Appendix.

Appendix. DUODECIMO.

6284 DRYDEN's Plays, 6 vol. *fair and neat*, 15s 1725
6285 Pope's Works, 9 vol. *elegantly bound, his own Edition*, 1l 11s 6d ——— ———
6286 Shadwell's 5 Plays, 2s ——— ——— 1743
6287 Wycherley's Plays, 2 vol. 3s ——— ——— 1720
6288 Farquhar's Plays, 2 vol. 2s 6d 1720
6289 Bysshe's British Parnassus, 2 vol. 3s ——— 1721
6290 Rehearsal, transposed by Marvel, 2 vol. 2s 6d ——— 1714
6291 Vaughan's Practica Walliæ, 3s ——— ——— 1672
6292 Anacreon, Gr. & Lat. Baxteri, *edit. opt.* 1s 6d ——— 1672
6293 Idem, Gr. & Lat. a Barnesio, 3s ——— *Lond.* 1710
6294 Aristophanis Comœdiæ, Gr. & Lat. a Scaligero, 2s *Cantab.* 1705
6295 Opera Sententiosa Vetust. Poetarum, Græce *Amst.* 1670
Antv. 1564—Reusneri Polyanthea sive Paradisus Poeticus *Bas.* 1568, 1s 6d
6296 Livius, a Ruddimanno, 4 tom. 8s ——— *Edinb.* 1751
6297 Catullus, Tibullus & Propertius, *cum fig. exemp. pulch. eleg. comp. fol. deaurat.* 6s ——— ———
6298 Æschylus, Gr. & Lat. 2 tom. *nov. & nit. comp.* 6s *Paris.* 1754
6299 Suetonius, cum Animadv. Grævii, *& fig.* 1s 6d *Glasg.* 1746
6300 Marc. Antoninus (Imp.) de Rebus Suis, Gr. & Lat. 1s 6d *Amst.* 1697
Glasg. 1744
6301 Catullus, Tibullus & Propertius, a Maittaire, 2s *Lond.* 1715
6302 J. Cæsar, *cum fig.* 2 tom. *exemp. pulch. eleg. comp. fol. marmor.* 10s
L. Bat. 1684
6303 Sulp. Severi Opera, 1s ——— *L. Bat. ap. Elzev.* 1635
6304 Q. Curtius, 2 tom. *cum fig. nit. comp.* 2s 6d *H. Com.* 1727
6305 Livius a Ruddimanno, 4 tom. *chart. opt.* 12s *Edinb.* 1751
6306 Plinii Epist. & Panegyricus, Notis Lallemand, *nit. comp. fol. marm.* 3s ——— ——— ———
Par. 1749
6307 A. Gellius, *comp. in membr.* 2s ——— *L. Bat.* 1644
6308 Horatius, *nit. comp.* 5s ——— ——— *Sedani* 1626
6309 Virgilius, *nit. comp.* 5s ——— ——— *ibid.* 1625
6310 Anacreon, Gr. & Lat. 2 tom. *nit. comp. min. formæ*, 2s *Edinb.* 1754
6311 Horatius, Juvenal & Persius, Terentius, Virgilius, Catullus, Tibullus & Propertius, Lucanus, 2 tom. Phædrus Lucretius Ovidius, 5 tom. Q. Curtius, 2 tom. C. Nepos, Sallustius, J. Cæsar, 2 tom. *Lond.* 1744, &c.

N. B. *The above Set of Classics, neatly printed by Brindley, in 20 vol. ruled with red lines, elegantly bound in yellow morocco, marble leaves*, 3l 3s

6312 Gyraldi Poematia, item Geraldini Bucolica *Bas.* 1543—Bonincontrus de Reb. Cœlestib. *Venet.* 1526 — Hericus de Vita Sti. Germani, 2s 6d ——— *Par. ap. Colin.* 1543
6313 Albinovani Elegiæ & Fragmenta, Notis Scaligeri & alio, 1s 6d
Amst. 1703
6314 Sautelis Annus sacer Poeticus, 2 tom. 2s 6d *Lugd* 1679
6315 ——— Lusus Poetici Allegorici, 1s 6d ——— *Par.* 1725
6316 Vanierii Prædium Rust. *exemp. pulch.* 2s ——— *Amst.* 1749
6317 Buchanani Poemata, 1s ——— *L. Bat. ap. Elz.* 1628

6318 Tragi.

6318 Tragi. Theat. Londini Celebrat. *cum effig.* 2s 6d *Amst.* 1649
6319 Miltoni Ars Logicæ, 1s —— —— *Lond.* 1672
6320 Dickinsoni Delphi Phœnicizantes *Oxon.* 1655—Smith Syntag. de Morib. Druidum, 5s —— —— *Lond.* 1644
6321 Nov. Test. Gr. 2 tom. *exemp. pulch. lineis rubr. nit. comp. fol. marm.* 6s —— —— *Lutet. ap. R. Steph.* 1549
6322 Nov. Test. Gr. *exemp. pulch.* 2s —— *L. Bat. ap. Elz.* 1641
6323 Nov. Test. Gr. *Lond,* 1701 —— Liturgia Eccles. Ang. Gr. 2s *Cantab. ap. Field*
6324 Nov. Test. Gr. & Lat. a Leusdeno, 2s — *Amst.* 1741
6325 Oeuvres Melees du Philosophe de Sans Souci, *avec fig.* 2 tom. *nouv. & fort bien relie,* 6s —— *suivant la Copie de Berl.* 1760
6326 Annales Politiques de l'Abbe de St. Pierre, 2 tom. *nouv. & fort bien relie,* 6s —— —— *Lond.* 1758
6327 Ocellus Lucanus, en Gr. & en Fr. par D'Argens, *nouv. & fort bien relie,* 2s 6d —— —— *Berlin* 1762
6328 Tacitus's Works, Engl. by Gordon, 5 vol. 12s 1753
6329 The same, 5 vol. *new and very neat,* 15s —— 1753
6330 Salmon's Peerage of Engl. *in boards,* 1s 6d —— 1751
6331 The same, *interleaved,* 2 vol. *in boards,* 2s —— 1751
6332 Rollin's Ancient Hist. 10 vol. *neat,* 1l 1s — *Edinb.* 1758
6333 Tour thro' Gr. Britain, 4 vol. *very fair,* 8s —— 1762
6334 The same, 4 vol. *new and neatly bound,* 12s —— 1762
6335 Orders, Reports, &c. of the House of Commons, *sewed,* 1s 1756
6336 Voltaire's Hist. of Charles XII. 1s 6d —— 1733
6337 History of the Duke of Marlborough, 2s —— 1741
6338 Life of Dr. Radcliffe, and his Last Will, 1s —— 1724
6339 Badeslade's Maps of the Counties in Engl. and Wales, 3s 1742
6340 Sallust, engl. by Rowe, 1s —— —— 1715
6341 Burnet's Essay on Queen Mary, 1s —— 1695
6342 Molyneux's Case of Ireland, 1s —— 1719
6343 Secret Hist. of K. Cha. II. and K. Ja. II. 1s —— 1690
6344 Ireland's Case briefly stated, 1s —— — 1720
6345 Boat's Nat. Hist. of Ireland, 2s —— 1652
6346 English, Scots and Irish Compend. with the Arms of the Nobility, 5 vol. *last edit.* 1l —— —— 1753, &c.
6347 Prior's Poems, 1s 6d —— —— 1741
6348 Addison's Poems, 1s 6d —— *Glasg.* 1750
6349 Juvenal and Persius, Engl. by Dryden, 2s
6350 Shakespear's Works, by Pope and Sewell, 10 vol. 15s 1728
6351 Dryden's Plays, 6 vol. 15s —— —— 1718
6352 Plautus's Amphitrion, Lat. and Engl. by Cooke, 1s 1746
6353 Guardian, a Comedy; Very Woman, Trag. Com. both by Massenger, 1s —— —— 1655
6354 Select Pieces of Drollery, 2 parts, 3s —— 1672
6355 Otway's Works, 2 vol. 3s 6d —— 1722
6356 Montfort's Plays, 2 vol. 3s —— —— 1720
6357 Sir Rob. Howard's Plays, 2s —— —— 1722
6358 Young Ladies Miscellany, 1s —— —— 1726
6359 Siege of Damascus, and four more Tragedies, 1s 6d
6360 Blind Lady, a Comedy — Fair Quaker of Deal, and three more Plays, 1s 6d
6361 Cartwright's Plays and Poems, 1s 6d —— 1651

6362 Sedley's

6362 Sedley's Works, 2 vol. 3s ——— — 1722
6363 Steele's Plays, 1s ——— ——— 1712
6364 Thyestes, a Tragedy, 1s ——— ——— 1674
6365 Troades, by Seneca, Engl. with Poems, by S. P. 1s 1660
6366 Hippolytus of Seneca, with Poems, by Prestwick, 6d 1651
6367 Lilly's Court Comedies, 1s 6d ——— 1632
6368 Swift's Works, 14 vol. *new and neat*, 2l 2s ——— 1760
6369 Rabelais's Gargantia and Pantagruel, 1s ——— 1653
6370 Hervey's Meditations, 2 vol. *very fair*, 4s ——— 1749
6371 Plato's Works abridged, with Notes, by Dacier, 2 vol. 3s 6d 1749
6372 Guardian, with the Engl. Motto's, 2 vol. 3s 6d *Dubl.* 1752
6373 Manners, translated into Engl. *in boards*, 1s ——— 1749
6374 Blounts's Micosmography, 1s ——— 1732
6375 Locke on Hum. Understand. abridged by Wynne, 1s 6d 1731
6376 Catholick Christian Instructed, 1s 6d ——— 1737
6377 Grosvenor's Essay on Health, 1s ——— 1716
6378 Blount's Oracles of Reason, and his other Works, 1s 6d 1695
6379 Scheme of Literal Prophecy, by Collins, 1s ——— 1726
6380 Ray's Collection of English Words, 1s ——— 1674
6381 Archbp. Laud's Sermons, 1s ——— 1651
6382 Cicero's Familiar Epistles, by Webbe, 1s 6d
6383 Bysshe's Art of Poetry, 2 vol. *new and very neatly bound*, 6s 1762
6384 Peregrine Pickle, 4 vol. *in boards*, 5s ——— 1751
6385 Journey through Life, 2 vol. 3s ——— 1754
6386 Euclid's Elements, Engl. by Barrow, 1s ——— 1714
6387 Pardie's Geometry, Engl. by Harris, 1s ——— 1717
6388 Fontenelle's Plurality of Worlds, 1s ——— 1719
6389 Faithorne's Art of Graving and Etching, *with cuts*, 1s 6d 1662
6390 Algarotti on Light and Colours, 2 vol. in 1, 2s 6d — 1742
6391 Count Saxe's Plan for Modelling the French Army, 1s 6d 1753
6392 Leslie's Account of Jamaica, 2s ——— *Edinb.* 1739
6393 Law on Trade in Scotland, 1s 6d ——— *Glasg.* 1751
6394 Stewart and Bruce's Index to Scotch Acts, 2 vol. 2s 6d *Edinb.* 1707 and 1726
6395 Histoire Ecclesiastique, par Fleury, 32 tom. 2l 10s *Brux.* 1723
6396 L'Esprit des Loix, 3 tom. *demi relie*, 6s — *Amst.* 1755
6397 Le meme, 4 tom. *nov. & fort bien relie*, par Johnson, 17s *Par.* 1757
6398 Le meme, 2 tom. *en 8vo, bien relie*, 8s ——— *Genev.*
6399 Histoire Ancienne des Egypt. par Rollin, 14 tom. *tres elegamen relie*, 2l 2s ——— ——— *Par.* 1737
6400 Hist. des Revolut. d'Angleterre, par D'Orleans, 4 tom. *fort bien relie*, 8s ——— ——— ——— *ibid.* 1737
6401 Memoires de le Marq. de Feuquiere, 4 tom. *fort bien relie*, 8s *Lond.* 1737
6402 Memorial de Paris & de ses Environs, 2 tom. *fort bien relie*, 4s *Par.* 1749
6403 Hist. de la Ligue de Cambray, 2 tom. 3s — *ibid.* 1728
6404 —— des Revolut. de Suede, par Vertot, 1s 6d *Amst.* 1722
6405 —— de Tite Live, trad. par Du-Ryer, 8 tom. en 4 vol. 8s *Lyon.* 1695
6406 Voyage au l'Amerique, par Labat, *avec fig.* 6 tom. *fort bien relie*, 18s ——— ——— ——— *Haye* 1724
6407 Henault Chronologiq. de Hist. de France, 2 tom. *nouv. fort bien relie*, 10s ——— ——— — *Par.* 1761

6408 Hist.

6408 Memoires du Maresch. de Tourville, 3 tom. *bien relie*, 6s *Amst.* 1742
6409 Hist. des Negociations, 3 tom. *bien relie*, 6s *Haye* 1757
6410 Memoires du Sr. de Pontis, 2 tom. *fort bien relie*, 4s *Par.* 1715
6411 Theatre de Quinault, *avec fig.* 5 tom. 7s 6d — *ibid.* 1715
6412 Oeuvres de Plaute, par Limiers, Lat. & Fr. 10 tom. 1l 5s *Amst.* 1719
6413 ——— de Horace, par Tarteron, 2 tom. 3s — *Par.* 1723
6414 ——— de Racine, 2 tom. *fort bien relie*, 4s — *ibid.* 1736
6415 ——— diverses de Rousseau, 2 tom. 3s 6d — *Brux.* 1732
6416 ——— de Moliere, *avec des fig.* 8 tom. *nouv.* 1l *Par.* 1760
6417 ——— de Racine, 3 tom. *nouv. & fort bien relie*, 7s 6d *ibid.* 1760
6418 Comedies d'Aristophane, trad. par Dacier, 2s — *ibid.* 1692
6419 Histoire de Gil Blas, *avec fig.* 5 tom. *nouv. & fort bien relie*, 12s 6d *ibid.* 1759
6420 Melanges de Litterature, d'Hist. & de Philosophie, 4 tom. 12s *Amst.* 1759
6421 Institut. d'un Prince, par M. Du Guet, 4 tom. *eleg. relie & doree sur les tranches, par Padeloup a Paris*, 10s —— *Lond.* 1740
6422 Bibliotheque Poetique, 4 tom. *fort bien relie*, 10s *Par.* 1745
6423 Contes & Nouvelles en Vers de Fontaine, 2 tom. 3s *Lond.* 1755
6424 Memoires du Comte de Grammont, 2s —— *Par.* 1746
6425 Amusemens de Spa, *avec fig.* 2 tom. 5s —— *Amst.* 1734
6426 Satyre de Petrone, *avec fig.* 2 tom. 2s —— *Colog.* 1694
6427 Prem. Livre de l'Iliade en Vers, par Reginer, 1s *Par.* 1700
6428 Lettres de Voltaire sur les Anglois, 1s 6d —— *Basle* 1734
6429 Grammaire, Fr. & Allemande, par Pepliers, 1s *Leipz.* 1752
6430 Synony. Francois, par Girard, *fort bien relie*, 2s 6d *Par.* 1740
6431 Gram. Fran. par Restaut, *fort bien relie*, 2s —— *ibid.* 1758
6432 Voyage Litterarie, en Fr. en Angleterre & en Holl. *fort bien relie*, 2s *Haye* 1736
6433 Grammaire Espagn. & Fran. par Sobrino, 1s — *Brux.* 1717
6434 Lettres du Card. Richelieu, 2 tom. *cousu*, 3s *Par.* 1696
6435 ——— Juives, 6 tom. *cousu*, 6s —— *Haye* 1742
6436 ——— de l'Abbe Le Blanc, sur les Anglois, 3 tom. *cousu*, 3s *Amst.* 1749
6437 Maniere d'Etudier les Belles Lettres, par Rollin, 4 tom. *cousu*, 5s *ibid.* 1745
6438 De la Sagesse, par Charron, *relie en maroq.* 1s —— *Par.* 1654
6439 Lettres d'une Religieuse au Chevalier, 1s — *Haye* 1716
6440 Hexameron Rustique, par La Mothe, 1s —— *Amst.* 1698
6441 Elite de Bon Mots recueillies des Livres in *Ana*, 2 tom. *fort bien relie*, 4s —— —— *ibid.* 1731
6442 Hist. du Chev. des Grieux & de Manon Lescaut, 2 tom. *nouv. & fort bien relie*, par Johnson, 5s —— *ibid.* 1756
6443 Les Visions de Pasquille, 1s —— —— 1547
6444 Hist. Nat. d'Irlande, par Boat, 1s —— *Par.* 1666
6445 Nouvelles Oeuvres de Voiture, *bien relie en maroq.* 1s *ibid.* 1665
6446 Maladies Veneriennes, par Astruc, 4 tom. *fort bien relie*, 8s *ibid.* 1755
6447 Alstoni Tyrocin. Botan. Edinburg. *sutus*, 1s — *Edinb.* 1753
6448 Opere di Metastatio, 9 vol. *cicuto*, 1l 10s — *Parig.* 1755
6449 —— di Machiavelli, 4 vol. *cicuto*, 10s —— *Haia* 1726
6450 Hist. della Guerra di Fiandra da Bentivoglio, 3 vol. 9s *Col.* 1635
6451 Rime di Petrarca, *cicuto*, 1s 6d —— *Venez.* 1739

6452 Polibio

6452 Polibio, tradotto per Domenichi, 5s — *Venet.* 1546
6453 Semplicita Ingannata di Galer. Baratotti, 1s — *Leida* 1654
6454 Obras y Relaciones de Ant. Perez, 1s — *Gen.* 1645
6455 Liturgia ſegun el uſo de la Yglesia Anglic. *elegantly bound in morocco, gilt leaves,* 2s 6d — — *Lond.* 1715

Books added. FOLIO.

6456 DUGDALE's Monaſticon Anglicanum, *cum fig.* 3 tom. *exemp. eleg.* — — *Lond.* 1655, &c.
6457 Johnſon's Engliſh Dictionary, 2 vol. *in rough calf,* 3l 10s 1755
6458 Platonis Opera, Gr. & Lat. a Ficino, *damaged,* 18s *Francf.* 1602
6459 Plutarchi Opera, Gr. & Lat. a Cruſerio & Xylandro, 2 tom. *exemp. pulch. comp. in membr.* 1l 1s — *ibid.* 1620
6460 Dr. Stukeley's Itinerarium Curioſum, and his Antiquities of Stonehenge and Abury, *with a great number of cuts,* 3 vol. in 2. *uniformly and finely bound, with a border of gold and marble leaves,* 1724, &c.
6461 Xenophontis Opera, Gr. & Lat. a Leunclavio, 7s 6d *Baſ.* 1572

Books added. QUARTO.

6462 SAUNDERSON's Algebra, 2 vol. *new and very neat,* 1l 7s
6463 Stukeley's Palæographia Britannica, 3 numb. *cuts* 1743—Stukeley's Palæographia Sacra, *very fair and neatly bound, marble leaves* 1736 10s 6d
6464 Don Quixote, tranſlated by Smollet, *with fine cuts deſigned by Hayman, new and elegantly bound, by Johnſon,* 2 vol. 2l 5s 1755
6465 Dr. Leland's Neceſſity of Divine Revelation, 2 vol. *new and neatly bound,* 1l 10s — — — 1763
6466 Robertſon's Hiſt. of Scotland, 2 vol. *large paper, new and elegantly bound, marble leaves,* &c. 2l 2s — 1759
6467 Philoſoph. Tranſactions, abridged by Lowthorp, Jones, Eames and Martyn, *compleat and neat,* in 12 vol. 5l 15s 6d 1722, &c.

Books added. OCTAVO and TWELVES.

6468 FLOYD's Synopſ. of Univ. Biography, 3 vol. *in boards,* 7s 6d — — — 1760
6469 Dictionary of Arts and Sciences, *with a great number of cuts,* 8 vol. 2l 2s — — 1754
6470 Dyche's English Dictionary, 3s 6d — 1744
6471 Bailey's English Dictionary, 3s — 1726
6472 Boyer's Fr. and Engl. Dictionary, 2s 6d — 1708
6473 The ſame, 2s 6d — — — 1720
6474 Young's Lat. and Engl. Dictionary, 4s — 1757
6475 Baretti's Introduction to the Italian Language, *in boards,* 2s 1755
6476 Bachinau's German Grammar, 2s — 1751
6477 Palermo's Italian Grammar, 2s — 1755
6478 Milles's Practical Grammar to the Lat. Tongue, 2s 1729
6479 Philipps's Compend. Way of Teach. Languages, 2s 6d 1750
6480 Mœridis Lexicon Atticum, cum Notis var. *nov. & nit. comp.* 6s *L. Bat.* 1759
6481 Ainſworth's Lat. and Engl. Dictionary, abridged by Thomas, 2 vol. *new and neatly bound,* 12s
6482 Vigerus de Præcipuis Græc. Diction. Idiotiſmis, cum Animadv. Hoogeveen, *exemp. pulch. nit. comp.* 4s — *L. Bat.* 1752
6483 Holmes's Grammar of the Lat. Tongue, 1s — 1737
6484 ——— Greek Grammar, 1s — — 1737
6485 Greenwood's Engl. Grammar, *neatly bound,* 1s 6d 1729
6486 Clarke's Grammar of the Lat. Tongue, *interleaved,* 1s 1733
6487 H. Stephani Ciceronianum Lexicon, Græco-Lat. *exemp. pulch. nit. comp. in cor. turc.* 6s — *Par. ap. H. Steph.* 1757
6488 ——— Paralepomena Grammat. Gr. Linguæ Inſt. 1581—Enocus de Puerili Doctr. Græcar. Literarum, *nit. comp.* 2s 6d *Oliva R. Steph.*
6489 Cellarii Orthographia Latina, *nit. comp.* 2s — *Halæ* 1704
6490 Aldi Manutii Ratio Orthographiæ, *nit. comp.* 1s 6d *Venet.* 1561
6491 Sewel's Dutch Grammar, 1s — *Amſt.* 1725
6492 Clavis Homerica, a Patrick, 3s — *Lond.* 1741
6493 Grammat. Ling. Græcæ, 1s — — *Edinb.* 1738
6494 Altieri's Ital. & Engl. Grammar, 2s — 1728
6495 Maitre Italien de Veneroni, par Placardi, 2s 6d *Baſ.* 1752
6496 Dictionaire Hiſtoriq. Litteraire & Critique, 6 tom. *nouv. & fort bien relie,* 1l 10s — — *Par.* 1758
6497 Dictionaire Univerſ. des Foſſiles, par Bertrand, 2 tom. en 1 vol. *nouv. & fort bien relie,* 6s — — *Haye* 1763
6498 Dr. Middleton's Miſcellaneous Works, 5 vol. *new and very neat,* 18s
6499 ——— ——— Works, 5 vol. *new and elegantly bound, by* Johnſon, 5 vol. 1l 4s
6500 ——— ——— Works and Life of Cicero, 8 vol. *new and very neat,* 1l 13s
6501 ——— ——— Works and Life of Cicero, *new and elegantly bound, by* Johnſon, 8 vol. 2l 2s

6502 Neal's

6502 Neal's History of New England, 2 vol. *new and elegantly bound, by* Johnson, 2 vol. 10s —— —— 1747

6503 Milton's Poetical Works, with Cuts and Notes by Bishop Newton, 4 vol. *new and elegantly bound, by* Johnson, 1l 7s

6504 Quintilliani Institut. Oratoria, a Rollin, *nov. & elegant. compact. per* Johnson, 7s

6505 Ciceronis Epist. ad Familiares, with Notes in English, by Dr. Ross, *beautifully printed,* 2 vol. *new and very neatly bound,* 12s *Cant.*

6506 The same, 2 vol. *new and elegantly bound, by* Johnson, 14s

6507 Law's Considerations on the State of Religion in the World, *last edition, with great additions, new and neatly bound,* 6s 1759

6508 Hurd's Political Dialogues, *new and neatly bound,* 5s 1762

6509 The same, *new and elegantly bound, by* Johnson, 6s — 1762

6510 The same, with the new Dialogues on Education and Travel, *new and elegantly bound,* 7s 6d

6511 Horace, Lat. and Engl. with Notes, by Hurd, 2 vol. *new and very neatly bound, best edition,* 8s —— —— 1757

6512 Cote's Lectures, published by Dr. Smith, *new and neatly bound,* 5s

6513 The same, *second hand,* 3s 6d —— — 1747

6514 Dr. Rutherfurth's Institutes of Natural Law, 2 vol. *new and elegantly bound,* 12s —— —— *Camb.*

6515 Universal History, from the earliest Account of Time, *cuts,* 21 vol. *in boards,* 5l —— —— 1747

6516 Sir W. Temple's Works, 4 vol. *in boards,* 10s 6d *Edinb.* 1754

6517 Jortin's Remarks on Eccles. Hist. 3 vol. 15s —— 1751

-18 Plutarch's Lives, with Dacier's Notes, 6 vol. *new and very neat,* 1l 10s —— —— —— 1758

9 Cicero's Letters, by Melmoth, 3 vol. *neat,* 10s 6d 1753

0 Keyslar's Travels, *with cuts,* 4 vol. *new and neatly bound,* 1l 1s

21 Leland's View of Deistical Writers, 2 vol. *new and neatly bound,* 12s —— —— —— 1763

522 Kennet's Antiq. of Rome, *cuts,* 2s 6d —— 1737

6523 Watts's Logick, 2s 6d —— —— 1751

6524 Essays on Morality and Nat. Religion, 2s 6d — *Edinb.* 1751

6525 Maclaurin's Algebra, 4s —— — 1748

6526 Keil's Astronomy, *cuts,* 3s 6d —— — 1748

6527 —— Natural Philosophy, 2s 6d —— 1745

6528 Sherwin's Mathemat. Tables, revised by Gardiner, 7s 6d 1741

6529 Musschenbroek's Natural Philosophy, Engl. by Colson, *cuts,* 2 vol. 6s —— —— —— 1744

6530 Dissertat. on the Numbers of Mankind, by Wallace, 2s 6d *Edinb.* 1753

6531 Biblia Hebraica, â Joh. Simone, 2 tom. *nitid. compact, fol. marm.* 12s —— —— —— *Halæ* 1752

6532 Heineccii Syntag. Antiq. Roman. Jurisprudent. 2 tom. 6s *Traj.* 1745

6533 ———— Hist. Juris Civilis Romani, *sutus,* 3s 6d *L. Bat.* 1748

6534 Grotius de Jure Belli ac Pacis, Notis Gronovii & Barbeyracii, 2 tom. *exemp. pulch.* 7s —— —— *Amst.* 1735

6535 Corpus Juris Civilis, 2 tom. *comp. in* 1 vol. *exemp. pulch.* 15s *Amst.* 1681

6536 Westenbergii Principia Juris, 5s —— *L. Bat.* 1745

6537 Quintiliani Opera, Notis varior. 2 tom. 10s — *ib.* 1665

6538 Cal-

6538 Callimachus, Gr. & Lat. Not. varior. & Ernesti, 2 tom. *nov. & nit. comp.* 1l 1s ——— ——— *L. Bat.* 1761

6539 Petronius Arbiter, Notis varior. *comp. russico;* 7s 6d *Amst.* 1669

6540 Tolandi Adeisidæmon, with his Apology, 2s 6d *H. Com.* 1709

6541 Linnæi Philosoph. Botanica, *cum fig.* 3s 6d — *Stock.* 1751

6542 ——— Genera Plantarum, 3s 6d ——— *Halæ* 1752

6543 Tableau de la Ville de Paris, *fort bien relie, marb. sur les tranches,* 4s *Par.* 1762

6544 Aminta di Tasso con le Annot. da Menagio, 2s 6d *Venez.* 1736

6545 Analyze des Echecs, par Philidor, *cousu,* 1s 6d *Lond.* 1749

6546 Richardson sur la Peinture & la Sculpture, 3 tom. *bien relie,* 6s *Amst.* 1728

6547 Lettres Provinciales, par Montalte, 2s —— *Colog.* 1684

6548 Recreations Mathematiq. par Ozanam, *avec plusieurs fig.* 4 tom. *nouv. & fort bien relie,* 12s ——— — *Par.* 1735

6549 Lettres Persanes, 2 tom. *nouv. & fort relie,* 3s 6d *Col.* 1721

6550 Cent Nouvelles de Gomez, 20 tom. en 10 vol. *nouv. & fort bien relie,* 1l 10s ——— ——— *Haye* 1762

6551 L'Esprit des Loix, par Montesquieu, 4 tom. *nouv. & elegamen. relie par* Johnson, 17s ——— —— *Paris*

6552 Oeuvres de Moliere, 8 tom. *avec fig. nouv. & elegam. relie par* Johnson, 1l 10s —— —— *ib.* 1762

6553 Abrege Chronolog. de l'Hist. de France, 2 tom. *nouv. & eleg. relie, par* Johnson, 13s ——— — *ib.* 1762

6554 Oeuvres de Destouches, *avec fig. nouv. & elegam. relie par* Johnson, 10 tom. 1l 16s ——— ——— *ib.*

6515 Bysshe's Art of Poetry, 2 vol. *new and elegantly bound by* Johnso 7s 6d —— —— ——— 17

6556 Gordon's Translation of Tacitus, *with Political Discourses,* 5 *new and elegantly bound by* Johnson, 18s ——— 17

6557 Brookes's Natural History, *with cuts,* 6 vol. *new and neatly bound,* 1l 1s ——— ——— ——— 176

6558 Horatius, *forma minor, exemp. splend. & elegant. comp. in corio turc. fol. deaur. & marm.* 2l 2s —— *Par. e Typogr. Regia* 176

6559 Phœdrus, *eleg. comp. in cor. maurit. fol. deaur.* 1l 7s *Par. e Typogr. Regia* 1729

6560 Anecdotes of Polite Literature, *beautifully printed,* 5 vol. *sewed,* 10s 1764

6561 The same, 5 vol. *bound,* 12s 6d

F I N I S.

1764

MUSÆUM THORESBYANUM.

A

CATALOGUE

Of the genuine and valuable

COLLECTION

Of that well-known Antiquarian the late

RALPH THORESBY, Gent. *F.R.S.*

Author of DUCATUS LEODIENSIS.

CONSISTING OF

Roman, Britiſh, Runic, Saxon, and Engliſh Coins and Medals in Gold, Silver, &c. Manuſcripts, Curioſities, Autographs, antient Deeds, original Letters and Signs Manual of Britiſh and foreign Kings and Queens, Cromwell the Protector and his Son Richard, Principal Nobility and eminent Perſons, for Two Centuries paſt.

All which will be

SOLD by AUCTION,

By *WHISTON BRISTOW*, Sworn Broker,

At the Exhibition Room, *Spring Gardens, Charing Croſs*;

On *Monday March* 5th, and the Two following Days, begining punctually at 12 o'Clock.

To be viewed on *Thurſday March* 1ſt, and the following Days, *Sunday* excepted.

Catalogues to be had *gratis* at the Place of Sale, and of W. BRISTOW [Publiſher of the *Public Ledger*] St. *Paul's Church yard*, who ſells by Commiſſion Eſtates, Medals, Books, Pictures, Curioſities, Stocks in Trade, and Houſhold Furniture.

CONDITIONS of SALE.

I. THE highest Bidder is the Buyer; and if any Dispute shall arise between Two or more Bidders, the Lot in Dispute is to be put up again, or decided by the Majority of the Company.

II. No Person to advance less than Sixpence under a Pound; above a Pound, One Shilling; above Five Pounds, Two Shillings and Sixpence; and so in Proportion.

III. Each Person to pay down Five Shillings in the Pound, as Earnest, in Part of Payment for each Lot they buy; and to give in his Name and Place of Abode, if required.

IV. The Lots to be taken away, with all Faults, at the Buyer's Expence; and the Remainder of the Purchase-Money to be paid on the Delivery, within Two Days after the Sale; otherwise the Money deposited is to be forfeited, and the Lots uncleared to be sold, by public or private Sale, and the Deficiencies (if any) to be made good by the First Purchasers.

Those Gentlemen who cannot attend the Sale, may depend on having their Commissions faithfully and punctually executed by

Their obedient humble Servant,

W. BRISTOW.

A CATALOGUE.

First Day's Sale.

Roman Brass.

1 A Large Parcel of *Roman* Coins of all Sizes

2 A Parcel of Paduans, and Casts of different Emperors

3 One Pupienus, 1 Theodohatus, and 19 more of different Emperors 21

4 One Antoninus, reverse Britannia, 1 Marius, 1 Allectus, and 9 more, small Brass 12

5 Valerianus, Salonina, Claudius, Quintillus, Aurelianus, Probus, Tacitus, and Florianus 21

6 Posthumus, Victorinus, Tetricus, Marius, Carausius, Allectus, Carus, Carinus, and Numerian 23

7 Carausius 7, Allectus 1 8

8 ~~*Roman*~~ Weights 4, of Antioch 2 small, dated 104 and 108 6

9 Philip 1, Alexander 1, Demetrius 1, Antiochus Epiph. 1, Alexander Bala 1, and Ptolemy 1 7

Roman large, middle, and small Brass.

10 Julius 3, Agrippa 1, Augustus 5, Tiberius 2, Drusus 2, Germanicus 1, Agrippina 1, Caligula 1, and 2 more,

A N° 84,

N° 84, 85, 86, 87. 93, 94, 95, 96, 97. 100, 101, 102, 103, 104, 105, and 106, in the Ducatus, p. 286, 287 18

11 Caligula 3, Claudius 4, Nero 8, Galba 2, Vitellius 1, Vespasian 5, *vide* Ducatus, N° 108, 109, 110. 113, 114, 115. 121. 125, 126, 127, 128, 129, 130. 132. 135, 139, 140. 153. 159, 160. 165, 166, and 167 23

12 Vespasian 2, Domitian 7, Agrippa 1, Nerva 2, Trajan 9, *vide* Ducatus, N° 176. 183. 201. 209, 210. 217, 218. 227. 229. 231. 233. 238, 239. 274, 275, 276. 279, 280. 284. 294 21

13 Hadrian 7, Sabina 1, Antoninus 15, *vide* N° 305. 315. 316. 323, 330, 331, 332. 341. 347. 350, 351, 352. 360, 362. 364. 369, 370, 371. 383, 384, 385, 386. and 388 24

14 Faustina 1, M. Aurelius 3, Faustina jun. 1, Verus 1, Lucilla 1, Commodus 5, Crispina 1, *vide* N° 389. 403. 406. 413. 422, 423. 439. 442. 444, 445, 446. 449, 450, and 457 14

15 Did. Julianus 1, Pesc. Niger 1, Sept. Severus 3, Caracalla 1, Jul. Mammea 1, Alex. Severus 3, Gordianus 3, *vide* N° 459. 460. 465. 468. 495. 530. 549. 558. 570, 571. 578, 579, and 581 13

16 Philip 2, Traj. Decius (a Medallion) 1, Salust Barbia 1, *vide* N° 600. 602, 607 and 610 4

17 Treb. Gallus 1, Æmilian 1, see N° 619 and 627 2

18 Diocletian, Constantius, Maximianus, Maximinus, Maxentius, Severus, Licinius, Magnentius, Constantine, and Crispus, middle Brass

19 Diocletian, Constantius, Maximianus, Maximinus, Severus, Maxentius, Magnentius, Decentius, Licinius, Constantine, Crispus, Constans, and Mag. Maximus, middle Brass

20 Diocletian, Maximianus, Helena, Theodora, M. Fausta, Constantinus, Crispus, &c. small 40

21 A *Jewish* Shekel, an Half Shekel, and a Selah, see N° 1, 2, and 3 3

22 A Silver Tetradrachm of Athens, and a Brass Coin of ditto, *vide* N° 4 and 6

23 Another Silver Tetradrachm of Athens with the Name of the Magistrate, and 1 Brass of the same Place, *vide* N° 5 and 7

24 Three Silver Coins of Neapolis, Achaia, and Velia, *vide* N° 8, 9, and 10 3

25 A

25 A Brafs Coin of Smyrna, 1 of Carthage, 1 of Antioch; and 1 more, *vide* N° 11, 12, 13, and 14 4

26 A Drachm of Amintas, 1 of Alexander, and 1 Tetradrachm of ditto, *vide* N° 15, 16, and 17 3

27 Two Brafs Coins of the Ptolemies, 1 of Alexander, and 1 of Antiochus Epiphan. *vide* N° 18, 19, 20, and 22 4

28 Three Brafs Coins of Antiochus, 1 of Alex. Bala, 1 of Tryphon, and 1 of Cleopatra, *vide* N° 23, 24, 25, 26, 27, alfo the Cafts 5

29 Six Antient Roman Weights, *vide* N° 1, 2, 3, 4, 5, and 6, p. 279

* 29 Four ditto, 1 Pertinax, large Brafs, 1 Ælius, 1 Adrian 7

Roman Silver Denarii.

30 A double Denarius, and a Quinarius, *vide* N° 7 and 8

31 Aburia, Acilia, Æmilia, Antonia, Aurelia, Calpurnia, Carifia, Caffia, Claudia, Coelia, and Cordia, *vide* N° 9 to 32 25

32 Cornelia, Fannia, Flaminia, Fonteia, Furia, Herennia, Hoftilia, Julia, Junia, Livinia, Lucilia, Lucretia, Mamilia, Manlia, Maria, and Minucia, *vide* N° 33 to 38 26

33 Muffidia, Naevia, Norbana, Papiria, Plautia, Plaetoria, Poblicia, Pompeia, Porcia, Pofthumia, Rubria, Rutilia, Scribonia, Sentia, Sergia, Sicinia, and Valeria 23

Roman Imperial.

34 Julius Cæfar 4, Auguftus 5, Tiberius 1, Caligula 1, Claudius 3, Nero 5, Galba 4, Otho 1, *vide* N° 80, 81, 82, 83. 88, 89, 90, 91, 92. 99. 111. 118, 119, 120. 122, 123, 124. 131. 134. 136, 137, 138. 141 and 142 25

35 Otho 5, Vitellius 5, Vefpafian 14, *vide* N° 143, 144, 145, 146, 147, 148, 149, 150, 151, 152, 154, 155, 156, 157, 158. 161, 162, 163, 164. 168, 169, 170, 171, and 172 24

36 Vefpafian 7, Titus 11, Jul. Titi 1, Domitian 6, *vide* N° 173, 174, 175. 177, 178, 179, 180, 181 182. 184, 185. 187, 188, 189, 190, 191, 192, 193, 194, 195, 196, 197, 198, 199, and 200 25

37 Domitian 21, *vide* N° 202 *to* 208, 211 *to* 216, 219 *to* 225, and 228 21

38 Domitia 1, Nerva 10, Trajan 14, *vide* N° 230. 232. 234. 236 *to* 257 25

39 Trajan 27, *vide* N° 258. 260 *to* 273, 278. 281 *to* 295 27

40 Trajan 4, Hadrian 21, *vide* N° 296 *to* 299, and 301 *to* 325 25

41 Hadrian 4, Sabina 1, Ælius 2, Antoninus Pius 17, *vide* N° 326 *to* 329, and 334 to 361 24

42 Antoninus Pius 16, Faustina 8, *vide* N° 363 *to* 368, 372 *to* 382. 390. 392 *to* 398 24

43 Mar. Aurelius 16, Faustina Aurel. 4, Verus 5, Lucilla 1, *vide* N° 402, 404, 405. 407 *to* 411, 414 *to* 417, 419 *to* 421, 426 *to* 429, 432 *to* 436, 441 27

44 Commodus 4, Crispina 1, Pertinax 1, Albinus 2, Sept. Severus 21, *vide* N° 448. 452, 453. 455, 456. 458. 461 *to* 464. 467. 469, 470 *to* 486 29

45 Sept. Severus 8, Julia Domna 5, Caracalla 13, *vide* N° 487 *to* 494, 496 *to* 513 25

46 Plautilla 1, Geta 6, Macrinus 2, Heliogabalus 13, Julia Paula 1, *vide* N° 514 *to* 519, 521 *to* 529, 531 *to* 536, 538 *to* 541 25

47 Julia Paula 2, Julia Aquilia 1, Julia Mæsa 2, Julia Mammea 2, Alex. Severus 15, *vide* No. 542 *to* 548, 550 *to* 563. 565. 567 24

48 Alex. Severus 1, Maximinus 4, Balbinus 1, Gordianus 10, Philippus 5, Ottacilla 2, Philip jun. 1, *vide* No. 569. 572 *to* 576. 580, 582 *to* 584, 586 *to* 591, 595 *to* 599, and 603 *to* 605 24

49 Traj. Decius 2, Etruscilla 2, Treb. Gallus 6, Volusianus 4, Æmilianus 1, Valerianus 6, Gallienus 9, *vide* No. 606, 611 *to* 617, 620, 621, 623 *to* 626, 628 *to* 642 30

50 Constantius 3, Julianus 3, Valentinian 4, Valens 2, Gratian 2, Mag. Maximus 2, Eugenius 1, Arcadius 2, Honorius 1, Theodosius 1 21

51 Gallienus 32, *vide* No. 644 *to* 675 (Brass) 32

52 Gallienus, Salonina, Valerianus, and Posthumus, *vide* No. 677 *to* 716 40

53 Posthumus, Victorinus, and Tetricus, *vide* No. 717 *to* 752 40

54 Tetricus and Claudius, *vide* No. 753 *to* 787 40

55 Carausius 4, Allectus 2, *some finely preserved* 6

56 One Allectus in Silver, 1 in Brass, and 1 Carausius, *fine Preservation* 3

57 Constantine, Crispus, Constans, Constantius, Licinius, and Magnentius 72

58 Probus, Tacitus, Florianus, Diocletian, Carausius, Allectus, Constantinus, and Magnentius 36

59 Quin-

59 Quintilius, Carauſius, Conſtantine, Valens, Valentinian, Gratian, Arcadius, and Honorius 43

60 Carauſius 7, Reverſe *Pax*, *Moneta*, *Salus*, *Hilaritas*, *Fides Militum*, *Virtus*, *and a Legion* 7

61 Carauſius 3, Allectus 2, *finely preſerved* 5

Engliſh Medals in Silver and Copper.

62 Three Jettons ſtruck in *Holland* alluding to the Aſſiſtance given them by Queen *Elizabeth*, and an engraved Counter of *James* I. No. 326, 327, 328, and 350 4

63 Eight Jettons and Medals of *Charles* I. No. 407, 408, 409, 410, 411, 412, and 415 8

64 An antient Copper Medallion of *John Kendal*, grand Turkopolier at the Siege of *Rhodes*, 1480, *vide* fol. 591, and No. 32. in the Plate of Antiquities

65 Three Medals of *Charles* I. No. 413, 414, and 416 3

66 Three Medals of the Earl of *Eſſex*, and 2 of Sir *Thomas Fairfax*, No. 418, 419, 420, and 421 5

67 Two Silver, and 1 Copper Medal of *James* I. and 5 of *Charles* I. No. 347, 348, 349. 422, 423, 424. 496, and 756 8

68 Three chaſed Medallions of *Charles* I. and II.

69 Two Medals of *Charles* II. on the Reſtoration and his *Scotch* Coronation Medal, No. 452, 453, and 760 3

70 A Medal of *Oliver Cromwell*, and one of *Fairfax* 2

71 A Pattern Piece by *Simmons* of *Charles* II.

72 The Coronation Medals of *James* II. and his Queen, No. 497, and 499 3

73 A Medal on the Birth of the Chevalier, *Hercules* ſtrangling Serpents in his Cradle, No. 500

74 One Silver and 2 Copper Jettons of the Chevalier, No. 501, 502, and 503

75 One Medal of *William* and *Mary*, and 4 of Queen *Anne* 5

76 Two Medals of Queen *Anne* and 2 of *George* I. 4

77 Six Medals of Queen *Anne* in Copper 6

78 One Half-penny, and 2 Farthings of Queen *Anne* 3

79 A Jetton of the Earl of *Saliſbury*, 1 of the Counteſs of *Pembroke*, 1 of Sir *Edmund Godfrey*, 1 of the Earl of *Lauderdale*, and 1 of Prince *Eugene*, No. 353. 491. 495, and 757 5

80 The famous and rare Medal of Col. *Lilburne*, No. 446

Foreign

Foreign Silver Coins and Medals.

81 Coins of *France*, *Flanders*, *Germany*, *Denmark*, *Sweden*, &c. at *per* oz.
82 Ditto,
83 Ditto,
84 Ditto, coarse Silver,
85 An *Arabian* Larin, 1 antient *Arabic*, and 10 more *Turkish* and *East Indian* Pieces in Silver and 19 in Lead and Copper 31
86 Four very rare and fine Talismans, and a Hebrew Shekel 5
87 A fine large Marriage Medal. 1 of *Luther*, and 9 more of *Sweden*, *Denmark*, *Germany*, and *Lorrain* 11
88 A Medal of *Henry* II. 7 *French* Jettons in Silver, and a fine Copper one gilt of *Lewis* XIII. 9
89 *Innocent*, X. *Clement* X. *Clement* XI. in Silver, *Clement* IX. *Clement* X. *Alexander* VII. *Gregory* XIII. and *Innocent* XII. in Copper, the last gilt 8
90 A Medal of the Battle of *Leipsick*, 4 more of *Germany*, and 1 ditto plated 6
91 Twelve *Dutch* and *Flemish* Jettons in Silver, and 16 more in Copper 28
92 Four Medals of the *United Provinces* on the Synod of *Dort*, Peace of *Munster*, Battle of *Newport*, and Prince *Maurice* 4
93 Eight *Roman* Catholick Pieces with the *Virgin Mary*, *Ignatius*, *Xavier*, &c. in Silver, and 8 in Brass 16

English, Roman, and Foreign Gold.

94 A Rose-noble of *Edward* IV. and an Angel of ditto, *vid.* No. 240, and 241
95 A Sovereign and Angel of *Henry* VIII. No. 261, and 269 2
96 A Half-sovereign of *Edward* VI. and an Angel of Queen *Mary*, No. 284, and 293 2
97 An Angel of Queen *Elizabeth*, a Half-sovereign and Double Rose Royal of ditto, 329, 330, and 331 3
98 A double Rose Royal of *James* I. No. 352
99 One of *Charles* V. and 8 more foreign Coins and Medals 9
100 A Gold Denarius of *Tiberius*, No. 98
101 Ditto of *Trajan*, No. 283
102 Ditto of *Joannnes Comnenus*, *vid.* p. 598

103 A Quarter Noble of *Edward* III. and a Noble of *Henry* VI. 2

Silver Roman.

104 From Auguſtus to Julianus 52

105 Auguſtus, Tiberius, Vitellius, Veſpaſian, Titus, Nerva, Trajan, Hadrian, Ælius, Antoninus, Fauſtina, Verus, Caracalla, and Julia Pia 25

106 Veſpaſian, Titus, Domitian, Nerva, Trajan, Hadrian, Antoninus, Fauſtina, Aurelius, Verus, Caracalla, Geta, S. Severus, and Julia Domna 26

107 Julian 2, Jovian 2, Valentinian 1, Valens 2, Mag. Maximus 2, Victor 1 10

108 Conſtantius 2, Julian 4, Valens 3, Gratianus 1, Arcadius 2, Honorius 2 14

Braſs, Copper, Lead, &c.

109 Sundry foreign Coins, and Jettons

110 Ditto

111 Sundry foreign Medals, &c. Copper and Pewter

112 Three Matrices of antient Seals

113 Ditto

114 Six Medals of *Charles Guſtavus*, and *Charles* XII. Kings of *Sweden*, the Duke of *Lorrain*, and Count *Teckley*, in hard Metal

115 *Lewis* XIV. William III. and Queen Mary, Queen Ann, the Emperors Joſeph and Charles VI. &c. 14

117 Jurieu, Cocceius, Le Tellier, Molinas, Wittichius, and the Duke of *Monmouth* in ditto

118 Sixty-one *Roman* Coins in large and middle Braſs in two Boards

~~*118 A Cabinet~~

119 A Parcel of Boards, with Cells for Coins

*119 Mr. Thoreſby's Ducatus Leodienſis, *full of Manuſcript Additions by the Author*

Second Day's Sale.

Pewter and Lead Medals.

120 COPPER, Lead, and Pewter Coins and Medals

*120 Copper, Pewter, Lead, and Iron ditto

121 Sundry Silver Coins, ~~at per oz.~~

122 Different Halfpence and Farthings, Engliſh and Iriſh 60

123 Fifty

Lot	Description	No.
123	Fifty Ditto	51
124	Fifty ditto	50
125	Town Pieces and Tradesmens Tokens	72
126	Ditto	72

British Coins, &c. D. L. p. 337.

Lot	Description	No.
127	One Electrum, 2 coarse Silver, *vid.* D. L. No. 1. 2. 4.	3
128	Two Copper, and 1 coarse Silver, D. L. No. 3. 5. 6.	3
129	One Gold, 1 Silver, No. 9 and 10	2
130	Four small Silver, 1 large ditto, No. 11, 12, 13, 14, &c.	5
131	Three Copper, 1 ditto small, *Quære*, if *British*, No. 7. 15, 16, 17	4

Saxons.

Lot	Description	No.
132	One supposed to be the Figure of the God *Thor*, the other probably of *Woden* or *Othin*, &c. see No. 18 and 19	2
133	One of the Peter Pence, and 1 supposed to be of K. *Edwin* of *Northumberland*, 617. *vid.* p. 340, No. 20. 23	2
134	One Penny of K. *Elfred*, as supposed of *Northumberland*, but more probably of *Alfred* the Great, No. 21	1
335	A St. *Peter's* Penny, No. 22.	1
136	A St. *Martin's* ditto, No. 24	1
137	Penny (*sancti Eadi*) No. 51	1
138	*Æthelstan* of *Kent*, 1 Penny, *Burgred* of *Mercia*, 3	4
139	*Burgred* 2, *Edmund* 2, and 2 *Irish* Pennies	6
140	Ten fine Stica of *Eadbert*, *Ethelret*, *Alred*, *Eanred*, and *Ethelred*, No. 25, 26, 27, 28, 29, 30, 31, 32, 33, 34	10
141	Ditto of *Ethelred*, &c. No. 35, 36, 37, 38, 40, 41, 42, 43, 44	10
142	Ditto of *Edilred*, *Ardvvlfsyning*, *Ethelhelm*, *Ethelread*, *Osbright*, &c. No. 45, 46, 47, 48, 49. 50. 53, 54. 59, 60	10
143	Ditto of *Osbright*, *Alla*, and *Eanred*, No. 61, 62, 63, 64, 65, 66, 67, 68, 69	10
144	Ditto of Edilred, and others, *uncertain*	13
145	Fourteen ditto	14
146	Alfred the Great, 1 Penny, No. 70, Æthelred, 1 ditto, No. 58	2
147	Athelstan the Dane 1, *vid.* 71. Edward, 4 ditto, 73, 74, 75, 76	5
148	Athelstan, No. 77. 78, 79, 80, 83	5
149	Athelstan, 3, 81, 82. 85	3
150	Athelstan, 2, No. 84 and 87	2
151	Athelstan, 2, 86 and 88, Ethelnoth, 1, 72	3

151 Eadred,

152 Eadred, 2, 89, 90. Eadgar, 3, 91, 92, 93 5
153 Eadweard, *Reverse, a Church,* No. 95 1
154 Eadweard ditto 1
155 Eadweard 3, 96, 95. 98 3
156 Canutus the Danish Kinig, 4, and 1 of Harold 3
157 Æthelred 3, 99, 100, 101. Canute, 1. Edward ditto, 105, 106, 107, &c. Burgred, 2 13

Coins from the Norman Conquest. D. L. p. 349.

158 Of William I. or II. 6 Pennies, 108, 109, 110, 111, 112, 113 6
159 Ditto 7, and 1 of Rufus, 15, 16, 17, 18, 19. 114. 120 8
160 Ditto
161 Henry I. *with Pax, very rare,* 1 Penny, and 1 of Henry II. 128, 129 2
162 Stephen and Henry, *exceeding scarce,* No. 130. 1
163 Eustachius, No. 131, *scarce* 1
164 Eustacius, *Reverse, Eboraci,* No. 132, *exceeding rare* 1
165 Stephen, 1 Penny, *scarce* 1
166 King John, 1 Penny, Henry III. 10. 133, 134, 135, 136, 137, 138, 139, 140, 141. 143 11
167 Richard I. *as supposed by Speed,* &c. No. 142, and 1 Piece of the black Money, *well preserved* 2
168 Henry III. 15 Pennies, from No. 144 to 155 15
169 Edward I. and II. Twelve Pence and Halfpence ditto, *some very rare* 12
170 Edward III. 1 Acquitaine Penny, No. 190, Henry VI. ditto 1 2
171 Edward I. II. and III. 44 Pennies 44
172 Edward III. 4 Groats, 2 Halves, and 2 Halfpence 8
173 Edward III. 1 Groat, London, 1 York, 1 Half Groat, York, and 1 Half Calais, *rare* 4
174 Richard II. 2 Pennies, 207, 208 2
175 Henry IV. and V. &c. Groats and Half Groats, &c. 209, 210, 211, 212, 213, 214, 215, &c. 10
176 Edward IV. 11 Groats, No. 226, 227. 230, 231 11
177 Ditto Dublin and Drogheda, *one with three Crowns,* and a scarce Half Groat, *with Star or Sun on Reverse,* No. 234, 235, 236, 237 4
178 Richard III. 1 Groat, *with the Rose,* No. 242, 1 ditto, *Boar's Head* 2
179 Henry VII. 5 Groats, 3 Half Groats, 4 Pennies, and a Farthing ditto 13
180 Ditto, and Henry VIII. 9 Groats, 8 Half Groats, 5 Pennies,

B

nies, &c. No 243, 244, 245, 246. 248. 250. 260, 261 24

181 Henry VIII. a Proof Piece for the Penny, *minted at Durham, wt.* 44 *Grains,* No. 259 1

182 Ditto a Shilling, Groat, and Half Groat, Penny and Halfpenny, and a Jetton, *vid.* No. 263

183 Edward VI. 2 Shillings side faced, one of which is the *Timor Domini,* with a Half Groat, side faced, *rare* 3

184 Edward VI. a Crown 1551, and a Half Crown, 6 Shillings, 2 Sixpences, and one Threepence of fine Silver, No. 281. 283 10

185 Queen Mary, a Shilling, with her Head, *Reverse, a Harp crowned,* Philip and Mary, 2 Six pences ditto *vide* No. 290, 291 3

186 Ditto 3 Shillings, and a Crown 1553, and a base Penny Edward VI. with some others, No. 281. 287, 288, &c. 9

187 Elizabeth the scarce Portcullis Shilling, and rare Sixpence, countermarked with the Belgick Lion, No. 294, 306 2

188 Elizabeth, Pledge of a Half-penny, and her Brass Money Ireland, 1602, No. 324, 325

189 Elizabeth, Crown, Half Crown, Shilling, &c. Sixpence, Threepence, Twopence, Penny, and Halfpenny, No. 295, 296, 297 18

190 Elizabeth's English and Irish Shilling and Sixpence, 2 Pennies, Halfpenny, and Copper Farthing, No. 300. 314, 322 8

191 King James I Crown, Half Crown, Shilling, and Sixpence, Two Pence, Penny, and Halfpenny, No. 332. 334, 335, 336, 337, 338. 362 7

*191 King James's English and Irish Coins, Shillings, Sixpences, and 7 smaller Coins, No. 333. 339, 340. 342, 343, 344. 346, &c. 10

**191 King *Charles* I Crown, Half Crown, 5 Shillings, a Sixpence, and Two-pence, *vide* D. L. No. 354. 5. 7. 8. 9. 37 8

192 Ditto, Sundry Coins minted at *York,* from the Half Crown to the Penny, *vide* D. L. No. 336. 9. 371. 393. 400. 1. 4. 5. 11

193 Ditto, Sundry Coins from the Half Crown to the Twopence, of the *Oxford* Exurgat Money, *vide* D. L. No. 363. 390, 1. 7. &c. 11

194 Ditto, Newark Siege Coins, &c. the Half Crown, Shilling, Nine-pence, Six-pence, Ormond Shilling, Sixpence,

pence, and Groat, and Shilling, 1645, *in the Legend vide* D. L. No. 365. 374. 381. 2. 7. 9

195 Ditto, A *rare* Siege Crown and Shilling, N. E. *vide* D. L. No. 360. 380 2

196 Ditto, The Carlisle Three Shilling, and Shilling Piece, *vide* D. L. No. 361. 375. 2

197 King *Charles* I. and II. 4 Pontefract Shillings, *vide* D. L. No. 377, 378. 426, 427 4

198 King *Charles* I. a ditto, and a Cork Six-pence, *vide* D. L. No. 366. 384 2

199 Ditto, a Scarborough Siege Coin, 2*s.* 3*d.* Plate Money, D. L. No. 367 1

200 Ditto, a Siege Coin stamped 1*s.* 4*d.* a Shilling ditto, Plate Money, *vide* D. L. 368. 376 2

201 Lord Baltimore's Shilling (a Proof Six-pence in Copper) and 3 New England Shillings, a Six-pence and Three-pence, *vide* D. L. 441. 3. 4. 5. 6 7

202 Commonwealth, a mill'd Six pence 1651, in fine *Preservation*, and very *rare*, *vide* D. L. No. 435 1

203 Ditto, a Crown, a Half Crown, 2 Shillings, a Six-pence, a Two pence, a Penny, and Half Penny, *vide* D. L. No. 430. 1, 2, 3, 4. 7 8

204 The Protector Oliver Cromwell's Crown, Half Crown, and Shilling, *vide* 436. 449. 451 3

205 King Charles II. hammered Money, Half Crown, Shilling, Six-pence, Four pence, Three pence, Two pence, and Penny, *vide* D. L. 456. 7, 8. 464 13

206 King James II. Crown, Half Crown, Shilling, Six-pence, Four-pence, Three-pence, Two-pence, and Penny 8

207 King William and Mary, ditto 8

208 King William, ditto 8

209 Queen Ann, a Vigo Crown, Half Crown, Shilling, Six-pence, Four-pence, Three pence, Two-pence, Penny, and 3 Shillings 11

Scotch Coins.

210 Alexander I. David I. Alexander II. Alexander III. John, Robert I. David II. and James I. Pence and Half Pence, *vide* D. L. 647 *to* 660. 672 *to* 699 16

211 David II. Robert III. sirnamed John Farne Zeir, and James II. Groats, Half Groats, and Pence, *vide* D. L. 660 *to* 667. 670 *to* 674 12

212 James II. III. and IV. Groats, Half Groats, &c. *vide* D. L. No. 675, 676. 680 *to* 683. 686, 687, and 684 11

213 Mary,

213 Mary, and Francis and Mary, from Shilling to Penny, *vide* D. L. 688, 689 to 702 15

214 Mary, a Shilling with her Head, and a Medal when Dowager of *France*, *vide* D. L. 703 to 709 2

215 Mary, Mary and Henry, a Crown (or 3 Pound Piece) the Half and Quarter ditto, *vide* D. L. 705, *to* 708 5

216 James VI. ditto, ditto, *vide* D. L. 710 *to* 716 7

217 James VI. and Charles, from the 30*s*. Piece to the smallest Coin, *vide* D. L. 717 *to* 726. 733 *to* 736. 740 *to* 751 27

218 Sundry English and Scotch Coins from Charles II. to Queen Ann inclusive, 40, 20, 10, and 5 Penny Pieces 23

219 Various Scotch Half Pence and Farthings, in Copper, *vide* D. L. 727, &c. 27

220 A Series of the Irish Gun Money of King James II. Crowns, Half Crowns, Shillings, and Six-pences 39

221 Pewter Pence, Half Pence, and Farthings, *well preserved* 9

222 King James II. Pewter Irish Crown, very *rare* and well *preserved* 1

223 Common Wealth, a Farthing, very *rare*, *vide* D. L. No. 438 1

224 Charles II. 2 scarce Farthings, or Patterns for such, *vide* D. L. 428, 429 2

225 Ditto, 1 Silver, 2 Copper, Farthings, *Quatuor Maria vindico*, Exergue, Britannia, *vide* D. L. p378 3

226 English Pewter Half Pence and Farthings of Charles, James, William and Mary 15

227 Ditto, Ditto 16

The Third Day's Sale.

Manuscripts, Curiosities, original Letters, Autographs, &c.

1 TWelve Vol. of Sermons, by *Topham*, *Byard*, &c. many of them preached before General *Fairfax* during the Civil Wars and the Interregnum, and some of them copied by the General in his own Hand

2 Twelve ditto

3 Twelve ditto with some Theological Tracts and single Sermons

4 A very

4 A very antient Exposition of the Creed, and 9 more

5 Lectures of *Roger Manhood*, Esq; Chief Baron, concerning Tithes, 1567——Sentence against Sir *T. Lake* and Sir *Francis Bacon*'s Speech, when he took Place as Lord Chancellor, (*vide* D. L. N° 119, P. 531,) and 5 others

6 Sir *J. Neltborp*'s Alphabetical Table of the Law, and 5 more

7 Historica Descriptio Vitæ Gul. Wickami, Winton. Episcopi, et 7 alii

8 Epigrams, Essays, &c. by Mr. *Geo. Farrant*, neatly wrote, and 5 more

9 The Will of *E. Allen*, Esq; with the Ordinances, Rules, and Statutes, for his College at *Dulwich*

10 Sapientia Solomonis Drama Comicotragicum—— N. B. This MS is finely preserved, and was formerly Queen *Elizabeth*'s own Book, and 4 more

11 Certain Tables shewing the Break of Day, the Rising and Setting of the Sun, &c. for ever, 1584, and 11 more

12 *Parlor's* Abridgment of Martial Disciplin, selected out of best Authors, and the Order of Fortifications and Approaches by Sea and Land

13 Miniatura, or the Art of Limning, by *D. Ring*, and 5 more

14 Letters of sundry Persons, in the Reigns of Queen *Elizabeth* and King *James*, and 3 more

15 Lives of *Jesus Christ* and of certain Saints, and 7 more

16 Ten Treatises upon Husbandry, Grafting of Trees, &c. *vide* D. L. N° 108, p. 530

17 An Account of *Witchcraft*, in the Family of E. *Fairfax* at *Leeds*——An Account of ditto, in the Family of *N. Starkie*, Esq; in *Lancashire*——Behaviour of Mr. *John Bradford*, Preacher, and of the young Man who suffered with him in *Smithfield* for the Testimony of *Christ*

18 A Treatise of the Sovereignty of *Scotland*, in *Latin*, wrote in a very fair Hand, and 1 more

19 A learned Treatise of Forest Laws, and 2 more

20 The History of *Bombay*, wrote upon *Indian* Paper, by *John Burnell*, Esq; Governor of *Dungary* Fort in that Island

21 Three Journals of Voyages to the *East Indies*, &c. and 4 more

22 Three Treatises of the Isle of Man, One of them finely wrote and beautifully illuminated

23 History of *Staffordshire*, by *Erdswick*

24 Instructions from Queen *Elizabeth* to Sir *F. Walsingham*, with several Letters in her Reign

25 The trew Coppye of the E. of *Arundel*, his Letters sent from the Tower to the Queen, 1585—Judge *Jenkyns*'s Answer

ſwer when Priſoner in the Tower, 1647—And King *Charles* I. Farewell to his Lords at *Newport*, 1648—*vide* D L. N° 123, p. 532, and 3 more

26 The State of *England*, *France*, *Spain*, and *Holland*——And Natural and Political Obſervations upon the State of *England*, with ſeveral Calculations on Land, Coin, Trade, Wool, &c. *vide* D. L. N° 93, p. 527, and 2 more

27 Nine Volumes containing the Names of all ſuch Perſons as have come from beyond the Seas, as alſo of the Places from whence they came, and where they intend to lodge, together with their Buſineſs, taken by Order of the Parliament, 1655

28 A Volume containing 152 Tracts, chiefly relating to King *James* and King *Charles* I. including a waggiſh Deſcription of *Scotland*

29 Queen *Elizabeth*'s Inſtructions to *H.* Earl of *Pembroke*, appointing him Preſident of the Principality of *Wales*, 1598, and 10 more

30 Parliamentary Tracts during the Reign of *Charles* I. and the Interregnum, with a brief Note of a Decree of the Star Chamber concerning Printing, *July* 11th 1637, 5 vol.

31 A Book of Survey made in the Sixth Year of Queen *Elibeth*, containig the State of Manors, Lands, and Tenements, in the Countie's of *York*, *Durham*, *Derby*, &c. with ſeveral Accounts of the Families of Lord *Eure* and Sir *John Dawnay*

32 Commiſſions of King *James* I. and King *Charles* II. with ſeveral other Liſts and Matters, *vide* D. L. N° 84. p. 525, and 2 more

33 Hiſtory of the Surprize of *Pontefract* Caſtle, *vide* D. L. N° 78. p. 525, and 9 more

34 An *Engliſh* Verſion of *Kirkby*'s Inqueſt, with ſeveral other Matters interſperſed——Names of the Monaſteries and Hoſpitals in the Dioceſs of *York*, likewiſe of what Prebends, Officers, &c. in the Gift of the Archbiſhop of *York*——An Inventory of the Jewels, Plate, &c. within *York* Cathedral, with other Liſts——Viſitation of *Yorkſhire* in Queen *Elizabeth*'s Reign, with Additions, by *R. Thoresby*——Miſcellanies chiefly relating to *York*——And a Rental or Computus of the Archbiſhop of *York*

35 Twelve Volumes of curious Tracts of the opulent and flouriſhing Town of *Leeds* in *Yorkſhire*, relating to its Cuſtoms, Privileges, and extenſive Manufactory in the Cloth Trade

36 Pedi-

36 Pedigrees of many of the Gentry of *Yorkshire*, concludes in Queen *Elizabeth's* Reign, with the Arms painted, *vide* D. L. N° 42. p. 521——Pedigrees of the Gentry of the West Riding of the County of *York*, *vide* D. L. N° 86. p. 526——And an Alphabetical List of the Names and Arms of the Nobility and Gentry in *Yorkshire*, and in the Bishoprick of *Durham*, with Additions, by *Fairfax*, *vide* D. L. N° 30. p. 518

37 The Pedigrees and Arms of the Nobility, drawn by *Perkins* of *Fishlake*, about the Year 1610 or 1620, the Coats of Arms handsomely express'd

38 A List of the Nobility, &c. as likewise of the Offices, Fees, &c. in *England*, *vide* D. L. N° 48. p. 521, and 1 more

39 Royal Descent of the Reigns from *Egbert* I. to Queen *Elizabeth*, with the Alliances between *England* and *France*, with their Arms coloured, *vide* D. L. N° 28. p. 518——Arms of the Nobility from *William* the Conqueror to *Edward* IV. with their Marriage and Issue, coloured, *vide* D. L. N° 29. p. 518——And an Alphabetical List of Crests belonging to several Families, Extracts from Domes-day Book relating to several Parts of *Yorkshire*——Fœdarium Honoris Pontefract

40 The Arms of Queen *Elizabeth* and the Knights of the Garter in the Year 1599, upon Vellum, finely painted and gilt, bound in Velvet, *vide* D. L. N° 132. p. 532

41 Corpus Christi Playe, in antique *English* Verse, *vide* D. L. N° 17. p. 517

42 Collection of Letters on Vellum, painted and gilt, *vide* D. L. N° 12. p. 515 —— Scali Mundi, and Catalogue of Popes, on Vellum, *vide* D. L. N° 13. p. 516

43 A Volume of very antient Music, by *R. Fairfax*, Doctor of Music, and 1 more

44 Cronica fratris Martini Papæ Penitentiani et Capellani, *vide* D. L. No. 104. p. 529, & 5 alii

45 Historia regum Britan. a Bruto ad Oswaldum, *vide* D. I No. 191. p. 538, & 3 alii

46 An ancient Breviary, & 4 alii

47 Baltasar Castalionis ad regem Henricum, de Guid. Monetario Urbini Duce, *vide* L. D. No. 194. p. 538, *illuminated*

48 A Missal upon Vellum, *finely painted and gilt*

49 St. Jerome's Latin Bible, *neatly* wrote upon Vellum, *vide* D. L. No. 3. p. 501

50 A Latin Bible, *neatly* wrote on Vellum, *vide* D. L. No. 4. p. 502

CURI-

CURIOSITIES.

51 Six Pieces of Ore and Flint, and 3 antient Boxes, 2 of Brass, and 1 of Wood, and an old Key

52 A Miniature Picture of King *Charles* I. a ditto of *Charles* II. 1 ditto of his Queen, and sundry Mochas, &c.

53 A Pair of white Gloves in 2 Walnut Shells, and several Dozen of Spoons, Knives, ~~and Forks~~ in a Cherry Stone

54 A Handkerchief of King *Charles* I. and 2 Pieces of Point Lace.

55 A Pair of King *James* I. Gloves embroidered with Gold, D. L. 481.

56 Four curious Purses, and 4 Gloves

57 An antient Manuscript Almanack, and 3 old printed ditto

58 Two old *Roman* Celts, 3 antient Rings, and sundry odd Things

59 A Loadstone, and a Prism

60 Sundry *Romish* Relicks, &c.

61 A Pair of Stone Buckles, a Pair of Clasps, a Silver Box, a Silver Bodkin, and sundry odd Things

62 Three Box Medals, and a Box Almanack, and an antient Coat of Arms in Wood

* 62 The House of *Parliament* curiously enameled upon Gold, *Thomas* Lord *Fairfax* the General of their Forces, upon *Chesnut* his Charging-Horse, with distant Prospects of Armies, Gladiators, &c. and in a Scroll, *Sic radiant Fideles:* Upon the other Side is the fatal Battle at *Naseby*. All three are expressed with so much Art, that the Metal, though Gold, is but as Dross compared with the Workmanship; in a Scroll is writ *non nobis*. The Whole comprised in an Inch and Half Diameter, yet so exquisitely performed, that the Countenances of particular Persons may be discovered. It was a Present from the *Parliament* to the *General*, and was purchased by Mr. *Thoresby*'s Father, with his noble Collection of Medals. *Materiam superabat opus, vide* D. L. p. 495

63 A very broad antique Gold Ring, p. 495.

64 A Miniature Picture set in Silver

65 A small *Thomas à Kempis*, a neat Pocket-book on Vellum, 2 Wooden Almanacks, a Hebrew and another Scroll.

66 A Parcel of Prints, Drawings, &c. and sundry odd Things

Antient

☞ Antient Deeds and original Letters of Kings, Queens, and sundry great Personages, &c.

67 Letters wrote by blind, deaf, and dumb Persons, and those without Arms, and several Curiosities in Writing; among which is an exceeding fine Piece of Penmanship, being the Letter of *Publius Lentulus* to the Senate of *Rome*, giving a Description of our Lord and Saviour *Jesus Christ*

68 Sundry old Deeds

69 Two Deeds in the Reigns of *Henry* VIII. and *Elizabeth*

70 Three Ditto in the Time of the Commonwealth

71 One ditto of *Richard Cromwell*, and Letters Patent under his Hand and Great Seal, as Lord Protector of the Commonwealth of *England*, for dissolving the Parliament, *April* 20th 1659

L E T T E R S.

72 An Autograph of *Martin Luther*, and a great Number of Letters of several eminent Divines

73 Sundry Letters of *Hugh Peters*, *Baxter*, and other dissenting Ministers

74 Letters and Autographs of Bishops, and eminent Divines

75 Commissions, Letters, &c. from 1502 to 1650, with Autographs of most of the principal Persons concerned in the Manegement of public Affairs during that Period

76 Another Parcel of ditto

77 Another Parcel of ditto

78 Another Parcel of ditto

79 Another Parcel of ditto; *N. B.* in this Lot are 20 Letters of General *Monk*

80 A Box containing a great Number of Letters by eminent Persons, among which are *Locke*, *Boyle*, *Prior*, *Steele*, *Flamstead*, *Halley*, *Woodward*, Sir *H. Sloane*, Sir *Christopher Wren*, *Brown Willis*, *Warburton*, and many others

Autographs, Letters, &c. of Kings, Queens, &c.

81 One of Queen *Katherine Parr*, 2 of King *Edward* VI. 1 of of Queen *Mary*, and 2 of *Mary Queen* of *Scots* to the Countess of *Shrewsbury*

82 One

82 One Letter and 1 Warrant of Queen *Elizabeth*

83 Two Letters and one Warrant of ditto

84 Two ditto of King *James* I. and four Commissions, &c. of King *Charles* I.

85 Nine Commissions, &c. of the Commonwealth

86 Two Letters from *Cromwell* the Protector to Captain *J. Pickering* near *Wakefield Yorkshire*—Instructions to Lord Viscount *Fauconberge* upon his Repair to the *French* King—A Letter to Lord *Wharton*, concerning the Loss of *Knottingly*—A Letter from *R. Cromwell* to the University of *Oxford*

87 A Letter to the Duke of *Newcastle*, and 7 Signatures of King *Charles* II.

88 Eight ditto of ditto

89 Three Letters and Signatures of King *James* II.—Four ditto of King *William*——Two ditto of Queen *Anne*——Two ditto of King *George* I. and a Letter from his late Royal Highness *Frederick* Prince of *Wales* to Queen *Caroline*

90 Several Letters of the King of France, the Prince of Orange (Grandfather to King William) Princess Sophia, and other foreign Princes

F I N I S.

Thomas Hearne

The son of the parish clerk of White Waltham in Berkshire, Thomas Hearne, born in 1678, was befriended by Francis Cherry, the Lord of the Manor, so that he was able to enter St Edmund's Hall, Oxford, where he graduated M.A. in 1703. He became janitor, and by 1712 second keeper, in the Bodleian Library, but his passionate adherence to the Jacobite cause led to his refusal to take the oaths of allegiance to the House of Hanover: his election to Architypographus and Esquire Bedell in Civil Law in 1715 was rescinded, and he was thenceforward refused admission to the Library, where new locks were installed to prevent him using the keys with which he had been issued, and which he retained. For the rest of his life he remained in St Edmund's Hall, a crabbed eccentric figure devotedly editing medieval chronicles and other texts which he published by subscription, and keeping a diary full of Oxford gossip and uninhibited comment on the many contemporaries he regarded as enemies, usually because they were not non-jurors like himself and could be characterized as (for instance) 'a great snivelling poor-spirited whigg and good for nothing that I know of'. 'I do not regard the ridicule of buffoons and jack-puddings', he wrote, but he enjoyed lampooning them in his diary. His work as an editor, however, has for all its quirks come to be recognized as an important contribution to historical studies, and his reputation stands today far higher than his contemporaries would have guessed. A sympathetic study of his work has been given by David Douglas in his *English Scholars,* 1939,

Chapter IX, and his *Diary* was published by the Oxford Historical Society in eleven volumes between 1884 and 1918. Extracts from his own library catalogue were published as *Bibliotheca Hearniana* in a limited edition of seventy-five copies by Beriah Botfield in 1848, and reprinted as Appendix XVII in Volume III of J. R. Smith's 1869 edition of Philip Bliss's *Reliquiae Hearnianae*.

Hearne was a bibliophile who had to build up his own working library after his exclusion from the Bodleian: writing to a friend in March 1728/29 he declined to lend a volume because 'being debarr'd the Bodleian library I am now confined to my own books, which I am every minute using'. He was interested in book prices, and kept a keen eye on any appreciation in the value of items he had bought cheap, and was justifiably proud of his library — 'Mr Murray told me t'other day', he wrote in 1723, 'that my collection of books was the oddest that he ever saw', with 'odd' of course being used in its earlier complimentary sense of 'extra-ordinary'. He died in 1735 and his library was sold together with that of 'another Gentleman of Note', so that it is impossible to assign at first sight any of the 6,776 lots specifically to Hearne, and pending an exhaustive collation of his own MS list with the sale catalogue one can hardly do more than guess at probabilities. We can be sure, however, that the 'FINE EDITIONS of the CLASSICKS', such as lot 2176, a Cicero *'lineis rubris, corio turcico, foliis deauratis'* would not be his, for as a poor scholar he wrote of a library sale in 1726 'People are in love with good binding more than good reading'.

The Gentleman of Note appears to have been a rich man of taste, interested not only in classical literature, in early editions or fine bindings, but in art and architecture, owning copies of Vitruvius, Palladio and Serlio in Italian and English, and Colen Campbell's *Vitruvius Britannicus,* 1717 (lot 803), together with other works on architecture and painting; to him too should presumably be assigned Montfaucon and the twenty-five volumes of the Graevius and Gronovius *Thesaurus* (lot 1). But most of the sections comprising *Rerum Britannicarum Scriptores*, and the 'History, Antiquities and Parliamentary Affairs of Great Britain' are likely to have been made up largely from Hearne's library, with Rymer's seventeen-volume *Foedera* (lot 265), Dugdale's *Monasticon* (lot 303), and the chronicles such as Holinshed, Froissart, Grafton, Fabian and Hall, as well as Inigo Jones and others on Stonehenge. The group of lots under *Bibliothecarii* could hardly have come from any other source. By kind permission the British Library copy (269.c.7) is reproduced: one other example has been traced in the Bodleian.

A

CATALOGUE

OF THE

VALUABLE LIBRARY

Of that GREAT ANTIQUARIAN

Mr. *THO. HEARNE*

Of OXFORD:

And of another Gentleman of Note.

Confifting of a very great Variety of UNCOMMON BOOKS, and fcarce ever to be met withal.

Among the reft are,

A very Large, Curious, and Valuable Collection of OLD TRACTS, and SCARCE PAMPHLETS; great Numbers relating to the Parliamentary Affairs of *Great-Britain* and *Ireland*.

The Hiftories of *France, Italy, Spain, Germany, Mufcovy, Poland, Sweden, Denmark, Afia, Africa* and *America*.

Muratori Rerum Italicarum Scriptores, 22 vol. *Rymer's* Fœdera, 19 vol. *Grævius* and *Gronovius's Greek* and *Roman* Antiquities, 25 vol. *Montfaucon's* Antiquities, 15 vol. *lar. pap.* The *Byzantine* Hiftorians, 31 vol.

All the FINE EDITIONS of the CLASSICKS. The *Elzevir* Claffıcks compleat, bound in 49 vol. in *Morocco*. Les Oeuvres de Plutarque, par *Amyot*, 13 vol. in *Turkey*.

All the Hiftories of the feveral Counties in England. A large Collection of Voyages, and Natural Hiftory. Moft of the Ancient and Modern Books of Phyfick, *&c.* Books of Sculpture, Architecture, Medals, Painting, Mathematicks, Law Civil and Common.

Which will begin to be fold very cheap, the loweft Price mark'd in each Book, at T. OSBORNE's Shop in GRAY's-INN, on *Monday* the 16th Day of *February* 1735-6.

CATALOGUES to be had at the Place of Sale, and Money for any Library or Parcel of Books.

INDEX CAPITUM.

FOLIO.

QUARTO.

OCTAVO, &c.

Architectura, Pictura, Sculptura, Numismata, Pompæ, Ceremoniæ, & Antiquitates. Lat. Folio.

1 GRævii & Gronovii Thesaurus antiquitatum Romanarum & Græcarum, 25 vol. *cum multis fig.* ——— *Lug. Bat.*
2 Thesaurus Antiquitat. & Historiar. Italiæ Mari Ligustico & Alpibus vicinæ, cura G. Grævii, 6 tom. 3 vol. *cum fig.* ———*ib.*1704
3 Begeri Thesaurus Brandenburgicus selectus, 3 tom. 2 vol. *Colon. Marchica.*1696
4 ———Thesaurus ex thesauro Palatino selectus. *Heidelb.*1685
5 Antiquitates sacræ & civiles Romanorum explicatæ, lat. & gal. cum fig. ——— *a la Haye.*1726
6 Putei Perspectiva Pictorum & Architectorum, 2 tom. 1 vol. cum fig. ——— *Roma.*1723
7 Numismata ærea selectiora maximi moduli e Museo Pisano olim Corrario.
8 Architectura civilis per E. Theil, 4 vol.—— *Augsperg.*1711
9 Brevis & particularis descriptio Urbium & Locorum totius Italiæ, 2 vol. cum multis fig. ——— *Haga Comit.*1724
10 Novum & magnum Theatrum Urbium Belgicæ Liberæ & Federatæ a J. Bleau, 2 vol. cum multis fig. *Amst.*
11 Veteres Arcus Augustorum triumphis insignes ex reliquiis quæ Romæ adhuc supersunt, cum notis Bellorii, cum fig. *Roma* 1690
12 Admiranda Romanorum Antiquitat. a veteris sculpturæ vestigia Anaglyphico a P. S. Bartolò cum notis Bellorii. *ib.*
13 Insignium Romæ Templorum prospectus exteriores interioresque a Celeber. Architectis inventi. ——— *ib.*1684
14 Villa Pamphilia ejusque Palatium, &c. cum ejusdem Villæ absolutæ delineatione. ——— *ib.*
15 Leon. Ch. Sturms prodromus Architecturæ Goldmannianæ. *Augsperg.*1714

B 16

16 Icones Legatorum qui nomine Pont. Max. Imperat. Regum ad Pacem universalem constituendam Osnaburgam. *Ant.* 1684

17 Romanæ magnitudinis monumenta cura D. de Rubeis. *Romæ.*

18 Arcus L. Septimii Severi anaglyphica cum explicat. J. Mariæ Suaresii. ——— ——— *ib.*1676

19 Appendix ad Theatrum Basilicæ Pisanæ. ——— *ib.*1723

20 Fragmenta vestigii veteris Romæ cum notis Bellorii, *corio turcico, foliis deauratis.* ——— *ib.*1673

21 Basilicæ S. Mariæ majoris delineat. & descript. a Paulo de Angelis. ——— *ib.*1621

22 Roma subterranea novissima Opera & studio P. Aringhi, 2 vol. cum multis fig. ——— *ib.*1651

23 J. Vaillant Numismata ærea Imperatorum Romanor. & Cæsarum. ——— *Paris.*1695

24 Gemmarum affabre Sculptarum thesaurus, digessit & recensuit J. Bajerus. ——— *Franc.*

25 J. de Sandrart Academiæ nobilissimæ artis Pictoriæ cum fig. elegantiss. ——— *Noribergæ* 1683

26 Cuperi de Elephantis in Nummis obviis exercitat. cum fig. *Hagæ Comit* 1719.

27 Gyraldi Opera omnia, 2 tom. 1 vol. cum fig. *Lug. Bat.* 1696

28 J. Sponii Miscellanea eruditæ antiquitatis ——— *Lug.* 1685

29 Occoni Imperatorum Romanorum Numismata a Pompeio magno ad Heraclium. ——— *Mediol.* 1683

30 Junius de Pictura Veterum. ——— *Rot.* 1694

31 C. du Molinet Hist. summorum Pontificum per eorum Numismata. ——— ——— *Lut.* 1679

32 Sculptura Historiarum & Temporum Memoratrix, cum multis fig. ——— *Nurnberg.*

33 Reinesii Syntagma Inscriptionum antiquarum cum primis Romæ veteris quarum omissa est recensio in vasto Gruteri Opere. ——— *Lipsiæ* 1682

34 Revelatio Ordinis SS. Trinitatis Redemptionis Captivorum, fig. elegantiss. ——— *Paris* 1632

35 Emblemata sacra e præcipuis utriusque Testamenti Historiis concinnata & a P. Vander Burgio, fig. illustrat. 1639

36 Pighii Annales Romanorum, 3 vol. — *Ant apud Plant.* 1615

37 Imperator. Romanor. Numismata descripta & enarrata per Patinum. ——— ——— *Argent.* 1671

38 Boldoni Epigraphica. ——— *August. Perusiæ.* 1660

39 Ædes Barberinæ ad Quirinalem a Comite Tetio descriptæ. cum fig. ——— ——— *Romæ.* 1642

40 Architectura curiosa nova per A. Becklern. — *Norimberg.*

41 Dempsteri de Etruria regali Lib. vii. curante T. Coke, *Mag. Britan. Armigero,* 2 vol. ——— *Florent.* 1723

42 Icones vitæ & elogia Imperator. Romanorum per H. Goltzium. ——— *Ant.* 1645

43

43 Familiæ Romanæ ex antiq. Numiſmat. ex bibliotheca F. Urſini. ——— ——— *Romæ*. 1577

44 Schilteri Theſaurus Antiquitatum Teutonicarum Eccleſiaſticar. Civilium, Literarium, 3 vol. cum fig. ——— *Ulmæ*. 1728

45 Novus Theſaurus Antiquitatum Romanorum congeſtus ab A. de Sallengre, 3 vol. cum fig. *ch. max. & minor.* — *Hagæ Comit*. 1716

46 Goltzii Numiſmata Græciæ, Cæſaris Auguſti & Tiberi, Faſti Romanorum, Sicilia & mag. Græcia, Imperatorum, 5 vol. *foliis deauratis.* ——— *Ant*. 1617

47 Bonanni Numiſmata Pontificum Romanor. a Martino V. uſque ad annum 1699, 2 vol. ——— *Romæ*. 1699

48 ——— Numiſmata ſummorum Pontificum Templi Vaticani Fabricam indicantia. ——— *ib*. 1715

49 Bavaria ſancta, 4 vol. cum fig. elegantiſſ. per *Ralph Sadelerum, Monachi*. 1624

50 D. de Neſſel breviarium & ſupplementum Commentariorum Lambecianorum, 2 vol. cum fig. ——— *Vindobonæ*. 1690

51 Regum & Imperator. Romanor. Numiſmata, aurea, argentea, ærea, cura illuſtriſſ. Caroli Ducis Croyiaci. *Ant*. 1654

52 Caſalii de Urbis ac Romani olim Imperii ſplendore Opus Eruditionibus Hiſtoricis, &c. illuſtrat. cum fig. *Romæ*. 1650

53 Stuckii Opera continens Antiquitatum Convivalium Lib. III. *Lug. Bat*. 1695

54 Raſponi de Baſilica & Patriarcho Lateranenſi, Lib. IV. cum fig. ——— ——— *Romæ* 1656

55 Ethruſcarum Antiquitatum fragmenta a C. Inghiramio, cum fig. *foliis deauratis.* ——— *Franc*. 1637

56 {
O. Panvinii xxvii Pontif. Maximor. Elogia & Imagines. *Romæ*. 1568
Imagines xxiv Imperatorum Romanorum.
Illuſtrium Jure-Conſultorum Imagines ad vivam Effigiem expreſſa. ——— *Romæ*. 1666
}

57 Statuta Hoſpitalis Hieruſalem, cum fig. elegantiſſ.

58 Deſcriptio Vaticanæ Baſilicæ veteris & novæ cum notis P. de Angelis, cum fig. ——— *Romæ* 1646

59 Evangelicæ Hiſtoriæ Imagines CLIII fig. Auctore H. Natali. *Ant*. 1593

60 Olai Wormi Danicorum Monumentorum Lib. VI. —*Hafniæ*. 1643

61 Gemmæ antiquæ cælatæ per B. Picart, lat. & gal. *Amſt*. 1724

62 Gruteri Corpus Inſcriptionum ex recenſione & cum Annotat. G. Grævii, 4 vol. *ch. max. & minor.* ——— *ib*. 1707

63 H. Pradi & J. Villalpandi in Ezechielem explanationes & apparatus Urbis, ac Templi Hieroſolymitani Comment. & Imaginibus illuſtratus, 3 vol. ——— *Romæ*. 1596

64 Beſſoni Theatrum Inſtrumentorum & Machinarum cum Beroaldi fig. ——— ——— *Lug*. 1578

65 Ceremoniale Epiſcoporum, cum fig. elegantiſſ. — *Romæ*. 1600

B 2 66

· 66 Hist. August. Imperator. Romanor. a Julio Cesare usque ad Josephum, Lotichii & Hofmanni tetrastichis. *Amst.* 1710
. 67 Marmora, Arundeliana cum variis Commentariis per M. Mattaire, cum fig. —— —— *Lond.* 1732
68 O. Panvinius de Ludis Circensibus & de Triumphis cum notis Argoli, cum fig. —— *Patav.* 1681
69 Begeri Specilegium Antiquitates.—— *Colon. Brandenburg.* 1692
• 70 Vita D. Thomæ Aquinatis Othoni Væni ingenio & manu delineata. —— —— *Ant.* 1610
• 71 H. Schmitz Theatrum Machinarum novum. *Col. Agrip.* 1662
72 Nummi antiqui Familiarum Romanor. perpetuis interpretat. illustrati per J. Vaillant, 2 vol. —— *Amst.* 1703
73 Antiquæ urbis splendor Opera & Industria J. Lauri. *Romæ.* 1612
•• 74 Herωologiæ Anglica, cum fig. elegantiss.
• 75 Theologorum qui Rom. Antichristum præcipue oppugnarunt effigies. —— —— *Hagæ Comit.* 1602
76 Marmora Arundeliana recensuit & perpet. Comment. H. Prideaux. —— —— *Oxon.* 1676
77 Ecclesiæ Anglicanæ Trophæa per B. de Cavalleriis æneis typis representatæ. —— *Romæ.* 1584
78 Serlii Architectura Lib. V. cum extraordin. Liber. *Venet.* 1569
79 Vitruvii Architectura cum notis var. digesta & illustrata a J. de Laet. —— *Amst. apud Elz.* 1649
80 Vetera Monumenta in quibus præcipue Musiva Opera sacrarum profanarumque Ædium Structura per Ciampinum. *Romæ.* 1690
81 Ciampini de sacris Ædificiis a Constantino magno constructis Synopsis Historica. —— —— —— *ib.* 1693
82 Symbolica Dianæ Ephesiæ Statua a C. Menetreio exposita, cum fig. —— —— —— ——*Romæ.* 1688
83 Panciroli notitia dignitatum cum Orientis tum Occidentis ultra Arcadii Honoriique Tempora, cum fig.——*Venet.* 1593
• 84 Columna Trojana a Ciacconio, *corio turcico, foliis deauratis, splendidiss. compacta.* —— —— ——*Romæ.* 1616
85 A. Augustini Archiepisc. Tarracon. Antiquitat. Romanar. Hispanarumque in Nummis Veterum Dialogi. —— *Ant.* 1617
• 86 Illustrium Medicorum Imagines.
87 B. Dietterlin Architectura in Ling. German. — *Norimb.* 1598
• 88 Freheri Theatrum Virorum eruditione clarorum, 2 vol. cum multis fig. —— —— —— *ib.* 1618
• 89 Boissardi Thesaurus Antiquitatum Romanarum, 2 vol. *Editio Opt. corio turcico.* —— —— *Franc.* 1627
90 J. Vaillant Numismata Græca. —— *Amst.* 1700
91 Putei Perspectiva Pictorum & Architectorum lat. & german. *Auspurg.* 1706
• 92 Fabretti de Columna Trajani Syntagma. —— *Romæ.* 1683
• 93 Begeri Lucernæ veterum Sepulchrales Iconicæ——*Colon. Marchicæ.* 1702

94

94 Marliani Urbis Romæ Topographia, *cum fig.* —*Rom.* 1543

95 Monumenta Illustrium Virorum & Elogiæ. *Traject. ad Rhen.* 1671

96 Lucæ Paeti de Mensuris & Ponderibus Romanis & Græcis Lib. 5. ——— ——— *Ven.* 1573

97 Vitruvius per Jocundum Solito Castigatior factus, *cum fig. ib.* 1511

98 Fabretti Inscriptionum Antiquar. quæ in Ædibus paternis asservantur. ——— *Romæ* 1702

99 Basilica SS. Udalrici & Afræ Imperialis Monasterii Aug. Vind. Hist. descripta, *cum fig.* —— *Aug.Vind.* 1653

100 Gyraldi de Deis Gentium varia & multiplex Historia. *Basil.* 1560

101 O. de Stradæ Vitæ & Icones Imperatorum Cæsarum Romanorum. ——— ——— *Franc.* 1615

102 O. Vredi Sigilla Comitum Flandriæ & Inscriptiones Diplomatum, cum Exposit. Historica. —— *Brug. Fland.* 1639

103 Musæum Calceolarianum Veronense a B. Ceruto Inceptum, & ab Chiocco descriptum & perfectum.——*Ver.* 1622

104 Antiquarum Statuarum Urbis Romæ, auct. J. de Caval.

105 Liceti de Lucernis Antiquorum reconditis Lib. 6. *cum fig. Pat.* 1662

106 G. Lloyd Series Chronologica Olympiadum, Pythiadum, Isthmiadum, Nemeadum quibus veteris Græci tempora sua metiebantur. ——— —— *Ox.* 1700

107 Imagines & Vitæ Srnctorum Augustanorum Vindelicorum æreis tabellis expressæ.——— *Ven.* 1594

108 Monumenta Sepulchrorum, cum Epigraphis Ingenio Excell. Virorum de Archetypis expressa.

109 Blondi Flavii Forliviensis Triumphis Romæ, *fol. deaur. Edit. antiq. sine anno & loco.*

110 O. Panvinii Romanor. Principum Lib. 4. Ejusdem de Comitiis Imp. Liber. ——— *Basil.* 1558
——Fastorum Lib. 5.——*Ven. ex Off. Valg.* 1558
——in Fastos Consulares Appendix. *ib. apud Valgr.* 1558

111 Sigonius, de antiquo Jure Populi Romani.——*Bon.* 1574

112 Robertellus de Vita, & victu Populi Romani.——*ib.* 1559

113 Epigrammata antiquæ Urbis. ——— *Romæ* 1521

114 Marmora Felsinea, per C. Malvasium, *cum fig.* *Bon.* 1690

115 Ælia Lælia Crispis non nata resurgens per eundem. *ib.* 1683

116 Monumenta Patavina S. Ursati, studio suisque Iconibus expressa. ——— ——— *Pat.* 1652

117 Puteani Bruxellæ Incomparabili exemplo Septenaria Gripho Palladio descripta. ——— *Brux.* 1646

Archi-

Architettura, Scoltura, Pittura, Medaglie, &c. Italici & Hispanici. Folio.

118 J. Cesare in Oro, in Argento, in Medaglioni, in Metallo grande raccolti nel Farnese Museo da P. Pedrusi, 8 vol. *fol. deaur* ——————————— *Parma* 1709
119 La Galleria di Minerva overe Notizie Universali, 7 vol *Ven.* 1696
120 Le Pitture antiche del Sepolcro di Nasonii nella Via Flaminia disegnate, ed intagliate di P. Bartoli. *Roma* 1680
121 Istorie Fiorentine di Scipione Ammirato, 2 vol. *Fir. nella Stamperia di P. Giunt.* 1600
122 Opere Istoriche di Daniello Bartoli, 5 vol. —— *Roma* 1663
123 Historie Cronologiche dell' Origine de gl' Ordine Militari e di tutte le Religione Cavaleresche nel Mondo da B. Giustinian, 2 vol. *con fig.* ——— *Venez.* 1692
124 { Discorso della Religione antiche di Romani da Choul, *con fig.* ——— *Lyone, appr. Rov.* 1559
——— sopra la Castrametatione di Romani con i Bagni antichi di Greci & Romani, par Choul. *ib. ib.* 1556 }
125 Il Tribunale della S. Rota Romana descritto da D. Bernino, *con fig.* ——— ——— *Roma* 1717
126 Vocabolario degli Accademici della Crusca, 2 vol. *Firenz.* 1691
127 La Gerusalemme di T. Tasso figurat. da B. Castello. *Gen.* 1617
128 Raccolti delle Navigatione & Viaggi, 3 vol. *Venet. nella Stamperia de Giunti* 1554
129 I Vestigi dell' Antichita di Roma raccolta & ritratti in Perspettiva da S. du Perac. ——— *Roma* 1575
130 La Sicilia di F. Parutade scritta con Medaglie, con Aggiunta da L. Agostini. ——— —*ib.* 1649
131 L'Historia Augusta da Giulio Cesare, a Constantino il Magno, da F. Angeloni. ——— *ib.* 1685
132 Saggi di Naturali Esperienze fatti nell' Academia del Cimento, *con fig.* ——— *Fir.* 1691
133 Utillissimo trattato dell' Acqua Correnti, studio e osservato da Carlo Fontana, *con fig.* ——— *Rom.* 1696
134 Vestigi delle Antichita di Roma Tivoli, Pozzuolo & alteri Luochi. ——— ——— *ib.* 1660
135 Monarchia Ecclesiastica o Historia Universal del Mundo, por Juan de Pineda, 4 vol. ——— *Barc.* 1620
136 Le Ricchezza della Lingua Volgare di F. Alunno. *Vineg.* 1543
137 Architettura Universale di V. Scammozzi. *Ven.* 1615
138 Fabriche & Edificii in Prospettiva di Roma Moderna. *Rom.*

139

139 Le antiche Lucerne Sepolcrali figurate, disegnate ed intagliate da P. Bartol. ——— ib. 1691
140 Iconografia cioe disegni d'Imagini de Famosiss. Monarchi, Regi, da Angelo Canini. ——— ib. 1669
141 Biblia Vulgare, *con fig.* ——— Ven. 1546
142 Opere di Dominico Cavalcha, *Edit. antica, sine anno & loco.*
143 Memorie del Museo del Conte Lodovico Moscardo, *con fig.* Ver. 1672
144 El Maranon y Amazonas Historia, por Rodriguez. *Madr.* 1684
145 L'Historia di Casa Orsina di F. Sansovino. *Ven.* 1565
146 Historia Pontifical y Catolica, por Gonzalo de Yllescas, 2 vol. ——— ——— *Madr.* 1613
147 Il Cortegiano del Conte B. Castiglione, *foliis deaurat.* *Ven. appres. Ald.* 1528
148 La Sacra Biblia Comment. da Diodati. ——— *Gen.* 1641
149 Descrittione di tutti i Paesi Bassi, *cum fig. depictis.* *Anvers.* 1567
150 Teatro d'Imprese di Giovan. Ferro. ——— *Ven.* 1623
151 Vite & Azzioni di Personaggi Militari, e Politici descritte dal Conte Gualdo Prioraro, *con fig.* ——— *Vien.* 1673
152 Inventioni d'Ornamenti d'Architettura e d'Intagli diversi inventati & intagliati da F. Passarini. *Rom.* 1698
153 Disegni di vari Altari e Capelle nelle Chiese di Roma. *ib.*
154 Palazzi di Roma de piu Celebre Architetti disegnati da P. Ferrerio, 2 vol. ——— *Roma.*
155 Raccolta di Statue antiche e moderne. ——— *ib.* 1704
156 L'Anfiteatro Flavio descritto e delineato dal Caval. Fontana. *nell Haia* 1725
157 L'Adone Poema del Caval. Marino. ——— *Parigi* 1623
158 Dante, con le Comment. di C. Landino, *foliis deaurat.* *Fir.* 1481
159 Il Regno di gli Slavi hoggi corrotamente dette Schiovani Historia di Don Mauro Orbini, *foliis deauratis.* *Pesaro* 1601
160 Statue antiche che sono poste in diversi Luoghi nella Citta di Roma. ——— *appr. G. Porro.*
161 Cronica breve de i fatti Illustri de Re di Francia, con le loro Effigie dal Naturale. ——— *Ven.* 1597
162 La Historia d'Italia di F. Guicciardini, *cor. turc. fol. deaur.* *Fior. appr. Tor.* 1561
163 Il primo Libro d'Architettura di S. Serlio, Ital. & Franc. *Paris* 1545
164 Arcano del Mare di D. Ruberto Dudleo Duca di Nortumbria, 2 vol. *ch. gr.* ——— *Fior.* 1661
165 I 4 primi Libri di Architettura di P. Cataneo. ——— *Vin.* 1554
166 L'Architettura di Andrea Palladio. ——— *Ven.* 1642
167 Regole della Prospettiva Pratica da Vignola. *Rom.* 1583
168 L'Architettura di Vitruvio, per B. Caporali. *Perug.* 1536

169

169 Il 3 Libro di S. Serlio, *con fig.* ——— *Ven.* 1540
Raccolti di Tempii & Sepolcri disegnato dall' Antica di B. Montano. ——— *Rom.* 1638
Traitte des 5 principales Sortes de Colonnes, par Ponsard. *Paris* 1617

170 Historia Oriental de las Peregrinaciones de Fernan Mendez Pinto. ——— ——— *Valen.* 1645

171 Trattato della Pintura di Lionardo da Vinci, *con fig.* *Parigi* 1651

172 Osservazioni sopra i Cimiteri de Santi Martyri ed antichi Christiani di Roma, *con fig.* ——— *Roma* 1720

173 L'Isole piu Famose del Mondo descritte da Tho. Porcacchi e intagliate da G. Porro. ——— *Ven.* 1572

174 Regola delli 5 Ordini d'Architettura da Vignola.

175 La Jerusalemme Liberata di T. Tasso. *Parigi, nella Stamperia Reale* 1664

176 Architettura di S. Serlio. ——— *Ven.* 1663

177 ———di Battista Montani, 5 Lib. ——— *Rom.* 1691

178 Racconto della Trasportatione del Corpo di Papa Paolo V. *con fig.* ——— *ib.* 1623

179 Li Giardini di Roma disegnate da Battista Falda con direttione di G. de Sandrart.

180 Architectura di Vitruvio. ——— *Mil.* 1521

181 Colonna Trajana disegnata & intagliata da P. Bartoli, 2 vol.

182 Roma Sotterranea di Ant. Bosio, *con fig.*

183 ———il medesimo, *corio turcico, foliis deauratis, splendid. compacta.*

184 Studio d'Architettura Civile sopra di Ornamenti di Porte e Fenestre tratti da alcuni Fabriche insigni di Roma, con le Misure, &c. Opera de piu Celebri Architette de Nostri Tempi. ——— ——— *Roma* 1702

185 Historia delle Guerre Civile di Francia di C. Davila, 2 vol. *Par. nella Stamp. Reale* 1644

186 Architettura d'Antonio Labacco.

187 Palazzi antichi & moderni di Genova raccolti e disignati da P. Paolo Rubens. ——— *Anver.* 1708

188 La Pratica di Prospettiva del Lorenzo Sirigatti. *Ven.* 1625

189 Historia Naturale di C. Plinio, tradotta per C. Landino. *Ven. appr. Jenson* 1476

190 Descrittione del Regno di Scotia & delle Isole sue adjacenti di Petruccio Ulbaldini. ——— *Anv.* 1588

Rerum Britannicarum Scriptores. Folio.

191 A. du Chesne Historiæ Francorum Scriptores Coetanei, 5 vol. ——— ——— *L.Par.* 1636

192 ———Historiæ Normannorum Scriptores antiqui. *ib.* 1619

193 Historiæ Anglicanæ Scriptores X. ——— *Lond.* 1652

194

194 Rerum Anglicarum Scriptores, post Bedam. *Franc.*1601
195 Camdeni Britannia, cum tabulis Geograph. *Lond.*1607
196 Alfordi Annales Ecclesiastici & Civiles Britannorum, Saxonum, Anglorum, 4 vol. — *Leod.*1663
197 Harpsfeldii Hist. Ecclesiæ Anglicanæ. — *Duac.*1622
198 Matthæi Paris Hist. Anglicana, editore W. Watts. *Lond* 1640
199 Historiæ Anglicanæ scriptores varii, Edit. J. Sparke. *ib.*1723
200 Spelmanni vitæ Ælfredi magni Anglorum Regis. *Oxon.*1678
201 Johnstoni Hist. rerum Britannicarum, *foliis deaurat.* — *Amst.* 1655
202 G. Burnet Hist. Reformationis Ecclesiæ Anglicanæ, 2 vol. *Genev.*1689
203 Spelmanni Concilia, 2 vol. — *Lond.*1639
204 A. du Monstier Neustria Pia, seu de omnibus & singulis Abbatiis & Prioratibus totius Normanniæ. — *Rothomag.*1663
205 W. Imhoff Regum Pariumque Magnæ Britanniæ Historia Genealogica. — *Norimb.*1690
206 R. Poli Cardinalis pro Ecclesiasticæ unitatis defensione Lib. IV. 1555
207 Historiæ Britannicæ, Saxonicæ, Anglo-Danicæ Scriptores XV. Opera T. Gale, 3 vol. — *Oxon.*1691
208 Reyneri Hist. & Antiquitates Monachorum nigrorum ordinis St. Benedicti in Regno Angliæ. — *Duaci.*1626
209 Camdeni Britannia cum Tabulis Geograph. — *Amst. apud J. Bleau.*1662
210 Numismata Anglo-Saxonica & Anglo-Danica breviter illustrata ab Andrea Fountaine Eq. Aur. — *Oxon.*1705
211 Registrum Honoris Richmond, *ch. max. & minor.* — *Lond.* 1722
212 M. Parkeri Hist. & Antiquitat. Ecclesiæ Anglicanæ accurant. S. Drake, *ch. max. & min.* — *ib.*1729
213 Vita & rebus gestis Mariæ Scotorum Reginæ Autores XVI. recensita a J. Jebb, 2 vol. *ch. max. & min.* — *ib.*1715
214 Whartoni Anglia Sacra, 2 vol. — *ib.*1691
215 Waræi rerum Hibernicarum Annales. — *Dublin.*1664
216 Denyaldi Rollo Northmanno-Britannicus. — *Rotomag.*1660
217 Jacobi Regis Opera, edita a J. Montacuto. — *Franc.*1689
218 Messinghami Vitæ & Acta Sanctorum Hiberniæ. *Paris.*1624
219 Skenæi Regiam Majestatem Scotiæ. — *Lond.*1613
220 Walsinghami Hist. Anglicana. — *ib.*
221 Parkeri Hist. de Antiquitate Britannicæ Ecclesiæ. — *Hanov.* 1605
222 Petri Blessensis Epistolæ, Editio antiq. sine anno & loco.
223 Hectoris Boethii Historiæ Scotorum. — *Paris* 1675
224 Balæi Scriptor. Illustr. majoris Britanniæ. — *Basil.*1559
225 Torfæi Hist. rerum Orcadensium. — *Hauniæ* 1697
226 Smithei Florum Hist. Ecclesiasticæ Gentis Anglorum Lib. VII. *Paris.*1654
227 Sibbaldi Scotia illustrata, cum fig. — *Edinburg.*1684

C 228

228 Polydori Virgilii Historia Anglicana. ——— *Basil*. 1556
229 Eadmeri Monachi Historia Novorum. ——— *Lond*. 1623
230 Buceri Scripta Anglicana. ——— *Basil*. 1577
231 Ant. a Wood Hist. & Antiquitates Universitatis Oxoniensis. *Oxon*. 1674
232 Bedæ Hist. Ecclesiasticæ Latine & Saxonice, cura & studio J. Smith, *ch max. & minor*. ——— *Cant*. 1722
233 D. Wilkins Leges Anglo-Saxonicæ Ecclesiasticæ & Civiles, *ch. max. & minor*. ——— *Lond* 1721
234 Buchanani Opera omnia, 2 vol. ——— *Edinb*. 1715
235 Usserii Hist. & Antiquitates Ecclesiæ Britannicæ. *Lond* 1685
236 Matthei Westmonasteriensis Hist. Anglicana. — *Franc*. 1601
237 Rerum Britannicarum Scriptores Vetustiores.—*Heidelb*. 1687

X ***Books relating to the History, Antiquities, and Parliamentary Affairs of Great-Britain and Ireland. Folio.***

239 Harris's History of Kent, cuts, lar. pap. ——— 1719
240* Salmon's History of Hertfordshire. ——— 1728
241 Atkyns's ancient and present state of Glostershire. 1712
242 Chauncy's historical Antiquities of Hertfordshire, cuts. 1700
243 Wright's Hist. and Antiquities of Rutland. ——— 1684
244 Prince's Worthies of Devon. ——— 1701
245 Leigh's natural History of Lancashire, and the Peak in Derbyshire, cuts. ——— 1700
246 Peck's antiquarian Annals of Stanford, cuts. ——— 1727
247 Plot's natural Hist. of Oxfordshire, lar. and sm. pap. cuts, rul'd. ——— 1677
248 ——natural Hist. of Staffordshire, lar. pap. cuts. 1686
249 Coker's Survey of Dorsetshire. ——— 1732
250 Somner's Antiquities of Canterbury, cuts. ——— 1703
251 King's Vale Royal of England. ——— 1656
252 Thoroton's Antiquities of Nottinghamshire, cuts.—— 1677
253 Morton's natural History of Northamptonshire, cuts. 1712
254 Leycester's historical Antiquities of Cheshire. ——— 1673
255 Phillipot's Survey of Kent. ——— 1659
256 Thoresby's Antiquities of Leeds. ——— 1715
257 Burton's Description of Leicestershire.
258 Dugdale's Antiquities of Warwickshire, cuts. ——— 1656
259 Enderbie's History of Wales. ——— 1661
260 Gunton's Hist. of the Church of Peterborough, lar. & sm. pap. ——— 1686
261 Lewis's History of Great-Britain. ——— 1729
262 Moll's Description of England and Wales, with Maps. 1724
N. B. This is a compleat Sett of the Counties, and are to be sold either together or separate.

263

263 Loggan's Description of all the Churches and Colleges in Oxford, cuts. ——— *Oxford*. 1675
264 Ashmole's Hist. of the most noble Order of the Garter, cuts, lar. & sm. pap. ——— 1672
265 Rymer's Fœdera, 17 vol. ——— *Lond.* 1727
266 Acta Regia, or an Abridgment of Rymer's Fœdera. *ib.*
267 Anstis's Register of the most noble Order of the Garter, 2 vol. 1724
268 Madox's Hist. and Antiquities of the Exchequer, lar. and sm. pap. ——— 1711
269 Madox's Formulare Anglicanum, or a Collection of ancient Charters and Instruments. ——— 1702
270 Winwood's Memorials of Affairs of State, 3 vol. lar. pap. 1725
271 Ephemeris Parliamentaria. ——— 1654
272 Collection of Proclamations in the time of King James the first.
273 Madox's Historical Essay concerning the Cities, Towns, and Burroughs of England, lar. pap. ——— 1726
274 Speed's History of Great-Britain. ——— 1611
275 Spelman's English Works, lar. and sm. pap. 1723
X276 Sir Wm. Pety's Maps of Ireland, very scarce. ———
277 Ogilby's Entertainment of K. Charles, in his Passage through the City of London, cuts. ——— 1662
278 Strype's ecclesiastical Memorials, 3 vol. lar. pap. 1721
279 Strype's Life of Arch-Bp. Grindal. ——— 1710
280 Spelman's posthumous Works. ——— 1698
281 Strype's Memorials of Arch-Bp. Cranmer. ——— 1694
282 ——Life of Arch Bp. Parker. ——— 1711
283 ——Life of Arch-Bp. Whitgift. ——— 1718
284 Collection of Tracts relating to the Forfeiture of the Charter of the City of London.
285 Sandford's History of the Coronation of King James the second, fine cuts. ——— 1687
286 Jones's, Charleton's, and Webb's Antiquities of Stone-Henge, cuts, lar. and sm. pap. ——— 1724
287 Jones's Antiquities of Stone-Henge. ——— 1655
288 Ogilby's description of the Roads of England, cuts, 1675
289 Saxton's Maps of England.
290 Speed's Maps of Great-Britain. ——— 1676
291 Oldmixon's Hist. of England during the Reigns of the royal House of Stuart, lar. pap. ——— 1730
292 Stowe's Survey of the Cities of London and Westminster, publish'd by Strype, 2 vol. cuts. ——— 1720
293 ——Survey of London. ——— 1633
294 ——Annals, or general Chronicle of England. 1631
295 Gibson's Codex Juris Ecclesiastici Anglicani, 2 vol. in one. 1713

296 Collyer's ecclesiastical History of Great-Britain, 2 vol. lar. and sm. pap. —— 1708
297 Prynne's Hist. of King John, K. Henry III. and K. Edward I. —— 1670
298 ——Supream ecclesiastical Jurisdiction. —— 1666
299 Burnet's Memoirs of the Dukes of Hamilton.—— 1677
300 ——History of the Reformation, 3 vol. —— 1681
301 ——History of his own Time, 2 vol. lar. and sm. pap. either Volume sold alone. —— 1724
302 Dugdale's Antiquities of Warwickshire, 2 vol. cuts, lar. and sm. pap. —— 1730
303 ——Monasticon Anglicanum, 3 vol. cum fig. —— 1682
304 ——The same in English, with Stevens's Continuation, 3 vol. cuts. —— 1718
305 ——Baronage of England, 2 vol. lar. and sm. pap. 1675
X 306 ——History of Imbanking and Draining the Fenns *.To this Book is added a curious MS. on the same Subject.* 1662
307 ——History of St. Paul's Cathedral. —— 1668
308 ——Short View of the Troubles in England. —— 1681
309 ——Discourse touching the Office of Lord Chancellor of England.
310 ——Summons to Parliament. —— 1671
311 ——Origines Juridiciales. —— 1680

N. B. This is a compleat Sett of Sir Wm. Dugdale's Works, and are to be sold either together or separate.

312 Compleat Collection of State-Tryals, 6 vol. —— 1730
313 ——The same, 12 vol. lar. pap. —— 1730
314 Wood's Athenæ Oxonienses, or the Hist. of the Oxford Writers, 2 vol. lar. and sm. pap. —— 1721
315 Guillim's Display of Heraldry, lar. and sm. pap. —— 1724
316 Clarendon's Hist. of the Rebellion, 3 vol. lar. and sm. pap. 1702
317 Dart's Hist. and Antiquities of Westminster-Abbey, 2 vol. fine cuts, large and small paper.
318 ——Hist. and Antiquities of the Cathedral Church of Canterbury, fine cuts, large and small paper. 1726
319 Camden's Britannia, publish'd by Gibson, lar. and sm. pap. 1695
320 ——The same, 2 vol. large and small paper. —— 1725
321 Sir S. D'Ewes Journal of the Parliaments in Q. Elizabeth's Time. —— —— 1628
322 Scott's Hist. of Scotland. —— 1727
323 Tryal of Coleman, Ireland. Pickering, and Grove, Green Berry, and Hill; five Jesuits; Langhorne, Reading, Wakeman, Marshall, Rumley, Corker, Jesuits Speeches, Oates's Narrative, History of the Plot.
324 Pearce's Laws and Customs of the Stannaries. —— 1725
325 Parr's Life of Arch-Bp. Usher. —— 1686
326 Pleadings and Arguments upon the Quo Warranto. 1690

327

327 Tryal of the VII Bishops. Sir R. Atkyns on the Power of Parliaments. Sir R. Atkyn's defence of Ld. Russel. Ld. Russel's Case. Sir R. Atkyns on the penal Laws. Ld. North's Argument. Arguments upon Monopolies. Duke of Norfolk's Case. Ld. Nottingham's Argument. Hawles's Remarks on Tryals, with other Tracts.

328 Remarkable Proceedings in Parliament. Appeal from the Country. Advice and Address to the Nobility. Letter from St. Omers, with several Narratives, Informations, and Depositions.

329 Naked Truth. Sir R. Atkyns's Speech. Allegations in defence of Mary Queen of Scots. Nostradamus, and other Predictions. Report of the Irish Forfeitures. Duke of Norfolk's Tryal. Pleadings on the Quo Warranto.

330 L'Estrange's Observators, 2 vol. — 1684

331 Lloyd's Memoirs of noble Personages. — 1668

332 Tryal of Popish Priests, Algernoon Sidney, of Cornish. Votes in 1680. Ld. Russel's Case. Sir R. Atkyns's Arguments. Clavell's Catalogue, and other Tracts.

333 Heylyn's Hist. of the Reformation. — 1661

334 Vincent's Discovery of Errors in Brooke's Heraldry, with the Arms colour'd. — 1622

335 Inett's Origines Anglicanæ, 2 vol. in one. — 1704

336 Arch-Bp. Laud's Hist. of his Troubles and Tryal, 2 vol. 1694

337 Power of Parliaments asserted. Father Paul of Beneficiary Matters. Tryal of Ld. Stafford, with his Speech. Votes in 1680. England bought and sold, with several other scarce Tracts.

338 Collection of all the Tracts relating to Layer's Plot, with several others.

339 Tryal of S. College. Account of the Earl of Essex's killing himself. Tryal of Walcot and others, with their Speeches. Tryal of Sir T. Armstrong, of Sir S. Bernardiston, with several other Parliamentary and Political Tracts.

340 Tryal of the Earl of Shaftsbury. Earl of Denby's Arguments. Duke of Norfolk's Case, with several relating to the Privileges and Liberties of the City of London.

341 Collection of Acts of Parliament in 1648, and 1649.

342 Collection of Proclamations.

343 Sir James Melvill's Memoirs. — 1683

344 List and Characters of the Lords High Stewards of England, together with Abstracts of several Tryals, and the manner of Proceeding before their Lordships, MS.

345 A perfect Collection of all the Messages, Addresses, &c. from the House of Commons to the King, in 1679. 1680

346 Proceedings of the House of Commons at Oxford in 1680. 1681

λ 347

347 Sir Edward Coke's Argument upon the Ld Buckhurst's Case in Chancery, MS.

348 Tryals of Stayley, Coleman, Ireland, Pickering, and Grove. Green, Berry and Hill, Reading, Langhorn, Sir G. Wakeman, and others.

349 Tryals of Coleman, Walcot, Hone and Russel, Boroky, Coningsmark, and others; of Sir Wm. Pritchard, Sir R. Grahme, and Ashton.

350 Milles's Catalogue of Honour. —— 1610

351 May's History of the Parliament in 1640. —— 1647

X 352 Sir Th. More's History of King Richard the Third, *black Letter.*

353 Martin's History of England, with the Succession of the Dukes and Earls of this Kingdom. —— 1638

354 Violet's Proposals to Oliver Cromwell. —— 1656

355 Sibbald's Hist. ancient and modern, of the Sheriffdoms of Fife and Kinross. —— 1710

356 Slayter's Hist. of Great Britain.

357 Stranguage's History of Mary Queen of Scots. —— 1724

358 Spotswood's Hist. of the Church of Scotland. —— 1655

359 Selden's Tracts. —— 1683

360 Treatise concerning the Nobility, and according to the Laws of England, MS.

361 Serj. Pemberton's Arguments concerning Dr. James Smith's being an Alderman of the City of London, and for a peremptory Writ or Mandamus to return him, MS.

362 Petition of Rights by Parliament 1638. Attorney General's Objections to the House of Commons Arguments about Liberty, Sir Edward Coke's Arguments, MS.

363 Cases of Barons, by Writ, MS.

364 Collection of curious parliamentary Tracts relating to the stating the publick Accounts, The occas. Conformity, and other very material Affairs.

365 Stillingfleet's Discourse on the Illegality of the late Ecclesist. Commission, Ravillac Redivivus, Vindic. of Titus Oates, Tryal of the 7 Bishops, and other Tracts.

366 Sprat's History of the Rye-House Plot. —— 1685

367 Sprigge's England's Recovery. —— 1647

368 Daniel and Trussel's History of England, 2 vol. —1617

369 Articles of Impeachment against Sir Wm. Scroggs, Popish Cruelties, Tryal of F. Smith Bookseller, of E. Cellier, Fitzharris, Tryal of Spiritual Courts, Tryal of John Hambden, Tryal of Swendsen, and others, for stealing Mrs. Pleasant Rawlins, with other Tryals.

370 Tryals of Ld Derwentwater and other Lords, Cranburne and Lowick, Sir H. Mackworth's Peace at home, Vindication of the Rights of the Lords and Commons, with other Tryals and parliamentary Tracts.

371

371 Tryals of Titus Oates, Ld Delamere, Charnock, King and Keys, Cooke, Rookwood, Sir J. Friend, Sir Wm Perkins, Cranburne and Lowick, with other Tryals.
372 Drayton's Poly-Olbion, cuts.
373 Case of the Earl of Shaftesbury, Articles against the Earl of Danby, Articles against the Dutchess of Portsmouth, Case of the Charter of the City of London, Tryal of Ld Delamere, Tryal of Ld Mohun, with several other Tryals and parliamentary Tracts.
374 Hanmer, Campion, and Spenser's History of Ireland. 1633
375 Kennet's History of England, 3 vol. cuts, *large and small paper.* 1706
376 ——— Register and Chronicle, Ecclesiastical and Civil. 1728
377 Fiddes's Life of Card. Wolsey, *large and small paper.* 1724
378 Echard's History of England, 2 vol. 1720
379 Tyrrell's Enquiry into the ancient Constitution of the English Government, *large and small pap.* 1718
380 Tyrrell's general History of England, 3 vol. compleat. 1698
381 State-Tryals, vol. 5th and 6th, to compleat Setts.
382 Baker's Chronicle of the Kings of England, to the End of George I. 1733
383 Cressy's Church of Britain. 1668
384 Hollinshed's Chronicle, *compleat, with the Castrations,* 2 *vol. large and small paper.* 1587
385 Castrations to Hollingshed's Chronicle sold alone.
386 Froyssart's Chronicle, *compleat and very fair.* 1525
387 Grafton's Chronicle, *compleat and very fair.* 1559
388 Polychronicon, *compleat and very fair.* 1527
389 Fabian's Chronicle, *compleat and very fair.* 1559
390 Hall's Chronicle, *compleat and very fair.* 1550
391 Ld Bacon's Works, 4 vol. 1730
392 Rushworth's Collections, 8 vol. *first Edition, very fair and uniform.* 1682
393 Ryley's Pleadings in Parliament, *large pap.* 1661
394 Johnston's Excellency of the English Monarchy, *large paper.* 1686
395 Le Neve's Essay towards deducing a regular Succession of all the principal Dignitaries in England and Wales. 1716
396 Collection of all the Reports, Speeches, &c. that were in relation to Layer's Plot. 1722
397 Fuller's History of the Worthies of England. 1662
398 ——— Church-History of Great Britain, 1656
399 The Antiquities of Middlesex, with several other curious Historical and Parliamentary Tracts, 2 vol. sold separate.
400 Tryal of the Earl of Macclesfield. 1725
401 Sammes's Antiquities of ancient Britain, *cuts.* 1676
402 Fox's Book of Martyrs, 3 vol. *white Letter.* 1684

403

403 Castelnau's Memoirs. ——— 1724
404 Walker's historical Discourses upon several Occasions. 1705
405 Barnes's History of Edward III. ——— 1688
406 Walker's Sufferings of the Clergy. ——— 1714
407 Trial of John Hambden in the great Case of Ship-Money. 1719
408 Trials of the Earl of Strafford, with several other remarkable Trials and Narratives.
409 ———of Titus Oates, of Edward Earl of Warwick, of Kirkby, Constable, &c. with several other Trials and Tracts relating to the Murder of Sarah Stout by Spenser Cowper.
410 The naked Truth, The State Prodigal, Observat. upon the Revolution, Tryal of Ld Stafford, with several other Narratives and parliamentary Tracts.
X 411 Tryal of the Earl of Strafford. *Note, This is not in the Collection of Tryals.* ——— 1700
412 Drummond's Life of King James, with his other Works. 1711
413 Stillingfleet's Origines Britannicæ. ——— 1685
414 State-Tracts in King Charles's Time. ———1689
415 Tryal of Dr. Sacheverell, with the Lords Protests, and all the other Papers relating to that Affair. ——— 1710
416 Sleyzer's Theatrum Scotiæ, being Cuts of all the King's Palaces, Churches, and other the most noted Buildings in Scotland. ——— ——— 1718
X 417 Sir T. More's Life of Picus Mirandola, Notes concerning K. Henry V. Censures pass'd by the Lords on the Bp of Lincoln, with several Tryals in the Court of Star-Chamber, with the Manner of proceeding in that Court, and other curious Tracts, MS.
X 418 Sandford's genealogical History of the Kings of England, *fine cuts.* ——— ——— 1677
419 Frankland's Annals of K. James and K. Charles the Second. 1681
420 Camden's Britannia, with Maps. ——— 1637
421 Cotton's Abridgment of the Records in the Tower, *large and small paper.* ——— ——— 1657
422 Ld Herbert's History of Henry VIII. ——— 1649
423 Complete Collection of all the Tryals, Narratives, and other Papers that were published about the Popish Plot, 4 vol.
424 Drummond's History of Scotland. ——— 1655
425 Collection of Kings Speeches, Addresses, and Proclamations in different Reigns.
426 Cuts of all the Cathedral and Conventual Churches in Engl. and Wales.
427 Report of the Committee concerning the Cottonian Library. 1732

428

428 Calderwood's Hist. of the Church of Scotland. —— 1680
429 Customs of London, or Arnold's Chronicle, *black Letter, compleat and very fair.*
430 Churchill's Remarks on the Kings of this Isle. —— 1675
431 { Cabala, or Mysteries of State, *best Edit.* —— 1663
{ Digges's compleat Ambassador. —— 1655
432 Brady's History of England, 3 vol. compleat. —— 1684
433 Yorke's Catalogue of the Nobility. —— 1612
434 Burton's Commentary upon Antoninus's Itinerary. —— 1658
435 Journey to Scotland, Tryal of Sir J. Friend, Proceedings of the Lords concerning the Scotch Conspiracy, with several Reports and other parliamentary Tracts.
436 History of the Civil Wars of Great Britain and Ireland. 1661
437 The hereditary Right of the Crown of England asserted, by Bedford. —— —— —— 1713
438 Blome's Description of the Kingdoms of England, Scotland, and Ireland. —— —— 1673
439 Broughton's Ecclesiastical History of Great Britain. 1633
440 Burchet's naval History, *cuts.* —— 1720
441 Heylyn's History of ABp Laud, —— 1671
442 Biondi's History of the Civil Wars of England. — 1641
443 Lediard's naval History of England, *cuts.* — 1735
444 Hacket's Life of ABp Williams. —— 1693
445 Tryal of Francis Higgins. —— 1712
446 Collection of Tracts relating to the Dispute between the Bp of Ely, and Dr. Bentley, very scarce.
447 Several Records, Deeds, Wills, and other authentick Writings, proving the Title of Catharine Bokenham to the Barony of Berners.
448 The happy future State of England. —— 1688
449 Husband's Collections of Orders, Ordinances and Declarations. —— —— 1646
450 Nalson's historical Collections, 2 vol. This is a Continuation of Rushworth's Collection. —— 1682
451 Weever's ancient funeral Monuments compleat, with the Table. —— —— 1631
452 Wake's State of the Church and Clergy of England. 1703
453 Compleat Collection of Gazettes, beginning with the Oxford Gazettes, and ending 1718 inclusive, 12 vol.
454 Lauderdale's Affairs of Scotland, with several other historial and parliamentary Tracts.
455 Wilson's History of Great Britain, —— 1653
456 Votes for 1710, 11, 13, 14, 17, 18, 20, 21, 22, and 23. 10 vol. sold separate.
457 Nicholson's English historical Library. —— 1714
458 Newcourt's History of the Diocese of London, 2 vol. 1708
459 Dutchess of Newcastle's Life of the Duke of Newcastle. 1667.

460 Goodwin's Hiſtory of Henry the Vth. —— 1704
461 Hiſtory of Edward the IId.— —— 1680
462 Bacon's Hiſtory of Henry the VIIth. — ——1641
463 Buck's Hiſtory of Richard the IIId. —— ——1646
464 Habington's Hiſtory of Edward the IVth. —— 1640
465 Sanderſon's Hiſtory of King Charles the Iſt.— — 1658
466 Several Tracts pro and con, relating to the Sequeſtration of the Lord Craven's Eſtate, with ſeveral Reports of the Commons, and Col. Blood's Narrative.

Law. Folio.

467 Year-Books, 8 vol. with Maynard's Edward the IId. beſt Edition. *N. B.* Maynard's Edward ſold alone to compleat Setts.
468 Statutes at large, 6 vol. laſt Edition, with the Acts of the laſt Seſſions.—— —— —1735
470 Murray's Scotch Law. —— ——1681
471 Aleyn's—— — ——1688
472 Anderſon's — ——1664
473 Benloe's and Dalliſon's—— ——1689
474 Bridgman's —— ——1659
475 Bulſtrode's —— ——1688
476 Coke's 13 parts, with References.——1697
477 Carter's—— ——1688
478 Carthew's —— —— 1728
479 Comberbatch's —— ——1724
480 Croke's, beſt Edition. —— 1683
481 Davis's—— ——1674
482 Dyer's —— —— 1688
483 Fitz-Gibbons's—— ——1732
484 Farreſley's—— —— 1725
485 Finch's —— ——1725
486 Hetley's —— ——1657 } Reports.
487 Hobart's — —— ——1725
488 Hardreſs's —— —— 1692
489 Hutton's—— — —1682
490 Jenkins's—— — —1733
491 Jones's, Sir William, —— 1675
492 Jones's, Sir Thomas, —— 1729
493 Keyling's —— ——1708
494 Keble's —— — 1685
495 Keilway's— —— —1688
496 Lee's —— — —— 1669
497 Lutwych's, 2 vol. —— 1704
498 Lane's— — ——1657
499 Latch's —— —— 1672
500 Levinz's —— — ——1722
501 Leonard's — —— 1687

502

502	Littleton's	1659	Reports.
503	Lilly's	1719	
504	Modern, 7 vol. beſt.	1720	
505	Moore's	1688	
506	Noy's	1669	
507	Owen's	1656	
508	Palmer's	1688	
510	Plowden's	1688	
511	Pollexfen's	1702	
512	Popham's	1688	
513	Raymond's	1696	
514	Roll's	1675	
515	Salkeld's, 3 vol. 3d ſold alone.	1724	
516	Skinner's	1728	
517	Saunders's	1722	
518	Savil's	1675	
519	Shower's, 2 vol.	1708	
520	Siderfin's	1714	
521	Styles's	1658	
522	Vaughan's	1677	
523	Ventris's	1726	
524	Vernon's, 2 vol.	1728	
525	Wynch's	1668	
526	Yelverton's	1735	
527	Danvers's, 2 vol. with Error.		Abridgment.
528	Nelſon's, 3 vol.		
529	Lilly's		
530	Rolles's		
531	Booth of real Actions.	1701	
532	Coke's 1ſt, 2d, 3d, and 4th Inſtitutes.	1681	
533	Cowell's Law-Dictionary.	1727	
534	Duke's Law of Charitable Uſes.	1676	
535	Hawkins's Pleas of the Crown, 2 vol.	1726	
536	Hearn's Pleader.	1657	
537	Jacob's Law-Dictionary.	1729	
538	Lilly's Conveyancer.	1719	
539	Modern Caſes in Law and Equity from 7 to 12 K. G.	1730	
540	Prynne's Animadverſions on Lord Coke's 4th Inſtitute.	1669	
541	Swinburn of Wills.	1728	
542	Vidian's exact Pleader.	1684	
543	Watſon's compleat Incumbent and Clergyman's Law.	1725	
544	Wood's Inſtitutes of the Laws of England.	1728	
545	——— Inſtitutes of the Imperial or Civil Law.	1730	
546	Jacob's common Law common plac'd.	1732	
547	Abridgment of Caſes in Equity.	1734	
548	Precedents in Chancery.	1733	
549	Liber Placitandi.	1674	
550	Townſend's Tables, 2 vol.	1667	
551	Maxims in Equity.	1728	

D 2 552

552 Shower's Cases in Parliament. —— —— 1698
553 Bridgman's Conveyances, 2 vol. —— —— 1725
554 Wynch's —— —— 1680
555 Officina Brevium. —— —— 1679
556 Modern, 2 vol. —— 1734
557 Coke's —— —— —— 1614
558 Brown's —— —— 1675
559 Registrum Brevium. —— —— 1687 } Entries.
560 Robinson's —— —— 1684
561 Rattell's —— —— —— 1670
562 Brownlow's —— —— —— 1693
563 Brevia Judicialia. —— —— 1662
564 The old Book of —— 1546
565 Domat's Civil Law translated by Strahan, 2 vol. *large and sm. pap.* —— —— —— 1722
566 Cawley's Laws. —— —— 1680
567 Cases in Chancery, 3 parts. —— —— 1735
568 Dalton's Office of Sheriffs. —— —— 1700
569 Coke's Reports English. —— 1680
570 Tables to all the Reports. —— —— 1719
571 Tremaine's Pleas of the Crown. —— —— 1723
572 Waterhouse's Comment upon Fortescue de Laudibus Legum Angliæ. —— —— —— —— 1663
573 Sheppard's Actions upon the Case for Deeds. —— 1663
574 Ashe's Tables to the Year-Books, 4 vol. *interleav'd.* — 1614
575 Table to Fitzherbert's Abridgment, *interleav'd.* —— 1565

Libri Classici, Grammatici, Critici, Poetici, & Lexicæ. Folio.

576 { Athenæus, gr. *lineis rubris.* —— *Venet. apud Aldum* 1514
G. Gemistus, Herodianus, Enarratiunculæ Antiquæ, *lineis rubris.* —— —— *ib. ib.* 1503
Philostrati Vita Apollonii Tyanei, gr. lat. *lineis rubris. ib. ib.* 1501 }
577 Appianus Alexandrinus, *foliis deauratis.* —— *Paris ex Officina Vascosan.* 1538
578 —— Gr. ex Bibliotheca Regia. *Lutetiæ apud C. Steph.* 1551
579 —— Gr. Lat. H. Steph. Annotationes. —— *Genevæ* 1592
580 —— Lat. *corio turcico.* —— —— *Venet.* 1477
581 Auli Gellii Noctium Atticarum Comment. *Brixiæ sine anno.*
582 —— Comment. per Bonfin. Asculanum, *lineis rubris, foliis deauratis.* —— —— —— *Venet.* 1517
583 { —— Idem. —— —— *ib.* 1509
Nestor Vocabalista. —— —— *ib.* 1496 }
584 Demosthenes, gr. cum Scholiis Græcis. *Lutetiæ apud J. Benenatum.* 1570

585

585 Demosthenes Gr. cum Comment. Ulpiani. *Basil. apud Hervagium* 1532

586 ———————Gr. Libanii Sophistæ in eas Orationes Argumenta, Vita Demosthenis per Libanium & Plutarchum, *foliis deaurat.*——— ———*Venet. apud Aldum* 1504

587 C. du Fresne Glossarium ad Scriptores mediæ & infimæ Latinitatis, 3 vol. ——— ——— *Lut. Paris* 1678

588 ———————Glossarium ad Scriptores mediæ & infimæ Græcitatis, 2 vol.——— ——— ———*Lug.* 1688

589 Stephani Doleti Comment. Linguæ Latinæ, 2 vol.——*Lug. apud S. Gryph.* 1536

590 Dionis Cassii Historia ex Xylandri Interpretat. gr. lat. *apud H Steph.* 1591

591 ———————Gr. ex Bibliotheca Regia, *foliis deauratis.*——*Lutetiæ apud R. Steph.* 1548

592 Dictionarium Latino-Gallicum.——*Lut. apud C. Steph.* 1552

593 Diogenes Laertius Aldobrandino Interpret. gr. lat. cum Notis Stephani & Casauboni, & Menagii Observat. *Lond.* 1664

594 Dictionarium Græcum, *foliis deauratis.*—*Venet. apud Aldum* 1597

595 Ovidii Metamorphosis, cum Comment. R. Regii & J. Micylli. ——— ——— ——— *Basil.* 1543

596 Oratores Græci, corio turcico. — *Venet. apud Aldum.* 1513

597 Robortelli de convenientia supputationis Livianæ. *Patav.* 1557

598 Somneri DictionariumSaxonico-Latino-Anglicum. *Oxon.* 1659

599 Calmet Dictionarium Biblicum, 2 vol. cum fig. — *August. Vindel.* 1729

600 Salmasii Plinianæ exercitat. in Caii Julii Solini Polyhistoria, 2 vol. ——— ——— *Paris.* 1629

601 Suetonius, J. Casaubonus recensuit & Animadverf. —*ib.* 1610

602 Stobæi Eclogæ Interpret. G. Cantero gr. lat. ——— *Ant.* 1575

603 Senecæ Tragœdiæ, foliis deauratis, Editio antiqua sine anno & loco.

604 Salustius per Pomponium emendata, & J. Britannicum revisa.——— ——— ——— ———*Brixiæ* 1470

605 Ferdinandi Episcopi Paderbornensis Poemata.——*Paris. e Typo. Regia.* 1684

606 Aristophanis Comœdiæ, gr. lat. notis Var. recensuit L. Kusterus, ch. max. & minor. ——— ——— *Amst.* 1710

607 ———————cum Scholiis antiquis, gr. lat.—— *Aureliæ Allobrog.* 1607

608 ———————gr. cum Scholiis Græcis, foliis deauratis.——*Venet. apud Aldum.* 1498

609 Hickesii Tesaurus Septentrionalium, 3 vol. ch. max. & minor. ——— ——— ——— ——— *Oxon.* 1705

610 Ciceronis Opera Gruteri, 2 vol. ch. max. & minor. *Lond.* 1681

611 ———————Orationes, Editio prima.

612 ———————Opera, 2 vol.——————— *Paris apud R. Steph.* 1538

613

613 Ciceronis Opera a D. Lambino emendata, 2 vol. *Lut. apud Turrisanum.* 1566

614 ——Opera, 2 vol. —— *Paris apud C. Steph.* 1555

615 ——Opera Gruteri, 2 vol. —— *Hamb.* 1618

616 ——Opera P. Victorii Comment. 4 vol. foliis deauratis. —— *Venet. apud Juntas.* 1537

617 —— Mannucciorum Comment. illustratus antiquæq; lectioni restitutus, 5 vol. foliis deauratis. *Venet. apud Aldum.* 1582

618 ——Orationes P. Manutii Comment. —— *ib. ib.* 1578

619 ——Epistolæ ad Atticum. —— *Romæ.* 1582

620 ——Epistolæ ad Familiares cum Comment. —— *Venet.* 1483

621 ——Epistolæ ad Familiares cum annotat. Doctissimornm XVII Virorum, foliis deuratis. — *Paris apud A. Parvum.* 1549

622 —— Tusculanæ Questiones. —— *Venet.* 1482

623 ——de Finibus, corio turcico. —— *ib.* 1471

624 ——Hotomanni Comment. in Orationes Ciceronis. *Oliva apud R. Steph.* 1554

625 ——Corradi Comment. in Ciceronis de claris Oratoribus, foliis deauratis. —— *Florent. apud Torrent.* 1552

626 ——Polentoni Comment. in Oration. Ciceron. foliis deauratis. —— *Patav.* 1413

627 ——Tusculanæ Questiones, Editio antiqua sine anno & loco.

628 Phavorini Lexicon Græcum. —— *Romæ.*

629 ——Idem, lineis rubris, foliis deauratis. — *Basiliæ.* 1538

630 P. Victorii Comment. in Lib. Demetrii Phalerei de Elocutione. —— *Florent. apud P. Juntam.* 1594

631 ——Variæ Lectiones. —— *ib. ib.* 1582

632 Pausaniæ Geographia cum notis Xylandri & Silburgii, gr. lat. *Hanov.* 1613

633 ——Romulus Amasæus vertit. —— *Florent. apud Torrentinum.* 1551

634 ——Græcæ. —— *Venet. apud Aldum.* 1516

635 Thesaurus Linguæ Latinæ, sive Forum Romanum, 3 vol. *Basiliæ apud Frobenium.* 1561

636 Aristotelis Opera gr. lat. G. du Val, 2 vol. ch. max. & min. *Lut. Par.* 1619

637 ——gr. lat. ex Bibliotheca Casauboni. *Aureliæ Allobrog.* 1605

638 ——gr. per Erasmum Roterodamum, 2 vol. *Basil.* 1531

639 ——gr. 6 vol. corio turcico. *Venet. apud Aldum.* 1491

640 ——lat. cum Comment. Averrois, 5 vol. *Venet. apud Juntas.* 1503

641 ——Organum, gr. —— *Venet. apud Aldum.* 1495

642 ——Victorii Comment. in Lib. Aristotelis de arte Dicendi. —— *Florent. ex Offic. Junct.* 1579

643 ——Victorii Comment. in Lib. Aristotelis de arte Poetarum. —— *ib. ib.* 1560

644

644 ——Robortelli in Lib. Aristotelis de arte Poetica explanationes. —— *Florent. apud Torrent.* 1548
645 Boetius de Consolatione Philosophiæ, & St. Thomæ Aquinatis in ejusdem Boetii Comment. Editio antiqua, sine anno & loco.
646 Aristidis Orationes, gr.—— *Florent. apud P. Juntam.* 1517
647 Aquini Lexicon militare, 2 vol. —— *Romæ.* 1724
648 Philostrati Opera, gr. lat. recensuit F. Morellus. *Paris.* 1608
649 ——Vita Appollonii Tyanei, gr. lat. lineis rubris, foliis deauratis. —— *Venet. apud Aldum.* 1502
650 Diodorus Siculus, Dictys Cretensis & Daryus Phrygius, lat. *Basil.* 1578
651 Propertius cum Comment. P. Beroaldi. —— *Bonon.* 1487
652 Pomponius Mela de Situ Orbis cum Comment. J. Vadiani. *Paris.* 1540
653 Corpus Poetarum Latinorum, 2 vol. —— *Lond.* 1713
654 Themistii Orationes, gr. lat. cum notis Harduini, foliis deauratis. —— *Paris.* 1684
655 ——& Alexandri Aphrodisiensis de anima, gr. —— *Venet. apud Aldum Manutium.* 1534
656 Terentius. —— *Paris apud R. Steph.* 1529
657 ——cum Comment. Donati. —— *ib. ib.* 1536
658 Corn. Taciti Historia, corio turcico, foliis deauratis. Editio antiqua sine anno & loco.
659 ——Opera, J. Lipsius recensuit. *Ant. apud Plantin.* 1627
660 ——Annales cum Comment. Lud. Dorleans. *Paris.* 1622
661 Thucydidis, gr. lat. cum notis Stephani & Hudsoni, recensuit & notas suas J. Wasse. —— *Amst.* 1731
662 ——gr. lat notis Hudsoni. —— *Oxon.* 1696
663 ——gr. lat. ex interpret. L. Vallæ, lineis rubris. *apud H. Steph.* 1564
664 Herodoti Hist. ex Interpret. L Vallæ, lineis rubris. *ib. ib.* 1566
665 Thucydides gr. foliis deauratis.—— *Venet. apud Aldum.* 1502
666 { Terentius. Horatius. Juvenalis & Persius. Virgilius. } *Paris e Typo. Regia.*
667 Hofmanni Lexicon universale, 4 vol. —— *Lug. Bat.* 1698
668 Suidæ Lexicon Græcum. —— *Mediol.* 1499
669 ——gr. foliis deauratis. —— *Venet. apud Aldum.* 1514
670 ——gr. lat. Interpret. Æ. Portus cum notis F. Porti. *Genev.* 1619
671 ——gr. lat. 3 vol. L. Kusterus. —— *Cant.* 1705
672 Senecæ Philosophi Opera cum Comment. & Scholiis Morelli. *Paris.* 1613
673 ——Virorum Doctor. Notis castigata, lineis rubris. *ib. apud J. Dupuys.* 1587

674

674 Platonis Opera Græca, lineis rubris, foliis deauratis. *Venet. apud Aldum.*1513

675 ——gr. lat. Interpret. & Notis J. Serrani, 2 vol.—— *apud H. Steph.*1578

676 R. Stephani Thesaurus Linguæ Latinæ, 4 vol. Editio opt. *Lug.*1573

677 Cardinalis Barberini Poemata, corio turcico, foliis deauratis. *Paris e Typo. Regia.*1642

678 B. de Montfaucon Palæographia Græca, sive de Ortu & Progressu Literarum Græcarum. —— *Paris.*1708

679 Catullus, Tibullus, & Propertius, notis Variorum, ch. max. *Lut. apud Morel.*1604

680 Eneæ Silvii Epistolæ, foliis deauratis. —— 1576

681 Enarrationes allegoricæ fabularum Fulgentii Placiadis, Editio antiqua sine anno & loco.

682 De Viridario August. Chigii Patritii senensis vera Libellus Galli Egidii Romani Poet. Laureat. —— *Romæ.*1511

683 Euripidis Tragœdiæ gr. lat. studio J. Barnes. —— *Cant.*1694

684 Æsopi Vita & Fabulæ, corio turcico.— *Venet. apud Aldum.* 1505

685 Nonnius Marcellus de proprietate Sermonum, corio turcico. *Brixiæ.*1483

686 Julii Pollucis Vocabularium, foliis deauratis. *Florent. apud B. Juntam.*1520

687 ——gr. lat. cum notis Variorum, 2 vol.—— *Amst.*1706

688 Budæi Comment. Ling. Græcæ. —— *Basil.*1557

689 Brodæi Epigrammata Græca, notis H. Stephani. *Franc.*1600

690 P. de Blarrorivo Nanceidos Opus de bello Nanceiano, cum fig. —— —— 1518

691 J. Davies antiquæ Ling. Britannicæ nunc vulgo dictæ Cambro-Britannicæ. —— *Lond.*1632

692 Pindari Opera gr. lat. cum notis. —— *Oxon.*1697

693 Annotationes Ling. Latinæ per J. Bap. Pium, foliis deauratis. *Florent. apud P. Giuntam.*1504

694 Valerius Maximus Leonici Comment. —— *Venet.*1482

695 Pereyræ Prosodia in Vocabularium trilingue Latinum, Lusitanicum & Castellanicum. —— *Ulissippona.*1669

696 Cæsaris Comment. cum notis S. Clarke, Tabulis Æneis ornata. —— —— *Lond.*1712

697 Josephi Opera, gr. lat. Hudsoni, 2 vol. ch. max. & minor. *Oxon.*1720

698 ——gr. lat. recensuit S. Havercampus, 2 vol. ch. max. *Amst.*1726

699 Virgilii Opera per Ogilvium, edita & Sculpturis Eneis adornata. —— —— *Lond.*1658

700 ——per Jacobum Pontanum, —— *Lug.*1604

701 ——cum XI Judic. Virorum Comment. cum fig. *Venet.* 1537

702 ——cum notis Servii. —— *Paris, apud R. Steph.*1532

I 703

703 Viegilii Opera, Editio antiqua, fine anno & loco.
704 ——cum notis Servii. —— *Venet.* 1584
705 Politiani Opera omnia, corio turcico. — *Venet. apud Aldum.* 1498
706 ——Idem. —— —— *Basil.* 1553
707 Thesaurus Cornucopiæ, & Horti Adonidis, foliis deauratis. *Venet. apud Aldum.* 1496
708 Cornucopiæ five Linguæ Latinæ Commentarii. — *Venet. apud Aldum.* 1513
709 Cato, Varro, Columella, &c. de Re Rustica, cum Comment. Beroaldi, corio turcico. —— *Bonon.* 1494
710 ——Idem. —— *Paris. apud J. Parvum.* 1533
711 Chauvini Lexicon Philosophicum, ch. max. & minor.— *Leovardiæ.* 1713
712 Hist. Romanæ Scriptores Latini veteres qui extant omnes, 3 vol. —— *Aureliæ Allobrog.* 1609
713 Vossii Etymologicon Linguæ Latinæ. —— *Amst.* 1662
714 Herodoti historia gr. foliis deauratis.— *Venet. apud Aldum.* 1502
715 ——ex Interpret. L. Vallæ. —— *apud H. Steph.* 1566
716 ——gr. lat. ab H. Stephano recognita. *apud P. Steph.* 1618
717 Plauti Comœdiæ cum Comment. Lambini.—— *Lut. apud. Macæum.* 1577
718 Horatii Opera cum Comment. Lambini, foliis deauratis. *ib. ib.* 1567
719 Plinii hist. naturalis J. Dalecampii. —— *Genev.* 1631
720 ——Idem. —— —— *Parmæ.* 1481
721 ——Idem, cum annotationibus, corio turcico.—— *Paris apud A. Parvum.* 1545
722 ——Idem, Editio prima, corio turcico. —— *Romæ.* 1470
723 ——Idem, foliis deauratis. —— *Parmæ.* 1476
724 M. Becichemi in Plinium prælectio. —— *Lut. Paris.* 1519
725 Nizolii Dictionarium, five Thesaurus Ling. Latinæ, 3 vol. *Venet.* 1551
726 ——vol. 2d. ch. max. —— *Basil.* 1613
727 Sylburgii Etymologicon magnum. —— 1594
728 Etymologicum magnum gr. Linguæ. —— *Venet.* 1549
729 Suiceri Thesaurus ecclesiasticus, 2 vol. —— *Amst.* 1728
730 Martialis Epigrammata Interpret. D. Calderino, foliis deauratis. —— *Venet.* 1552
731 ——foliis deauratis, Editio antiqua.
732 Dionysii Halicarnassei Opera, ex Bibliotheca Regia, lineis rubris. —— *Lut. apud R. Steph.* 1546
733 ——gr. lat. Opera & Studio F. Sylburgii.— *Franc.* 1586
734 Diogenes Laertius, corio turcico. —— —— *Venet.* 1493
735 ——Idem, corio turcico. — *Venet. apud N. Jenson.* 1475
736 Plauti Comœdiæ cum Comment. B. Saraceni, cum fig. *Venet.* 1511
237 ——Idem. —— *Paris apud R. Steph.* 1530

738 Plutarchi Opera gr. 2 vol. —— *Venet. apud Aldum.* 1519
739 Homeri Opera cum Comment. Eustathii, 4 vol. *Romæ.*
740 ———gr. lat. cum notis Spondani. ——— *Basiliæ.* 1606
741 Luciani Opera gr. lat. Bourdelotii, ch. max. & minor.—*Lut. Paris.* 1615
742 ———lat. lineis rubris. —— *Paris, apud Vascosan.* 1546
743 ———gr. foliis deauratis. —— *Venet. apud Aldum.* 1503
744 ———lat. cum notis Micylli. —— *Franc.* 1543
745 Livii Historia. ——— —— *Venet.* 1498
746 ———foliis deauratis. ——— *Venet. apud Aldum.* 1520
747 ———cum notis Rhenani & Gelenii. —— *Paris, apud A. Parvum.* 1543
748 ———a C. Sigonio emendata.—*Venet. apud Manutium.* 1555
749 Lancini Curtii Epigrammata, 2 vol. foliis deauratis.——*Mediolani.* 1439
750 Lucii Apulei Opera, Editio prima, foliis deauratis.
751 Scapulæ Lexicon. ——— —— *Lug. Bat. apud Elz.* 1652
752 Rhodigini Lectiones antiquæ, foliis deauratis.——*Venet. apud. Aldum.* 1516
753 Justini Historia. ——— *Venet.* 1478
754 Isocratis & Aristidis Orationes gr. *Venet. apud A. Manutium & P. Juntam.* 1534——1517
755 Cooperi Thesaurus Ling. Romanæ & Britannicæ. *Lond.* 1578
756 N. Biffii in Claudii Claudiani Lib. de Raptu Proserpinæ Comment. ——— *Mediolani.* 1684
757 Conciones sive Orationes ex Græcis Latinisque Historicis excerptæ. ——— *apud H. Steph.* 1570
758 Cæsaris Commentarii. ——— *Paris apud Vascosan.* 1543
759 Tusani Lexicon Græco-Latinum. ——— *Paris.* 1552
760 Thesaurus Tullii Ciceronis. *Paris, apud C. Steph.* 1556
761 Theodori Introductivæ Grammatices, Lib. IV. —— *Venet. apud Aldum.* 1595
762 Spelmanni Glossarium Archaiologicum, Editio opt. *Lond.* 1687
763 Strabonis Geographia gr. lat. J. Casaubonus recensuit. 1587
764 ———gr. lat. notis Variorum, 2 vol.—— *Amst.* 1707
765 ———gr. foliis deauratis.—— *Venet. apud Aldum.* 1516
766 Labbæi Glossaria Latino-Græca & Græco-Latina. —— *Lut. Paris.* 1679
767 Dictionarium Historicum, Geographicum, Poeticum per N. Lloydium. ——— *Lond.* 1686
768 Skinneri Etymologicon Linguæ Anglicanæ, ch. max. & min. *ib.* 1671
769 Calepini Dictionarium VIII Linguæ, 2 vol.—— *Lug.* 1656
770 Quinciliani Institutiones Oratoriæ. *Paris, apud Vascosan.* 1549
771 ———foliis deauratis, Editio antiqua sine anno & loco.
772 Q. Curtius, foliis deauratis, Editio antiqua sine anno & loco.
773 Ludolfi Grammat. Æthiopica. ——— *Franc. ad Man.* 1702
774 Xenophontis Opera Leunclavii, gr. lat. *Lut. Paris.* 1625

775

775 Xenophontis Opera. —— *Franc. apud Wechelium.* 1596
776 ————gr. —— *Venet. apud Aldum.* 1525
777 ————Omissa, G. Gemistus, Herodianus, Enarratiunculæ antiquæ, foliis deauratis. —— 1503
778 Exceptæ e Dione Hist. ab J. Xiphilino gr. lat. ex Interpret. G. Blanci. —— *apud H. Steph.* 1592

English Books of Architecture, Painting, Antiquities, Voyages and Travels, Divinity, Dictionaries, Physick, Surgery, Natural History, Poetry, and Miscellanies. Folio.

779 Selden's Works, 6 vol. lar. and sm. pap. —— 1726
780 Harris's Collection of Voyages and Travels, 2 vol. cuts. 1705
781 Holy Bible, 2 vol. *black letter.*——Printed by *Barker.* 1613
782 Collection of Voyages and Travels, 6 vol. lar. and sm. pap. 1732
783 Calmet's Dictionary of the Bible, 3 vol. cuts. 1732
784 Ovid's Metamorphosis, translated by Garth, cuts. 1717
785 Religious Ceremonies and Customs of all Nations in the World, 3 vol. with cuts, by *Picart.* —— 1731
786 Sanson's Maps, being 38 in number. —— 1692
787 Collection of Maps describ'd by Sanson, and corrected by Berry.
788 Several Traities of Mathematiques by the Royal Academy of Sciences, being part of the King of France's Cabinet, and printed at his expence.
789 Pitts's English Atlas, 4 vol. —— *Oxford.* 1680
790 Continuation of the Hist. of Animals, being part of the King of France's Cabinet, at his expence.
791 The Cartoons at Hampton-Court, Painted by *Rubens,* and graved by Sir *N. Dorigny,* with two other Cuts, painted by *Poussin,* and grav'd by *Frey,* all of them of the first Impressions.
792 The four Seasons, and ten other Cuts, painted by *Watteau,* with the King of France's Tapestry, painted by *Le Brun,* and grav'd by *Picart.*
793 Several Cuts, painted by *Poussin* and *Albanus,* grav'd by *Baudett, Picart,* and Sir *N. Dorigny.*
794 The King of France's Tapestry, being part of his Cabinet, and printed at his expence.
795 Thirty six Views, painted by *Vander Muelen,* and *Sylvester,* being part of the King of France's Cabinet, and printed at his expence; bound in Turky Leather, and gilt on the Leaves.
796 Collection of Cuts upon different Subjects, by *Michael Angelo, Bella, Holbens,* and others the most celebrated Masters.

797 Several Cuts belonging to the King of France's Cabinet, sew'd together in boards.
798 Several Plans and Uprights of the Royal Palace of Claigny.
799 Burnet's Theory of the Earth. ——— — 1691
800 Leybourn's Dialling. —— ——— ——— 1682
801 Brigg's Logarithmetical Arithmetick. ——— 1631
802 Atlas Maritimus & Commercialis, or a general View of the World, so far as relates to Trade and Navigation. 1728
803 Cambel's Vitruvius Britannicus, containing the Plans, Elevations, &c. of the most noted, publick and private Buildings in Great-Britain, 3 vol. large and sm. pap. 1717
804 The Loves of Cupid and Psyche, painted by Ralph Urbin, and grav'd by Salamanca.
805 Description of the Grotto of Versailles, being part of the K. of France's Cabinet, and printed at his expence.
806 Ovid's Metamorphosis in Latin and English, with cuts, by Picart. ——— ——— ——— ———1732
807 Bedford's Scripture Chronology, lar. and sm. pap. 1730
808 Tenier's Gallery, being a large Collection of Cuts, painted by that eminent Painter, gilt on the leaves. —— 1684
809 Laurence's compleat Body of Husbandry and Gardening. 1726
810 Palladio's Architecture, publish'd by Leoni. —— *Lond.* 1721
*810 ———the same, English, Italian, and French, 5 vol. 1715
811 Alberti's Architecture, publish'd by Leoni, in English and Italian, 3 vol. ——— ——— 1726
812 The Life and Miracles of St. Benedict, express'd in Figures, with several other Cuts on Scripture-Subjects.
813 Collection Cuts on several Subjects by Salamanca, and other eminent Masters.
814 Selden's Right and Dominion of the Sea. ——— 1663
815 Carkesse's Book of Rates. ——————— 1726
816 Gesner's History of Four-footed Beasts, Serpents, and Insects, with cuts. ——— ——— ——— 1658
817 Davila's History of the Civil Wars of France. ——— 1647
818 Prior's Poems. —— ——— ———1718
819 Pool's Annotations on the Holy Bible, 2 vol. ——— 1700
820 Raleigh's History of the World. ——— ——— 1614
821 Sir Wm. Davenant's Works. ——— ——— 1673
822 Chaucer's Works, black letter, very fair.
823 Collyer's great Historical, Genealogical, and Poetical Dictionary, with the Supplement and Appendix compleat, 4 vol. lar. and sm. pap. ——— ——— 1701
824 Fiddes's Body of Divinity, 2 vol. lar. pap. ——— 1718
825 Blome's History of the old and new Testament, fine cuts. 1701
826 Vertot's Hist. of the Knights of Malta, with LXXI Heads of the grand Masters, grav'd by the best Hands in France, 2 vol. lar. and sm. pap. ——— —— 1728

827

817 Vingboon's Architecture. —— —— 1674
828 Collection of Cuts, being Views of ancient Buildings and Ruins.
829 Collection of ſeveral Cuts of Antiquities, Temples, and illuſtrious Perſons, by *Michael Angelo*, and others the moſt eminent Painters.
830 The Works of the Author of the Whole Duty of Man. 1695
831 Collection of curious Cuts, painted by Correge, Le Brun, Albanus, Mignard, Coypel, and other eminent Painters, (together with Cuts of the King of France's Cabinet) and grav'd by the moſt celebrated Gravers.
832 Scott's Works, 2 vol. —— 1718
833 The Sphere of Manilius, tranſlated with notes by Sherburne. 1675
834 Views of the Noblemen's and Gentlemen's Seats.
835 Crooke's deſcription of the Body of Man, cuts. —— 1631
836 Diſney's View of the Laws againſt Immorality and Profaneneſs. —— —— 1729
837 King Charles's Works, 2 vol. —— 1662
838 Account of the Reception of Mary de Medicis into Amſterdam, fine cuts. —— *Amſt.* 1639
839 Pliny's natural Hiſtory, tranſlated by Holland. —— 1635
840 Sandrat's Academy of Architecture, Sculpture, and Painting, in High Dutch, cuts. —— 1675
841 The Ship of Fools, with cuts very fair and compleat.
842 Manley's Hiſtory of the Wars in Denmark. —— 1670
843 Ben. Johnſon's Works. —— —— 1640
844 The true Effigies of the moſt eminent Painters, large paper. 1694
845 Mezeray's general Hiſtory of France. —— 1683
846 Tillotſon's Sermons, publiſh'd in his life-time. —— 1707
847 Collection of Cuts, painted by Perelle, and graved by Viſſcher.
848 Livy's Roman Hiſtory, with Freinſhemius's Supplement. 1686
849 Cæſar's Commentaries, tranſlated by Edmondes, cuts.
850 Caſſandra, the fam'd Romance. —— 1661
851 Cotgrave's French Dictionary. —— 1631
852 Bp. Hall's Works. —— 1625
853 Hornius's ancient Geography, rul'd, with the Maps colour'd, and gilt on the leaves. —— 1700
854 Statues and Buſts in the King of France's Gardens, being part of his Cabinet, and grav'd at his expence.
855 Collection of Maps, by Ortelius and others.
856 L'Eſtrange's Joſephus, 2 vol. lar. pap. —— 1702
857 Lucan's Pharſalia, tranſlated by Rowe, lar. pap. —— 1718
858 The Engliſh Pilot. —— —— 1701
859 Tallent's Chronological Tables.
860 Ayliffe's new Pandect of the Roman Civil Law, large paper 1734

861

861 Ayliffe's Commentary on the Canons and Conftitutions of the Church of England, lar. pap. ——— 1726
862 The Holy Bible, 2 vol. lar. pap. *Oxford, Printed by Baskett.*
863 ———the fame, fmall pap. bound in turky leather, rul'd, and gilt on the leaves.
864 ———the fame, with curious cuts by Viffcher, bound in turky leather, rul'd and gilt on the leaves, 2 vol. large pap. Printed at *Cambridge* by Field. ——— 1666
865 Chaucer's Works, publifh'd by Urry, lar. pap. ——— 1721
866 Ifaacfon's Chronological Tables. ——— 1633
867 Collection of Voyages and Travels, vol. 5th and 6th, large and fm. pap. to compleat Setts. ——— 1732
868 Pomona, or the Fruit-Garden illuftrated, by Langley, with cuts, lar. pap. ——— 1729
869 Collection of Prints of Architecture, grav'd by Mariette.
870 Ogilby's defcription of Africa, with curious cuts. ——— 1670
871 Collection of Cuts, being Ornaments for Architecture, by Le Pautre.
872 { Vignola's five Orders of Architecture.
Labacco's Architecture, beft Edition.
Several Cuts, being Ornaments for Architecture.
Collection of the antique Vafes, grav'd by Salamanca. }
873 Collection of curious Cuts, being Defigns for Iron-Work, Shields, Plat-forms for Gardens, and other things.
874 Francine's Architecture, tranflated by Pricke. ——— 1669
875 Collection of Cuts, being an Account of the Ceremonies and Proceffions ufed at the Coronation of a Pope.
876 Collection of antique-Heads for defigning.
877 Hiftory of Papal Ufurpation, Tyranny, and Perfecution. 1712
878 Drayton's Poly-Olbion, and Spencer's Works.
879 The ancient, famous, and honourable Hiftory of Amadis de Gaule. ——— ——— ——— 1619
880 Hobbes's Leviathan. ——— ——— 1651
881. Common-Prayer for the Ufe of the Church of Scotland. 1637
882 Cave's Lives of the Primitive Fathers, 2 vol. ——— 1687
883 King Edward the VIth Common-Prayer, *compleat and very fair.* ——— ——— 1552
884 Leybourn's Curfus Mathematicus. ——— 1690
885 Howel's Englifh, French, Italian and Spanifh Dictionary.
886 Englifh and Portuguefe, and Portuguefe and Englifh Dictionary. ——— ——— ——— 1701
887 Fryer's Travels to Eaft-India and Perfia. ——— 1698
888 Locke's Effay on Human Underftanding. ——— ——— 1694
889 The Cuts to Salvian's Hiftory of Fifhes.
890 Howell's French and Englifh Dictionary. ——— 1673
891 Memoirs of Litterature, 4 vol.
892 Ribadeneira's Lives of the Saints, 2 vol. *cuts.* ——— 1669
893 Du Pin's Ecclefiaftical Hiftory for 16 Centuries, 3 vol. 1723
894 Perrier's Statues, *beft Edition, gilt on leaves.* ——— 1638

895

895 Taylor's Life of Christ and the Apostles, *cuts*. ——— 1684
896 Wanley's Wonders of the little World, or a general View of Man. ——— ——— 1678
897 Moll's Geography, with Maps. ——— ——— 1723
898 Rycaut's History of the Turks, 3 vol. ——— ——— 1687
899 Bates's Works. ——— ——— 1700
900 Hammond's Works, 4 vol. ——— ——— 1684
901 Saurin's Dissertations on the Old and New Testament. 1723
902 Salmon's English Herbal, or History of Plants, *cuts*. — 1710
903 L'Estrange's Josephus. ——— ——— 1702
904 Breval's Travels, *cuts*. ——— ——— 1726
905 Prideaux's Connection of the Old and New Testament, 2 vol. 1723
906 Palladio's Architecture MS.
907 Rycaut's Lives of the Popes. ——— ——— 1688
908 Several Cuts of Architecture, by different Masters, bound together.
909 Leslie's Theological Works, 2 vol. ——— 1721
910 Taylor's Cases of Conscience. ——— ——— 1696
911 Echard's Ecclesiastical History. ——— 1702
912 Hill's State of the Ottoman Empire, *cuts*. — 1709
913 Blome's Cosmography and Geography. ——— 1684
914 Book of Homilies. ——— ——— 1683
915 The Holy Bible. ——— *printed by Barker* 1607
916 Bayle's general Historical and Critical Dictionary, in 13 vol. *the whole containing the History of the Illustrious Persons of all Ages and Nations, particularly those of Great Britain and Ireland, distinguish'd by their Ranks, Actions, Learning, and other Accomplishments*
917 Spon's Hist. of the City and State of Geneva. ——— 1687
918 Samuel Johnson's Works. ——— ——— 1710
919 Cudworth's intellectual System with the Sacrament, *best Edition*. ——— ——— ——— 1678
920 Bingham's Antiquities, 2 vol. ——— 1726
921 Sir William Temple's Works, 2 vol. ——— ——— 1731
922 Thuanus's History of his own Times, translated by Wilson. 1729
923 Gordon's Life of Pope Alexander the VIth and his Son Cæsar Borgia. ——— ——— ——— 1729
924 Kidder's Demonstration of the Messias. ——— 1726
925 Scott's Christian Life. ——— ——— 1729
926 Kempfer's History of Japan, 2 vol. *cuts*. ——— 1728
927 Motraye's Travels, 3 vol. *cuts*. ——— ——— 1732
928 ——— Voyages and Travels, vol. 3d, *to compleat Setts*. 1732
929 Giannoni's Hist. of the Kingdom of Naples, translated by Ogilvie, 2 vol. ——— ——— 1729
930 Patrick's and Lowth's Commentaries, 4 vol. ——— 1727
931 Whitby's Commentary on the New Testament, 2 vol. 1727

932

932 The Holy Bible, *black letter, compleat and very fair, printed by Grafton.* ——— ——— —1539
933 Miege's French Dictionary. ——— ———1688
934 Pozzo's Perspective, English and Latin. —— ——1707
935 The Holy Bible, *bound in turky leather, gilt on the leaves:* *Oxford* 1680
936 Montfaucon's Antiquities, with the Supplement, translated by Humphreys, 7 vol. *cuts.* ——— 1721
937 ————Antiquities of Italy, *cuts.* —— 1725
938 Bishop Smalridge's Sermons. —— —— 1727
939 Hooker's Ecclesiastical Polity, with his Life of Walton. 1723
940 Homer's Iliad, translated by Ogilby, *fine cuts.* —— -1669
941 The Common-Prayer, *black letter, large pap. bound in turky leather, gilt on the leaves.* —— ——1662
942 General Description of the Royal Hospital of Invalids, *fine cuts, being part of the King of France's Cabinet, and printed at his Expence.* ——— —— 1683
943 Description of the Church of the Invalids, *being part of the King of France's Cabinet, and printed at his Expence, bound in turky leather, gilt and marbled on the leaves*
944 The Pleasures of the inchanted Island, *being part of the King of France's Cabinet, and printed at his Expence, bound in vellum, and gilt on the leaves.*
945 The Pourtraits of Illustrious Men, *Painted by Van Dyck, the cuts of the first Impression.*
946 Le Moyne's Gallery of Heroick Women, *fine cuts, gilt on the leaves.* ——— ——— ——1652
947 Collection of very scarce and curious Political Poems.
948 Parkinson's Herbal, *cuts.* ——— ———1640
949 The Holy Bible, *with curious cuts by Vischer.* ———1672
950 The Songs in the Opera of Radamisto set to Musick
951 Ludolphus's History of Ethiopia, *cuts.* — — 1682
952 Rycaut's State of the Ottoman Empire, *cuts.* ——1670
953 Father Paul's History of the Council of Trent, *best Edition.* 1676
954 Bishop Andrews's Sermons. ——— ———1635
955 Mason's Vindication of the Church of England, by Lindsay. 1728
956 Comber's Companion to the Temple, —— 1688
957 Pococke's Comment. on Micah, Malachi, Joel, and Hosea, *compleat.* ——— ——— ———1692
958 Webster's displaying of supposed Witchcraft. ———1677
959 Wheatly's Illustration of the Common-Prayer. ———1720
960 Hammond's Paraphrase on the New Testament ——1653
961 Voyages and Adventures of Fernand Mendez Pinto. ——1653
962 Gerrard's Herbal, *cuts.* ——— ——1597
963 Wesley's Life of Christ, *cuts.* ——— 1693
964 Malebranch's Search after Truth. ——— 1694
965 The Loves of Cupid and Psyche, by Salamanca, *very fair.*

966

966 Compleat Table of the Duties upon Wines and Vinegar. 1721
967 Tobacco batterr'd and the Pipes shatter'd.
968 Hist. of the Life of Duke Espernon. —— 1670
969 Croft's Musica Sacra, or select Anthems in score, 2 vol.
970 Stackhouse's compleat Body of Divinity. —— ——1734
971 Dryden's Juvenal.—— —— 1693
972 Pope's Works. —— —— ——1717
973 The Holy Bible, *black letter.* —— 1539
974 Bartholomeus de Proprietatibus Rerum, English. ——1582
975 Fowler's History of the Troubles in Swethland and Poland. 1656
976 Strada's History of the Low-Countrey Wars.——1650
977 Topsell's History of Serpents. — —— 1608
978 Pearson's Exposition of the Creed. —— ——1710
979 Dutchess of Newcastle's Letters and Poems.——1678
980 The History of Justin, translated by Wilkins. ——1606
981 H. Stephens's Apology for Herodotus. ——*Edinburgh* 1608
982 The Holy Bible, *black letter, cuts.*—— ——1602
983 Taylor the Water-Poet's Works, *very fair.*—— —1630
984 Homer in a Nut-Shell, with several other curious Poems.
985 Knox's History of the Island of Ceylon, *cuts.* ——1681
986 Rea's Flora, *cuts.* —— ——1676
987 Hector Boethius's History of Scotland, black letter, *very fair.*
988 Scheffer's History of Lapland, *cuts.*—— ——1674
989 Burton's Anatomy of Melancholy. —— 1660
990 Maimbourg's History of the Crusade, translated by Nalson. 1685
991 Relation of the French Conquests in the Netherlands, in 1672 and 1673.
992 The Shepard's Kalendar, *black letter, cuts.* ——
993 Blackmore's King Arthur.—— ——1697
994 Hooke's Micrographia, with the Louse and Flea, compleat. 1665
995 Leybourne's compleat Surveyor.—— ——1722
996 Parkinson's Flower-Garden, *cuts.*—— ——1656
997 The Common-Prayer, *black letter; printed by Jugge.*
998 The Common-Prayer in Portuguese, *printed at the Expence of the East-India Company.* —— 1695
999 Sir Tho. Brown's Works. —— ——1686
1000 Selden's Tracts. —— —— —1683
1001 The Dyctes and notable wyse Sayenges of the Philosophers, *printed by Caxton, very fair.*
1002 The Holy Bible, *black letter, very fair.* — 1566
1003 Stebbing's Polemical Tracts. —— ——1727
1004 Hackluyt's Voyages, with the Voyage to Cadiz compleat, 2 vol.—— —— ——1598
1005 Evelyn's Discourse of Medals.—— ——1697
1006 Holyday's Juvenal, *cuts.* —— —1673

F 1647

1007 Selden's Titles of Honour. — — 1631
1008 De Gray's compleat Horseman and expert Farrier. — 1639
1009 Nalson's History of the Holy War. — — 1686
1010 Tavernier's Voyages, *cuts.* — — 1678
1011 Du Bastas's Works. — — 1641
1012 Collection of curious Cuts, *painted by Le Brun, Rubens, Mignard, Lanfranc, Raph. Urbin, and Van Dyck, and grav'd by Audran, Drevet, Dorigny, Ragot, Vanden-Enden, and Edelinck.*
1013 Kettlewell's Works, 2 vol. — — 1719
1014 De la Quintinye's compleat Gardener. — — 1693
1015 Boccalini's Parnassus. — — — 1674
1016 L'Estrange's Alliance of Divine Offices. — — 1699
1017 Burnet's Exposition on the 39 Articles. — — 1705
1018 Stillingfleet's Sermons. — — 1707
1019 Tillotson's Works, 3 vol. — — 1735
1020 Bp. Beveridge's Works, 2 vol. — — 1729
1021 Mather's Ecclesiastical History of New England. — 1702
1022 Le Brun's Voyages, *fine cuts.* — — 1702
1023 Farindon's Sermons. — — 1674
1024 Blackhall's Works, 2 vol. — — 1723
1025 Lhuyd's Archæologia Britannica. — — 1707
1026 Evelyn's Discourse of Forest-trees. — — 1729
1027 Sidney's Discourses concerning Government. — 1698
1028 Machiavel's Works. — — — 1720
1029 Chillingworth's safe way of Protestants. — — 1638
1030 Barrow's Treatise on the Pope's Supremacy. — 1683
1031 Nicholls's Commentary on the Common-Prayer. — 1712
1032 Cave's Lives of the Primitive Fathers, *cuts, large and sm. pap.* — — — 1716
1033 Fiddes's Sermons. — — 1720
1034 Barrow's Works, 2 vol. — — 1722
1035 Howell's general History of the World, 3 vol. — 1680
1036 Pricke's Ornaments of Architecture. — — 1674
1037 Bonet's Guide to the practical Physician. — — 1684
1038 Mariana's general History of Spain. — — 1669
1039 The Historical Library of Diodorus the Sicilian, by Booth. 1700
1040 Freart's Parrallel of ancient and modern Architecture, by Evelyn. — — — 1733
1041 Perrault's Treatise of the five Orders of Architecture, by James. — — — 1708
1042 Josephus's Works, translated by Lodge. — — 1670
1043 Ayliffe's Comment. on the Canons and Constitutions of the Church of England. — — 1734
1044 Dryden's Virgil, *cuts.* — — 1697
1045 Douglas's Virgil in Scottish Verse. — — 1710
1046 Common-Prayer, *rul'd, and bound in turky leather, gilt on the leaves.* — — — 1706

1047

1047 Holyoake's Latin and English Dictionary. ——— 1677
1048 Harris's Lexicon Technicum, 2 vol.——— ——— 1736
1049 Willughby's History of Birds, *cuts.*
1050 Wilson's compleat Christian Dictionary. ——— 1661
1051 The Sentiments of the most excellent Painters concerning the Practice of Painting. ——— 1688
1052 Grimeston's general History of the Netherlands. ——— 1627
1053 Pope's Homer's Iliad, 6 vol. ——— 1715
1054 Cowper's Anatomical Treatise on the Muscles, *large pap.* 1724
1055 ——— the same, *large pap. bound in Russia Leather.* 1734

Theologia & Historia Ecclesiastica, Gr. Lat. Folio.

1056 Biblia sacra Polyglotta, cum Castelli Lexicon, 8 vol. *Lond.* 1657
1057 Biblia sacra, 8 vol. ——— *Paris e Typo. Regia* 1642
1058 Bulli Opera omnia, *ch. max.* ——— 1703
1059 Testamentum Græcum, *lineis rubris, foliis deauratis. Par. e Typo. Regia*
1060 Vitringæ Comment. in Lib. Prophetiarum Jesaiæ, 2 vol. *ch. max.* ——— ——— *Leovard.* 1724
1061 Eusebii, Sozomeni, & Evagri Hist. Ecclesiastica, gr. lat. cum Notis Valesii & G. Reading, 3 vol. *chart. max. & min.* ——— ——— *Cant.* 1720
1062 Usserii Annales veteris & novi Testamenti, *ch. max.*
1063 Ven. Hildeberti Opera, *chart. max. & min. Paris* 1708
1064 S. Athanasii Opera, gr. lat. 3 vol. ——— *ib.* 1698
1065 S. Basilii Magni Opera, gr. lat. 3 vol.——— *ib.* 1721
1066 S. Chrysostomi Opera, gr. lat. 11 vol.——— *ib.* 1718
1067 S. Irenæi Opera, gr. lat. ——— *ib.* 1710
1068 S. Anselmi Opera. ——— *ib.* 1721
1069 S. Cypriani Opera.——— ——— *ib.* 1726
1070 S. Gregorii Opera, 4 vol. ——— *ib.* 1705

(1063–1070: Studio Monachorum Ordinis S. Benedicti.)

1071 Biblia sacra, 2 vol. *foliis deauratis. Lug. apud S. Gryph.* 1550
1072 Anastasius Bibliothecarius de Vitis Pontificum, 3 vol. *Romæ* 1718
1073 Testamentum Syriacum & Latinum. *apud H. Steph.* 1569
1074 B. de Montfaucon Hexaplorum Origines, gr. lat. 2 vol. *Paris* 1713
1075 Biblia sacra Latina, 2 vol.——— *ib. apud* R. *Steph.* 1540
1076 F. Amato Pouget Institutiones Catholicæ in Modum Catacheseos, 2 vol. ——— ——— *Par.* 1725
1077 Justini Martyris Opera, cum Notis Thirlbii, gr. lat. *Lond.* 1722
1078 Angeli Rocca Episcopi Tagestan Opera omnia, 2 vol. *Rom.* 1719

1079 A. Franci Synopsis Annalium Societatis Jesu in Lusitania. *August. Vindel.* 1726

1080 Codex Constitutionum quas summi Pontifices ediderunt in solemni Canonizatione Sanctorum. ———— *Rom.* 1729

1081 P. a Limborch Comment. in Acta Apostolorum. *Rot.* 1711

1082 Lactantii Opera. *corio turcico, foliis deauratis.*—— *Ven.* 1478

1083 P. a Limborch Theologia Christiana. ———— *Amst.* 1700

1084 Psalterium Spirensium ad usum Orandi & Cantandi.

1085 { Sirenius de Fato. ———— ———— *Venet.* 1563
Ant. Nata de Deo. ———— *ib.* 1559
———— de Pulchro. ———— ———— *ib.* 1562 }

1086 Animadversiones & Responsiones super III Miracula post Obitum Sanationis Pueri Hectici, ex Gratia vidend. *foliis deauratis.*

1087 E. Browne Fasciculus Rerum expetend. & fugiendar. 2 vol. *Lond.* 1690

1088 Biblia sacra, cum duplici Translat. & Scholiis F. Vatabli, 2 vol. ———— ———— *Salm.* 1584

1089 ———— cum Concordantiis veteris & novi Testamenti, S. Hieronimo Interprete.———— ———— 1500

1090 Gianii Annales sacri Ordinis Fratrum Servorum, 2 vol. *Florent.* 1618

1091 Theophylacti Opera, gr. ———— *Romæ* 1542

1092 Clerici & Hammondi Comment. in totam Scriptur. 6 vol. *Amst.* 1710

1093 Pii Secundi Pont. Max. Epistolæ. ———— *Mediolan.* 1481

1094 Manfredi de Cardinalibus sanctæ Romanæ Ecclesiæ Liber. *Bonon.* 1564

1095 Vossius de Theologia Gentili. ———— *Amst.* 1668

1096 Biblia sacra, Scholiis illustrat. ab J. Tremellio & F. Junio. *Lond.* 1693

1097 Arnobius adversus Gentes, *foliis deauratis.*———— *Rom.* 1542

1098 Grotii Opera omnia Theologica, 4 vol. ———— *Basil.* 1632

1099 Trommii Concordantiæ Græcæ, 2 vol.———— *Amst.* 1718

1100 C. Meichelbeck Historia Frigensis, 2 vol. *August. Vindel.* 1724

1101 Sancti Vincentii Ferrerii Opera. ———— *ib.* 1729

1102 P. a Jacobi Epitome Bibliothec. Sanctorum Patrum, 2 vol. *ib.* 1719

1103 Lactantii Opera, *MS. in Pergameno.*

1104 Platina de Vitis Pontificum, *corio turcico, edit. prima.*

1105 Saavedræ Symbola Christiano-Politica. ———— *Brux.* 1649

1106 Macedi Divi tutelaris Orbis Christiani Opus singulare. *Ulissipone* 1687

1107 Symonetæ de Christianæ Fidei & Romanorum Pontificum Persecutionibus. ———— ———— *Basil.* 1509

1108 Vitæ Sanctorum Gothorum Sueonumque, Opera J. Vastovii. *Col. Agrip* 1623

1109

1109 Lactantii Opera, *foliis deauratis, editio antiqua, sine anno & loco.*

1110 E. Scheltrate Antiquitatis Ecclesiæ Opus Chronologicum. *Romæ* 1692

1111 Cortesii Lib. de Cardinalatu. ——— 1510

1112 Martyrologium Romanum. ——— *Par.* 1613

1113 S. Augustinus de Civitate Dei. ——— *Venet.* 1470

1114 Clementis Alexandrini Opera, gr. ex Bib. Medicea. *Florent. apud Torrentin.* 1550

1115 Eusebii Historia Ecclesiastica & de Preparatione Evangelica, gr. 2 vol. ——— *Lut. Par. apud R. Steph.* 1544

1116 Biblia sacra, ex S. Castelionis Interpret. ——— *Franc.* 1697

1117 Oudini Comment. de Scriptoribus Ecclesiasticis, 3 vol. *ib.* 1722

1118 Schmidii Concordantiæ. ——— *Lips.* 1717

1119 Biblia sacra vulgatæ Editionis, *lineis rubris. Venet. apud Juntas* 1557

1120 S. Irenæi Opera. ——— *Lut. Par.* 1675

1121 Agricolæ Hist. Provinciæ S. Jesu Germaniæ Superioris. *Aug. Vindel.* 1727

1122 Ughelli Italia sacra, 8 vol. ——— *Venet.* 1717

1123 Morini Comment. de sacris Ecclesiæ Ordinationibus. *Par.* 1655

1124 H. de Noris Hist. Pelagiana, & Dissertatio de Synodo 5 Oecumenica. ——— *Lovan.* 1702

1125 H. Vonderhart in Jobum Hist. Populi Israelis in Assyriaco Exilio. ——— *Helm.* 1728

1126 T. Delbene de Officio S. Inquisitionis circa Heresim, 2 vol. *Lug.* 1680

1127 P. Halloix Illustrium Ecclesiæ Orientalis Scriptorum secund. Seculi Vitæ & Documenta. ——— *Duaci* 1636

1128 N. Testamentum Gr. *lineis rubris, foliis deauratis. Lutet. apud R. Steph.* 1550

1129 Crux triumphans & gloriosa, a J. Bosio descripta. *Ant. ap. Plantin.* 1617

1130 Annales Minorum, Auctore Luca Waddingo, 6 vol. *Romæ* 1731

1131 Justini Martyris Opera, gr. ex Bibliotheca Regia. *Lutet. ap. R. Steph.* 1551

1132 T. Ruinart Acta primorum Martyrum sincera & selecta. *Amst.* 1713

1133 Clementis XI. Pont. Max. Opera omnia. ——— *Franc.* 1729

1134 Biblia sacra, *lineis rubris.* ——— *Lug. apud Tornesium* 1556

1135 Scriptores Ordinis Prædicatorum recensiti. ——— 1719

1136 Historia Episcopatuum Fœderati Belgii. ——— *Lug. Bat.* 1719

1137 Cotelerii Patres Apostolici, 2 vol. ——— *Amst.* 1724

1138 Petavii Dogmata Theologica, 3 vol. ——— *Ant.* 1700

1139 Thesaurus Monumentorum Ecclesiasticorum & Historicor. sive Canisii Lectiones antiquæ, 6 vol. ——— *Amst.* 1725

1140

1140 Natalis Alexandri Opera omnia, 8 vol. ——— *Par.*1714
1141 Centuriatores Magdeburgici, 3 vol. ——— *Basil.*1624
1142 Philonis Judæi Opera omnia, gr. *Par. apud Turneb.*1552
1143 Tertulliani Opera Rigaltii.——— ———*Lutet.*1634
1144 J. Goar Rituale Græcorum.——— ———*Venet.*1730
1145 Fromondi Comment. in ſacram Scripturam.— *Roth.*1709
1146 Critici ſacri, 10 vol. ——— ———*Lond.*1660
1147 S. Raymundi Opera. ——— *Par.*1720
1148 S. Ephraim Syrus, gr. ——— *Oxon.*
1149 S. Cypriani Opera, recognita a J. Fello. ——— *Amſt.*1700
1150 Clementis XI. Pont. Max. Orationes Conſiſtoriales, *cum fig.* *Romæ* 1722
1151 Hiſt. & Monumenta J. Hus atque H. Pragenſis. *Norimberg.* 1715
1152 Novum Teſtamentum Græcum, Studio J. Millii. *Lipſ.*1723
1153 Euſebii Nierembergii Hieromeliſſa Bibliotheca. *Lug.*1661
1154 S. Nili Epiſtolæ, gr. lat. Interpret. L. Allatio. *Romæ* 1668
1155 Tertulliani omniloquium Alphabeticum rationale tripartit. Opera C. Moreau, 3 vol. ——— *Par.*1658
X 1156 Paperbrochii Conatus Chronico-Hiſtoricus ad Catalogum Romanorum Pontificum, *cum fig.* ———*Ant.*1685
1157 Marci Abaudini Paradiſus Theologicus. ———*Lug.*1673
1158 Magni Gerhoii Comment. in Pſalmos & Cantica Ferialia. *Aug. Vindel.*1728
1159 Vitæ Sanctorum Siculorum, Opus poſthumum O. Cajetani. *Panorm.*1657
1160 C. du Pleſſis d'Argenter Collectio Judiciorum de novis Erroribus, 2 vol. ——— *Lut. Par* 1728
1161 Theodoreti Epiſcopi Opera, tom. 5.——— ———*ib.*1684
1162 Biblia ſacra, gr. lat. ſecundum LXX. 3 vol. *ib. apud N. Buon* 1628
1163 Divinæ Scripturæ, nempe veteris ac novi Teſtamenti omnia. *Franc.*1597
1164 C. de Arembergh Icones, Vitæ & Geſta Virorum illuſtrium Ordinis Fratrum Minorum, 2 vol.——— *Col. Agrip.*1642
1165 S. Cypriani Opera, a J. Fello, ——— *Oxon.*1682
1166 Teſtamentum Græcum, ſtudio J. Gregorii.———*ib.*1703
1167 S. Athanaſii Magni Opera, gr. lat.——— ———*Par.*1627
1168 Biblia ſacra, gr. lat. ſecundum LXX. Interpret. 3 vol. *Lut. Par. apud Sonnium* 1628
1169 Innocentii III. Epiſtolæ, S. Baluzius edidit, 2 vol. *Par.*1682
1170 Menologium, Regula, Conſtitutiones, & Privilegia Ordinis Ciſtercienſis.——— ———*Ant. apud Plant.*1630
1171 G. Cave Scriptorum Eccleſiaſticorum Hiſtoria Litteraria. *Genev.*1705
1172 Clementis Alexandrini Opera, gr. lat. emendat. a F. Sylburgio.——— ——— *Lut. Par.*1641
1173 Pricæi Comment. in varios novi Teſtamenti Libros. *Lond.* 1660

1174

1174 Simonis Episcopii Opera Theologica, 2 vol. —*Amst.* 1690
1175 Scacchi sacrorum Elæochrismat, Myrothecia tria. *ib.* 1701
1176 T. a Kempis de Imitatione Christi, *Par. e Typo. Regia* 1640
1177 Cardinalis de Lugo Opera omnia, 3 vol.—— *Lug.* 1670
1178 Philonis Judæi Opera, gr. lat. Gelenii & aliorum Interpret. *Franc.* 1691
1179 Biblia Sacra, vulgatæ Editionis. —— *Lug.* 1684
1180 St. Irenæi Opera cum notis Var. J. Grabe.—— *Oxon.* 1702
1181 Testamentum Græcum studio J. Millii. —— *ib.* 1707
1182 Ismael Abul-Feda da Vita & rebus gestis Mohammedis, Arab. & Lat. notis J. Gagnier. —— *ib.* 1723
1183 Vetus Testamentum juxta LXX Interpretes, cura E. Grabe. *Oxon.* 1707
1184 B. de Montfaucon collectio Græcorum Patrum. *Paris.* 1706
1185 Natali Adnotationes & Meditationes in Evangelia, cum multis fig. —— —— *Ant.* 1607
1186 Biblia Sacra, vulgatæ Editionis, lineis rubris. *Paris, apud Colinaum.* 1541
1187 Alciati & Cotto Vitæ de SS. Martyribus. —*Mediolan.* 1657
1188 St. Optati Opera. —— *Paris.* 1679
1189 Theophanis Archiepiscopi Homiliæ gr. lat.— *Lut. Par.* 1644

Libri Mathemat. Itinera, Philosophia, Juridici, Medici, Hist. Naturalis, Hist. Var. Gentium, Bibliothecarii, Hist. Byzantina & Miscellanæi. Folio.

1190 Historiæ Byzantinæ Scriptores, 36 vol. *Paris e Typo. Regia.*
1191 Marianæ Hist. de Rebus Hispaniæ Lib. XXX accedunt J. Emmanuelis Minianæ continuat novæ Lib. X. 2 vol. cum fig. ——— *Haga Comit.* 1733
1192 Theatrum Machinarum Hydrotechnicarum, Arithmetico-Geometricum, Hydraulicarum, Staticum, Pontificiale, 8 vol. ——— 1726
1193 Thuani Historia sui Temporis, 7 vol, *Lond. apud S. Buckley.* 1733
1194 Ptolemæi Cosmographia.—— —— —— —— 1481
1195 J. Marianæ Hist. de Rebus Hispaniæ Lib. XX. corio turcico. —— —— —— —— — *Toleti.* 1592
1196 Struvii Corpus Historiæ Germanicæ, 2 vol.—*Jena.* 1730
1197 J. Wallis Opera Mathematica, 3 vol. ——— *Oxon.* 1695
1198 Constantini Observationes Forenses practicabiles, 3 vol. *Rom.* 1701
1199 Diogenes Laertius, gr. lat. Aldobrandino Interpret. & cum observat. Menagii. —— —— —— *Lond.* 1664
1200 T. de Bry descriptio Indiæ Orientalis & Occidentalis, 4 vol. cum fig. elegantiss. —— —— —— *Franc.*
1201 Possevini Gonzaga, Calci Operis addita Genealogia totius Familiæ. ——— *Mantuæ.* 1628

3 1202

1202 Renaldini ars Analytica Mathemat. 3 vol. — *Florent*. 1665
1203 Lindenbrogi Scriptores rerum Germanicarum Septentrionalium. — — — — *Franc*. 1630
1204 Pontani rerum & Urbis Amstelodamensium Historiæ. *Amst*. 1610
1205 Novarini omnium Scientiarum anima, 3 vol. — *Lug*. 1644
1206 Hospiniani Opera omnia, 4 vol. — *Genev*. 1681
1207 Wolfii Lectiones Memorabiles & Reconditæ, 2 vol. *Franc*. 1671
1208 Jus Domaniale ex Celeberrimor. Jurisconsultorum, 2 vol. *ib*. 1701
1209 { Germanicarum rerum IV. Celebriores Vetustioresque Chronographi. — *ib*. 1566
B. Rhenani rerum Germanicarum Lib. III. — *Basil*. 1501 }
1210 Æneæ Sylvii Historia rerum Frederici III. Imperatoris. *Argent*. 1685
1211 C. Clavii Opera Mathematica, 4 vol. — *Mogunt*. 1612
1212 Reuberi Historia Imperatorum, 2 vol. — *Franc*. 1726
1213 Baccetii Septimianæ Historiæ Lib. VII. — *Romæ*. 1724
1214 Nicolai primi Pont. Max. Epistolæ. — *ib*. 1542
1215 Becani Origines Antwerpianæ. — *Ant*. 1569
1216 Goldasti rerum Alamannicarum Scriptores. — *Franc*. 1661
1217 Torfæi Historia rerum Norvegicarum, 4 vol. *Hafniæ*. 1711
1218 Manzii Bibliotheca aurea, Juridico, Politico-Theoretia practica, 3 vol. — *Franc*. 1695
1219 Carusii Bibliotheca Historica Regni Siciliæ, 2 vol. *Panorm*. 1723
1220 J. Zahn Oculus artificialis Teledioptricus — *Norimb*. 1702
1221 Telesii de rerum Natura juxta propria Principia. *Neap*. 1587
1222 Freheri Hist. rerum Bohemicarum. — *Hanov*. 1602
1223 Joannis Magni Historia Gothorum, corio turcico. *Rom*. 1554
1224 Isthuansi Historia de rebus Ungaricis. — *Col. Agrip*. 1622
1225 Bucherii de Doctrina Temporum Comment. — *Ant*. 1634
1226 Scriptores rerum Lusaticarum antiqui & recentiores, 2 vol. *Lipsiæ* 1719
1227 Gesta Dei per Francos, sive Orientalium expeditionum & Regni Francorum Hierosolymitani Historia, corio turcico. *Hanov*. 1611
1228 Justiniani Emp. Constitutiones gr. — *apud H. Steph*. 1558
1229 Antiquitatum Romanarum P. Manutii Liber de Legibus. *Venet*. 1557
1230 Indices rerum ab Aragoniæ Regibus gestarum ab initiis Regni ad annum 1610 a H. Surita. — 1678
1231 Vasæi Chronici rerum memorabilium Hispaniæ, tomus prior. — *Salmanticæ*. 1652
1232 Photii Bibliotheca gr. D. Hoeschelius edidit. *Aug. Vindel*. 1601
1233 ——— Epistolæ, gr. lat. — *Lond*. 1651
1234 De Aureis & Argenteis Cimeliis in arce Perusina effossis hoc anno 1717 Epistolæ. 1235

1235 Rerum Moscoviticarum Auctores varii. —— *Franc.*1600
1236 Subtilissimi Decretis Anglici Suiser Lib. calculat. sine anno & loco.
1237 Statuta Almæ Urbis Romæ. —— *Romæ.*1580
1238 Stephanus de Urbibus, gr. —— *Basil.*1568
1239 Kircheri China, Monumentis, cum fig. —— *Amst.*1667
1240 De Nominibus propriis Pandectæ Florentinæ cum Ant. Augustini Archiepiscopi Tarraconensis Notis. *Tarracon.*1579
1241 Kyriandri Augustæ Trevirorum Annales. —— 1619
1242 Hist. expositiones geminæ de Nobiliss. & Antiquiss. Welforum prosapia a Reineccio. —— *Franc.*1581
1243 F. de Rosieras Stemmatum Lotharingiæ ac Barri Ducum. *Paris.*1580
1244 B. Rhenani rerum Germanicarum Lib. III. *Basil.*1531
1245 Jani Suaningii Chronologia Danica. —— *Hafniæ.*1650
1246 Reidani Belgarum aliarumque Gentium Annales. *Lug. Bat.* 1633
1247 Euclidis Elementa Lib. XXX. in Ling. Arabicam. *Romæ*1594
1248 Pithoei Historia Francorum. —— *Franc.*1596
1249 Sexti Empirici Opera, gr. lat. —— *Genev.*1621
1250 Hippocratis Opera per Fabium & aliorum Latinitate donata. *Basil.*1526
1251 Vossii & clarorum Virorum ad eum Epistolæ. *Lond.*1690
1452 Chifletii de Ampulla Remensi disquisitio. —— *Ant.*1651
1253 Thomæ Mori Opera omnia. —— *Franc.*1689
1254 Kircheri Musurgia universalis. —— *Romæ.*1650
1255 Cluverii Germania antiqua, cum fig. — *Lug. Bat.*1666
1256 Valdesii de dignitate Regum Regnorumque Hispaniæ Lib. *Granatæ.*1602
1257 Photii Bibliotheca, gr. lat. —— 1611
1258 Julii Solini Polyhistor. & Pomponius Mela de Situ Orbis. *Basil.*1538
1259 Guidi Ubaldi e Marchionibus Montis de Cochlea Lib. IV. *Venet.*1615
1260 Archimedis Opera, gr. lat. —— *Paris, apud Morel.*1615
1261 Apollonii Pergæi Conicorum Lib. IV. cum Pappi Alexandrini Comment. —— *Bonon.*1566
1262 Chiromantiæ. —— —— *ib.*
1263 { Joannis Grammaticus in Lib. de Generatione & Interitu. / —Comment. in Lib. de Anima Aristotelis. } *apud Aldum.*
1264 Navigatio ac Itinerarium Hugonis Linschotani, cum fig. *Amst.*1614
1265 Ludolfi Historia Æthiopica, 2 vol. cum fig. — *Franc.*1681
1266 Procopii Arcana Historia, gr. lat. —— *Lug.*1623
1267 Appendix Bibliothecæ Gesneri. —— *Tiguri.*1555
1268 Lindenbrogi Codex Legum Antiquarum, 2 vol. *Franc.*1613
1269 Corpus universæ Historiæ præsertim Byzantinæ. *Lut.*1567
1270 Hippocratis Opera, gr. —— *Basil.*1538

G 1271

1271 Diophanti Alexandrini Arithmetica, gr. lat. *Lut.Par.*1621
1272 B. Portæ Phytognomonica, cum fig. —— *Neap.*1588
1273 Cujacius de Feudis. —— *Lug.*1566
1274 P. Maffeii Historia Indicarum. —— *Col.Agrip.*1589
1275 Dominici Marii Nigri Geograph. Comment. Lib. XI.—*Basiliæ.*1557
1276 Diogenes Laertius de dogmatis & vitis Philosophorum, Editio antiqua sine anno & loco.
1277 Guidi Ubaldi e Marchionibus Montes Mechanicorum Liber. *Pisauri.*1577
1278 Meyeri Annales rerum Flandricarum. —— *Ant.*1561
1279 H. Blanca Aragonensium rerum Comment. *Cæsar Augustæ.* 1588
1280 G. Leibnitz Codex Juris Gentium Diplomaticus. *Hanov.* 1693
1281 J. Anton. Pilaiæ Decisiones Pontificiæ, 2 tom. 1 vol. *Messanæ.*1667
1282 J. de Laet Americæ utriusque descriptio, cum fig. *Lug. Bat.*1633
1283 Bocharti Geographia. —— *Cadomi.*1646
1284 Tychonis Brahæ Astronomiæ instauratæ Mechanica. *Noriberg.*1602
1285 Galeni Opera gr. 5 vol. —— *Venet. apud Aldum.*1525
1286 Equinarii ad omnes partes Pandectarum Juris Enucleati Manualium Liber singularis, 3 vol. *Lutetiæ apud Vascosan.* 1562
1287 Connani Comment. Juris Civilis, 2 vol. lineis rubris, foliis deauratis. —— —— *ib.ib.*1553
1288 Paparellæ Opera omnia. —— *Maceratæ.*1582
1289 Lyndwoodi Provinciale, seu Constitutiones Angliæ. *Oxon.* 1679
1290 Freheri Origines Palatinæ. —— 1613
1291 Garsiæ a Saavedræ tractat. de Hispanorum Nobilitate. *Com. pluti.*1597
1292 Marinæi de rebus Hispaniæ memorabilium.—— 1533
1293 Faleti Orationes, foliis deauratis.
1294 Beringii Florus Danicus. —— *Hauniæ.*1709
1295 Rudbekii Atlantica sive Manheim, cum fig. *Upsalæ.*1679
1296 Julii Firmici & aliorum Astronomica. —— *Venet.*1499
1297 Historia Ducum Styriæ, cum fig. —— 1728
1298 Mutius de Germanorum prima Origine, foliis deauratis. *Basil.*1539
1299 Velseri rerum Augustanar. Vindelicar. Lib. VIII. foliis deauratis.
1300 Conradi Abb. Urspergensis Chronicum. —— *Basil.*1569
1301 Leoni Historia Prussiæ. —— *Brunsberg.*1725
1302 Nattæ de Pulchro Lib. VI. corio turcico.—— *Papiæ.*1553

1303

1303 { Simplicii Comment. in Ariſtotelis de Anima. *Venet. apud Aldum.* 1527
Alexandri Aphrodiſienſis Naturalis de Anima Morales. 1536 }

1304 De Locis ſolidis Ariſtæi Senioris ſecunda Divinatio V. Viviani. —— —— —— *Florent.*

1305 In Mediceam Monarchiam Coſmi Medicea Geſta, corio turcico. —— —— 1527

1306 Aventini Annales Bojorum ſive veteris Germaniæ Lib. VII. *Franc.* 1627

1307 Mariani Scoti Opera. —— *Baſil.* 1559

1308 Plukenetii Hiſtoria Stirpium, Icones, Tabulis Æneis, 4 vol. *Lond.* 1691

1309 Syntagma Hiſtorico-Genealogicum Domus Comitum, & Baronum Woracziczkiorum. —— *Praga.* 1708

1310 { Saxonis Grammatici Hiſtoria Danica. —— 1646
S. Johannis Stephani Notæ in Hiſtoriam Danicam Saxonis Grammat. —— —— 1645 }

1311 Guicciardini Inferioris Germaniæ Regionum deſcriptio, cum fig. —— —— *Amſt.* 1624

1312 Bartholomeus de proprietatibus rerum. —— 1519

1313 Procopii Hiſtoria. —— *Baſil.* 1531

1314 Genealogiæ Ducum Saxonicum a Leorino, cum fig. 1610

1315 Turco-Græciæ Lib. VIII. a M. Cruſio. *Baſil.*

1316 Knipſchiltii de Nobilitate Sagata & Togata antiqua & nova, 2 vol. —— —— *Campoduni.* 1693

1317 J. And. de Georgio repetitiones Feudales ineditæ ad rubricas. —— —— *Neapoli.* 1724

1318 Pingonii Inclytorum Saxonicæ Sabaudiæque Principum Arbor Gentilitiæ. —— *Aug. Taurinor.* 1581

1319 Scriptores rerum Epiſcopatus Bambergenſis cura J. Ludewig, tom. 1 vol. —— *Franc.* 1718

1320 Hiſt. Domus Auſtriacæ. —— *Oenepenti.* 1660

1321 Guiliarum Opus H. Herboni. —— 1539

1322 Albertini Muſſati Hiſt. Auguſt. Henrici VII Cæſaris & alia quæ extant Opera. —— *Venet.* 1636

1323 Epitome Bibliothecæ Conradi Geſneri. —— *Tiguri.* 1555

1324 Chronici Ditmari Epiſcopi Merſepurgii Lib. VII. *Franc.* 1580

1325 Solemnia Electionis & Inaugurationis Leopoldi Imp. cum fig. —— —— *ib.* 1660

1326 Haræi Annales Ducum Bræbantiæ totiuſque Belgii, 2 vol. *Ant.* 1623

1327 M. Gosky Divi Auguſti Ducis Brunoviæ Vita & Fama, cum fig. —— —— *Franc.* 1693

1328 Strada de Bello Belgico, 2 vol. cum fig. —— *Roma.* 1640

1329 Selden de Jure Naturali & Gentium. —— *Lond.* 1640

1330 Obſidio Bredana, cum fig. —— *Ant.* 1639

1331 De Chales Curſus Mathematicus, 3 vol. —— *Lug.* 1674

1332 Winſemii rerum Friſicarum Lib. VII. —— *Leovardia.* 1646

1333 Corpus Francicæ Hist. veteres & sinceræ.—— *Hanov.* 1613
1334 Gesneri Bibliotheca. —— *Tiguri.* 1583
1335 Irenici Exegesis Historiæ Germaniæ.—— *Hanov.* 1728
1336 Nova, & Amœnior de admirando Fontium Genio Philosophia. —— —— *Ferrar.* 1659
1337 Hipparchi Bithyni in Arati & Eudoxi Phenomena Lib. III. gr. —— *Florent. in officina Juntarum.* 1567
1338 Arithmetica Logarithmetica. —— *Lond.* 1624
1339 N. Upton de Studio Militari. —— *ib.* 1654
1340 L. Howel Synopsis Canonum SS. Apostolorum, 2 vol. *ib.* 1708
1341 Cromeri de Origine & Rebus gestis Polonorum Lib. XXX *Basil.*
1342 Rerum Hungaricarum Scriptores varii. —— *Franc.* 1600
1343 J Fontani de Bello Rhodio Lib. III. corio turcico, foliis deauratis.
1344 Paschalius de viribus Patriæ potestatis. —— *Franc.* 1718
1345 Aristotelis Hist. Animalium Lib. IX. T. Gazæ & Alcyonio Interprete. —— *Paris, apud Colinaum.* 1524
1346 Originum ac Germanicarum Antiquitatum Lib. Opera J. Herold, corio turcico. —— *Basil.*
1347 Denola Opusculum, Distinctum, Plenum, Clarum, Doctum, Pulcrum, Verum, Grave, Varium, & Utile, corio turcico, *Venet.* 1514
1348 Ptolemæi Cosmographia, Editio antiqua sine anno & loco.
1349 Ramnusii de Bello Coustantinopolitano & Imp. Comnenis Historia. —— —— *Venet.* 1634
1350 Bertrandi de Tholosanor. Gestis ab Urbe condita, corio turcico. —— —— *Tholosa.* 1515
1351 Rondeletius de Piscibus, foliis deauratis. —— *Lug.* 1554
1352 Passerini tractat. de Electione Canonica ——*Col. Agrip.* 1694
1353 A. Tacquet Opera Mathematica. —— *Ant.* 1707
1354 E. Speckham Opera omnia Juridico-Politico-Historico-Medica. —— —— *Franc.* 1695
1355 Theophrasti Hist. Plantarum, gr.
1356 Synesii Episcopi de Regno ad Arcadium Imp. *Paris, apud Turnebum.* 1553
1357 Feyrabendii Annales rerum Belgicarum. —— *Franc.* 1580
1358 Digestum vetus, seu Pandectæ Juris Civilis, 5 vol *Par.* 1565
1359 Collectio Conciliorum Hispaniæ. —— *Madriti.* 1593
1360 Justelli Bibliotheca Juris Canonici veteris, 2 vol *Lut. Paris.* 1661
1361 Authores varii de Morbo Gallico, 2 vol. —— *Venet.* 1566
1362 Vivæ Imagines partium Corporis Humani æreis formis expressæ.—— —— —— *Ant. apud Plantin.* 1566
1363 Pauli Jovii de Romanis Piscibus Libellus. —— *Basil.* 1533
1364 Mag. Hippocrates Prosperi Martiani Opus desideratum. *Patav.* 1719
1365 M. de Heredia Opera Medica, 2 vol. —— *Ant.* 1690

1366

1366 M. de Lobel Plantarum ſeu Stirpium Hiſtoria. *Ant. apud Plantin.* 1576
1367 J. Voſſii Epiſtolæ. ——— *Lond.* 1693
1368 Conſtitutiones Concilii Provincialis Moguntinæ. *Mogunt.* 1549
1369 Argenterii Medici de Morbis, Lib. XIV. —— *Florent.* 1556
1370 Alexandri ab Alexandro Genialium Dierum Lib. VI. *Paris.* 1549
1371 Antiqua & Recentiora nomina Piſcium, &c. in Jovii Comment. continentur. ——— *Roma.* 1524
1372 O. Brunf de Herbis. ——— *Argent.* 1532
1373 Curtii Hortorum Lib. XXX ——— *Lug.* 1560
1374 Catalogus Plantarum Horti Piſani, cum fig. — *Florent.* 1723
1375 Petri de Creſcentiis Ruralium Commodorum. —— 1574
1376 Index Bibliothecæ Cardinalis Barberinæ, 2 vol.— *Romæ.* 1681 ×
1377 Briſſonius de Verborum ſignificatione. ——— *Paris.* 1596
1378 Avicennæ Arabum Medicorum principis Canon Medicinæ. *Venet. apud Junt.* 1608
1379 Hippocratis Opera gr. lat. H. Mercuriali. ——— *ib. ib.* 1588
1380 Plantæ per Galliam, Hiſpaniam, & Italiam obſervatæ Iconibus æneis exhibitæ a J. Barreliero. ——— *Paris.* 1714
1381 Heſperides ſive de Malorum aureorum cultura & uſu B. Ferrarii Lib. IV. cum fig. ——— *Romæ.* 1646
1382 { Dioſcoridis de Medicinali Materia Lib. —— *Paris.* 1516
{ Oribaſii Medici de Simplicibus Lib. V. —— *Argent.* 1533
1383 Hippocratis Opera per F. Calvum Lat. donata. *Romæ.* 1595
1384 Speculi Intellectualis Regiſtrum, foliis deauratis, ligatura Grolieriana.
1385 Mag. Oecumen. Conſtantienſe Concilium, 4 vol. *Franc.* 1708
1386 Auguſtini Archiepiſcopi Tarraconenſ. de Legibus & Senatus Liber. ——— *Paris.* 1584
1387 Index Librorum Prohibitorum. ——— *Matriti.* 1667
1388 Æginetæ Opera gr. ——— *Venet. apud Aldum.*
1389 Gorræi definitiones Medicæ. *Franc* 1601
1390 Tacuini Ægritudinum & Morborum ferme omnium Corporis Humani. ——— *Argent.* 1532
1391 Corteſii practicæ Medicinæ, 3 vol. ——— *Meſſanæ.* 1635
1392 G. Hertman Clavis eccleſiaſticæ Diſciplinæ. — *Paris.* 1693
1393 Lambard de priſcis Anglorum Legibus. —— *Cant.* 1644
1394 Petiti Leges Atticæ. ——— *Paris.* 1635
1395 Deciſiones Regni Aragonum Authore J. de Seſſe. *Venet.* 1612
1396 E. Chiſhull Antiquitates Aſiaticæ. ——— *Lond.* 1728
1397 Hortii Reſponſa, & Deductiones. ——— *Franc.* 1729
1398 Adrichomii Theatrum Terræ Sanctæ, cum fig. *Col. Agrip.* 1628
1399 Moriſoni Hiſt. Plantarum, 2 vol. ——— *Oxon.* 1715
1400 Eraſmi Epiſtolæ omnes, 2 vol. ch. max. — *Lug. Bat.* 1706
1401 F. Suarez tractat. de Legibus ac Deo Legiſlatore. *Lond.* 1679
1402 Concilia Rotomagenſis Provinciæ ſtudio G. Beſſin. *Rotomag.* 1717

1403

1403 Rerum Sicularum Scriptores. ——— Franc.1679
1404 Sammarthani Gallia Christiana in Provincias ecclesiasticas distributa, 2 vol. ——— Paris, e Typo. Regia.1716
1405 Menckenii Scriptores rerum Germanicarum præcipue Saxonicarum. ——— Lipsiæ.1728
1406 Ruellii de Natura Stirpium Lib. III. lineis rubris, ch. max. Paris, apud Colinæum.1536
1407 Alphabethi ex Diplomatibus & Codicibus Thuricensibus specimen publicat. a J. Scheuchzer. —— Tiguri.1730
1408 Repertorium Conciliorum N. Nigrand. ——— 1579
1409 Pithæi Observat. ad Codicem & Novelas Justiniani Imp. ejusdem Codex Canonum, 2 vol. ch. max. & min. Paris, e Typo. Regia.1689
1410 Hispania illustrata, 3 vol. ——— Franc.1603
1411 A. Baudrand Geographia, 2 vol. ——— Paris.1682
1412 Hortus Indicus Malabaricus, 12 tom. 6 vol. cum multis fig. elegantiss. ——— Amst.1686
1413 D. de Faria additiones ad Covarruviam, 2 vol. Col. Allobrog. 1726
1414 Gesneri Opera omnia, cum fig. ——— Franc.1604
1415 Malpighii Anatome Plantarum, 2 vol. cum fig. Lond.1675
1416 S. Bochart de Animalibus Sacræ Scripturæ, 2 vol. ib.1663
1417 Connani Comment. Juris Civilis, 2 tom. 1 vol. Neap.1724
1418 Guazzini tractat. de Confiscatione Bonorum. — Lug.1676
1419 Aristotelis Hist. de Animalibus J. C. Scaligero Interpret. cum ejusdem Comment. ——— Tolosa.1619
1420 Cujacii Opera omnia, 10 vol. ——— Lut. Paris.1658
1421 Tamburinus de Jure & Privilegiis Abbatum, 4 tom. 2 vol. Aug. Vindel.1698
1422 Codicis Legum Wisigothorum Lib. XII. ex Bibliotheca Pithœi. ——— —— Paris.1579
1423 Corpus Juris Appanagii & Paragii cura Meieri.— Lemgoviæ. 1727
1424 Silesiacarum rerum Scriptores, 3 vol. —— Lipsiæ.1729
1425 M. Alting descriptio secundum Antiquos Agri Batavi & Frisii, ch. max. cum fig. ——— Amst.1697
1426 Euclidis Elementa gr. lat. ex recensione D. Gregorii. Oxon. 1703
1427 E. Martene veterum scriptorum & Monumentorum Historicor. Dogmaticor. Moralium ampliss. collectio. 3 vol. Paris.1724
1428 J. Valenzuela Velasquez Concilia sive Juris Responsa, 2 vol. Col. Allobrog.1727
1429 G. a Hermosilla Notæ, Additiones & Resolutiones ad Glossas Legum Partitarum D. G. Lopetii, 2 vol. —— ib.1726
1430 Apollonii Pergæi Sectiones Conicæ E. Hallæus, ch. max. Oxon.1720
1431 J. Lipsi Opera omnia, 4 vol. cum fig.— Ant. apud Plantin. 1637

1432

1432 Fabroti Basilicus gr. lat. 7 vol. — *Paris apud Cramoisy*. 1647
1433 Spelmanni Concilia, 2 vol. ——— *Lond* 1664
1434 Capitulariæ Regum Francorum edidit S. Baluzius, 2 vol. *Paris*. 1677
1435 Mangeti Bibliotheca Anatomica, 2 vol. cum fig. *Genev*. 1685
1436 J. Friend Opera omnia Medica, ch. max. & minor. *Lond*. 1733
1437 Codex Justiniani, Accurtii & Contii Comment. 2 vol. *Paris*. 1676
1438 Valentini Corpus Juris Medico-Legale. —— *Franc*. 1722
1439 Pharmacopœia Londinensis, ch. max. ——— *Lond*. 1721
1440 Barlæi rerum per Octennium in Brasiliæ & alibi nuper Gestar. sub C. Mauritio, ch. max. cum multis fig. *Amst*. 1647
1441 Lazius de Gentium aliquot Migrationibus. —— *Franc*. 1600
1442 Caponi Controversiarum Forensium utriusque Juris & Fori. *Col. Allobrog*. 1732
1443 Goldasti Politica Imperialia. ——————— *Franc*. 1614
1444 Corpus Juris Civilis, Notis Gothofredi, 2 vol. —— *Lug*. 1650
1445 Sabellici Historia Veneta, corio turcico, foliis deauratis. *Venet*. 1487
1446 S. Vaillan Botanicon Parisiense, cum fig. —— *Amst*. 1727
1447 Uffenbachii Thesaurus Chirurgiæ. ———— *Franc*. 1610
1448 W. Imhoff Excellentium Familiarum in Gallia Genealogiæ. *Norimberg*. 1687
1449 Metalliotheca Vaticana M. Mercati, cum fig. — *Romæ*. 1717
1450 Simonetæ rerum gestarum F. Sphortiæ Mediolan. Ducis, corio turcico, foliis deauratis. ——— *Mediol*. 1479
1451 Sweertii rerum Belgicarum Annales. ——— *Franc*. 1620
1452 P. Jovii Historia sui Temporis, ch. max. *Florent. apud Torrent*. 1550
1453 Aimoini Lib. V. de gestis Francorum. ——— *Paris*. 1603
1454 P. Jovii Historia sui Temporis, 2 vol. — *Lut. apud Vascosan*. 1553
1455 Helvici Theatrum Historicum & Chronologicum. *Marpurg*. 1638
1456 Possevini Bibliotheca Selecta. ——— —— *Romæ*. 1593
1457 G. Reading Bibliothecæ Cleri Londinensis in Collegio Sionensi Catalogus. ——————— *Lond*. 1724
1458 Acta Conciliorum & Epistolæ Decretales, ac Constitutiones summorum Pontificium studio J. Harduini, 12 vol. *Paris*. 1715
1459 Sacrosancta Consilia ad Regiam Editionem exacta studio P. Labbei, & G. Cossartii, 17 vol. ——— *Lut. Paris*. 1672
1460 L. Muratori rerum Italicarum scriptores, 23 vol. —— 1723
1461 Delectus Actorum Ecclesiæ universalis, 2 vol. —— *Lug*. 1706
1462 Ortelii Theatrum Orbis Terrarum, cum tabulis Geographi. depictis. ——————————— *Ant*. 1575
1463 Hansizii Germania Sacra, cum fig. —— *August. Vindel*. 1727
1464 Eusebii Thesaurus Temporum, Opera J. Scaligeri. *Amst*. 1658.

1465 Phyfiologia Kircheriana experimentalis cum fig. *Amft.*1680
1466 G. Bidloo Anatomia Humani Corporis CV Tabulis. *ib.*1685
1467 Spigelii Opera omnia, ch. max. cum fig. ——— *ib.*1645
1468 Hortus Eyftetenfis. ——— ——— ——— 1613
1469 Danubius Pannonico-Myficus obfervat. Geograph. Aftronom. Hydrograph. perluftratus & in 6 tom. digeftus ab a Ferd. Comite Marfilii. ——————— *Hagæ Comit.*1726
1470 M. Fifini Philofophi Platonici Opera, 2 vol.——*Paris.*1641
1471 Blanchini Hefperi & Phofphori Nova Phænomena.*Rom.*1728
1472 Antoniana Margarita Opus, 2 vol.———————1554
1473 Mauroceni Hiftoria vetera.——————— *Venet.*1623
1474 Cafferii Placentini de vocis auditufque Organis Hift. Anatomica, cum fig. ——————— *Ferrariæ.*1601
1475 Willughbeii Ornithologiæ Lib. III. cum fig.—— *Lug.*1676
1476 Pifonis Hift. Naturalis Brafiliæ, cum fig. —— *Lug.Bat.*1648
1477 Breynii Exoticarum aliarumque minus cognitarum Plantarum Centuria, cum fig. ——————— *Gedani.*1678
1478 Romani Collegii Societat. Jefu Mufæum celeberrimum, cum fig. ——————————— *Amft.*1678
1479 Kircheri Ars magna Lucis & Umbræ, cum fig.——*ib.*1671
1480 ———Ars magna Sciendi.——————— *ib.*1669
1481 Bauhini Hift. Plantarum univerfalis, 3 vol. *Ebroduni.*1650
1482 Cronica cum Figuris & Imaginibus ab Initio Mundi.
1483 J. Commelin rariorum Plantarum Horti Medici Amftelodamenfis Defcriptio & Icones, 2 vol.——— *Amft.*1697
1484 Cæfii Minerologia, five Naturalis Philofophiæ Thefauri. *Lug.* 1636
1485 M. Sibilliæ Merian de Generatione & Metamorphofibus Infectorum Surinamenfium, cum fig.depictis.*Hagæ Com.*1726
1486 Aldrovandi Hift. de Quadrupedibus, de Avibus, de Serpentibus & Draconis, de Pifcibus & de Cetis, de Infectis, de Mollibus, de Cruftaceis, de Teftaceis, de Zoophitis, de Monftris, & Mufei Metallici Dendrologiæ, 13 vol. cum multis fig. foliis deauratis.
1487 Vefalii Anatomia, cum fig. —— *Bafiliæ per Oporinum.*1555
1488 Diophanti Alexandrini Arithmetica cum Comment. Bacheti, gr. lat. ——————————— *Tolofæ.*1670
1489 F. Schannat veterum Monumentor. ad Germaniam Sacram præcipue fpectantium Collectio. ——— *Lipfiæ.*1723
1490 Salviani Hiftoria Aquatilium, cum fig. elegantiff. *Rom.*1554
1491 C. Sheiner Rofa Urfina, five Sol ex admirando facularum & macularum fuarum Phænomeno varius, cum fig.*Bracciani.* 1629
1492 Euftachii Taoula Anatomica ——————— *Romæ.*1714
1493 Florilegium Em. Sweertii.———————*Franc.*1612
1494 Mafenii Antiquitat. & Annalium Trevirenfium, Lib. XXV. *Leodii.*1670
1495 Galeni Opera lat. 5 vol.——— *Venet. apud Juntas.*1597
1496 Mufeum Wormianum, feu Hiftoria rerum rariorum, cum fig. ——————————— *Lug. Bat.*1655

1497 Anthologia Magna, seu Florilegium novum. *Franc. ex Officina Brijana.* 1626
1498 P. de Sorbait universæ Medicinæ Opera. —— *Noriberg.* 1672
1499 Ant. de Herrera descriptio Indiæ Occid. cum fig. *Amst.* 1622
1500 Catalogus Manuscriptorum Angliæ & Hiberniæ. *Oxon.* 1697
1501 Harduini Opera Selecta. —— *Amst.* 1709
1502 Rerum Suevicarum Scriptores veteres, ex Bibliotheca Goldasti. —— —— *Ulm.* 1727
1503 Alverni Mathematici & Philosophi Opera omnia, *lineis rubr. cor. turc. fol. deaur.* —— *Ven.* 1591
1504 Canones SS. Apostolorum Conciliorum generalium & provincialium, cum Comment. T. Balsamonis, gr. lat. *Lut. Typ. Regiis* 1620
1505 Pontani Historia Celrica, cum fig. —*Amst.* 1639
1506 Catalogus Libror. MSS. Bibliothecæ Cottonianæ. *Oxon.* 1696
1507 Cornelius Celsus. —— —— *Ven.* 1497
1508 C. Commelin Horti Malabarici Catalogus. ——*L.B.* 1696
1509 Launoii Epistolæ omnes. —— *Cant.* 1689
1510 Laurentii Hist. Anatomica Humani Corporis.——*Par.*
1511 Marsilii Dissertat. de Generatione Fungorum, *cum fig. Rom.* 1714
1512 Stephanus de Urbibus, gr. lat. cum Notis Holstenii. *Lug. Bat.* 1694
1513 Besleri Gazophylacium rerum Naturalium e Regno Vegetabili, &c. —— —— 1642
1514 B. Guesnay Provinciæ Massiliensis ac Reliquæ Phocensis Annales. —— —— —— *Lug.* 1657
1515 Bucholceri Chronologia. —— —— 1584
1516 Hist. Naturalis Hassiæ Inferioris, *cum fig.*—— 1719
1517 Legatus F. de Marselaer ad Philippum IV. Hispaniar. Regem. —— —— *Ant.* 1666
1518 Cæsaris Bulengeri Opera, 3 vol. ——*Lug.* 1619
1519 P. Æmylius & A. Ferronus de gestis Francorum, *lin. rubr. Lut. apud Vasc* 1566
1520 Valentini Aphitheatrum Zootomicum Tabulis æneis quam plurimis exhibens Hist. Animalium Anatomicam. *Franc.* 1720
1521 Scardionii de Antiquitat. Urbis Patavii, lib. 3. *Basil.* 1560
1522 Fabricii ab Aquapendente Opera Chirurgica, *cum fig. Lug. Bat.* 1723
1523 Morisotti rerum in Mari & Littoribus Historia, *cum fig. Div.* 1643
1524 A. Cesenati rariores Plantæ Horti Farnesiani, *cum fig. Rom.* 1625
1525 Simsonii Chronicon Catholicum ex recens & cum Animad. P. Wesseling. —— *L.B.* 1729
1526 Annales Francorum Faldensis.

H 1527

1527 Cirini var. Lect. de Urbe Roma ejusque conditore Romulo Lib. singul. ——— ——— *Panor.* 1665

1528 P. de Marca, Marca Hispanica, sive Limes Hispanicus. *Par.* 1688

1529 Johnstoni Hist. de Quadrupedibus, de Piscibus, de Exanguibus, de Avibus, de Insectis, & de Serpentibus, *cum fig.* ——— ——— *Amst.*

1530 Epistolæ Melancthonis, Mori & Vivis. —— *Lond.* 1642

1531 Thuani Historiar. sui Temporis, pars 1. *Paris, apud Patis.* 1604

1532 Launoii Opera omnia, 10 vol. ——— *Col. All.* 1731

1533 Mongitori Bibliotheca Sicula, sive de Scriptoribus Siculis. *Panor.* 1707

1534 Theatrum Triumphale Mediolanensis Urbis, per Vitalem. *Mediolan.*

1535 Fonteii de Prisca Cæsiorum Gente Comment.—*Bon.* 1582

1536 F. Schannat. Corpus Traditionum Fuldensium. *Lips.* 1724

1537 Lazius de Republica Romana & Græcà.——*Franc.* 1598

1538 Compend. R. Gaguini Francorum Gestis. ——*Par.* 1598

1539 Thuani Historia sui Temporis, 3 vol. —— *Gen.* 1620

1540 Sirmondi Opera varia, 5 vol. *ch. max. & minor. Paris, e Typ. Reg.* 1696

1541 Pandectæ Florentinæ, 2 vol. *fol. deaur. Florènt. apud Torrent.* 1503

1542 P. Jovii Opera, ——— *ibid.* 1501

1543 Chronica Bossiana, *corio turcico, foliis deauratis. Mediolan.* 1628

1544 Cluverii Sicilia antiqua, Germania antiqua, & Italia antiqua, 3 vol. cum multis fig. ——— *L. Bat.* 1624

1545 Successores S. Bárnabæ Apostoli in Ecclesia Mediolanensi. *Mediol.* 1628

1546 { Talicotii de Curtorum Chirurgia per insitionem, lib. 2. cum fig. ——— *Ven.* 1597
Minadoi de Humani Corporis Turpitudinibus Cognoscendis & Curandis Lib. 3. ——— *Pat.* 1600 }

1547 Bibliotheca Telleriana. ——— *Paris, e Typ. Reg.* 1693

1548 Ugolini Verini de Illustrat. Urbis Florentiæ, Lib. 3. *foliis deaur.* ——— *Lut. apud Patis.* 1583

1549 T. Hyde Catalogus Bibliothecæ Bodleianæ. ——*Ox.* 1674

1550 De Dignitate Genuensis Reipublicæ disceptatio. *Gen.* 1646

1551 Bibliotheca Coisliniana olim Sequeriana, Opera B. de Montfaucon, *ch. max. & min.* ——— *Par.* 1715

1552 Aretini Historia Florentina. ——— *Argent.* 1610

1553 Dionis Chrysostomi Orationes, gr. lat. *ch. max. Lut. apud Morell.* 1604

1554 Ripamontii Hist. Mediolani, 5 vol. —— *Med.*

1555 Sigonii Hist. de Regno Italiæ. —— *Bon.* 1580

1556 Fazelli de rebus Siculis Decades. —— *Panor.* 1560

1557 Calvisi Opus Chronologicum. ———*Franc.* 1650

1558

1558 Theophanis Chronographia, gr. lat. *ch. max. Paris, e Typ. Regia* 1655

1559 Laonici Chalcondylæ Hist. gr. lat. *ch. max.* —— *ib. ib.* 1650

1560 C. du Fresne Historia Byzantina, — *Lut. Par.* 1682

1561 Theophylacti Semocatæ, gr. lat. *ch. max. Paris, e Typ. Regia* 1647

1562 Annæ Comnenæ Porphyrogenitæ Cæsarissæ Alexias, gr. lat. *ch. max.* —— —— *ib. ib.* 1651

1563 Ducæ Michaelis Ducæ Nepotis Hist. Byzantina, gr. lat. *ch. max.* —— —— *ib. ib.* 1649

1564 J. Cantacuzeni Historia, gr. lat. —— *ib. ib.* 1645

1565 G. Cedreni Compend. Historiarum, gr. lat. ch. max. 2 vol. *ib. ib.* 1647

1566 P. Labbe Corpus Byzantinæ Historiæ, gr. lat. *ch. max. ib. ib.* 1648

1567 Nicetæ Acominatæ Choniatæ Historiæ, gr. lat. *ch. max. ib. ib.* 1647

1568 G Acropolitæ Magni Logothetæ, & Ducæ Michaelis Ducæ Nepotis Historia Byzantina, gr. lat. *ch. max. ib. ib.* 1651

1569 Anastasii Bibliothecarii Hist. Ecclesiastica & de Vitis Pontificum, gr. lat. *ch max.* —— *ib. ib.* 1649

1570 G. Pachymeris Historia, gr. lat. 2 vol. *ch. max.* *Rom.* 1666

1571 G. Codinus Curopolata de Officiis & Officialibus, Curiæ & Ecclesiæ Constantinopolitanæ, gr. lat. *ch. max. Paris, e Typ. Regia* 1648

1572 Laonici Chalcondylæ Atheniensis Historia, gr. lat. *ch. max. ib ib.* 1650

1573 C. Manassis Breviar. Historicum & G. Codinus de Originibus Constantinopol. gr. lat. *ch. max.* —— *ib. ib.* 1655

1574 J. Cinnami Imp. Grammat. Historia, gr. lat. *ch. max. ib. ib.* 1670

1575 Aretæi Opera, gr. lat. J. Wigan, *ch. max.* —— *Oxon.* 1723

Livres d'Architecture, Peinture, Sculpture, Antiquitez, Mathematique, Voyages, Philosophie, Medecine, Hist. Naturelle & des different Nations, Dictionaries, Theologie, &c. en Francoise. Folio.

1576 Genealogie de la tres illustres, tres ancienne & autrefois Souveraine Maison de la Tour, par Flacchio, 3 vol. *avec fig.* —— *Brux.* 1709

1577 Hist. Militaire du Prince Eugene de Savoye, du Prince & Duc de Marlborough, & du Prince de Nassu Frise, avec gr. nomb. des fig. 2 vol. —— *a la Haye* 1729

1578 Lettres du Card. d'Ossat, *gr. pap. regle.* —— *Par.* 1641

1579 Medailles sur les principaux Evenemens du Regne de Louis le Grand, *dore sur tranche. Paris, de l'Imprim. Royale* 1702

H 2 1580

1580 Hist. de la Ville de Paris, par Felibien, reveu par Lobineau, 5 vol. *avec des tres belles fig.* ——— *Paris* 1725
1581 Plan de plusieurs Batimens de Mer, avec leur Pavillons & Enseignes, *tres propremens en lumine.* ——— *Amst.* 1700
1582 Theatre du Piemont & de la Savoye, 2 vol. *avec gr. nomb. des fig.* ——— *a la Haye* 1725
1583 ——— des Etats de son Altesse le Duc de Savoye, 2 vol. *avec gr. nomb, des fig.* ——— *ib.* 1700
1584 Veues & de Facades principal dans la Ville & aux Fauxbourgs de Vienne.
1585 Hist. de Joseph, traduite par Genebrarde, 2 vol. *gr. pap. regle.* ——— *Paris* 1646
1586 Bibliotheque Historique de la France, par Le Long. *ibid.* 1719
1587 L'Antiquité expliquee et representee en Figures par Montfaucon, avec le Supplement, 15 vol. *grand papier. ibid.* 1722
1588 Les Monumens de la Monarchie Francoise, par Montfaucon, 5 vol. *gr. & pet. pap. avec fig.* ——— *ib.* 1729
1589 Nouveau Coustumier Generale, ou Corps des Coustumes generales et particuliers de France, avec les Notes, 8 vol. *ib.* 1724
1590 Oeuvres diverses de P. Bayle, 4 vol. ——— *a la Haye* 1725
1591 Hist. generale des Plantes, par Dalechamp, 2 vol. *Lyon.* 1653
1592 Le Cabinet de la Bibliotheque de Sainte Genevive, par du Molinet, *avec fig.* ——— *Par.* 1692
1593 Les Histoires d'Herodote, par du Ryer. ——— *ib.* 1645
1594 Ancienne et nouvelle Discipline de l'Eglise touchant les Benefices et les Beneficiers, par Thomassin, 3 vol. *Par.* 1725
1595 Recueil des Commentateurs anciennes et modernes sur les Coutumes generale de France, 2 vol. ——— *ib.* 1726
1596 Histoires des Archevesques de Rouen. ——— *Rouen* 166[illegible]
1597 Hist. Genealogiques de la Maison de Harcourt, par Andre de la Roque, 4 vol. ——— *Par.* 1662
1598 Les Coustumes et Statutes particulieres de tous les Bailliages du Royaume de France, *en lettres Gothiques. ib.* 1540
1599 Les Histoires de Justin, traduite par Seyssel. *Paris, apud Vasc.* 1559
1600 L'Hist. de Thucydide, par Seyssel. ——— *ib. ib.* 1559
1601 Discours de la Religions des anciens Romaines, par du Choul, *avec les Medailles.* *Lyon, par Roville* 1556
1602 Illustrations de la Gaule Belgique, *en lettres Gothiques. Par.* 1531
1603 Hist. de la Peinture ancienne extraite de Pline. *Lond.* 1725
1604 Panegyrique de Pline a Trajan, fr. et lat. avec des Remarques, par Coardi de Quart. ——— *a la Haye* 1726

1605

1605 Le grand Dictionnaire, Geographique et Critique, par Bruzen dela Martiniere, 5 vol. —— *a la Haye* 1726
1606 Hist. entiere des Poissons, par Rondelet, *avec fig.* *Lyon.* 1558
1607 Traite des Fougeres de l'Amerique, par Plumier, *avec fig.* *Par. de l'Imprim. Royale* 1705
1608 Architecture de Palladio, par Leoni, avec des Notes d'Inigo Jones, 2 vol. —— —— *a la Haye* 1726
1609 Hist. de Dauphine et des Princes qui ont porte le nom de Dauphin, 2 vol. —— —— *Gen.*1722
1610 Trophees tant sacres que profanes du Duche de Brabant, par Butkens, 4 vol. *avec fig gr. & pet. papier. a la Haye* 1724
1611 Hist. Naturelle des plus rares Curiositez de la Mer des Indes, *avec les fig. tres proprement Peintee.* ——*Amst.* 1717
1612 Le grand Dictionnaire de la Bible, par Simon, 2 vol. *Lyon.* 1717
1613 Les Memoires du Duc de Nevers, par Gomberville, 2 vol. *Par.*1665
1614 Hist. de Bretagne, par Lobineau, 2 vol. *avec de tres belles fig.* —— *ib.*1707
1615 L'Histoire et Memoires du Cardinal Duc de Richelieu, 3 vol. —— *ib.*1660
1616 Les Decades de Tite Live, par Vigenere, 2 vol.——*ib.*1583
1617 Dictionnaire de la Langue Francoise, ancienne et moderne, par Richelet, 3 vol. —— *Lyon* 1728
1618 Le Coutumier de Vermandois, 2 vol. —— *Par.*1728
1619 Les Oeuvres de Plutarque, traduite par Amyote, 2 vol. *ib.* 1582
1620 Le Dictionnaire de l'Academie Francoise, 3 vol. *gr. & pet. pap.* —— *ib.*1694
1621 Hist. de la Maison Royale de Savoye, par Guichenon, 3 vol. —— *Lyon* 1660
1622 La Saincte Bible. —— *Anvers* 1578
1623 Les Essais de Montaigne, *gr. pap.* —— *Par.*1640
1624 Les Pratiques du S. Fabre sur l'Ordre et Regle de Fortifier, Garder, Attaquer et Deffendre les Places, avec fig. *ibid.* 1629
1625 Hist. naturelle de l'Or et de l'Argent. —— *Lond.*1729
1626 ——de la Province d'Alsace, par Laguille, avec fig. *Stras.* 1727
1627 Les Triomphes des Louis le Juste, fr. et lat. avec fig. *Par.* 1649
1628 Annales de la Monarchie Francoise, par Limiers, 3 tom. 1 vol. —— *Amst.*1724
1629 L'Histoire et Chronique du Froissart, *le bonne Edit.* *Lyon* 1559
1630 Le Cronique de Monstrelet, 2 vol. —— *Par.*1572
1631 L'Histoire des Successeurs de Alexandre le Grand. *ib.*1530
1632

1632 Les Oeuvres Poetiques de P. le Moyne, avec fig.—*Par.*1672
1633 Les Histoires de Polybe, traduite par du Ryer.— *ib.*1655
1634 Le Ceremonial Francois, par Godefroy, 2 vol.— *ib* 1649
1635 Les Croniques et Annales de France, par Belleforests. *ib.* 1617
1636 Les Memoires d'Olivier de la Marche. ——— *Lyon* 1562
1637 Les Conquestes et les Trophees des Normans-Francois, par du Moulin, *doree & marbre sur tranche. Rouen* 1658
1638 Les Ambassades et Negotiations du Card. du Perron. *Par.* 1625
1639 Voyages faits en Perse, Moscovie et en Tartarie, par Olearius, avec fig.——— *Amst.*1727
1640 Description Geographique et Historique de la Moree, par Coronelli, avec grand nombres des fig. ——*Par.*1687
1641 Hist. des IX Roys Charles de France, par Belle-forests. *ib.* 1568
1642 Etat de la France, par Boulainvilliers, 3 vol.—*Lond.*1727
1643 L'Histoire Sainte du Nouveau Testament, par Talon, 2 vol. *gr. pap.* ———*Par.*1669
1644 Hist. de l'Abbaye Royale de Saint Germain, par Bouillart, avec fig.——— *ib.*1724
1645 La Bibliotheque du Sieur de la Croix du Maine. *ib.*1685
1646 Les Oeuvres d'Architecture d'Anthoine de la Pautre. *ib.*
1647 Relation des divers Voyages curieuses. par Thevenot, 2 vol. avec fig.———*ib.*1696
1648 Les Histoires de Polybe, traduite par du Ryer, *ch. max. ib.*1655
1649 Le Parlement de Bourgogne, par Palliot —— *Dijon* 1649
1650 Les Hist. et Chroniques du Monde, par Zonaras, traduite par Maumont, *regle & dore sur tranche. Par. par Vasc.* 1561
1651 Les Loix Civiles dans leurs Ordre naturel, par Domat. *Par.*1713
1652 Artifices de Feu, et divers Instruments de Guerre, avec fig. ——— *Rouen* 1648
1653 Architecture de Philibert de l'Orme. ——*Par.*1656
1654 Les Negotiations de le President Jeannin. ——*ib.*1647
1655 Histoire Grecque, par Marcassus.——— *ib.*1659
1656 Les Memoires de Castelnau, 2 vol. ——— *ib.*1726
1657 Dictionnaire Universelle de la France, ancienne et moderne. 3 vol.——— *ib.*1638
1658 Hist. de Bretagne, par d'Hozier. ——— *ib* 1639
1659 Hist. Genealogique de la Maison de Bethume, par du Chesne. *ib.*1638
1660 { Hist. de Bretagne, par d'Hosier.——— *ib* 1640
{ ———-Bearn, par P. de Marca.——— *ib.*1663
1661 Maniere de Bien Bastir, par Muet.——— *ib.*1685
1662 Les 5 Ordres d'Architecture, par Scamozzi.——— 1663

1663 Hist. de Concile de Trent, traduite de P. Soave Polan, par Diodati. —— *Par.* 1655
1664 L'Hist. du vieux et du nonveaux Testament, par Royaumont, avec fig. —— *ib.* 1723
1665 Memoirs pour servir a l'Hist. de Dauphine. —— *ib.* 1711
1666 Les Origines de la Ville de Clairmont, par Durand. *ibid.* 1662
1667 Hist. Universel du S. Aubigne. —— 1626
1668 La Bibliotheque d'Antoine du Verdier. —— *Lyon* 1585
1669 Histoire de l'Eglise, par Basnage, 4 tom. 2 vol. —*Rot.* 1699
1670 Lettres et Memoirs d'Etat, par Ribier, 2 vol.—*Par.* 1666
1671 Trophez a l'Antique dessine par le Pautre. —— *ib.* 1680
1672 Traite de la Perspective, par Courtonne. —— *ib.* 1725
1673 Ordonnances des 5 Especes de Colonnes, par Perrault. *ib.* 1683
1674 Memoires Ecclesiastiques et Histoire des Empereurs, par Tillemont, 15 tom. 7 vol. —— *Brux.* 1712
1675 Hist. de tous les Cardinaux Francois de Naissance, par du Chesne, 2 vol. —— *Par.* 1600
1676 Trent Pieces d'Architecture tirees de Scamozzi.
1677 Le Theatre de Corneille, 2 vol. ——*Rouen* 1663
1678 Les Vies des Saints, par Giry, 3 vol. —— *Par.* 1719
1679 La Dissection des Parties du Corps Humain, par C. Estienne, *avec fig. regles.* —— 1546
1680 Hist. des Provinces-Unies des Pay-Bas, per Wicquefort, *gr. pap.* ——*a la Haye* 1719
1681 Memoires de Sully, *la bonne Edition.*
1682 Hist. generale d'Espagne, par Turquet. —— *Par.* 1608
1683 L'Hist. de la Decadence de l'Empire Grecque, par Vigenere, avec fig. —— *ib.* 1612
1684 Le veritable Inventaire de l'Histoire de France, par de Serres, 2 vol. *gr. pap.* ——*ib.* 1648
1685 Les plus excellents Bastimens de France, par Cerceau. *ib.* 1607
1686 Architecture, Peinture et Sculpture de la Maison de Ville d'Amsterdam, reprensentee en cx fig. ——*Amst.* 1719
1687 Dictionnaire Historique, Critique, Chronologique, Geographique et Litteral de la Bible, par Calmet, 4 vol. avec fig. —— *Par.* 1730
1688 Traite du Jardinage, par Boyceau, avec fig. ——*ib.* 1638
1689 Annales Genealogiques de la Maison de Lynden, par Butkens, avec fig. —— *Anvers* 1636
1690 Diverses Pieces pour la Defence de la Royne Mere, 2 vol. *gr. pap.* —— 1644
1691 Commentaires Historiques, par Tristan. —— 1635
1692 Hist. du Roy Louis le Grand par les Medailles, par Menestrier. —— *Par.* 1691
1693 Le Cabinet des beaux Arts, *tres belles fig.* ——*ib.* 1690
1694 L'Architecture des Voutes, par Derand, *gr. pap.* —*ib.* 1643
1695

1695 Les 10 Livres d'Architecture de Vitruve, par Perrault. *Par.* 1673

1696 Les Images, ou Tableaux de Platte Peinture, par Vigenere, *avec des belles fig.* —— *ib.* 1637

1697 Hist. d'Angleterre, d'Escosse, et d'Irelande, par Larrey, 4 vol. avec fig. —— —— *ib.* 1637

1698 Journal du Palais, ou Recueil des principales Decisions de tous le Parlemens et Cours souverains de France, 2 vol. *Par.* 1713

1699 { Memoirs de l'Histoire de Lyon, par Paradin. *Lyon* 1573
Chronique de Savoye, par Paradin. —— 1602 }

1700 Hist. Genealogique des Comtes de Chamilly de la Maison de Bouton, par Palliot, *avec fig.* —— *Dijon* 1671

1701 Les grandes Croniques de Bretaigne, *en lettres Gothiques, dore sur tranche.* —— —— 1532

1702 Traites des Manieres de dessiner les Ordres de l'Architecture antique, par Bosse. —— *Par.*

1703 Parallele de l'Architecture, antique et de la moderne. *ib.* 1702

1704 Coutume d'Orleans commentee, par de Lalande, 2 vol. *Orleans* 1704

1705 Ornamens et autres Oeuvres d'Architecture, par Marot. *Paris.*

1706 Recueil tire des Procedures Civiles faits en l'Officialte de Paris, par de Combes. —— *ib.* 1705

• 1707 La Genealogie et les Alliances de la Maison d'Amanze, par Palliot. —— —— *Dijon* 1659

1708 Discours Historial de l'Antiquite et Illustre Cite de Nismes, par Poldo. —— —— *Lyon* 1560

• 1709 Le Cabinet des plus beaux Portraits, faits par le fameux Antoine Van Dyck. —— *a la Haye* 1723

1710 Une Frise faite de Stuc soubs la Conduite et sur les Desseins de Jule Romain.

1711 Commentaire du Droict Civil, par Terrien.—— *Rouen* 1654

1712 L'Architecture a-la-mode, ou sont les nouveaux Dessins pour la Decorations des Batimens et Jardins, 3 vol. *Par.*

• 1713 Figures des Histoires de la Saincte Bible. *ib.* 1683

• 1714 Voyages au Levant, par le Brun, *avec grand nombres de tres belles fig.* —— —— *ib.* 1714

1715 Considerations Morales tirees des Ouvrages de la Nature et de l'Art, par Moreau. —— *Liege* 1686

1716 Histoire de l'Abbaye Royale de Saint Denys, par Felibien, avec fig. —— —— *Par.* 1706

• 1717 Hist. et Recherches des Antiquites de la Ville de Paris, par Sauval, 3 vol. —— —— *ib* 1724

• 1718 Recueil des Planches, de Plans, Profils, et Elevations de plusieurs Palais, Chateaux, Eglises, Sepulcres, Grottes et Hotels des Sieurs Marot Pere et Fils.

1719 Art de bien Bastir, par Leon. —— —1553

1720

1720 Recueil des Plans, Profiles, & Elevations de plusieurs Eglises, Sepulteurs, Grotes, & Hostels dans Paris.

1721 Le Theatre Moral de la Vie humaine representee en plus de C. Tableaux, par Otho Venius. ——— Brux. 1678

1722 Description de l'Afrique, par Leon African, regle. Lyon 1556

1723 Description des Indes Occidentales, par Ant. de Herrera, *avec fig.* ——— *Amst.* 1622

1724 Journal du Voyage du Chev. Chardin en Perse & aux Indes Orientales, *avec fig.* ——— *Lond.* 1686

1725 L'Hist. Naturelle & Generaille des Indes, Isles, & Terre ferme de la Grand Mere Oceane. *Paris apud Vascosan* 1556

1726 Hist. Ecclesiastique & Civile de Lorrain, par Calmet, 3 vol. *cum fig.* ——— *Nancy* 1728

1727 Hist. de Malte avec les Statutes & les Ordonnances de l'Ordre, par Baudoin, *avec fig.* ——— *Paris* 1659

1728 Hist. de Naples & de Sicily, par Turpin. ——— *ib.* 1630

1729 { La Perspective avec la Raison des Ombres & Miroirs, par de Caus. ——— *Franc.* 1612
Hortus Palatinus, a S. de Caus. ——— *ib.* 1620
Les Raisons des Forces mouvantes avec diverses Machines, par de Caus. ——— *ib.* 1615
Institution Harmonique, par de Caus. ——— *ib.* 1615 }

1730 Leçons de Perspective positive, par du Cerceau. *Par.* 1576

1731 Hist. de Barbarie & de ses Corsairs, par P. Dan. *ib.* 1649

1732 Cours d'Architecture, par Blondel, 2 vol. ——— *Amst.* 1698

1733 Livre d'Architecture de J. Androvet du Cerceau. *Par.* 1611

1734 Hist. d'Angleterre, d'Escosse, & d'Irlande, par du Chesne, 2 vol. *grand pap.* ——— *ib.* 1641

1735 La Vie de Michel de Ruyter Amiral d'Hollande, *avec fig.* *Amst.* 1698

1736 Les Memoires du Martin du Bellay. ——— *Par.* 1582

1737 Description exacte des Isles d'Archipel, par Dapper, *avec fig.* ——— *a la Haye* 1730

1738 De la Primaute en l'Eglise, par Blondel. ——— *Gen.* 1641

1739 La veritable Origine de la tres-illustre Maison de Sohier, *avec fig.*

1740 Voyages da la Corneille le Brun par la Moscovie, en Perse, & aux Indes Orientales, *avec fig.* ——— *Amst.* 1718

1741 Hist. de Charles VIII. Roy de France par Godefroy. *Par.* 1684

1742 Hist. de Berry, par Chaumeau. ——— *Lyon.* 1566

1743 Hist. d'Angleterre, d' Escosse, & d'Irlande, par du Chesne. *Par.* 1641

1744 Hist. de Charles VII. de France, par Godefroy. ——— *ib.* 1661

1745 Atlas de la Navigation & du Commerce. ——— *Amst.* 1715

1746 Grand Art d'Artillerie par Cisimir Siemienowicz, avec fig. *Franc.* 1676

1747 L'Origine des Bourgognons, & Antiquitez des Estats de Bourgogne par du Saincte Julien. ——— *Paris.* 1581

I 1748

1748 Tableau de l'Histoire des Princes & Principaute d'Orange par dela Pise. —————— *a la Haye*.1639
1749 Hist. des Comtes de Tolose par Catel. —— *Tolose*.1623
1750 Recherches curieuses des Monoyes de France par Bouteroue. *avec fig.* ——— ——— *Paris*.1666
1751 Hist. Metallique de la Republique d'Hollande par Bizot. *ib.* 1687
1752 Les Oeuvres de Chirurgie de J. Guillemeau.—— *Roven*.1649
1753 La Coustume reformee du Pays & Duche de Normandie par Berault. ——— ——— *ib*.1632
1754 L'Instruction & Nourriture du Prince du Catin d'Osforio traduite par Brisson. ——— *Paris*.1583
1755 L'Hist. de la Nature des Oyseaux par Belon, *avec fig. regle, doré sur tranche.* ——— ———*ib*.1555
1756 Hist. de France par P. Æmyle traduite par Regnart.*ib*.1598
1757 Les Antiquitez de la Ville d'Amiens par de la Morliere. *ib.* 1642
1758 Diverses Pieces pour la defence de la Royne Mere par Matthieu de Morgues.
1759 Le Compört & Kalendrier de Berger, en lettres gothiques, avec fig. ——— ——— *Paris*.1500
1760 Le grand Cronique de Bretagne, en lettres gothiques.*ib*.1509
1761 Dictionaire Etymologique de la langue Francoise par Menage. ——— ——— *ib*.1694
1762 ————Historique & Critique par Bayle, 2 vol. *Rot*.1697
1763 Hist. du Mareschal de Matignon par De Cailliere. *Par*.1661
1764 Hist. Genealogique de la Maison de Gondi par Corbinelli, 2 vol. *avec des tres belles fig.* ——— *ib*.1705
1765 Hist. de Charles VI. Roy de France par Laboureur, 2 vol. *Paris*.1663
1766 Hist. de Charles VI. Roy de France par Godefroy. *ib*.1653

Libri Italici & Hispanici. Folio.

1767 Historia di Leopoldo Cesare di Gualdo Priorato, *con fig. Vienna*.1670
1768 La Coronica general de Espana. ——— 1574
1769 Libro de grandezas y cosas memorabiles de Espana. 1549
1770 Annales de la Corona de Arragon por Curita, 7 vol. *Caragoza*.1610
1771 Historia di Ferdinando III. Imperatore di Gualdo Priorato, *con fig.* ——— ——— *Vienna*.1672
1772 Curia Filipica. ——— —— *Madrid*.1725
1773 Biblioteca Napolitana di N. Toppi. ——— *Napoli*,1678
1774 Crisis Politica. ——— *Madrid*.1719
1775 Comment. de los Hechos de los Espanoles par Herrera. *ib.* 1624
1776 Compend. Historial de las Chronicas y universal Historia de todos los Reynos de Espana par Roman, 4 vol. *Barcelon.* 1628

1777 Hiſtoria general de Eſpana por Mariana, 2 vol. *Madrid.* 1635

1778 La Cronica del Rey Don Juan el Segundo. *Salamanca.* 1517

1779 Illuſtraciones Genealogicas de los Catolicos Reyes de Eſpana por Garibay. ——— ——— *Madrid.* 1596

1780 Teatro Hiſtorico Genealogico y Panegyrico de la Caſa de Souſa, con fig. elegantiſſ. foliis deauratis.—— *Paris en la Emprenta Real.* 1694

Books relating to the Law, Hiſtory, Antiquities, and Parliamentary Affairs of Great-Britain and Ireland. Quarto.

1781 ANderſon's Collections relating to the Hiſtory of Mary, Queen of Scotland, 4 vol. lar. pap. ——— 1727

1782 Arguments on the Statutes of the Univerſity of Cambridge. 1727

1783 Francis Atterbury on the Original of the Reformation, Mr. Lock's laſt Will and Teſtament, with other Tracts.

1784 Avesbury in Wiltſhire, the Remains of a Roman Work, erected by Veſpaſian and Julius Agricola.

1785 Anſtis's Obſervations upon the Knighthood of the Bath. 1725

1786 An Apology for the Clergy of Scotland, oppos'd to the Calumnies of a late Presbyterian Vindicator ——— 1693

1787 Account of Mr. Parkinſon's Expulſion from the Univerſity of Oxford.——————————1689

1788 The ancient Land-Mark, Skreen or Bank betwixt the Prince and People of England and a Speech in the Houſe of Commons againſt Penſioners.

1789 Account given to Parliament by the Miniſters ſent by them to Oxford. ——————————— 1647

1790 Anſwer to the Letter written to a Member of Parliament upon the Occaſion of ſome Votes againſt their Speaker and others. ——————————— 1695

1791 An Apologetick for the ſequeſtred Clergy of the Church of England. Printed at Munſter in the year of Confuſion.

1792 Several Tracts relating to the Impriſonment of Richard Stafford. Collins's Diſcourſe on Salt and Fiſhery, and Selden de Nummis.

1793 K. James's Apology for the Oath of Allegiance, Tortus Lyes confuted, and an Apology for the Oath of Allegiance against the Pope's Breves.

1794 Answer to the Earl of Strafford's Conclusion, 13 April, 1641

1795 Langbane's Answer to the Chancellor, Masters, &c. of the University of Oxford. —— 1649

1796 True Account of that dreadful Fire which happen'd in London. —— 1687

1797 True Account of the bewitching of John Tonken of Pensans, in Cornwall. —— 1686

1798 Several Tracts relating to the Proceedings against the Bp. of London in 1686.

1799 Abridgment of Summary of the Scots Chronicle.

1800 Appeal to the Parliament, or Sion's Plea against the Prelacy.

1801 History of the renowned Prince Arthur and his Knights of the round Table. —— 1601

1802 Answer to the Design for bringing a navigable River from Rickmansworth to the St. Giles's. —— 1641

1803 Detection of Mary Q. of Scots. The Case of Allegiance consider'd. Advice to the Protestant Brethren going against the Irish Rebels. Politicks of France, and Buchanan de Jure Regni apud Scotos, in English.

1804 The Speeches and Prayers of Barkstead, Okey and Corbet, with Animadversions on them.

1805 The Life of Sir Tho. Bodley, Founder of the publick Library of Oxford.

1806 Account of Mr. Blunt's Book, entituled, K. William and Q. Mary, Conquerors. —— 1693

1807 Collection of Parliamentary Tracts, by Bagshaw, Herbert, Atwood, Williams, Cawley, Hare, Stamford, and Delamere.

1808 The Prophecy of Tho. Becket, Arch-Bishop of Canterbury. 1666

1809 Hymn to the Pillory in 1703. Vindicat. of the University of Oxford. Relation of the dreadful Tempest in 1703. with several Tracts about Nonconformists.

1810 Brooks's Discovery of Errors in the much commended Britannia, 2 vol. —— 1724

1811 Bp. Parker's Examination of a Declaration in Defence of the Ministers of London refusing to wear the Apparel prescrib'd by the Laws. Collection of slanderous Articles given out by the Bishops. The Character of the Beast, or the false Constitution of the Church. The Examinations of Barrow, Greenwood and Berry, with their Answers.

1812 Sir W. Brereton's Letter concerning the Surrender of Chester. Advice to both Houses of Parliament. A horrible Plot to murder Sir T. Fairfax and others. Inditement against John Moore, Esq. Ld. Lambert's Letter, with several other Parliamentary Tracts.

1813

1813 Church of England's Complaint againſt the Irregularities of its Clergy, and the Norfolk Ballad.

1814 The Lord Protector's Speech, with a large collection of Ordinances, Acts and other Parliamentary Tracts.

1815 Collection of Papers relating to the preſent Juncture of Affairs in England, in 12 parts compleat. ——————— 1689

1816 View of the late Tryals in Oates's Plot, with the Speeches of thoſe that have been executed.

1817 Charge of the Scottiſh Commiſſioners againſt Canterbury, and the Lieutenant of Ireland. ——————— 1641

1818 The City of Bath deſcrib'd, with Obſervations on its Waters, by Chapman. ——————— 1673

1819 The Caſe of Spenſer Cowper. Caſe of Mary Stout. Reply to the Hertford Letter. The Hertford Letter, containing Obſervat. on the Tryal concerning the Murder of Sarah Stout, and Obſervations on the Tryal of Spenſer Cowper.

1820 The Caſe of Margret Clark, lately executed for Firing her Maſter's houſe. ——————— 1680

1821 The glorious Life and honourable Death of Sir John Chandos, by Wirley.

1822 Stone Henge reſtor'd to the Danes by Charleton. ——— 1663

1823 True Catalogue of the ſeveral Places and moſt eminent Perſons in the three Nations, where and by whom Richard Cromwel was proclaim'd.

1824 Husband's Collections of Declarations, Votes, Orders, Ordinances, &c. ——————— 1643

1825 Umbra Comitiorum, or Cambridge Commencement in Types, Re-printed at Oxford, for the famous Univerſity of Cambridge.

1826 Carleton's thankful Rememembrancer of God's Mercy, with curious cuts. ——————— 1627

1827 Relation of Mr. Cook's Paſſage by Sea from Wexford to Kinſale, in that great Storm, Jan. 5th. ——— 1650

1828 A Cenſure of the Book of W. P. entituled, the Univerſity of Oxford's Plea refuted. ——————— 1648

1829 The Caſe of the Univerſity of Oxford, in a Letter to Mr. Selden. ——————— 1648

1830 Copy of the Speaker's Letter to the Vice-Chancellor of Oxford. ——————— 1642

1831 Reaſons why the Kings of England ſhould give over all further Treaty, and enter into War with the Spaniard. 1624

1832 The Croſſes Caſe in Cheapſide, whether its Militia, the ſetting of it in a poſture of Defence, be according to Law. 1642

1833 Coryate's Crudities, compleat and very fair. ——— 1611

1834 Whitbourne's Diſcovery of Newfound-Land, 1620. The Surrey Impoſtor, in Anſwer to the Surrey Demoniack. 1697

1835 Carew's Survey of Cornwal, bound in turky leather, gilt on the leaves. ——————— 1723

1836

1836 Relation between the Ld. of a Mannor and the Copyholder his Tenant. Denshall's Readings on the Statute de Finibus. Articles against the Justices of the King's Bench and Barons of the Exchequer. Argument to prove that each Subject hath a propriety in his Goods. Arguments on the Habeas Corpus. Cotton's Abstract of the Records. Bacon's Cases of Treason. Leigh's Considerations on the Court of Chancery.

1837 Honour of the London Apprentices. Ld. Fairfax's Remonstrance. Packet of Letters from Scotland. Articles of the Army against 80 Parliament Men, with other Parliamentary Tracts.

1838 Coke's compleat Copyholder. —— 1641

1839 Chronicle of the Kings and Description of the Kingdom and and Isles of Scotland.

1840 Collection of Transactions in Parliament in relation to the Impeachment of the Earl of Danby —— 1695

1841 Coppinger's, Pym's, and Maynard's Speeches in Parliament, and Ld. Strafford's Speech on the Scaffold.

1842 Considerations upon Ld. Russel's Speech. —— 1683

1843 Abridgment of Camden's Britannia, with the Maps of the Counties. —— 1626

1844 Collection of Acts of Parliament, relating to the Universities of Oxford and Cambridge. —— 1657

1845 Collection of the Antiquities of the English Franciscans, commonly call'd Gray Fryers. —— 1726

1846 Cooper's Chronicle, compleat and very fair. —— 1565

1847 A Censure of the Hist. of the Royal Society. Independency of England maintain'd.

1848 Character of a Trimmer. War Horns make room for Bucks.

1849 Case of Exeter College, related and vindicated. —— 1691

1850 Camden's Remains concerning Britain. —— 1657

1851 Tracts, pro and con, concerning the Attainder of the Earl of Strafford. Duke Hamilton and Ld. Capel's Speeches. Mr. St. John's Speech. Arguments upon the Habeas Corpus, with other Tracts.

1852 Dale's Hist. and Antiquities of Harwich and Dover-Court. Cuts, lar. and fin. pap. —— 1730

1853 Dodridge's Hist. of Principalities of Wales, Cornwall, and Chester. —— 1630

1854 Declaration of great Lucifer, Prince of the Air, and of Devils, and of all the damn'd Crew in Hell. Declaration of Vice-Admiral Batten.

1855 Sir C. Cornwallis's Discourse of the illustrious Prince Henry, late Prince of Wales. —— 1641

1856 Articles of Treason against the Ld. Kimbolton, Pym, and others. Sir S. Ducy's Speech. Speech of Wm. Perpoynt, and Articles against the Justices of the King's Bench, and Barons of the Exchequer.

1857 Ld Digbie's Design to betray Abingdon, and Declaration of Prince Rupert.

1858 Account of all the Triumphs, Ceremonies, &c. observ'd at the Marriage of K. Charles with the Princess Henrietta-Maria of Bourbon. ——— 1625

1859 Sir S. Dewe's Speech in Parliament. ——— 1641

1860 Daniel's History of the Civil Wars between the Houses of York and Lancaster. ——— 1609

1861 God's Justice upon Treason exemplified in the Life and Death of the Duke of Hamilton. ——— 1649

1862 Treasons attempted and committed by the Earl of Essex, and his Accomplices. ——— 1605

1863 Miserable Captivity of Wm Davis Barber-Surgeon of London, under the Duke of Florence. 1614

1864 General Demands concerning the late Covenant, with the King's Declaration.

1865 Defence of the Rights and Privileges of the University of Oxford. ——— 1690

1866 Ld Digby and Ld Fienne's Speech, The King's Answer to the Petition of the Commons, and Articles exhibited against Dr. Heywood.

1867 The Form and Order of the Coronation of K. Charles II. at Scoon in Scotland. ——— 1651

1868 Enquiry into the Murder of the Earl of Essex, Dialogue between a Williamite and a Jacobite, with several other curious parliamentary Tracts.

1869 The English Pope, or a Discourse wherein the late mystical Intelligence betwixt the Courts of England and Rome is discovered. ——— 1641

1870 The Fore-runner of Revenge, being two Petitions to the King's Majesty. ——— 1643

1871 Examinations of Barrow, Greenwood and Penry.

1872 Collection of Tracts relating to the secluded Members.

1873 The King's, and Sir J. Eliot's Speeches in Parliament. 1641

1874 Eng. New Chains discovered, London's Liberties, Inquisitio Anglicana, Liberties and Customs of the City of London, Temporalities nor Tythes not due to Bishops.

1875 Relation of the late Traverses of State in England, under the Mask of the good Old Cause. ——— 1659

1876 English Coins from Henry the VIIIth, to Oliver Cromwell.

1877 List of the Army under the Command of Robert Earl of Essex. ——— 1642

1878 Freedom of parliamentary Elections justified, True Narrative of the illegal Sufferings of the Fanaticks, Declaration of the Bishops concerning the scandalous Proceedings of the Clergymen.

I 1879

1879 Collection of Histories no less profitable than necessary. 1576

1880 Articles of Impeachment against Col. Fiennes, with his Reply.

1881 The History of the Lives and Deaths of two Weavers, who affirmed themselves the two great Prophets who should come in the End of the World.——1642

1882 Particular Charge of Impeachment against Sir Tho. Fairfax.——1642

1883 Description of the future Hist. of Europe, from 1650, to 1710, Declarations of Treasons, Blasphemies, &c. spoken by that great Wizard Wm Lilly, Becket, Usher, and the Quakers Prophecies.

1884 Reply to the Hertford Letter, wherein the Case of Mrs. Sarah Stout's Death is considered.——1699

1885 Gibson's View of the ancient and present State of the Churches of Door-Home, Lacy and Hempsted.——1727

1886 Speeches of Col. John Gerhard, and Peter Vowel, who were executed.——1654

1887 Gerrard's Collections of such Intermarriages as have been in the Lines of Engl. and Spain since the Conquest. 1624

1888 Godwin's Catalogue of the Bishops of England.——1615

1889 The religious and loyal Protestation of Dr. Gauden, sent to the Ld Fairfax.——1648

1890 The Speech of Mr. John Gibbons on Tower-Hill. 1651

1891 Last Will and Testament of Sir Th. Gresham Kt.

1892 Haward's Life of K. Henry IV.——1595

1893 Declaration of A. Henderson Commissioner from the Kirk to the Parliament.——1648

1894 The High-Court of Justice, or Cromwell's new Slaughter-house in England.——1651

1895 Howard's Lives of the 4 Norman Kings of England. 1613

1896 Have with you to Saffron-Walden, or Gabriel Harvey's Hunt is up.——1599

1897 Humble Address both of Church and Poor, against the Uniting of Churches, and the Ruin of Hospitals. 1641

1898 Don Juan Lamberto, or a comical History of the late Times, 2 parts, cuts.——1661

1899 Narrative of the Election of Dr. Hough, President of St. Mary Magdalen College Oxon 1687.

1900 Gesta Grayorum, Narrative of the finding St. Edward's Crucifix and gold Chain, Case of erecting a Hospital at Highgate vindicated, London lampoon'd.

1901 Mr. Hide's Argument, Answer to an infamous Pamphlet, A Declaration of the Commons, Ld Clarendon's Settlement and Sale of Ireland.

1902 Hayward's Life of Edward VI.——1630

1903

1903 Poem in Latin and Eng. on the Chalybeate Well, Violet the Goldſmith's two Petitions.
1904 A Hand-Kirchief for loyal Mourners, Prince Charles's Declaration, with other Speeches and Declarations.
1905 Hiſtory of the Church of Great Britain. —— 1674
1906 Hardyng's Chronicle.
1907 Speech of Denzel Holles concerning Sir R. Crew. 1641
1908 The Liberty of the Subject againſt Impoſitions, by Hakewell. —— 1641
1909 Hiſt. of the Wars, Treaties, Marriages, and other Occurrences between England and Scotland. —— 1607
1910 Compariſon between the Days of Purim, and that of the Powder-Treaſon, The Nativity of Wm Lilly aſtrologically perform'd, and other Tracts.
1911 Hiſtory of the military Government of the City of Glouceſter. —— 1647
1912 Anglo-Judæus, or the Hiſtory of the Jews whilſt here in England. —— 1656
1913 The Iriſh Maſſacre ſet in a clear Light. —— 1714
1914 True Information of the Beginning and Cauſe of all our Troubles, how they have been hatched, and how prevented. —— 1648
1915 Ireland's Complaint againſt Sir George Ratcliffe. —— 1641
1916 Dr. Rainolde's Judgment touching Epiſcopacy, View of the Life of Henry the IIId. Hakewell's Liberty of the Subject, Character of a Trimmer, with ſeveral other Tracts.
1918 Authority arraign'd, or the Remonſtrance and humble Appeal of Tho. Ivie Eſq; —— 1654
1919 Proceedings of the Commiſſioners at Whitehall, dedicated to the Ld Protector. —— 1654
1920 Judge Jenkins's Plea delivered to the Earl of Mancheſter. 1647
1921 The Judgment and Doctrine of the Clergy of the Church of Eng. concerning penal Laws. —— 1687
1922 The Judges Reſolutions concerning Statute-Law for Pariſhes. —— 1641
1923 Journal of the Proceedings in that memorable Parliament begun at Weſtminſter 1640. —— 1657
1924 Journal of remarkable Paſſages in the Houſe of Commons relating to the Eaſt-India Trade, and the Management of the War with France conſidered.
1925 Kilburne's Survey of Kent. —— 1659
1926 Narrative of the Proceedings of G. Keith at Coopers-Hall in the City of Briſtol. —— 1700
1927 The Kingdom's brief Anſwer to the Declaration of the Houſe of Commons. —— 1648
1928 Kennet's Parochial Antiquities. —— 1695

K 1929

1929 The King and Queen's Entertainment at Richmond in 1636.

1930 Hist. of the Kentish Petition, Danger of the Church of England, The Hertford Letter, Life of Capt. Whitney, Account of the Sessions of Parliament in 1692, with several other curious historical and parliamentary Tracts.

1931 The Life of Mrs. C. Brettergh, Dialogue concerning the Ceremonies of the Church of England, A. Nevylli ad Walliæ proceres Apologiæ, Apology for Women, Conspiracies against Q. Elizabeth, with other Tracts.

1932 The King's Message to the Prince of Wales, The glorious and living Cinque-Ports of our Island, Relation of a Conspiracy in Worcestershire, Duke of York's Victory over the Dutch, and other Tracts.

1933 Jonah's Cry out of the Whale's Belly, by Col Lilburne.

1934 Col. Lilburne's apologetical Narration relating to his Sentence, and the fundamental Liberties of the People of Eng. asserted by Lilburne.

1935 Defensive Declaration of Col. John Lilburne.

1936 The Tryals of Col. John Lilburne, together with all the Papers and Pamphlets which was wrote or publish'd by him, in 3 vol.

1937 Lambarde's Perambulation of Kent.————1596

1938 Calculation of the tyrannical Exactions, Taxations, &c. during the four Years of this unnatural War.————1647

1939 Compleat Collection of Lilly's Prophecies, and Astronomical Predictions and Calculations.

1940 Lhoyd's Hist. of Cambria, now called Wales.

1941 Verstegan's Restitution of decay'd Intelligence, cuts. 1634

1942 Actio in Proditores, *Lond.* 1606. Leycester's Commonwealth, 1641. Vita Henrici Chichele, Naunton's Fragmenta Regalia.————1641

1943 Letter to a Member of the Convocation concerning the Case of a late Fellow of University College. —— 1699

1944 The Lieutenant of the Tower's Speech and Repentance. 1615

1945 Letter concerning the disabling Clauses, Attempt for healing the Animosities in England, Orders and Rules of the Company of Stationers, and the Triers and Tormenters tried and cast.

1946 A Collection of Tracts, written by Sir Roger L'Estrange.

1947 Mr. Lesley's Letter to the Bishop of Sarum.

1948 Lewis's History and Antiquities of the Isle of Thanet, *cuts*. 1723

1949 The Lepanto of James VI. K. of Scotland.

1950 Magna Britannia & Hibernia, antiqua & nova, or a Survey of Great Britain and Ireland, 5 vol. ———— 1720

1951 Speeches of two Orphans, Eng. and Scotl. Covenant, The Army's Plea, Apology for Christians, Ld Strafford's Speech, with other Tracts.

1952 Mercurius Elencticus, *or the Proceedings at the head Quarters of Westminster.*

1953 Mercurius Aulicus, *being Intelligence from Westminster.*

1954 Mercurius Pragmaticus, *being the Designs, Humours and Conditions of the Kingdom.*

1955 The Mirrour for Magistrates, containing the Falles of the first infortunate Princes of this Land, *in verse, black letter.* ———— 1575

1956 Capt. Audley Mervin's Speech. ———— 1641

1957 A merry Dialogue between Band, Cuff, and Ruff. — 1615

1958 Three Letters from the Ld General Monck. ———— 1659

1959 The Cuckoo's Nest at Westminster, The Parliament Kite, and Mercurius Psiticus.

1960 Milton's History of Britain, now called England. —— 1671

1961 The Manner of holding Parliaments in England, collected from ancient Records. ———— 1641

1962 A modern Account of Scotland. ———— 1679

1963 Memorial of the Church of England, Life of Mr. Locke, Priest-Craft, Locke's Paraphrase on the Epistle to the Galatians.

1964 The Life and strange Prophecies of Ambrosius Merlin. 1641

1965 Nicanor's Epistle, Matters concerning the Realm of Scotl. Hist. of the King's Affairs in Scotland, with other Tracts relating to Scotland.

1966 Bp Merck's Speech in Parliament.

1967 Mistriss Parliament brought to bed of a monstrous Child of Reformation. ———— 1648

1968 Two Letters from Mr. Montague to the Lord Treasurer. 1679

1969 Malice display'd, or a Tray of coarse Stuff made up in Newgate, and an Account of the Conspiracy against K. William.

1970 Nicolson's Letter to Dr. Kennet, in Defence of the Eng. historical Library. ———— 1702

1971 Letter sent to Bp Laud, Life of the Earl of Strafford, and the Earl of Strafford's Letter.

1972 The new Testament of our Lords and Saviours the new Parliament at Westminster. ———— 1648

1973 Case of the Commonwealth of England, Journal of the Parliam. of Irel. Fair Warning for Engl. Remonstrance of the State of the Kingdom.

1974 Narrative of the Discovery of a College of Jesuites at Come in Hereford. ———— 1679

1975 Naunton's Fragmenta Regalia. ———— 1672

1976 Names of all the Market Towns, Villages, &c. in Eng. and Wales. ———— 1668

1977 Nordon's Description of Middlesex and Hertfordshire. 1723

1978 Norden's Description of Cornwall, large pap. —— 1728
1979 ——the same, printed upon Vellum, bound in turkey, gilt on the leaves. —————— 1728
1980 A Nose-gay for the House of Commons, J. White's Defence, Judge Jenkins's Answer, with other Tracts.
1981 A New-Year's Gift for the Welch Itinerants.——1654
1982 Articles concerning the Surrender of Oxford. ——1646
1983 The good old Cause explain'd, revived, and asserted.
1984 Memorandums of a Suit between Sir H. Everard, and J. Oswald. —————— 1702
1985 Propositions concerning the Sale of Delinquents Lands, with other Tracts.
1986 History of K. James for the first 14 Years.——1651
1987 The Order of the Creation of Prince Henry, Tethy's Festival, or the Queen's Wake.
1988 Ordinance of the Lords and Commons.—— 1646
1989 Ordinance of the Lords and Commons for the Visitation of Oxford. ———— 1647
1990 Tryals of Ld Macquire, J. Streater, and of J. Twyn, Duke Hamilton's Case and Speech, with other Tracts.
1991 Prynne's Refutation of J. Lilburne's miserable mistated Case. 1645
1992 ——Mount-Orgueil, or divine and profitable Meditations. 1641
1993 { ——Discovery of some prodigious Blazing-Stars. 1646
——Popish Royal Favourite. —— 1643
——Relation of the Imprisonment of Colonel Fiennes. 1644 }
1994 ——seasonable, legal, and historical Vindation.—1655
1995 ——Players Scourge, or Actors Tragedy. 1633
1996 ——Plea for the Lords and House of Peers.— 1658
1997 ——Health's Sickness, Oxford Plea refuted, Irenarchus Redivivus, Plea for the Lords, Speech in Parliament, Declaration and Protestation, Concordia Discors, Vindication of the secluded Members, Narrative; all by Prynne.
1998 Account of Mr. Prynne's Refutation of the Oxford Plea. 1648
1999 The Vision of Pierce Plowman, Dialogue between Experience and a Courtier, Heywood's Works, all black letter.
2000 Collection of Tracts writ by the Quakers.
2001 Parliamentary Transactions, *cuts*; Commonwealth's great Ship, *cuts*; London's Blame, if not its Shame.
2002 Present Interest of Engl. Letter to Sir T. Osborn, Scotch Mist, Scotland's Grievances, Hist. of Indulgence, Last Speech of J. Hicks, and other Tracts.
2003 The Parliament Porter. ———— 1648
2004 Relation of the great Sufferings of Henry Pitman, Relation of some remarkable Passages in Cheshire.

2005

2005 Pugh's British and Outlandish Prophecies. —— 1658
2006 The Parliament's Petition to the Devil. —— 1648
2007 Parliament's Answer to the Petitions of the County of Buckingham, and Remonstrance of the State of the Kingdom.
2008 The Papist's Petition in England to their diabolical Center of Impiety the Pope. —— 1642
2009 England's Independency upon the papal Powers, by Sir J. Davis. —— —— 1674
2010 Indictment of J. Price Esq; Receiver-General in Ireland.
2011 University of Oxford's Plea refuted, by Prynne. —— 1689
2012 An Owl at Athens, or a Relation of the Entrance of the Earl of Pembroke into Oxford. —— 1647
2013 The old, old, very old Man, or the Life of Thomas Parr. —— 1648
2014 Earl of Pembroke's Speech, with his last Will and Testament. —— ——
2015 The Pope's Letter to the Prince, in Latin, Spanish, and English. —— —— 1648
2016 Presbyterian Inquisition, as it was practised against the Professors of the College of Edinburgh. —— 1623
2017 No Protestant Plot, 3 parts. —— 1691
2018 England's Reformation needing to be reform'd. —— 1681
2019 The Complaint and Declaration of 1200 Freeholders in Lincoln, with other Tracts. —— 1661
2020 Declaration of J. Pen Esq; Mr. St. John's Argument of Law.
2021 Last of John Presbyter, Battaile between a Presbyterian Cock and a Craven; No martial Law, but Advice for the Grand Jury.
2022 Large Collection of historical, political, parliamentary, and theological Tracts, by Prynne, and others, bound together.
2023 Declaration of the Bishops, Treasons of the Earl of Essex, Levett's Manner of ordering Bees, Town-Talk, and other Tracts.
2024 The Repertory of Records. ——
2025 The Rebels Warning-piece. —— 1631
2026 Reply to the Reflector on the Gloucestershire Petition, with several other Tracts. 1650
2027 New Map of Eng. or 46 Queries, Labyrinth of Man's Life, Reflex. upon the Reformers, Articles of Impeachment against Gibbons and Yeardley, with other Tracts.
2028 Impartial Relation of the whole Proceedings against Mary Magdalen College in Oxon, in 1687.
2029 Sir W. Rawleigh's Ghost, or England's Forewarner. 1626
2030 Walker's History of the Independency of Parliaments. 1648

2031

2031 Reasons against a Registry for Lands. —— 1678

2032 Robinson's Proposals for new modelling the Laws, and for the Peoples Freedom. —— —— 1652

2033 Roswell's Relation of what passed in the Church of Rochester. —— —— 1656

2034 Relation of the unparallel'd Oppression of the Gentlemen Prisoners in the Tower. —— 1647

2035 Divers remarkable Passages concerning the Church and Kingdom of Ireland. —— —— 1642

2036 Relation of the Gleanings of the Idiotisms and Absurdities of Miles Corbet. —— —— 1646

2037 Remarks on the present State of Affairs, Case of Tolerat. stated, with several other Tracts relating to stand. Armies.

2038 The royal Legacies of K. Charles I. —— 1649

2039 Charge against the D. of Argyle, Reflections on the Conspiracy, Account of what past in the House of Commons, Oct, 28. 1689, with several other Tracts.

2340 Journal of the three Campaigns of King William in Ireland. 1690

2041 Loyalty's Tears flowing after the Blood of Charles I.

2042 Stowe's Annals of England, very fair.

2043 Considerations on the Affairs of England, and the true Protestant Subject.

2044 Sprat's History of the Royal Society. —— 1667

2045 The Subject's Sorrow, or Lamentations for the Death of King Charles. —— —— 1649

2046 Speeches of the Regicides, Tryal of Sir H. Vane, and John James.

2047 Mercurius Melancholicus.

2048 Story's impartial History of the Wars in Ireland; *cuts.* 1693

2049 Collection of Tracts, pro and con, in relation to the Affair of ABp Laud.

2050 Discourse of the Life and Death of Catherine Stubbs. 1664

2051 Comment. upon the Foundation, and Affairs of Balliol College, Defence of the Rights of the University of Oxford, and Notitia Oxoniensis.

2052 Symmons's Vindication of K. Charles. —— 1649

2053 Examinations, Arraignment, and Conviction of Geo. Sprot. 1608

2054 Account of Queen Mary's Methods for introducing Popery. 1681

2055 Proceedings and Votes of the Parliament of Scotland. 1689

2056 The Case of Ship-Money discours'd, with several other Law and Parliamentary Tracts.

2057 Spelman's Villare Anglicum, *interleav'd with MS. Notes.* 1656

2058 Smith's Commonwealth of England. —— 1621

2059

2059 The Year of Jubilee, or England's Releasement. —1646
2060 Great Satisfaction concerning the Death of the Earl of Strafford.
2061 Subjects Joy for the King's Restoration, The Beacons quenched, with other Tracts.
2062 Present State of Christendom, and the Interests of England. — — — 1678
2063 Satyrical Catechism, Prince Charles's Letter, Packet of Letters from Scotland, The Junto's Memento, and Propositions sent to Scotland.
2064 Somner's Antiquities of Canterbury. — 1640
2065 Description of the King's Palace at Loo, Life and Character of Locke, Practices and Treasons of the Earl of Essex.
2066 Entertainm. of Prince Charles by the K. of Spain, with other Tracts on the same Subject.
2067 Treleinie's Treatise of Tithes, Letter to a Member of Parl. and other Tracts.
2068 Large Collection of Tracts relating to Trade, History, and parliamentary Affairs, bound together.
2069 The mistaken Murderer, Life and Death of the young Maid at Desmond, Relat. of a League made with the Devil, The Dewitting of Glencoe, Q. Elizabeth's Speech, with several other parliamentary Tracts.
2070 True Account of the Baptism of Prince Frederick, Prince of Scotland and Wales. — 1603
2071 True Report of the Arraignment of a Popish Priest named Drewice. — — 1607
2072 Time-serving Proteus, and Ambidexter Divine uncased to the World. — — 1650
2073 Treatise of Taxes and Contributions, Protestant Mask taken off from the Jesuited Englishman.
2074 Rudyard's Speech in Parliament, Judgment of the Lords against Morrice and others, The whole Business of Sindercome, Relation of the Disorders committed upon the Goods of Tho. Hubbert.
2075 Vox Populi, or Gondomir appearing in the Likeness of Machiavell.
2076 Vox Populi, Fax Populi, Letter from a Person of Quality to his Friend in the Country.
2077 Vox Plebis, or the People's Outcry against Tyranny.
2078 Presbytery display'd, The Jacobites Hudibras, with other Tracts.
2079 Vowell's Catalogue of the Bishops of Excester, *black lett.* 1584
2080 Votes of the Parliament touching no Address to the King. 1647
2081 Bp Usher's Prophecy, Votes of the Parliament of Scotland, Fundam. Liberties of the People of England, A Primer for the Scholars of Europe.

2082

2082 Collection of State-Tracts, by Le Vassor, Addison, and others.
2083 Vindication of his Majesty's ecclesiastical Commissioners. Remarks on the Letter to a Dissenter.
2084 The Life and Death of Sir Henry Vane, Knight. —— 1662
2085 The Hearse of the Earl of Essex. Treatise of Altars, Altar-Furniture, Altar-cringing, and Musick.
2086 Verstegan's Restitution of decay'd Intelligence, curious cuts. 1628
2087 God in the Mount, or England's Parliamentary Chronicle. 1644
2088 The Case of Glocester Hall in Oxford.
2089 Brown Willis's Survey of the Cathedrals, cuts. —— 1727
2090 A learned Oration disburthened from H. Walker, a quondam Ironmonger. —— 1642
2091 Declaration of Great-Britain and Ireland, shewing the down-fall of their Princes. —— 1649
2092 Monuments of Honour deriv'd from Antiquity, and celebrated in London. —— 1624
2093 Speech of J. White, Counsellor at Law, concerning Episcopacy. —— 1641
2094 Bp. Wren's Petition to the Parliament in Defence of Episcopacy. —— 1642
2095 Publick Conference betwixt 6 Presbyterian Ministers and some independent Commanders. —— 1646
2096 Sir G. Paule's Life of Arch-Bp. Whitgift. —— 1612
2097 Mr. Waller's Speech in the House of Commons. —— 1643
2098 The Life and Death of Ralph Wallis, the Cobler of Glocester. 1670
2099 The true and wonderful History of Perkin Warbeck. 1618
2100 Mr. Waller's Speech in Parliament at a Conference. 1641
2101 A Whip for the present House of Lords. The Recantation of Col. Lilburne. Proceedings of Col. Lilburn and his Associates.
2102 Warmington's moderate Defence of the Oath of Allegiance. 1612
2103 The Life of Cardinal Woolsey, compos'd by one of his Servants.
2104 Plea of the Fellows of Winchester College, against the Bp. of Winchester. —— 1711
2105 Life and Actis of the maist Illuster and Vailzeand Campion, Wm. Wallace, in verse, black Letter. —— 1601
2106 Warner's Albion's England. —— 1602

Libri Classici, Grammatici, Poetici, Critici, & Lexici. Quarto.

2107 Æliæ Aristidis Opera omnia, gr. lat. recensuit & observat. S. Jebb, 2 vol. *ch. max, & minor.* —— *Oxon.* 1722

2108 Aurelius Victor recensitus ab And. Schotto. —— *Paris.* 1579
2109 Antiqui Rhetores Latini ex Bib. Pithoei. —— *ib.* 1599
2110 Arratei Phænomena gr. cum Scholiis Græcis. *Paris, apud Morel.* 1559
2111 Adagia,, sive Proverbia Græca ab And. Schotto gr. lat. *Ant. apud Plantin.* 1612
2112 Arriani & Hannonis Periplus, Plutarchus de Fluminibus, Strabonis Epitome gr. —— *Basil apud Froben.* 1533
2113 Auctores Latinæ Linguæ in unum redacti Corpus, cum notis Gothofredi. —— 1602
2114 Appianus Alexandrinus. —— *Venet.* 1477
2115 Ausonii Burdigalensis Opera, cum Comment. Æ. Veneti. *Burdigalæ.* 1580
2116 Æsopi Vitæ & Fabellæ gr. lat. Aldi Manutii interpret. *Lovan.* 1517
2117 F. Arretini Epistolæ, *foliis deauratis.* —— *Florent.* 1487
2118 Æliani varia Historia, gr. —— *Romæ.* 1545
2119 Ammianus Marcellinus ex Bib. Lindenbrogi. *Hamburg.* 1609
2120 L. Apulei Apologia, J. Casaubonus recensuit. 1594
2121 Anthologia Magna gr. lat. Interprete E. Lubino. —— 1603
2122 Æschyli Tragœdia septem Thebana gr. lat. *Lut. apud Morel.* 1585
2123 Aristotelis de Republica Interpret. & enarratione J. Genesio, *lineis rubris, foliis deauratis.* *Paris, apud Vascosan.* 1548
2124 ——— de Ortu & Interitu, J. Benedictino Interpret. & Interpret. —— *ib. apud Richardum* 1550
2125 ——— Cathegorias Institut. P. Aquini Comment. *Patav.* 1557
2126 ——— Meteorologia, J. Perionio Interpret. & Observat. *Paris, apud Richardum* 1552
2127 ——— Rhetorica Interpret. H. Barbaro, & Comment. D. Barbari. —— *Venet.* 1544
2128 ——— de Moribus Lambino Interpret. & Annotat. *Basil.* 1566
2129 ——— Organum gr. —— *Franc. apud Wechelum.* 1577
2130 ——— de Generatione & Corruptione D. Bannes Comment. & Quæstiones. —— *Venet.* 1587
2131 ——— Prædicamenta gr. —— *Lovan.* 1523
2132 N. Bocherii Apologia adversus Audomari Talæi explicat. in primum Aristotelis Ethicum Lib. —— 1562
2133 Aristophanis Opera Græca cum Scholiis græcis, *corio turcico, foliis deauratis.* —— *Florent. apud Juntas* 1525
2134 ——— Comœdiæ XI. gr. —— *Basil.* 1532
2135 ——— Cereris sacra celebrantes gr. cum Scholiis Græcis. —— *Paris, apud Tiletanum,* 1545
2136 ——— Comœdia Vespæ gr. —— *ib. apud Wechelum.* 1540
2137 ——— Comœdiæ Equites gr.
2138 ——— Comœdia Plutus gr. lat. cum Comment. Giraldi. *Paris.* 1549

k 2139

2139 Broukhusii Poemata Edit. D. Hoogstratano. —— *Amst.* 1711
2140 Boetius de Consolatione Philosophiæ, cum duplici Comment.
2141 T. Bezæ Vezelii Poemata varia. —— 1597
2142 G. Bergeri de naturali Pulchritudine Orationis. *Lipsiæ.* 1700
2143 Borrichii Cogitationes de variis Latinæ Linguæ ætatibus. *Hafniæ.* 1675
2144 Cluverii Geograghia notis var. —— *Amst.* 1729
2145 Crispini Lexicon Græco-Latinum. —— *Col. Allobrog.* 1615
2146 D. Chimhi Grammatica Hebræa. *Paris apud C. Steph.* 1554
2147 Catullus, Tibullus, & Propertius. —— *Lut. Paris.* 1723
2148 Catullus, & in eum J. Vossii Observationes. —— *Lond.* 1684
2149 Casæ Latina Monimenta, *corio turcico. Florent. apud Juntas.* 1564
2150 Cortonæi varia Carmina Græca. *Venet. apud J. Gryphium.* 1555
2151 Chytræi Chronologia, Hist. Herodoti & Thucydidis. *Helmæstad.* 1585
2152 Callimachus, *litteris majusculis.*
2153 ———— cum Scholiis. —— *Basil.* 1532
2154 Ciceronis Opera notis var. recensuit J. Verburgius, 3 vol. *Amst.* 1724
2155 ———— Opera recognita ab J. Gronovio, 2 vol. — *Lug. Bat.* 1692
2156 ———— Opera accurant. Schrevelio. *Amst. apud Elz.* 1661
2157 ———— de officiis. —— *Paris, apud Richardum.* 1562
2158 ———— de oratoria. —— *ib. ib.* 1547
2159 ———— de Senectute. —— *ib. ib.* 1550
2160 ———— Oratio pro Milone. —— *ib. ib.* 1548
2161 ———— Topica. —— *ib. ib.* 1549
2162 ———— de Amicitia. —— *ib. ib.* 1550
2163 ———— Oratio pro Planco. —— *ib. apud Vascosan.* 1539
2164 ———— Oratio pro Lege Manilia. —— *ib. ib.* 1541
2165 ———— Oratio pro Rege Dejotaro. —— *ib. ib.* 1547
2166 ———— Epistolæ ad Octavium. —— *ib. ib.* 1536
2167 ———— de Fato. —— *ib. ib.* 1550
2168 ———— Oratio pro C. Rabirio Posthumo. —— *ib. ib.* 1537
2169 ———— Oratio contra Rullum. —— *ib. ib.* 1540
2170 ———— Oratio secunda contra Rullum. —— *ib ib.* 1540
2171 ———— Actionum in Verrem Lib. IV. —— *ib. ib.* 1539
2172 ———— Oratio pro Ligario. —— *ib. ib.* 1547
2173 ———— Epistola ad Octavium. —— *ib. ib.* 1549
2174 ———— Oratio contra Rullum. —— *ib ib.* 1540
2175 ———— de Amicitia. —— *Ant.* 1604
2176 ———— Pardoxa, *lineis rubris, corio turcico, foliis deaurat. Lug. apud L. Cloquemin.* 1579
2177 ———— de Somnio Scipionis, *lineis rubris, foliis deauratis. ib ib.* 1579
2178 ———— Oratio pro Marcello. *Paris, apud Tiletanum.* 1539
2179 ———— de Legibus. —— *ib. ib.* 1533

2180

2180 Oratio pro Val. Flacco. —— *apud Bad. Ascensium.*
2181 ——Oratio pro Cornelio Baldo. —— *ib.ib.*
2182 ——Oratio pro Roscio. —— *ib.ib.*
2183 ——Oratio pro Milone. —— *ib. apud Macaum.* 1538
2184 —— Brutanæ Quæstiones. —— *ib. apud Bogardum.* 1547
2185 ——Quæstiones Academicæ A. Talei Comment. *Basil.* 1575
2186 ——de Officiis cum Comment. P. Marsii.
2187 Deogenes Laertius de Vitis, Dogmatis & Apophthegmatis Philosophorum gr. lat. notis var. 2 vol.—— *Amst.* 1692
2188 Dionis Nicæi Historiæ Epitome, Author. J. Xiphilino, ex Bib. Regia, gr. —— *Lut. apud R. Steph.* 1551
2189 Delrii Syntagma Tragœdiæ Latinæ. —— *Lut. Paris.* 1620
2190 Demosthenis Orationes gr. —— *Oxon.* 1597
2191 Dion. Halicarnassei de Thucydidis Historia Judicium, Duditio Interprete. —— *Venet.* 1560
2192 Eclogæ Legationum gr. —— *Aug.Vindel.* 1603
2193 Erasmi Moriæ Encomium, Declamatio.
2194 Eschenbachi Epigenes de Poesi Orphica.—— *Noriberg.* 1702
2195 Ennii Poetæ Vetustissimi Fragmenta. —— *Neapoli.* 1599
2196 L. Florus cum Comment. E. Veneti. —— *Pictavis.* 1563
2197 Fasti Romanorum Liviani. —— *Gedani.*
2198 Tanaquilli Fabri Epistolæ, 4 vol. —— *Salmurii.* 1659
2199 R. Whitintoni Grammatica, *in ædibus Winandi de Worden.*
2200 L. Gambaræ rerum sacrarum Liber, Carmina, *cum fig. Ant.* 1577
2201 Homeri Ilias gr. lat. cum notis S. Clarke, 2 vol. *Lond.* 1729
2202 ——Ilias & Odyssea gr. lat. Opera & Studio J. Barnes, 2 vol. —— *Cant.* 1711
2203 ——Ilias gr. lat. Scholia Dydimi.—— *Cant.* 1689
2204 Horatius Bentleii. —— *Amst.* 1728
2205 ——cum Comment. Veteris & Cruquii. —— 1611
2206 ——de Arte Poetica Grisoli Interpret. explicatus. *Florent.* 1550
2207 Hickesii Institutiones Grammaticæ Anglo-Saxonicæ. *Oxon.* 1689
2208 De Theæ Villa Capta M. Hospitali Carmen. *Paris, apud Morel.* 1558
2209 Harveii Ciceronianus. —— *Lond.* 1577
2210 Hesiodi Opera & Dies gr. —— *Venet.* 1537
2211 Hesychii Lexicon cum variis doctorum Virorum notis. *Lug. Bat.* 1668
2212 Hederici Lexicon Græcum. —— *Lond.* 1727
2213 Harpocrationis Dictionarium in Decem Rhetores. *Paris.* 1614
2214 Justini Historia, L. Florus Epitome, & S. Ruffi de Hist. Romana Opus.
2215 G. Knowles Materia Medica Botanica Carmen. *Lond.* 1723
2216 Luciani de Morte Peregrini Libellus gr. lat. cum notis T. Fabri. —— *Paris.* 1653

L 2 2217

2217 ———Piſcator Bilibaldo Pirkheymero Interpret. *Nurenberg*: 1517

2218 Dialogi, gr.

2219 Littleton's Dictionary. ——— *Lond.* 1678

2220 Livii Hiſtoria, Decades prim. cum notis Glareani. *Paris, apud Vaſcoſan.* 1549

2221 Laurent. Vallæ elegantia Ling. Latinæ. *Paris, apud Colinæum.* 1532

2222 Lib. de re ruſtica Scriptores. — *Florent. apud Juntas.* 1515

2223 Ludolfi Lexicon Æthiopico-Latinum. —— *Lond.* 1661

2224 Lycophronis Alexandra gr. lat. cum Comment. J. Tzetzis. 1601

2225 ————Alexandra gr. *interfoliata.* —— *Oxon.*

2226 Longinus de Sublimitate gr. lat. Z. Pearce.—— *Lond.* 1724

2227 ————de Sublimitate gr. lat. J. Tollius. *Traject. ad Rhen.* 1694

2228 Lucretius cum explanat. & animadverſ. J. Nardii. *Florent.* 1647

2229 ————Lambini. —— *Lutetiæ apud Bene-Natum.* 1570

2230 ————T. Fabri. ——— *Salmurii.* 1662

2231 Grammatica in Carmen Auth. P. Megango, *lineis rubris, corio turcico.* ——— *Paris. apud Vaſcoſan.* 1549

2232 Moſchopuli de ratione exanimandæ Orationis Libellus. *Lut. apud R. Steph.* 1545

2233 Maſſoni Elogia Renati Biragæ Carmen. —— *Paris.* 1583

2234 Manethonis Apotelesmaticorum Lib. VI. gr. lat. cura Gronovii. —— —— *Lug. Bat.* 1698

2235 Madii Italicæ Grammatices Inſtitutio. —— *Venet.* 1601

2236 Natalis Comitis Mythologiæ. ——— *ib.* 1581

2237 Nicandri Alexipharmaca gr. lat.—— *Paris apud Morel.* 1557

2238 Ovidii Opera cum notis variorum, cura Burmanni, 4 vol. *Amſt.* 1727

2239 Oppianus de Piſcibus & de Venatione gr. lat.——*Paris, apud Morel.* 1555

2240 ————de Venatione Bodino Interpret.——*Lut. apud Vaſcoſan.* 1555

2241 Plutarchi Opera gr. lat. recenſuit. Bryanus gr. lat. 5 vol. *Lond.* 1729

2242 { ———de primo Frigido gr.— *Paris, apud Turnebum.* 1552
———de Liberorum Inſtitutione gr. *ib: apud Morel.* 1561 }

2243 Poetæ Latini Minores cum notis var. curante Burmanno, 2 vol. ——— ——— *Leidæ.* 1731

2244 Virgilius, Horatius, Catullus, Terentius, 4 vol. *Cant.*

2245 Ptolemæi Geographia a Bilibaldo Pirckheymerio tranſlata. *Venet.* 1562

2246 ————Sententiæ a Pontano Græco in Lat. tranſlatæ. *ib. apud Aldum.* 1519

2247 { Pomponius Mela de Situ Orbis. ——— 1512
Solinus de Memorabilibus. }

2248

2248 Cicero de Oratore, 2 vol. —— *Paris*.1687
2249 ——Orationes, 3 vol. —— *ib*.1684
2250 ——Epistolæ ad Familiares. —— *ib*.1685
2251 Panegyrici Veteres, corio turcico, foliis deauratis. *ib*. 1676
2252 Ovidii Opera, 4 vol. —— *Lug*.1689
2253 Lucius Apuleius, 2 vol. —— *Paris*.1688
2254 Horatius. —— *ib*.1691
2255 Plautus, 2 vol. —— *ib*.1679
2256 Phædri Fabulæ. —— *ib*.1675
2257 Eutropius. —— *ib*.1683
2258 Terentius. —— *ib*.1675
2259 Cornelius Nepos. —— *ib*.1675
2260 Suetonius. —— *ib*.1684
2261 Plinii Hist. Naturalis, 5 vol. —— *ib*.1685
2262 Cæsaris Comment. —— *ib*.1678
2263 Aurelius Victor. —— *ib*.1681
2264 Boetius de Consolatione Philosophiæ. —— *ib*.1695
2265 Virgilius. —— *ib*.1726
2266 Juvenalis & Persius. —— *ib*.1684
2267 Justinus. —— *ib*.1677
2268 Sullustius. —— *ib*.1674
2269 Lucius Florus. —— *ib*.1674
2270 Ausonii Burdigalensis Opera. —— *ib*.1730
2271 Claudianus. —— *ib*.1677
2272 Dictys Cretensis, & Dares Phrygius.—— *Amst*.1702
2273 Manilius. —— *Paris*.1679
2274 Martialis Epigrammata. —— *ib*.1680
2275 Quintus Curtius. —— *ib*.1678

(2248–2275: in usum Delphini.)

N. B. The above Delphins are all sew'd up in boards, and not cut on the leaves.

2276 Phædri Fabulæ notis illustravit in usum Principis Nassavii, cum fig. ch. max. & minor. —— *Amst*.1701
2277 Petronius Arbiter ex Museo Ant. Gonsali de Salas. *Franc*. 1629
2278 Portii Dictionarium Latinum, Græco-Barbarum & Litterale. —— *Lut. Paris*.1635
2280 Palmeri exercitat. in optimos fere Autores Græcos. *Lug.Bat*. 1668
2281 Passeratii Kalendæ Januariæ Carmen. *Lutetiæ apud Patisson*. 1597
2282 Ex Libris Polybii selecta de Legationibus gr.—— *Ant. apud Plant*.1582
2283 Pisidæ Opus sex Dierum gr. lat.—— *Lut. apud Morel*.1584
2284 Pindari Opera gr. lat. J. Benedictus. —— *Salmurii*.1620
2285 ——Opera gr. cum Scholiis Græcis. —— *Romæ*. 1599
2286 ——Opera gr. lat. ——
2287 ——Opera gr. cum Scholiis græcis. —— *Franc*.1542
2288 Purschii Grammaticæ Latinæ Auctores antiqui.*Hanov*.1605

2289

2289 Persii Satyræ studio Freigii. ——— *Basiliæ.*
2290 Propertius cum notis variorum. ——— *Amst.*1702
2291 Phile de Animalium Proprietate gr. lat. a C. de Paaw. *Traject. ad Rhen.*1730
2292 Platonis Epistolæ a P. Ramo latinæ factæ. ——— *Paris.*1549
2293 ———Timeus cum Comment. J. Meursii. *Lug.Bat.*1617
2294 ———de Republica gr. lat. M. Ficino Interprete. *Paris.* 1544
2295 Polybii, Diodori Siculi, N. Damasceni, Dion. Halicar. Appiani Alexand. Dionis & Antiocheni excerpta gr. lat. notis Valesii. ——— ——— *Paris.*1634
2296 Plauti Comœdiæ cum notis Paræi. ——— *Franc.*1523
2297 ———Lambini. ——— *Col. Allobrog.*1622
2298 Q. Curtius cum notis var. curavit H. Snackenburg. *Lug. Bat.* 1724
2299 Quinquarborei de re Grammatica Hebræorum Opus. *Paris.* 1582
2300 Quintiliani Opera Burmanni, 4 vol. ——— *Lug.Bat.*1720
2301 ———Opera ex recensione Obrechti, 2 vol. *Argent.*1698
2302 ———Opera. ——— *Paris, apud R. Steph.*1542
2303 ———Institutiones Oratoriæ E. Gibson. ——— *Oxon.*1693
2304 ———Idem, corio turcico, foliis deauratis. *Paris, apud F. Gryph.*1539
2305 ———Declamationes Scholiis illustratæ. *ib. apud Morel.* 1563
2306 ———Institutiones Oratoriæ. *ib. apud Richardum.*1554
2307 ———Idem, corio turcico, foliis deauratis. ——— *ib. apud Vascosan.*1542
2308 ———Idem. ——— *ib. apud Colineum.*1542
2309 Poetæ Latini Rei Venatici Scriptores notis var. *Lug. Bat.* 1728
2310 Ruæi Tragœdiæ & Carmina, cum fig. ——— *Lut.Paris.*1680
2311 Rapini Hortorum Lib. IV. ——— *Paris e Typo. Regia* 1665
2312 Robertsoni Thesaurus Græcæ Linguæ. ——— *Cant.*1676
2313 Rivoli Dictionarium Armeno-Latinum. ——— *Lut.Paris.*1633
2314 Suetonii Opera S. Pitisci, 2 vol. ch. max. & minor. *Leovardiæ.*1714
2315 ———ad usum Josephi Portugalensis per Almeidam. *Hagæ Comit.*1727
2316 Senecæ Tragœdiæ notis var. ch. max. & minor. *Delphis.*1728
2317 Silius Italicus notis var. ch. max. & minor. *Traject. ad Rhen.* 1717
2318 Seberi Index Vocabulorum in Homeri. ——— 1604
2319 Sulpitius de Divino Judicio, foliis deauratis. ——— *Romæ.*1506
2320 Stobæi collectiones Sententiarum, gr. ——— *Venet.*1535
2321 Statii Opera notis var. cura & Comment. Crucei. *Par.*1618
2322 Sylvii in Linguam Gallicam Isagogæ. *ib. apud R. Steph.*1531
2323 Sophoclis Tragœdiæ Philoctetes gr. lat. *Lutetiæ apud Morel.* 1586

2324

2324 Sophoclis Tragœdiæ VII. gr.—*Paris, apud Turnebum.*1553
2325 ———Tragœdiæ VII. gr. ——— *Franc.*1544
2326 Terentius notis var. curavit. Westerhovius, 2 vol. ch. max. & minor. ——— *Hagæ. Comit.*1726
2327 ———Bentleii. ——— *Amst.*1727
2328 ———Donati. ——— *Paris, apud R Steph.*1541
2329 ———Paræi. ——— *Neapoli.*1619
2330 ———Badii Ascensii. ——— *Lug.*1502
2331 Themistii Orationes gi. lat. notis Patavii. *Paris, apud Morel.*1618
2332 Theocriti Idyllia gr. ——— *ib.ib.*1585
2333 Tremellii Grammatica Chaldea & Syria.*apud H. Steph.*1569
2334 Taciti Opera notis var. ex recensione Gronovii, 2 vol. *Traject. Batav.*1721
2335 Annales Thucydidei & Xenophontei, præmittitur apparatus ab H. Dodwello. ——— *Oxon.*1702
2336 Tibullus cum notis var. & fig. ——— *Amst.*1708
2337 Tomasini Livius Patavinus. ——— *Patav.*1630
2338 Valerii Flacci Arganautica notis var. curante Burmanno. *Leidæ.*1724
2339 Virgilii Opera notis var. recensuit Masvicius, 2 vol. *Leovardiæ.*1717
2340 ———cum notis var. ——— *Amst.*1646
2341 ———Taubmanni. ——— ——— 1618
2342 Ursini Elegiæ de Peste. ——— ——— *Viennæ.*1541
2343 Vossii de Rhetoricæ Naturæ ac Constitutiones Lib. II. *Hagæ Comit.*1658
2344 L. Vallæ de Latina Elegantia.—*Paris, apud R. Steph.*1533
2345 ———de falso credita & ementita Constantini Donatio Libellus. ——— ——— ——— 1520
2346 Valerii Sermonetani Opera, foliis deauratis.——— *Romæ.*1514
2347 Vivarii descriptio Aurei Velleris Carmen. ——— *Pragæ.*1585
2348 C. Wase Strícturæ Nonianæ. ——— *Oxon.*1685
2349 Xenophontis de Cyri Institutionæ Lib. VIII. gr. lat. T. Hutchinson. ——— ——— ——— ——— ——— *ib.*1727
2350 ———Idem, gr. ——— *Etonæ.*1613
2351 Zeni in Concionem Periclis & Lepidi Comment. *Venet.*1569
2352 Homeri Ilias gr. cum fig. ——— ——— *ib* 1526

Libri Italici & Hispanici. Quarto.

2353 Orlando Furioso di Ariosto, con le fig. di Rame da G. Porro. *Venet. appres. Valgrisi.*1580
2354 ———Il Medesimo con le annotat. di Ruscelli, con fig. *Venet.*1556
2355 ———Il Medesimo. ——— *ib. appres. Giolit.*1543
2356 ———Il Medesimo con le Argumenti di L. Dolce. *Venet.* 1602
2357 Le Gemme antiche figurate di L. Agostini, 2 vol. ch max. & minor. ——— ——— ——— *Rom* 1686

2358 Trattato di Scientia d'Arme, con un Dialogo di Filosofia di Camillo Agrippa, con fig. ——— *ib.*1553
2360 Lezioni di Benedetto Averani sopra il IV Sonetto del Petrarca. *Ravenna.*1707
2361 Los Dialogos de Amor de Leon Arbanel. —— *Venet.*1568
2362 Scuole sacre del Conte Palatino Domenico Aulisio. *Nap.*1723
2363 Descrittione di tutta Italia di L. Alberti. ———*Venet.*1568
2364 Discorsi sopra il modo d'Alzar Acque da Luoghi Bassi, con fig. ——— ——— —*Parma.*1567
2365 Della famosissima Compagnia della Lessina Dialogo. — 1598
2366 Ragionamento dello Academico Aldeano sopra la Poesia Giocosa. ——— ——— ——— *Venet.*1634
2367 Historia delle Guerre d'Europa della comparsa dell' Armi Ottomani nell Hungaria 1683 di Beregano, 2 vol. *ib,*1698
2368 Disegni delle piu illustri Citta & Fortezze del Mondo raccolta da Ballino. ——————— *ib.*1569
2369 La Biblia Espanola.———————————1569
2370 Documenti d'Amore di F. Barberino. ——— *Roma.*1640
2371 Relationi del Cardinal Bentivoglio. ——— *Colonna.*1630
2372 Hist. della Vita, Miracoli, Traslatione e Gloria di S. Nicolo il magno da Bari. ——————— *Neapoli.*1645
2373 Il Decameron di Boccaccio.
2374 ———Il Medesimo da Rolli. ——— *Lond.*
2375 Discursos sopra la Pintura de J. de Butron.—— *Madrid.*1626
2376 Lisnoetti di Burchiello. ——————— *Venet.*1485
2377 Ragguali di Parnasso di Boccalini. ——— *ib.*1612
2378 Le XII Pietre Pretiose di A. Bacci.——— *Roma.*1587
2379 Di Herone Alesandrino de gli Automati, overo Machine se moventi tradot del Greco. ——— *Venet. apres. Porro.*1589
2380 Comment. Istorico Erudito da G. Baruffaldi. *Ferrara.*1704
2381 Guerras Civiles de Inglaterra Tragica Muerte de su Rey Carlos, por Mayolino. ——— *Barcelona.*1673
2382 Terremoto Dialogo di Ant. Buoni. ——— *Modena.*
2383 L'Historia delle Guerre Civili d'Inglaterra del F. Biondi, 3 vol. ——— *Bolog.*1647
2384 Istorici delle Cose Veneziane i quali hanno scritto per publico decreto cioe A. Sabellico, P. Bembo, P. Paruta, A. Morosini, B. Nani, M. Foscarini, 10 vol.—— *Venez.*1718
2385 Elogii d'Huomini Letterati scritti da L. Crasso, 2 vol. con fig. ——— ——— *ib.*1666
2386 Essemplari del disegno principiante nell' Arte della Pictura & Scultura da Agostino. ——— *Roma.*
2387 Scelta de Medaglioni piu rari nella Bibliotheca di G. Carpegna. ——— ——— *ib.*1679
2388 Istoria della Citta d'Avignone di S. Fantoni Castrucci. *Venet.* 1678
2389 Compend. del Istoria del Regno di Napoli di Collenuccio, Roseo, & Costo, *ib.*1613
2390 Dizzionario Italiano-Todesco e Todesco-Italiano da Castelli. 1728

2391 L'Iſtoria di Milano da B. Corio. —— Vineg. 1554
2392 Poetica d'Ariſtotele vulgarizatta & ſpoſta per L. Caſte.vetro. —— —— Baſil. 1576
2393 Iſtoria della Diſtruttione dell' Indie Occidentali di B. dal'e Caſe. —— —— Venet. 1626
2394 Poema Tragico del Amor Laſcivo por D. de Leon. Madrid. 1654
2395 Lettere Familiare del Annibal Caro. —— Venet. 1592
2396 L'Eneide di Virgilio del Annibal Caro. ib. appreſ. Giunti. 1581
2397 Dialogos della Pintura por V. Çarducho. —— Madrid. 1634
2398 Impreſe di diverſi Principi, &c. di L. Dolce. —— Venet. 1615
2399 Hiſtoria Venetiana di Doglione. —— ib. 1598
2400 La Comedia di Dante con ſpoſitione di Velutello. Vineg. 1544
2401 Trattatò di S. Erizzo dell' Inſtrumento & Via inventrice de gli antichi. —— —— Venet. 1554
2402 Diſcorſo di S. Erizzo ſopra le Medaglie de gli antichi. Vineg. 1568
2403 Teſoro Britannico overo il Muſeo Nummario da F. Haym, 2 vol. —— —— Lond. 1719
2404 Politica overo ſcienza civile ſecundo la Dottrina d'Ariſtotele da F. Figliucci. —— —— Venet. 1583
2405 Fili di Sciro.
2406 Govierno general, Moral, y Politico. —— Barcelona. 1696
2407 Dyalogo de miſer ſanto Gregorio Papa, *Editio antica.*
2408 Il Gelio di F. Giambulari. —— Fiorenz. 1546
2409 Il Paſtor Fido di Guarini. —— Parigi appreſ. Cramoiſy. 1650
2410 La Hiſtoria d'Italia di Guicciardini. —— Venet. 1590
2411 Il Paſtor Fido di Guarini, *con fig. corio turcico, foliis deaurat.* ib. appreſ. Ciotti. 1602
2412 ——Il Medeſimo per Altieri. —— Lond. 1728
1413 Rime di Guarini. —— Venet. appreſ. Ciotti. 1598
2414 Lettere di Guarini. —— ——ib. 1593
2415 Prediche di Hieronymo da Ferrara ſopra Ezechiel.
2416 Los Hermitanos mos Opueſtas. —— Madrid.
2417 Hiſt. della Conquiſta di Portugal. —— Valencia. 1586
2418 Dottrina Chriſtiana tradot. della Italiana nella Lingua Hebrea. —— —— Roma. 1658
2419 Raccolta di Targhe diſegnate, ed intagliate di F. Juvarra. ib. 1722
2420 Le Deche di T. Livio tradot. de J. Nardi, 2 vol. Vineg. 1574
2421 Croniche de gli Ordini inſtituti dal Franceſco, 2 vol. Venet. 1606
2422 Lettere familiare del Conte Magalotti. —— Venez. 1719
2423 Soledades de la Vida y deſenganos de el Mundo Novelas exemplares por Lozano. —— Madrid. 1713
2424 Rime e Proſe di S. Maffei. —— Venez. 1719
2425 Declaracion Magiſtral ſobre las Emblemas de Alciato. Valenc. 1655

M 2426

2426 Obras Poeticas di G. Lobo. —— *Pamplona*.1729
2427 Silvia de varia Leccion por Pedro Mexia.—— *Madrid*. 1673
2428 Succesos y Prodigios de Amor novelas por Montalvan. *Zarogaca*.1665
2429 Compendio de contratos publicos por Melgareio. *Madrid*. 1728
2430 Le Vite di V. ultimi Imperadori Turchi da Majolino. *Genova*. 1654
2431 Obras en Prossa y Verso de Jacinto Polo de Medina. 1670
2432 La Guerra de Granada de Don Diego de Mendoza. *Madrid*. 1674
2433 Tratos y Contratos de Mercaderes por Tho. de Mercado. *Salamanca*.1569
2434 L'Arte Critica Diplomatica. —— *Mantova*.1727
2435 Historia di Corfu descritta da A. Marmora. —— *Venet*.1672
2436 Tutte le Opere di Machiavelli. —— *Geneva*.1550
2437 Historia di Siena da Malavolti. —— *Siena*.1574
2438 Descrittione del Regno di Napoli di Mazzella.—*Napoli*.
2439 Chronica di Mantua. —— —— 1521
2440 Libro Historico Politico solo Madrid por Nunez de Castro. *Barcelona*.1698
2441 Historia della Republica Veneta di B. Nani, 2 vol. *ch. gr. Venet*.1576
2442 Le Storie della Citta di Firenze di J. Nardi.——*Firenz*.1584
2443 Osservazioni sopra alcuni Medaglioni antichi di Gran-Duca di Toscana. —— —— *Roma*.1698
2444 Istoria delle Rivoluzioni d'Inglaterra di Orleans. *Venez*.1724
2445 Discorso della Natura e Proprietate di diversi Uccelli, con le figure dal Tempesta. —— *Roma*.1622
2446 Le Origine de Padova di L. Pignorio.—— *Padova*.1625
2447 Discorsi Politici di Paolo Paruta. —— *Venet*.1599
2448 Discorsi di P. Paolo Magni sopra il modo di Sanguinare, con fig. —— —— —— *Roma*.
2449 Discorsi di P. Paolo Magni sopra il modo di fare i Cauteri, con fig. —— —— *ib*.1588
2450 { Discorsi di P. Paolo Magni intorno al Sanguinar i Corpi Humani, con fig. —— —— *ib*.1584
P. Martyris Troni de Ulceribus & Vulneribus Capitis. *Ticini*.1584
Frascati de Aquis Riturbii Ticinensibus Comment. *ib* 1575 }
2451 Funerali antichi di diversi Popoli & Nationi descritte da Porcacchi con le fig di Porro. —— *Venet*.1574
2452 Prodomo Apologetico alli Studi Chircheriani Opera di Petrucci, con fig. —— —— *Amst*.1677
2453 J. Donneschi di fetti di G. Passi. —— *Venet*.1618
2454 Historia de Lisseno y Fenissa. —— *Madrid*.1701
2455 Il Petrarcha. —— —— 1470
2456 ——Il Medesimo con l'Espositione di Velutello. *Vineg*. 1538

2457

2457 ——— Il Medesimo. ——— *ib. appres. Giolito.* 1547
2458 ——— Il Medesimo con l'Espositione di B. Daniello. *ib.* 1541
2459 Historia de Hippolito y Aminta por F. de Quintana. *Madrid.* 1673
2460 Tradato de Levas por F. de Oya y Ozores. ——— *ib.* 1734
2461 Obras de Francesco de Quevedo, 3 vol. ——— *Amberes.* 1699
2462 Raccolta di Scritture seguite nelli presenti Motti d'Italia.
2463 Rime di Bernardino Rota. ——— ——— *Neap.* 1572
2464 Noche de Invierno Conversacion sin Naypes por F. de Rozas. ——— ——— *Madrid* 1662
2465 Discorsi di Ant. Agostini sopra le Medaglie. ——— *Roma.* 1592
2466 Ritratti & Elogii di Capitani Illustri. ——— *ib.* 1635
2467 Le imprese illustri con Espositione & Discorsi di Ruscelli. *Venet.* 1566
2468 Invettive, Orationi & Discorsi di C. Rao. ——— *Vineg.* 1587
2469 Il Re Gernando Tragedia di L. Rota.
2470 Iconologia di Cesare Ripa, con fig. ——— *Padova.* 1611
2471 Le Memorie Bresciane, Opera Historica, e Simbolica di O. Rossi, con fig. ——— ——— *Brescia.* 1693
2472 Tutte le Opere di F. Redi, 6 vol. ——— *Firenz.*
2473 Varias Poesias Sagrades y Profanas. ——— *Madrid.* 1716
2474 Vite de Principi della Casa Othomana per Sansovino. *Venet.* 1573

2475 {
Natura & Virtu delle dose che Nutriscono & delle cose non naturali. ——— *ib.* 1575
Tramutatione Metallica di B. Nazari, con fig. *Brescia.* 1599
Il Diamerone Giornata di Giamboli. ——— *Venet.* 1589
}

2476 Governo de Regni & delle Republiche antiche & moderne di Sansovino. ——— ——— *ib.* 1567
2477 Statuti e Constitutione del l'Ordine de Cavalieri di S. Stefano. *Firenz. appres. Giunti.* 1577
2478 Trattato contra all' Aversita della Fortuna. ——— *ib.* 1730
2479 Avvertimenti della Lingua sopral Decamerone di Salviati. *Venez.* 1584
2480 Il 7 Libro d'Architettura di Serlio, interfoliata. *Venet.* 1584
2481 Tutte l'Opere d'Architettura di S. Serlio, 7 Lib. ——— *ib.* 1619
2482 ——— Il Medesimo, 6 Lib. ——— *ib.* 1584
2483 Aminta de Tasso. ——— *Par. appres. Cramoisy.* 1656
2484 Annali di C. Tacito tradot. da G. Dati. ——— *Venet.* 1598
2485 Arminia Ecloga di G. Visconte. ——— *Milano.* 1599
2486 Gerusalemme Conquista di T. Tasso. ——— *Roma.* 1593
2487 Lettere Miscellanee di B. Vanozzi. ——— *Bologna.* 1617
2488 La Dialettica di Tito Giovanni Scandianese. *Vineg. appres. Giolito.* 1563
2489 Historia Veneta di Vianoli, 2 vol. ——— *Venet.* 1680
2490 Viagge di F. Villa in Dalmatia, e Levante. ——— *Torino.* 1668

M 2 1491

2491 Novedades antiquas de Espana por T. de Vargas. *Madrid.* 1624
2492 Discorsi di Enea Vico sopra le Medaglie de g'i antiche. *Venet. appres. Giolito.* 1558
2493 Obras en Verso del Homero Espanol que recogia Juan Lopez de Vicuna. ———— *Madrid.* 1627
2494 Li X Libri della Pirotechnia per Vanuccio Biringoccio, con fig. —— ———— ———— 1559
2495 Trattati di tutti le Vici Humani, Editio antica.
2496 Hist. de la Persecution de Inglaterra y de los Martyrios por Diego de Yepes. ———— ———— *Madrid.* 1599
2497 Sommario Istorico del Dottor M. Zappulo. —— *Nap.* 1609
2498 Obras Historicas, Politicas, Filosoficas, y Morales por de Zabaletta. ———— ———— *Barcelona.* 1704
2499 L'Idea del Segretario dal Sig. B. Zucchi, 2 vol. *Venet.* 1614
2500 Dell' Anno & Giorno della morte di Christo, di M. de Capella. ———— ———— *ib.* 1579
2501 Novelas de Dona Maria de Zayas y Sotomayor. *Madrid.* 1664

Livres d'Architecture, Peinture, Sculpture, Antiquitez, Mathematique, Voyages, Philosophie, Medecine, Hist. Naturelle & des different Nations, Dictionaries, Theologie, &c. en Francoise. Quarto.

2502 Apologie faicte par un Serviteur du Roy, contre les Calomnies des Imperiaux sur la descente du Turc. *Paris. par C. Estienne.* 1552
2503 Histoire de Melun par Rovillard. —— *Paris.* 1628
2504 Argumens & Reflexions sur la sainte Bible, 2 vol. *Neufchatel.* 1720
2505 Anciennes & Nouvelles Discipline de l'Eglise touchant les Benefices & les Beneficieres. ———— *Paris.* 1717
2506 Les Tables Astronomiques du Comte de Pagan. —— *ib.* 1681
2507 Sommaire de tout ce qui s'est passe de plus memorables en Angleterre depuis l'Annee 1640 jusques 1650. —— *ib.* 1650
2508 Les Antiquitez de la Ville, Comte & Chatelenie de Corbeil. *ib.* 1647
2509 Abrege de l'Hist. des Vicontes & Ducz de Milan par P. Jove. *ib. par C. Estienne.* 1552
2510 Les 4, 5, 6, & 7 Livres d'Amadis de Gaul. —— *Anvers.* 1573
2511 Apologie des Estats du Royaume de Boheme. —— 1619
2512 Hist. des Derniers Revolutions d'Angleterre par Burnet, gr. pap. ———————— *a la Haye.* 1725
2513 Le Theatre des Grecs par Brumoy, 3 vol. pr. pap. *Paris.* 1730
2514 Cronique des faicts illustres des Roys de France avec leurs Pourtraits au Naturel. ———— —— *Venise.* 1597

2515 Hist. du vieux & du Nouveau Testament par Basnage, avec fig. *relie en Maroquin, doree sur tranch.* —— *Amst.* 1706
2516 La sainte Bible. ———— *Genev.* 1705
2517 ———le meme par Sacy, 2 vol. *avec fig.*——— *Mons.* 1713
2518 La Theorie & la Pratique du Jardinage par Le Blond, *avec fig.* ———— ———— *Paris.* 1722
2519 Hist. des grands Chemins de l'Empire Romain par Bergier, 2 vol. *avec fig.* ———— *Brux.* 1728
2520 Bibliotheque de Medicine & de Chirurgerie par Bonet, 2 vol. *avec fig.* ———— —— *Genev.* 1708
2521 Defence du droit de la Compagnie Hollandoise des Indes Orientales par Barbeyrac. —— *a la Haye.* 1725
2522 Oeuvres de Boileau, *avec fig.* —— *Paris.* 1713
2523 Le Tableau des Riches Inventions par Beroalde, *avec fig.* *ib.* 1600
2524 Elemens de Geometrie de Monf. le Duc de Bourgogne. *ib.* 1705
2525 Projet d'une nouvelle Mechanique par Varignon. *ib.* 1687
2526 Hist. de P. d'Aubusson Grand-Maitre de Rhodes par Bouhours. ———— ———— *ib.* 1676
2527 Nouvelle Maniere de fortifier les Places par Blondel, *avec fig.* ———— ———— *ib.* 1699
2528 Hist. de Blois par Bernier. ———— *ib.* 1682
2529 Le Dessein de l'Histoire de Reims par Bergier.—*Reims.* 1635
2530 Les Voyages Fameuz de Vincent Le Blanc.——— *Paris.* 1649
2531 Hist. des Chevaliers de Malte par Boissat, 2 vol. *Lyon.* 1612
2532 Les Oeuvres Poetiques de J. Dubellay, *regle & dore sur tranche.* ———— *Paris, par Morel.* 1561
2533 Les Reglets de J. Dubellay. ———— *ib. ib.* 1559
2534 L'Art universel des Fortifications Francoise par De Bitainvieu, *avec fig.* ———— *ib.* 1671
2535 Balet Comique de la Royne par de Beaujoyeulx, *avec fig.* *ib.* 1542
2536 Traicte des Chevaulx par Baret. ———— *ib.* 1660
2537 Hist. des Pays & Comte du Perche & Duche d'Alencon par Gilles Bry. ———— *ib.* 1620
2538 Le Fort inexpugnable de l'Honneur du Sexe Femenin par Billon. —— ———— *ib.* 1555
2539 Les Relations du Card. Bentivoglio traduite par Gaffardy. *ib.* 1642
2540 Les Observations des plusieurs Singularitez trouvee en Grece & aileurs, par Belon. ——— *ib.* 1588
2541 Cours d'Architecture par Daviler, 2 vol. ——— *ib.* 1691
2542 Defense pour le Roy contre Jaques Omphalius. *ib. par R. Estienne.* 1544
2543 Les Oeuvres Poetiques de R. Belleau, *relie en Maroquin, dore sur tranche.* —— *ib. par Patisson.* 1576
2544 Les Poemes de P. De Brach. ——— *Bourdeaux.* 1576
2545 Hist. Romaine par Catroue & Roville, 16 vol. *avec fig* *Paris.*

2546 Hist. Romaine, tom. 9, 10, 11, & 12. gr. pap.——*ib.*
2547 Hist. de Polybe par Toilliard, avec une Commentaire, 6 vol. *avec fig.* ———— —— *ib.*1727
2548 Hist. des Anabaptistes par Catrou. ———— *ib.*1706
2549 Hist. de l'Eglise du Japon par Crasset, 2 vol. avec fig. *ib.* 1715
2550 Hist. du Monde par Chevreau, 2 vol.———— *ib.*1686
2551 Commentaire litteral sur tous les Livres de l'Ancien & du Nouveau Testament par Calmet, 23 vol. ——— *ib.*1715
2552 Nouveau Traite de toute l'Architecture par Cordemoy. *ib.* 1714
2553 Commentaire sur l'Analyse des Infinimens petits par Crouzas. ——— ——— ———*ib.*1721
2554 L'Origine de l'Imprimerie de Paris, dissertation Historique & Critique par Chevilier. ———— *ib.*1694
2555 Le Commerce rendu facile par Claircombe.—— *Lond.*1722
2556 La Pharmacie Theorique par Chesneau. ——— *Paris.*1682
2557 Les Commentaires de Cesar traduite par Ablancourt. *ib.*1652
2558 Histoire de Tournay par Cousin. ———— *Douay.*1620
2559 Pharmacopee Royale, Galenique & Chemique par Charas. *Lyon.*1704
2560 Les Memoires de Castelnau. ———— *Paris.*1621
2561 Coustumes du Pais de Normandie. ——— *Rouen.*1588
2562 La Sophonisbe & 13 autres Comedies Francoise.
2563 Explications du plusieurs Textes difficiles de l'Ecriture, avec fig. ———— ———— *Paris.*1730
2564 Les Oeuvres de St. Cyprien par Lombert, 2 vol. *Rouen.*1716
2565 La Vie de St. Martin Evesque de Tours, par Gervaise. *Tour.* 1699
2566 De la Saintete & des Devoirs de la Vie Monastique, 3 vol. gr. pap. ——— ———— *Paris.*1683
2567 Discours au Roy sur l'Ancien Estat de la Ville de Rochelle. 1628
2568 La Vie du Pierre Dan.———————— *Paris.*1731
2569 Hist. de la Milice Francoise par Daniel, 2 vol. avec fig. *Amst.* 1724
2570 Hist. de France per Daniel, 10 vol. avec fig.— *Paris.*1729
2571 ————le meme abrege par Daniel, 6 vol.——*ib.*1727
2572 Lettres du Card. D'Ossat avec les notes par Amelot de la Houssaie, 2 vol. ———————————— *ib.*1698
2573 Combinaison generale des Changes des principales Places de l'Europe par Darius, 3 vol.———————— *ib.*1728
2574 Les Vies des Hommes illustres de Plutarque par Dacier, 8 vol. ———————————————— *ib.*1721
2575 Oeuvres d'Horace avec des Remarques par Dacier, 4 tom. 2 vol. ———————————— *Hamb.*1735
2576 Les Loix Civiles dans leurs ordre naturelle par Domat, 3 vol. ————————————— *Paris.*1695
2577 Hist. de l'Eglise de Meaux par Du Plessis, 2 vol. *ib.*1731

2578

2578 La Discipline ecclesiastique des Eglises reformees de France. *Amst.* 1710
2579 Bibliotheques des Autheurs ecclesiastique par Du Pin, 19 tom. 8 vol. —— *Utrecht.* 1731
2580 Dissertations preliminaires sur la Bible per Du Pin. *Amst.* 1701
2581 Hist. des Demelez de la Cour de France avec la Cour de Rome, par Desmarais. —— 1707
2582 Traite de la Grammaire Francoise par Desmarais. *Paris.* 1705
2583 Le parfait Procureur par Duval, 2 vol. —— *Lyon.* 1705
2584 Traite des Changes Etrangeres par Dernis. —— *Paris.* 1726
2585 Les Notes de Charles du Moulin sur les Coutumes de France. *ib.* 1715
2586 Hist. de Constantin le grand, par De Varenne. —— *ib.* 1728
2587 Remarques sur la Navigation par Radouay. —— *ib.* 1727
2588 Memoires concernant les Arts & les Sciences par Denis. *ib.* 1672
2589 Paraphrase sur la Politique d'Aristote par de Benevent. *ib.* 1621
2590 Nouvelles Observations & Conjectures sur l'Iris, par de la Chambre. —— *ib.* 1662
2591 La Nature de la Lumiere exterieure par de la Chambre. *ib.* 1662
2592 Traite generale du Commerce par Ricard. —— *Amst.* 1721
2593 Hist. du Cambray & du Cambresis par Carpentier. *Leyde.* 1664
2594 Hist. d'Allemagne par de Prade. —— *Paris.* 1677
2595 Le Theatre des Antiquitez de Páris par Du Breul. —— *ib.* 1612
2596 Chronique Bourdeloise par De Lurbe. —— *Bourdeaux* 1619
2597 Discours de la Religions des anciens Romains par du Choul, avec fig. —— *Lyon.* 1581
2598 Les Oeuvres de Alain Chartier. —— *Paris.* 1617
2599 La Physique reformee par de Rochas. —— *ib.* 1648
2600 L'Homme de Rene Descartes avec les Remarques par de la Forge. —— *ib.* 1664
2601 Contredits touchant le Comte de S. Paul par de la Guesle. *ib.* 1634
2602 Les Merveilles des Indes Orientales & Occidentales par de Berquen. —— *ib.* 1661
2603 Dictionnaire Francois-Latin. —— *ib.* 1674
2604 Hist. d'Herodian par J. Des Comtes de Vintemille. *ib.* 1599
2605 Les Chroniques & Annales de Flandres par d'Oudegherst. *Anvers.* 1571
2606 Declaration du Roy Jaques pour les Droits des Roys. *Lond.* 1615
2607 Le parfaict Mareschal par de Solleysel. —— 1679
2628 L'Anatomie des Romans & des Grandeurs Mondaines. *Stetin.* 1728
2609 Oeuvres de St. Evremond, 2 vol. gr. pap. —— *Lond.* 1705
2610 Eloges Historiques des Archevesques de Paris par de Harlay, avec des tres belles fig. —— *Paris.* 1698

I 2611

2611 Elemens de la Geometrie de l'Infini. *Par. de l'Imprimerie Royale* 1727
2612 Hist. de l'Edit de Nantez, 5 vol.—— ———————*Delft* 1693
2613 Nouveaux Elemens de Geometrie.————————*Par.*1667
2614 Le Droit de la Guerre & de la Paix, par Grotius, traduite par Barbeyrac, 3 vol. *gr. pap.* ————————*Amst.*1724
2615 ——— le meme, traduite par Courtin, 2 vol.— *Par.*1687
2616 Stile universelle de toutes les Cours de France, par Gauret, 2 vol. ——————————————————— *Par.*1702
2617 Recueil d'Oraisons funebre, prononcee par Gaudin, Anselme, Bossuet, Bourdaloue, & de la Broue.—— ————*ib.*1690
2618 Hist. de la Vie du Duc d'Espernon, par Girard.——*ib.*1730
2619 Hist. du Conseil du Roy, par Guillard.————————*ib.*1718
2620 Recueil d'Ouvrages curieux de Mathematique & Mechaniq. par de Serviere. ————————————————————*Lyon* 1719
2621 Hist. Ecclesiastique, par Fleury, 34 vol.——— *Par.*
2622 Journal des Observations Physiques, Mathematiques, & Botaniques, par Feuille, 2 vol. *avec fig.*———— *ib.*1714
2623 Idee de la Perfection de la Peinture, par Freart. *Mans* 1662
2624 Hist. de le Medicine, par J. Friend. —————*Par.*1728
2625 Funerailles des Romains, Grecs, & autres Nations, par Guichard, *relie en maroquin, & doree sur tranche. Lyon* 1581
2626 Les nouveaux Styles du Parliament de Paris, par Gastier. *Par.*1666
2627 Hist. d'Artus III. Duc de Bretaigne, par Godefroy. *ib.*1622
2628 Les Antiquitez & Histoires Gauloises & Francoises, par Fauchet. ———————————————————*Genev.*1611
2629 Hist. du Pays & Duche de Nivernois, par Coquille. *Paris* 1611
2630 La Venerie de Jacques de Fouilloux, *avec fig.*———*ib.*1640
2631 De la primitive Institution des Roys, Herauldz, & Poursuivantes d'Armes, par le Feron.———————*ib.*1555
2632 Entretiens sur les Vies & sur les Ouvrages des plus excellens Peintres anciens & modernes, par Felibien, 6 vol. *ib.* 1666
2633 Essay des Merveilles de Nature & de plus nobles Artifices, par Rene.—— ——————————————*Rouen* 1621
2634 Principes de l'Architecture, de la Sculpture, de la Peinture, avec un Dictionaire des Termes des Arts, par Felibien. *Par.*1676
2635 La Pratique de la Geometrie d'Oronce, revue par Forcadel. *ib.*1586
2636 Discours des Os de Cheval, par Heroard, *avec fig. ib.*1599
2637 Hist. de l'Academie des Inscriptions & Belles Lettres, 8 vol. *ib.*1717
2638 Conjectures Physiques, par Hartsoeker. ———*Amst.*1706
2639 Cours de Physiques, par Hartsoeker.——— *a la Haye* 1730
2640 Principes de Physique, par Hartsoeker.———— *Par.*1696

2641

2641 Hist. de l'Imprimiere & de la Libraire, *relie en Maroquin. ib.*1689
2642 Hist. du Diocese de Bayeux, par Hermant. ——*Caen* 1705
2643 Hist. des Ordres Monastiques, *avec fig.* ——*Doway* 1714
2644 Hist. du Peuples de Dieu, par Berruyer, 7 vol. *Par.*1728
2645 Hist. des Papes, 4 vol.——*a la Haye* 1732
2646 Arithmetique pratique & raisonnee, par Irson.—— *ib.* 1696
2647 Pratique generale & methodique des Changes Etrangers, par Irson.——*ib.* 1696
2648 Recueil des Inscriptions, par Jodelle.——*ib.* 1558
2649 Le Jubilee de l'An 1700, *avec fig.*——*Amst.*1701
2650 Hist. abrege de Portugal & des Algarves. —— *ib.*1724
2651 Hist. de l'Inde, par F. Lopez de Castagneda. *Paris par Vascosan.*1553
2652 Les Playdoyez & Haranguez de Mr. le Maistre.—— *ib.* 1660
2653 Hist. de la Concile de Pise, par Lenfant, *gr. & pet. pap. Amst.*1724
2654 Hist. du Concile de Constance, 2 vol. *gr. & pet. pap. ib.* 1727
2655 Le Nouveau Testament, par Beausobre & Lenfant, 2 vol. *ib.*1718
2656 Lettres Pastorales addresses aux Fideles de France. *Rot.* 1689
2657 Antiquite des Temps retablie & defendue contre les Juifs. *Par.* 1687
2658 Traite universel des Drogues simples, par Lemery. *ib.* 1693
2659 Traite analytique des Sections Coniques, par le Marq. de l'Hospital. ——*ib.*1707
2660 Relation Historique d'Abissinie du J. Lobo, traduite par Le Grand. ——*Par.*1728
2661 Hist. des Gaules & Conquestes des Gaulois, par de Lestang. *Bourdeaux* 1618
2662 Memoire contre l'Erection de l'Evesche de Cambray en Archevesque.—— *Par.* 1695
2663 Memoires pour servir a l'Hist. du xviii. Siecle, par Lamberty, 12 vol.——*a la Haye* 1731
2664 De l'Excellence du Gouvernement Royal, par Loys le Roy. *Par.*1575
2665 La Legende de Flammans, *en lettre Gothique.*——*ib.*1552
2666 Description de toute l'Isle de Chypre, par F. Estienne. *ib.* 1580
2667 Discours sur les Medailles, par le Poys, *avec les Medailles.*
2668 Traite de l'Aiman. ——*Liege* 1691
2669 Oeuvres de Clement Marot, 4 vol. *gr. pap. a la Haye* 1731
2670 —— de Moliere, 6 vol. *avec fig.*——*Par.*1734
2671 Medailles sur les principaux Evenements du Regne de Louis le Grand, *relie en Maroquin.*——*ib* 1702
2672 Oeuvres de Mariotte, *avec fig.*——*Leide* 1717
2673 Hist. de Henry de la Tour d'Auvergne Duc de Bouillon, par Marsollier. ——*Par* 1719

2674 Ouvrages posthumes de Jean Mabillon & de T. Ruinart, 3 vol. ib. 1724
2675 Hist. du Calvinisme, par Maimbourg.—— ib. 1682
2676 Hist. de la Decadence de l'Empire, par Maimbourg. ib. 1686
2677 Traite des Maladies des Femmes grossez, par Mauriceau, *avec fig.*—— ib. 1694
2678 De la Mature des Vaisseaux.—— ib. 1728
2679 Memoires pour servir a l'Hist de France & de Bourgogne. ib. 1729
2680 Hist. generale des Pays de Gastinois, Senonois, & Hurepois, par Morin.—— ib. 1630
2681 Les Origines de la Langue Francoise, par Menage. ib 1650
2682 Journal des Voyages de Mr. Monconys, 3 vol. *avec fig.* *Lyon* 1665
2683 L'Afrique de Marmol, 3 vol.—— *Par.* 1667
2684 Antiquitez, Histoires & Choses plus remarquable de la Ville d'Amiens, par de la Morliere, *doree sur tranche* —ib. 1627
2685 La Perspective speculative & pratique, par Aleaume. ib. 1643
2686 Memoires de Philippe de Mornay, 5 vol. —— 1624
2687 Opuscules posthumes de Mr. Menjot.—— *Amst.* 1697
2688 La Poetique de Jules de la Mesnardiere. —— *Par.* 1640
2689 Emblemes, ou Devises Chretienne, par Damoiselle Gorgette de Montenay.—— *Lyon* 1571
2690 Traicte des v Ordres d'Architecture, traduit du Palladio par Muet.—— *Par.* 1645
2691 Relation du Voyage de Moscovie, Tartarie, & de Perse, par Olearius. —— ib. 1656
2692 Hist. des Revolutions d'Angleterre, par Orleans, 3 tom. 1 vol. *gr. & pet. pap.*—— *a la Haye* 1729
2693 Dictionaire Mathematique, par Ozanam. —— *Par.* 1691
2694 Traite d'Optique, par Newton, traduite par Coste. ib. 1722
2695 Propositions importantes pour l'Apologie de la Relig. 4 vol. ib. 1719
2696 Oeuvres de Physiques & de Mechanique, par Perrault, 2 vol. *avec fig.*—— *Leide* 1721
2697 Nouveaux Elements de Mathematiques, par Prestet, 2 vol. *Par.* 1689
2698 Hist. de l'Academie Françoise, par Pellison, 2 tom. 1 vol. ib. 1729
2699 Les Oeuvres de Thevenin, Chirurgien du Roy.—*Lyon* 1691
2700 La Pratique du Theatre.—— *Par.* 1657
2701 Hist. du Concile du Trent, par Pierre Soave Polan. *Genev.* 1621
2702 Les trois Mondes, par de la Popelliniere. —— *Par.* 1582
2723 Discours d'Ambroise Pare sur la Mumie, des Venins, de la Licorne, & de la Peste.—— ib. 1582
2704 Systeme de la Religion Protestant, par Pegorier.— *Rot.* 1718
2705 Instruction pour les Jardins Fruitiers & Potagers, par de la Quintinye, *avec fig.*—— *Par.* 1730

2706

2706 Recueil de l'Origine de la Langue & Poesie Francoise, par Fauchet. —————— ib. 1581
2707 Le Romant des trois Pelerinages, *en lettres Gothiques.*
2708 Les Satyres & autres Oeuvres de Regnier, avec des Remarq. *Lond.* 1729
2709 Les Ruses Innocentes, *avec fig.* —————— *Par.* 1660
2710 La Religion des Gaulois tiree de l'Antiquite, 2 vol. *avec fig.* *ib.* 1727
2711 Hist. d'Angleterre, par Rapin Thoyras, 10 vol. *a la Haye* 1727
2712 Les Comparaisons des Grands Hommes de l'Antiquite. par Rapin, 2 vol. —————— *Par.* 1684
2713 Oeuvres Posthumes de Rohault. —————— *ib* 1682
2714 Dictionaire Francois, par Richelet. —————— 1688
2715 Systeme de la Philosophie, par Sylvain Regis, 3 vol. *Paris* 1690
2716 Diverses Poesies de Jean Regnault de Segrais. —— *ib.* 1658
2717 Les Hymnes de P. de Ronsard. —————— *ib.* 1555
2718 Recueil des Antiquites Gauloises & Francoises. —— *ib.* 1579
2719 Le parfait negotiant, par Savary, 2 vol. —— *ib* 1721
2720 Observations Mathematiques faits par les Jesuites aux Indes & a la Chine, *avec fig.* —————— *ib* 1729
2721 Dissertations Historiques & Critiques sur la Chevalerie ancienne & moderne. —————— *ib.* 1718
2722 Nouvelles Observat. sur le Nouveau Testament, par Symon. *ib.* 1695
2723 Nouvelle Methode pour apprendre la Langue Italienne, par Stanglini. —————— *Lond.* 1724
2724 Discours politiques des Rois, par Scudery. —— *Par.* 1647
2725 Les Oeuvres de St. Amant. —————— *ib* 1629
2726 Le Siege de Mets en l'Anne 1552 —*ib. par C. Estienne* 1553
2727 Description de la Limagne d'Auvergne, par Symeon. *Lyon* 1561
2728 Les illustres Observations antiques, par Symeon.— *ib.* 1558
2729 Essai d'une Hist. des Provinces Unies, par de Sallengre. *a la Haye* 1728
2730 Sonnets & Quatrains d'Admirations. —————— 1614
2731 Les Discours Philosophiques de Pontus de Tyare, *reglee & doree sur tranche.* —————— *Par.* 1587
2732 Relation d'un Voyage fait au Levant, par de Thevenot. *Rouen* 1665
2733 Traite de l'Etude des Conceils & de leurs Collections. *Paris* 1724
2734 Dictionaire Francois-Latin, par Tachard. —— *ib.* 1689
2735 Relation d'une Voyage du Levant, par Tournefort, 2 vol. *avec fig.* —————— *Amst.* 1718
2736 Le Voyage du Roy au Pays Bas de l'Empereur en l'An 1554. *Par. par C. Estienne* 1554

N 2 2737

2737 La Philosophie Morale explique en Tables par de Lesclache. 1651

2738 Eclaircissemens sur l'Analyse des Infinement petits, par Varignon. ——— 1725

2739 Traicte des Droicts & Libertez de l'Eglise Gallicane. *ib.* 1612

2740 Discours de la Nature du Monde & de ses Parties, par Pontus de Tyard. ——— *ib. apud Patisson* 1578

2741 Explanation de la Genealogie du Roy Henry IV. *ib.* 1595

2742 Tresor politique. ——— *ib.* 1608

2743 Voyage de Levant, fait par le Commandement du Roy en l'Annee 1621.

2744 Hist. des Revolutions arrivees dans l'Europe en Matiere de Religions, par Varillas, 4 vol. ——— *Par.* 1686

2745 Observations de l'Academie Francoise sur les Remarques de M. de Vaugelas. ——— *ib.* 1704

2746 Traicte de l'Ancien Estat de la Petite Bretagne, par Vignier. *ib.* 1619

2747 Hist. des Chevaliers de Malte, par Vertot, 4 vol. *ib.* 1726

2748 La Henriade de Mr. de Voltaire, *avec fig.* ——— *Lond.* 1728

2749 Ebauche de la Religion Naturelle, par Wollaston. *a la Haye* 1726

2750 L'Hist. de Geoffroy de Ville Hardovyn Mareschal, *d'un coste en son vieil Language, & de l'autre en un plus moderne,* par Vigenere. ——— *Par.* 1584

2751 Memoires & Instructions pour les Ambassadeurs, par Walsingham. ——— *Amst.* 1700

2752 Dictionaire de la Langne sainte, par Leigh. ——— *ib.* 1703

English Books of Architecture, Painting, Antiquities, Voyages and Travels, Divinity, Dictionaries, Physick, Surgery, Natural History, Poetry, and Miscellanies. Quarto.

2753 Albin's Natural History of Birds, 2 vol. *colour'd to the Life.* 1731

2754 ——— Natural History of English Insects, *colour'd to the Life.* ——— 1735

2755 ——— Natural History of Spiders, *colour'd to the Life.* 1736

2756 Addison's Works, 4 vol. ——— 1721

2757 The shortest Way with the Dissenters exemplified, being the Case of Abraham Gill, a Dissenting Minister in the Isle of Ely. ——— 1707

2758 Atlas Geographus, or a complete System of Geography, ancient and modern, 5 vol. ——— 1711

2759 Sermons by Altham, Hickeringill, Brady, Twisse, and others.

2760

2760 The Life of that learned and victorious King Almansor. 1627
2761 The abolishing of the Book of Common Prayer by reason of above fifty gross Corruptions in it. 1641
2762 Killing no Murder. 1659
2763 The Art of Defence represented in Figures.
2764 Ascham's Discourse on the Affairs of Germany, his Toxophilus, and his School-Master.
2765 Ashmole's Theatrum Chemicum Britannicum. 1652
2766 The Accidence of Armory. 1576
2767 Alexis's Secrets. 1580
2768 Description and Explanation of 268 Places in Jerusalem. 1653
2769 A Treatise concerning the Payment of Tythes and Oblations in London. 1641
2770 An Abstract of some special foreign Occurrences. 1638
2771 Treatise concerning the Payment of Tythes, and a Decree for Tythes.
2772 The Processe upon the Body, Picture, and Bookes of Antonius de Dominis after his Death. Pope Joan, a Dialogue.
2773 The Anatomy of the English Nunnery at Lisbon. 1622
2774 Boerhaave's Elements of Chemistry. 1735
2775 The Courtier, by Baldassar Castiglione, English and Italian. 1727
2776 Jherome of Brunswicke's Surgery, *black letter.* 1525
2777 Brooke's Abridgment. 1570
2778 Bibliotheca Anatomica, Medica, Chirurgica, &c. 3 vol. *cuts.* 1711
2779 The Holy Bible, *black letter.* 1599
2780 ——— the same, in the German Language. *Leips.* 1705
2781 Brownlow's and Goldesborough's Reports. 1675
2782 ——— Declarations, Counts, and Pleadings. 1654
2783 The Holy Bible, 5 vol. *interleav'd.* 1629
2784 The Doway Bible and Rhemish Testament, 3 vol. 1609
2785 Shaw's Abridgment of Boyle's Philosoph. Works, 3 vol. 1725
2786 Bradford's Sermons at Boyle's Lectures.
2787 Boyle's Experiments touching Cold. 1683
2788 ——— Experiments touching the Air. 1662
2789 No Sacrilege nor Sin to purchase Cathedral Lands. 1660
2790 The History of the Bible *in Cuts rul'd and gilt on the leaves.*
2791 A Sermon of Repentance, preach'd before the House of Commons. 1660
2792 The Canticles or Ballads of Solomon in Metre, by Baldwin. 1549
2793 Ticho-Brahe's Astronomical Conjecture of the much-admir'd Star in 1572. 1586
2794 A brief Account of antient Church-Government. 1685
2795 Browne's Lecture of Anatomy, the Apostate Protestant, and a Letter to the Bishop of Salisbury.

2795

2796 Cumberland's Treatise of the Laws of Nature, by Maxwell. 1727

2797 Cibber's Plays, 2 vol. 1721

2798 Bradwell's Physick for the Sickness call'd the Plague. 1636

2799 The Apostolick Way of Preaching, Jesus Christ the great Wonder, The Lord of Hosts, and other Tracts.

2800 Butler's English Grammar. 1633

2801 Relation of the wicked Plots and perfidious Practises of the Spaniards. 1624

2802 The elder Brother, with 7 other old Plays.

2803 Monsieur Thomas, with 8 other old Plays.

2804 A Remonstrance against the Non-Residents. 1642

2805 Barrough's Method of Physick. 1651

2806 The Common Prayer, with cuts. 1590

2807 Blundeville's Art of Riding. 1583

2808 Boetius's Comfort of Philosophy, by Coldervel, *black letter*. 1561

2809 Collection of Tracts, by Burnet.

2810 Collection of Cuts for Architecture.

2811 Collection of curious Cuts.

2812 Virgil's Eneids, translated and printed by Wm. Caxton.

2813 Tully, translated and printed by Caxton.

2814 Callis's Readings upon Sewers. 1686

2815 Discovery of a Shell-Fish, found in the Severn. The Dissenters new Plot, with other Tracts.

2816 The compleat Clerk. 1677

2817 Common-Place-Book to the Holy Bible. 1735

2818 Comber's Historical Vindication of Tythes. 1685

2819 The Case of Founder's Kinsmen.

2820 Collection of Tracts concerning Wedlock and Divorce.

2821 The Castle of Knowledge, *black letter*.

2822 A Coal from the Altar. The dead Vicar's Plea, and Antidotum Lincolniense.

2823 Carion's Chronicle, *black letter*. 1550

2824 Bp. Bonner's Catechism, *black letter*.

2825 Conference between the Marquiss of Worcester and King Charles. 1651

2826 Jurisdiction by Carlton. Funeral Sermon on the Earl of Dorset. Discourse against Husbands beating their Wives. Tryal of Sprot, with other Tracts.

2827 Discourse on Usury. Legacy of J. Wilmer, and a Letter concerning the French Invasion.

2828 Stubbe's Censure of the Hist. of the Royal Society. 1670

2829 The Curate's Conference, Impropriations purchas'd, and an Answer to a Letter written at Oxford.

2830 Conferences between Separatists and Independents. 1650

2831 The ancient Hist. of the Destruction of Troy, *black letter*. 1617

2832 Caveat against Flattery and Profanation. 1689

2833

2833 Ld. Falkland's Discourse of Infallibility. —— 1651
2834 Discovery of the unobserv'd Dangers of ignorant Practisers in Physick. —— ——
2835 The Countryman's Recreation, or the Art of Planting, Graffing, and Gardening. —— 1612
2836 Eight Tracts, for and against Tythes. 1640
2837 The True Character of an untrue Bishop. —— 1641
2838 The famous Hist. of the 7 Champions.
2839 Conference with Campion the Jesuite, and Articles of Peace between K. Charles and Philip of Spain.
2840 Clarke's Lives of the Fathers, *with curious cuts.* —— 1650
2841 Doctrina Placitandi. ——
2842 Vindication of deprived Bishops, with other Tracts. 1677
2843 The Book named Tectonicon, by Digges, *black letter.*
2844 Aurenzebe, with 6 other Plays.
2845 Dodwell of Separation. —— ——
2846 Sir F. Drake revived, The World encompass'd by Drake, Sir F. Drake's West-Indian Voyage. 1679
2847 The Question of Questions. ——
2848 ABp. Cranmer's Defence of the Doctrine of the Sacrament, *black letter.* 1686
2849 Discovery of infinite Treasure, hidden since the World's Beginning. —— ——
2850 Lord's Discovery of the Sect of the Banians, and Religion of the Persees. —— —— 1639
2851 Directory for the publick Worship of God 1630
2852 Danæus's wonderful Workmanship of the World, *black letter.* —— —— 1646
2853 Donne's Defence of Self-Murder. 1578
2854 The Duello, or single Combat. ——
2855 Deacon and Walker's Discourse of Devils and Spirits. 1610
2856 The World's Resurrection, or the general calling of the Jews, by Drake. —— 1601
2857 The Caveat for Archippus, by Dyke. —— 1609
2858 Edwards's Preservative against Socinianism. —— 1620
2859 The Epistles and Gospels, with a Postill on them, *black letter.* 1698
2860 Elstob's English Saxon Grammar. ——
2861 Ld. Elsemere's Privileges of the Court of Chancery, Englishman's Birthright, Bacon's Cases of Treason, the City Law, and Dyer's Readings upon the Statutes. 1715
2862 Elderfield's Civil Right of Tythes. —— ——
2863 Erasmus's Praise of Folly, translated by Sir T. Chaloner, black letter. —— —— —— 1650
2864 Fitzherbert's Natura Brevium. —— 1549
2865 Fleury's Ecclesiastical History, 4 vol. —— 1730
2866 Fruit-Walls improv'd, by a Member of the Royal Society. 1727
2867 Fitzherbert's Grand Abridgment. —— 1695
1577
2868

2868 Falkner's Seamons. ——— ——— 1684
2870 Fuller's rational Account of eruptive Fevers. ——— 1730
2871 Folkingham's Epitome of Surveying. ——— 1610
2872 Torset's comparative Discourse of the Bodies Natural and Politique. ——— ——— 1606
2873 Full and plain Declaration of ecclesiastical Discipline, black letter. ——— ——— 1574
2874 A joyful Jewel, by L. Fioravantie, and Fioravantie's Discourse upon Chirurgerie, both black letter.
2875 Tythes vindicated from Anti-Christianisme, by Firmin. 1659
2876 Fuller's Lives and Deaths of modern Divines, fine cuts. 1651
2877 The reformed Politick. Answer to the Jesuit's Challenge. More Work for a Masse-Priest, and yet more Work for a Masse-Priest.
2878 Doctor Flud's Answer to Foster. ——— ——— 1631
2879 French's Art of Distillation, and the London Distiller.
2880 The Hero, by Baltasar Gracian. ——— ——— 1726
2881 Greenhill's Art of Embalming, cuts.
2882 Godolphin's Orphans Legacy. ——— ——— 1701
2883 ———Repertorium Canonicum. ——— 1687
2884 The Gentleman's Journal. ——— ———1692
2885 The Charitable Physician. ——— ——— 1639
2886 The simple Cobler of Aggawan in America. ——— 1647
2887 The Ground-Work of Conny-Cathing. ——— 1592
2888 Giffard's Dialogue concerning Witches and Witchcrafts. 1603
2889 The Civile Conversation of Stephen Guazzo. ——— 1586
2890 Good Works if they be handled. ——— 1641
2891 Life and Death of Mrs. Catharine Stubbes, with other Tracts.
2892 Slight Healers of publick Hurts, by Gauden. ——— 1660
2893 The heroick Life and deplorable Death of Henry IV. 1612
2894 Virginia's Cure, or an abusive Narrative concerning Virginia. ——— ——— ——— 1662
2895 Hughe's Grand Abrigment, 3 vol. ——— 1662
2896 Collection of Parliament Sermons, 2 vol.
2897 Hody's Case of vacant Sees. ——— ——— 1693
2898 Hatton's Merchant's Magazine. ——— 1726
2899 The Hind and Panther, with other Tracts.
2900 Lord Clarendon's Survey of Hobbes's Leviathan.——— 1676
2901 A Counter-snarle for Ishmael Rabshacbeh, a Cecropidan Lycaonite. ——— ——— 1613
2902 Explanation of the curious Dyal set up in the King's Gardens at London, *cuts*. ——— ——— 1673
2903 The Book of Homilies, *black letter*. ——— 1547
2904 Treatise of the Ministry of England, *black letter*.
2905 Hill's Art of Gardening and ordering Bees. ——— 1608
2906 Hist. of Passive Obedience. ——— 1689
2907 Harcourt's Voyage of Discovery to Guiana. ——— 1613
2908 Heylyn's Hist. of St. George of Cappadocia. ——— 1631
2909 James's Theory and Practice of Gardening, *cuts*. 1712

2910

2910 The Bathes of Bathes Ayde, with other Tracts.
2911 The Jesuit's downfal. The Sacke of Rome. The Pope's Parliament, with other Tracts.
2912 Bale's Image of both Churches, *black letter.* —— 1550
2913 Jorden's Discourse of Bathes and Mineral Waters. 1632
2914 Enoch's Walk and Change, by Jacombe. —— 1656
2915 Kirkby's Arithmetick. —— —— 1735
2916 Keyser's Lapis Philosophorum, with other Tracts.
2917 Collection of Sermons, by Kennet, and others.
2918 Confutation of the horrible Heresies of the Family of Love. 1579
2919 Bundy's Introduction to the Holy Scriptures, *cuts.* 1723
2920 Lenfant's Hist. of the Council of Constance, 2 vol. 1730
2921 Locke's Paraphrase on the Epistles. —— 1733
2922 Lowth's Comment upon Jeremiah. —— 1718
2923 Collection of curious Cuts, by Tempest.
2924 Lodge's Treatise of the Plague. —— 1603
2925 Ley's defensive Doubts, Hopes, and Reasons. —— 1641
2926 Hartlib's Legacy. —— 1651
2927 Bp. Latimer's Sermons, *black letter.*
2928 A Saxon Treatise concerning the Old and New Testament. 1633
2929 The London Distiller. —— 1667
2630 Letter relating to the Martyrdome of Ketaban. 1633
2931 True experimental Discourse upon the happy Recovery of Breda. —— —— 1637
2932 Milton's Poetical Works, 2 vol. —— 1720
2933 Morgan's compleat Hist. of Algiers, 2 vol. *lar. pap.* 1728
2934 Malcolm's System of Arithmetick. —— 1730
2935 Muggleton's Acts of the Witnesses of the Spirit. —— 1699
2936 Morgan's Language of Arms by Colours and Metals. 1666
2937 A Novelty, or a Government of Women distinct from Men.
2938 Moxon's Mechanick Exercises. —— 1683
2939 —— Mechanick Powers. —— 1696
2940 —— Tutor of Astronomy and Geography. —— 1699
2941 The Voyages and Travels of Sir J. Mandeville, *cuts.*
2942 Tryals of several Witches executed in New-England. 1693
2943 The Medal, a Satyre, with several other Poems.
2944 Mountague's History of Tythes. —— 1621
2945 The Charter of Maryland.
2946 Enquiry whether St. Peter was ever at Rome. 1687
2947 March's Reports. —— —— 1675
2948 The Life of St. Teresa. —— —— 1611
2949 Markham's Master-piece, with the compleat Jockey. 1681
2950 Silk-worms and their Flies described in Verse. 1599
2951 Milton's Paradise-Lost, first Edit. —— 1669
2952 Health's Improvement, by Muffett; and Butler's History of Bees.
2953 Answer to the Jewish Part of the Hist. of Tythes.

O 2954

2954 The new Gospel not the true Gospel, by Norice.——1638
2955 Night-Walker, or Evening Rambles in search after lewd Women. —— —— 1698
2956 Collection of old Novels, 2 vol. black letter.
2957 Noli me Tangere.
2958 A necessary Doctrine of Erudition, black letter.
2959 The Overthrow of Stage-Plays. —— 1599
2960 Collection of Tracts relating to Government.
2961 The Pilgrimage of Perfection, black letter. ——1526
2962 Patrick's Comment. upon Genesis, Exodus, Numbers, Deuteronomy, Samuel, Judges, and Ruth, 6 vol. sold separate.
2963 Sermon preach'd at the Coronation of K. James and Queen Mary. —— —— 1685
2964 Eusebius's Ecclesiastical History, by Parker.—— 1729
2965 Parsons's Book of Cyphers. —— 1704
2966 Pemberton's View of Sir I. Newton's Philosophy.——1728
2967 The Iliad of Homer, by Pope, 6 vol. ——1715
2968 Common-Prayer. —— 1719
2969 Virgil's Eneidos, translated by Phayer, black letter. 1607
2970 Pegasus taught by Bankes's Ghost to dance in the Dorick Mode. —— —— 1648
2971 Prynne's short Examination of the Common-Prayer. 1661
2972 Poole's seasonable Apology for Religion. —— 1673
2973 The Papacy of Paul the IVth, or Restitution of Abbey-Lands. —— —— 1673
2974 The Worth of a Penny, or a Caution to keep Money. 1677
2975 Sprat's History of the Royal Society.—— 1734
2976 The Politicks of the French King discover'd.——1689
2977 Pliny's Panegyrick, translated by Sir R. Stapylton. 1644
2978 The new Testament in the Irish Language. —1681
2979 Regimen Sanitatis Salerni, translated by Paynel, bl. letter. 1541
2980 Collection of Tracts relating to Attorneys, Taxes, Debts, &c.
2981 The Holy Bible, *printed at Cambridge, by Field.* —1668
2982 Protestation of Prince Lodowicke, with other Tracts.
2983 Common-Prayer and Psalms, black letter.——1627
2984 The wonderful and extraordinary Fits of Mr. T. Spachett, who was under Witchcraft. —— 1693
2985 Ten considerable Queries concerning Tithes. ——1659
2986 Collection of Tracts written by Sir W. Penn.
2987 The Pollution of University Learning. ——1642
2988 The poor Man's Plaister-Box. —— 1634
2989 Purchas's Theatre of political flying Insects.——1657
2990 The Lord's Prayer in above a hundred Languages. 1700
2991 Philosophical Transactions from the beginning, to the Year 1730 inclusive.

I 2992

2992 Hooke's philosophical Lectures. ——— 1674
2993 Lowthorpe, Jones, Eames, and Martyn's Abridgm. of the Philosophical Transactions, 8 vol. ——— 1732
2994 Lowthorp's Abridgment, 3 vol. *lar. pap* ——— 1705
2995 Eames and Martyn's Abridgment, 3 vol. sold separate to compleat Setts.
2996 Collection of ancient Obelisks and Columns in Rome.
2997 Religious Philosopher, 3 vol. *cuts.* ——— 1734
2998 The poor Vicar's Plea for Tythes. ——— 1720
2999 Randolph's present State of the Morea. ——— 1686
3000 Discourse upon prodigious Abstinence, occasioned by the 12 Months Fasting of M. Taylor, by Reynolds. 1669
3001 Relation of the Funeral Pomp of Gustavus the Great. 1633
3002 Ridley's View of the Civil and Ecclesiastical Law.—1607
3003 The jealous Lovers, with 11 other Plays.
3004 Peter Ramus's Geometry. ——— 1636
3005 Godwin's Roman Antiquities. ——— 1648
3006 Stevens's Spanish Dictionary. ——— 1726
3007 The Koran, commonly called the Alcoran, by Sale. 1734
3008 Snell's divine Authority of the Christian Religion. 1728
3009 Shakespear's Works, by Pope, 7 vol. ——— 1725
3010 Somner's Treatise of Gavel-kind, with his Life, by Kennet. 1726
3011 Selden's Table-Talk. ——— 1689
3012 ———Fleta. ——— ——— 1685
3013 ———History of Tithes. ——— 1618
3014 Stillingfleet's Unreasonableness of Separarion. ——— 1682
3015 Wells's Specimen for the easy understanding the Scripture- 1709
3016 Sherly's Travels into Persia. ——— 1613
3017 Staunford's Pleas of the Crown, fr. ——— 1560
3018 Sympson's Book of Cyphers. ——— 1727
3019 Collection of Tracts, by Stillingfleet.
3020 Compleat Body of the Sea-Laws.
3021 Compleat Collection of all the Sermons both in Print and MS. that ever were preach'd before the Sons of the Clergy, 2 vol.
3022 Sheppard's Touch-stone of common Assurances. ——— 1648
3023 Life's Preservative against Self-killing, by Sym. ——— 1637
3024 Smith's Description of Virginia, Proceedings of the English Colony in Virginia, The new Life of Virginia, and the present State of Virginia.
3025 Sinclar's Hydrostaticks. ——— 1672
3026 Saviolo's Treat. of the Use of the Rapier and Dagger. 1595
3027 Tythes too hot to be touch'd, by Spelman.
3029 The Spyder and the Fly, a Poem, in black letter, *cuts.*
3030 Great Britain's Salomon. ——— 1625

3031 Conſtitutions and Canons of the Church of Ireland. 1635
3032 Spicer's Tables of Intereſt. —— 1693
3033 Hiſtory of the nine Women Worthies, with other Tracts.
3034 Sparrow's Canons. —— —— 1684
3035 The Lives of the Saints.
3036 Scotch Presbyterian Eloquence. —— 1692
3037 Sermons by Sherlock, Atterbury, Morley, Pelling, and Smalridge.
3038 The Spaniards perpetual Deſigns to univerſal Monarchy. 1624
3039 Scott's Aphoriſms of State. —— 1624
3040 Account of marvellous Cures performed by the ſtroaking of the Hands of Valentine Greatarick. —— 1666
3041 Several Tracts relating to the Quakers, bound together.
3042 Tournefort's Voyage to the Levant, 2 vol. *cuts.* —— 1718
3043 The new Teſtament, by Beza, with Notes, *bl. letter.*
3044 Tyſon's Anatomy of a Pigmy, with *cuts.* —— 1699
3045 Trapp's Virgil, 2 vol. —— 1718
3046 The new Teſtament in the Indian Language. —— 1661
3047 —— with Notes and Cuts.
3048 Treatiſe touching the Eaſt-Indian Trade. —— 1664
3049 Sermon preach'd at Dublin, at the Funeral of the Bp of Armagh. —— —— 1663
3050 Tilleſley's Anſwer to Selden's Hiſtory of Tythes. —— 1619
3051 Book of Judgments in real, perſonal, and mixt Actions. 1664
3052 Top's Olive-Leaf, or univerſal Abce. —— 1603
3053 Philoſophical Tranſactions, by the Philadelphian Society. 1697
3054 The Loves of Troylus and Creſida, engliſh and lat. *Oxon.* 1635
3055 Tuſſer's 500 Points of good Husbandry. —— 1620
3056 Treatiſe of Cleanneſs in Meats and Drinks. 1682
3057 Taxes no Charge. —— 1690
3058 Collection of Tracts in Popiſh Controverſy, chiefly on the Proteſtant ſide, 8 vol.
3059 Vox Populi, or News from Spain. —— 1620
3060 The Epiſtle to the Miniſters, Moon-ſhine, or Reſtauration of Jews-Trumps and Bag-Pipes.
3061 A Looking-glaſs for Malignants. —— 1643
3062 Winſlow's Anatomy. —— 1734
3063 Maimbourgh's Hiſtory of Arianiſm, by Webſter, 2 vol. 1728
3064 Wiſe's Confutation of Atheiſm, 2 vol. —— 1706
3065 Waller's Eſſays of natural Experiments, *cuts.* —— 1684
3066 Woodford's Paraphraſe upon the Pſalms. —— 1667
3067 Obſervations of the Engliſh Spaniſh Pilgrim, &c. —— 1630
3068 Wats's Mortification apoſtolical. —— 1637

3069

3069 Sir R. Williams's Actions of the Low-Countries. — 1618
3070 Whitfeld's Discovery of the present State of the Indians in New England. — — 1651
3071 The History of Travayle in the West and East-Indies, *bl. letter.* — — — 1577
3072 The English Myrror, The Bellman's second Night's Walk, with his O per se O, both black letter.
3073 The Passions of our Saviour in Cuts, grav'd by Le Clerc.

Rerum Britannicarum Scriptores Latini. Quarto.

3074 Antonini Iter Britanniarum Comment. T. Gale.—*Lond.* 1709
3075 Certamen Seraphicum Provinciæ Angliæ, cum fig. *Duaci* 1649
3076 F. Godwin Annales Hen. VIII. Edward. VI. & Mariæ. *Lond.* 1628
3077 Galfridi Monumetensi Hist. Anglicana. fol. deaur. —1517
3078 Britannia Rediviva, Carmen. — *Ox.* 1660
3079 Camerarius de Scotorum Fortitudine. — *Par.* 1631
3080 C. Tonstalli contra Impios Blasphematores Prædestinationis Opus. — *Ant.* 1555
3081 Camdeni Britannia, cum Chartis Geograph.
3082 ——— Insignia Carmen. — *Ox.* 1624
3083 Capelli adversus prætensum Primatum Ecclesiasticum Regis Angliæ Lib. — — *Bon.* 1610
3084 Clementis a Lybeo Monte Trinobantiados Augustæ Carmen. *Lond.* 1636
3085 Panegyrici Cromwello scripti, unus a Legato Portugallici Regis, alter a quodam Jesuita. — 1654
3086 D. Calderwood Ecclesiæ Anglicanæ Politia. —*L.B.* 1708
3087 Historia Ecclesiastica Gestis Scotorum, Dempsteri. *Bonon.* 1627
3088 Seldeni Marmora Arundeliana. — *Lond.* 1628
3089 P. Jovii Descriptio Britanniæ, Scotiæ, Hiberniæ, & Orchadum, fol. deaur. — *Ven.* 1548
3090 Leslæi de Titulo & Jure Principis Mariæ Libellus. *Rhem.* 1583
3091 Dempsteri apparatus ad Historiam Scoticam Lib. 2. *Bonon.* 1622
3092 Gibsoni Chronicon Saxonicum. — *Oxon.* 1692
3093 A. Gil Logonomia Anglica, Literæ a Conventu Theologorum in Anglia, anonymus Persa de Siglis Arabum & Persarum Astronomicis.
3094 Osullevani Hist. Catholicæ Iberniæ. — *Ulissip.* 1621
3095 Hatveii Musarum Lachrymæ. — *Lond.* 1578
3096 Arcis Sammartinianæ obsidio & fuga Anglorum a Rea Insula. — — *Par.* 1629
3097 Leslæus de Origine, Moribus, & Rebus Gestis Scotorum. *Romæ* 1578

3098

3098 Lilii Anglorum Regum Chronicon. —— *Franc.*1565
3099 Historia Majoris Britanniæ, per J. Majorem.——1521
3100 T. Mori Epistola ab Academia Oxon. ——*Oxon.*1633
3101 De Proditione in Magn. Brit. Regem, Antimartinus. Tobias Græce, cum multis aliis.
3102 Nonæ Novembris Æternitati Consecratæ. ——*ib.*1607
3103 Notitia Oxoniensis Academiæ. —— *Lond.*1675
3104 O Flaherti Ogygia, seu rerum Hibernicarum Chronologia. *ib.*1685
3105 Pitseus de Rebus Anglicis. —— *Par.*1619
3106 Prisei Historiæ Brytannicæ Defensio. —— *Lond.*1573
3107 Jacobi Regis Declaratio pro Jure Regio. ——*ib.*1616
3108 Stanihurstius de Rebus in Hibernia Gestis. —— *Ant.*1584
3109 Vitæ G. Wicami Episcopi. —— *Oxon.*1690
3110 Usserii Antiquitates Ecclesiæ Britanniæ. ——*Dub.*1639
3111 Regni Angliæ Religio Catholica, Prisca, Defæcata. *Lond.* 1729

Libri Mathemat. Itinera, Philosophia, Juridici, Medic. Hist. Naturalis, Hist. var. Gentium, Theologia, Bibliothecarii & Miscellanæi. Quarto.

3112 Goesii Rei Agrariæ, auctores legesque variæ, *cum fig. Amst.* 1674
3113 Arsenii in Porphyrii 5 universalia Dilucidationes. *Flor. apud Junt.*1599
3114 Abbot de Suprema potestate Regia, contra Bellarminum. *Lond.*1619
3115 De Alchemia, Rosarium Philosophorum.
3116 Alcoranus Muhammedis, in Ling. Turc. —— *Hamb.*1694
3117 Arnobius adversus Gentes. —— *Romæ* 1583
3118 Æmyliani Naturalibus de Ruminantibus Historia. *Ven.*1584
3119 Arnobius adversus Gentes. —— *L.B.*1651
3120 Aristotelis de Optimo Statu Reipub. Lib. 8.gr. *Paris, apud Morel.*1556
3121 L. Allatii de Symeonum scriptis Diatriba.——*Par.*1664
3122 Muratorii Anecdota, Græc. —— ——*Pat.*1709
3123 Siculi & Alii de Agrorum Conditionibus limitum. *Par. apud Turneb.*1554
3124 P. Alpinus de Plantis Ægypti, cum Observat. Veslingii. *Pat.*1640
3125 Euclidis Phænomena Scholiis antiquis. —— *Rom.*1591
3126 Goesii Rei Agrariæ auctores legesque variæ, cum Notis Rigaltii, *cum fig.* —— *Amst.*1674
3127 Actuarii Johannis Filii Zachariæ Methodi Medendi, Lib. 6. *Ven.*1554
3128 Aselii Lacteis Venis 4 Vasorum Mesaraicorum genere. *L. Bat.*1640

3129

3129 Antidotarium Bononiense, corio turc. —— *Bon.*1574
3130 Augenii de ratione Curandi, per Sanguinis Missionem, Lib. 10. —— *Taur.*1584
3131 Amorum Emblemata, fig. Othonis Væni. —— *Ant.*1608
3132 Academiæ Cæsareo Leopoldinæ Carolinæ Naturæ Curiosorum Ephemerides. —— *Norib.*1719
3133 Mindererus de Calcantho. —— *Aug. Vind.*1617
3134 J. Friend Opera omnia Medica. —— *Par.*1735
3135 Bebelii Antiquitates Germaniæ, *corio turcico.* *Argent.*1669
3136 Cæsalpinus de Metallicis —— *Norib.*1602
3137 F. Albertini Mirabilia Romæ. —— *Lug.*1520
3138 B. Angeli de admirabili Viperæ Natura Lib. *Norib.*1603
3139 Acerra Medico-Chymica. —— *Lipf.*1713
3140 Alberti Tentamen Lexici Realis. —— *Halæ Mag.*1727
3141 ——Introductio in universam Medicinam. —— *ib* 1718
3142 ——de Re Ædificatoria. —— *Par.*1512
3143 Ad nummum Anniæ Faustinæ Dissertatio Apologetica. *Pat.* 1713
3144 Germani Audiberti Venetiæ Carmen. —— *Ven.*1583
3145 { Argenterius de Somno & Vigilia. —— *Flor.*1556
R. a Fonseca de Hominis Excrementis. —— *Pisis* 1613 }
3146 Altesserra Ordinum Rei Monasticæ, Lib. 10. —— *Par.*1674
3147 B. à Mallinkrot de ortu ac progressu Artis Typographicæ Dissertat. —— *Col. Agrip.*1640
3148 Athenagoras de Resurrectione Mortuorum, gr. lat. *Par. ap. Wech.*1541
3149 Apologia de Sententia Christianissimi Francorum Regis. *Lut.* 1551
3150 Adolphi de Aere, Aquis & Locis Lipsiensibus. —— *Lipf.*1725
3151 Historia Tamerlanis, Arabice. —— *L. Bat.*1636
3152 Rei Accipitraria Scriptores. —— *Lut.*1612
3153 { Alchabitius, cum Comment. —— *Ven.*1502
Albumazar Introduct. in Astronom. *cum fig.* *Aug. Vind.* 1489 }
3154 Augustini Archiepisc. Dialogi. —— *Par.*1607
3155 Alfonsus Sanctius de Rebus Hispaniæ. —— *Compl.*1634
3156 Michaelis Apostoli Proverbiæ, gr. lat. —— *L. B.*1653
3157 Bayfius de Captivis, & de Re Navali, *lin. rubr.* *Par. apud R. Steph.*1536
3158 Bellum & Excidium Trojanum, a Begero, *cum fig.* *Lipf.* 1699
3159 Bibliotheca Cordesiana. —— *Par.*1643
3160 Augustini Itinera, Notis var. curante Wesselingio. *Amst.* 1735
3161 Boecleri Opera, 4 tom. 3 vol. —— *Franc.*1733
3162 G. Britonis Morici Philippidos Lib. —— 1657
3163 Balbus de Civili & Bellica Fortitudine, fol. deaurat. *Romæ* 1526
3164 Bucclini Rhetia sacra & prophana Topo-Chrono-Stemmata Graphica. —— *Aug. Vind.*1666

3165 Bissarii Cardinalis Opuscula, *foliis deauratis, Editio antiqua.*
3166 Balduini Relatio ad Henricum Andium Ducem Magnum. *Par.* 1570
3167 Officina Barbarina. ——— *Ven.* 1569
3168 { Vitæ & Icones Sultanorum a Boissardo.——— *Franc.* 1596
Pannoniæ Historia.——— *ib.* 1596 }
3169 Boissardi Theatrum Vitæ Humanæ, cum fig.—— *ib.* 1596
3170 ———Emblemata. ——— *Metis* 1588
3171 Batillii Emblemata.——— *Franc.* 1596
3172 Bartholini Acta Medica & Philosophica Hafniensia, 4 vol. *Hafn.* 1673
3173 Boissardi Bibliotheca Chalcographica.——— *Franc.* 1650
3174 Historia Chronologica Pannoniæ, *cum fig.*——— *ib.* 1608
3175 J. de Bie Numismata.——— *Ant.* 1615
3176 Barzizii & Guiniforti Filii Opera. —— *Romæ* 1723
3177 Commentatio de Personis vulgo Larvis seu Mascharis. *Franc.*
3178 Achillis Bocchii Emblemata. ——— *Bonon.* 1574
3179 Banduri Bibliotheca Nummaria.——— *Hamb.* 1719
3180 Bayeri de Nummis Romanis Comment.——— *Lipf.* 1722
3181 Biblia Græca ex Versione 70 Interpret. *Lond. apud Daniel.* 1653
3182 Burnet de Statu Mortuorum.——— *Lond.* 1723
3183 ———de Fide & Officiis Christianorum. ——— *ib.* 1722
3184 Buxtorfi Dissertationes Philologico-Theologicæ.—*Baf.* 1662
3185 Basilii Exhortationes, gr. ——— *Lut. apud Morel.* 1583
3186 Breviarium Romanum, 2 vol. ——— *Ant. apud Plant.* 1682
3187 Baluzii Hist. Tutelensis.——— *Par. e Typ. Regia* 1717
3188 Borellus de Motu Animalium.——— *Romæ* 1683
3189 Bredenburgii Euervatio, tractat. Theologico-Politici. *Rott.* 1675
3190 Bynæus de Calceis Hebræorum.——— *L.B.* 1724
3191 Balianus de Motu Naturali Gravium, Solidorum & Liquidorum. ——— *Gen.* 1646
3192 Bulfingeri Dilucidationes Philosophicæ de Deo. *Tubingæ* 1725
3193 Beutheri Fastorum Antiquitatis Romani Opus absolut. *Spiræ* 1600
3194 R. Boyle Opera varia, 4 vol. ——— *Gen.* 1714
3195 Synopsis variar. Historiar. a Creatione Mundi ad Captam Constantinopolim, gr.
3196 Bugenhagii Pomerania. ——— *Gryph.* 1728
3197 Burgundi Historia Bavarica. ——— *Helm.* 1705
3198 ——— Belgica. ——— *Halæ Mag.* 1708
3199 S. a Berneck Historia Motuum & Bellorum in Rhetia Excitatorum & Gestorum. ——— *Col. All.* 1629
3200 Bynkershoeck Observationes Juris Romani.——— *Franc.* 1723
3201 Boerhaave Elementa Chemiæ, 2 vol. ——— *Par.* 1733

3202

3202 Barchusen de Medicinæ Origine & Progressu Dissertat. *Traj. ad Rhen.* 1723
3203 J. Broen Opera Medica. ——— *Rott.* 1703
3204 Declamatio ad N. Beraldum Oratorem. ——— *Lut.*
3205 Bibliotheca Bentesiana. ——— *Amst.* 1702
3206 Banacosus de Laudibus Heraclis Estensis. ——— *Ven.* 1555
3207 Liturgia Belgica, gr.
3208 F. Deo Bez Historia Regum Francorum. ——— *Par.* 1577
3209 Baysius de Captivis & de Re Navali. ——— *Bas.* 1537
3210 Portnerii Vita & Elogia H. Bignonii. ——— *Par.* 1657
3211 J. Broen Animadversiones Medicæ. ——— *Neap.* 1721
3212 Bocconi Descript. rariorum Plantarum Siciliæ, Melitæ, Galliæ & Italiæ. ——— *Ox.* 1617
3213 Mannii Senensi de Balneis Sancti Cassiani Tractat. *Senis* 1674
3214 Bartholinus de Causis contemptæ à Danis adhuc Gentilibus Mortis. ——— *Hafn.* 1689
3215 Bauhini Hist. Novi & Admirandi Fontis Bollensis. 1598
3216 Bossueti de Natura Aquatilium Carmen, cum fig. *Lug.* 1558
3217 Bossiell ad Legem Molinæam de Testibus Comment. *Pict.* 1582
3218 De Dominio Genuensis in Mari Ligustico. ——— *Romæ* 1641
3219 Bibliotheca Juris Imperantium quadripartita. *Noriberg.* 1727
3220 Brissonius de Formulis & Solemnibus Populi Romani Verbis. ——— *Mog.* 1649
3221 Beverigii Codex Canonum Ecclesiæ Primitivæ Vindicat. *Lond.* 1678
3222 Meliagridis & Ætolia ex Numismate Kyrieon apud Goltzium. ——— *Col. Brand.* 1696
3223 Biblia Græca ex versione 70 Interpret. cura L. Bos. *Franeq.* 1709
3224 ——— Vulgatæ Editionis, cum fig. *Ven. apud Junt.*
3225 Bynæi de Morte Christi Comment. ——— *Amst.* 1691
3226 Barlaami Monachi Logistices, gr. lat. ——— *Par.* 1600
3227 Bellopoelii de Pace inter Henricum Galliarum & Edwardum Angliæ Reges. ——— *Lond.* 1552
3228 Bauhini Theatri Botanici. ——— *Basiliæ.* 1671
3229 Baieri Horti Medici Acad. Altorf. Historia. ——— *Altorfi.* 1727
3230 Bornitii Tractatus Politicus. ——— *Franc.* 1612
3231 Boecleri Cynosuræ Materiæ Medicæ continuata. *Argent.* 1729
3232 B. Bossuet Defensio declarationis Cleri Gallicani. *Luxemb.* 1730
3233 Praxis Francisci Clarke. ——— 1684
3234 Bellini Opuscula. ——— *Lug Bat.* 1724
3235 ——— Exercitationes Anatomicæ. ——— *ib.* 1726
3236 Bellissimum Ovidii Theatrum, lineis rubris, foliis deauratis. *Norimb.* 1685

P 3237

3237 Bellinus de Urinis & Pulsibus. ——— *Franc.* 1698
3238 Borcholten in 4 Institut. Juris Civilis Lib. Comment. *Genev.* 1653
3239 Bertrandi de Juris-Peritis Lib. II. ——— *Tolosa.* 1617
3240 Burchelati Comment. memorabilium multiplicis Historiæ Tarvisinæ. ——— *Tarvisii* 1616
3241 De Aquis Medicamentis nova Methodus Bauhini. ——— 1607
3242 Bergerus de Thermis Carolinis. ——— *Lipsiæ.* 1709
3243 Boetii de Boodt Gemmarum & Lapidum Historia. *Hanov.* 1609
3244 Brunnerii Consiliorum Medicorum Lib. ——— *Franc.* 1727
3245 Cardelinus de Origine Foetus. ——— *Vincent.* 1628
3246 G. Bidloo Exercitat. Anatomicæ, cum fig. *Lug. Bat.* 1708
3247 Brunnemanni tractat. de Cessione Actionum & Versuris. *Franc.* 1721
3248 Braunius de Comitiis Regni Poloniæ. ——— *Colon.*
3249 Bulla in Cena Domini 1523. ——— *Rom.* 1523
3250 Barlaami de Papæ principatu Libellus, gr. lat. ——— *Oxon.* 1592
3251 Lusus Amatorius, Fides Ecclesiæ Anglicanæ vindicatus.
3252 Biblia Sacra Scholiis Tremellii & Junii. ——— *Lond.* 1585
3253 Batei Vitæ select. Virorum. ——— *ib.* 1681
3254 St. Barnabi Apostoli Epistola Catholica gr. lat. ——— *Par.* 1645
3255 Battelli exposit. aureæ Numismatis ex Museo Clementis XI. *Romæ.* 1702
3256 Manuale sacrarum Cærimoniarum. ——— *Venet.* 1673
3257 Septali Labyrinthi Medici extricati. ——— *Genev.* 1687
3258 Boxhornii Quæstiones Romanæ. ——— *Lug. Bat.* 1637
3259 Broweri Antiquitates Fuldenses, cum fig. ——— *Ant.* 1612
3260 Cotelerii Ecclesiæ Græcæ Monumenta, 3 vol. *Lut. Paris.* 1677
3261 Conradi Annales Schirenses. ——— *Argent.* 1716
3262 Spinosæ Arcana Atheismi Revelata. ——— *Rot.* 1676
3263 Charletoni Onomasticon Zoicon, cum fig. ——— *Lond.* 1668
3264 Selectiora Numismata in ære max. Moduli e Museo F. de Camps interpret. per Vaillant. ——— *Paris.* 1695
3265 Crassus de Cæremoniis Cardinalium & Episcoporum in eorum Diœcesibus. ——— *Venet.* 1582
3266 Historia Scholastica, excellens Opus. ——— *ib.* 1729
3267 Gesenii de Igne Purgatorio Dissertat. ——— *Helmestad.* 1650
3268 Cumberland de Legibus. ——— *Lond.* 1672
3269 Noris de Cruce stationali investigatio Historica; cum fig. *Rom* 1694.
3270 B. Crippæ in Aristotelis de Animalium. ——— *Venet.* 1566
3271 Bregnii Prodromus Fasciculi rariorum Plantarum. *Gedani.* 1689
3272 Capacii Puteolana Historia. ——— *Neapoli.* 1604
3273 Geographia Papæ Pii ——— *Venet.* 1503
3274 G. Courtin de tribus Principiis, Auro Potabili. *Paris* 1579
3275 Coccell Jus Civile Controvers. 2 vol. ——— *Franc.* 1729

3276

3276 Confideratio Caufarum hujus belli quod anno 1618 in Bohemia. —— —— —— 1647

3277 { Contarenus de Rebus in Etruria Geftis. —— Lug. 1562
Capella de Rebus geftis pro Reftitutione Francifci II. Mediolanenfium Ducis. }

3278 Cataneus de Arte Bellica, *cum fig.* —— 1600

3279 Callimachus de Ludis Scenicis Mimorum & Pantomimorum Syntagma. —— *Patav.* 1713

3280 Corradini vetus Latium Profanum & Sacrum, 4 vol. *cum fig.* —— —— *Romæ.* 1704

3281 Collenucci Apologia. —— *ib.* 1526

3282 Columbus de rebus geftis Valentinorum & Dienfium Epifcoporum. —— —— *Lug.* 1628

3283 Cæpollæ tractat. de Servitutibus. —— *Amft.* 1686

3284 Cafus Medicinales 26 fele̳ctiores. —— *Lipfiæ.* 1725

3285 Cowperi Glandularum defcriptio, *cum fig.* —— *Lond.* 1702

3286 Cornarius de Re Medica. —— *Bafiliæ.* 1529

3287 Cofchwitz Organifmus & Mechanifmus in Homine vivo obvius & ftabilitus, 2 vol. —— *Lipfiæ.* 1725

3288 Contii Opera omnia. —— *Paris.* 1616

3289 Tulli in Leges quafdam Carnutum Municipales Comment. *ib.* 1560

3290 Contatori Hiftoria Terracinenfe. —— *Romæ.* 1706

3291 Contelorus de Præfecto Urbis, *cum fig.*

3292 Ramazzini de Contagiofa Epidemia differtat. —— *Lipfiæ* 1713

3293 Camarri de Teate antiquo Lib. III. —— *Romæ.* 1651

3294 Clivoli de Balneis Naturalibus. —— *Lug.* 1552

3295 Fabius Columnus de Purpura. —— *Kiliæ.* 1675

3296 Conringius de Finibus Imperii Germanici. —— *Franc.* 1680

3267 Colomefii Gallia Orientalis. —— *Hagæ Comit.* 1665

3268 Coleri Decifiones Germaniæ. —— *Franc.* 1610

3269 Cæcus de Origine Juris. —— *Bonon.* 1563

3300 De Nutritione Fœtus in Utero Paradoxa. —— *Dantifci.* 1655

3301 Capacii Hiftoria Neapolitana. —— *Neapoli.* 1607

3302 Corvini Juris-prudentiæ Romanæ fummarium. —— *Amft.* 1655

3303 Confuetudines Aurelian. & Turonen. —— *Paris.* 1520

3304 Liber Juris Civilis Urbis Veronæ. —— *Veronæ.* 1728

3305 Controverfiæ Mantuanæ, *corio turcico.* —— *Franc.* 1629

3306 Cofmianarum Actionum Lib. V. —— *Florent.* 1578

3307 Paftorii Hiftoria Belli Scythico-Cofaici. —— *Dantifci.* 1650

3308 Ciampini Sacro-Hiftorica difquifitio de duobus Emblematibus. —— —— *Romæ.* 1691

3309 Practica nova in Medicina. —— *Lug.*

3310 Caftellionæi Antiquitates Mediolanenfes, *cum fig. Mediol.* 1625

3311 Cinnami de Rebus geftis Imp. Conftant. Joannis & Manuelis Comnenorum Lib. IV. gr. lat. —— *Traject. ad Rhen.* 1652

3312 Cenfura quorundam Scriptorum veterum. —— *Lond.* 1614

3313 Cochlæus adverfus Lutherum. —— *Colon* 1525

3314 Ricoldus adverfus Sectam Mahumeticam. —— 1511

P 2 3315

3315 Donati Roma vetus ac recens, *cum fig.* —— *Romæ.*1665
3316 Origenis de Oratione Libellus, gr. lat. —— *Basil.*1694
3317 Dempsteri Antiquitates Romanæ. —— *Genev.*1558
3318 Dickensoni Physica vetus & vera. —— *Lond.*1702
3319 Dania ad Exteros de perfidia Suecorum.
3320 Deusingii de vero Systemate Mundi Dissertatio. *Amst.*1643
3321 P. de Dusburg Chronicon Prussiæ. —— *Jenæ.*1679
3322 Delphinus de Nobilitate. —— *Perusiæ.*1590
3323 Maccius de Historia. —— *Venet.*1613
3324 Dionysii Orbis Ambitus gr. —— *Paris apud Morel.*1559
3325 Duellii Miscellanea, 2 vol. —— *August.Vindel.*1723
3326 Dannhaweri Disquisitiones sacræ, 2 vol. —— *Lipsiæ.*1700
3327 Du Pin de Antiqua Ecclesiæ Disciplina Dissertationes Historicæ. —— —— *Paris.*1686
3328 Scrivineri Apologia S. Ecclesiæ Patribus. —— *Lond.*1672
3329 A. Driessen Lumen & Doctrina Conscientiæ & Homo vetus & novus. —— —— *Groningæ.*1728
3330 Dallæus de Scriptis quæ sub Dionysii Areopagitæ & Ignatii Antiocheni nominibus circumferuntur Lib. — *Genev.*1666
3331 H. a Deventer Operationes Chirurgicæ. —— *Lug.Bat.*1701
3332 Diaria de Bello Carolino.
3333 Severini Idea Medicinæ Philosophicæ. —— *Basil.*1571
3334 Digbeius de Arte Natandi, *cum fig.* —— *Lond.*1587
3335 Propeduemata Aphoristica J. Dec. —— *ib.*1568
3336 Diemerbroeck Opera omnia Medica & Anatomica, 2 vol. *Genev.*1687
3337 Ant. de Dominis suæ profectiones Consilium exponit. *Lond.* 1616
3338 Epinicium Ludovico Francorum Regi Christianiss. *Rom.*1628
3339 Drusii de Sectis Judaicis Comment. —— *Arnhem.*1619
3340 Proverbia Ben Siræ. —— *Franeq.*1597
3341 D'Outremanni Constantinopolis Belgica. —— *Tornaci.*1643
3342 Dodwell de veteribus Græcorum Romanorumque Cyclis. *Oxon.*1701
3343 Veterum Interpretum Græcorum in totum vetus Testament. Fragment. a Drusio. —— *Arnhem.*1622
3344 Drusii in Voces Ebraicas Novi Testamenti Comment. duplex. *Franek.*1616
3345 ——ad Loca difficiliora Josue &c. Comment. —— *ib.*1618
3346 Valent ab Eickset Epitome Annalium Pomeraniæ. —— 1728
3347 Epistolæ diversorum Philosophorum gr. *Venet. apud Aldum.*
3348 Electa Rei Nummariæ. —— *Hamb.*1709
3349 Epistola Regis Christianiss. ad ampliss. sacri Imperii Ordines. *Paris, apud C. Steph.*1553
3350 Eusebii Chronicon. —— *Paris.*1511
3351 Ernesti de Franckenau Bibliotheca Hispanica. — *Lipsiæ.*1724
3352 Elenchus Tabularum Pinacothecarum atque nonnullorum Cimeliorum in Gazophylacio L. Vincent. —— *Harlem.*1719
3353 Hare Epistola Critica. —— *Lond.*1726

3354

3355 Engelbrechti Epistola, *corio turcico, foliis deaur. Basil.* 1515
3356 Eckhardi Dissertat. de Templo Capadociæ. *Coman.* 1721
3357 Basilii Magni & aliorum Epistolæ, gr. *Ven. apud Ald.* 1499
3358 Epiphanie Medicorum.———————— 1506
3359 { Eustachius de Gentibus. ——————*Ven.* 1563
{ J. Rueff de Conceptu & Generatione Hominis, *fig.* 1554
*3359 Eyndii Convivialis Senatus super Pace Hispana. *L. Bat.* 1640
3360 Frischi Exercitationes Juris Publici.—— *Ingolstad.* 1667
3361 Enenckelius de Privilegiis Juris Civilis. ——*Ratisb.* 1720
3362 Fontani Medicina Arithmetica.—— ——*Lug.* 1657
3363 Fontanini Vindiciæ Antiquorum Diplomatum.—*Romæ* 1705
3364 ——— de Antiquitatibus Hortæ. ———— *ib.* 1708
3365 Fabricii Bibliotheca Græca, 12 vol. ——— *Hamb.* 1708
3366 Frontini de Aquæduct. Urbis Romæ Comment. *Pat.* 1722
3367 Ferettus de Jure & Re Navali.————*Ven.* 1579
3368 Hemmingi Astrologiæ rationes & experientia refutatæ. *Ant.* 1583
3369 Farbii Opuscula Geometrica. ——— ———*Romæ* 1659
3370 Victoris Fausti Veneti Orationes, *corio turcico, foliis deaurat. Venet.* 1559
3371 And. Max. Fredro-Henricus primus Rex Polonorum. *Dantisci* 1659
3372 Fersii de Præfectura, S. Prætorii Tractat.—— *Franc.* 1611
3373 Flacii Comment. de Vita & Morte. ————*ib.* 1584
3374 Ferrarius de Veterum Acclamationibus & Plausu. *Med.* 1627
3375 Forcatuli Polonia Felix. —— ————*Lug.* 1574
3376 Facii Politica Liviana. ——— ——— *Altenburg.* 1617
3377 —— Epitome Felini de Regibus Siciliæ & Apuliæ. *Hanov.* 1611
3378 Fischeri de Terra Medicinali Tokayensi Tractat. *Wratislaviæ* 1732
3379 Fieni Chirurgia.————————*Lond.* 1733
3380 M. Faber Strychnomiæ, *cum fig.*—— *Aug. Vindel.* 1677
3381 Franciotti Tractat. de Balneo Villensi.———— 1552
3382 Volckameri Flora Nebrigensis, *cum fig.*——*Noriberg.* 1700
3383 Fransi Emblemata.————————*Lond.* 1588
3384 Ferrarius de Re Vestiaria, *cum fig.* ——*Patav.* 1654
3385 Gyraldus de Sepultura, ac vario Sepeliendi Ritu. *Helmestad* 1676
3386 Geographia antiqua, edente Gronovio. gr. lat. *Lug. Bat.* 1697
3387 Geudii & Sarravii Epistolæ ————*Ultraject.* 1697
3388 De Germaniæ Miraculo opt. max. Typis Litterarum Dissertat.—————————— *Lipsiæ*
3389 Malquytii Ictorum Philosophia.—— *Halæ Magdeburg.* 1727
3390 { Gaurici de Sculptura Liber. ————*Ant.* 1609
{ Gorlæi Dactyliotheca.————*ib.* 1609
3391 Glissonii Tractat. de Natura Substantiæ energetica. *Lond.* 1672

3392

3392 Gulielmini Opera omnia Mathematica, Hydraulica, Medica; & Physica, 2 vol. ———————— *Genev.* 1719
3393 Gravesande Physices Elementa Mathematica, 2 vol. *Lug. Bat.* 1720
3394 Goldastus de Bohemiæ Regni. ———————— *Franc.* 1627
3395 Guillimannus de Rebus Helvetiorum. ———————— 1598
3396 Grandi Geometrica Demonstrario Theorematum Hugenianor. *Florent.* 1701
3397 Gemmæ & Sculpturæ antiquæ depictæ, ab L. Agostino. *Romæ*
3398 C. Gemma de Arte Cyclognomica, *foliis deauratis. Ant.* 1569
3399 Galluccius de Bello Belgico, 2 vol. ———— *Bambergæ* 1705
3400 Gorlæi Dactyliotheca, cum Explanat. J. Gronovii. *Lug. Bat.* 1707
3401 Guidotti de Thermis Britannicis Tractat. *cum fig. Lond.* 1691
3402 Egineta de tuenda Valetudine, G. Copo Interprete. *Lovan.* 1518
3403 Grulingii Florilegii Hippocrateo-Galeno-Chymici novi. *Lipf.* 1665
3404 Philostorgii Historia Ecclesiastica J. Gothofredi. *Gen.* 1642
3405 Galeni Ars Medica. ———————— *Par.* 1543
3406 Garisch Considerat. de Saliva Humana. ———— *Lipf.* 1723
3407 Gassendi Vita Tychonis Brahei. ———— *Hagæ Comit.* 1655
3408 Oswaldi Grembs Arbor integra & ruinosa Hominis. *Franc.* 671
3409 Gyraldi Hist. Ducis Atestinis. ———————— *Ferrar.*
3410 Glandorpii Opera omnia. ———————— *Lond.* 1729
3411 D. Georgii de antiquis Italiæ Metropolibus Exercitat. *Romæ* 1722
3412 Gandlingii de Emptione Uxor. Dote & Morgengaba ex Jure Germanico Lib. ———————— *Lipf.* 1731
3413 Galeratus de Titulis Philippi Austrii Regis Catholici. *Bononiæ* 1573
3414 Ordinum Hollandiæ ac Westfrisiæ Pietas. —— *Lug. Bat.* 1613
3415 Glasii Opuscula Christiologia Mosaica. ———— *ib.* 1700
3416 Grotii Annotationes in Vetus & Novum Testamentum. *Lond.* 1727
3417 Schematismus Anatomiæ Hodiernæ Romanæ Ecclesiæ. *Colon.* 1531
3418 Gosselini Vita F. Gonzagæ Principis Molfettæ. — *Venet.* 1579
3419 Galenus de Diebus Decretoriis. ———— *Lug.* 1559
3420 Gronovius de Sestertiis. ———————— *Lug. Bat.* 1691
3421 Gatakeri de novi Instrumenti Stylo Dissertatio. *Lond.* 1648
3422 Horatii Guicciardi Sermon. Spiritual. ———— *Bonon.* 1586
3423 Blanchini de Lapide Antiati Epistola. ———— *Romæ* 1698
3424 A. Massa Gallesii contra Usum Duelli. ———— *ib.* 1554

3425

3425 Theophilo antecessore Græco Interpret. — Gen. 1620
3426 Giphanii de Ordine Judiciorum Tractat. — 1628
3427 Hygini Gromatici & Polybii de Castris Romanis quæ exstant. — — Amst. 1660
3428 Nobilitas Ecclesiæ Moguntinæ. — Mogunt. 1614
3429 Ulugh Beighi Tamerlanis Magni Nepotis Tabellæ Stellarum Fixarum. — — Oxon. 1665
3430 Harduini Nummi antiqui Populorum et Urbium illustrat. Par. 1684
3431 Rechenbergi Hist. Rei Nummariæ veteris. Amst. 1692
3432 Hankii Monumenta. — — Lipf. 1718
3433 Henckelius de Bello Gustavi Adolphi Regis Suecorum. Stet. 1631
3434 Hasii Doliorum Dimensiones. — Vitem. 1728
3435 Hugenii Systema Saturnium. — Haga Comit. 1659
3436 Hannemanni Pharus ad Ophir Auriferum. — Lub. 1725
3437 Hugenii Opuscula posthuma, 2 vol. cum fig. — Amst. 1728
3438 Harduinus de Nummis antiquis. — — Par. 1689
3439 ———Chronologiæ Prolusio de Nummis Herodiadum. ib. 1693
3440 Harprechti Tractat. Academici de Successionibus, 4 vol. Ulmæ 1698
3441 ————de Usufructu Statuario Materno. Tub. 1720
3442 Hilleri Comment. in loca Scripturæ sacræ quæ Plantarum faciunt Mentionem. — Traject. ad Rhen. 1725
3443 Hugenii Opera varia, 2 vol. — L.B. 1724
3444 Hermanni Phoronomia, cum fig. — Amst. 1716
3445 Hankii de Silesiorum majoribus Antiquitates. — Lipf. 1702
3446 Heuteri rerum Belgicarum Lib. 15. — Ant. 1598
3447 Henelii Silesiographia Renovata. — Lipf. 1704
3448 Harveii Exercitationes de Generatione Animalium, cum fig. Lond. 1651
3449 Hermanni Paradisus Batavus, cum fig. — L.B. 1698
3450 S. Cyrilli Catechesis, gr. lat. — Par. 1609
3451 Pontani Vita Christiani III. Regis Daniæ. — Han. 1729
3452 Hoferi Hercules Medicus, sive Locorum Communium Liber. — — Norib. 1675
3453 Hannemanni Tantalus Chemicus. — Hamb. 1717
3454 Hartungii Differtat. Juris Civilis. — Gief. 1729
3455 Hoepfneri de Justificatione Hominis pacatores coram Deo. Lipf. 1728
3456 Hasæi de Lapide Fundamenti cui olim Arca Fœderis imposita fuit Differtat. — — ib.
3457 Bap. Van Helmont Opera omnia. — Haf. 1707
3458 Hadrianus VI. sive Analecta Historica de Hadriano VI. collegit & notis C. Burmannus. — Traj. ad Rhen. 1727
3459 Horstii Opera Medica, 3 vol. — Goudæ 1661

3460

3460 Hippocratis de Morbis Popularibus, gr. lat. Comment. J. Freind. —— Lond. 1717
3461 Hosemiani Curionis Hermotimus. —— Basil. 1570
3462 Hoffmanni Notæ ad Hartmani Praxin Chymiatricam Lib. 2 vol. —— Lips. 1728
3463 Heyll Comment. in Galen. Lib. de Artis Medicæ. Mogunt. 1534
3464 Hankii de Silesiis indigenis Eruditis post Literarum Culturam. —— Lips 1707
3465 ——de Silesiorum rebus ab anno 550, ad 1170, exercitat. ib. 1705
3466 Haddoni Orationes & Epistolæ. —— Lond. 1657
3467 Huberi Prælectiones Juris Civilis, 3 vol. —— Lips. 1725
3468 ——Digressiones Justinianeæ. —— Franeq. 1696
3469 ——de Jure Civitatis. —— ib. 1694
3470 ——Institutiones Historiæ Civilis. —— ib. 1703
3471 Ursini Illustrium Imagines. —— Ant. 1606
3472 Ittigii de Hæresiarchis Dissertatio. —— Lips. 1703
3473 P. Jovii Novocomensis. Hist. Patriæ, Lib. 2. —— Ven. 1629
3474 T. Bezæ Icones Virorum Doctrina simul & pietate illustr. Gen. 1580
3475 Ingrassiæ de Purgatione per Medicamentum. —— Ven. 1568
3476 Imp. Theodosii, Valentiniani, &c. novellæ Constitutiones. Lut. apud R. Steph. 1571
3477 H. Jungken Corpus Pharmaceutico Chymico-Medicum. Franc.
3478 Icones Historiarum Veteris Testamenti. —— Lug. 1547
3479 Jacchini Praxis, sive in 9 Lib. Rasis Comment. ib. 1622
3480 Institutionum Forensium Lib. 4. —— Par. 1543
3481 Jesu Christi SS. Evangelia Gothice & Anglo-Saxonice. Dord. 1665
3482 S. Ignatii Epistolæ genuinæ, gr. lat. Notis Pearsoni. Oxon. 1709
3483 Adriani Isagoge in S. Scripturam. —— Aug. Vind. 1602
3484 Icones Arborum, Fruticum, Hebarum, &c. —— L. B.
3485 Falconerii Notæ ad Inscriptiones Athleticas. —— Romæ. 1668
3486 Weberi Thermarum Wisbadensium Descriptio. —— 1617
3487 Joelis Opera Medica, 3 vol. —— Rost. 1630
3488 Kircheri Scrutinium Contagiosæ Luis quæ dicitur Pestis. Lips 1671
3489 ——Splendor & Gloria Domus Joanniæ Descripta. Amst. 1672
3490 ——Iter extaticum 2. qui & Mundi Subterranei dicitur. —— Romæ 1657
3491 ——Iter extaticum Cœleste. —— Herb. 1671
3492 G. Kolbs Series Romanorum Imperator. cum Reflectionib. Historicis. —— Aug. Vind. 1727
3493 Runæ in Nummis vetustis, Nummi diversi ex Argent. Præstantiss. Nummorum in Hibernia.

3494

3494 Kreſſii Comment. in Conſtitut. Criminal. Caroli V. Imperatoris. ——— *Han.* 1730

3495 Krulli Tractat. de Regali Monitarum Jure. —— *ib.* 1728

3496 Kergeri de Fermentatione Liber Phyſico-Medicus. *Witteb.* 1663

3497 Kulmi de vera Monſtroſi Fœtus Conſtitutione. *Ged.* 1724

3498 Kyperi Anthropologia Corporis Humani Contentorum. *Lug. Bat.*

3499 Kitzelii Tractat. de Jure Monetarum. ——— *Marp.* 1632

3500 Lochneri Nerium, ſive Rhododaphne vet. & recentiorum: *Norib.* 1716

3501 Lipſi Admiranda, ſive de Magnitudine Romana Lib. cum fig. ——— *Ant.* 1605

3502 Landi ſelect. Numiſmatum præcipue Romanor. Expoſitiones. ——— *L.B.* 1695

3503 Lydii Syntagma Sacrum de Re Militari, *cum fig. Dord.* 1698

3504 Lomeiri de veterum Gentilium Luſtrationibus Syntagma. *Ultr.* 1681

3505 Loemelii Apologia. ——— *Aud.* 1631

3506 Epiſtolæ Magni Turci Laudinio editæ.

3507 Laeti rerum Danicarum Lib. 11. ——— *Franc.* 1582

3508 Leopardi Emendationes & Miſcellaneæ. ——— *Ant.* 1568

3509 Loccenii Hiſt. Suecanæ Lib. 9. ——— *Franc* 1676

3510 B. de Lezana allegatio pro Cathedralitate Eccleſiæ Sanctæ Mariæ del Pilar. ——— *Lug.* 1656

3511 Theſaurus Reliquiarum Electoralis Brunſvico-Luneburgicus. *Han.* 1713

3512 Lanciſii Diſſertat. Hiſtorica de Bovilla Peſte. —— *Romæ* 1715

3513 ——— de Nativis Romani Cœli Qualitatibus Hiſt. *ibid.* 1711

3514 Froereiſenii Comment. Theolog. de Ædificio Spirituali. *Argent.* 1728

3515 Lutherus de Servo Arbitrio contra Eraſmum. —— *ib.* 1707

3516 Hugonis Falcandi Siciliæ Hiſtoria, *lineis rubris. Par. apud Du-puys* 1550

3517 Leuſden tranſlat. Hebraica omnium Textuum Chaldaicorum. ——— *L. Bat.* 1685

3518 M. Schoti Liber Phiſionomie, Regimen Sanitatis Salerni.

3519 P. de Leyden tractat. Juridico-Politici. ——— *Amſt.* 1701

3520 Catalogus Libror. MS. Teniſoniana, & Dugdaliana. *Oxon.* 1692

3521 L. Regii Oratio ad Henricum II. Francorum Regis. *Paris, apud Morel.* 1559

3522 Cenſorinus de Die Natali, notis Lindenbrogii. *Hamb.* 1614

3523 Catalogus Nummorum, &c. in Muſeo Graingeriano. *Lond.* 1728

3524 Arcana Naturæ detecta, ab A. Van Leeuwenhoeck, *cum fig.* ——— *Delph. Bat.* 1695

4 3525 Lipsi Saturnalium Sermonum Lib. 2. qui de Gladiatoribus, *cum fig.* — *Ant.* 1598
3526 S. Loyens Hist. Ducum Brabantiæ. — *Brux.* 1672
3527 Miscellanea Chiffletiana, 4 vol. — *Amst.* 1688
3528 Masii Dissertationes Academicæ, 2 vol. — *Hamb.* 1719
3529 M. Phoebonii Historia Marsorum. — *Neap.* 1678
3530 Miscellanea Curiosa Medico-Physicæ Academiæ Naturæ Curiosorum ab anno 1670, ad annum 1688, 11 vol.
3531 Morhofi Polyhistor Literarius Philosophicus & Practicus, 2 vol. — *Lub.* 1714
3532 — Notitia Auctorum & Rerum Comment. — *ib.* 1688
3533 Merchlini Tractat. Physico-Medicus de Incantamentis. *Noriberg.* 1715
3534 Miscellanea Berolinensia, *cum fig.* — *Berol.* 1710
3535 Michelloti de Separatione Fluidorum in Corpore Animali Dissertat. *ch. max.* — *Ven.* 1721
3536 Manfredii de Annis Inerrantium Stellarum Aberrationibus. *Bonon.* 1729
3537 Rerum Amorfortiarum Scriptores duo inediti. *Lug. Bat.* 1693
3538 Matthæus de Auctionibus. — *Traject. ad Rhen.* 1653
3539 Mascampii Institutiones Historicæ. — *Amst.* 1711
3540 B. Mallinckrot de Archi-Cancellariis Sacri Romani Imperii. — 1640
3541 Menteli de vera Typographiæ Origine Parænesis. *Par.* 1640.
3542 Thomistica Mathesis vel Philosophicum Antelucanum. *Flor.* 1660
3543 Marmor Pisanum de Honore Bisellii. — *Bonon.* 1666
3544 M. Mattaire Annales Typographici, 4 vol. *ch. max. Hagæ Comit.* 1719
3545 Comment. Academiæ Scientiarum Imperialis Petropolitanæ. *Petrop.* 1728
3546 E. Martene veterum Scriptorum & Monumentorum collectio. — *Roth.* 1700
3547 Miræi de Bello Bohemico Comment. — *Brux.*
3548 Meyer vera Emmanuelis Generatio ex Virgini viro Desponsata, heb. & lat. — *Amst.* 1723
3549 Vitoni & Hidalfi Hist. Mediani in monte Vosago Monast. Ordinis S. Benedicti. — *Argent.* 1724
3550 Morestelli Philomusus. — *Lug.* 1605
3551 J. Mabillon Italicum, *cum fig.* 2 vol. — *Lut. Par.* 1724
3552 Monumenta Paderbornensia, ex Hist. Rom. Franc. Saxonica eruta, *cum fig.* — *Franc.* 1713
3553 Antiquitat. Romanar. P. Manuccii Liber de Civitate Romana. — *Romæ* 1585
3554 Magneni Exercitationes de Tabacco. — *Ticini* 1648
3555 Malpighii Dissertat. Epistolica de Bombyce, *cum fig.* *Lond.* 1669

3556

3556 Muntingii de vera Antiquorum Herba Britannica Differtat. *Amst.* 1681
3557 Pici Mirandulæ de Septiformi Sex Dierum Geneſeos enarr. *Edit. antiq. ſine anno & loco.*
3558 Malpighii de Viſcerum Structura Exercitat. Anatomica. *Bonon.* 1666
3559 Libri Moyſi V, cum Annotat. Hebraicis. *Paris, apud R. Steph.* 1541
3560 Manuale ad uſum Eccleſiæ Sariſburienſis, *foliis deauratis.* 1529
3561 Maſſoni de Epiſcopis Urbis qui Rom. Eccleſiam rexerunt. — *Par.* 1586
3562 Manſi Ærarium Evangelicum, 2 vol. — *Colon.* 1668
3563 Monumenta Pietatis & Literaria virorum. — *Franc.* 1701
3564 S. Merian Erucarum Ortus, Alimentum & Paradoxa Metamorphoſis, *cum fig.* — *Amſt.*
3565 Chaldæa Jonathæ in 6 Prophetas Interpret. *Paris, apud C. Steph.* 1559
3566 E. Martene Comment. in Regulam S. Benedicti. *Paris* 1690
3567 Marianus de Etruria Metropoli. — *Romæ* 1728
3568 Erici Mauritii Diſſertationes et Opuſcula. — *Argent.* 1724
3569 J. a Mele Notitia majorum plurimas Lubecenſium. *Lipſiæ* 1707
3570 Maccii Emblemata. — *Bonon.* 1628
3571 Leonis Imp. Tactica, gr. lat. notis Meurſii. — *L.B.* 1612
3572 Morgagni adverſaria Anatomica omnia, 2 vol. — *Pat.* 1719
3573 ——— Epiſtolæ Anatomicæ duæ. — *L.B.* 1728
3574 Methodus Medendi Homoboni Piſonis. — *Pat.* 1726
3575 H. Mercurialis de Arte Gymnaſtica Lib. 6. — *Par.* 1577
3576 Miſcellanea Medico-Phyſica Academiæ Naturæ Curioſorum Germaniæ, *cum fig.* — — *ib.* 1672
3577 Mabillon de Liturgia Gallicana. — *Lut. Par.* 1685
3578 Muleni Numiſmata Danorum et Vicinarum Gentium, edit. a F. Bartholino. — — *Hafn.* 1670
3579 Miſſæ aliquot pro Sacerdotibus itinerantibus in Anglia. 1615
3580 Maffei Hiſt. Indicarum Lib. 16. — *Berg.* 1690
3581 Malpighii Opera poſthuma. — *Amſt.* 1700
3582 Meurſi Cecropia, et Areopagus. — *L.B.* 1722, & 24
3583 ——— Miſcellanea Laconica. — *Amſt.* 1661
3584 ——— Panathenæa et Græcia Feriata. *L.B.* 1619
3585 ——— Piſiſtratus et Themis Attica. *ib.* 1623, & 84
3586 ——— Fortuna Attica. — *ib.* 1622
3587 ——— Regnum Atticum. — *Amſt.* 1633
3588 ——— Atticæ Lectiones, et Archontes Athenienſes. *L.B.* 1617, & 22
3589 ——— de Regno Laconico, & Piræeus. *Ult.* 1687, & 6
3590 ——— Hiſtoria Danica. — *Hafn.* 1630
3591 Noris de Epochis Syromacedonum Diſſertat. — *Lipſ.* 1696

3592 Magni August. Niphi Opuscula. ——— *Venet.* 1535
3593 Newtoni Principia Philosophiæ, *ch. max.* —— *Lond.* 1726
3594 Osiandri Theologia moralis. ——— *Tubingæ.* 1678
3595 Olearii Bibliotheca Scriptorum ecclesiasticorum. *Jenæ.* 1711
3596 M. de l'Obel Stirpium illustrationes. ——— *Lond.* 1655
3597 Oricellarii de Bello Italico Comment. *ch. max.* —— *ib.* 1724
3598 Oroseii annotat. in Interpretes Ætii.
3599 Onosandri Strategicus gr. lát. ——— 1600
3600 Pitcarnii Opuscula Medica. ——— *Rot.* 1714
3601 Exercitatio de Pauli in Urbem Romam Ingressu. *Jenæ* 1731
3602 Promptuarium, Icones. —— *Lug. apud Rovill.* 1581
3603 Icones & Vitæ Professorum Patavii. ——— *Patav.* 1682
3604 Liber Psalmorum Davidis Arab. & Lat. —— *Romæ.* 1614
3605 Plantavitii Chronologia præsulum Lodovensium. *Aramontii.* 1634
3606 Plexiaci Lexicon Philosophicum. —— *Hagæ Comit.* 1716
3607 Ptolomæi Liber de Analemmate Commandini notis. *Romæ.* 1562
3608 Bap. Portæ de refractione Optices Lib. IX. — *Neapoli.* 1593
3609 Pezelii præcepta Genethliaca. ——— *Franc.* 1607
3610 Poleni Epistolarum Mathematicarum fasciculus. *Patav.* 1729
3611 Papaver ex omni Antiquitate erutum. —— *Noriberg.* 1718
3612 L. Portii de Sestertio, Talentis & Ponderibus antiquis. *Basil.*
3613 Zucchi nova de Machinis Philosophia ——— *Romæ* 1649
3614 Nemesius de Natura Hominis. —— *Lug. apud S. Gryph.* 1538
3615 Natalis Comitis Historia sui temporis. —— *Venet.* 1572
3616 Naugeri Patritii Veneti Orationes duæ. —— *ib.* 1530
3617 Nova Polonica ex Comitiis Grodnensibus de Legatis Pont. Max. & Regis Mag. Britanniæ. ——— *Colon.* 1728
3618 D. Wrenn Numismatum Antiquorum Sylloge. *Lond.* 1708
3619 P. Nenter Fundamenta Medicinæ Theoretico-Practica, 4 vol. *Argent.* 1718
3620 Nardii Noctes Geniales. ——— *Bonon.* 1656
3621 Noris de Cruce stationali Investigatio Historica, *cum fig.* *Romæ* 1694
3622 Thesaurus Numismatum Antiquorum cum Comment. Oiseli. ——— ——— *Amst* 1677
3623 Bonanni Observat. circa Viventia, quæ in rebus non viventibus reperiuntur. ——— *Romæ.* 1691
3624 Outram de Sacrificiis. ——— *Lond.* 1677
3625 Origenis de Oratione, Liber gr. lat. G. Reading. — *ib.* 1728
3626 Pignorius de Servis & eorum apud Veteres Ministeriis. *Patav.* 1694
3627 Pancratii Justiniani Epistolæ. —— *Venet.* 1534
3628 Philelfi Epistolæ Familiares, *Editio antiqua, sine anno & loco.*
3629 Silvestri a Petra sancta Symbola Heroica. ——— *Amst* 1682
3630 Peyeri de Ruminantibus & Ruminatione Comment. *Basil.* 1685

3631

3631 Pfalterium Ethiopicum.
3632 Hulfii Numifmata. ——— *Spiræ.* 1595
3633 Pufendorf de Jure Naturæ & Gentium.——— *Amft.* 1704
3634 Paullini Cynographia curiofa, feu Canis Defcriptio. *Noriberg.* 1685
3635 Julius Pontederus de Floris Natura. ——— *Patav.* 1720
3636 Polemo-Middinia Carmen Macoronicum.——— *Oxon.* 1691
3637 Salomonii Agri Patavini Infcriptiones facræ & prophanæ. *Patav.* 1696
3638 Poftellus de Etruria Regione, *foliis deaurat.* *Florent* 1551
3639 Palladius de Gentibus Indiæ & Bragmanibus gr. lat. *Lond.* 1665
3640 Medici antiqui Græci J. Paulo lat. donati. ——— *Bafil.* 1581
3641 Pancratii de præclaris Venetæ Ariftocratiæ Geftis Liber. *Venet.* 1527
3642 Cavitelli Patritii Cremonen. Annales. ——— *Cremonæ.* 1588
3643 Ponteceræ Differtationes Botannicæ 11. *cum fig.*——— 1719
3644 Pearfonii Opera pofthuma Chronologica, &c. — *Lond.* 1688
3645 Petiti Mifcellaneæ. ——— *Paris, apud Morel.* 1630
3646 Henrici VIII. Pia & Catholica Chriftiani Hominis Inftitutio. ——— ——— *Lond.* 1544
3647 Proceffionale ad ufum Ecclefiæ Sarisburienfis.
3648 Petiti in Aretæi Cappadocis Lib. Comment. *ch. max.* *Lond.* 1726
3649 Priolus de Rebus Gallicis. ——— *Par.* 1665
3650 Palmarii Conftantini de Morbis Contagiofis Lib. VII. *ib.* 1578
3651 Fragmenta Vet. Juris Auctorum. *Lut. apud* R. *Steph.* 1573
3652 Pujolii Carmen de Pace. ——— *Paris.* 1559
3653 Pfalterium Davidis Æthiopice & Latine. ——— *Franc.* 1701
3654 Tractat. de Origine Hebræorum eorumque Regimine. *Venet.* 1588
3655 Panegyris de memorabili confederatorum aliquot Chriftianorum Principúm. ——— *Argent.* 1572
3656 Gaffendi Vita Fabricii. Kirsky *Hagæ Comit.* 1655
3657 Tomafini Vitæ Virorum illuftrium.——— *Patav.* 1644
3658 Procli Sphera gr. lat. ——— *Lond.* 1620
3659 Hiftoria Dynaftiarum Arab. Lat. E. Pocock. ——— *Oxon.* 1663
3660 Portiforium feu Breviarium ad ufum Ecclefiæ Sarisburienfis. 1556
3661 Peritfol Itinera Mundi Heb. Lat. notis T. Hyde. *Oxon.* 1691
3662 Petiti variæ Lectiones. ——— *Paris, apud Morel.* 1633
3663 S. Nili Epiftolæ gr. lat. *foliis deauratis.* ——— *Paris, e Typo. Regia.* 1657
3664 Hybneri Loci Theologiæ. ——— 1670
3665 Rutilii Orationes tres. ——— *Romæ.* 1536
3666 De Ignibus Feftivis, Jocofis, Artificialibus, & feriis variifque eorum ftructuris. ——— 1611
3667 Rochii de Infignibus Familiarum Lib. XI. ——— *Lucæ.* 1576

3668

3668 Roffin Comment. omnium a Creato Orbe Historiar. *Lut. apud Bene-Natum*. 1571

3669 Richerii Historia Consiliorum generalium, 2 vol. *ch. max. Colon*. 1683

3670 Renealmi Specimen Historiæ Plantarum, cum fig. *Par*. 1611

3671 Rotgersius de Successione Legitima. —— *Lug. Bat*. 1727

3672 Rigaltii Glossarium. —— —— *Lut*. 1601

3673 Rabirii Hastarum & Auctionum Origo, Ratio & Solennia. *Lut. apud C. Steph*. 1534

3674 Auctores Finium regundorum Rigaltii observat. & notæ. *Lut*. 1614

3675 Riccii rerum Italicarum sui Temporis narrationes. *Venet*. 1655

3676 Redmanni de Justificatione Opus. —— *Ant*. 1555

3677 Richerii de Rebus Turcarum ad Fran. Gallorum Regem Christianiss. Lib. V. —— *Paris, apud R. Steph*. 1540

3678 Rulandi Lexicon Alchemiæ. —— 1612

3679 Rueffus de Conceptu & Generatione Hominis. *Franc*. 1580

3680 Rivii Rerum Francicarum Decades IV. —— *Brux*. 1651

3681 B. de Roa de Cordubæ in Hispania Betica principatu Lib. *Lug*. 1617

3682 Meteorologia de Igneis, Aereis, Aqueisque Corporibus Auth. F. Resta Talleocotio.

3683 J. Roffensis Episcopus contra Lutherum. —— *Colon*. 1525

3684 Salmasii duarum Inscriptionum Veterum explicatio. *Lut. Par*. 1619

3685 Selecta Numismata antiqua ex Museo Seguini. —— *ib*. 1666

3686 Severinus de Viperæ Natura, cum fig. —— *Patav*. 1651

3687 Salmasii de Re Militari Romanorum Liber. *Lug. Bat*. 1657

3688 Spigelii Isagoges in Rem Herbariam, Lib. II. *Patav*. 1606

3689 Scaligeri in Lib. Aristotelis de Plantis. —— *Lut* 1556

3690 Sturmii Collegium experimentale sive curiosum. *Noriberg*. 1677

3691 Psalterium Davidis Lat. Saxonicum vetus a J. Spelmanno. *Lond*. 1640

3692 Sbaragli Anima sensitiva Brutorum demonstrata contra Cartesium. —— —— *Bonon*. 1716

3693 Piscium querelæ & vindiciæ expositæ a Scheuchzero. *Tiguri*. 1708

3694 Seldeni Uxor Ebraica. —— *Franc*. 1673

3695 Scheuchzeri Graminum, Juncorum, Cyperorum, Cyperoidum iisque affinium Historia, *cum fig*. —— *Tiguri*. 1719

3696 Schurigii Seminis Humani consideratio Physico-Medico Legalis. —— —— *Franc*. 1720

3697 Sigonius de Antiquo Jure Provinciarum. —— *Venet*. 1568

3698 Seldeni Liber de Nummis. —— *Lond*. 1675

3699 —— de Synedriis. —— —— *Amst*. 1679

3700 Salmasii Epistolæ. —— —— *Lug. Bat*. 1646

3701 Sigonius de Antiquo Jure Civium Romanorum. —— *Venet*. 1563

3702

3702 Serry Exercitationes Hist. Criticæ Polemicæ de Christo ejusque Virgine Matre. ——— ——— ib. 1719
3703 Serletti Philosophia Naturæ. ——— ——— Berolini. 1694
3704 Severus Alexandrinus de Ritibus Baptismi. ——— Ant. 1572
3705 Schomeri Exegesis in Epistolas Pauli ad Hebræos. Rostoch. 1729
3706 Goelicke Spiritus Animalis merens exul. ——— Franc. 1731
3707 Syngeli de laudibus divi Dionysii Lib. Paris, apud R. Steph. 1547
3708 Zanichelli de Ferro ejusque Nivis Preparatione Dissertatio. Venet. 1719
3709 Specimen Censuræ Regnerianæ. ——— Gissæ Hassorum.
3710 Sidonii Episcopi Opera. ——— Paris. 1652
3711 Sadoleti Orationes duæ. ——— Venet. 1561
3712 Schelstrate tractat. de Sensu & Auctoritate Decretorum Constantiniensis Concilii. ——— Rom. 1686
3713 Schotti Thaumaturgus Physicus, 2 vol. ——— 1659
3714 Santanelli Magicæ Magneticæ Mummialis Scientiæ explanatio. ——— ——— Colon. 1723
3715 Sturmii Prælectiones Academicæ. ——— Franc. 1722
3716 Santanelli Lucubrationes Physico-Mechanicæ — Venet. 1698
3717 Laus augustiss. Conjugum Magni Leopoldi & Magdalene. 1724
3718 Serrarii Historia Moguntina. ——— Mogunt. 1604
3719 Smithi Vitæ Illustrium Virorum. ——— Lond. 1707
3720 Struvii Syntagma Historiæ Germanicæ, 2 vol. Jenæ. 1716
3721 H. Spoor Favissæ utriusque Antiquitatis tam Romanæ quam Græcæ. ——— Ultraject. 1707
3722 Sperlingii Dissertatio de Nummis non Cusis tam veterum quam recentiorum. ——— Amst. 1700
3723 Scaliger de Subtilitate. ——— Lut. 1557
3724 Scheuchzeri Itinera Alpina, *cum fig.* ——— Lond. 1708
3725 Sylloges Epistolarum a Viris illustribus Scriptarum collect. per Burmannum, 5 vol. *ch. max.* ——— Leidæ. 1727
3726 Spanhemii dissertat. de præstantia & usu Numismatum antiquorum. ——— Amst. 1661
3727 Struvii Syntagma Juris Feudalis. ——— Franc. 1726
3728 ———Antiquitatum Romanorum Syntagma.——Jenæ. 1707
3729 Smetii Antiquitates Neomagenses, cum fig. Noviomag. 1678
3730 Schilteri Codex Juris Alemannici Feudalis.— Argent. 1697
3731 Scaligeri Opuscula varia. ——— Paris. 1610
3732 Walchini decas Fabularum Humani Generis. Argent. 1609
3733 Spanhemii Orbis Romanus. ——— Lond. 1703
3734 Sommeri Regum Vannianum antiquam Silesiam complectens. ——— ——— Vratislaviæ. 1722
3735 A. de Savissy de Mysticis Galliæ Scriptoribus. Paris. 1639
3736 Scribani Antverpiæ. ——— Ant. 1610
3737 S. de Ludwiger Dissertat. Politico-Historica de Ordine Fœminarum Equestri. ——— ——— ———Halæ

3738

3738 Antonii de Symeonibus de Bello Transylvanico & Pannonico Lib. vi. ——— *Romæ* 1713
3739 Sonnemanni Usus Modernus Novellarum Constitutionum Divi Justiniani. ——— *Franc.* 1725
3740 Regimen Sanitatis Salerni, *editio antiqua, sine anno & locó.*
3741 Schultingii Dissertationes de Recusatione Judicis. *Franeq.* 1708
3742 Schurigii Chylologia Historico-Medica. ——— *Dresdæ* 1725
3743 Deleboe Sylvii Opera Medica. ——— *Amst.* 1679
3744 Vegetii Mulomedicina. ——— *Basil.* 1574
3745 Schamsky Promptuarium parvum Medico-Practicum. 1714
3746 Sanctorii Methodi vitandor. Errorum omnium qui in Arte Medica contingunt. ——— *Genev.* 1630
3747 Schmidt Miscellaneorum Physicorum Fasciculus.
3748 Struvii Schediasma de Partu supposito & Custodia Corporis Fœminarum illustrium. ——— *Jenæ* 1732
3749 Schachtii Exercitatio Medico-Practica. ——— *Herbornæ* 1624
3750 Spigelii Anatomia, *cum fig.* ——— *Franc.* 1632
3751 Schroderi Pharmacopœia Medico-Chymica. ——— *Lug.* 1649
3752 Seldenus de Successionibus in Bona defuncti. ——— *Lond.* 1631
3753 ——— Eutychii Origenes Comment. ——— *ib.* 1642
3754 Scaligeri Epistola de Vetustate & Splendore Gentis Scaligeræ. *Lug. Bat.* 1694
3755 Schotti Observationum Humanarum Lib. V. — *Hanov.* 1615
3756 Sigonii Hist. Occidentalis Imperii. ——— *Basil.* 1579
3757 Origenis Philocalia, gr. lat. ——— *Par.* 1619
3758 Turretini Nubes Testium. ——— *Franc.* 1720
3759 Servetus de Trinitate.
3760 Telesius de Rerum Natura. ——— *Neapoli* 1570
3761 C. Thomas Manuductio ad Globum Artificialem Cælestem, *cum multis fig.* ——— *August. Vindel.* 1731
3762 Tuberonis Comment. de Temporibus suis. ——— *Franc.* 1603
3763 Tomasini Gymnasium Patavinum, Lib. v. ——— *Utini* 1654
3764 Academia Gissena restaurata, *corio turcico.* ——— *Gissæ* 1652
3765 Tractatus de Curia Pisana. ——— 1548
3766 Tonsi Vita Emanuelis Philiberti Allobrogum Ducis. *Mediol.* 1602
3767 Theatrum Mulierum, *cum fig.* ——— *Franc.* 1586
3768 Tomasini Petrarcha redivivus. ——— *Patav.* 1650
3769 Themis Romano-Suecica. ——— *Gryphiswaldiæ* 1729
3770 Theophili Antecess. Institutiones, gr. lat. ——— *Lug.* 1608
3771 Cautelæ circa Præcognita Juris-prudentiæ in Usum Auditorii Thomasiani. ——— *Halæ* 1720
3772 Thesaurus Secretorum curiosorum. ——— *Col. Allob.* 1709
3773 Alexand. Turamini ad Rubricam Pandect. de Legibus Comment. ——— *Florent.* 1592
3774 Tractatus de Libertatibus Ecclesiæ Gallicanæ. ——— *Leodii* 1684
3775 N. Testamentum in Ling. Arab.

3776

3776 Tozzi in Hippocratis Aphorismos Comment. 2 vol. *Neapoli* 1693
3777 Teichmerii Institutiones Legales vel Forenses. *Jenæ* 1723
3778 ——— Institutiones Chemiæ dogmaticæ & experiment. *ib.* 1729
3779 Twyni Antiquitatis Academiæ Oxoniensis Apologia. *Oxon.* 1608
3780 Teisserii Catalogus Auctorum & Bibliothecar. cum Labbæi Bibliotheca Nummaria. ——— *Genev.* 1686
3781 Tonstallus de Veritate Corporis & Sanguinis Dom. Nostri J. Christi in Eucharistia. ——— *Lutet.* 1554
3782 Fasciculus Similitudinum sacræ Scripturæ.
3783 Tournefort Institutiones Rei Herbariæ, 3 vol. ——— *Par.* 1719
3784 Tollii Epistolæ Itinerariæ, *cum fig.* ——— *Amst.* 1700
3785 Vaillant Numismata Imperatorum August. & Cæsarum. *Lut. Par.* 1698
3786 Schramm de Vitis & Scriptis famosi Athei Julii Cæsaris Vanini. ——— *Custrini* 1709
3787 Heideri Orationes 11 de Vulpeculis Scholasticis. *Lub.* 1728
3788 Ant. Viperani de Bello Melitensi Historia. ——— *Perus.* 1576
3789 Inscriptiones antiquæ Augustæ Vindelicorum, cum Notis Velseri. ——— *Venet.* 1590
3790 Veteris Philosophi profundiss. Physica restituta. *Tub.* 1725
3791 Verdries Physica. ——— *Gissæ* 1728
3792 Vignolii Dissertat. de Anno primo Imperii Severi Alexandri. *Romæ* 1712
3793 Contarenus de Frumentaria Romanorum Largitione. *Venet.* 1609
3794 Oratio P. Victorii in Maximilianum II. Cæsarem mortuum. *Florent. apud Juntas*
3795 Velschii Dissertatio Medico-Philosophica de Ægagropilis. 1666
3796 Ursini Antiquitates Hebraicæ Scholastico-Academicæ. *Hafniæ* 1667
3797 Vinnii Tractatus v. de Jurisdictione, &c. *Traject. ad Rhen.* 1697
3798 Liber Pontificalis de Gestis Romanorum Pontificum. *Romæ* 1724
3799 Vander-Muelen Exercitat. in Titulum Digestorum de Justitia & Jure. ——— *Traject. ad Rhen.* 1723
3800 Vinnii in iv. Lib. Institutionum Imperialium Comment. *Amst.* 1655
3801 Veslingii Syntagma Anatomicum, cum Comment. *ib.* 1666
3802 Veschius de Dracunculis Veterum, *cum fig. Aug. Vindel.* 1674
3803 Veri Rerum Venetarum Lib. iv. ——— *Patav.* 1638
3804 Vossii variæ Observationes. ——— *Lond.* 1685
3805 Vallerioli Comment. in vi. Galeni Lib. de Morbis & Symtomatis. ——— *Lug. apud S. Gryph.* 1540

3806 Æ. Vici omnium Cæsarum verissimæ Imagines.—— 1544
3807 ——— Augustarum Imagines. ————Lut. Par. 1619
3808 Usserii de Græca LXX. Interpretum Versione Syntagma. Lond. 1655
3809 Sarcoma e Pudendo Muliebre resectum———Vitemb.
3810 P. Vergilius de Inventoribus Rerum.
3811 Vaillant Numismata Imperatorum Romanorum. *Lut. Paris.* 1694
3812 Æ. Vici Comment. in vetera Imperator. Romanor. Numism. *Venet.* 1560
3813 Pierii Hieroglyphica.——————*Col. Agrip.* 1631
3814 Legenda aurea.———————————1507
3815 T. Willis Pharmaceutice Rationalis.————*Oxon.* 1674
3816 Waltheri Exegesis Epistolæ Apostoli Judæ.
3817 Wagenselii Exercitationes varii Argumenti. *Norimb.* 1719
3818 Weidleri Tractatus de Machinis Hydraulicis. *Witemberg.* 1728
3819 Wagenselii de Re Monetali veterum Romanorum Dissertat. 1723
3820 Diversarum Gentium Histor. antiquæ Scriptores tres. *Hamb.* 1640
3821 Weismanni Dissertationes varii Argumenti. *Tubingæ* 1725
3822 Wallini de Sancta Genouefa Disquisitio.———*Witteb.* 1723
3823 Wuchereri Vindiciæ Æternæ Divinitatis Jesu Christi contra Whiston.——————————*Jenæ* 1732
3824 Walchii Primitiæ sacræ Jenenses. ———*ib.* 1726
3825 Signa antiqua e Museo J. de Wilde.————*Amst.* 1700
3826 Waserus de antiquis Nummis Hebræorum, Chaldæorum, & Syrorum.————————*Tiguri* 1605
3827 Wedelii Dissertationes Medicæ Selectæ. ———*Jenæ* 1686
3828 S. Winton Episcopi ad M. Bucerum de Impudenti ejusdem Pseudologiæ Conquestio.————————*Lovan.* 1544
3829 Willisii Pathologiæ Cerebri Nervosi Generis Specimen. *Oxon.* 1667
3830 Wolfii Elementa Matheseos universæ. ————*Genev.* 1732
3831 Wasi Senarius, sive de Legibus & Licentia Veterum Poetarum. *Oxon.* 1687
3832 Weismanni Dissertationes varii Argumenti.—*Tubingæ* 1725
3833 Schenckii Isagoge Historica eaque generalis.—— *Franc.* 1684
3834 { Ars Medica Jo. Dominici Sala Patavini. ——— *Patav.* 1641
Alexand. de Vicentinis de Calore per Motum excitat. *Veron.* 1634
Claudinus de Ingressu ad Infirmos.————— *Venet.* }
3835 Portius de Coloribus, de Dolore, Maggius de Vulnerum Sclopetorum.
3836 Jenisii Annebergæ Misniæ Urbis Historia. —*Dresdæ* 1605
3837 Lindenbrogii Hypotyposis Arcium, Palatiorum, Libror. &c. *Franc.* 1592
3838 Thobiæ Sacro sanctæ Hist. Elegiaco Carmine.——*Basil.* 1563

3840

3840 Caii Orationes. ——— *Romæ* 1623
3841 Cyriaci Ducatus Mantuæ. ——— 1629

Libri Classici. Octavo.

Notis Variorum.

3842 Erasmi Colloquia. ——— *Amst.* 1693
3843 Minucius Felix. ——— *Lug. Bat.* 1672
3844 Cæsaris Comment. ——— *ib.* 1713
3845 L. Florus. ——— *Amst.* 1702
3846 Hesiodus. ——— *ib.* 1701
3847 Terentius. ——— *ib.* 1686
3848 Senecæ Tragœdiæ. ——— *ib.* 1682
3849 Pervigilium Veneris. ——— *Hagæ Comit.* 1712
3850 Phædri Fabulæ. ——— *Amst.* 1698
3851 Velleius Paterculus. ——— *Lug. Bat.* 1719
3852 Ovidii Opera, 3 vol. ——— *Amst.* 1683
3853 Alexander ab Alexandro, 2 vol. ——— *Lug. Bat.* 1673
3854 Grotius de Jure Belli ac Pacis. ——— *Amst.* 1680
3855 Polyæni Strategemata. ——— *Lug. Bat.* 1690
3856 Corn. Nepos. ——— *ib.* 1675
3857 Q. Curtius. ——— *Hagæ Comit.* 1708
3858 Plauti Comœdiæ. ——— *Lug. Bat.* 1644
3859 Lactantii Opera. ——— *ib.* 1660
3860 Appianus Alexandrinus, 2 vol. ——— *Amst.* 1670
3861 Æliani varia Historia. ——— *Lug. Bat.* 1701
3862 Ausonii Opera. ——— *Amst.* 1671
3863 Sulpitius Severus. ——— *Lug. Bat.* 1647
3864 Sallustius. ——— *ib.* 1649
3865 Mythographi Latini. ——— *Amst.* 1681
3866 Virgilii Opera, 3 vol. ——— *Lug. Bat.* 1680
3867 Juvenalis & Persius. ——— *ib.* 1648
3868 Plinii Hist. Naturalis, 3 vol. ——— *ib.* 1669
3869 ——— Panegyricæ. ——— *ib.* 1675
3870 ——— Epistolæ. ——— *ib.* 1669
3871 Luciani Opera, 2 vol. ——— *Amst.* 1687
3872 Lucanus. ——— *ib.* 1658
3873 Justini Historia. ——— *Lug. Bat.* 1719
3874 Ciceronis Opera, 11 vol. ——— *Amst.* 1699
3875 ——— Epistolæ. ——— *Hagæ Comit.* 1725

R 2 3876

3877 Ciceronis Opera omnia, 10 vol.——1642
3878 Horatii Opera, 3 vol. ——1639
3879 Virgilii Opera. ——1636
3880 Venatici Scriptores.——1643
3881 Terentius.——1635
3882 Livii Hist. Romana, 6 vol.——1634
3883 Sallustius. ——1634
3884 Quintus Curtius. ——1633
3885 Cæsaris Comment.——1635
3886 Plinii Hist. Naturalis, 3 vol.——1635
3887 —— Epistolæ & Panegyricus.——1640
3888 Lucius Florus. ——1638
3889 Senecæ Opera, 3 vol.——1639
3890 Claudiani Opera, 2 vol.——1650
3891 Erasmus. ——1636
3892 Barclaius.——1630
3893 Sulpitius Severus. ——1635
3894 Prudentius.——1656
3895 Justinus.——1640
3896 Cornelius Tacitus, 2 vol.——1640
3897 Velleius Paterculus. ——1639
3898 Ovidii Opera, 3 vol.——1629

(Elzev.)

N. B. *The above Books are all extremely fair, and are very nicely cover'd in Morocco and gilt on the Leaves, they make an entire Sett of the old Elzevir Classicks. The Louvre Edition of Suetonius is added to them, it being of the same Size, and beautifully printed.*

3899 Alexander ab Alexandro. ——*Franc.*1591
3900 ——Idem. ——*Paris apud Parvum* 1549
3901 Apollonii Rhodii Argonautica, gr. lat. Comment. & Notis illustrat.——*Lug. Bat.*1641
3902 —— Interpretatio antiqua. —— 1541
3903 Alphabetum Græcum. ——*Paris apud Wechel.*1530
3904 Aratei Phænomena, gr. Aratosthenis & Dionysii Hymnos, gr. ——*Oxon* 1672
3905 Anthologia, sive Epigrammat. Græcorum.——*ib* 1724
3906 Æschynis & Demosthenis Orationes, gr. lat. Explicat. P. Foulkes & J. Friend. ——*ib.*1725
3907 Andronici Rhodii Ethica, gr. lat. Interpret. Heinsii. *Cant.* 1679
3908 Aristotelis Opera, Gr. Lat. 2 vol.——1607
3909 —— Politica, gr. lat. cum Paraphras. Heinsii. *Lugd. Bat.*1621
3910 —— Physica, gr. 2 vol.——*Venet. apud Aldum* 1551
3911 —— Rhetorica, gr. lat. Not. Var. ——*Cant.*1728
3912 —— de Moribus, gr. ——*Argent.*1556
3913 —— de Arte Dicendi, gr.——*Paris apud Vascosan.*1549
3914 —— Prædicamenta Porphyrii Explanat.——*ib. ib.*1548
3915 —— & Theoprastus, gr.—— *Par. apud H. Steph.*1557

3916

3916 Aristotelis Organon, gr. ———— Bas. 1559
3917 Æsopi Fabulæ, gr. lat. ———— ib. apud Frob. 1524
3918 ———Idem, lat. ————Lut. apud R. Steph 1545
3919 ———Idem, lat. studio C. Daumi.———— Lips 1724
3920 ———Idem, Lat. notis F. Nilant. ————L.B 1709
3921 ——— Idem, lat. —— ———— Ant. 1724
3922 ———Idem. gr. lat. ———— L.B 1626
3923 ———et Abstemii Fabulæ.——— Lug. apud S. Gryph. 1540
3924 ———Idem. —— ———— Argent. 1523
3925 ———Fabularum Delectus, gr. lat. ch. max.—— Ox. 1690
3926 Batrachomyomachia, gr. lat. M. Mattaire. ——Lond. 1721
3927 Barberini postea Urbini VIII. Poemata. ————. Ox. 1726
3928 Boethius de Consololatione Philosoph. cor. turcico, fol deaur.
3929 ————Idem. ———— Par. 1640
3930 Bosi Animadversiones ad Scriptores quosdam Græcos. Franc.
1715
3931 Burtoni veteris Linguæ Persicæ qui apud Priscos Scriptores Græc. & Lat. reperiri potuerunt. ———— Lub. 1720
3932 Busbeii Hebraicæ Grammatices Rudimenta. Lond. 1717
3933 Bezæ Vezelii Poemata. ———— apud H. Steph. 1569
3934 Clenardi Tabula in Grammat. Hæbr. ———— Par. 1552
3935 Cebetis Thebani Tabula, gr. —— Par. apud Wech 1537
3936 Couleii Poemata Latina. ———— Lond. 1668
3937 Claudi Claudiani Poemata, recensuit C. Barthius. Hanov.
1612
3938 Clarke Christiados Carmen. ———— Brug. 1670
3939 Q. Curtius, M. Mattaire, ch. max. & minor. Lond. 1716
3940 ——notis Erasmi. ————' Lug apud S. Gryph. 1541
3941 ——Idem. ———— Par apud Colin. 1543
3942 Catullus, Tibullus, & Propertius, cum Comm. A. Mureti.
Ven. apud Ald. 1558
3943 ——Idem, M. Mattaire, ch. max. & minor Lond 1715
3944 ——Idem. ———— Ven. apud Ald 1515
3945 ——Idem, recensuit J. Scaliger. Lutetiæ, apud Patisson.
1557
3946 ——Idem, accesserunt C. Galli Fragmenta. Lug. apud S.
Gryph. 1542
3947 —— Idem. ———— Par. apud Colin. 1529
3948 Cæsaris Comment. M. Mattaire, ch. max.—— Lond. 1716
3949 ——Idem, cum notis, ex Biblioth. F. Ursini. Ant. apud
Plant. 1570
3950 ——Idem. ———— Lut. apud R. Steph. 1544
3951 ——Idem. ———— Ven. apud Aldum 1519
3952 ——Idem, ab Aldo Manutio Emendat. & Scholiis illustrat.
ib. ib. 1575
3953 ——Idem, 2 vol. lineis rubris. Lug. apud S. Gryph. 1546
3954 ——Idem, notis Glareani. ———— ib. ib. 1536
3955 ——Idem. ———— Flor. apud Junt. 15[illegible]4

3956

3956 ——Idem. ——— — *L.B.*1619
3957 ——Idem, *cor. turc. fol. deaur.* ——— 1569
3958 Ciceronis Opera, 8 vol. *corio turcico, fol. deauratis. Paris, apud R. Steph.*
3960 ————Opera, Gronovii, 11 vol. —— *L.B.*1692
3961 ————Opera, notis var. recensuit J. Verburgius, 16 vol. *Amst.*1724
3962 ————Tusculanæ Disputationes, cum Comment. Davisii. *Cant.*1730
3963 ————Rhetorica & de Inventione. —— *Ant.*1585
3964 ————Idem, variæ Lectiones. *Paris, apud Colinæum.* 1545
3965 ————Idem, ex Castigat. Boulierii, *lin. rubr. fol. deaur. Lug.*1560
3966 ————Idem, ex Castigat. Victorii & Manutii. *Lug. apud S. Gryph.*1548
3967 ————Epistolæ Familiares.—— *Lut. apud Patiss.*1578
3968 ————Idem, P. Manutii Scholia. *Paris, apud R. Steph.* 1550
3969 ————Idem, recensuit Cellarius. ——— *Lips.*1722
3970 ————Idem, cum Comment. diverſ. *apud. H. Steph.* 1577
3971 ————Idem, Lambino Emendata. — *Lond.*1591
3972 ————Idem, ex recensione Grævii. ——— *Amst.*1689
3973 ————Idem, notis P. Manutii. *Ant. apud Plantin.* 1568
3974 ———— Idem, notis Manutii. ——— *Amst.*1626
3975 ————Idem. ——— *Ven. apud Ald* 1522
3976 ———— Philosophia, 2 vol. *fol. deaur. ligat. Grolieriana, exempl. nitidiss.* ——— — *ib.ib.*1523
3977 ———— Idem, 2 vol. ——— *Par. apud Colin.*1549
3978 ————Idem, ex castigatione Boulierii, 2 vol. *lin. rubr. fol. deaur.* ——— ——— *Lug.*1562
3979 ————Philippicas, emendat. P. Manutii. *Paris, apud R. Steph.*1543
3980 ————de Natura Deorum, notis var. recensuit Davisius. *Cant.*1723
3981 ————de Oratore Lib. 3. ——— *Lug.*1560
3982 ————Idem, recensuit T. Cockman.——— *Oxon.*1706
3983 ————de Partitione Oratoria, notis Sturmii. *Argent.* 1571
3984 ————Idem. ——— *Paris, apud R. Steph.*1528
3985 ————Epistolæ ad Atticum, Emendat. L. Malæspinæ. *Ven.*1564
3986 ————Idem, cum Latina eorum Interpret. *Paris, apud Colin.*1532
3987 ———— Idem, Emendat. Lambini. *Lutetiæ, apud Dupuys.* 1573

3988

3988 ——— Idem, P. Manutii Comment. *Venet. apud Aldum* 1547

3989 ———Idem, P. Manutii Comment. *Paris, apud R. Steph.* 1543

3990 ——— Idem, ex castigat. Boulierii, *lineis rubris, foliis deauratis.* ——— *Lug.* 1561

3991 ———de Officiis, notis Tooly, ch. max. & min. *Oxon.* 1717

3992 ———Idem, ex recensione Grævii.——— *Amst.* 1699

3993 ——— Oratio pro Cœlio Comment. Tistini. *Par. apud Colin.* 1534

3994 ———Oratio, pro Sextio P. Manutii Comment. *cor. tur. fol. deaur.* ———*Ven. apud Aldum* 1559

3995 ———Orationes, cum Comment. Asconii.——*Lug.* 1551

3996 ———Orationes Selectæ, Cellarii. ——— *Jenæ* 1708

3997 ——— Orationes, 2 vol. — *Paris, apud R. Steph.* 1543

3998 ——— Orationes Selectæ. ———*Amst.* 1657

3999 ———Fragmenta, Sigonii Collecta & Scholiis illustrat. *Ven.* 1559

4000 ———de Legibus, notis var. recensuit Davisius. *Cant.* 1727

4001 ———de Somnio Scipionis, *foliis deauratis. Ven. apud Aldum* 1528

4002 ———Philippicas, P. Manutii Emendat.—— *ib. ib.* 1542

4003 ———Epistolæ Selectæ, recensuit Schoderus, interfoliat. *Delph. Bat.* 1721

4004 ———Idem, cura J. Ingnad. ——— *Lipf.* 1728

4005 ———Idem, P. Lagneri.—— *Lut. apud R. Steph.* 1548

4006 ———Castigationes P. Victorii. ———*Lug.* 1562

4007 Dictionarium universale Latino-Gallicum. *Hagæ-Comit.* 1731

4008 Dionysii Descriptio Orbis, cum Comment. Eustathii, gr. lat. ——— ——— *Ox.* 1710

4009 Dodwelli Annales Velleiani, Quintilianei, Statiani. *ib.* 1698

4010 Dicta Septem Sapientum, gr. lat. *Par. apud Morel.* 1563

4011 Disticha de Moribus nomine Catonis Inscripta, cum lat. & gal. Interpretat. *lineis rubris. Paris, apud R. Steph* 1544

4012 Dion. Cassius, Æ. Spartianus, J. Capitolinus, Æ. Lampridius, Vel. Gallicanus, notis Egnatii. ———*ib ib.* 1544

4013 Diogenes Laertius, gr. cum notis H. Steph. *apud H. Steph.* 1570

4014 ———Idem, gr. lat. notis Casauboni.——— *Gen.* 1615

4015 Eutropius, cum Metaphrasi Græca Pæanianii, recensuit Cellarius. ——— ——— *Jenæ* 1716

4016 Euripidis Tragœdiæ 18, gr. 2 vol. ——— *Bas.* 1537

4017 ———Tragœdiæ 9. ——— *ib.* 1537

4018 ———Tragœdiæ 19, gr. lat. Interpret. Æ. Portus. *Heid.* 1597

4019 ———Tragœdiæ 17, 2 vol. *foliis deauratis. Venet. apud Ald* 1503

2

4020 Euripidis Tragœdiæ 19. ——— *Ant apud Plant.* 1571
4021 ———Hecuba & Iphigenia Lat. tralatæ Erasmo Interpret. ——— ——— *Ven. apud Aldum* 1507
4022 Scholia in 7 Euripidis Tragœd. ——— *Ven.* 1534
4023 Egnatius de Cæsaribus, &c. *foliis deauratis. Florent. apud Juntas* 1519
4024 Epigrammata Græca, Selecta ex Anthologia Interpret. ab H. Steph. gr. lat. —— *apud H. Steph.* 1570
4025 ———Idem, a F. Christiano Selecta, & Lat. versa. *Lut.* 1608
4026 Epicteti Enchiridion, cum Cebetis Thebani, accèssere Arriani Comment. omnia, H. Wolfio Interpret. *Cant.* 1655
4027 ———Enchiridion, lat. Versibus Adumbratum, per E. Ivie, gr. lat. *ch. max. & min.* ———*Ox.* 1715
4028 ——Enchiridion & Cebetis Thebani Tabula, gr. lat. *ib.* 1680
4029 Erasmi Apopthegmata. —— *Paris, apud Colin.* 1532
4030 ———Idem. —— *Lug. apud S. Gryph.* 1548
4031 ———Colloquia, notis P. Rabi. — *Rott.* 1693
4032 ———Moriæ Encomium. — *Bas.* 1551
4033 ——— Dialogus cui Titulus Ciceronianus. ——*Oxon.* 1693
4034 ——— Apopthegmata. — *Ant. apud Plant.* 1564
4035 Anacreontis Odæ, gr. H. Steph. Observat. *fol. deaur. Paris, apud C. Morel.* 1556
4036 ———Idem, gr. lat. notis J. Barnes. *Cant.* 1721
4037 Ausonius. ——— *Ven. apud Ald.* 1517
4038 ———Opuscula varia. — *Lug. apud S. Gryph.* 1549
4039 Apollodorus de Deorum Origine, gr. lat. Spoletino Interpr. *Amst.* 1669
4040 Græcorum Epigrammatum Florilegium novum, interfoliat. *Lond.* 1718
4041 Orthographiæ Ratio, ab Aldo Manutio collecta. *Ven. apud Aldum* 1566
4042 Arrianus Alexandrinus, gr. lat. B. Facio Interpr. *Bas.*
4043 Æschyli Tragœdiæ 6. *lin. rubr. fol. deauratis. Paris, apud Turn.* 1552
4044 Achilles Tatius, gr. lat. ——— *L.B.* 1640
4045 Ausonii Popmæ de differentiis Verborum, Lib. 4. *Amst.* 1654
4046 Aristophanis Comœdiæ 11, gr. lat. ——— *ib.* 1670
4047 ———Idem, gr. lat. Emendat. J. Scaligeri. —*L.B.* 1624
4048 Buxtorfius de Abbreviaturis Hebraicis. — *Herb.* 1708
4049 Baudii Epistolæ. ——— *L.B.* 1620
4050 ——— Epistolæ, Orationes & Libellus de Foenore. *ibid.* 1650
4051 Boeclerus de Scriptoribus, gr. & lat. *Ultr.* 1700
4052 Buchanani Poemata. — —— *L.B.* 1628
4053 Becmani de Originibus Ling. Lat. —— 1613
4054 Bebelianæ Facetiæ. —— —— *Franc.* 1590

4055

4055 Bonii nova Ling. Lat. Exercitatio. — *Ven.* 1608
4056 Boissardi Poemata. — — *Metis* 1589
4057 Borbonii Tabellæ, *cor. turc. fol. deaur. Paris, apud Colin.* 1539
4058 Barlæi Poemata. — *Amst. apud Bleau* 1645
4059 Baldi Poemata. — — *Colin.* 1646
4060 Crisogoni de Sermone Latino & Modis Latine Loquendis. *Ven.* 1561
4061 Hegendorphini Lib. Dialecticæ Legalis V. *cor tur fol deaur. Par. apud R. Steph.* 1535
4062 Clerici Epistolæ Criticæ & Ecclesiasticæ. *Amst.* 1700
4063 Cortesii Volantillæ, Carmen, *cor. turc. fol. deaur. Par. apud Colin.* 1533
4064 Lami a tol' Ajam Carmen Tograi Poetæ Arabis Doctiss. una cum Versione Lat. & Notis, Opera Pocockii. *Oxon.* 1661
4065 Comelini Janua Ling. reserrata. — *Amst.* 1649
4066 Crucii Orationes varii Argumrnti. — *ib.* 1675
4067 Cocalii Poetæ Mantuani Macoronicorum Poemata, cum fig. *Ven.* 1561
4068 Comicorum Græcorum Sententiæ, *cor. turc.* 1569
4069 J. Casaubon de Satyrica Græcorum Poesi. — *Par* 1605
4070 ———de 4 Linguis Comment. — *Lond.* 1650
4071 Conciones & Orationes ex Historicis Latinis excerpta. *Lips.* 1699
4072 Carmina 5 illustrium Poetarum. *Florent. apud Torrentinum.* 1549
4073 ——— illustrium Poetarum Italorum, — *Lut.* 1576
4074 Cruci Epistolæ. — *Lub.*
4075 De variis Particulis Græcæ Linguæ Liber. —*Amst* 1700
4076 Demosthenis Orationes, gr. 3 vol. *Venet. apud Aldum* 1554
4077 Epitome Sex Aurel. Victoris. — *Par. apud Colin* 1544
4078 Donati Comment. Grammatici tres. *Paris, apud R. Steph.* 1543
4079 Dictionarium Poeticum quod vulgo inscribitur Elucidarius Carminum. — *Ant.* 1534
4080 Dion. Hallicarnassei Opuscula S. Hovio Lat. donata. *Lut. apud R. Steph.* 1556
4081 ——— Opera Gelenio Interpret. *lineis rubr. fol. deaurat. Lug* 1561
4082 Enchiridion Grammatices, gr. — *Flor. apud Junt.* 1516
4083 Espencæi Sacrarum Heroidum Liber. *Paris, apud Moreil.* 1564
4084 Epistolia, Dialogi breves, Oratiunculæ, Poematia, gr. lat. *ap. H. Steph.* 1576
4085 Erpenii Grammatica Syra & Chaldaica. —— *L. B* 1619
4086 Epistolæ Clarorum virorum. — *Lug.* 1561
4087 Ælianus de Animalibus, gr. lat. P. Gilio Interpret. — 1611

S 4088

4088 Valerius Flaccus, *foliis deauratis*. *Florent. apud Juntas.* 1517
4089 ——Idem, recensuit N. Heinsius. — *L.B.*1724
4090 V. Flaccus & Pomp. Festus de Verborum Significat. *Ven.* 1565
4091 Faerni Centum Fabulæ Explicat. cum fig. ——*Brux.*1682
4092 Gratii Falisci Cynegeticon, notis T. Johnson.— *Lond.*1699
4093 Florilegium diversorum Epigrammat.vet. gr.lat. E. Lubino Interpret. —— —— *Rostochii.*1607
4094 L. Florus accurant. Freinshemio. —— *Argent.*1655
4095 Gronovii Observationes. —— *Lug. Bat.*1639
4096 Gregorii Gyraldi Dialogi II. de Poetis nostrorum Temporum. *Florent.*1501
4097 Gruteri Epistolæ & Apologia. —— *Lug. Bat* 1611
4098 ——Epistolar. Centuria secunda. —— *Amst.*1629
4099 Gnomologia Demosthenica H. Wolfii Collecta. —*Basil.*1570
4100 Laurent. Gambaræ Poemata. —— *Ant. apud Plant.*1569
4101 Hortus Epigrammat. F. Morello Interpret. corio turcico, foliis deauratis. —— *Lut.*1595
4102 Grævii Præfationes & Epistolæ, —— *Hamb.*1707
4103 Heinsii Orationes. —— *Lug. Bat. Elz.*1620
4104 Wottoni Grammat. Septentrional. —— *Lond* 1708
4105 H. Hugo de prima scribendi origine. *Ant. apud Plant.*1617
4106 Hieroclis Comment. in aurea Pythagoreorum Carmina.*Par.* 1583
4107 ——Idem, gr. lat. Curterio Interpret. —— *Lond.*1654
4108 Heroicæ Poeseos Deliciæ ad unius Virgilii Imitationem, foliis deauratis. —— *Paris* 1646
4109 Hist. Augustæ Scriptores VI. —— *Lug.*1620
4110 Hercules tuam fidem. —— *Lug. Bat.*1608
4111 Knauthii Cheiragogus Grammaticus. —— *Dresdæ.*1722
4112 J. Leusden Synopsis Hebraica & Chaldaica. —— *Traject. ad Rhen* 1667
4113 Longolii Epistolæ, foliis deauratis. —— *Paris.*1526
4114 Laurembergii Cynosura Bonæ Mentis. ——*Rostoch.*1638
4115 Lycophronis Cassandra gr. lat. notis Canteri. *Genev.*1596
4116 G. Mayr institutiones Ling. Hebraicæ. —— *Lug.*1649
4117 Manilius J. Scaliger recensuit. —— *Lut. apud Patisson* 1579
4118 Hieropoematium F. Morello Auctore, corio turcico, foliis deauratis. —— *Lut. apud Morell.*1600
4119 Morelli Prosopopœia, corio turcico, foliis deauratis. *ib ib.* 1611
4120 Menagii Poemata, corio turcico, foliis deauratis. *Amst. apud Elz.*1663
4121 Meursii elegantia Latini Sermonis.
4122 Marcellus de Proprietate Sermonis. —— *Paris* 1583
4123 ——Idem. —— *Ant. apud Plantin.*1565
4124 Duesii nova Nomenclatura 4 Linguarum. —— *Amst.*1663
4125 Naufragium Joculare.

4126

4126 Oratorum Græcorum Orationes. —— Patav. 1688
4127 Orationes ex Salluftii, Livii, Curtii, & Taciti Hift. collect. Paris 1721
4128 Maurocordati Liber de Officiis gr. lat. —— Lond 1726
4129 Orthographia Romana. —— Vitemberg. 1707
4130 P. Olivier differtat. Academici de Oratoria, Hiftoria, & Poetica. —— —— Cant. 1674
4131 Opufcula Mythologica, Ethica, & Phyfica, gr. lat. Cant. 1671
4232 Panegyrici veteres. —— Paris. 1655
4133 Obfervationes Pintiani. —— Ant. 1547
4134 Pi&eti Græcorum Sententiæ. —— Amft. 1700
4135 L. Florus M. Mattaire, ch. max. —— Lond. 1715
4136 Fabricii Bibliotheca Latina. —— Lond 1703
4137 Grævii Orationes. —— Delphis 1721
4138 Aulus Gellius. —— Venet. apud Aldum 1515
4139 ——Idem. —— Flcrent. apud Juntas. 1513
4140 Gazæ Introductionis Grammat. Lib. IV. —— Bafil 1523
4141 Aulus Gellius. —— Lug. apud S. Gryph. 1550
4142 ——Idem. —— Lug. apud Ant. Gryph. 1565
4143 Hogæi Paraphras Poetica in Miltoni Poemata. —— Lond. 1690
4144 Hiftoriar. Fabularumque delectus gr. lat. —— ib. 1726
4145 Hift. Poeticæ Scriptores antiqui. —— Paris 1675
4146 Herodotus Hift. ex Interpret. L. Vallæ. —— Franc. 15`4
4147 ——Idem, lineis rubris, foliis deauratis. Lug. apud S. Gryph. 1542
4148 Hefiodi Opera gr. lat. ftudio Schrevelii. —— Lug. Bat. 1653
4149 ——Idem. —— Lipfiæ. 1730
4150 Homeri Ilias gr. lat. —— Cant. 1686
4151 ——Ilias gr.—— —— Paris, apud Turneb. 1554
4152 ——Ilias lat. per L. Vallenfen. —— Colon. 1522
4153 ——Opera gr. 2 vol. ch. max. —— Lovanii. 1535
4154 ——Opera gr. lat. ftudio & cura Giphanii, 2 vol. Argent.
4155 ——Ilias gr. Scholia Dydimi. —— Oxon.
4156 ——Odyffea gr. lat. curante Berglero. —— Amft. 1707
4157 ——Odyffea gr. lat.
4158 ——Odyffea gr. —— apud Crifpinum. 1567
4159 ——Lexicon Auth. L. Coulon. —— Paris. 1643
4160 ——Clavis. —— —— Lond. 1647
4161 Horatius Cunninghamii, 2 vol. —— Hagæ Comit. 1721
4162 ——Idem, notis E. a Zurck. —— Harlem.
4163 ——Idem & Juvenalis. —— Paris apud R. Steph. 1642
4164 ——Idem, M. Mattaire, ch. max. —— Lond 1715
4165 ——Idem, cum notis. —— Venet. 1563
4166 ——Idem, notis Heinfii. —— Lug. Bat. 1612
4167 ——Idem, in ufum Delph. —— Tolofæ. 1683
4168 ——Idem, notis Bentleii. —— Cant. 1713
4169 ——Idem, Scholiis illuftrat. ab H. Stephano. Lut. apud R. Steph. 15.9

4170 ———Idem, corio turcico, foliis deauratis. *Venet. apud Aldum.* 1501
4171 ———Idem, variæ Lectiones, lineis rubris, corio turcico, foliis deauratis. —— *Paris, apud R. Steph.* 1544
4172 Herodiani Hist. gr. lat. ab A. Politiano. —— *Lond.* 1639
4173 ———Idem, lat. A. Politiano Interpret. ——*Paris, apud R. Steph.* 1544
4174 ——— Idem, lat. —— *Venet. apud Aldum,* 1524
4175 ———Idem, ab A. Politiano lat. donati, corio turcico, foliis deauratis. —— *Paris, apud Colinæum.* 1539
4176 ———Idem, lat.—— *Lug. apud S. Gryph.* 1551
4177 Julii Pollucis Onomasticon, R. Gualthero interpret, *Basil.* 1541
4178 Isocratis Orationes VII. & Epistolæ gr. lat. G. Batie. *Cant.* 1729
4179 ———Idem, gr. lat. H. Wolfio Interpret. —— *ib.* 1686
4180 ———Idem, gr. lat. —— *apud P. Steph.* 1604
4181 ———Opera gr. lat. Wolfio Interpret. —— *Basil.* 1587
4182 ———Opera gr. —— *ib.* 1561
4183 Juvenalis & Persius, M. Mattaire, ch. max.— *Lond.* 1716
4184 ———Idem, cum Comment. *Lug. apud Paganum.* 1557
4185 ———Idem, variæ Lectiones. *Lut. apud R. Steph* 1544
4186 ———Idem, notis T. Marshall. —— *Lond.* 1723
4187 ———Idem, notis Lubini.
4188 ———Idem, Martialis, Ausonius. *Venet. apud Aldum.* 1535-18-17
4189 Justini Historia. —— *Florent. apud Juntas.* 1510
4190 ———Idem, notis illustrat. —— *Oxon.* 1705
4191 ———Idem, ex recensione Grævii. *Traject. ad Rhen.* 1708
4192 ———Idem, cum notis & variarum Lectionum Libellus —— ——*Paris, apud Du Val.* 1581
4193 ———Idem, recensuit T. Faber. —— *Salmurii.* 1671
4194 ———Idem, cum Scholiis. ——*Col. Agrip.* 1576
4195 ———Idem. —— *Venet. apud Aldum.* 1522
4196 ———Idem, Sallustius, Fenestella, P. Lætus. *Lut. apud R. Steph.* 1543-44-49
4197 J. Ker Selectarum de Ling. Latina observat.—— *Lond.* 1709
4198 Livii Historia. —— *Lug. apud S. Gryph.* 1554
4199 ———Idem, 5 vol.—— *Venet. apud Aldum.*
4200 ———Idem, M. Mattaire, 6 vol. —— *Lond.* 1722
4201 ———Idem, T. Hearne, 6 vol. ch. max. *Oxon.* 1708
4202 ———Historiarum Corpus concinnius. *Dordrecht.* 1711
4203 Lucretius M. Mattaire, ch. max. & min. —— *Lond.* 1713
4204 ———Idem, notis Lambini. —— *Franc.* 1583
4205 ———Idem. —— *Florent. apud Juntas.* 1512
4206 ———Idem, —— *Lug. apud S. Gryph.* 1540
4207 ———Idem. corio turcico, foliis deauratis. *Venet. apud Aldum.* 1515

4208

4208 Lucretius, notis T. Fabri. —— —— *Cant.* 1686
4209 ——Idem, Lambini, lineis rubris, foliis deauratis. *Par. apud Rovillium.* 1565
4210 Lucanus M. Mattaire, ch. max. & min. —— *Lond.* 1719
4211 ——Idem, recensuit G. Cortius. —— *Lipsiæ.* 1726
4212 ——Idem, variæ Lectiones.—— *Lut. apud R. Steph.* 1545
4213 ——Idem, foliis deauratis. — *Venet. apud Aldum.*
4214 ——Idem, —— *Lug. apud S. Gryph.* 1542
4215 ——Idem, lineis rubris, foliis deauratis. —— *Lug.* 1560
4216 ——Idem. —— *Paris. apud Colinæum.* 1543
4217 Luciani Opera gr. lat. 2 vol. —— *Basil.*
4218 ——Pseudosophista gr. notis Grævii. —— *Amst.* 1668
4219 D. Laertius, foliis deauratis. —— *Lug. apud S. Gryph.* 1541
4220 ——Idem, gr. lat. cum notis H. Stephani. —— *apud H. Steph.* 1570
4221 Lactantii Opera. —— —— *Cant.* 1685
4222 ——Idem, notis Thomasii.—— *Ant. apud Plan.* 1570
4223 ——Idem, Tertullianus.——*Venet. apud Aldum.* 1515
4224 Longinus de Sublimitate gr. lat. cum notis.—— *Oxon.* 1730
4225 Mellificium Oratorium Opera Meyfarti & Steinbruccii, 2 vol. *Franc.* 1701
4226 Moeris Atticistæ de Vocibus Atticis & Hellenicis. *Oxon.*
4227 Musæ Anglicanæ, 2 vol. —— *Oxon.* 1699
4228 Macrobii de differentiis & societatibus Græci Latinique Verbi Libellus, corio turcico, foliis deauratis. *Paris apud Du Val.* 1588
4230 ——Opera. —— *Paris.* 1585
4231 ——Idem. —— *Lug. apud S. Gryph.* 1556
4232 Manutii de Quæsitis per Epistolam Lib. III.——*Venet.* 1576
4233 ——Epistolæ, —— —— *ib.* 1560
4234 ——Idem notis Kirchmanni. —— *Lipsiæ* 1669
4235 Val. Maximus, corio turcico, foliis deauratis. *Venet. apud Aldum.* 1502
4236 ——Idem, ——*Paris, apud Colinæum.* 1535
4237 ——Idem, per S. Pighium.— *Ant. apud Plant.* 1574
4238 ——Idem, —— *Florent. apud Juntas.* 1517
4239 ——Idem, per Pighium. —— *Ant.* 1713
4240 Martialis, corio turcico, foliis deauratis. *Venet. apud Aldum.* 1501
4241 ——Idem. —— *Lug. apud S. Gryph.* 1553
4242 ——Idem, cum Comment. interfoliata. *Sedani.* 1624
4243 ——Idem, M. Mattaire, ch. max. —— *Lond.* 1716
4244 ——Idem, foliis deauratis. —— *Paris.* 1528
4245 ——Idem, cum notis variorum Doctor.——*Lug.* 1567
4246 ——Idem, ——*Paris, apud Colinæum* 1533
4247 P. Mela, J. Solinus, Itinerar. Anton. Vibius Sequester Prisiano interpret. —— *Venet. apud Aldum.* 1518
4248 ——Idem, —— *Florent. apud Juntas* 1526
4249 Pomp. Mela de Situ Orbis, notis Olivarii. *Paris, apud Colinæum.* 1539

4250 Macrini Hymnorum Lib. VI. corio turcico, foliis deauratis. *Paris, apud R. Steph.* 1537
4251 ——— Idem, Lib. III. —— *Lut. apud Vascosan.* 1550
4252 Cornelius Nepos, ch. max. —— *Oxon.* 1697
4253 ——— Idem. —— —— *Patav.* 1721
4254 ——— Idem, M. Mattaire, ch. max. —— *Lond.* 1715
4255 ——— Idem, cum Comment. H. Ernesti. *Lipsiæ.* 1707
4256 ——— Idem, lat. & german. —— *Auspurg.* 1717
4257 Ovidii Opera, M. Mattaire, ch. max. & min. *Lond.* 1715
4258 ——— Idem, 3 vol. —— *Lug. apud S. Gryph.* 1554
4259 ——— Idem, 3 vol, corio turcico. *Venet. apud Aldum.* 1502
4260 ——— Idem, Heinsii & Burmanni, 3 vol. —— *Lipsiæ.* 1715
4261 ——— Idem, 3 vol. —— *Paris, apud Colinæum.* 1541
4262 ——— Idem, Fastorum, Tristium, & de Ponto Lib. *Matriti* 1707
4263 ——— Metamorphosis, notis Bersmanni. —— *Lond.* 1655
4264 ——— Fastorum, Tristium de Ponto Lib. —— *Paris.* 1507
4265 ——— Opera Heinsii. —— *Amst.* 1647
4266 ——— Metamorphosis, notis Juvency, 2 vol. —— *Paris.* 1725
4267 Oppiani Venatione gr. corio turcico, foliis deauratis. *Florent. apud Juntas.* 1515
4268 De Poematum Cantu & Viribus Rythmi. —— *Oxon* 1673
4269 Plato de Rebus divinis gr. lat. —— *Cant.* 1683
4270 Polybii Hist. lat. Perotto Interp. —— *Basil.* 1557
4271 Pinonis de anno Romano Carmen. —— *Paris.* 1615
4272 Peckii ad Rem Nauticam pertinentes Comment. *Lug. Bat.* 1647
4273 Imagines Philostrati gr. —— *Venet. apud Juntas.* 1535
4274 Passeratii Præfatiuncula. —— *Lut. apud Patisson.* 1594
4275 Petronii Arbitri Fragmentum —— *Lut. Paris.* 1664
4276 Phile de Animalium proprietate gr. lat. —— 1596
4277 Phædri Fabulæ notis T. Fabri. —— *Amst.* 1712
4278 Porphyrogennetæ de Thematibus Occidentalibus F. Morellus interpret. —— *Lut. apud Morell.* 1609
4279 Parabata Vinctus Tragœdia. —— *Lut apud Patisson* 1595
4280 S. Pagnini Institutiones Hebraicæ, corio turcico, foliis deauratis. —— *Lut. apud R. Steph.* 1546
4281 Pedonis Albinovani Elegiæ & Fragmenta. —— *Amst.* 1703
4282 Persii, Juvenalis, & Sulpicii Satyræ cum vet. Comment. corio turcico, foliis deauratis. *Lut. apud Patisson.* 1585
4283 Prisciani Opera, corio turcico, foliis deauratis. *Venet. apud Aldum.* 1527
4284 Pontani Opera. —— *ib. ib.* 1527
4285 ——— Idem. —— *Basil.*
4286 ——— Idem. —— *Lug.* 1514
4287 Plinii Hist. naturalis, 3 vol. —— *Venet. apud Aldum.* 1536
4288 ——— Epistolæ. —— *Paris, apud H. Steph.* 1519
4289 ——— Idem. —— —— *Basil* 1521
4290 ——— Idem, lineis rubris, foliis deauratis. *Venet. apud Aldum.* 1508

4291 —— Idem. —— —Lug. Bat. 1653
4292 —— de Viris illustribus. —— Par. apud Colin. 1545
4293 —— Vita, par Masson. —— —Amst. 1709
4294 —— Panegyricus Trajano dictus, in Usum Delph. Lond. 1716
4295 —— Epistolæ & Panegyricus, Notis illustrat. —Oxon. 1677
4296 Plauti Comœd. xx. *corio turcico. foliis deauratis. Ven. apud Aldum* 1722
4297 —— Comœd. xx. Studio Camerarii. ——*Basil.*
4298 —— Comœd. xx. 2 vol.——*Lug. apud S. Gryph.* 1637
4299 —— Comœd. xx.——*Florent. apud Juntas* 1514
4300 —— Comœd. xx. ex Recensione Buchneri.—*Franc.* 1652
4301 —— Comœd. xx. Opera Sambuci, 8 vol. *Ant. apud Plant.* 1566
4302 —— Comœd. xx. ——*Lug. apud S. Gryph.* 1549
4303 Pindari Opera.—— ——*Venet. apud Aldum* 1513
4304 —— Idem, gr. lat. —— *Basil.* 1526
4305 —— Idem, gr. ——*Paris apud Morel.* 1623
4306 —— Idem, gr. lat. 2 vol. *lineis rubris. apud H. Steph.* 1560
4307 Quilleti Callipædia. —— ——*Lond.* 1708
4308 Quintiliani Institutiones Oratoriæ. *Florent. apud Juntas* 1515
4309 —— Idem, *corio turcico, foliis deauratis. Venet. apud Aldum* 1514
4310 —— Idem, Notis Turnebi. ——*Lond.* 1714
4311 —— Declamationes, cum Notis.——*Oxon.* 1692
4312 —— Ibid. ——*Lutet. apud Patisson* 1580
4313 —— Institut. Orator.——*Lug. apud S. Gryph.* 1540
4314 —— Lib. de Re rustica, *foliis deauratis. Florent. ap. Juntas* 1515
4315 —— Idem, *foliis deauratis. Venet. apud Aldum* 1514
4316 —— Idem.—— ——*Par. apud R. Steph.* 1543
4317 Rhetores selecti, gr. lat.—— ——*Oxon.* 1676
4318 Rudimenta Grammat. Hebrææ.—— ——*Venet.* 1681
4319 Ravisii Textoris Dialogi & Epigrammat.——*Rot.* 1652
4320 Rapini Hortorum Lib.—— ——*Par.* 1666
4321 Robortelli Annotat. tam in Græcis quam Latinis Authorib. *Venet.* 1544
4322 Rami Scholæ in 3 liberales Artes.——*Franc.* 1581
4323 Schrevelii Lexicon. ——*Lond.* 1725
4324 Sectani Satyræ, cum Comment. ——*Amst.* 1700
4325 Santolii selecta Carmina.—— —*Par.* 1670
4326 Sulpicius Severus, Notis Giselini.—*Ant. apud Plant.* 1571
4327 —— Idem, Sigonii Comment. ——*Hanov.* 1602
4328 Sententiæ, gr. lat. ——*Paris apud R. Steph.* 1540
4329 Schickardi Horologium Hebræum.——*Lond.* 1639
4330 Sybillina Oracula, Castalione Interpret. —— *Basil.*
4331 Johnii Pernassi Silesiaci. ——*Wratislaviæ* 1728
4332 Sciopii Minerva Sanctiana. ——*Patav.* 1663

4333

4333 Synopsis commun. Locorum, ex Latinis Poetis collecta. *Lond.* 1719
4334 A. Mariæ a Schurman Opuscula.——— *Lug. Bat.* 1648
4335 Sanadonis Carmina. ——————— *Lut. Par.* 1725
4336 H. Stephani Pseudo-Cicero Dialogus.— *apud H. Steph.* 1577
4337 Sabæi Epigrammata. ——————— *Romæ* 1556
4338 Siberi Ludus Litterarum.——— ——— *Lipsiæ* 1569
4339 Sententiæ veterum Poetarum. ——— *Ant. apud Plant.* 1566
4340 Stobæi Sententiæ.——————— *Lug. apud S. Gryph.* 1555
4341 Suetonius, Studio Pulmanni.——— *Ant. apud Plant.* 1574
4342 ——— Idem.——————— *Par. apud R. Steph.* 1543
4343 ——— Idem.——— ——— *Florent. apud Juntas* 1510
4344 ——— Idem, *lineis rubris.*——— *Venet. apud Aldum.* 1516
4345 ——— Idem Erasmi. ——— *Par. apud Colinæum* 1535
4346 ——— Idem, ex recensione Grævii. ——— *Amst.* 1697
4347 ——— Idem.——— ——— *Par. e Typo. Regia.* 1644
4348 ——— Idem, *lineis rubris. Lug. apud Frellonium* 1559
4349 Cæsarum Vitæ post Suetonium, *lineis rubris, foliis deaurat. Lug. apud S. Gryph.* 1551
4350 Sallustius. ——————— *Lug. apud S. Gryph.* 1540
4351 ——— Idem Pacis Querelæ. *Venet. apud Aldum* 1509-18
4352 Strozii Portæ Pater & Filius. ——————— *ib. ib.* 1513
4353 ——— Idem. ——————— *Paris apud Colinæum* 1530
4354 Senecæ Questiones, Notis Fortunati. *Venet. apud Aldum* 1522
4355 ——— Sententiæ singulares, Notis Gruteri. *Lug. Bat.* 1708
4356 ——— Tragœdiæ, var. Lect.——— ——— 1589
4357 ——— Idem, Studio Gruteri. ——————— 1604
4358 ——— Idem.——————— *Lug. apud S. Gryph* 1554
4359 Sannazarii Opera omnia. ——————— *Amst.* 1648
4360 Sophoclis Tragœdiæ vii. gr.
4361 ——— Idem, gr. Opera Canteri.——— *Lug. Bat.* 1593
4362 J. Scaligeri Epistolæ. —— ——— *ib.* 1627
4363 ——— Poemata. —— —— 1574
4364 ——— de Subtilitate. —— *Franc.* 1560
4365 ——— de Causis Ling. Lat. ——— 1623
4366 ——— Florilegium.——— *Lut. apud R. Steph.* 1607
4367 Statius.——— ——— *Paris apud Colinæum* 1530
4368 ——— Idem, recensuit Gevartius.——— *Lug. Bat.* 1616
4369 ——— Idem.——— ——— *Lug.* 1514
4370 ——— Idem, Val. Flacci Argonautica. *Venet. apud Aldum* 1523-24
4371 Scævolæ Sammarthani Pædotrophiæ.——— ——— *Lond.* 1708
4372 Terent. Varonis de Ling. Lat. J. Scaliger Conjectanea. *Par. apud R. Steph.* 1565
4373 Theocriti Opera, gr. ——————— *Romæ*
4374 Theodori Grammatices Introductionis Lib. iv. *Florent. ap. Juntas* 1520

4375

4375 Themistii Orationes, gr. lat. notis Pantini. *L. Bat.* 1614
4376 ———Idem, gr. ——— *apud H. Steph.* 1562
4377 Turselini de particulis Latinæ Orationis. *Lips.* 1700
4378 Theognidis Megarensis Sententiæ, gr. lat. ——1583
4379 Thesaurus Phrasium Poeticarum, Opera Buckleri. *Amst.* 1671
4380 Thesauri Carmina, *corio turcico, foliis deauratis.* *Oxon.* 1637
4381 Taciti Annales, *corio turcico, foliis deauratis.* *Venet. apud Ald.* 1534
4382 ———Hist. & Annales, notis Lipsii. *Ant. apud Plant.* 1574
4383 ———Opera, recensuit Lipsius. ——— *Gen.* 1619
4384 ———Idem. ——— *Amst. apud Bleau* 1649
4385 ———Annales, *lineis rubris, foliis deauratis.* *Lug. apud S. Gryph.* 1559
4386 Theophrastus, gr. lat. notis Casauboni, recensuit P. Needham. ——— ——— *Cant.* 1712
4387 Terentius, Mureto Emendat. *Venet. apud P. Manut.* 1555
4388 ———Idem, Comment. Antesignani. —— *Lug.* 1560
4389 ———Idem, notis Juvencii. ——— *Par.* 1716
4390 ———Idem, M. Mattaire. ——— *Lond.* 1713
4391 ———Idem, variæ Lectiones. —— *Cant.* 1723
4392 ———Idem, notis Mureti. ———*Lug.* 1576
4393 ———Idem, corio turcico, fol. deaurat. *Paris, apud R. Steph.* 1540
4394 Terentii Varronis Opera, 2 vol. corio turcico, fol. deauratis. 1581
4395 Theocritus, gr. cum Græcis Scholiis.——— *Lond.* 1729
4396 ——Idem, gr. cum Græcis Scholiis. ——*Ox.*
4397 Tibullus, Scholia Mureti. —— *Ven. apud P. Manut.* 1558
4398 Supplementa & Observat. ad Vossium de Historicis Gr. & Lat. ——— ——— *Hamb.* 1709
4399 Vossii Grammatica Latina. —— *L. B.* 1644
4400 Vivis Colloquia. ——— *Flor. apud Junt.* 1568
4401 Vigeri de præcipuis Græcæ Dictionis Idiotismis & Particulis. ——— ——— *Lond.* 1695
4402 Vegetius de Re Militari Comment. Stewechii. *Vesaliæ* 1670
4403 Vidæ Opera. ——— *Lug. apud S. Gryph.* 1541
4404 ——Idem. —— ——— *Ant.* 1536
4405 ——Bombycum, Lib. 2. —— *Ox.* 1701
4406 ——Opera. ——— *Lug. apud S Gryph.* 1536
4407 ——Opera. ——— *ib. apud Ant. Gryph.* 1592
4408 ——Christiados. Lib. 6. ——— *Oxon.* 1725
4409 Ursini Institut. Plenissimarum, 2 vol. ——*Ratis* 1701
4410 Vorstius de Latinitate falso suspecta. ——*Lips.* 1703
4411 Hosschii, Wallii & Becani Poemata, 2 vol. —— *Par.* 1723

T 4412

4

4412 B. Walton Introductio ad Lectionum Linguarum Oriental. *Lond.* 1655

4413 Væni Emblemati Horatiana, cum fig. —*Amſt.* 1684

4414 Aurelius Victor, cum fig. — *Ant. apud Plant.* 1579

4415 L. Vallæ de Ling. Lat. Elegant. —— *Col. Agr.* 1577

4416 Virgilius, M. Mattaire, *ch. max. & min.* *Lond.* 1715

4417 ———Idem, *corio turcico, foliis deauratis.* *Venet. apud Aldum* 1545

4418 ———Idem, Scholia H. Steph. —— 1683

4419 ———Idem, in uſum Delph. —— *Hagæ-Comit.* 1723

4420 ———Idem, notis Eobani Heſſi. —— *Ant.* 1544

4421 ———Idem, P. Rami prælect. —— *Par.* 1555

4422 ———Idem, notis Erythræi. —— *Lug.* 1608

4423 ———Idem, *lineis rubris.* — *Lug. apud S. Gryph.* 1554

4424 ———Idem, *corio turcico, foliis deauratis.* *Lut. apud R. Steph.* 1549

4425 ———Idem. —— *Sedani* 1625

4426 Velleius Paterculus, M. Mattaire, *ch. max.* *Lond.* 1718

4427 ———Idem, recenſuit J. Scheckius. — *Pat.* 1590

4428 ———Idem, Lipſi Animadverſ. —— *Lug.* 1592

4429 Valerius Maximus, variæ Lectiones. *Lut. apud R. Steph.* 1544

4430 ———Idem, per Pighium, *lineis rubris, foliis deauratis.* *apud Criſp.* 1602

4431 ———Idem, *corio turcico, foliis deauratis.* *Paris, apud Colin.* 1543

4432 Xenophon de Cyri Inſtitutione, gr. lat. Hutchinſon. *Lond.* 1730

4433 ———Idem, gr. lat. J. Leunclavii Interpret. —*ib.* 1713

4434 Methodus Ruſtica. —— *Baſil.*

Engliſh Divinity. Octavo and Twelves.

4435 Aſheton's Apology for the Honours of the Clergy. 1676

4436 ———on Laſt Wills and Teſtaments. —— 1696

4437 St. Auguſtine's Hiſtory of his own Life. —— 1660

4438 St. Athanaſius's Orations againſt the Arians, 2 vol. 1713

4439 Bellarmin's Art of dying well. —— 1720

4440 Art of Contentment. —— 1675

4441 Atterbury's Rights of an Engliſh Convocation. 1700

4442 Abbadie's Art of knowing one's ſelf. —— 1697

4443 Addiſon's Evidences of the Chriſtian Religion. 1733

4444 Bull's Vindicat. of the Church of Engl. —— 1719

4445 ——Theſaurus Theologicus, 4 vol. —— 1711

4446 Bury's conſtant Communicant. —— 1681

4447 Beveridge on the Church-Catechiſm. —— 1705

4448 ———on publick Prayer. —— 1714

4449 ———private Thoughts, 2 vol. —— 1728

4450 Balguy's Moral and Theological Tracts. —— 1734

4451

4451 Browne's Defence of the Religion of Nature. — 1732
4452 Brokesby's Hist. of the Governm. of the primit. Church. 1712

4453 Bennet's Confutation of Quakerism. — 1709
——on the 39 Articles. — 1715
——Abridgm. of the London Cases. — 1728
——Confutation of Popery. — 1728
——Rights of the Clergy. — 1711
——on set Forms of Prayer. — 1708
——on the Common-Prayer. — 1709
——Letter to Dr. Robinson. — 1710
——Directions for Study. — 1727
——Discourse of Schism. — 1716
——Discourse on the Trinity. — 1718

4454 ——against the Nonjurors, with other Tracts. 1716
4455 ——on the Common Prayer. — 1709
4456 ——Christian Oratory, 2 vol. — 1732
4457 Brett's Letter of Advice to a Friend. — 1715
4458 Bray's Bibliotheca Parochialis. — 1707
4459 Bourne's Antiquities of the common People. 1725
4460 Broughton's Nature of the rational Soul. — 1703
4461 Burnet's Faith and Duties of Christians. — 1733
4462 ——State of departed Souls. — 1733
4463 ——Hist. of the Rights of Princes. — 1682
4464 Bates's Saints everlasting Rest. — 1701
4465 ——on the Existence of God, and the Immortality of the Soul. — — 1677
4466 Boyle's Motives to the Love of God. — 1692
4467 Basire's Sacrilege arraigned and condemned. 1668
4468 Barrow's Duty and Reward of Bounty to the Poor, 1677
4469 Baylie's Certamen Religiosum. — 1649
4470 Bramhall's Castigations of Hobbes's Animadversions. 1658
4471 Bale's Apology against a ranke Papyst.
4472 Bradford's Examinations, *black letter*.
4473 Collection of several scarce Pieces of Divinity, by different Authors, *black letter*.
4474 Barrow's Exposition on the Lord's Prayer. — 1681
4475 Blount's Opinion concerning Man's Soul. — 1679
4476 Bunny's Answer to Father Parsons. — 1589
4477 Bernard's private Devotion. — 1704
4478 Clark's Essays on Baptism, Confirmation, and Repentance. 1699
4479 ——Scripture-Doctrine of the Trinity. — 1732
4480 ——on the Attributes. — 1732
4481 ——Paraphrase on the Evangelists, 2 vol. — 1729
4482 ——Letter to Dodwell. A Cat may look at a Queen, with other Tracts.

T 2 4483

4483 Collection of Tracts relating to the Protestant Mission in India.
4484 Collyer's sacred Interpreter, 2 vol. —— 1732
4485 Collection of Cases against the Dissenters, 2 vol. 1718
4486 Christians Duty, *bound in turkey. gilt on the leaves.* 1730
4487 Character of a primitive Bishop. —— 1714
4488 Calumny refuted by Conybeare, in a Letter to Dr. Holmes. 1735
4489 Comber on Ordination. —— 1699
4490 ——Discourse on Offices. —— 1696
4491 ——Companion to the Temple, 2 vol. — 1679
4492 ——Discourse on the Common-Prayer. —— 1684
4493 Christian's best Guide. —— 1716
4494 Christian Religion, as professed by a Daughter of the Ch. of England. —— —— 1705
4495 Chamberlayne's Arguments of the Old Testament, 2 vol. 1716
4496 Causes of the Decay of Christian Piety. — 1667
4497 Cave's Primitive Christianity. —— 1682
4498 Christianity as old as the Creation, by Tyndal. — 1732
4499 Christianity no Enthusiasm, against the Quakers. 1678
4500 Catholick Faith maintained in the Church of England, by Saul. —— 1676
4501 Cry from the Desert. —— 1707
4502 Ld Capel's Contemplations. —— 1683
4503 Dodwell's Reply to Baxter on Separation. 1681
4504 ——Defense of the Epistolary Discourse. 1707
4505 ——on the Mortality of the Soul. — 1706
4506 ——four Letters to Bp Burnet. — 1713
4507 ——Case in View considered. —— 1705
4508 ——Prospect of the Case in View. 1707
4509 ——on Marriages in different Communions. 1702
4510 ——Scripture Account of eternal Rewards or Punishments. — —— 1708
4511 ——Discourse concerning one Altar. —— 1683
4512 ——Lawfulness of instrumental Musick in Churches. 1700
4513 ——Discourse against the Romanists. 1676
4514 ——Occasional Communion. —— 1705
4515 Defence of Pluralities. —— 1703
4516 Discovery of false Churches. —— 1707
4517 Discourse of Free-Thinking. —— 1713
4518 Dryden's Life of St. Xavier. —— 1688
4519 Ditton's Discourse on the Resurrection. — 1727
4520 Deacon's Discourse against Purgatory. — 1718
4521 Echard's Ecclesiastical History, 2 vol. —— 1729
4522 Epistles of Barnabas, Ignatius, Clement, and Polycarp. 1693
4523 Essay towards a Proposal for Catholick Communion. 1704

4524

4524 End of the World, and second Coming of Christ. 1582
4525 Fleetwood's Essay upon the Miracles. —— 1701
4526 Fox's new Testament, with References, 2 vol. 1722
4527 Elstob's English-Saxon Homily. —— 1709
4528 Field's Life of Dr. Field Prebendary of Windsor. — 1716
4529 Fleury's Account of the Manners of the Christians. 1698
4530 Minucius Felix, translated by Combe. — 1703
4531 Fleetwood's relative Duties. —— 1723
4532 Finishing Stroke, or a Vindication of the Patriarch. Scheme. 1711
4533 Foxes and Firebrands, or a Specimen of the Danger of Popery. —— 1682
4534 Fell's Life of Dr. Hammond. —— 1661
4535 Fryth's Answer to More's Letter, *black letter.* 1546
4536 The Fall of the Romyshe Church, *black letter.*
4537 Following of Christ, *black letter.* —— 1585
4538 Gretton's Vindication of the Doctrines of the Church of England. —— —— 1725
4539 Gentleman Instructed, by Dorrell. —— 1716
4540 Gastrell's Christian's Institutes. —— 1707
4541 General Delusion of Christians. —— 1713
4542 Garenciere's general Instructions. —— 1728
4543 Granada's Memorial of a Christian Life. — 1688
4544 Gentleman and Ladies Calling. —— 1677
4545 Gavin's Master-Key to Popery, 3 vol. —— 1725
4546 Gifforde's Country Divinity, *black letter.* — 1581
4547 Grascombe's Certamen Religiosum. —— 1704
4548 Grabe's Defence of the Greek Church. — 1721
4549 Howardin's true Church of Christ, in Answer to Lesly, 2 vol. —— —— 1715
4550 Horneck's Crucified Jesus. —— 1689
4551 ——great Law of Consideration. —— 1721
4552 Hingeston's dreadful Alarm.
4553 Howe's History of the Bible, 3 vol. *cuts.* 1725
4554 Howell's Living Temple, 2 vol. —— 1702
4555 Hoadley's common Rights of Subjects. 1719
4556 Holy David, and his old English Translators cleared. 1706
4557 Hopkins's Doctrine of the two Sacraments.—— 1712
4558 Hutcheson's Enquiry into the Ideas of Beauty and Virtue. 1729
4559 History of Ecclesiastical Revenues. —— 1685
4560 Humphrey's hist. Account of the Society for the Propagat. of the Gospel. —— 1730
4561 Hickeringill's Works, 3 vol. —— 1716
4562 Hale's Contemplations, 3 parts, and Burnet's Life of him. 1705
4563 Hist. Collections concerning the Succession during the three first Centuries,—— 1713
4564 Harryson's Course at the Romyshe Foxe.

4565

4565 History of the Church, by Dupin, 4 vol. —— 1724
4566 Hist. of the modern Protestant Divines, *curious cuts.* 1637
4567 Hosius's Hist. of the Heresies of our Time. —— 1565
4568 Hickes's Treatises of Christian-Priesthood, 2 vol. —— 1711
4569 ——— Tracts. ——— —— 1709
4570 ——— divine Right of Episcopacy asserted. —— 1708
4571 ——— Constitution of the Catholick Church. —— 1716
4572 ——— Devotions in the ancient way of Offices, 2 vol. 1712
4573 Image of both Churches, Hierusalem and Babel. 1623
4574 Julian's Arts to undermine Christianity. ——— 1689
4575 Ignatius's Inthronization in a late Election in Hell. — 1611
4576 Life of Ignatius Loyala. ——— 1616
4577 Kenner's Case of Impropriations. ——— 1704
4578 ——— Ecclesiastical Synods. ——— 1701
4579 King's Constitution of the primitive Church. —— 1712
4580 Law's serious Call to a Holy Life. ——— 1729
4581 Lewis's Scourge in Vindication of the Church of England. 1720
4582 Lady's Calling. ——— 1677
4583 Lux Orientalis. ——— —— 1682
4584 Lesly's Snake in the Grass against the Quakers. —— 1698
4585 ——— Defence of the Snake in the Grass. ——— 1700
4586 ——— Case stated. ——— —— 1714
4587 Life of Gregory Lopez. ——— 1675
4588 Locke's History of our Saviour. ——— 1705
4589 Lauder's ancient Bishops considered. ——— 1707
4590 Luther's Last Will and Confession, *bl. letter.*
4591 Memoirs of Des-Ecotais, stiled the most venerable Father Cassianus of Paris. ——— 1677
4592 De la Militiere's Victory of Truth. ——— 1654
4593 More of the Immortality of the Soul. ——— 1659
4594 Norris's Letters concerning the Love of God. —— 1695
4595 Nelson's Companion for the Feasts and Fasts. —— 1732
4596 New Manual of Devotions. ——— 1729
4597 Nalson's Countermine against the Presbyterians. —— 1677
4598 Nelson's Practice of true Devotion. —— 1724
4599 ——— Address to Persons of Quality, large paper. 1715
4600 Owen's Nature of Apostasy. ——— 1676
4601 Parker of Religion and Loyalty, 2 vol. —— 1684
4602 Principles of the leading Quakers considered. —— 1732
4603 Patrick's Discourse on the Lord's Supper. —— 1717
4604 ——— on the Proverbs. ——— 1683
4605 ——— Christian Sacrifice. ——— 1720
4606 ——— on the Psalms, 2 vol. ——— 1680
4607 Prideaux's Connection, 4 vol. cuts. ——— 1729
4608 Pearson's Exposition of the Creed abridg'd. —— 1705
4609 Placette's Christian Casuist. ——— 1705

4610

4610 Primer set furth by K. Henry VIII. *bl. letter.*
4611 Prayer-Book, with the Pystels and Gospels, *bl. letter.*
4612 Primer in Latin, for the Use of Salisbury, *bl. letter.*
4613 Psalms, translated by K. James.
4614 Polyander against the Adoration of Reliques. —— 1611
4615 Parable of the wicked Mammon, *bl. letter.*
4616 Reflections upon Fleetwood of Miracles. —— 1706
4617 Reply to the Snake in the Grass. —— 1702
4618 Rights of the Christian Church, by Collins. —— 1707
4619 Ross's View of all Religions in the World. —— 1672
4620 Romish Horse-leech. —— 1674
4621 Reply to Waterland's Defence of his Queries. —— 1722
4622 Reflections on the Devotions of the Romish Church. 1674
4623 Rogers's Discourse of the visible and invisible Church. 1721
4624 Rye's Treatise against the Nonjurors, 2 vol. —— 1719
4625 Revelation examin'd with Candour, 2 vol. —— 1733
4626 Richardson's Canon of the New Testament vindicated. 1700
4627 Stanhope on the Epistles and Gospels, 4 vol. —— 1726
4628 ——St. Augustine's Meditations. —— 1728
4629 ——Kempis, or Christian Pattern, 2 vol. 1708
4630 ——Principles of the Christian Religion. —— 1719
4631 Sparrow's Rationale on the Common-Prayer. —— 1684
4632 Smalbrooke's Defence of Christianity. —— 1725
4633 Packet of Letters to Dr. Waterland. —— 1721
4634 Smith's Preservative against Quakerism. —— 1732
4635 Sykes's Authority of the Clergy vindicated. —— 1720
4636 Spelman's Hist. and Fate of Sacriledge. —— 1698
4637 Simon's religious Customs of the Eastern Nations. 1685
4638 Saurin's Dissertations on the Old and New Testament. 1720
4639 Stratford's Dissuasive from Revenge. —— 1684
4640 Spiritual Communion recommended from Scripture. 1725
4641 Savage's Power of the Sovereign, and the Right of the Liberty of Conscience. —— 1708
4642 Staynoe's Salvation, by Jesus Christ alone, 2 vol. —— 1704
4643 Steele's Romish Ecclesiastical History. —— 1714
4644 Spincke's sick Man visited. —— 1731
4645 ——Companion in the Closet. —— 1731
4646 ——Trust in God. —— 1714
4647 Smalbrook's Vindication of the Miracles, 2 vol. 1729
4648 Spelman de non Temerandis Ecclesiis, engl. 1668
4649 Selden on the Birth-Day of our Saviour. —— 1661
4650 Stillingfleet of English Convocations. —— 1702
4651 Sale's Introduction to a devout Life. —— 1614
4652 Savage's Vindication of Christianity. —— 1683
4653 Sherling's Life of St. Agnes. —— 1677
1654

4654 Sherlock's Discourse on Judgment. —— 1731
4655 ———on divine Providence. —— 1725
4656 ———on Death. —— —— 1731
4657 Stillingfleet's miscellaneous Discourses. — 1735
4658 ———Discourse on the Idolatry of the Ch. of Rome. 1672
4659 ———Ecclesiastical Cases. —— 1702
4660 ———Discourse on Christ's Satisfaction. ——1696
4661 Collection of Tracts in Divinity, 12 vol. sold separate.
4662 Tallent's History of Schism, and Moderation in fashion.
4663 Toland's Letters to Serena. —— 1704
4664 Treatises concerning the Worship of Mahomet. ——1719
4665 Taylor's Contemplations. —— 1684
4666 ———Worthy Communicant. —— 1701
4667 ———Holy Living and Dying. —— 1686
4668 Tryal of the Witnesses of the Resurrection, Whiston's Answer to Ld Nottingham, and Absolom and Achitopel, lat.
4669 Trapp's Doctrine of the Trinity proved.
4670 Tillotson's Rule of Faith. —— 1688
4671 Second Thoughts concerning human Soul. —— 1704
4672 Tillinghast's Generation Work. —— 1655
4673 Tyndall's Essay on the Power of the Magistrate.—— 1697
4674 Thorndike on the Primitive Government of Churches. 1650
4675 Vindication of the Church of England. — 1710
4676 Usher's Power of the Prince. —— 1710
4677 Veneer on the 39 Articles, 2 vol. —— 1730
4678 ———on the Common-Prayer. —— 1727
4679 ———Companion for the sincere Penitent. 1728
4680 Vindication of the Doctrine and Worship of the Ch. of England. —— 1733
4681 Woolston's Works, 5 vol. —— 1729
4682 ——— Moderator, and Discourse of the Miracles, compleat.
4683 Wilkins's Discourse on Prayer and Preaching. 1678
4684 Woodford's Paraphrase on the Psalms. — 1678
4685 Warren's impartial Church-man. —— 1728
4686 Wall's Hist. of Infant-Baptism. —— 1705
4687 Wake's Principles of the Christian Religion. 1700
4688 Ward's Controversy of Ordination illustrated. 1719
4689 Woodward's fair Warnings to a careless World. 1707
4690 Wesley's History of the Old and New Testament, 3 vol. cuts. —— —— 1716
4691 Wilson's Discourse of Religion. —— 1694
4693 Worthington's Duty of Self-Resignation. 1714
4694 Whiston's Primitive Christianity reviv'd, 4 vol. 1711
4695 Welton's Sufferings of the Son of God, 2 vol. 1720
4696 Waterland's Vindic. of Christ's Divinity. — 1719

4697

4697 Principles and Duties of Chrsstianity, by the Bp. of Sodor. 1707
4698 Ward on the Attributes of God. —— 1677
4699 Waring against the Papists, black letter.
4700 F. Atterbury's, 2 vol. —— —— 1734
4701 Bayly's, 2 vol. —— —— 1721
4702 Bradford, Smalbroke, Willis, and others.
4703 Bramston, Pearse, Bullock, and others.
4704 Burton's, 2 vol. —— —— 1684
4705 Burnet's —— —— 1713
4706 Bullock's —— —— 1730
4707 Bishop's —— —— 1726
4708 Brady's, 3 vol. —— —— 1730
4709 Blackhall on the Lord's Prayer. —— 1727
4710 Blackhall's, 8 vol. lar. and fin. pap. —— 1717
4711 Bull's, 4 vol. lar. pap.
4712 Brooke's and Bailie's, black letter.
4713 Clarke's, 10 vol.
4714 Clagett's, 2 vol. —— —— 1720
4715 Calamy's —— —— 1715
4716 Colet's —— —— 1661
4717 Dawes's, 3 vol. —— —— 1733
4718 Davies's —— —— 1720
4719 Delaune's —— —— —— 1728
4720 Friend, Gooch, Archer, and others.
4721 Gale's, 4 vol. —— —— 1726
4722 Hickman's, 2 vol. —— 1706 Sermons.
4723 Hoadly's, with other Tracts.
4724 Innes's —— —— 1726
4725 Kettlewell's —— —— 1708
4726 Lucas's, 2 vol. —— —— 1699
4727 Gace's —— —— —— 1578
4728 Latimer's, black letter. ——
4729 Moss's, 5 vol. —— —— —— 1732
4730 Markland's, 2 vol. —— —— 1729
4731 Nervlin's, 2 vol. —— —— —— —— 1720
4732 Peirce's —— —— —— 1728
4733 Pearse, Adamson, Bedford, and others.
4734 Payne's, Mangey, Chishull, and others.
4735 Piggott's —— —— —— 1714
4736 Reeves's —— —— 1729
4737 Sanderson's, 3 vol. —— —— —— 1722
4738 Sheridan's, 3 vol. —— —— 1720
4739 Stanhope, Willis, West, and others.
4740 Wise, Swynfen, Derby, and others.
4741 Smalridge, Potter, Sacheverel, and others.
4742 Sprat's —— —— —— 1722
4743 Sherlock's —— —— —— 1725
4744 Trebeck's —— —— —— 1730

U 4745

4745 Wise's — — — — 1727 } Sermons.
*4745 Wilder's
4746 Fleetwood's — — 1712
4747 Atterbury, Clarke, Roberts, and others.
4748 Common Prayer, Eng. and Irish.
4749 Cardinals Intrigues in chusing Popes. — 1721
4750 Common Prayer, Fr. and Eng. — 1717
4751 Blackmore's Summary of Christian Antiq. 2 vol. 1722
4752 The Old and New Testament, translated by Tindale, 2 vol. black letter.
4753 Lives and Acts of the Apostles, cuts. — 1700
4754 Collins's Grounds and Reasons of the Christian Relig. 1724
4755 Jones's Body of Divinity, 2 vol. — 1713
4756 Cancellar's Path of Obedience, black letter.
4757 Toile for two-legged Foxes. — — — 1600
4758 Protestant Hist. of the Pope's Pastoral Charge in Britain.
4759 Several curious Divinity Tracts, black letter, sew'd together.

Livres en Theologie. Octavo & Infra.

4760 Defense de la Libertez des Eglises reformees de France, 2 vol. — — — *Amst.* 1688
4761 Politique tiree de l'Ecriture sainte par Bossuet, 2 vol. *Brux.* 1721
4762 Ritraitte spirituelle par Bourdaloue, 2 vol. — *Paris.* 1721
4763 Oeuvres posthumes de Mr. Claude, 5 vol. — *Amst.* 1690
4764 Catechisme de Montpelier, 4 vol. — *Paris.* 1719
4765 Vie de St. Jean Chrysostome. — *Lyon.* 1683
4766 Les Visites Charitables par Drelincourt, 3 vol. *Amst.* 1731
4767 Defense des Ordinations Angloises par Courayer, 4 vol. *Brux.* 1726
4768 Exposition de J. Daille sur les Epistres, 2 vol. — *Genev.* 1660
4769 Essais de Morale, 4 vol. — 1673
4770 Hist. ecclesiastique par Fleury, 26 vol — *Brux.* 1723
4771 Panegyriques & autres Sermons par Flecher, 2 vol. *ib.* 1696
4772 Les Oeuvres de Granade, 9 vol. — *Paris.* 1675
4773 Hist. de l'Image & de la Chapelle de Notre Dame. *Saumur.* 1651
4774 Apologie pour Herodote. — 1566
4775 Preservative contre la Reunion par l'Enfant. — *Amst.* 1723
4776 Abus de la Critique en Matiere de Religion par de Laubrussel, 2 vol. — — *Paris.* 1710
4777 Les Larmes de St. Pierre & autres Verses, relie en maroquin, dore sur tranche. — *ib. par Estienne.* 1606
4778 Hist. de Notre Dame de Hale. — *Mons* 1697
4779 Traite des Etudes Monastiques par Mabillon. — 1691
4780 L'Excellence de la Foy par Martin, 2 vol. — *Amst.* 1710
4781 Oeuvres de Mestrezat, 4 vol. — *Genev.* 1651
4782 Hist. de l'Arianisme par Maimbourg, 2 vol. 1683

4783 Traitte de l'Aumon par Placette. ——— Amst.1699
4784 Traitte du Serment par Placette. —— a la Haye.1701
4785 Penses de Pascal sur la Religion. ——— Amst.1699
4786 Responce au nouv. Reformat, de l'Eglises. —— Paris.1562
4787 Entretiens de l'Abbe Jean & du Prestre Eusebe.——ib.1674
4788 Le vraye Commuuicant par Superville. ———Rot.1722
4789 Le Triomphe de la Providence par Abbadie, 4 vol. Amst.1723
4790 La Verite de la Religion reformee, 2 vol. —— Rot.1718
4791 Le Nouveau Testament. ——— Mons.1672

Libri Italici & Hispanici. Octavo & Infra.

4792 Avisi di Parnasso di Boccalini. ——— Venet.1619
4793 Anfiteatre e singolarmente de Veronesa.——— Verona.1728
4794 La Ulyxea de Homero en Leng. Castellana por Gonçalo Perez. Anvers.1556
4795 Hist. de el Cardenal Ximenez. ——— Leon.1712
4796 Horacio Espanol consegrad. a la individua Trinidad. ib. 1682
4797 Institutione del Prencipe. ——— 1545
4798 Osservazzioni sopra Poggiana. ——— Venez.1721
4799 Las Obras del Poeta Mosen Ausias March. Valladolid 1555
4800 Poesie Dramatiche di Ant. Moniglia, 2 vol.——Firense.1698
4801 Discorsi di Agost. Mascardi ——— Torino 1629
4802 Il Principe de N. Machiavelli. ——— 1537
4803 L'Adone del Marino, 4 vol. foliis deauratis. Parigi.1678
4804 Lettere di Manutio. ——— Venet.1556
4805 Rime di Marino. ——— ib 1602
4806 Le Metamorphosi di Ovidio, 3 vol. foliis deauratis. ib 1624
4807 ———Il Medesimo, con fig. ——— Lione.1584
4808 Mirtia di L. Paterno, 2 vol. ——— Napoli.1564
4809 Il Petrarcha.
4810 ———Il Medesimo, foliis deaurat. Lione par Rovillio. 1550
4811 ———Il Medesimo, 3 vol. foliis deaurat.——Venet.
4812 Il Pastor Fido, con fig. ——— Parigi.1677
4813 ———Il Medesimo con fig. ——— Amst.1662
4814 La Pazzia de gli Huomini di Corte. ——— Venet.1608
4815 Rime del Mauro & d' altri Auttori. ——— ib 1537
4816 Prediche di Savonarola. ——— ib 1544
4817 La Liturgia Ynglesa. ——— Lond 1707
4818 Compendio delle Virtu Heroiche di Leti, 2 vol. Amst 1700
4819 Ragguali di Parnasso di Boccalini. ——— Venet.1669
4820 Rime del Monte Magno da Pistoria. —— Roma.
4821 Rime di diversi Autori, 2 vol.—— Vineg. per Gielito.1564
4822 Scielta di Stanze di divers Autori Toscani. ——Venet.1571
4823 La Selva di varia Lettione di P. Messia. ——— ib.1544
4824 Rime Scelte di Poeti Ferraresi. ——— Ferrara.1713
4825 Dialogi d'Amicizia di L. Salviati. ——— Firenz.1564

4826 L'Italia Libertata da Goti di G. Trissino, 3 vol. *Parigi* 1729
4827 L'Aminta di Tasso difeso da Fontanini. —— *Rom.* 1700
4828 Aminta di Tasso, foliis deauratis. —— *Parigi.* 1678
4829 La Gierusalemme di Tasso, con fig. —— *Genova.* 1604
4830 ——Il Medesimo, corio turcico, foliis deauratis. *Venet.* 1609
4831 Discorsi sopra Tacito del Malvezzi. —— *ib.* 1665
4832 L'Humore Dialogo di B. Targio. —— *Milano.* 1564
4833 Tiempó de Regozijo y Carnestolandos de Madrid. *Madrid.* 1627
4834 Del Regno d'Italia sotto i Barbari Epitome di E. Tesauro. *Venet.* 1680
4835 Il Tesoro della Sanita di C. Durante. —— *ib.* 1589
4836 Hist. de Vicere di Napoli, 3 vol. —— *Napoli.* 1692
4837 Sonetti di B. Varchi. —— *Fiorenz.* 1555
4838 Poesie Italiane di Rimatrice viventi. —— *Venez.* 1716
4839 Le Visione Politiche. —— *Germania.* 1671
4840 Satire e Rime di Ariosto con le annotat. di Rolli. —— 1732
4841 Gli Opuscoli di Scipione Ammirato. —— *Fiorenz.* 1583
4842 L'Anthropologia di G. Capella, foliis deauratis. *Venet. per Aldo.* 1533
4843 Orlando Furioso, foliis deauratis. —— *Venet.* 1577
4844 Il Decameron di Boccacci, 2 vol. —— *Amst.* 1679
4845 Poesie Toscane del Card. Barberino. —— *Roma.* 1640
4846 Il Filocolo di Boccacio. —— *Firenz. per Giunti.* 1594
4847 Baccanali di Baruffaldi. —— *Venez.* 1722
4848 Lettere di Bentivoglio. —— *Roma.* 1654
4849 La Hist. del Mondo nuovo di Benzoni. —— *Venet.* 1565
4850 Il Cardinalismo di S. Chiesa, 2 vol. 3 vol.
4851 Conclavi di Pontifici Romani, 3 vol. —— *Col.* 1691
4852 Lettere di And. Calmo. —— *Vineg.* 1580
4853 La Chiave del Calandaro Gregoriano. —— *Lione.* 1583
4854 Chronologia ecclesiastica di Baldini. —— *Bolog.* 1690
4855 Le Secreti di L. Fioravanti. —— *Venet.* 1591
4856 Auroras di Diana por Pedro de Castro. —— *Madrid.* 1637
4857 Il Cortegiano di Castiglione, lineis rubris, corio turcico, foliis deauratis. —— *Lione per Rovillio.* 1562
4858 Dante, foliis deauratis. —— *Venet. per Aldi.* 1502
4859 ——Il Medesimo, lineis rubris, foliis deauratis. *Lione.* 1547
4860 ——Il Medesimo, 3 vol. foliis deauratis. —— *Venet.* 1620
4861 Leucadia del Droghi. —— *Bolog.* 1598
4862 Epistolas de Ant. de Guevara. —— *Anversa.* 1552
4863 Eleganze de la Ling. Toscana e Latina. —— *Venet.* 1575
4864 Lettere di L. Groto. —— *Vineg.* 1616
4865 Rime & Prose della Casa. —— *Fiorenz.* 1564
4866 Hist. di Giovanni Capriata. —— *Genev.* 1644
4867 Opere di Giovan della Casa, 2 vol. *Stampata in Pergameno.* 1727
868 Concetti di G. Garimberto. —— *Venet.* 1559

4869

4869 Comment delle Cose di Turchi di P. Giovio, foliis deauratis Vineg. per Aldi. 1539
4870 Dialoghi Politichi, 2 vol. ——— Roma. 1666
4871 Filli di Sciro. ——— Parigi. 1678
4872 ———Il Medesimo, ch. granda. ——— Lond. 1728

Theologia & Hist. Ecclesiastica. Octavo & Infra.

4873 St. Augustini Sententiæ. ——— Paris. 1649
4874 ———Opuscula quædam selecta, 3 vol.—L. Paris. 1726
4875 Allacii Vindiciæ Synodi Ephesinæ & Cyrilli.——Roma. 1661
4876 ——de Purgatorio. ——— ib. 1655
4877 —— de Octava Synodo Photiana. ——— ib. 1661
4878 Apollinarii interpret. Psalmorum versibus Heroicis gr. Paris. apud Turneb. 1552
4879 Aristæi Hist. LXXII. Interpretum gr. lat. ——— Oxon. 1692
4880 Athanasii Dialogi de Trinitate gr. lat. apud H. Steph 1570
4881 Vecsei Analytica D. Johannis Apost. S. Apocalypseos Paraphrasis adornata. ——— Franeq. 1690
4882 Buddei Prudentiæ Civilis Rabbinice Specimen.—Jena. 1694
4883 Biblia Sacra, 3 vol. —— ——Lut. apud R. Steph. 1545
4884 ———Idem, 2 vol. foliis deauratis. ——— Lug. 1549
4885 ———Idem. ——— Ant. 1572
4886 ———Idem, vulgatæ Editionis, corio turcico, foliis deauratis. ——— Col. Agrip. 1646
4887 ———Idem, ex Castellionis Interpret. 4 vol. Lond. 1726
4888 ———vulgatæ Editionis, 4 vol. lineis rubris.—— apud S. Gryph. 1550
4889 ———vulgatæ Editionis, 5 vol. ——— Col. Agrip. 1670
4890 ———vulgatæ Edit. lineis rubris, 3 vol. —Paris, apud Col. 1525
4891 ———Græcæ LXX Interpret.—Cant. apud Field. 1665
4892 ———Idem, 2 vol. ——— Lond. apud Daniel. 1653
4893 ———Idem, recensuit D. Millius, 2 vol.——Traject. ad Rhen. 1725
4894 Breviarium Romanum. ——— Venet. 1592
4895 Bilibra Veritatis & Rationis de Verbo Dei. ——— 1700
4896 Bulengeri Institutiones Christianæ. ——— Lut. Paris. 1560
4897 Bulfingeri de Origine & Permissione Mali. ——— Franc. 1724
4898 Burnet de Statu Mortuorum. ——— Lond. 1727
4899 ———de Fide & Officiis Christianorum. ib. 1723
4900 Brantii Hist. & Vita J. Arminii. ——— Amst. 1724
4901 T. Beza de Hereticis. ——— apud R. Steph. 1554
4902 Barnesii Catholico-Romanus Pacificus. Oxon. 1680
4903 J. Bastwick Flagellum Pontificis. ——— Lond 1641
4904 St. Barnabæ Epistola Catholica gr. lat. ——— Ooxn. 1685
4905 Declaratio J. Sergeantii. ——— Duaci. 1677
4906 D. Carthusianii contra Alcoranum & Sectam Machometicam Lib. ——— ——— Colon. 1533

4907

4907 Calvini Infernus adversus Polyandrum.—— *Ant.*1608
4908 Camuzat Promptuarium sacrarum antiq. 1610
4909 Calvini Defensio Fidei de sacra Trinitate.*apud R. Steph.*1554
4910 Cassiodori Opera, Lat. per Pamelium. ——*Ant.*1566
4911 Coleri Epistolæ varii Argumenti. —— *Lipf.*1725
4912 B. Conner Evangelium Medici. —— ——*Jenæ* 1724
4913 Raderi Vita Canisii. —— ——*Monachii* 1614
4914 Alcimus Episc. de Origine Mundi, &c.—— *Basil.*1545
4915 S. Castellionis Dialogi. —— *Goudæ* 1613
4916 Canones & Decreta Concilii Tridentini. ——*Rom.*1595
4917 Eusebii Dialogi. —— *Edinb.* 1574
4918 Doctrina de administrando Sacramento Penitentiæ, Opera Theologorum Belgarum. —— — *Lovan.*1701
4919 Dodwelli Dissertationes Cyprianic. —— Oxon.1684
4920 C. Daubuz pro Testimonio F. Josephi de Jesu Christo. *Lond.* 1706
4921 Dodwelli Dissertationes in Irenæum. ——Oxon.1689
4922 Drusii in Prophetam Hoseam Lectiones. ——1599
4923 —— in Prophetam Amos.—— ——1600
4924 Drelincurtii Orationes. —— *Lug. Bat.*1689
4925 Ebarti Enchiridion Theologicum Positivo-Polemicum. *Jenæ* 1690
4926 Espencæi Elegia, Eucharistia, Ænigma. *Paris apud Morel.* 1563
4927 Basilii Magni Epist. selectæ. —— *ib. apud Colinæum* 1531
4928 R. Ford Christianæ Religionis Comment. ——*Lond.*1720
4929 Frontonis Epist. & Dissertat. Ecclesiastic. —— *Hamb.*1720
4930 Flaminii in Lib. Psalmorum Explanat. *foliis deaurat. Venet. apud Aldum* 1545
4931 Gilberti Syntagma Dictorum Scripturæ cccc. *Franc.*1729
4932 Gregentii Disputat. cum Herbano Judæo. *Lut. apud Morel.* 1586
4933 Hymni v. in B. Deiparum, gr. lat. *Lut. apud Morel.*1591
4934 Colloquium Jesuiticum, Clenardi Tabula in Grammatic. Hebræam.
4935 Grotius de Cœnæ Administratione—— ——*Lond.*1685
4936 —— Animadvers. in Animadvers. Riveti.—— ——1642
4937 —— de Veritate Religionis Christianæ.——*Amst.*1662
4938 Gurtleri Synopsis Theologiæ Reformatæ.——*Marburg.*1731
4939 —— Hist. Templariorum. —— *Amst.*1703
4940 Vetus Testamentum juxta lxx. Interpretes, cura E. Grabe, 8 vol. —— —— *Oxon.*1707
4941 Heptateuchus, Liber Job, & Evangelium Nicodemi Anglo-Saxonic. —— —— *Oxon.*1698
4942 J. Hommey Supplementum Patrum. —— *Par.*1696
4943 Politica sacra, sive de Imperio Dei ejusque Juribus Comment. *Lubecæ* 1720
4944 Justini Martyris Apologia, gr. lat. —— *Oxon.*

4975

4975 Kenkeni Aphorismi. ———— Lips. 1730
4976 S. Martyris Ignatii Epistolæ, gr. lat. Par. apud Morel. 1562
4977 Julius Secundus, Dialogus. ———— Oxon. 1680
4978 Justini Martyris, cum Tryphone Judæo Dialogus, gr. lat. Edit. a S. Jebb. ———— Lond. 1719
4979 T. a Kempis de Imitatione Christi, *cor. tur. fol. deaurat.* Colon. 1682
4980 Lectiones Hebreæ, per Bomberg.
4981 Launoii Differt. de Auct. Librorum de Imitatione Christi. Lut. Par. 1663
4982 ———de Mente Concil. Trident. circa Contrit. & Attrit. Par. 1653
4983 Lactantii Opera, & Comment. a T. Spark. — Oxon. 1684
4984 Catechesis D. Martini Lutheri Minor. ——— Viteberg. 1572
4985 Cyrilli Patriarchæ Confessio Christianæ Fidei. ——— 1645
4986 Jonas Illustratus per Paraphrasin Chaldaicam, a J. Leusden. Traj. ad Rhen. 1692
4987 Latitudinarius Orthodoxus. ———— Lond. 1697
4988 Maraccii Prodromus ad Refutationem Alcorani, 4 vol. Romæ 1691
4989 J. Melchioris Fundamenta Theologiæ Didascalicæ. Marburgi. 1727
4990 C. Stresi Meditat. in Pauli Apostoli Epistolam ad Colossenses. Amst. 1708
4991 Massoni Jani Templum Christo Nascente reseratum. Rot. 1700
4992 P. de Marca Dissertationes posthumæ. ——— 1669
4993 Marii Mercatis Opera, Notis Baluzii. ———— Par. 1684
4994 Mysteria Patrum Jesuitarum. ———— Lamprop. 1633
4995 G. Nazianzeni Orationes, gr. *fol. deaurat.* Ven. apud Ald.
4996 ———Arcana. ———— ———— Lug. Bat. 1591
4997 Optatus Afrus de Schismate Donatistarum, contra Parmenianum. ———— Lond 1631
4998 Officium B. Mariæ Virginis. ——— Ant. 1692
4999 Origenis de Oratione, gr. lat. ——— Oxon.——
5000 Picteti Medulla Theologiæ Christianæ. ——— Gen. 1711
5001 Pomponatius de Immortalite Animæ. ———— 1534
5002 Breviarium, ad usum Sarum. ———— Par. 1532
5003 Liber Precum Eccles. Cathedral. Christi Oxon.— Oxon.——
5004 Psalterium, ad usum Sarum.
5005 Pfaffii Dissertatio de Genuinis Librorum Nov. Testament. Amst. 1709
5006 N. Testamentum Græcum. ———— Lond. 1633
5007 Pacificatorium Orthodoxæ Theologiæ Corpusculum, *cor. turc. foliis deaurat.* ——— ——— Lond. 1683
5008 F. Perrin Manuale Theologicum, 2 vol. ——— Par. 1714
5009 Psalmorum Davidis Paraphras. Poetica, a G. Buchanano, *cor. tur. fol. deaurat. lin. rub.* apud H. Steph.——
5010 Liturgia seu Liber Precum. ———— Lond. 1670

5011

5011 Liber Psalmorum Davidis tralatio. *apud R. Steph.* 1559
5012 ——Idem, gr. —— *Par. apud Morel.* 1618
5013 Compendium Moralis Evangelicæ, 8 vol. —— *Par.* 1694
5014 Richerii Hist. Conciliorum Generalium, 2 vol. *Col.* 1683
5015 Ribadeneiræ Illustrium Scriptorum Religionis S. Jesu Catalogus. —— —— *Ant.* 1608
5016 Rufini Liber de Fide Studio Sermondi. —— *Par.* 1650
5017 Rittangelius de Trinitate & Christo.—— *Franeq.* 1699
5018 Spicelegium Patrum E. Grabe, 2 vol. *ch. max.* *Oxon.* 1698
5019 Collectanea de S. Cyrillo Patriarcha, Aut. T. Smith. *Lond.* 1707
5020 Spenseri Dissertat. de Urim et Thummim.— *Cant.* 1669
5021 J. Stearne de Obstinatione Opus posthumum. *Dub.* 1672
5022 Sirmondus de Heresibus. —— *Par.* 1643
5023 Lemnii Herbar. Bibl. explicatio. —— *Ant.* 1569
5024 Savanorolæ Meditat. in Psalmos. — *Tubingæ* 1621
5025 Synopsis Locorum Sacræ Scripturæ Patrum. *Amst.* 1650
5026 Testamentum Græcum. — *Cant. apud Buck.* 1632
5027 ——Idem, M. Mattaire, *ch. max.* —— *Lond.* 1714
5028 ——Idem, variæ Lectiones. —— *Oxon.* 1675
5029 Idem. studio Curcelæi. —— *Amst.* 1658
5030 ——Idem, 2 vol. —— *Par.* 1715
5031 ——Idem, 2 vol. *cor. turc. fol. deaurat.* *Lond.* 1701
5032 ——Idem. —— *Lug. Bat. apud Elz.* 1641
5033 ——Idem. —— *Lut. apud R. Steph.* 1569
5034 ——Idem. —— *Sedani* 1628
5035 ——Idem, Lat. —— *Par. apud Ruel.* 1554
5036 ——Idem, vulgatæ Editionis. *Lug. apud S. Gryph.* 1555
5037 Delherri Eclogæ Sacræ N. Testament. Syriacæ, gr. lat. *Jenæ* 1662
5038 Theodoreti Episcopi de Providentia Sermones, gr. *Romæ* 1545
5039 Tolandi Adeisidæmon. —— *Hagæ Comit.* 1709
5040 Tertulliani Liber de Pallio, recensuit Salmasius. *Lug. Bat.* 1666
5041 Zouch tractat. de Politia Ecclesiæ Anglicanæ. *Lond.* 1705
5042 Maximi Tyrii Dissertat. gr. lat. ex interpret. D. Heinsii. *Cant.* 1703
5043 Uvigandus Episc. de Peccatis et Peccatoribus. —— 1580
5044 Cæsaris Vanini Dialogi. —— *Lut.* 1616
5045 ——Amphitheatrum Æternæ Providentiæ Divino Magicum. —— —— *Lug.* 1615
5046 Whartoni Hist. de Episcopis & Decanis Londinensibus. *Lond.* 1695
5047 Weismanni Orationes Academicæ. —— *Tubingæ* 1729
5048 Wormii Hist. Sabelliana. —— *Franc.* 1696
5049 Walchii Comment. de Concilio Lateranensi. — *Lips.* —
5050 Zosimi Hist. nova Notis illustrat. gr. lat. *Oxon.* 1679
5051 ——Idem, ex recensione Sylburgii. — *Jenæ* 1729

Books

Books relating to the History, Antiquities, and Parliamentary Affairs of Great-Britain and Ireland. Octavo & infra.

5052 Annals of Queen Anne, 11 vol. —— 1703
5053 Acta Regia, or an Abridgment of Rymer's Fœdera. 1731
5054 Earl of Arlington's Letters, 2 vol. —— 1701
5055 Ashmole's Hist. of the Order of the Garter. —— 1715
5056 Anderson's Essay, shewing the Crown of Scotland is Independent. —— —— 1705
5057 Account of Scotland. —— 1702
5058 Aleyn's Hist. of Henry the VII. —— 1638
5059 Abridgement or Summary of the Scots Chronicles. 1653
5060 Augustus Anglicus, or the Life of Charles II. 1686
5061 Aulicus Coquinariæ, or a Vindicat. of the Court and Character of King James. —— 1650
5062 Bulstrode's Memoirs of the Reigns of King Charles I. and II. 1721
5063 Bohun's Privileges and Customs of London. —— 1723
5064 ——Character of Queen Elizabeth. —— 1693
5065 Budgel's Letter to the King of Sparta.
5066 Baronettage of England, 2 vol. —— 1720
5067 Buchanan's Hist. of Scotland, 2 vol. —— 1722
5068 Barwick's Life of Dr. Barwick Dean of St. Paul's. 1724
5069 Brown's Collection of State-Treatises. —— 1702
5070 Burchet's Memoirs of Transactions at Sea. —— 1703
5071 Sir Thomas Brown's posthumous Works, *cuts.* —— 1712
5072 Brown's Lives of the Princes of Orange. —— 1693
5073 Bridall's View of London. —— —— 1676
5074 Bibliotheca Regia. —— —— 1659
5075 Brodrick's compleat Hist. of the late War, *cuts.* — 1713
5076 Bacon's Remains. —— —— 1679
5077 Barnard's Life of Dr. Heylin. —— 1683
5078 Monasticon Britannicum. —— 1655
5079 Account of the Family of the Butlers. —— 1716
5080 British Curiosities in Art and Nature. —— 1721
5081 Bernard's Life of Bp. Usher. —— 1656
5082 Boate's Natural Hist. of Ireland. —— 1652
5083 Broughton's Memorial of Great-Britain. —— 1650
5084 Brown's Discourse on the sepulchral Urns found in Norfolk. 1658
5085 Boscobel, or an Account of the King's Escape. 1680
5086 Bale's Acts of the English Votaries.
5087 Burton's Wars of England, Scotland, and Ireland. 1684
5088 Batchiler's Life and lamentable Death of Susanna Perwich. 1661

X 5089

5089 Burnet's Abridg. of his Hiſt. of the Reformation. 1683
5090 ——— Life of the Earl of Rocheſter. —— 1680
5091 ——— Eſſay on the Memory of Queen Mary. 1695
5092 ——— Life and Death of Sir M. Hale. —— 1682
5093 ——— Vindication of the Church of Scotland. —— 1673
5094 Craftſman, being a Critique on the Times, 2 vol. 1727
5095 Clarendon's Hiſt. of the Rebellion, 7 vol. *cuts.* 1705
5096 Chamberlen's preſent State of England. —— 1735
5097 Camden's Britannia abridg'd, 2 vol. —— 1701
5098 Caveat againſt the Whigs, compleat. —— 1714
5099 Cockburn's Remarks on publick Affairs, occaſional Hiſtorian, and Guy's laſt Will.
5100 Critical Hiſt. of England. —— 1724
5101 Copy of the Journal-Book of the Houſe of Commons. 1680
5102 Carrington's Life and Death of Oliver Cromwel. 1659
5103 Caſtlemaine's Catholique Apology. —— 1674
5104 Court and Character of King James. —— 1650
5105 Cromwell's Bloody Slaughter-Houſe. —— 1660
5106 Chronicle of Sir John Oldcaſtle, *black letter.*
5107 Caſe ſtated concerning the Judicature of the Houſe of Peers 1675
5108 Defence of the Scots abdicating Darien, with other Tracts.
5109 Drake's Hiſt. Anglo-Scotica. —— 1703
5110 Dying Speeches, being an Appendix to the State-Trials. 1720
5111 Dodridge's Hiſt. of the Principalities of Wales, Cornwal, and Cheſter. —— —— 1714
5112 Duck's Life of Arch-bp. Chichéle. —— 1699
5113 Drake's Memoirs of Dudley Earl of Leiceſter. —— 1706
5114 Debate at large concerning the Word Abdicated. 1710
5115 Defence of the Scots Settlement at Darien anſwer'd. 1699
5116 Drummond's Hiſt. of Scotland. —— 1682
5117 Doleman's Conference on the Succeſſion. —— 1681
5118 Defenſio Legis, or England defended. —— 1674
5119 Davies's Hiſt. of the Oxford and Cambridge Writers, 3 vol. 1716
5120 Dryden's Year of Wonders. —— 1667
5121 Dunſtar's Deſcription of England. —— 1699
5122 Drayton's England's Hiſt. Epiſtles. —— 1599
5123 Sir G. Downing's Diſcourſe in Vindication of King Charles. 1672
5124 Duncan's Life of the Lady Falkland. —— 1653
5125 Dugdale's ancient Uſage of bearing Arms. —— 1682
5126 Enquiry into the State of the Union of Great-Britain. 1717
5127 England's black Tribunal. —— 1703
5128 England's Miſeries ſet forth in a true Light. —— 1692
5129 England's Remembrancer. —— 1682
5130 England's Remarques. —— 1682

5131

5131 Fortescue's Difference between Absolute and Limited Monarchy. — — 1714
5132 Fleetwood's Chronicon Preciosum. — 1707
5133 Fanshaw's original Letters. — 1702
5134 Ferguson's Vindication of the Scots Design against Darien. 1699
5135 Faulkland's Hist. of King Edward II. — 1680
5136 Full and clear Answer to Sir William Petit. — 1681
5137 General Collection of Treaties of Peace, 2 vol. 1710
5138 Grand Question concerning Bishop's Right to vote in Cases Capital. — — 1680
5139 Gildas's Description of Great-Britain. — 1652
5140 Hist. of the English College at Doway, with other Tracts.
5141 Hist. of England, 4 vol. *cuts*. — 1722
5142 Hist. of the present Parliament 1711. — 1711
5143 Historical Register compleat, 22 vol.
5144 Higgons's Remarks on Burnet's History. — 1727
5145 Higden's View of the English Constitution. — 1709
5146 Howell's Medulla Hist. Anglicanæ, *cuts*. — 1734
5147 Hist. of the most remarkable Trials of Great-Britain. 1725
5148 Hist. of the Clemency of our English Monarchs. 1717
5149 Hawkin's Life of Bp. Ken. — 1713
5150 Herbert's Memoirs of the two last Years of K. Charles I. 1712
5151 Hist. of the last Parliament in 1700. — 1702
5152 Harmer's Errors in Burnet's Hist. of the Reformation. 1693
5153 Herne's History of the Charter-House. — 1677
5154 Hollis's Remains concerning the Judicature of Bishops. 1682
5155 Howard's Life of King Richard II. — 1681
5156 Hist. of the English and Scotch Presbytery. — 1659
5157 Hinde's Life and Death of John Bruen, Esq; — 1641
5158 Hist. Collections concerning the Reformation. 1674
5159 Hist. of the Commons War of England. — 1662
5160 Hobbes's History of the Civil Wars of Engl. — 1679
5161 Heylin's Help to English History. — 1709
5162 Hist. of the Antiquities of Great Britain, *cuts*. — 1716
5163 Hallifax, and its Gibbet-Law placed in a true Light. 1708
5164 History of Henry the VIIIth, and Clark's Life of Queen Elizabeth.
5165 Hist. Memoirs of the Reigns of Q. Elizabeth and K. James. 1658
5166 Heydon's prophetical Trumpeter to England. — 1655
5167 Hist. of the Reign of K. James II. — 1689
5168 Hist. of K. Charles II. — 1660
5169 Hakewill's Manner of passing Bills in Parliament. — 1641
5170 Heywood's Life and Troubles of Q. Elizabeth. — 1641
5171 Jebb's History of Mary Queen of Scots, large paper. 1725

5172 Jebb's Life of Robert Earl of Leicester, large and small pap. —— 1727
5173 Ignoramus, a Comedy acted before K. James. —— 1658
5174 Izacke's remarkable Antiquities of the City of Exeter.
5175 Information against the Oppressors of the poor Commons, bl. letter.
5176 Impartial Account of the Affairs of Scotland. —— 1705
5177 Just Defence of the Royal Martyr King Charles the Ist. 1699
5178 Jewel's View of Pope Pius Quintus's seditious Bull, black letter. —— 1582
5179 Knight's Life of Dr. Colet. —— 1724
5180 Lives of all the Lords Chancellors of England, 2 vol. 1708
5181 Life of K. Henry II. —— 1702
5182 Letter from the Earl of Marr to the King. —— 1715
5183 Lilburne's Exceptions to a Bill of Indictment. —— 1653
5184 Libel of Spanish Lyes. —— 1596
5185 Langhorne's Introduction to the History of England. 1676
5186 Lambard's Perambulation of Kent. —— 1656
5187 Leycester's Common-wealth, by Father Parsons. —— 1641
5188 Leigh's England described. —— 1659
5189 L'Estrange's Hist. of the Times, compl. —— 1687
5190 Life of St. Thomas, ABp of Canterbury. —— 1639
5191 Lhancarvan's History of Wales. —— 1697
5192 Life of Richard Hooker. —— 1665
5193 Lhuyd's Breviary of Britain, bl. letter.
5194 Life of Dr. Harris. —— 1660
5195 Memoirs of the Earl of Castlehaven. —— 1680
5196 —— of the Viscount Dundee, and the Highland Clans. —— 1714
5197 —— of John Ker of Kersland, 3 vol. —— 1726
5198 —— of the Affairs of Scotland. —— 1706
5199 —— Brit sh and Foreign. —— 1712
5200 —— of the Couduct of Queen Anne's Ministry, with other Tracts.
5201 —— of the Marquis of Clanricarde. —— 1722
5202 —— of the Earl of Anglesey. —— 1693
5203 Monastical History of Ireland, cuts. —— 1722
5204 Mackenzie's Defence of the Royal Line of Scotland. 1685
5205 Martyrology, or the bloody Assize under Lord Jefferies. 1689
5206 Martyrology of England. —— 1608
5207 Milton's History of England. —— 1695
5208 Mainwaring's Legitimacy of Amicia, Daughter of the Earl of Chester. —— 1679
5209 —— Defence of Amicia. —— 1673
5210 May's Hist. of the Parliament of England. —— 1689

5211

5211 Nalson's common Interest of King and People. —— 1678
5212 Non-such Charles's Character. —— 1651
5213 Nicholson's Irish historical Library. —— 1724
5214 Narrative of the Proceedings of Cromwell's Commissioners against the ejected Ministers. —— 1660
5215 Noy's Treatise of the Rights of the Crown. —— 1715
5216 Ogilby's Roads of England, 2 vol. —— 1720
5217 Old England, or the Government prov'd Hereditary. 1705
5218 Observations on Sir J. Finett's Reception of Ambassadors. 1656
5219 Oglio of Traytors, including the Tryal of the King.
5220 Orders of the Hospitals of St. Bartholomew, Christ's, Bridewell, and St. Thomas's. —— 1557
5221 Order of the Lord-Mayor and Aldermen for wearing their Apparel. —— 1696
5222 Penitent Life of the woeful J. Atherton Bishop of Waterford.
5223 Proceedings of the Court of Justice against King Charles. 1654
5224 Pointer's Chronolog. Hist. of England, 3 vol. —— 1714
5225 Proceedings against the Earl of Clarendon. —— 1700
5226 Peerage of England, 4 vol. —— 1717
5227 Parker's Hist. of his own Time, by Newlin. —— 1727
5228 Petty's political Survey of Ireland. —— 1719
5229 Paul's Life of ABp Whitgift. —— 1699
5230 Proceedings against Sir John Fenwick. —— 1698
5231 Parkhurst's Life of Burkitt. —— 1704
5232 Relation of the Expedition to Kent, Essex, and Colchester. 1650
5233 Rapin's History of England, 15 vol. cuts.
5234 Rosewell's Arraignment and Tryal. —— 1718
5235 Royal Treasury of England, or an hist. Account of Taxes. 1725
5236 Roman Stations in Britain, according to the Imperial Itinerary. —— 1726
5237 Report of the Lords concerning the publick Records. 1719
5238 Rebels no Saints, or the Speeches of Persons executed 1661
5239 Relation of defeating Mazarine's and Cromwell's Design on Ostend. —— 1666
5240 Southouse's Monasticon Favershamiense. —— 1671
5241 Skinner's Life of General Monk. —— 1724
5242 ——Hist. of the late Troubles in England. —— 1685
5243 State-Tryals, vol. 7, 8, and 9, to compleat Setts.
5244 Short Hist. of the Regal Succession.
5245 Smith's Annals of University-College. —— 1728
5246 Staveley's History of the Churches in England. —— 1712
5247 Summary of all the religious Houses in England and Wales. 1717

5248

5248 Somner's Treatise of the Roman Ports and Forts in Kent. 1693
5249 Sandwich's Letters.
5250 Secret History of the Reigns of K. Charles and James II. 1690
5251 Sprat's Observations on Sorbiere's Voyage to England. 1665
5252 Secret Hist. of the Dutchess of Portsmouth.——— 1690
5253 Salmon's Examin. of Burnet's Hist. 2 vol.———1724
5254 ———Hist. of Great Britain.——— 1725
5255 ———Chronological Historian.——— 1733
5256 Strype's Life of Bp Aylmer.——— 1701
5257 Storm, or the most remarkable Disasters which happen'd in the late dreadful Tempest. ———1704
5258 Superiority of the Crown of England over Scotl.——1704
5259 Stowe's Chronicle abridg'd, with Howe's Continuation. 1611
5260 State of the publick Records.———1723
5261 Stock's Lamentation for the Loss of the Godly.——1614
5262 Supplication to K Henry VIII. bl. letter.
5263 Sober Inspections into the long Parliament.——— 1655
5264 Taubman's Memoirs of Naval Transactions.———1710
5265 Treasons against Q. Elizabeth, and the Crown of Engl. 1572
5266 Tour through the whole Island of Great Britain, 3 vol. 1724
5267 Temple's Letters, 2 vol.——— 1700
5268 View of London, 2 vol. ——— 1708
5269 Vox Cœli, or News from Heaven.——— 1624
5270 View of the State of Religion in the Diocese of St. David's. 1721
5271 Vernon's Life of Dr. Heylin.——— 1682
5272 Vindication of Robert King of Scotland, from the Imputation of Bastardy.
5273 Udall's Life of Mary Queen of Seots.———1636
5274 Willis's Hist. of the mitred parliamentary Abbies in Engl. 2 vol. large pap.——— 1718
5275 ———Notitia Parliamentaria. ———1715
5276 Warwick's Memoirs of Charles I.——— 1703
5277 Wotton's Shabath and Eruvan, and Lewis's Life of Bp Wickliffe.
5278 Winstanley's England's Worthies. ——— 1660
5279 Ward's England's Reformation. ——— 1719
5280 Wallace's Description of the Isles of Orkney.———1693
5281 Willie's Description of Scarborough Spaw, and the Virtues thereof. ——— 1660
5282 Life of Tho. Wilson Minister of Maidstone. ——— 1672
5283 Risdon's Survey of Devonshire.———1714
5284 Hist. of the Cathedral Church of Rochester. ———1717

5285

5285 Natural Hist. and Antiq. of Surrey, 5 vol. ———— 1719
5286 Survey of the Roman Antiq. of England. ——— 1726
5287 Butcher's Survey of the Town of Stamford. —— 1717
5288 Hist. and Antiquities of the Church of Salisbury.— 1719
5289 Survey of the Cathedral Church of Landaff. ——— 1719
5290 Willes's Survey of the Church of St. Asaph. ——— 1720
5291 ——Survey of the Church of St. David's. ——— 1716
5292 Ashmole's Antiquities of Berkshire, 3 vol. lar. and sm. pap. 1719
5293 Antiquities of the Church of Worcester.———— 1717
5294 Antiquities of the Church of Hereford. ———— 1717
5295 Hist. of the Insurrection of Wat Tyler. ———— 1654
5296 Copy of the Journal Book of the House of Commons. 1680
5297 His Majesty's Instructions to his Son Prince Henry. 1603
5298 Life of Bp Rainbow. —— —— 1688
5299 Eikon Basilike. ——— —— 1648
5300 Present State of the Free-School at Whitney. ——— 1721
5301 Life of Anthony a Wood, Historiographer. — 1710
5302 Life and Death of that holy Preacher J. Machine. 1671
5303 Le Neve's Lives of the Protestant Arch-bishops, lar. pap. 1720
5304 Jeffrey of Monmouth's British History, large and sm. pap. 1718
5305 Historical Account of English Money. ——— 1726
5306 Toland's Defence of Milton's Life.———— 1699
5307 Conspiracy of Sir J. Croke and H. Larimore against the Life of R. Hawkins. ——— 1728
5308 Selden's Treatise on single Combat.
5309 Brokesby's Life of Dodwell, with an Account of his Works, 2 vol. ——— ——— 1715
5310 Two Centuries of Paul's Church-yard.
5311 Tryal of the 29 Regicides. ——— —1679
5312 Journey through England and Scotland, 3 vol. ——1732
5313 History of the Prince of Orange. —— 1689
5314 Tong's Life of Bp Shower. —— 1716
5315 Tryal of Dr. Sacheverell. ——— — 1710
5316 Debates on the present Constitution under King William. 1696
5317 Antiquities of the Abbey-Church of Westminster.— 1711
5318 Case of Charles Dean, who was executed at Tyburn. 1711
5319 Ancient Rights and Monuments of the Church of Durham. 1672
5320 History of the Principality of Wales. ——— 1695
5321 Life of Sir Tho. Smith, Secretary of State to Edward VI. 1698
5322 Narrative of the Proceedings against the Bp of St. Asaph. 1702

5323

5323 Memoires of the Family of the Stuarts, and Mackenzie's Jus Regium.
5324 Temple's Hiſtory of the Iriſh Rebellion. —— 1679
5325 Life and Death of Edmund Stanton. —— 1673
5326 Compleat Hiſtory of the Affair of Dr. Sacheverell. —1711
5327 Life and Death of Mr. Edmund Trench. ——1693
5328 ——of Anthony Earl of Shafteſbury. —— 1683
5329 Tradeſcant's Collection of Rarities preſerved at Lambeth. 1656
5330 Lockhart's Memoirs of Scotland. —— 1714
5331 Secret Hiſtory of Whitehall, 2 vol. —— 1717
5332 Hiſtory of Sir John Perrot. —— 1728
5333 Life and penitent Death of John Mawgridge. 1708
5334 His Majeſty's Property and Dominion on the Britiſh Seas aſſerted. —— —— 1672
5335 Le Neve's Monumenta Anglicana, 2 vol. —— 1718

Libri Medici & Chirurgici. Octav. and Twelves.

5336 Animadverſiones in Thruſtoni Diatribam de Reſpirationis Uſu primario. —— *Lond.* 1685
5337 Argenterius de Urinis, *cor. turc. fol. deaur.* — 1591
5338 ——de Collegiandi ratione Liber. *Florent. apud Torr.* 1551
5339 Avicennæ de Morbis Mentis Tractatus.—— *Par.* 1659
5340 Acturius de Urinis, A. Leone Interpret. — *ib.* 1549
5341 Pharmacopœia Amſtelredamenſis. —— *L.B.* 1701
5342 Blancardi Anatomia Reformata, cum fig. —— *ib.* 1688
5343 Bidloo Exercitat. Anatom. Chirurg. & Friend Emmenologia.
5344 Gerard. Bergen. de Preſervat. & Curat. Morbi Articularis, Sylvius de Morbi Articularis Curatione, Ferrerus de Morbo Gallico.
5345 Bartholini Specimen Hiſt. Anatomicæ, *Amſt.* 1601
5346 Boerhaave Praxis Medica, 5 vol. —— *Petav.* 1728
5347 ——Inſtitutiones Medicæ. —— *L.Bat.* 1734
5348 ——Aphoriſmi. —— *ib.* 1728
5349 ——Methodus dicendi Medicinam. *Lond.* 1726
5350 ——Hiſtoria Plantarum. —— *Romæ* 1727
5351 J. Broen de Duplici Bile veterum. —— *L B.* 1685
5352 Praxis Barbettiana. —— —— *ib* 1669
5353 Cornelius Celſus. —— *Ven. apud Aldum* 1528
5354 Chalmetei Enchiridion Chirurgicum.
5355 Chymiæ Naturalis Specimen. —— *Hagæ* 1707
5356 Eſſai ſur la Sante, par Cheney. —— *Par.* 1725
5357 Charletoni Inquiſitiones Medico-Phyſicæ. ——*L.B.* 1686
5358 Cæſar Cremoninus de Calido Innato & Semine.——*ib.* 1634
5359 Liſter Diſſertatio de Humoribus. *Lond.* 1709

5360

5360 Doringius de Medicina & Medicis. — Gief. 1611
5361 Entii Apologia pro Circuitione Sanguinis. Lond. 1685
5362 Elsholtii Anthropometria. — Franc. 1663
5363 Friend Emmenologia. — Lond. 1720
5364 ——— Prælectiones Chymicæ. — Paris 1727
5365 Fienus de Flatibus, Kraftheim Concilia Medicinal. Saracenus de Peste, & Tussanus de Febribus.
5366 Furstenau desiderat. circa Morbos eorumque Signa. Amst. 1712
5367 Fischeri Corpus Medicinæ Imperiale. — 1680
5368 Pharmacopeia Galenica. — Lond 1719
5369 Fernelii Febrium Curandarum Methodus generalis. Franc. 1577
5370 Falloppii Observationes Anatomicæ. — Ven. 1561
5371 Franbesarii Scholæ Medicæ. — L. B 1628
5372 Franci Veronica Theezans. — Lipſ.
5373 Groenvelt Differtat. Lithologica. — Lond. 1687
5374 Gulielmini de Salibus Differtatio. — L. B. 1707
5375 Diatriba de Febribus. — 1683
5376 Galenus de Sectis & de Plenitudine. Paris, apud Colin. 1528
5377 ——— de Ossibus, de Motu Musculorum, & de Febribus.
5378 Traite des Operations de Chirurgie, par Garengeot, 2 vol. Paris 1720
5379 Heisteri Compend. Anatom. cum fig. — Amst. 1723
5380 Pharmacopeia Hermetica. — Lond. 1719
5381 Thaddæi Hagecii Aphorismi. — Franc. 1584
5382 Jacksoni Enchiridion Medicum. — Brux. 1705
5383 Kircherus de Pestis. — Lipſ. 1659
5384 Lower Tractatus de Corde. — L. B. 1728
5385 Responsio ad Middletoni de Medicorum apud veteres Romanos digentium conditione Differtat. — Lond 1727
5386 Praxeos Mayernianæ, 2 vol. — ib 1690
5387 Mortoni Exercitat. de Phthisi. — ib 1689
5388 Mizaldi Hortus Medicus. — Lut. apud Morel. 1565
5389 Albertus Magnus de Secretis. — Arg. 1625
5390 Methode d'Operations de Chirurgie. — Par 1693
5391 Valla de Urinæ Significatione. — Arg 1528
5392 Prævotii Opera Medica posthuma, 2 vol. — Han. 1666
5393 Quercetani Pestis Alexiacus. — 1615
5394 Riverius Reformatus. — Gen. 1696
5395 Authores varii de Re Medica.
5396 Riolani Scholæ Medicæ, Horstii Introduct. ad Medicinam, & Walæi Methodus Medendi.
5397 Schenckii Opera omnia, 7 vol. — Frib. 1599
5398 F. Schreiber Element. Medicinæ. — Franc. 1731
5399 Strother Pharmacopœia Practica. — Lond. 1719
5400 Officina Chymica Londinensis. — 1685

Y 5401

5401 Sculteti Morbus Pilaris Mirabilis Observat. — Norib. 1658
5402 Scribonii Largi de Composit. Medicament Liber. — 1529
5403 Tabor Prælectiones Medicæ. — Lond. 1724
5404 Thrustoni de Respirationis usu primario Diatriba. L. Bat. 1708
5405 Hippocratis Opera omnia, à Vander Linden, gr. lat. 2 vol. Ib. 1665
5406 Des Natures & Complexiones des Hommes, par Aubert. Par. 1572
5407 Anatomia Artificialis Oculi Humani. — Amst. 1680
5408 Waldschmiedt Institutiones Medicinæ Rationalis. Lug. Bat. 1641

Historia variarum Gentium, Lat. Gal. & Ital. Octavo & infra.

5409 Almoinus de Gestis Francorum. — Par. 1567
5410 Advertissement sur la Faulsete de plusieurs Mensonges semez par les Rebelles. — ib. apud Morel. 1564
5411 Aretinus de Bello Italico. — ib. apud Colin. 1534
5412 L'Hist. du Card. Mazarin, par Aubery, 2 vol. — Par. 1695
5413 Actes & Negociationes de la Paix de Ryswick, 3 vol. a la Haye 1699
5414 Ambassade du Mareschal de Bassompiere, 3 vol. — Col. 1668
5415 Description de la Ville de Paris, 2 vol. avec fig. Paris 1717
5416 Card. Baronii Tractat. de Monarchia Siciliæ. — ib. 1609
5417 Le Belezze della Citta di Firenze. — Firenz. 1677
5418 Descrittione di Gaeta. — Napoli 1697
5419 Cronique de Comines. — Par. 1563
5420 Fleur de la Maison de Charlemagne, par Fauchet. ib. 1601
5421 Declin de la Maison de Charlemague, par Fauchet, regle & dore sur tranche. — ib. 1602
5422 Memoires pour servir a l'Hist. de Louis XIV. par l'Abbe de Choisy. — Amst. 1727
5423 Cellarii Descriptio Regni Poloniæ, cum fig. — ib. 1659
5424 Recherches sur les Antiquitez de la Ville de Vienne, par Chorier. — Lyon 1659
5425 Hist. delle Guerre della Germania Inferiori di Connestaggio. 1634
5426 Bibliotheque des Autheurs qui ont escrit l'Hist. de la France, par du Chesne. — Par. 1627
5427 Li Pregi della Nobilta Veneta. — Venez. 1682
5428 Description de la Ville, avec fig. — Rouen 1621
5429 Regles du Droit Francois. — Par. 1730
5430 Vertot Hist. des Revolutions de Suede, 2 vol. — ib. 1722
5431 ——— Revolutions de Portugal. — ib. 1728
5432 ——— Romaine, 3 vol. — ib. 1727

5433

5433 Vertot Hist de l'Etablissement des Bretons dans les Gaules, 2 vol. ——— ib. 1720
5434 Ceccervitii Carminum de Rebus Danicis Lib. 4. *Stetini* 1581
5435 Abrege de l'Hist. de France, par Daniel, 9 vol. *Par.* 1731
5436 Eringii Vita Ernesti Pii Ducis Saxoniæ. ——— *Lipf.* 1704
5437 Hist. de France, par Larrey, 9 vol. ——— *Amst.* 1718
5438 Nouvelle Description de la France, par de la Forge, 6 vol. avec fig. ——— *Par.* 1718
5439 L'Etat de la France, 3 vol. ——— *ib.* 1718
5440 Histoire de France, 3 vol. ——— *ib.* 1720
5441 Petri de Frisiorum Antiquitate & Origine. ——— *Franq* 1698
5442 Hist. de la Vie du Duc d'Espernon, par Girard, 4 vol. *Par.* 1730
5443 Lib. de la Republica di Vinitiani, per Donato.
5444 Les Memoires d'Henri de Lorraine Duc de Guise. *ibid.* 1681
5445 Hist. du Siege d'Ostende. ——— *ib.* 1604
5446 Hotomanni Franco-Gallia. ——— 1576
5447 Hauberi Primitiæ Schauenburgicæ. ——— 1728
5448 Hist. du Regne de Louis XIII. par Vassor, 18 vol. *Amst.* 1701
5449 ——— de la Province d'Alsace, 8 vol. ——— *Straf* 1727
5450 Olai Hist. Suecorum Gothorumque ——— *Holm.* 1654
5451 Abrege Chronologique de l'Hist. de France, par Mezeray, 9 vol. ——— ——— *Amst.* 1723
5452 Matharelli Italogallia. ——— — 1578
5453 Memoires de Langallerie. ——— *a la Haye* 1686
5454 Memoires de Clermont Marquis de Montglat, 2 vol. *Amst.* 1727
5455 Meslanges Historiques, par Camuzat. ——— *Troyes* 1619
5456 Persecutio Eccles. Vallis Angrun. ——— *Gen.* 1501
5457 Machiavelli Hist. Florentina. ——— *Hag. Comit.* 1658
5458 Ant. Nebrissensis Hist. Hispaniæ. ——— 1550
5459 S. Nieupoort Hist. Republ. & Imperii Romanorum, 2 vol. *Traj ad Rhen.* 1723
5460 Zampinus de Origine & Atavis Hugonis Capeti. *Par.* 1581
5461 Pii II. Descriptio & Asiæ & Europæ. ——— *ib.* 1534
5462 Clusii Notæ in Garciæ Aromatum Historiam. ——— *Ant.* 1582
5463 Puffendorfius de Foederibus in Sueciam & Galliam, lat. gal. *Haga* 1708
5464 De Justitia Armorum Christianiss. Regis. ——— 1637
5465 Hist. du Ministere du Card. Mazarin. ——— *Amst* 1671
5466 Memoirs pour l'Hist. du Card. Richelieu, 5 vol. *Col.* 1667
5467 La Vie du Card. Richelieu, 2 vol. ——— *ib.* 1694
5468 Riccobani de Historia Comment. ——— *Ven.* 1568
5469 Relation des Divertissemens dans le Parc de Versailles. *Par.* 1664

5470 Harangue de P. de la Rame. —— 1557
5471 La Recep. de la Royne Catholique. —— 1559
5472 Hist. de Geneve, par Spon, 4 vol. —— *Gen.* 1730
5473 Sommaire des Histoires de Naples —— *Par.* 1546
5474 Strada de Bello Belgico, 2 vol. cum fig. —— 1658
5475 Schoockii Descript. Reip. Federati Belgii. —— *Amst.* 1652
5476 Stellæ Elogia Venetor. Navali pugna Illustrium. *Venet.* 1558
5477 Taraphæ de Origine, ac rebus gestis Regum Hispaniæ Lib. *Ant.* 1553
5478 Tursellini Romani Historiar. Epitome. —— *Ultr.* 1718
5479 Gregorii Turonici Hist. Francorum Lib. 10. —— *Par.* 1561
5480 Memoires de la Chretiente, par Temple. —— *Amst.* 1708
5481 Raupachii de præsenti Rei Sacræ & Literariæ in Dania Statu. —— *Hamb.* 1717
5482 Hist. de Charles XII. Roy de Suede, par Voltaire. —— 1731
5483 Lettres & Memoires de Vargas. —— *Amst.* 1700
5484 Lettres & Negociations de Jean de Witt, 5 vol. —— *ib.* 1724
5485 Coccinii de Bellis Italicis.
5486 Several Volumes of the Republicks sold separate.

History of different Nations. Octavo and Twelves.

5487 Ablancourt's Memoirs. —— 1703
5488 Memoirs for the Hist. of Anne of Austria, 5 vol.
5489 Aretin's Hist. of the Wars in Italy, *bl. letter.*
5490 Several Tracts relating to the Persecution of the Protestants in France.
5491 Memoirs of Philip de Comines, 2 vol. —— 1723
5492 Hist. of the Civil Wars of France. —— 1655
5493 Daniel's History of France, 5 vol. —— 1726
5494 Dauncey's Chronicle of the Kingdom of Portugal. —— 1661
5495 Echard's Roman History, 5 vol. —— 1713
5496 ——Gazetteer. —— 1731
5497 History of the House of Este. —— 1681
5498 ——of France, 2 vol. —— 1702
5499 The Laws and Statutes of Geneva, *bl. letter.*
5500 Life and Actions of Bernard Van-Gale. —— 1680
5501 History of the German Empire, 2 vol. —— 1731
5502 ——of the Transactions of the Court of Spain. 1691
5503 Hautevill's Account of Poland. —— 1698
5504 Hind's History of Greece. —— 1707
5505 Account of the Troubles during the Wars of Paris. 1686
5506 Impartial Enquiry into the Management of the War in Spain. —— 1712
5507 Pezron's Antiquities of Nations. —— 1706
5508 Kennet's Roman Antiquities.
5509 Hist. of Lewis XIV. King of France. —— 1709

5510

5510 Memoirs of the Duke of Bouillion and Marefchal Turenne.

5511 Temple's Memoirs of Chriftendom. ———— 1693
5512 Maimbourg's Hift. of the League, by Dryden. —— 1692
5513 Hift. of Cardinal Mazarine, 2 vol. ———— 1684
5514 Catrou's Roman Hiftory, by Ozell, 2 vol. ———— 1691
5515 Lives of the Princes of Orange. ———— 1725
5516 Puffendorff's Introduction to the Hift. of Europe. —— 1734
5517 Potter's Antiquities of Greece, 2 vol. *cuts*. ———— 1706
5518 Richer's Hift of the Royal Genealogy of Spain. —— 1728
5519 Brown's Method to underftand the Roman Hiftory. 1724
5520 Relation of the Differences between Spain, John of Auftria, and Cardinal Nitard. ———— 1731
5521 Savage's compleat Hift. of Germany. ———— 1678
5522 Parthenay's Hift. of Poland. ———— 1702
5523 Sandeval's Hift of Charles V. ———— 1734
5524 Stephen's Hift. of Portugal. ———— 1703
5525 Salmon's Modern Hiftory, vol. 7, 8. 9, 10 and 12, fold feparate. 1698
5526 Chronological Tables of Europe, grav'd by Sturt.
5527 Toland's Account of the Courts of Pruffia and Hanover.

5528 Vertot's Hift. of the Revolutions of Rome, 2 vol. —— 1714
5529 Hift. of the Revolutions in Spain, 5 vol. ———— 1732
5530 Vertot's Hift. of the Revolutions in Sweden. ———— 1724
5531 ——— Revolutious in Portugal. ———— 1729
5532 ——— Eftablifhment of the Britons among the Gauls. 1735
5533 Hift. of the Wars of the King of Sweden. ———— 1722
5534 Hift. of the Treaty of Utrecht, 2 vol. ———— 1720
5535 Le Vaffor's Hift. of Lewis XIII. 4 vol. ———— 1715
1700

Hiftoria & Antiquitates Magnæ Britanniæ & Hibern. Lat. & Gal. Octavo & infra.

5536 Antiquitates Rutupinæ, *ch. max.* ———— 1711
5537 Afchami Epiftolæ, *ch. max.* ———— *Oxon.* 1703
5538 Afferii Annales Ælfredi Magni, recenfuit F. Wife, *ch. max. et minor.* ———— *ib.* 1722
5539 Baxteri Gloffar. Antiquitat. Roman. ———— *Lond.* 1726
5540 Abrege chronologique de l'Hift. d'Angleterre, 8 vol. *Amft.* 1730
5541 Itinerarium Antonini Augufti. ———— *Col. Agrip.* 1600
5542 Batei Elenchus Motuum nuperorum in Anglia. *Lond.* 1663
5543 Buchanani Rerum Scoticarum Hiftoria. ———— *Edin* 1643
5544 P. Barwick Vita Johannis Barwick. ———— *Lond.* 1721
5545 Apologia Ecclefiæ Anglicanæ. ———— *Romæ* 1562
5546 Afchami Apologia pro Cœna Dominica, &c ———— 1578
5547 Oclandi Anglorum Prælia. ———— *Lond.* 1582

5548

5548 Episcopus Roffen. adversus Lutherum. —— *Ant.* 1537
5549 Lettres du Card. d'Ossat, avec des Notes, par Amelot de la Houssaie, 5 vol. —— *Amst.* 1732
5550 Basinstochii Hist. Britanniæ, lib. x. —— 1602
5551 ——Orationes. —— *Atrebati.* 1596
5552 Hist. Mariæ Reginæ Scotorum.
5553 Camdeni Annales. —— *Franc.* 1616
5554 ——Britannia. —— *Lond.* 1586
5555 Catalogus Martyrum e Collegio Anglorum Duacino. *Duaci* 1630
5556 S. Thomæ Cantuariensis Monomachia de Libertate Ecclesiast. —— *Col. Agrip.* 1626
5557 Campiani Orationes. —— *Ant.* 1631
5558 F. Clarke Praxis Curiæ Admiralitatis Angliæ. —— 1667
5559 Jacobi IV. V. et Mariæ Regum Scotorum Epist. 2 vol. 1722
5560 Rerum nuper in Regno Scotiæ Gestarum Historia. *Dantisci* 1641
5561 Disciplina Ecclesiastica. —— 1574
5562 Everardi Angligenarum in Collegio Romano vitæ ratio. *Lond.* 1611
5563 Fizerberte de Antiquitate et Continuatione Catholicæ Religionis in Anglia. —— *Romæ* 1608
5564 ——Descriptio Oxoniensis Academiæ. —— *ib.* 1602
5565 Hist. of the Martyrdom of xii. Priests. —— 152
5566 Froissardi et Comenii Historia. —— *Franc.* 1584
5567 Gildas de Calamitate, Excidio et Conquestu Britanniæ.
5568 Herbert de Expeditione in Ream Insulam. —— 1656
5569 Horni Rerum Britannicarum, lib. vii. —— *Lug. Bat.* 1648
5570 Heutzneri Itinerarium Germaniæ, Angliæ, Galliæ, Italiæ. *Norib.* 1629
5571 Hist. secrette de la Duchesse de Portsmouth. —— 1690
5572 Hoornbeck Epist. ad Duræum. —— *Lug. Bat.* 1660
5573 Harmari vindiciæ Academiæ Oxoniensis. —— *Oxon.* 1662
5574 De Rebus Gestis Britanniæ Comment, —— *ib.* 1640
5575 Irvini Hist. Scoticæ Nomenclatura. —— *Edin.* 1682
5576 Justitia Britannica. —— *Lond.* 1584
5577 Ignoramus Comœdia coram Rege Jacobo. —— 1731
5578 Vindiciæ Catholicorum Hiberniæ. —— *Par.* 1650
5579 Lelandi de Rebus Britannicis Collectanea, edidit T. Hearne, 6 vol. —— *Oxon.* 1715
5580 ——de Scriptoribus Britannicis, 2 vol. —— *ib.* 1709
5581 Langhornii Antiquitates Albionenses. —— 1720
5582 Langueti Epistolæ. —— *Lug. Bat.* 1646
5583 G. Musgrave Antiquitates Britan. 4 vol. —— 1720
5584 Memoria Balfouriana. —— *Edinb.* 1698
5585 Prophetia Anglicana. —— *Franc.* 1608
5586 Metamorphosis Anglorum. —— 1653
5587 Literæ Cromwelli à Miltono. —— 1676

5588

5588 G. Neubrigensis Hist. Anglicana. —— Par. 1610
5589 De furoribus Norfolciensium Ketto Duce, *fol. deaurat.* *Lond.* 1582
5590 Votum Candidum Vivat Rex. —— *Ib.* 1669
5591 Parkeri de Rebus sui Temporis Comment. *ch. max.* 1726
5592 Prælectiones Academicæ in Schola Historices Camdeniana. *Oxon.* 1692
5593 Analecta de Rebus Catholicorum in Hibernia. *Colon.* 1619
5594 Pontici Virunii Britannicæ Historiæ lib. vi. —— *Lond.* 1585
5595 Rossi Warvicensis Hist. Regum Angliæ T. Hearne, *ch. max. corio turcico, foliis deaurat.* —— *Oxon.* 1716
5596 Symeonis Monachi Hist. Ecclesiæ Dunhelmensis edidit T. Bedford. —— *Lond.* 1732
5597 Remarques sur la Conduite de la Grand Bretagne. *Amst.* 1729
5598 T. Rosæ de Jacobi Regis virtutibus enarratio. *Lond.* 1608
5599 Sheringhami de Anglorum Gentis Origine. —— *Cant.* 1670
5600 Roberti Huntingtoni Epistolæ. —— *Lond.* 1704
5601 Smith de Republica Anglorum. —— *ib.* ——
5602 Sanderus de Schismate Anglicano. —— *Col. Agrip.* 1610
5603 Jani Anglorum *facies altera.* —— *Lond.* 1681
5604 Maria Scotor. Regina Innocens, a cæde Darleana. *Ingolstadt.* 1588
5605 Hist. de Maria Stuarda del Causino. —— *Ven.* ——
5606 Trivetii Annales edidit A. Hall, 2 vol. —— *Oxon.* 1719
5607 Le Triomphe Royal a l'Honneur de Guillaume III. *aves fig.* —— *a la Haye.* ——
5608 Theatrum Tragicum Londini celebrat. *cum fig. Amst.* 1640
5609 Lettres sur les Anglois, par Voltaire. —— 1734
5610 Polydorii Vergilii Hist. Anglicana, 2 vol. —— *Gand.* 1556
5611 Waræi Antiquitates Hiberniæ. —— *Lond.* 1658

Physick, Surgery, and Chimistry. Octavo and Twelves.

5612 Barbett's Chirurgical and Anatomical Works, *cuts.* — 1676
5613 Blackmore on the Spleen and Vapours. —— 1725
5614 Bradley's Lectures on the Materia Medica. —— 1730
5615 Bellinger's Discourse on the Nutrition of the Fœtus in the Womb. —— 1717
5616 Boerhaave's Treatise of Medicine. —— 1720
5617 Bates's Dispensatory, by Salmon. —— 1706
5618 Blancard's Physical Dictionary. —— 1697
5619 Boyle's Reconcileableness of Specifick Medicines. —— 1685
5620 ——Medicinal Experiments. —— 1718
5621 Brown's Treatise on the King's Evil, gilt on the leaves. 1684
5622 Busschoff's Treatise of the Gout. —— 1676
5623 Bayfield's Treatise of Diseases of the Head. —— 1663
5624 Cheyne's Essay on Health and long Life. —— 1725

5625

5625 Cheyne's English Malady. — 1733
5626 Le Clerc's History of Physick. — 1699
5627 Pitt's Craft and Frauds of Physick. — 1702
5628 Dionis's Surgery, cuts. — 1733
5629 Duncan's Advice against the Abuse of hot Liquors. 1706
5630 Floyer's Preservative of old Men's Healths. — 1724
5631 ——— Treatise of the Asthma. — 1717
5632 Gibson's Anatomy. — 1697
5633 Collection of Tracts in Surgery, bl. letter.
5634 De la Boe Sylvius's Practice of Physick. — 1675
5635 Graunt's Observations on the Bills of Mortality. — 1665
5636 Little Venus unmask'd, by Harvey — 1702
5637 Memoirs of the Plague. — 1722
5638 Morgan's philosophical Principles of Medicine, l. and s. p. 1725
5639 Mead's Discourse on the Plague, l. and sm. p. — 1722
5640 Tournefort's Description of simple Medicines. — 1716
5641 Morton's Treatise of Consumptions. — 1694
5642 Marten's Theory of Consumptions. — 1720
5643 Modern Quack, Lover's Week, Life of Palleotti.
5944 Maynwaring's Treatise of Physique. — 1679
5645 Marlow's Letters to a sick Friend. — 1682
5646 The Myrrour or Glasse of Helth, *bl. letter.*
5647 Observations in the Practice of Physick. — 1715
5648 Pitcairne's Works. — 1715
5649 Paxton's Essays on the Body of Man. — 1702
5650 Purcell's Treatise of Vapours. — 1707
5651 The Regimen of Life, *bl. letter.*
5652 Quinton's Observations in Physick and Surgery. — 1707
5653 Quincy's Dispensatory. — 1733
5654 Alleyn's English Dispensatory. — 1733
5655 Robinson's Method of treating Consumptions. — 1727
5656 Pharmacopœia Radcliffeana. — 1716
5657 Read's Manual of Anatomy. — 1655
5658 Strother's Materia Medica, 2 vol. — 1727
5659 ——— Essay on Sickness and Health. — 1725
5660 ——— Discourse on Causes and Cures. — 1718
5661 Salmon's Family-Dictionary. — 1710
5662 ——— practical Physick. — 1692
5663 ——— Doron Medicum. — 1683
5664 Turner on the Venereal Disease. — 1732
5665 ——— on the Diseases of the Skin. — 1714
5666 Tauvry's Treatise of Medicines. — 1700
5667 Theory of acute and slow-continued Fevers. — 1722
5668 Twisden's Answer to Medela Medicinæ. — 1666
5670 Wiseman's Surgery, 2 vol. — 1734
5671 ——— Treatise of Wounds. — 1672
5672 Woodward's State of Physick. — 1718

5673

5673 White's Obſervations on Fevers. —— 1712
5674 Wilſon's Chimiſtry, 2 vol. interleaved with Notes.—1709

Voyages, Travels, and Books relating to the Hiſt. of the Eaſt and Weſt-Indies. Octavo and Twelves.

5675 Addiſon's Travels. —— —— 1733
5676 Voyage to Arabia the Happy. —— 1726
5677 Engliſh Empire in America. —— 1685
5678 Cruelties of the Dutch at Amboyna. —— 1651
5679 Ball's Antiquities of Conſtantinople. —— 1729
5680 Bernier's Hiſt. of the Mogol Empire. —— 1671
5681 Blome's Deſcription of Jamaica. —— 1678
5682 Isbrand's Journey from Moſcow over Land to China. 1698
5683 Burnet's Travels. —— —— 1686
5684 Reflexions on Burnet's Travels. —— 1688
5685 Cooke's Voyage round the World, cuts. —— 1712
5686 Drury's Hiſt. of Madagaſcar. —— 1731
5687 Gordon's Geographical Grammar. —— 1733
5688 Geddes's Church-Hiſtory of Ethiopia. ——1696
5689 Gage's Survey of the Weſt-Indies. —— 1677
5690 Guillatierre's Voyage to Athens. —— 1676
5691 View of the Engliſh Acquiſitions in Guinea. ——1686
5692 Glanius's Voyage to the Eaſt-Indies. —— 1682
5693 Herrera's Hiſt. of America call'd the Weſt-Indies, 6 vol. cuts. 1725
5694 Hatton's Treatiſe of Geography. —— 1732
5695 Journey through the Auſtrian Netherlands. —— 1732
5696 Philipps's Conference with the Malabarians. 1719
5697 Relation of the Country of Janſenia. —— 1668
5698 Joſſelyn's New-England's Rarities diſcovered. 1672
5699 Kolben's preſent State of the Cape of Good-Hope, 2 vol. cuts. —— 1731
5700 Voyage into the Levant. —— 1664
5701 Sir J. Mandeville's Travels. —— 1725
5702 Maundrell's Journey from Aleppo to Jeruſalem, *cuts.* 1732
5703 Relation of a Voyage into Mauritania. —— 1671
5704 Maſſey's Travels and Adventures. —— 1733
5705 Northleigh's Voyages. —— 1702
5706 New Voyage to the Northern Countries. ——1674
5707 Ockley's Hiſtory of the Saracens, 2 vol. ——1708
5708 Voyage round the World, or a Pocket-Library.
5709 Hiſt. of the Revolutions of Perſia, 2 vol.——1733
5710 Rogers's cruiſing Voyage round the World. ——1718
5711 ——four Years Voyages. —— 1726

Z 5612

5712 Earl of Carlisle's Embassy to Muscovy. — 1669
5713 Stevens's Hist. of Persia. — 1715
5714 Short Way to know the World, cuts. — 1712
5715 Sadeur's Discovery of Terra Incognita Australis. — 1693
5716 History of Timur-Bec, or Tamerlane the Great, 2 vol. 1723
5717 Lithgow's nineteen Years Travels. — 1682
5718 Terry's Voyage to East-India. — 1659
5719 The Traveller of Jerome Turler, *bl. letter.* 1575
5720 Varenius's compleat System of Geography, 2 vol. cuts. 1734
5721 Wells's historical Geography of the Old Testament, 4 vol. cuts. — — 1709
5722 ——— antient and present Geography. — 1726
5723 Windus's Journey to Mequinez. — 1725
5724 Williams's Key into the Language of America. 1643

Trade, Husbandry, Gardening and Natural History. Octavo and Twelves.

5725 Allen's natural History of the Purging Waters in England. 1699
5726 Account of new Inventions and Improvements.
5727 Art and Mystery of Vintners and Wine-Coopers. — 1680
5728 Builder's Dictionary, 2 vol. cuts. — 1734
5729 Bradley's Improvements in Planting and Gardening, cuts. 1731
5730 Blair's Botanick Essays. — 1720
5731 Touchstone of Gold and Silver-Wares. — 1677
5732 Crouch's compleat View of the British Customs. — 1725
5733 Book of Rates. — — 1702
5734 Account of all the Gold and Silver Coins ever used in Engl. 1718
5735 Lister's Art of Cookery.
5736 Cook of Forest-Trees. — 1724
5737 Curiosities of Nature and Art in Husbandry and Gardening. 1707
5738 Complete Gardener, by London and Wise, cuts. — 1701
5739 Cumberland of Jewish Weights and Measures. — 1686
5740 Castaigne's Book of Interest. — 1720
5741 Dictionarium Polygraphicum, 2 vol. *cuts.* — 1735
5742 ——— Rusticum, 2 vol. — 1726
5743 Davenant of Grants and Resumptions. — 1700
5744 ——— Essays on Peace at home, and War abroad. 1704
5745 Derham's Account of Ilmington Waters. — 1685
5746 Compleat English Tradesman, 2 vol. — 1727
5747 Evelyn's philosophical Discourse of Earth. — 1676
5748 Free Trade, or the Means to make Trade flourish. — 1622

5749

5749 Solitary or Carthusian Gardener. ——— 1706
5750 Guidott's Discourse of Bath. ——— 1676
5751 Gentleman's Recreations. ——— 1686
5752 Gentleman Farrier. ——— ——1732
5753 Treatise of the Ipswich Spaw. ———1717
5754 Hatton's Tradesman's Companion. ——— 1716
5755 Herefordshire Orchard, a Pattern for all England. —1657
5756 Compleat Horseman, by Sir W. Hope. ——1706
5757 Huet's View of the Dutch Trade. ——— 1722
5758 Jorden's Discourse of Mineral Baths and Mineral Waters. 1669
5759 Laurence's Duty and Office of a Land-Steward. 1731
5760 Lamb's Royal Cookery. ——— 1731
5761 Clergyman's Recreation, Lady's Recreations, and Fruit-Garden Kalender.
5762 Lovell's Hist. of Animals and Minerals. —1661
5763 Latham Spaw, and Cures effected by it. —1670
5764 Manner of making Coffee, Tea, and Chocolate. —1685
5765 City and Country Purchaser and Builder's Dictionary. 1726
5766 Olivet's Dissertation on Bath-Waters. —— 1716
5767 Pechey's complete Herbal. ——— 1707
5768 Plat's Garden of Eden. ——— 1675
5769 Perfect Directions for all English Gold.
5770 Retir'd Gardener, by London and Wise, 2 vol. 1706
5771 Essay for the Amendment of the Silver Coins. 1695
5772 Nobleman, Gentleman, and Gardener's Recreations.—1715
5773 Sharrock's Hist. of Vegetables, interleav'd. —— 1672
5774 Stubbes's Discourse on Chocolate. ——— 1672
5775 Simpson's Discovery of the Scarborough Spaw. 1670
5776 Worlidge's Treatise of Cyder ——— 1678
5777 Waller's Essay on the Value of Mines. —— 1698
5778 Wittie's Description of the Scarborough Spaw.—— 1667
5779 Worth's Art of Brewing. ——— 1692

Livres Francoise. Octavo & Infra.

5780 Dequisemens des Auteurs. ——— *Par.*1690
5781 Bibliotheque Raisonnee des Ouvrages des Scavans, 15 vol. *Amst.*1730
5782 ————des Gens de Cour, 3 vol. ——*Par.*1722
5783 ————des Dames, par Steele, 3 vol.——— *Amst.*1727
5784 Recueil des Discours, par Barbeyrac, 2 vol. ——*ib.*1731
5785 Lettres de M. Bayle, 3 vol. ——— *ib.*1729
5786 Le Bibliothequarie Universel, par Jacob. —*Par.*1668
5787 Reflexions sur le Ridicule, par Bellegarde.——*Amst.*1707
5788 Lettres Curieuses, par Bellegarde. ——— *ib.*1707
5789 Modelles de Conversations, par Bellegarde. *ib.*1702
5790 Regles de la Vie Civile, par Bellegarde.——— *ib.*1707
5791 Lettres Choisies, par Balzac.

5792 Apologie pour Balzac.—— ———————— Roven.1663
5793 Considerations Politique sur l'Etat de l'Europe, 3 vol. 1688
5794 Hist. du Monde par Chevreau, 4 vol. ——— *a la Haye*.1687
5795 Les Conseils de la Sagesse.—— ——— *Paris*.1683
5796 Le parfait Courtisan par Castillion, *dore sur tranche*.— *Lyon*. 1580
5797 Lettres de Mr. de la Chambre.
5798 L' Apparat Royal ou Diction. fr. & lat. —— *Roven*.1729
5799 Dictionnaire Francois-Aleman-Latin.——— *Leyden*.1642
5800 Des Causes de la Corruption du Goust par Dacier. *Paris*. 1714
5801 La Disputation de l'Asne contre frere Anselme.
5802 Traite du Choix des Etudes par Fleury.——— *Brux*.1687
5803 Le Heros de B. Gracien.———————— *Paris*.1725
5804 Hist. de l'Academie Royale des Sciences, 34 vol. *Amst*.1715
5805 Traicte des plus belles Bibliotheques par Jacob. *Paris*.1634
5806 Jugemens des Savans par Baillet, 16 vol.—— *Amst*.1725
5807 Journal Literaire, 13 vol. ———— *a la Haye*.1713
5808 La Science des Personnes de la Cour, 4 vol.—— *Amst*.1723
5809 Lettres de Loridano fr. & ital.———— *Brux*.1712
5810 Les Essais de Montaigne.———— *Paris*.1602
5811 Nouvelle Grammaire Grecque. ———— *ib*.
5812 Hist. de l'Academie Royale des Inscriptions & Belles Lettres, 9 vol.———————— *Amst*.1719
5813 Melanges d'Histoire & de Literature par Marville, 2 vol. *Roven*.1700
5814 Memoire pour servir a l'Hist. des Hommes illustres, 2 vol. *Paris*.1727
5815 Hist. de l'Exil de Ciceron par Morabin. ——— *ib*.1726
5816 Le Mausolie de la Toison d'Or.———— *Amst*.1689
5817 La Maniere de bien Penser.———— *ib*.1709
5818 Memoire pour l'Hist. des Sciences & des beaux Arts. *Trevoux*.
5819 Mercure Historique & Politique, 4 vol. —— *Parma*.1686
5820 Nouvelles Litteraires, 10 vol.———— *a la Haye*.1715
5821 Methode pour Apprendre la Langue Latin par Mess. du Port Royale.———————— *Paris*.1655
5822 Des Orateurs. ———————— *ib*.1722
5823 Introduction a l'Hist. de l'Europe par Puffendorf, 4 vol. *Amst*. 1710
5824 Le plaisant Jeu du Dodechedron de Fortune.—— *Lyon*.1581
5825 La Politique des Jesuites.———————— *Col*.1699
5826 Les Devises Heroiques de Paradin. ——— *Anvers*.1567
3827 Hist. des Juifs par Prideaux, 5 vol.——— *Amst*.1722
5828 Recueil generale des Pieces concernant le Procez entre Madame Cadiere & Girard, 7 vol. —— *a la Haye*.1731
5829 Recueil des Harangues prononcez dans l'Academie Francoise, 2 vol.———————— *Amst*.1709
5830 Recueil des Discours Politiques ——— ——1632

I 5831

5831 Recueil des plusieurs Pieces d'Eloquence. —— *Paris.* 1723
5832 Reflexions sur la Rhetorique & sur la Poesie par Fenelon, 2 vol. —— *Amst.* 1730
5833 Lettres de Madame de Savigne, 4 vol. —— *Paris.* 1734
5834 Traductions diverses pour former le Gout de l'Eloquence. *ib.* 1712
5835 Les Elemens de l'Histoire par Vallemont, 3 vol. *Amst.* 1701
5836 La Pratique de l'Education des Princes par Varillas. *ib.* 1684
5837 Recueil des Chansons mises au Musique, 8 vol. *Paris.* 1712
5838 Lettres sur toutes sortes de Sujets par Vaumoriere, 2 vol. *ib.* 1706
5839 Traitte des Societes civiles par Villette. —— *Lond.* 1727
5840 Appian Alexandrin traduitte par Seyssell. —— *Paris.* 1559
5841 Les Apophtegmes ou bons Mots des Anciens par Ablancourt. *ib.* 1694
5842 Les Amours des grands Hommes par Villedieu. *Amst.* 1688
5843 Amitiez, Amours, & Amourettes par le Pays. —— *ib.* 1665
5844 L'Argenis de Barclay, *avec fig. regle & dore sur tranche.* *Paris.* 1625
5845 Traite du Poeme Epique par Bossu. —— *ib.* 1708
5846 Les Oeuvres du Bellay. —— *Paris, par Morel.* 1569
5847 Le Brutus Trgedie par Voltaire. —— *Lond.* 1731
5848 Les Oeuvres de Tho. & P. Corneille, 10 vol. *avec fig.* *Paris.* 1723
5849 Quinte Curce traduite par Vaugelas. —— *Amst.* 1665
5850 Hist. de Dion. Cassius abrege par Xiphilin, 2 vol. *Paris.* 1674
5851 Traduction des Colloques de Cordiere. —— *Amst.* 1729
5852 La Pratique par d'Aubignac, gr. pap. —— *ib.* 1715
5853 Les Oeuvres d'Horace avec des remarques par Dacier, 10 vol. *ib.* 1727
5854 L'Iliade & L'Odyssee d'Homere avec des remarques par Dacier, 7 vol. *avec fig.* —— *ib.* 1731
5855 Hist. des Juifs par Joseph traduite par d'Andilly, 5 vol. *Brux.* 1701
5856 Essai d'une Nouvelle Traduction d'Horace. —— *Amst.* 1727
5857 Explication Historique des Fables. —— *Paris.* 1711
5858 Contes & Nouvelles en Vers par de la Fontaine, 2 vol. *avec fig.* —— *Amst.* 1732
5859 Les Fontenes de Pouges de Raymond de Massac. *Paris.* 1605
5860 Les Fantomes & le Jaloux Comedies Ital. & Franc. *Oxford.* 1731
5861 Epitome de l'Histore Romaine. —— *Paris.* 1670
5862 Contes & Nouvelles en Vers par de la Fontaine, *avec fig.* *Amst.* 1685
5863 Hist. de Guzman d'Alfarache, 3 vol. *avec fig.* — *Brux.* 1705
5864 L'Homme detrompee de B. Gracian, 2 vol. *a la Haye.* 1708
5865 Hist. d'Herodote traduite par du Ryer, 3 vol. — *Paris.* 1713
5866 Hist. de Salluste. —— *ib.* 1713

5867

5867 Le Jugement de Paris.—————— *Roven*.1650
5868 Les Oeuvres d'Amadis Jamyn, *regle & dore sur tranche*. *Paris, par Patisson*.1577
5869 Les Decades de Tite Live avec les Supplemens de Freinshemius traduite par du Ryer, 10 vol. ——— *Amst* 1700
5870 Lucien de la Traduction d'Ablancourt, 3 vol.—*Paris*.1707
5871 Les Lunettres des Princes, *en lettres Gothiques*.— *ib*.1527
5872 Oeuvres de Clement Marot, 6 vol.——— *a la Haye*.1731
5873 ————le meme. ———— *Paris*.1536
5874 Marguerites de la Marguerites de Princess & Royne de Navarre, regle. ———— *Lyon*.1547
5875 Les Oeuvres de Moliere, 8 vol. *avec fig*.——— *Paris*.1730
5876 Le Moyen de Parvenir.
5877 Les Propheties de Nostradamus.——— *Amst*.1668
5878 Les Metamorphoses d'Ovide, *avec fig*.——— *Roven*.1651
5879 Les Metamorphoses d'Ovide par du Ryer, 3 vol. *avec grand nombres des fig. dore sur tranche*.——— *Amst* 1718
5880 Oeuvres diverses du Sr. R * * *. ——— *Soleure*.1719
5881 Les Comedies de Plaute fr. & lat. par Marolles, 4 vol. *avec fig* ———— *Paris*.1658
5882 Les Oeuvres de Plutarque par Amyot, 13 vol. *relie en Maroquin, livres tres rare*.——— *Paris, par Vascosan*.1567
5883 Hist. de l'admirable Don Quichotte de la Mancha, 12 vol. *avec fig*.——— *Paris*.1733
5884 Les Oeuvres de Ronsard, 5 vol.——— *Lyon*.1592
5885 Oeuvres de l'Abbe de St. Real, 3 vol. —— *a la Haye*.1726
5886 L'Hist. des Hommes illustres de Plutarque abrege, 2 vol. par de la Serre. ——— *Paris*.1664
5887 Les Oeuvres de Scarron, 6 vol.——— *Amst*.1717
5888 Les Sentences Illustres de Ciceron par Belleforestes. *Paris*. 1574
5889 Tacite, avec des notes par Amelot de la Houssaie, 2 vol. *a la Haye*.1692
5890 ———le meme par Ablancourt, 3 vol.——— *Lyon*.1661
5891 Les Avantures de Telemaque, 2 vol. *avec fig*.— *Paris*.1717
5892 ———le meme, *avec fig*. ——— *Hamb*.1731
5893 Les Oeuvres Poetiques de Tyssot, 3 vol.——— *Amst*.1727
5894 Le Nouveau Theatre Italien, 6 vol. ——— *Paris*.1733
5895 L'Eneide de Virgil par Segrais, 3 vol. *avec fig*. *Amst*.1700
5896 Oeuvres de Voltaire, 3 vol.——— *ib*.1732
5897 Les Oeuvres de Virgile par Vallemont, 4 vol.— *Lyon*.1721
5898 Hist. du Theatre Italien par Riccoboni, *avec fig*.
5899 La Henriade, *avec fig*.——— *Lond*.1730
5900 Odes sur les Affaires du Tems, 5 vol. ——— *Liege*,1731

English Miscellanies. Octavo & Infra.

5901 Athenian Oracle, 4 vol. ——— 1728
5902 Astry's Royal Politician, 2 vol. *cuts*. ——— 1700

5903

5903 Athenian Sport. 1707
5904 Altieri's Italian Grammar. 1728
5905 Agrippa's Vanity of Arts and Sciences. 1676
5906 Ascham of the Confusions and Revolutions of Government. 1649
5907 Life and Death of Arminius, Episcopius. Essay on critical and curious Learning.
5908 Athenagoras's Discourse on the Resurrection of the dead, *bl. letter.*
5909 Atalantis, 4 vol. 1720
5910 Baily's Etymological Dictionary. 1727
5911 Boyer's French Dictionary. 1728
5912 Cole's Latin Dictionary. 1693
5913 Bentley's Answer to Boyle. 1699
5914 Boyle's Answer to Bentley. 1699
5915 High-Church turn'd Presbyterian, Account of a Dream at Harwich, with other Tracts.
5916 Dr. Bernard's Catalogue.
5917 Boulainvillier's Life of Mahomet. 1731
5918 Blandy's Chronological Tables.
5919 Prince of Conti's Works. 1711
5920 Bruyere's Characters. 1700
5921 Bulstrode's miscellaneous Essays. 1724
5922 Baker's Reflections upon Learning. 1714
5923 Letters from the Living to the Dead. 1703
5924 Letters from the Dead to the Living. 1703
5925 Sir T. Brown's Miscellaneous Tracts. 1684
5926 Burnet's Hist. of the Rights of Princes. 1682
5927 Burman's Oration, and Tasso's Amintas, ital. and eng.
5928 Bayle's occasional Reflections. 1665
5929 Bp. Barlow's genuine Remains. 1693
5930 Balzac's Letters. 1658
5931 Banner on Simony, Plague at Athens, and Directions for Brewing.
5932 Brightland's English Grammar. 1712
5933 Pattern for Students in the University. 1729
5934 Barnes's Discovery of a little People call'd Pigmies. 1675
5935 The Boke of Wysdome, *bl. letter.*
5936 Casaubon's Treatise proving Spirits and Witches. 1672
5937 Chronicle of the Success of Times, *bl. letter.* 1611
5938 Sir R. Cotton's posthumous Works. 1672
5939 Vivier's French Grammatical Dictionary. 1705
5940 Colerus's Life of Benedict Spinosa. 1706
5941 Clergyman's Vade-mecum. 1709
5942 Catalogue of Graduates in Divinity, Law, and Physick. 1705
5943 The famouse Game of Chesse.
5944 The fearful Fancies of the Florentine Cooper. 1599
5945 Collection of Foreign Coins.

5646

5946 Somner's English Saxon Vocabulary. —— 1701.
5947 Charron of Wisdom, 2 vol. —— 1697
5948 Comazzi's Morals of Princes, by Hatchet. —— 1729
5949 Poetical Dialogues. Comment on Tom Thumb. Way to be wiser, and other Tracts.
5950 Collier's Essays, 3 vol. —— 1698
5951 The Courtier, by Balthasar Castiglione. —— 1724
5952 Parrhasiana, or, Thoughts on Subjects, by Le Clerc. 1700
5953 Dodwell's Considerations how far Romanists may be trusted. 1675
5954 Williams's Catalogue of printed Books in the Welch Language. —— 1717
5955 Consolidator, or Memoirs from the World in the Moon. 1705
5956 Dictionary of all Religions, ancient and modern. —— 1723
5957 Antonius de Dominis's Manifestation, with his Sermon, with several other Tracts.
5958 Dublin Scuffle, being a Challenge sent by J. Dunton of London, to P. Campbel at Dublin. —— 1699
5959 Royal Marriage, King Lemuel's Lesson. —— 1722
5960 De Pyle's Art of Painting, and Lives of the Painters. 1706
5961 Fresnoy's Art of Painting, by Dryden. —— 1716
5962 Remarks on the Life of Kennet. Character of the Earl of Wharton, and other Tracts.
5663 Discourse concerning having many Children. —— 1695
5964 Discourse of the Empire, and of the Election of a King of the Romans. —— 1658
5965 The Deaf and Dumb Man's Tutor. —— 1680
5966 The Devil's Patriarch, or, an Account of the Life of Pope Innocent XI. —— 1683
5967 The surest Way to destroy the Ottoman Empire. —— 1687
5968 Sir Evremond's Works, 3 vol. —— 1728
5969 Emblems for the Entertainment of Youth, in 62 Copper-Plates.
5970 Dr. Eachard's Works. —— 1705
5971 Locke's Thoughts concerning Education. —— 1693
5972 Walker of Education. —— 1687
5973 Essay upon Civil Government. —— 1722
5974 The Boke named the Governour, by Sir T. Elyot, *bl. letter*.
5975 Fuller's Directions, Counsels, and Cautions. —— 1725
5976 Freke's select Essays. —— 1693
5977 Fleury's Method of Studies. —— 1695
5978 Frontinus's Stratagems of War, *bl. letter*. —— 1539
5979 Sir R. Filmer on the natural Power of Kings. —— 1680
5980 Geddes's Miscellaneous Tracts, 3 vol. —— 1730
5981 Glanville of Witches. —— 1726
5982 Guy's last Will and Testament, *bound in Turky*. —— 1725
5983 Grabe's Essay on two Arabick Manuscripts. —— 1711
5984 Courtier's Manual Oracle, by Gracian. —— 1685

5985

5985 Gentleman's Dictionary. ——— 1705
5986 Greave's Discourse on the Roman Foot and Denarius. 1647
5987 Gildas's Epistles. ——— 1638
5988 Universal, Historical, Geographical, Chronological and Poetical Dictionary, 2 vol. ——— 1703
5989 Hickeringill's Works, 3 vol. ——— 1716
5990 Huarte's Trial of Wits. ——— 1698
5991 Honesty in Distress. Reply to Colebatch, and other Tracts.
5992 Hutchinson's Essay concerning Witchcraft. ——— 1718
5993 Historical Account of the Life and Writings of Mr. J. Hale. 1719
5994 Hist. of the Seven Wise Masters. ——— 1683
5995 Inventers and Instituters of the famous Arts in the World. 16 6
5996 Critical Hist. of Pamphlets. ——— 1715
5997 Lives and Amours of the Empresses. ——— 1723
5998 Idea of Jansenism, both historick and dogmatick.—1669
5999 The Jewish Kalendar.
6000 Kelly's Collection of Scotish Proverbs. ——— 1721
6001 Lewis's Antiquities of the Hebrew Republick, 4 vol. 1724
6002 Leigh's Observations of all the Roman Emperors.— 1664
6003 Ludwig's German Grammar. ——— 1717
6004 Langbaine's Account of the English dramatic Poets. 1691
6005 Loveday's Letters. ——— 1676
6006 Lightfoot's Miscellanies, Christian and Judaical.—— 1629
6007 Longinus on the Height of Eloquence.———1652
6008 Memoirs of Literature, 8 vol. ——— 1722
6009 New Memoirs of Literature. ——— 1725
6010 Moyle's Works, 2 vol. ——— 1726
6011 Montaigne's Essays, 3 vol. ——— 1685
6012 Meige's French Dictionary. ——— 1699
6013 Flecher's Life of Theodosius the Emperor. —— 1693
6014 Malard's French and Protestant Companion. ——— 1719
6015 Sir Toby Matthew's Letters.
6016 Mauger's French Grammar. ——— 1725
6017 Maynwaring's Means of enjoying Health. ———1683
6018 Compleat Hist. of Magick, Sorcery and Witchcraft, 2 vol. 1715
6019 The Rehearsal transpros'd. ——— 1673
6020 Hytholoday's Discourse concerning the best State of a Common-wealth, *bl. letter.*
6021 Sir George Mackenzie's Moral Essay on Solitude.
6022 Discourse of the Possession and Dispossession of seven Persons in Lancashire. ——— 1600
6023 Newton on University Education. ——— 1726
6024 Nicolson's Scotish Library. ——— 1702
6025 Newcome's Sermons, 2 vol. ——— 1712
6026 Nichodemus's Gospel.

A a 6027

6027 Nourse's Discourse on the Nature and Faculties of Man. 1686
6028 Oswestry of the Heart, and its Right Sovereign.—— 1678
6029 Observations and Reflections, Moral and Political.— 1710
6030 Ockley's Account of the Arabick Manuscripts. —— 1712
6031 Osborn's Works. ———————— 1658
6032 The Plain-Dealer, 2 vol. ———————— 1734
6033 Pointer's Miscellanies. ———————— 1718
6034 Fresnoy's Method of studying History, 2 vol. *lar. and sm. pap.* ———————— 1728
6035 Palmer's Essays on the English, Scotch, and Foreign Proverbs. ———————— 1710
6036 Prideaux's Directions to Church-Wardens. *interleav'd.* 1723
6037 Pettit's Visions of Government. ———— 1684
6038 Persian Letters. ———————— 1735
6039 Percey's compleat Swimmer, or, the Art of Swimming. 1658
6040 Rollin's Method of studying the Belles Letters, 4 vol. 1734
6041 Present State of the Republick of Letters, vol. 9.—10.
6042 Rogissard's French Grammar. ———— 1734
6043 Several Tracts relating to K. Edward VIth's Liturgy.
6044 Several Tracts by Caleb D'Anvers, Budgel, and others.
6045 Cambridge Phrases. ———————— 1693
6046 Ray's Collection of English Proverbs. ———— 1678
6047 ————Collection of English Words used in the Northern and Southern Counties.
6048 Record of ancient Histories, entitled, in Latine Gesta Romanorum, *bl. letter.* ———————— 1663
6049 Robertson's Gate to the Holy Tongue.
6050 Campanologia improv'd, or, the Art of Ringing.— 1733
6051 Spectators, 8 vol. ———————— 1733
6052 ——the same, 16 vol. *lar. letter.* ———— 1724
6053 Guardians, 2 vol. ———————— 1734
6054 Tatlers, 4 vol. ———————— 1733
6055 Englishman. ———————— 1714
6056 Lover and Reader. ———————— 1723
6057 Freeholder. ———————— 1723
6058 Homourist. ———————— 1720
6059 Free-Thinkers, 3 vol. ———————— 1733
6060 Turkish Spy, 8 vol. —— ——— 1718
6061 Shaftesbury's Characktericks, 3 vol. ———— 1732
6062 Tryals of the Rioters at Bristol, Life of W. Fuller, Dying Speeches, Tryal of Hendley, Rochester, and Kelly's Speech, with several other Tracts.
6063 Seneca's Morals, by L'Estrange. ———— 1722
6064 Salmon's Family-Dictionary. ———— 1710
6065 Strauchius's Chronology. ———— 1704
6066 Case of Catiline, View of London, Bestuchef's Memorial, and Spirit and Conduct of several Writers.

6067

6067 Queen of Scot's Letters, with other Tracts relating to the Affair of Dr. Sacheverell

6068 Selden's Table-Talk. —— —— 1716

6069 Spelman de non Temerandis Ecclesiis. —— 1613

6070 Deaf and dumb Man's Discourse, Aretini Dialogus, and La Visiera Alzata Hecatoste.

6071 Strange Metamorphosis of Man transform'd into a Wilderness. —— —— 1634

6072 Thynn's Histories concerning Ambassours. —— 1651

6073 Discovery by Sea with a Wherry from London to Salisbury. 1623

6074 A thousand notable Things of sundry sorts. —— 1650

6075 Terræ Filius, or the secret History of the Univ. of Oxford. 1726

6076 Tatlers, vol. 1, 2, 3, imperial pap.

6077 Tillemont's Life of Apollonius Tyaneus. —— 1702

6078 Smith's Vanity of Conquests and Universal Monarchy. 1705

6079 The Art of Speaking, by Messieurs du Port-Royal. 1676

6080 Swan Tripe-Club, Letter of R. Walpole Esq; in the Tower, Battle of Audenard, and several other Tracts.

6081 Staynoe on the Education of Children. —— 1717

6082 Mystery of Rhetorique, unvail'd by Smith. —— 1657

6083 History of the Lives of the Highwaymen, 3 vol. —1714

6084 Evelyn's Hist. and Art of Chalcography. —— 1662

6085 Universal Library, or a compleat Summary of Science, 2 vol. —— —— 1722

6086 Uvedale's Italian Grammar. —— 1711

6087 Wotton's History of Rome. —— 1701

6088 ———Remains. —— —1651

6089 ———Reflexions upon Learning. —— 1694

6090 Walker's Memoirs of the Life of Sally Salisbury. —1723

6091 Worthington's Miscellanies. —— 1704

6092 Wars of the Elements, Republican Procession, Metamorphosis of the Town, Amorous War, with several other Tracts.

6093 Wagstaffe's Works. —— —— 1726

6094 Whear's Method of reading History. —— 1698

6095 Willymote's peculiar Use and Signification of Words. 1705

6096 Walker's Treatise of English Particles. —— 1695

6097 ———Phrases. —— 1670

6098 The Bowman's Glory, or Archery reviv'd.———1682

6099 Walker's Greek and Roman History of Coins and Medals. 1692

6100 Webb's Essay to prove that the Language of China is the primitive Language. —— 1669

6101 Wheeler's Account of the Churches of the primitive Christians, cuts. —— —— 1689

6102 Monarchy asserted, by Wren.

6103 Wilson's Discourse on Usury. —— 1572
6104 Pleasant Treatise of Witches. —— 1673

Law, Civil, Canon, and Common, Eng. Lat. and Fr. Octavo and Twelves.

6105 Abridgment of the Statutes, 6 vol. —— 1708
6106 Ashby and White. —— —— 1705
6107 Averani Interpretationes Juris. —— *L.B.* 1716
6108 Astry's Charge to Grand Juries. —— 1703
6109 Hale's Analysis of the Law. —— 1713
6110 Attorney's Pocket-Companion. —— 1733
6111 Nicholson's Border-Laws. —— —— 1705
6112 Statutes at Large concerning Bankrupts. —— 1728
6113 Compleat Arbitrator. —— 1731
6114 Ancient Tenures of Land, and jocular Customs. —— 1679
6115 Brown's Treatise of Fines and Recoveries. —— 1725
6116 ————Entring Clerk's Vade Mecum. —— 1626
6117 Methodus novissima Intrandi Placita Generalia. —— 1699
6118 Bohun's English Pleader. —— 1734
6119 ————English Lawyer. —— 1732
6120 ————Law of Tythes. —— 1731
6121 ————Declarations and Pleadings. —— 1733
6122 ————Cursus Cancellariæ. —— 1715
6123 ————Institutio Legalis. —— 1732
6124 Blackerby's Cases in Law. —— 1717
6125 ————Justice, 2 vol. —— 1730
6126 Benincasii Tractat. de Paupertate ac ejus Privilegiis.
6127 Branchii Observationes ad Jus Romanum. 1721
6128 Brissonii Comment. de Spectaculis & Feriis. *Goudæ* 1695
6129 Compleat Sheriff. —— —— 1727
6130 Cases of Settlements. —— 1732
6131 Common and Statute-Laws relating to Tryals in Treasons. 1700
6132 Clerk's Tutor in Chancery. —— 1694
6133 Covert's Scrivener's Guide, 2 vol. —— 1716
6134 Corpus Juris Civilis, 2 vol. —— *Amst.* 1700
6135 Curson's Office and Duty of Executors. —— 1728
6136 ————Law of Estates Tail. —— 1703
6137 ————Mysteries of Clerkship explained. 1705
6138 Charter of Romney-Marsh. —— 1686
6139 Clerk's Assistant. —— —— 1683
6140 Hughe's Abridgment of Croke's Reports. —— 1665
6141 Compendium of the Laws. —— 1712
6142 Compleat Parish-Officer. —— 1709
6143 Caborii Disputat. var. Juris. —— *Han.* 1598
6144 Collection of Statutes relating to High-Treason. —— 1723
6145 Degges's Parson's Counsellor. —— 1709

6146

6146 Doctor and Student, *bl. letter.*
6147 Fitzherbert's Natura Brevium. —— 1718
6148 Fornerii rerum Quotidianarum Lib. 3. ——*Par.* 1600
6149 Fortescue de Laudibus Legum Angliæ, with Notes by Selden. —— —— 1672
6150 Greenwood's Method of keeping Courts. —— 1730
6151 Grey's System of English Ecclesiastical Law. —— 1730
6152 Green's Privileges of the City of London. —— 1722
6153 Godolphin's View of the Admiral Jurisdiction. 1661
6154 Alberi Gentilis de Legationibus Lib. 3. *Han.* 1607
6155 Hawkins's Abridgment of the Pleas of the Crown, 2 vol.
6156 Higgs's Guide to Justices. —— 1728
6157 Hale's History of the Common Law. —— 1734
6158 Hughes's Grounds of the Laws of England. —— 1713
6159 The Mirrour of Justices. —— —— 1656
6160 Johnston's Collection of Ecclesiastical Laws, 2 vol. 1646
6161 Jacob's accomplished Conveyancer, 3 vol. —— 1720
6162 ——Clerk's Remembrancer. —— 1714
6163 ——Compleat Court-Keeper. —— 1714
6164 ——Student's Companion. —— 1713
6165 ——Laws of Appeals and Murder. —— 1734
6166 Instructor Clericalis, vol. 1, 2, 3. —— 1709
6167 Bonefidii Juris Orientalis Lib. 3. *lineis rubris, fol. deaurat. apud H. Steph.* 1707
6168 Kilburn's choice Precedents. —— 1573
6169 Kitchin's Jurisdiction of Courts. —— 1715
6170 Les Loix Civiles dans leur Ordre Naturel, par Domat, 5 vol. —— —— 1657
6171 Legal Judicature in Chancery stated. —— *Par.* 1695
6172 Law of Actions. —— —— 1727
6173 Law of Errors, and Writs of Errors. —— 1710
6174 Lambard's Comment. on the Courts of Justice.—— 1703
6175 Legal Provision for the Poor. —— —— 1635
6176 Littleton's Tenures. —— —— 1710
6177 Molloy de Jure Maritimo. —— —— 1627
6178 Modern Conveyancer, 3 vol. —— 1701
6179 Abridgment of the Irish Statutes. —— 1725
6180 Magna Charta. —— —— 1700
6181 Nelson's Justice. —— —— 1602
6182 ——Rights of the Clergy. —— 1726
6183 ——Lex Maneriorum. —— 1709
6184 ——Laws of England concerning the Game. 1733
6185 Rules and Orders collected out of the Journals of the House of Commons. —— —— 1732
6186 Obrechti Tractat. de Principiis Juris. ——*Arg.* 1717
6187 Praxis Almæ Curiæ Cancellariæ, 2 vol. —— 1619
6188 Practical Register in Chancery. —— —— 1725
6189 Prideaux's Original and Right of Tithes. —— 1714

1710

6190

6190 Report of Cases in Chancery, 3 vol. —— 1693
6191 Readings upon the Statute-Law, 5 vol. — 1723
6192 Rules and Orders of the Court of King's Bench. 1734
6193 Ridley's View of the Civil and Ecclesiastical Law. 1675
6194 The Right of Tithes re-asserted. —— 1680
6195 Scroggs of Courts Leets and Courts Baron. —— 1728
6196 Styles and Lilly's practical Register, 3 vol. 1710
6197 Collect. of Statutes relating to the Stamp-Duties. 1716
6198 Sheppard of Corporations and Guilds. —— 1659
6199 De Virginitate, Virginum Statu & Jure, Tractat. Jucundus. 1669
6200 Treatise of Trespasses Vi & Armis. —— 1704
6201 Tryals per Pais. —— —— 1702
6202 Treleine's Discourse of Tithes. —— 1708
6203 Tenant's Law. —— —— 1735
6204 Triglandii Pedia Juris. —— —— 1710
6205 Glanville Tractat. de Legibus Regni Angliæ.— *Lond.* 1677
6206 C. Van Eck Vindiciæ Juris Academici. ——*Franc.* 1688
6207 Vaughn's Practica Walliæ. —— 1672
6208 Wood's Institute of the Civil Law. —— 1704
6209 Wilkinson of Courts. —— 1703
6210 Williams's Excellency of the Laws of England. —— 1680
6211 Wingate's Briton. —— —— 1640

Philosophy, Mathematicks, and Astrology. Octavo and Twelves

6212 Agrippa's Vanity of Arts and Sciences. —— 1684
6213 Artificial Embellishments. —— — 1665
6214 Aleandri's Book of calculating Nativities. *bl. letter.*
6215 Burnet's Theory of the Earth, 2 vol. —— 1726
6216 Barrow's mathematical Lectures. —— 1734
6217 ——— Geometrical Lectures. —— 1735
6218 Boethius's Consolation of Philosophy, by Lord Preston. 1695
6219 Bayle's Reflections on the Comet, 2 vol. 1708
6220 Boyle's Experiments touching Cold. —— 1665
6221 Brown's Description of the Triangular Quadrant, and his Art of Dyalling.
6222 ——— Arithmetica Infinita. —— 1718
6223 Regnault's Philosophical Conversations, by Dale, 3 vol. cuts. 1731
6224 Mercurius Trismegistus his divine Pymander. —— 1657
6225 Fletcher's Arithmetick. —— —— 1727
6226 Gregory's Elements of Astronomy, 2 vol. —— 1715
6227 Gravesand's Elements of natural Philosophy. —— 1721
6228 Green's Principles of natural Philosophy. —— 1712
6229 Sir G. Wharton's Works, by Gadbury. —— 1683

6230

6230 Glanvill's Discourse of Experimental Philosophy. — 1671
6231 Gaffarel's unheard-of Curiosities. — 1650
6232 The Book of Knowledge and Prognostication for ever, *bl. letter.* — — — 1671
6233 Hodgeson's Treatise of practical Gauging. — 1689
6234 Hatton's mathematical Manual. — 1728
6235 ——— Index to Interest. — 1711
6236 Holder's Treatise of Harmony. — 1731
6237 Hill's Art of Physiognomy. — 1613
6238 Henshaw's Register for the Air. — 1684
6239 Hunt's Recreations. — — 1651
6240 John's Essay towards the Theory of the intelligible World.
6241 List of the Royal Society. *N.B. most of them suppressed.*
6242 Leybourne's sure Guide for Purchasers. — 1693
6243 ——— Introduction to Astronomy and Geography. 1675
6244 Lock of Human Understanding, abridg'd. 1696
6245 Logick, or the Art of Thinking. — 1702
6246 Mandey's universal mathematical Synopsis. — 1702
6247 ——— Marrow of Measuring. — 1717
6248 Miscellanea Curiosa. — — 1705
6249 Moxon's mechanick Exercises. — 1703
6250 Malcolm's Treatise of Musick. — 1721
6251 Meteorological Essays, cuts. — 1715
6252 De Moivre's Value of Annuities upon Lives. — 1725
6253 The Man in the Moon, or a Discourse of a Voyage there. 1657
6254 Newton's Optical Lectures. — 1728
6255 Oughtred's mathematical Recreations. — 1653
6256 Patridge's Description of the Double Scale, and the Loves of the Philosophers.
6257 Saunders's Secrets of Palmistry. — 1669
6258 Robinson's natural History of this World of Matter. 1696
6259 Ray's Wisdom of God in the Creation. — 1701
6260 Simpson's Hydrological Essays. — 1670
6261 Sharrock's Hist. of the Propagation of Vegetables. 1660
6262 Taylor's Treasury of the Mathematicks. — 1707
6263 Things divine and super-natural conceiv'd by Analogy, with Things natural and human. — 1733
6264 Wells's Art of Shadows. — 1635
6265 Whiston's Astronomical Lectures. — 1715
6266 Ward's young Mathematician's Guide. — 1734
6267 Wilkins's mathematical Magick. — 1680
6268 ——— swift Messenger. — — 1694
6269 Williams's occult Physick. — 1660
6270 Wingate's Arithmetick. — 1694
6271 Witty's Survey of the Heavens. — 1685

Philosoph.

Philosoph. Mathemat. & Hist. Naturalis. Octavo & infra.

6272 Ariſtarchus de Magnitudinibus & Diſtantiis Solis & Lunæ, gr. lat. notis Pappi Alexandrini. ——Ox.1688
6273 Alimari Longitudinis aut Terra aut Mari Inveſtigandæ Methodus. —— —— *Lond.*1715
6274 La Philoſophie Occulte de C. Agrippa, 2 vol. *a la Haye* 1727
6275 T. Burnet Archæologiæ Philoſophicæ. ——*Lond.*1728
6276 L'Ecole des Arpentures. —— *Par.*1728
6277 Oughtredi Clavis Mathematicæ. ——*Lond.*1631
6278 Traite de la Science des Nombres, par Brunot. *Paris* 1723
6279 Bernardus de Menſuris & Ponderibus Antiquis. *Oxon.* 1688
*6278 Trattato dell' Agricoltura di P. de Creſcenzi, 2 vol. *Nap.* 1724
*6279 Caius de Canibus Britannicis. ——*Lond.*1729
6280 ——de Ephemera Britannica. —— *ib.*1721
6281 Nouveau Syſteme du Monde, par Le Clerc.—— *Par.*1706
6282 Canon Triangulorum. —— —— *L.B.*1626
6283 Ciaconius de Ponderibus, Menſuris & Nummis. *Romæ* 1608
6284 Cluſii Hiſtoria Stirpium. —— *Ant.*1583
6285 P. de Croſa Phyſicæ Utilitate Diſſertat. Philoſophica. *Gron.* 1725
6286 Lecons Phyſico-Mechaniques. —— *Lond.*1717
6287 Dodwelli Diſſertat. de Ætate Phalandis & Pythagoræ. *ib.* 1704
6288 Raii Synopſis Methodica Stirpium Britannicarum. *Lond.* 1724
6289 Luidii Lythophylacii Britannici Ichnographia. ——*ib.*1699
6290 Elemens de Botanique, par Tournefort, avec gr. nomb. des fig. ———— *Par.*1694
6291 Le nouveau Livre des Changes, par Barreme, 2 vol. *ib.*
6292 Traite de la Conſtruction & des principaux Uſages des Inſtrumens de Mathematique, par Bion. *ib.*1716
6293 Brenkmani de Eurematicis Diatriba. ——*L.B.*1711
6294 L'Excellente Jeu de Pythagoras dict Rythmomachie, fr. & lat. ———— *Lut.*1556
6295 Diſcours ſur les Eaux Chaudes & Bains de Plombiere. *Nan.* 1615
6296 Jordani Bruni Acrotiſmus. —— *Vit.*1588
6297 Euclidis Elementa, J. Barrow. ——*Lond.*1678
6298 Wolfgangus de Unicornu. —— 1598

6299

6299 Blondel Descriptio Thermarum Aquisgranensium H. de ab Heers de Acidulis Spadanis, & Observat. Medicæ, Tractat. de Fontibus Medicatis Angliæ.
6300 Boyle de Coloribus. ——— *Amst.* 1667
6301 Berckringerus de Cometis. ——— *Ultraject.* 1665
6302 J. Caii Opera omnia. ——— *Louanii.* 1556
6303 Observations sur les Eaux Minerales par du Clos. *Paris.* 1675
6304 Pratique de la Geometrie par le Clerc, 2 vol. — *Amst.* 1713
6305 Clerici Physica. ——— ——*ib.* 1696
6306 Lumen novum Phosphorus accensum. ——— *ib.* 1717
6307 Cozzandus de Magisterio antiquorum Philosophorum, Lib. 6. *Genev.* 1684
6308 Contarini de Frumentaria Romanorum Largitione Liber. *Vesaliæ.* 1669
6309 P. Dube de Mineralium Natura in Universum. *Paris.* 1649
6310 Goedartii Hist. naturalis Insectorum, *cum fig.*
6311 Curiositez inouyez sur la Sculpture Talismanique par Gaffarel. ——— ——— 1637
6312 Galenus de Urinis, gr.
6313 Magiri Physiologiæ Peripateticæ Lib. VI.——— *Cant.* 1642
6314 J. Newton Optice. ——— ——— *Lond.* 1719
6315 Nemesius de Natura Hominis gr. lat.——— *Oxon.* 1671
6316 B. Portæ Phytognomonica. ——— *Franc.* 1608
6317 J. Woodward naturalis Hist. Telluris. ——— *Lond.* 1714
6318 Gronovii Origenis Philosophumena gr. lat. ——— *Hamb.* 1706
6319 G. du Val. Phytologia sive Plantarum. ——— *Paris.* 1647
6320 J. Scaliger de Subtilitate. ——— *Franc.* 1665
6321 Usserii de Macedonum & Asianornm Anno Solari dissertat. *Lond.* 1648
6322 Caius de Canibus Britannicis, ch. max. ——— *ib.* 1729
6323 Abrege de la Philosophie de Gassendi par Bernier, 7 vol. *Lyon.* 1678
6324 Les Meditations Metaphysiques de Rene d'Escartes, 2 vol. *Paris.* 1724
6325 Discourse Philosophique sur la Creation du Monde. *Amst.* 1700
6326 Dialogues Rustiques. ——— *Leyden.* 1612
6327 M. Fehr de Absinthio Analecta. ——— *Lipsiæ.* 1668
6328 L. Arithmetique en sa Perfection par le Gendre. *Lyon.* 1699
6329 Sturmius Mathesis Juveniles, 2 vol. ——— *Noriberg.* 1702
6330 J. Alexandri Synopsis Algebraica. ——— 1693
6331 Gemini de apparentiis Cælestibus Lib. gr. lat.——— *Lug.* 1603
6332 T. Hobbs Elementa Philosophica. ——— *Amst.* 1669
6333 La Clavicule ou la Science de Raymond Lulle par Jacob. *Paris.* 1647
6334 Synopsis Philosophiæ moralis. ——— *Franc.* 1692
6335 Kircheri Magneticum Naturæ Regnum.——— *Amst.*
6336 Lemnius de Miraculis occultis Naturæ.——— *Ant.* 1581
6337 Traite des Eaux Minerales. ——— *Par.* 1723

6338 Macer de Herbis Carmen.
6339 Pretiosa Margarita Novella de Thesauro, ac Pretiosissimo Philosophorum Lapide.
6340 Cocklearia Curiosa, de Natura Alcidi, Hist. Nitri, Introit. Apertus ad Occlusum Regis Palatium, Aurora Chymica.
6341 Mercurius Botannicus. —— *Lond.* 1634
6342 Mizaldi Ephemerides Æris perpetuæ. —— 1554
6343 Nova Geometria practica super Charta & Solo. *Amst.* 1692
6344 Syrbii Institutiones Philosophiæ primæ. —— *Jenæ.* 1726
6345 Scaligeri Animadvers. in Hist. Theophrasti. —— *Lug.* 1584
6346 Scheibleri Philosophia Compendiosa. —— *Lond.* 1685
6347 Hist. des Plantes par Tournefort. —— *Par.* 1692
6348 P. Virgilii de rerum Inventoribus Lib. 8. —— *Lug. apud S. Gryph.* 1546
6349 Pratum Lacus Arundinetum. —— *Par. apud Colinæum.* 1543
6350 Reinhardi Synopsis Philosophiæ primæ. —— *Lipsiæ.* 1730
6351 Catalog. Viror excell. in Arte Astrolog. —— *Ant.* 1580
6352 Specimen Artis ratiocinandi Naturalis & Artificialis ad Pantosophiæ principia Manuducens. —— *Hamb.* 1684
6353 R. Steph. Index Plantarum. —— *Par.* 1536
6354 M. Thruston de Respirationis usu primario Diatriba. *Lug. Bat.* 1708
6355 Priezaci Dilucida de Coloribus dissertat. —— *Par.* 1657
6356 Bitumen & Lignum Fossile Bituminosum descript. *Altenburg.* 1674
6357 Procli, Cleomedis, Arati, & Dyonysii de Sphæra, &c. *Basil.* 1547
6358 Phinellæ Nevorum Lib. de signis in Unguibus Salium Empyricum.
6359 W. Payer de Thermis —— *Lipsiæ.* 1614
6360 Horti Regii Parisiensis Catalogus. —— *Amst.* 1691
6361 Strauchii Tabulæ Sinuum, Tangentium, Logarithmorum. *ib.* 1700
6362 J. Sarisberiensis de Nugis Curialium & Vestigiis Philosophorum Lib. —— *Lug. Bat.* 1639
6363 Traite des Oranges & Citronniers. —— *Par.* 1692
6364 J. Sachs Oceanus Macro-Microcosmicus.
6365 Tesoro delle Gioie Trattato curioso. —— *Padov.* 1630
6366 Hexameron Rustique. —— *Amst.* 1698

Poetry, Novels, and Translations. Octavo & Infra.

6367 Husbands's Miscellany of Poems. —— 1731
6368 The Dancing Master, 3 vol.
6369 Daniel de Foe's Works. —— 1703
6370 Dunster's Horace, Latin and English. —— 1712
6371 Sir George Etherege's Works. —— 1704
6372 English Adventures. —— 1676
6373 La Fontaine's Fables and Tales, fr. and eng. —— 734

6374

6374 Fontenelle's Dialogues of the Dead. —— 1708
6375 Lucius Florus, lat. and eng. by Clarke.
6376 Pastor Fido, translated by Sir R. Fanshawe. —— 1664
6377 The French Rogue. —— 1672
6378 Dryden's Fables. —— 1721
6379 Oppian's Nature of Fishes and Fishing of the Ancients. 1722
6380 Swift's Miscellanies, vol. 3d. —— 1732
6381 Plutarch's Lives abridg'd. —— 1712
6382 Rochester's Poems, with the Tragedy of Valentinian. 1696
6383 Pills to purge Melancholy, 6 vol. —— 1719
6384 Iliad of Homer, with Dacier's Notes. —— 1714
6385 The Loves of Charles Duke of Mantua. —— 1669
6386 Lansdowne's Poems. —— —— 1732
6387 Lee's Plays, 3 vol. —— —— 1734
6388 Virgil, translated by Ld. Lauderdale, 2 vol.
6389 Daniel's poetical Works, 2 vol. —— 1718
6390 Dryden's Virgil, 3 vol. cuts. —— 1721
6391 Hughes's Poems, 2 vol. —— 1735
6392 Gay's Fables, cuts. —— —— 1728
6393 Gulliver's Travels, 2 vol. —— 1726
6394 Whig and Tory, The Conscious Lovers, and Key to the Lock.
6395 Hudibras. —— —— —— 1700
6396 The Irish Hudibras. —— —— 1689
6397 Earl of Surrey's Poems. —— —— 1717
6398 The Intelligencer, by Swift. —— —— 1729
6399 Lee's Plays, 2 vol. —— —— 1713
6400 Herodotus, translated by Littlebury, 2 vol. —— 1723
6401 Erasmus's Colloquies, by Lestrange. —— 1725
6402 L'Estrange's Æsop, 2 vol. —— 1708
6403 Quevedo's Visions, by L'Estrange. —— 1696
6404 Creech's Lucretius. —— —— 1683
6405 Mitchell's Poems, 2 vol. —— 1729
6406 De la Mott's Tales and Fables, fr. and eng. —— 1729
6407 Miscellany Poems and Translations. —— 1712
6408 Swift's Miscellanies. —— —— 1713
6409 Miscellanies in Prose and Verse. —— 1729
6410 Poems by Dryden, Granville, and others. —— 1701
6411 Amours of the Kings of France. —— 1695
6412 Beggars Opera. Polly, an Opera. Beggars Wedding. Country Burial. Jovial Crew, and the Chambermaid.
6413 Lady Winchelsea's Poems. —— 1727
6414 Fenton's Poems. —— —— 1717
6415 Prior's Poems. —— —— 1709
6416 Corn. Nepos, translated by several Hands. —— 1684
6417 Ovid's Epistles, by several Hands. —— 1693
6418 Allan Ramsay's Poems. —— 1720
6419 Pliny's Panegyrick. —— 1686
6420 Rymer's short View of Tragedy. —— 1693

6421 Horace, translated by several hands. —— 1680
6422 The Rambler, an Anti-heroick Poem. —— 1682
6423 Southerne's Play, 2 vol. —— 1721
6424 Spencer's Redivivus. —— 1687
6425 The Musical Miscellany, 6 vol. —— 1729
6426 Heywood's Novels, 4 vol. —— 1732
6427 Incognita, or Love and Duty reconcil'd. —— 1713
6428 London Gentleman. Wormwood Lectures. Horn-Fair Fumbler's-Hall, Noble Cuckold, and others.
6429 The gallant Hermaphrodite. —— 1687
6430 Heroine Musquetier, or the Female Warrior. 1678
6431 Shakespear's Works, by Theobald, 7 vol. —— 1733
6432 Telemachus, by Ozel, 2 vol. *cuts*. —— 1735
6433 Wicherley's Plays. —— —— 1731
6434 Plain-Dealer. Rehearsal. Provok'd Wife, and Careless Husband.
6435 Virgil Travestie. —— —— 1678
6436 Terracon's Dissertation on Homer's Iliad, 2 vol. 1722
6437 Tibullus, translated by Dart. —— 1722
6438 Thompson's Seasons. —— —— 1729
6439 Terence's Comedies, by several hands. —— 1694
6440 Tacitus's Annals and History, 3 vol. —— 1698
6441 Homer's Battle of the Frogs, Revenge, Rape of the Lock, Chit-Chat, Essay on Poetry, and Busiris.
6442 Collection of Operas.
6443 Hamlet, Cato, Victim, and Rehearsal.
6444 Bysshe's Art of Poetry, 2 vol. —— 1718
6445 Bossu's Treatise of Epick Poetry, 2 vol. —— 1719
6446 Collection of diverting Songs, ancient Histories, &c. collected by Tho. Hearne, 3 vol.
6447 Morell's Poems. —— —— 1732
6448 Provok'd Husband, Trip through London, Beggars Opera, Memoirs of Mackheath.
6449 Sophocles's Tragedies, by Adams, 2 vol. —— 1729
6450 Arrian's History of Alexander's Expedition, by Rooke, 2 vol. —— —— 1729
6451 London Spy, 2 vol. —— —— 1709
6452 Behn's Plays, 4 vol. —— —— 1724
6453 Aristotle's Art of Poetry. —— —— 1705
6454 Waller's Poems, with *cuts*. —— 1711
6455 Collyer's short View of the English Stage. —— 1698
6456 Vanbrugh's Plays, 2 vol. —— —— 1719
6457 Truth in Fiction, or Morality in Masquerade. —— 1708
6458 Swift's Tale of a Tub. —— —— 1711
6459 Steele's Plays. —— —— 1732
6460 Dryden's Fables, 6 vol. —— 1717
6461 Drayton's Poems.
6462 Lives of all the Roman Emperors. —— 1636
6463 Gildon's Art of Poetry, 2 vol. —— 1724

6464

6464 Diana de Caſtro.
6465 Moliere's Plays, fr. and eng. 8 vol.
6466 ——— the ſame, in eng. 6 vol. 1732
6467 Motteux's Don Quixote, 4 vol. *cuts.* 1714
6468 Mountfort's Plays. 1733
6469 Adventures of Pomponius, and Nunnery-Tales. 1720
6470 The merry Muſician, 2 vol.
6471 Mirth diverts all Care. 1730
6472 Collection of wiſe and ingenious Sayings. 1708
6473 Poetical Honey, by Roſs.
6474 Merry Jeſts concerning Popes, Monks, and Friars. 1642
6475 Meroveus, a Novel. 1617
6476 Paradiſe regain'd. 1682
6477 The ten Pleaſures of Marriage. 1713
6478 The Tragedie of Gorbdodue, *black letter.* 1683
6479 Art of making Love, and fatal Beauty. 1565
6480 The Novels of Queen Elizabeth. 1688
6481 Rocheſter's Poems. 1680
Antwerp
6482 Ovid's Metamorphoſis, by ſeveral Hands, *cuts.* 1727
6483 Collection of Novels, 6 vol.
6484 Telemachus. 1729
6485 Juſtin, lat. and eng. by Bailey. 1715
6486 Blackmore's King Alfred. 1732
6487 Cotton's Poems. 1723
6488 Antoninus's Meditations, by Collier. 1689
6489 Tully de Finibus, by Collier. 1726
6490 Eutropius, lat. and eng. by Clarke. 1702
6491 Collection of Poems, by ſeveral hands. 1728
6492 Æſop naturaliz'd. 1693
6493 Cleveland's Works. 1711
6494 Pope's Homer's Iliad, 6 vol. 1687
6495 Prior's Poems, 3 vol, 1720
6946 Rocheſter's, Roſcommon's, and Dorſet's Works. 1733
6497 Tamerlane, Meaſure for Meaſure, and Careleſs Husband. 1731
6498 Ambitious Step-Mother, Tamerlane, Fair Penitent, and Jane Shore.
6499 Rowe's Lucan, 2 vol.
6500 Callipædia, or, the Art of getting pretty Children. 1722
6501 Croxal's Æſop, *cuts.* 1710
6502 Horace, tranſlated by ſeveral hands. 1731
6503 Latin and Engliſh Songs. 1671
6504 Poems ſacred and ſatyrical, and Edom and Babylon againſt Jeruſalem. 1685
6505 Swift's Miſcellanies, 4 vol.
6506 Tom Brown's Works, 4 vol. 1733
6507 Life and Adventures of Mr. Cleveland, 4 vol. 1715
6508 Creech's Horace. 1734
6509 Collection of old Ballads, 3 vol. *cuts.* 1720
6510 Cotton's Poetical Works, *cuts.* 1725
1725
6511

6511 Cowley's Works, 3 vol. ———— 1721
6512 Cupid's Addrefs to the Ladies, *cuts*. ——— 1683
6513 Cotton's Poems. ———— 1654
6514 Collect. of Comical and Tragic Novels. ——— 1703
6515 Ovid's Epiftles, tranflated by Turberville, *black letter*.
6516 Ogilby's Virgil. ———— 1665
6517 Sir Thomas Overbury's Wife. ——— 1664
6518 Amours of Alcippus and Lucippe, a Novel. ——— 1704
6519 Witty Apopthegmes, by K. Charles and others. — 1669
6520 Xenophon's Inftitutions, *bl. letter*. ——— 1657
6521 Drunken Barnaby's Itinerary, lat. and engl. with other Tracts.
6522 Butler's pofthumous Works, 3 vol. ——— 1716
6523 The Scourge of Villany, 3 Books of Satires. ——— 1598
6524 Norris's Mifcellanies. ———— 1717

Afia, Africa, America, & Itinerar. Lat. Gal. & Ital. Octavo & infra.

6525 Hift. de la Conquefte de Mexique, par Ant. de Solis, 2 vol. *avec fig*. ——— ——— *Par*. 1730
6526 Befoldi Hift. Conftantinopolitana, 2 vol. ——— *Argent*. 1634
6527 Belloni Obfervationes. ——— *Ant*. 1589
6528 Hift. de Jean de Brienne, Roy de Jerufalem. — *Par*. 1727
6529 Busbequii Epiftolæ. ——— *Lovan*. 1630
6530 Dionyfii Defcriptio Orbis, gr. lat. a G. Hill. ——— *Lond*. 1679
6531 A. Contzen. Hift. Regis Abiffini. ——— *Col. Agrip*. 1628
6532 Varenii Geographia. ——— *Cant*. 1681
6533 Libanii Sophiftæ Legatio ad Julian Imp. gr. *lin. rub*. — *Par. apud Morel*. 1611
6534 Mabilloni Itineris Germanici Defcriptio. ——— *Hamb*. 1717
6535 Yvonis Belli facri Chriftian. adverfus Barbaros, gr. *lin. rub*. *Par*. 1620
6536 De l'Utilite des Voyages, par Darival, 2 vol. *Rouen*. 1727
6537 Geographiæ Veteris Scriptores Græci minores, gr. lat. 4 vol. ———— *Oxon*. 1698
6538 Nouveau Voyage au tour du Monde, par Dampier. 5 vol. *avec fig*. ——— ——— *Amft*. 1711
6539 Hift. de la Conquefte des Ifles Moluques, 3 vol. *avec. fig*. *ib*. 1706
6540 Geographie de Mr. de Robbe, 2 vol. *a la Haye*. 1704
6541 P. Maffei Hift. Indicarum, lib. xvi. ——— *Col. Agrip*. 1590
6542 Pii II. Pont. Max. Afiæ & Europæ. ——— 1531
6543 Vadiani Geographia. ——— *Tiguri*. —
6544 Hift. Sinica. ——— ——— ——— 1699
6545 T. Smith de Moribus Turcarum. ——— *Oxon*. 1674
6546 G. Artus Hift. Indiæ Orientalis. ——— *Col. Agrip*. 1608
6547 Levini Apollonii de Peruvia Regionis Hift. — *Ant*. 1567

6548

6548 Itinera Italiæ. —— —— Vicent. 1601
6549 Viagii Fatti da Vinetia in Persia. —— Vineg. 1545
6550 Geufræi Descriptio Turciæ, 2 vol. —— Basil. ——
6551 Rerum a Societate Jesu in Oriente Gestarum Comment. Diling. 1571
6552 Leonhardii Gorecii Bellum Ivoniæ. —— Franc. 1578
6553 Mundus Alter & Idem. —— —— ib. ——
6554 Cellarii Geographia, 2 vol. —— Jenæ 1716
6555 Cuspinianus de Turcarum Origine, —— Lug. Bat. 1654
6556 De Turcarum Moribus Epitome. —— Lug. 1578
6557 Martinii de Bello Tartarico Hist. —— Romæ 1655
6558 Frolichii Bibliotheca seu Cynosura Peregrinantium. Ulmæ 1643
6559 Description du Royaume de Siam, par Loubere, 2 vol. *avec fig.* —— —— Amst. 1713
6560 Nouvelle Relation de l'Afrique Occidentale, par Labat, 5 vol. *avec fig.* —— —— Par. 1728
6561 Italiæ brevis & accurata Descriptio. —— Ultraj. 1650
6562 Totius Orbis Descriptio.

Architectura, Pictura, Sculptura, Numismata & Antiquitates. Octavo & infra.

6563 Antiquitates Urbis Romæ ab And. Palladio, lat. & ital. Oxon. 1709
6564 Maniere de Graver sur l'Arain, par A. Bosse. —— Par. 1645
6565 Maniere Universelle de Mr. Desargues pour pratiquer la Perspective, par Bosse. —— ib. 1648
6566 C. Fleetwood Inscriptionum Antiquarum Sylloge. Lond. 1691
6567 Leo Allatius de Templis Græcorum. Col. Agrip. 1645
6568 Baxteri Glossar. Antiquitat. Roman. —— Lond. 1726
6569 Alciati Emblemata, *fol. deaurat.* —— Lug. 1551
6570 Saavedra Symbola Politica. —— Amst. 1659
6571 Religiosæ Kijovienses Cryptæ. —— Jenæ 1675
6572 Hadriani Junii Emblemata. —— Ant. 1565
6573 Entretiens sur les Vies & sur les Ouvrages des Peintres, par Felibien, 2 vol. —— Lond. 1705
6574 Julii Cæsaris Portus Iccius Illustratus. Oxon. 1694
6575 Alberici Gentilis de Armis Romanis Lib. Hanov. 1612
6576 Theodorus de Mensibus. —— Par. apud Colin. 1535
6577 Julius Cæsar Nomismaticus. —— Lond. 1678
6578 Gruchius de Comitiis Romanorum. —— Ven. 1559
6579 L. Faunus de Antiquitatibus Urbis Romæ, *fol. deaurat.* ib. 1549
6580 Dissertation sur Nigrianus. —— Par. 1704
6581 Baysius de re Vestiaria, Vascularia et Navali, *cor. turc. fol. deaurat.* —— —— Lut. apud C. Steph. 1553
6582 Iscrizioni di Palermo. —— Paler. 1721

6583

6583 T. Belli Roma Reſtituta. —— *Amſt*.17[illegible]
6584 Budæus de Aſſe et partibus ejus. —— *Colon*.15[illegible]
6585 Vocabula Menſurarum et Rei Nummariæ.—— *Franc*.1573
6586 Nigronus de Caliga Veterum. —— *Lug. Bat*.1711
6587 Saubertus de Sacrificiis Veterum. —— *Jenæ* 1659
6588 Philandri in Lib. Vitruvii de Architectura Annotat.—*Romæ* 1554
6589 Cuperi Harpocrates. —— *Amſt*.1676
6590 Gutherius de Jure Manium. —— *Lipſ*.1671
6591 Sperlingii de Furia Sabina Diſſertat. —— *Amſt*.1688
6592 Bartholini de Armillis Veterum. —— *Hafniæ* 1647
6593 P. Rami de Militia Julii Cæſaris. —— *Franc*.1584
6594 Almeloveeni Faſti Conſulares. —— *Amſt*.1705
6595 Vitruvii Architectura, lib. x. *cor. turc. fol. deaurat. Venet. apud Juntas*.1522
6596 Deſcription des Tableaux du Palais Royale. *Par*.1727
6597 J. Vitalis Epitaphium, cum Notis criticis Dodwelli, et Comment. Dodwelli. —— 1711
6598 Conſtantini Imp. de Adminiſtrando Imperio. *Lug. Bat*.1661
6599 Thwiteſii Notæ in Anglo-Saxonum Nummos. *Oxon*. 1708
6600 Habiti Antichi et Moderndi di tutto il mundo. —— 1598
6601 Rivii Hiſt. Navalis Antiqua. —— 1633
6602 Valdkirchiani Icones Illuſt. Virorum.—— *Baſil*.1599
6603 Recueil d'Emblemes diverſes, par Baudoin. 1638
6604 Monumenta Antiqua Judaica. —— *Aug. Vind*.1686
6605 Maniere Univerſelle de Mr. Deſargues pour poſer l'Eſſieu, par Boſſe. —— —— *Par*.1643
6606 Bulengerus de Spoliis Bellicis, et O. Panvinius de Ludis Circenſibus. —— —— 1601
6607 J. Cæſaris Bulengeri de Theatro Ludiſque Scenicis. 1603
6608 L'Architecture de Savot. —— *Par*.1685
6609 Opſopæi Sibyllina Oracula. —— *ia*.1606
6610 Traite de Perſpective, par Lamy. —— *ib*.1701
6611 T. Lydiat Canones Chronologici. —— *Oxon*.1675
6612 Vegetius de Re Militari, cum Comment. *Lug. Bat*.1592
6613 Sleoogtius de Sepulturis. —— *Jenæ* 1722
6614 { Poſtellus de Originibus. —— *Baſ*.1553
{ Gyraldus de Annis & Menſibus. —— *ib*.1541
6615 Spanhemii Hiſt. Imaginum reſtituta. —— *Lug. Bat*.1656
6616 Popmæ de Operis Servorum Liber. —— 1608
6617 Nicii Erythræi Pinacotheca Imaginum. —— *Lipſ*.1712
6618 Illuſtrium Imagines. —— *Romæ* 1517
6619 Cenali Menſurarum ad Ponderibus ratio. —— *Par*.1547
6620 Cantelii de Re Militari & Civili Romanor. *cum fig. Lug. Bat*.1726
6621 Cellarii Antiquitates Romanæ. —— *Halæ Mag*.1730
6622 Ruinarum Romæ, Epigrammata. —— *Bonon*.1641
6623 Icones et Vitæ Pontificum Romanor.
6624 De Lipſii Latinitate Palæſtra. —— *Franc*.1695

I 6625

6625 Nouvelle Explication d'une Medaille d'Or. —— *Par.* 1699
6626 Le Antichite della Citta di Roma. —— *Ven.* 1562
6627 Antiquitatum Romanar. P. Manutii Liber de Legibus. *Col. Agrip.* 1570
6628 Aurogallus de Hebræis Urbium, Locorum, Populorum, &c.
6629 Seldenus de Dis Syris. —— *L.B.* 1629
6630 Le Pittura di Bologna. —— *Bol.* 1663
6631 Thomassinus de Tesseris Hospitalitatis.
6632 Pignorius de Servis, cum fig. —— *Amst.* 1674
6633 Gaurici de Sculptura Libellus. —— *Ant.* 1528
6634 Patinæ Introductio ad Historiam Numismatum. *Amst.* 1683
6635 Ricquii de Capitolio Romano Comment. —— *L.B.* 1669
6636 Nicolaus de Triumphis Romanorum. —— *Franc.* 1696
6637 { Lipsius de Cruce. —— *Amst.* 1670
Niqueti Hist. Titulis S. Cruci. —— *Ant.* 1670 }
6638 Brissonius de Jure Connubiorum. —— *Amst.* 1662
6639 Balduinus de Calceo & Nigronius de Caliga veterum. 1667
6640 Kirchmannus de Funeribus Romanorum. —— *L.B.* 1672
6641 —— & Alii de Annulis. —— *ib.* 1672
6642 Les Sculptures, ou Graveurs sacres. —— 1553
6643 Paradini Symbola Heroica. —— *Ant.* 1563
6644 A Book of ancient Coins.

Biliothecarii & Miscellanei. Octavo & infra.

6645 Bibliotheca Duboisiana, 4 vol. —— *a la Haye* 1725
6646 Grotii Epistolæ ad Gallos. —— *Lips.* 1674
6647 Galeni Chronologia, Meursi Criticus Arnobianus, & Procli Sphæra.
6648 Francii Orationes. —— *Amst.* 1705
6649 Dattii de Venditione Liberorum Diatriba. —— *Ulmæ* 1700
6650 Erasmi Dialogus. —— *Ox.* 1693
6651 H. Brenkman de Eurematicis Diatriba. —— *L.B.* 1711
6652 J. Antiocheni Cognomento Malalæ Hist. Chronica. *Oxon.* 1691
6653 Catalogus Bibliothecæ Selectæ. —— *Amst.* 1722
6654 Bibliotheca Carlsoniana. —— *Hagæ-Comit.* 1711
6655 Erasmi Stultitiæ Laus, fig. Holbenianis. —— *Bas.* 1676
6656 De Coma Dialogus. —— 1645
6657 M. Antonini Meditationes, gr. lat. —— *Lond.* 1643
6658 Leonis Hebræi de Amore Dialogi 3. —— *Ven.* 1564
6659 Amundi Ziericsiensi Chronica. —— *Ant.* 1534
6660 Censorinus de Dei Natali, & Meursi de Ludis Græcorum.
6661 Cruci Epistolæ. —— *Delph.* 1633
6662 Politicæ Succinctæ ex Aristotelis erutæ. —— *Jenæ* 1658
6663 Bibliotheca Bariniana. —— *Amst.* 1709
6664 Apicii Coelii de Arte Coquinaria. —— *ib.* 1709

C c 6665

6665 Cassiodori Opera. — Lug. 1595
6666 Bibliotheca Bremeriana. — Rott. 1713
6667 Caselii Epistolæ — Franc. 1667
6668 Caborii Disputationes. — Par. 1593
6669 Beverlandus de Fornicatione. — Aug. 1697
6670 Celarii Orationes Academicæ. — Lipſ. 1714
6671 Bibliotheca Bigotiana. — Par. 1706
6672 ——— Anonymiana. — L.B. 1716
6673 ——— Almeloveeniana. — Amſt. 1713
6674 De Vita & Scriptis Ehingeri Comment. Bruckeri. Aug. Vind. 1724
6675 Hugonis Juriſprudentia particularis Germanica delineata. 1708
6676 Fortii de ratione Studii Liber. — Rot. 1702
6677 Bibliotheca Baldæana. — L.B. 1711
6678 Bodini Artis Hiſtoricæ Penus. — Baſ. 1579
6679 Bibliotheca Baluziana, 2 vol. — Par. 1719
6680 Candelarii Parthenia. — Roth.
6681 B. Caſtilionis de Curiali Lib. — Cant. 1713
6682 Conſtantini Porphyrogeniti de Thematibus Occidentalis, lineis rubris, corio turcico, foliis deauratis. Lut. apud Morel. 1609
6683 Leonis Allatii Apes Urbanæ. — Hamb. 1711
6684 E. Burgravii Panoplia Phyſico-Vulcania. — Amſt.
6685 Bibliotheca J. Galloys. — Par. 1710
6686 Heliodori Hiſtoria, gr. lat. — 1596
6687 Exemplar. Literarum a quodam Sacerdote Collegii Anglor. Duaceni. — Duaci 1617
6688 Fabricii Bibliotheca Latina, 2 vol. — Hamb. 1708
6689 Heinſii Opera Hiſtorica. — L.B. 1673
6690 Buchanani Epiſtolæ. — Lond. 1711
6691 Panegyrici veteres. — Ant. 1596
6692 Bartholini de Libris Legendis Diſſertat. Hagæ Comit. 1711
6693 Hegeſippus de Bello Judaico. — Col. 1575
6694 Bibliotheca Kryſiana. — Hagæ-Comit. 1727
6695 Lambecii Bibliotheca, 2 vol. — 1712
6696 Bibliotheca Klefekeriana. — Hamb. 1717
6697 Kulpis de Legationibus Statuum Imperii Comment. Gieſ. 1679
6698 Cruci Orationes varii Argumenti. — Amſt. 1675
6699 Colomeſii Opuſcula. — ib 1700
6700 Contareni de Frumentaria Romanorum Largitione Liber. Veſ. 1669
6701 Marianæ de Rege & Regis Inſtitutione, Ejuſdem de Ponderib. & Menſuris. — Mog. 1605
6702 Lipſii Politica. — Jenæ 1667
6703 Jani Antiquæ & Pervulgatæ de 4 Monarchiis Sententiæ. Franc. 1728

2 6704

6704 Arcana Bibliothecæ Thomanæ Lipsiensis Sacra. *Lipsiæ* 1703
6705 J. Lipsi Electorum Liber. ——— *Ant* 1580
6706 Meursi Criticus Arnobianus Lib. & Lycophronis Cassandra.
6707 Catalogus Librorum, J. Bridges. ——— *Lond.*1725
6708 Bibliotheca Hulsiana, 4 vol. ——— *Hagæ* 1730
6709 R. South Opera posthuma. ——— *Lond* 1717
6710 Abelardi & Heloisæ Epistolæ. ——— *ib.*1718
6711 L. Bos Exercitationes Philologicæ. ——— *Franc.*1713
6712 Bibliotheca Cordesiana.
6713 ———Schalbruchiana. ——— *Amst.*1723
6714 M. Mattaire Hist. Stephanorum. ——— *Lond* 1709
6715 Gibboni Introductio ad Latinam Blasoniam. ——— *ib.*1682
6716 Bibliotheca Maarseviana. ——— *Amst.*1704
6717 Chronicon Carionis. ——— ———1617
6718 Noordkerki Observationes. ——— *Amst* 1731
6719 Comment. de Bello Aphrodisiensi Lib. 5. auctore Horatio Nucula Interamnate, fol. deaur. ——— *Romæ* 1552
6720 H. de Monte de Finibus Regundis. ——— *Norib.*1610
6721 H. Mercurialis variæ Lectiones. ——— *Basil* 1576
6722 Bibliotheca Thuanea, 2 vol. ——— *Par.*1679
6723 Paschalii Coronæ. ——— ———*L.B.*1671
6724 Aristæneti Epistolæ, gr. lat.
6725 Alciati Hist. Mediolani. ——— *Med* 1625
6726 T. Philips Dissertationes varii Argumenti. ——— *Lond* 1715
6727 Ruperti Observationes ad Hist. Universalis. *Norib.*1659
6728 Struvii Collectanea Manuscriptorum, 3 vol. ———*Jenæ* 1713
6729 Rosæi Institutio Principis. ——— *Arg.*1608
6730 Bibliotheca Sarraziana. ——— *Hagæ-Comit.*1715
6731 E. Steenberch Cognoscendi Methodus. ——— *Davent.*1697
6732 Servius de Unguento Armario. ——— *Romæ* 1643
6733 Sigonius de Republica Hebræorum. *Franc.*1585
6734 Marbodei Galli Dactyliotheca. ——— *Basil.*1555
6735 Meursii Elegantiæ Latini Sermonis.
6736 Mori Enchiridion Ethicum. ——— *Amst.*1695
6737 Bibliotheca Maddiana.
6738 ———Hartsoekeriana. ——— *Hagæ-Com.*1727
6739 Buschii Vita Commentarius. ——— *Franc.*1719
6740 Athenæ Lubecensis, 2 vol. ——— *Lubec.*1719
6741 Bibliotheca Marckiana. ———*Hagæ Comit.*1712
6742 Oligenii Dissertat. de primariis precibus Imperialibus. *Frib.* 1707
6743 Albertus Magnus de Secretis. ——— *Amst.*1662
6744 Malvezzi Princeps. ——— ——— *L.B.*1636
6745 Thesaurus Ridendi & Jocandi. ——— ———1648
6746 Puffendorfii Introductio ad Historiam Europeam. *Ultraj.* 1702
6747 ———de Officio Hominis & Civis. *Cant.*1682

6748

6748 Excerpta e Statutorum Universitatis Oxoniensis. —— 1691
6749 Græcorum Sententiæ. —— *Amst.* 1706
6750 J. Pacii Artis Lullianæ Emendatæ Lib. 4. —— *Valent.* 1618
6751 Prosperi Aquitanici Opera. —— *Colon.* 1540
6752 C. Van-Eck Vindiciæ Juris Academici. —— *Franc.* 1683
6753 Vite di Quattro Huomini Illustri. —— *Fir.* 1580
6754 Scaligeri Epistolæ. —— *Lut. apud Patis.* 1582
6755 Schultingii Enarrationes. —— *L.B.* 1720
6756 Salmasius de Modo Usurarum. —— *ib.* 1639
6757 Scaligeriana. —— —— *Gron.* 1669
6758 Horni Historia Mundi. —— *L.B.* 1668
6759 Beroadi Declamationes.
6760 Præ-Adamitæ. —— —— 1655
6761 Propylæum Sapientis & Felicis Principis. —— *Lipsiæ* 1708
6762 Puteani Comus. —— —— *Ox.* 1634
6763 Leonici de varia Historia Lib. 3. *Lug. apud S. Gryph* 1555
6764 Bibliotheca Heukelomiana. —— *Hagæ-Com.* 1730
6765 Lipsius de Constantia, *corio turcico, foliis deauratis. Amst.* 1631
6766 Bibliotheca Vander-Hemiana. —— *Hagæ-Comit.* 1730
6767 Thomasi Orationes. —— *Lipsiæ* 1683
6768 Pselli de Operatione Dæmonum Dialogus. *Lut. Par.* 1615.
6769 Stapletoni Orationes. —— *Ant.* 1576
6770 Bibliotheca Winckleriana. —— *Hamb.*
6771 Orrwini Principia Juris. —— *Franc.* 1719
6772 Discours de la Possessions de Religieuses Urselines de Lodun. —— —— 1634

Libri Omissi.

6773 Fabri Thesaurus Eruditionis Scholasticæ, cura a M. Gesnero, 2 vol. —— *Hagæ-Comit.* 1735
6774 Hippocratis & Galeni Opera, gr. lat. recensuit R. Charterius, 13 tom. 9 vol. —— *Lut. Par.* 1679
6775 Ciceronis Opera, Verburgii, 2 vol. —— *Amst.* 1724
6776 Historia General de las Indias Ocidentales, por Herrera, 4 vol. —— —— *Amberes* 1728

F I N I S.

George Vertue

George Vertue was an artist and engraver, whose antiquarian studies, pursued with unswerving single-mindedness for the whole of his working life, were directed to one subject only, the history of painting in England from the earliest times. The forty note-books which he filled with information on this subject were bought by Horace Walpole from Vertue's widow after his death in July 1756 at the age of seventy-two, and before his library was publicly sold in March 1757. These then formed the basis of the *Anecdotes of Painting* published by Walpole at Strawberry Hill in four volumes between 1762 and 1771, and have since been published in their original form by the Walpole Society in volumes XVIII to XXX of its publications (1930–55). There were only 120 lots in the book sale of 18–19 March 1757, but the British Museum Print Room copy of the printed catalogue, reproduced here by kind permission, has a MS. note recording that Vertue's prints, drawings and books of prints were sold by the same auctioneer between 16 and 22 March: a copy of this catalogue is also in the Print Room. It was from this part of the sale that Walpole must have bought 'a large piece of Philip and Mary, from the original at Woburn' and Vertue's 'drawings taken from Holbein'.

Vertue was a Roman Catholic, and his parents had been servants in the royal household of the exiled James II at St Germain. He soon became noted as a portrait engraver; he worked under Kneller and was encouraged by Harley,

Coleraine and Winchilsea, and was a leading spirit in the founding of the Society of Antiquaries of London in 1717, to which he was official engraver. He designed and engraved the Oxford Almanacs from 1723 to 1751, and apart from his portraits made valuable archaeological drawings, including the *Vetusta Monumenta* engraved for the Society of Antiquaries up to 1756. One notable set made for Lord Winchilsea in 1725 is now the only (and clearly a very accurate) record of a vanished hoard of elaborate Thracian silver-work from the island of Sark (D. F. Allen, *Arch.*, CIII, 1971, pp. 1–31).

His small library contained, as might be expected, a fair number of books on the theory and practice of painting and engraving, and a few on sculpture and architecture: English, French and Italian authors are represented and reflect his Continental background. There are a certain number of the expected antiquarian books — Stow, Weever, Gibson's 1695 Camden (lot 85), Sammes's *Britannia Antiqua Illustrata,* 1676, (lot 100, second day's sale) — while Stukeley's *Itinerarium Curiosum,* 1724 (lot 113), and Alexander Gordon's *Itinerarium Septentrionale,* 1726 (lot 97, second day), probably relate to friendships made in the new Society of Antiquaries, where Stukeley was the first, and Gordon, in 1735, a later Secretary. Hadrian's Wall is represented by John Warburton's rather lightweight book, the *Vallum Romanum* (lot 52) of 1753.

A group of books seem at first to reflect not Vertue's antiquarian, nor even art historical interests, but an appreciation of English literature, until we realize that it was the illustrations engraved by himself and others that must account for Theobald's eight-volume Shakespeare (1752), for instance, as well as the complete Milton, Pope's *Iliad* (six volumes, 1720), Spenser in as many volumes (1718) and Swift in fourteen (1751). Here too we must presumably group the poems of the Earl of Surrey, Waller, Rochester, Sedley, and others, and the 1710 edition of the poems of Mrs Katherine Philips, 'the Matchless Orinda'. But the separate edition of *The Shepheard's Calendar* (lot 6, first day's sale), and that of Skelton's poems are more unexpected; Vertue also had a copy of John Earle's *Microcosmography* (lot 10), catalogued anonymously and so presumably one of the seventeenth-century editions from 1628 onwards, the authorship not being acknowledged until that of 1732. We may have here a glimpse of Vertue's personal literary tastes.

Finally, lot 108, sold on the second day, is a MS. item in fourteen volumes, consisting of the accounts for labour, materials and other expenses incurred in the building of the 'Fifty New Churches' under the Act of 1711 and the supervision of Nicholas Hawksmoor and John James: these, presumably purchased at the sale, were presented to Lambeth Palace Library in 1759 (E. G. W. Bill, *Cat. MSS. Lambeth Palace Library*, 1972, p. 263).

A

CATALOGUE

Of the Entire and Genuine

LIBRARY of BOOKS

OF

Mr GEORGE VERTUE,

ENGRAVER,

Late of *Brownlow-Street*, deceas'd.

CONSISTING OF

Scarce and valuable Editions in Hiſtory, Antiquity, Painting, Architecture, &c.

Which will be Sold by AUCTION,

By Mr. FORD,

At his Great Room, the upper End of St. *James's Haymarket*,

On *Friday* and *Saturday*, the 18th and 19th of this Inſtant *March*, 1757.

The BOOKS *may be viewed with his Prints and Drawings every Day till to the Hour of Sale, which will begin each Day exactly at Twelve o'Clock.*

CATALOGUES to be had *gratis* at Mr. FORD's.

CONDITIONS of SALE.

1*st*, THE *highest Bidder* to be the *Buyer*; and if *any Dispute* arises between any *two* or *more Bidders*, the LOT so *disputed* to be *put up again*.

2*dly*, No *Person* to advance *less* than 6*d. above* a *Pound* 1 *s. above* Five Pounds 2*s.* 6*d.* and so on *in Proportion*.

3*dly*, The *Purchasers* are to give in their *Names* and *Places of Abode*, and *positively* to pay down 2 *s.* 6 *d. in the Pound* in Part of Payment of the *Purchase Money*, in Default of which, the LOT or LOTS *so purchased*, to be *immediately put up again, and resold*.

4*thly*, The Books to be taken as perfect without collating, those that are known to be otherwise being mention'd in the Catalogue.

5*thly*, To *prevent* the INCONVENIENCIES that *too frequently attend* LONG and OPEN ACCOUNTS, the *Remainder* of the *Purchase Money* to be ABSOLUTELY Paid ON or BEFORE the *Delivery*.

6*thly*, Upon *Failure of complying* with the *above* CONDITIONS, the Money so *deposited in Part* of *Payment*, shall be *forfeited*; the LOTS *uncleared* within the Time aforesaid, shall be *resold*, by *public* or *private Sale*, and the *Deficiency* (if any) *together with the Charges attending such Re-sale*, shall *be made good* by the *Defaulters* at this SALE.

Firſt Day's Sale, *Friday, March 18th*, 1757.

O C T A V O, &c.

1 ODES of Horace—Ward's reformation, 2 vol.—Hudibras, 3 vol.
2 Prior's poems—Waller's poems—Vida's art of poetry—Davies on the ſoul
3 Milton's paradiſe loſt—Garth's diſpenſary—Waller's poems—Rocheſter's works
4 Cartright's poems and 5 more
5 Earl of Surry's poems—Sedley's works—Fenton's Poems—Mariamne
6 Spenſer's ſhepherd's calendar—Moleſworth's poems—Pattiſon's poems—Pilkington's poems
7 Young's love of fame—Skelton's poems—Milton's paradiſe loſt
8 Waller's poems *large paper*, 1711—Mrs. Philips's poems *large paper*, 1710
9 Gardiner on the ſacrament *and* 10 *other books in black letter*
10 Burnet's travels——Microcoſmography——Vol. of plays and poems——Pancirollus—Keill's anatomy—Examiners
11 Telemachus, 2 vols.——Pointer's hiſtory of England, 3 vols
12 Collection of epigrams——Hallifax's miſcellanies——Howard's plays
13 Pope's Homer's iliad, 6 vols —— 1720
14 Spectators, 8 vols —— —— 1718
15 Spenſer's works, 6 vols —— 1718
16 Bulwer's chirologia and chiromania——Somner's Roman ports and forts of Kent——Survey of Newcaſtle——Doddridge's account of Wales
17 Sadler's letters and 5 more
18 Swift's works, 14 vols —— 1751
19 View of London, 2 vol and 4 more
20 Catalogus bibliothecæ Harleianæ, 5 vols 1743
21 Shakeſpear's works by Theobald, 8 vols —— 1752
22 Hiſtory of France, 2 vols——Hiſtory of Spain——Higgons's remarks on Burnet
23 Winſtanley's England's worthies——Sandys's worthies of England——Herne's account of the Charter-houſe

24 Salmon's

24 Salmon's examination of Burnet's hiſtory, 2 vols——Boccalini's advertiſements from Parnaſſus, 2 vols
25 Vidæ poemata, 3 tom——Barberini poemata
26 Atalantis, 4 vols——King's heathen gods——Parker's own time
27 Antiquities of Weſtminſter abbey, 2 vols——Richardſon's notes on Milton——Memorials of Engliſh affairs
28 Baronettage of England, 2 vols——Brodrick's hiſtory of the late war, 2 vols
29 Johnſton's notitia Anglicana, 2 vols——Willis's notitia parliamentaria
30 Collins's Peerage of England, 4 vol —— 1730
31 Milton's paradiſe loſt—Eraſmus on folly—Parſons analogy
32 Antiquities of Saliſbury——Antiquities of Rocheſter—Antiquities of Worceſter——Antiquities of Exeter
33 Hiſtory of the rebellion in verſe *with cuts*, 3 vols 1713
34 Athenian oracle, 4 vols —— 1706
35 Echard's Roman hiſtory, 5 vols —— 1713
36 Fanſhaw's letters and 9 more
37 King's works, 2 vol——Byſhe's art of poetry——Aſhmole's order of the garter——Heath's Chronicle
38 Mercure François, 10 tom —— *Paris* 1611
39 Hiſtorical regiſters 23 vols
40 Life of Barwick——Lives of the archbiſhops——Sparrow's rationale——Perrault's lives of illuſtrious men
41 Life of the black prince——Life of Milton—Life of Cromwell——Life of king Charles——Jacob's lives of the poets, 2 vols

QUARTO.

42 ANtiquitates Middletonianæ
43 Folkes's tables of ſilver and gold coin —— 1745
44 Wollaſton's religion of nature —— 1738
45 Tomlinſon's art of dancing——Weaver's ditto
46 Caſley's catalogue of the manuſcripts in the king's library 1734
47 North's examen——Lives of lord North, Sir Dudley North, and Dr. North
48 Wright's travels, 2 vol. —— —— 1730
49 Wotton's ſhort view of Hickes's theſaurus, by Shelton 1735
50 Lambarde's deſcription of England and Wales —— 1730
51 Collins's Engliſh baronage —— —— 1727
52 Warburton's Vallum Romanum —— 1753
53 Waller's poems —— —— 1729

54 Vrays portraits des roys de France —— *Paris* 1633
55 Metamorphoses d'Ovide, *avec fig.* —— *ib.* 1676
56 Haym's Tesoro Britannico, 2 vol. —— 1719
57 Ames's account of printing in England —— 1749
58 Fresnoy's art of painting——Aglionby's lives of the painters
59 Widmore's history of Westminster abbey —— 1751
60 Dale's antiquities of Harwich —— 1732
61 Magna Britannia et Hibernia, 6 vol. —— 1720
62 Castiglione's courtier——Dunciad variorum
63 Reresby's memoirs and 8 more
64 Stow's annals and 9 more
65 Three vol. of plays
66 Godwin and Rous's antiquities and 11 more
67 Milton's history of England and 13 more
68 Present state of Europe, 6 vol.
69 Lord Bacon's letters——Boccace's amorous Fiametta—— Nisbett on armories ——Two 2 Junius on painting
70 Littleton and 3 other dictionaries
71 Dutch book of psalms and 13 more
72 Simon's account of Irish coins —— —— 1749

F O L I O.

73 GIBBS's architecture —— 1728
74 Speed's maps——Speed's history of Britain—Ogilby's Homer's iliad
75 Historia Arthuri regis——Historia Lanceloti du Lac, *MSS. on vellum, with* 87 *miniature paintings*
76 Wood's Athenæ Oxonienses, 2 vol. —— 1721
77 Histoire d'Angleterre, par Larrey, 4 tom. *Amst.* 1723
78 Sandford's coronation of king James II. *with cuts* 1687
79 Wise catalogus nummorum antiquorum Scriniis Bodleanis 1750
80 Lord Strafford's state letters, 2 vol. —— 1739
81 Froyssart's chronicle —— —— 1523
82 Peck's annals of Stanford —— —— 1727
83 Description du Manege moderne, par d'Eisenberg 1727
84 Sandford's genealogical history of England —— 1677
85 Camden's Britannia, by Gibson —— 1695
86 Anderson's genealogical tables —— 1736
87 Favine's theatre of honour——Milles's catalogue of honour 1610 Vincent's errors in Brooke's heraldry—— York's heraldry —— — 1622
88 Ashmole's order of the garter —— 1672

89 Grimestone's

89 Grimeston's history of France——Heylin's cosmography—Stow's survey of London——Martin's history of England
90 Johnston on monarchy——Newcourt's repertorium—Camden's Britannia——Moll's geography
91 Weever's funeral monuments —— 1631
92 Dugdale's monasticon in English —— 1718
93 Anderson diplomata & numismata Scotiæ
94 Churchill's divi Britannici—Lloyd's worthies—Broughton's history of Britain——Dugdale's view of the troubles in England
95 Brooke's heraldry with the arms colour'd —— 1622
96 Drayton's poems——Chaucer's works, *imperfect*
97 Brady's history of England, 3 vol. —— 1684
98 Fabian's chronicle —— —— 1533
99 Herbert's life of Henry VIII.——Camden's Elizabeth——Sanderson's life of Mary queen of Scots——Udall's life of Mary queen of Scots
100 Higden's polycronycon —— 1527
101 Sir Thomas More's works, *gilt leaves* — 1557
102 Gower de confessione amantis——Boccace's fall of princes 1554
103 Fuller's history of the worthies of England, *imperfect* 1662
104 Marsilii dissertatio de generatione fungorum *Romæ* 1714
105 Vies des hommes illustres, par Thevet — *Paris* 1584
106 Dart's antiquities of Canterbury —— 1726
107 Ross's Silius Italicus —— —— 1661
108 Prynn's history of king John —— 1670
109 Blomefield's history of Norfolk, 2 vol. —— 1739
110 Echard's history of England, 3 vol. 1707
111 Rapin's history of England, with the heads and monuments of the kings, &c. of England, 2 vol. *in morrocco, and gilt leaves*, 1732. Note, *The above book is printed on a fine paper, and Mr.* Vertue *has added a number of heads of eminent men to it*
112 Dugdale's view of the troubles——Stow's chronicle——Walker's historical discourses——Frankland's annals of James and Charles
113 Stukeley's itinerarium curiosum —— 1724
114 Brown's art of painting——Lives and heads of the painters
115 Hollandi Herwologia Anglica
116 Evelyn on medals —— —— 1697
117 Hackluyt's voyages and 6 more
118 Ogilby's Virgil and 5 more
119 Architettura da Vignola, 1607——Architettura di Palladio 1601

The Second Day's Sale, *Saturday*, *March* 19.

OCTAVO, &c.

1 ROLLIN's arts and ſciences, 2 vol. and 9 more odd vols.
2 Illuminato di Venezia and 4 more Italian
3 Le pittura di Bologna——Le minere della pittura——Dialogo di pittura——Indice delle ſtampe de Roſſi——Studio di pittura——Diſennos y eſtampas de San Lorencio del Eſcurial
4 Habiti antichi & moderni —— *Venet.* 1590
5 Boyer's French dictionary——Eraſme de la folie——Livre intitule, Internelle conſolation —— 1522
6 Houbraken's lives of the painters in Dutch, 2 vol.
7 Catalogue du cabinet de Crozat——Catalogue de deſſeins de Monſ. Huls——Catalogue du cabinet de M. Quentin——Memorial de Paris
8 Vies des peintres, par Felibien, 5 tom. —— *Lond.* 1705
9 Traité de la peinture, par Richardſon, 2 vol.——Reflexions ſur la poeſie & ſur la peinture, 2 vol.
10 Cabinet d'architecture, peinture, &c. par le Comte, 4 vol 1702
11 Maniere de graver en taille douce, par Boſſe——Deſcription du tableaux du palais royal——Cours de peinture, par de Piles——Vies des peintres, par de Piles
12 Traité de peinture en mignature—— L'academie de la peinture——Sentimens des diverſes manieres de peinture, par Boſſe—Deſcription de divers ouvrages de peinture——Diſſertation ſur les ouvrages des plus fameux peintres
13 Eloge de Monſ. le Clerc——Vie de pierre Mignard——Conference de Monſ. le Brun——Pratique de geometrie, par le Clerc——Les monumens de Rome
14 Epigrams upon paintings——La Motte's eſſay on poetry and painting——Samber's Roma illuſtrata —— Evelyn's idea of painting——Tradeſcant's rarities——Salmon's Polygraphice
15 Judgment of Hercules——Elſum's art of painting ——Painter's voyage of Italy——Evelyn's idea of painting——Neri's art of glaſs——Bull's eſſay on painting
16 Richardſon's treatiſe of painting, 3 vol.
17 Evelyn's art of chalcography——Faithorne's art of graving, &c.

18 De

18 De Pile's art of painting——Fresnoy's art of painting
19 Da Vinci on painting——Monier's history of painting, &c.
20 Norden's declineation of Northamptonshire
21 Charter of the society of antiquaries——Ames's catalogue of English heads
22 Cowdrey's description of lord Pembroke's pictures, &c. 1751
23 Gambarini's description of lord Pembroke's pictures, *with some MSS. remarks and drawings by Mr.* Vertue 1731
24 Reges, reginæ, nobiles, & alii in ecclesia Westmonast. sepulti 1603
25 Treatise of dancing, *MSS.*
26 Officium Beatæ Mariæ Virginis, *on Vellum* *Lugd.* 1499
27 The same book, *MSS. on Vellum, with several miniatures*
28 Large collection of old books in English, &c.
29 Vidæ poemata, per Owen, *Oxon.* 1733——Reliquiæ Baxterianæ Barberini poemata —— 1726
30 Vidæ hymni de rebus divinis, *Chart. Mag.* *Oxon.* 1733
31 Vidæ poemata Tristram & Owen, 2 vol. ——*ib.* 1733
32 Ditto, 3 vol. —— —— *ib.* 1733
33 Parcel of pamphlets
34 Ditto
35 Les images de la mort —— *Lyon* 1562
36 Imagines mortis —— —— *Lugd.* 1545
37 Catalogue Raisonnee de plus belles cabinets, par Monf. Gersaint, 8 vol. —— *Paris* 1745, &c.
38 Of the new lands and people found by the messengers of Emanuel king of Portugal, *black letter* *printed by J. Desborow*
39 Knight's life of Dr. Collet——Bearcroft's account of the Charter-house
40 Knight's life of Erasmus —— 1726
41 Lewis's life of Caxton, *large paper* —— 1737
42 Collection of curious discourses by eminent antiquarians 1720

QUARTO.

43 THE images of the old testament *Lyons* 1549
44 Icones Livianæ, 1572——Icones historiarum veteris testamenti —— *Lugd.* 1547
45 The heads of the kings of England on wood prints with some of their principal acts by T. Timms, with Mss. additions —— —— 1597
46 Holben's death's dance with a Mss. account of it by Mr. *Vertue* —— —— *Franc.*

47 Wright's

47 Wright's Louthiana — — 1748
48 Ædes Walpolianæ — — 1747
49 Boiffardi Icones illuftrium virorum, fig. de Bry *Franc.* 1597
50 Biblia Latina — *Venet.* 1478
51 Polygraphie, et univerfelle ecriture cabaliftique par Trithieme 1561
52 Traite Hiftorique des monnoyes de France, par le Blanc 1692
53 Epitome thefauri antiquitatum, ex mufæo de Strada—Promptuarium Iconum—Van Goch's money of Europe in Dutch
54 Vita del Cav. Bernino — *Firenz.* 1672
55 Notizia de profeffori del defegno, di Baldinucci *Firenz.* 1688
56 L'Abcedario Pittorico — *Bologn.* 1719
57 Le vite de Pittori Veneti dal Ridolfi *Venet.* 1648
58 Vormandir's Lives of the painters in Dutch *Amft.* 1618
59 Vies des plus fameux peintres, 2 tom *Paris* 1745
60 Traité fur la peinture, par du Puy — 1700
61 Le vite de pittori, fcultori, &c. da Baglione *Roma* 1649
62 Due Trattati di Cellini — *Firenz.* 1731
63 Vite de pittori, &c. di Vafari tom 1, and 4 more
64 Gardner's hiftory of Dunwich, in fheets 1754
65 The fame book in fheets — 1754
66 Simon's medals, coins, great feals, &c. by Mr. Vertue 1753
67 Martyn's unlawfulnefs of priefts marriages 1553—Sir Thomas More's dialogue of comfort 1554 — Erafmus's praife of folly 1549—Bifhop Gardiner againft Joye 1546
68 Milton's paradife loft *firft edition* — 1668
69 Spenfer's fairy queen — 1596
70 Lifle's Saxon monuments—Brown's travels—Plat's jewel houfe of art and nature—Hankfbee's experiments
71 Lord Pembroke's medals
72 Collins's account of the Oxford family—Catalogue of lord Oxford's coins, medals, &c. *with the prices and names of the buyers*—Catalogue of lord Oxford's pictures, *with the prices and the names of the buyers*—Catalogue of the countefs of Oxford's miniatures, enamel and limned pictures taken by Mr. *Vertue*, Mfs. In this book is contained *drawings of feveral of the curiofities by Mr.* Vertue

F O L I O.

73 EVELYN's parallel of architecture—Manclere's architecture—Serly's architecture
74 Tindal's bible

B 75 Polydor.

75 Polydor. Virgilius, and 3 more
76 Voyage de Charles II. a Hollande——Histoire de l'entre de la Reyne Mere de la Grande Bretaigne——Lord Castlemaine's embassy to the Pope
77 Monumens de la monarchie Francoise, par Montfaucon, tom 5 —— —— *Paris* 1733
78 Time's storehouse and 9 more
79 Caxton's chronicle *imperfect*
80 Grafton's chronocle —— —— 1568
81 Hall's chronicle *imperfect*
82 Collection of poems in mss. on vellum
83 Fructus temporum, by Pynson —— 1510
84 Lomatius on painting——Sanderson's art of painting
85 Hollingshed's chronicle and 8 more
86 Monumenta illustrium virorum——Barlandi Hollandiæ comitum historia —— —— 1684
87 Erasmi opera and 4 more
88 Grew's rarities of Gresham college—Browne on the muscles
89 Chaucer's works and 4 more
90 Rushworth's collections, 4 vols
91 Histoire naturelle de l'Or et de l'Argent——Histoire de la peinture ancienne —— —— 1725
92 Goltzii Icones imperatorum Romanorum *Antwerp* 1645
93 Spelmanni vita Alfrædi magni —— 1678
94 Fiddes's life of cardinal Wolsey —— 1726
95 Collins's historical collections of several noble families 1752
96 Wright's antiquities of Rutland——Tent of Darius explained——Forbes's state papers, vol. 1.
97 Gordon's itinerarium septentrionale —— 1726
98 Ward's lives of the professors of Gresham college 1740
99 Motraye's travels, 3 vol. —— 1723
100 Sammes's Britannia and 3 more
101 Æsopi fabulæ——Lives of the saints, *imp.* *Mediolan.* 1480
102 Morant's history and antiquities of Colchester, *in sheets* 1748
103 Julii Clovii thesaurus artis pictoriæ —— 1733
104 Biblia Latina, *MSS. on vellum, with a great number of fine miniature paintings*
105 Biblia Latina, *bound in velvet* —— *Venet.* 1478
106 Exposition de l'institution nouvelle en mathematique, par Chazeyrat, *MSS. on vellum, and bound in velvet*
107 Elsyng's ancient manner of holding parliaments, MSS. *This was* Peter le Neve's *book*

108 Accounts

108 Accounts of the works of the ſeveral workmen, the materials and labour, with all the ſums of money, bills and payments for the pariſh churches, chapels and cemeteries, with the parſonage houſes, built by the commiſſioners of the new churches, in MSS. 14 vol.

109 Pope's works, vol. 2. ——— 1735

110 Sandrart academia artis pictoriæ ——— *Noria.* 1683

111 Catalogue of king Charles the Firſt's collection of pictures, enamels, medals, &c. Note, *Part of this is printed, and the printed part is to go with the MSS.*

112 Tratados del matrimonio, pretendido por el principe de tales con la infanta le Eſpana, Mſs.

113 Catalogue of the nobility in England in the time of James the firſt

114 Collection of Mſs on various ſubjects 15 vol Mſs

115 Two account books of work done by Mr. Stone maſter maſon to James and Charles the firſt with a vol. of deſigns by him, Mſs.

116 A catalogue of king James the ſecond's pictures at Whitehall and other palaces, Mſs.

117 Collection of arms of foreign princes, nobility, &c. *with the the arms coloured*, 2 vols

118 Copy of Shakeſpear's laſt will, Mſs.

119 Catalogue of the officers of the crown for the years 1597, 1626, 1633, &c. 2 vols. Mſs.

120 Of the union of England and Wales, Mſs.

F I N I S.

William Stukeley

William Stukeley is remembered as probably the best known antiquary of the eighteenth century, who if not the discoverer of Stonehenge and Avebury, first introduced them in detail to the learned world, and who was also responsible for inventing most of the nonsense about Druids that pervaded the last two centuries and indeed is still with us today. Born in 1687, he was first a physician-antiquary, beginning professional life as a Doctor of Medicine and bringing to the study of antiquities the empirical approach of the Royal Society, but later he became a parson-antiquary who used his archaeology in religious controversy of a curiously fanciful kind. A biography of him by the writer was published in 1950 (*William Stukeley: An Eighteenth Century Antiquary*).

He collected books from his undergraduate days. From Grantham in 1727 he wrote to a friend 'I have now fitted up my library (& 'tis just full), so I may properly say I begin to live'. He added, as many a book collector has done, 'I have done buying books' but the sale catalogue of his library shows (again not for the first time) that books continued to be added, reaching a total of around 1,000 lots if one excludes MSS. and duplicate copies of his printed works. At the end of his life he was living in London, Rector of St George's, Queen's Square, and his library was sold a year after his death, in April 1766: in the copy of the British Library, Department of Manuscripts, here reproduced with their kind permission, there is a note that his coins, antiquities and fossils were sold a month later. Of this latter sale catalogue there is a copy in the Department of Coins and Medals, the British Museum: a second copy of the catalogue of the library has been traced in the Bodleian.

Stukeley's library represents fairly enough the stages of his professional life, and the changes in emphasis of his continuing antiquarian interests as the cautious Doctor gives way to the speculative Rector. There are a fair number of medical books, particularly on specialized subjects in which he had a personal interest, such as the gout. Architectural interests are represented by Vitruvius, Wood and other titles, for Stukeley liked to design whimsical eye-catchers for his own garden or his friends' estates; here too is a copy of Dürer's *De symmetria* of 1534 (lot 701). The standard classics, more Latin than Greek, are here, but recent literature is scarcely represented by more than Milton, Sir Thomas Browne, *Hudibras* (lot 88), Florio's *Montaigne* and a volume of Molière. Naturally, the strength of the library was in its historical and antiquarian books. There are perhaps more of the former than might be expected from one of the first field archaeologists; the printed catalogues of the Cotton and Harley MSS. for instance, and the third volume of Hickes's *Thesaurus,* 1703 (lot 544), which was in fact Humphrey Wanley's catalogue of Anglo-Saxon MSS.; Wharton's *Anglia Sacra,* 1691 (lot 1086); the *Decem Scriptores* of Twysden and others (1652, lot 1048) and the comparable *Historiae Anglicanae Scriptores* of Thomas Gale (1684–91, lot 1047) as well as Joseph Sparke's *Scriptores Varii,* 1723 (lot 1051), though perhaps his friendship with the younger Gales, and the fact that Sparke was concerned with Peterborough documents, and so with a region familiar and dear to him, may carry weight here. But with Montfaucon's great seven-volume *Antiquities,* 1721, Gibson's 1695 Camden, Horseley's *Britannia Romana,* 1732 (lot 1055), and Rowlands' *Mona Antiqua Restaurata,* 1766 (lot 1026), we are within the mainstream of the antiquarian literature of the day, with the eccentricities not far away, such as Aylett Sammes and Verstegan. The 1709 edition of Aelfric's Homily by 'the Saxon nymph', Elizabeth Elstob, appears under the theological section of the catalogue, but claims a place here.

Stukeley's numismatic interests are reflected in several works, some sound and some (like Pettingal on British coins) as eccentric as his own views, and with the theological books from the Church Fathers to the pamphlets of the Deists, come the books on Druids, from Guenebauld's *Chyndonax,* 1621 (lot 825), and Schedius' *De Diis Germanis,* 1648 (lot 794), to Pelloutier's *Histoire des Celtes,*

1750 (lot 766), which were to play so important a part in his later theories. And it is interesting to find not only several copies of Charles Bertram's forgery, the alleged Roman Itinerary of Britain transcribed by a medieval Richard of Cirencester which had deceived Stukeley and deluded the whole learned world when published in 1757, but copies of his English–Danish grammar and textbook of 1753, reminding us that Bertram was a young student in Copenhagen when he produced that light-hearted *jeu d'esprit* from which he derived no profit save the joy of hoaxing so many of the gravely learned of his day.

(No. 18,1766) 

A

CATALOGUE

Of the GENUINE

LIBRARY

OF

BOOKS,

In PRINT and MANUSCRIPT,

And COLLECTION of

PRINTS and DRAWINGS,

Of the late Revd. and Learned

William Stukeley, M.D.

Fellow of the College of Physicians,
and of the Royal and Antiquary Societies,
Deceased;

Including the Remainder of the Impressions of
his Works.

Which will be sold by AUCTION,

By *SAMUEL PATERSON*,

At *Essex House*, in *Essex Street*, *in the Strand*,

On *Monday*, *April* 28, 1766, and the Five
following Evenings,

To begin each Evening exactly at Six o'Clock.

To be viewed on *Thursday* the 24th Instant, and to the
Time of SALE.

CATALOGUES may be had *gratis* at *Essex-House* aforesaid.

Conditions of SALE.

I. THE higheſt Bidder is to be the Buyer; but if any Diſpute ſhall ariſe between two or more Bidders, the Lot in Diſpute is to be put up again.

II. No Perſon is to advance leſs than 3d, under Ten Shillings; above Ten Shillings, 6d. above One Pound, 1s.

III. Every Purchaſer is to pay down Five Shillings in the Pound, in part of Payment, and to give in his Name and Place of Abode, if required.

IV. The Books are preſumed perfect, unleſs otherwiſe expreſſed in the Catalogue; but if upon collating, at the Place of Sale, any ſhall prove imperfect, the Purchaſers ſhall be at Liberty to take or refuſe them.

V. The Lots are to be removed, with all Faults, at the Expence of the Buyers, within three Days after the SALE is ended, and the Remainder of the Purchaſe Money to be then abſolutely paid; in default of which, the Depoſit is to become forfeited, the Lots reſold, and the Deficiencies, if any, are to be made good by the firſt Purchaſers.

First Evening's Sale, *Monday*, *April* 28.

OCTAVO et Infra.

Lot

1 SUNDRY old Books of ſmall Value
2 Webb of the Primitive Language — 1669
3 Walton de Linguis Orientalibus — *Lond.* 1655
4 Udall's Key of the Holy Tongue *Leyd.* 1593
5 Capellus de Literis Ebræorum — *Amſt.* 1644
6 Bellarmini Inſtitutiones Linguæ Hebr. 1619—Schickardi Horologium Hebræum — *Lond.* 1675
7 Holloway's Primævity and Pre-eminence of the Sacred Hebrew ——— *Oxf.* 1754
8 Caſaubon de Ling. Hebr. et de Ling. Saxonica ——— ——— *Lond.* 1650
9 Buxtorfii Lexicon Hebr. et Chald *Baſ.* 1615
10 Verr. Flaccus et Pompeius Feſtus de Verbor. Significatione ——— ——— *Ven.* 1559
11 Bowles's Inſtitution of the Latin Tongue *Oxf.* 1740
12 Richards's Welch-Engliſh Dictionary and Grammar ——— ——— ——— *Briſtol* 1753
13 Another Copy ——— ——— 1753
14 Boyer's French and Engliſh Dictionary 1715
15 Bertram's Royal Engliſh-Daniſh Grammar, Ethics, and View of the Engliſh Tongue and Style *Copenh.* 1753
16 Hugo de Prima Scribendi Origine et Rei Literariæ Antiquitate ——— *Antv.* 1617
17 Baker's Reflections upon Learning ——— 1708
18 Ainſworth Monumenta Vetuſtatis Kempiana *Lond.* 1720
19 ——— *Muſeum Woodwardianum* *ib.* 1728
20 Catalogue of the MSS of Tho. Rawlinſon, Eſq; 1734
21 Another Copy ——— ——— 1734
22 Bibliotheca Harleiana, 5 tom. — *Lond.* 1743
23 ——— Meadiana, 1754—Muſeum Meadianum 1755
24 ——— Coll. Medicor. Londinenſis 1757
25 Bibliotheque Britannique, 2 tom. *Haye* 1737-1741
26 Felton on the Claſſics 1713—and 2 more
27 Homeri Ilias et Odyſſea Gr. & Lat. *Gen.* 1629
28 ——— Ilias et Odyſſea Gr. & Lat. 2 tom. *Cant.* 1664
29 ——— Batrachomyomachia Gr. a Maittaire *Lond* 1721

B 30 Orphei

30 Orphei Argonautica, Hymni & de Lapidibus Gr. & Lat. Eſchenbachii ——— *Traj.* 1689
31 Callimachus Gr. & Lat. Friſhlini, *Baſ.* 1589—and 2 mo
32 Anacreon Gr. & Lat. per Baxter *Lond.* 1710
33 Pindarus et octo Lyrici Gr. & Lat. *Oliv. P. Steph.* 1626
34 Poetæ Græci Lyrici, Gr. & Lat. *ap. Commelin* 1598
35 Euripidis Tragoediæ Gr. & Lat. per King, 2 tom. ——— ——— ——— *Cant.* 1726
36 Euripides Lat. Melanthonis, *Baſ.* 1558
37 Lucianus Gr. et Lat. Sambuci, 4 tom. *Baſil.* 1602
38 Longinus Gr. et Lat. ——— *Ox.* 1710
39 Ariſtotelis Op. Gr. et Lat. Pacii 2 tom. *Gen.* 1597
40 PlatonisDialogi Gr. et L. per North, *Cant.* 1673—2 mo
41 Epictetus Arriani Gr. et Lat. a Wolfio, *Cant.* 1659
42 Xenophontis Opuſc. Gr. et Lat. per Wells, *Oxon.*
43 Iſocrates Gr. et Lat. Wolfii, *Baſ.* 1631 — Æliani Variæ Hiſtoriæ Gr. et Lat. Kuhnii, *Arg.* 1685
44 Herodotus Lat. Vallæ, *Francof.* 1584—Diodorus Siculus Lat. Rhodomani, *Hanov.* 1611—Dion Caſſius Lat. Xylandri, *Ludg* 1559
45 Herodianus Gr. et Lat H. Stephani, *Lugd.* 1611—2 mo
46 Plutarchi Opera Lat. Xylandri, 2 to. *Baſ.* 1572 —4 mo
47 Plutarch's Lives with Dacier's Notes v. 1. 2. 3. 5. 6. 7. ——— ——— 1727
48 Plutarch's Lives, vol. 3. ——— 1703
49 Sundry ſmall Claſſics
49*Ditto
50 Juſtinus Grævii, ——— *L. B.* 1701
51 Pollio, Vopiſcus, &c. *ap. R. Steph. Par.* 1544
52 Livii Hiſt. ——— *ap Elz. Amſt.* 1678
53 Jul. Cæſaris Commentarii Grævii *Amſt.* 1697
54 Jul. Cæſar in Uſ. Delph. ——— *Lond.* 1706
55 Jul. Celſus de Vita Jul. Cæſaris — *Lond.* 1697
56 Suetonius, ——— *ap. Juntam* Flor. 1510
57 Hiſtoriæ Auguſtæ Scriptores Schrevelii, *L. B.* 1661
58 Ammianus Marcellinus, ——— *L. B.* 1732
59 Vell. Paterculus, ——— *ap. Elz.* L. B. 1654
60 ——— ——— ——— ——— *Oxon* 1711
61 Cicero de Officiis, ——— *L. B.* 1603
62 ———- Natura Deorum Daviſii, *Cant.* 1723
63 ———- Oratore, per Pearce ——— 1716
64 Macrobius Gronovii ——— *Lond.* 1694
65 Plinii Epiſtolæ ——— *Par.* 1518
66 ——— Epiſt et Panegyr. *ap. Elz.* L. B. 1640
67 Seneca Opera 2 tom. ——— *Gen.* 1665
68 Aulus Gellius ——— *Amſt.* 1666

69 Horatius per Jones ——— *Lond.* 1736
70 Horatius per Baxter, C. M. *Lond.* 1725 *with a remarkable Paragraph relating to the Interment of* Mr. John Underwood *of* Naffington, *a great lover of* Horace 1733
71 Maffon Horatii Vita, ——— *L. B.* 1708
72 Ovidius Cnippingii, 3 tom. ——— *Amft.* 1702
73 Ovidii Fafti a Schrevelio ——— *Lond.* 1699
74 Maffon Ovidii Vita, ——— *Amft.* 1708
75 Sundry old Books
76 Lucretius Fabri, *Cant.* 1686—Martial, *ap Gryph. Lugd.* 1547
77 Lucanus Grotii, *L. B.* 1627—Valerius Flaccus, *Flor.* 1503
78 Manilius Scaligeri *apud Patiffon, Paris* 1579
79 Statii Sylvæ per Stephens, *Cant.* 1651—Prudentius, *Antv.* 1545
80 Hygini Fabulæ Munckeri ——— *Hamb.* 1674
81 Hiftoriæ Poeticæ Scriptores Gr. & Lat. per Gale, ——— ——— ——— *Par.* 1675
82 Opufcula Mythologica Gr. & Lat. per Gale, *Cant.* 1671
83 Opufcula Mythologica, Phyfica et Ethica Gr. & Lat, per Gale ——— *Amft.* 1688
84 Apuleius, 2 tom. *Lugd.* 1604—Alciati Emblemata, *L. B.* 1608
85 Erafmi Colloquia Schrevelii — *L. B.* 1664
86 Allatii Exercitationes, *Col.* 1645—Gutberlethi Opufcula, *Franek.* 1701
87 Edwards's Canons of Criticifm ——— 1750
88 Butler's Hudibras, 8vo. ——— 1704
89 Milton's Paradife Loft, 8vo. ——— 1707
90 Richardfon's Notes on Milton ——— 1734
91 Letters concerning Poetical Tranflations and Virgil's and Milton's Arts of Verfe ——— 1739
92 Wotton's Works ——— ——— 1672
93 Ofborn's Works ——— ——— 1701
94 Hoadly on Government ——— 1710
95 Hufbands's Poems ——— *Oxf.* 1731
96 Sundry Magazines, &c.
97 Guarini, *Il Paftor Fido* ——— *Amft.*
98 Oeuvres de Moliere, tom. 4, *Amft.* 1701—Oeuvres de Rapin, tom. 1, *Amft.* 1686

QUARTO.

QUARTO.

98* BRerewood on Languages — 1622
99 Postellus *de Originibus, seu de Hebr. Lingtæ et Gentis Antiquitate,* — Paris, *apud Lescuier* 1538
100 Loescherus de Causis Linguæ Ebrææ *Francof.* 1706
101 Hottingerus de Usu Linguarum Orientalium in Rebus Sacris —— —— *Heidel.* 1658
102 Buxtorfii Commentarius Masorethicus — *Bas.* 1620
103 Manwaring's *Stichology,* or a Recovery of the Latin, Greek, and Hebrew Numbers —— 1737
104 Gothofredi Auctores Latinæ Linguæ — 1595
105 Gouldman's Latin and English Dictionary, —— —— —— *Cambr.* 1674
106 Analecta Literarum, tom. 1.2. —— *Lip.* 1725
107 Boyer's Fr. and Eng. Dictionary *Amst.* 1719
108 Veneroni, Dictionaire Ital. & Fr. *Par.* 1710
109 Maittaire Miscellanea Græcorum Carmina Gr. & Lat. —— —— *Lond.* 1722
110 Vossii Opuscula, 2 tom.
111 Merulæ Opera Varia, —— *L. B.* 1684
112 TRACTS. *The Phœnix of these late Times: or the Life of Mr.* Henry Welby, Esq; *who lived at his House in* Grub Street 44 *Yeares, and in that Time was never seen by any,* aged 84; 1637—The Arrival and Entertainment of the Morocco Embassador, 1637—Dunton's *Journal of the Sally Fleet,* 1637—Lithgow's *Siege of* Breda, 1637—Blunt's Voyage into the Levant, 1637—*A Description of his Majesty's Royal Ship built this Yeare* 1637 at Wooll-witch in Kent—Taylor's old, old, very old Man, or the Age and Life of Tho. Parr, 1635—Juvenal's 5th Satire, by Chapman, 1629—Russel's Poems on the Battles and Death of Gustavus Adolphus, 1634.
113 Huetii Demonstratio Evangelica, *Lips* 1766
114 Lamy Harmonia Evangelica & Apparatus Biblicus, 2 tom. in 1. —— —— *Paris.* 1699
115 Sermons and Tracts, 3 vol.
116 Moebii Exercitationes Sacræ, —— *Lips.* 1686
117 Hottinger Historiæ Creationis Examen, *Heid.* 1659
118 Heinsii Exercitationes Sacræ, —— *Cant.* 1640
119 Wachteri Naturæ & Scripturæ Concordia, *Lips.* 1752
120 Vossii Chronologia Sacra, —— *Hag.* 1659
121 Casaubonus de Rebus Sacris et Ecclesiasticis, *Gen.* 1654

122 Stilling-

122 Stillingfleet's *Irenicum* and *Origines Sacrae* 1662
123 Bampfield's Tracts on the Creation and Sabbath 1692
124 Fabricius de Veritate Religionis Christianæ, — — — — — *Hamb.* 1725
125 Scharpii Symphonia Prophetarum & Apostolorum — — — — *Gen.* 1625
126 Cartwriti Harmonia Evangelica — 1630
127 Heidegger de Hist. Sacra Patriarcharum, 2 tom. — — — — *Amst.* 1688
128 Bunting's Travels of the Patriarchs, 1623
129 The Lives of the Primitive Fathers, *cuts* 1640
130 Ecclesiastical Hist. of France — — 1676
131 Wollaston's Religion of Nature — 1725
132 Hill against Lord Bolingbroke — 1755
133 Sundry Tracts
134 Ditto

FOLIO.

135 BIblia Sacra — *Antv.* 1534
136 Biblia Sacra Tremellii & Junii *Francof.* 1579
137 ——— *interfol.* Han. 1603
138 The Holy Bible, B. L. *printed by* Barker 1585
139 ——— *printed for* Tho. Guy *Oxf.* 1682
140 ——— *with Head and Tail Pieces, bound in Russia, printed by* Basket — *Oxf.* 1717
141 Musculus in Psalmos — *Bas.* 1618
142 Hildersam's Lectures upon the 51st Psalm 1642
143 Wither's Preparation to the Psalter — 1619
144 Marloratus in Psalmos — *Gen.* 1585
145 Calvini Prælectiones in Jeremiam & Lament. *ib.* 1563
146 Wesley Dissertationes in Jobum — *Lond.* 1736
147 Aretius in Nov. Testamentum — *Gen.* 1618
148 Hammond on the New Testament — 1689
149 Whitby on the New Testament, 2 vol. 1727
150 Calvini Harmonia Evangelica — *Gen.* 1582
151 Davenantius in Epistolam D. Pauli ad Colossenses — — *Cant.* 1630
152 Toinard Evangeliorum Harmonia Græco-Lat. — — — *Par.* 1707
153 Lightfoot's Harmony of the New Testament 1655
154 The Harmony of the N. Test. by Dr. Stukeley, *Ms.*
155 A Kalendar to the Evangelical Hist ry, *Ms.*
156 Prints and Drawings of the O. & N. Testament

157 Bernard's

157 Bernard's *Thesaurus Biblicus* —— 1644
158 The Cambridge Concordance —— 1720
159 Whiston's Josephus, 2 vol. L. P. —— 1737
160 Lee's Temple of Solomon —— 1659
161 Didacus del Castillo de Ornatu et Vestibus Aaronis, —— —— *Antv.* 1671
162 Leydeckerus de Republica Hebræorum, 2 tom. —— —— *Amst.* 1710
163 Martini Pugio Fidei adversus Mauros & Judæos —— —— —— *Par.* 1651
164 Hospinianus de Templis, &c. —— *Tig.* 1587
165 —— Origine Festorum —— *ib.* 1592
166 Clemens Alexandrinus Gr. & Lat. Sylburgii, *Lut.* 1629
167 —— *Col.* 1687
168 Tertulliani Opera —— —— *Bas.* 1539
169 S.Thomæ Aquinatis Summa Theologiæ, *Col. Ag.* 1622
170 Hittorpius de divinis Officiis & Mysteriis Catholicæ Ecclesiæ —— —— *Par.* 1623
171 Flaccii Clavis Scripturæ, 2 tom. *Bas.* 1567
172 Usserii Annales V. Testamenti, 2 tom. *Lond.* 1650
173 Usher's Body of Divinity —— 1658
174 Barrow's Works, vol. 2, 3. —— 1686
175 Taylor's Course of Sermons — 1653
176 Common Prayer, *in Morocco*, damaged 1715
177 —— —— *Lond.* 1745
178 —— —— *Cambr.* 1748
179 The Communion Service, *with some Drawings of sacred Edifices, by* Dr. Stukeley, *in Turkey*
180 Hooker's Ecclesiastical Politie
181 Bulengeri Opuscula — *Lugd.* 1621
182 Mede's Works —— 1677
183 Homes's Exercitations —— 1661
184 Claude's Catholic Doctrine of the Eucharist 1684
185 Hist. Ecclesiast. Scriptores Antiq. Eusebius, &c. Gr. & Lat. Valesii, 3 tom. —— *Mognut.* 1677
186 Ancient Ecclesiastical Histories of Eusebius, &c. 1636
187 Eusebii Præparat. & Demonstr. Evangelica, Lat. —— *Ven.* 1536, et *Col.* 1539
188 Eusebii Thesaurus Temporum Scaligeri, *L. B.* 1606
189 Du Pin's Ecclesiast. Hist. 9 *Centuries*, in 3 vol. 1695
190 Tillemont's Ecclesiastical Memoirs of six first Centuries by Deacon, 2 vol. —— 1733
191 Eachard's Ecclesiastical History — 1719
192 Cave Hist. Literaria, tom. 2. — *Oxon.* 1743
193 ——'s Lives of the Apostles and Primitive Fathers, 2 vol. —— —— 1687

194 Taylor's Life of Chrift, and Cave's Lives of the Apoftles ——— ——— 1678
195 Perefius de divinis Apoftolicis atque Ecclefiafticis Traditionibus ——— — *Col.* 1549
196 Montagu's Acts and Monuments of the Church, 1642
197 Montacutii Exercitationes Ecclefiafticæ *Lond.* 1622
198 Chemnicii Examen Confilii Tridentini *Gen.* 1614
199 Papal Ufurpation and Perfecution ——— 1712
200 Szegedini Theologiæ finceræ Loci communes ——— ——— *Baf.* 1608
201 Fuller's Pifgah-Sight of Paleftine — 1662
202 A Marriage Regifter Book

Second Evening's Sale, *Tuefday April* 29th.

OCTAVO & Infra.

LOT
203 GRegorii Lexicon Sanctum, Heb. & Lat. *Hanov.*
204 N. Teft. Gr. & Lat. Montani, *ap Plantin. Antv.* 1583—Paforis Lexicon, Gr. & Lat. N. Teft. *Amft.* 1641
205 Nov. Teft. Gr. & Lat. *ap. Buck, Cant.* 1632—Paforis Lexicon, Gr & Lat. N. Teft. *Lond.* 1644
206 N. Teft. Lat. Bezæ, *Amft.* 1673—R. Stephani Index V. & N. Teft. *Par.* 1537
207 El Teftamento Nuevo ——— 1596
208 Theophylactus in 4 Evangelia Lat. *Col.* 1536—Junii Parallelorum Sacrorum Libri tres, *ap. Commelin*, 1610
209 Whifton's Tranflation of the New Teft. 1745
210 ——— Sacred Hift. of the O. and N. Teft. vol. 1. 5. ——— ——— 1745
211 Wall's Critical Notes on the O. Teft. 2 vol. 1734
212 *A Commentarye upon the Prophet* Mycha, *written by* Anthony Gilby, B. L. *imprinted by* Ihon Daye 1551
213 Bate on Genefis Ch. 3d ——— 1741
214 Wells's Geography of the O. Teft. vol. 1. 1711—Well's Geography of the N. Teft. 1708
215 Pfalterium Gr. Lat. *Par.* — Genebrardus in Pfalmos, *Ludg.* 1592

216 Robertfon's

216 Robertson's Hebrew Psalms and Lamentations, ——— ——— *Cant.* 1685
217 Whiston's Accomplishment of Scripture Prophecies ——— ——— ——— 1724
218 Warburton's Divine Legation of Moses, 3 v. 1738-41
219 Morgan's Examination of Warburton's Divine Legation ——— ——— 1742
220 Tillard's Reply to Warburton's Appendix 1742
221 Sykes agt. Warburton ——— 1744
222 Bott's Answer to Warburton's Divine Legation 1743
223 Kennedy's Scripture Chronology ——— 1751
224 Brett's Scripture Chronology 1729—Twells's Critical Examinat. of the Gr. and Eng. Test. 2 parts 1731
225 Hutchinson's Glory or Gravity ——— 1733
226 ——— Covenant in the Cherubim 1734
227 Prideaux's Connexion, 3 vol. ——— 1718
228 Shuckford's Connexion, vol. 1. 2. 1728
229 Censorinus de Die Natali, *Cant.* 1695—Butler of the true Year of Christ's Birth 1671
230 Mann of the true Years of Christ 1733
231 Locke's Hist. of Jesus Christ ——— 1705
232 Reading's Hist. of Jesus Christ, with the Lives of the Apostles ——— ——— 1726
233 Kidder on the Messiah, vol. 1. 1684—Lavaur, Conference de la Fable avec l'Hist. Sainte, tom. 1. *Par.* 1730
234 S. Clementis Epist. 2. ad Corinthios, Gr. & Lat. per Wotton, 2 tom. ——— *Cant.* 1718
235 Dodwell Dissertationes Cyprianicæ, *Oxon.* 1684
236 ——— in Irenæum, *Ox.* 1689—Athenagoræ Apologia Gr. & Lat. *ap H. Steph.* 1557—Lactantii Opera *Cant.* 1685
237 Jack's Mathematical Principles of Theology 1747
238 Bradley's View of Christianity, with the Life of Apollonius Tyanæus 1699—Whitby of Idolatry 1674
239 Delany on Revelation, 2 vol. ——— 1733
240 Rogers's Necessity of Revelation ——— 1729
241 Nicholls's Conference with a Theist, 2 vol. 1723
242 Smith's Cure of Deism, 2 vol. ——— 1736
243 Chandler (Edw.) agt. Collins's Grounds and Reasons, ——— ——— 1725
244 West on the Resurrection ——— 1747
245 Warburton's Alliance between Church and State, 1736
246 Warburton's Julian ——— 1751
247 ——— Doctrine of Grace, 2 vol. 1763

248 Woolston's

248 Woolston's six Discourses on the Miracles and Defence ——— — ——— ——— 1728
249 Herbert's (Lord) Ancient Religion of the Gentiles ——— ——— ——— 1711
250 Clarke on the Attributes ——— 1711
251 ———— Trinity ——— 1719
252 Owen on the Trinity 1669—Nye on the Trinity 1701
253 Waterland's Importance of the Doctrine of the Trinity ——— ——— 1734
254 *Alkibla* ——— ——— 1740
255 Propositions and Principles of Divinitie, 1595—Allix against the Unitarians 1699
256 Bull's (Bp.) Works, by Holland, 2 vol. 1730
257 Pighii Themis Dea, seu de Lege divina, *Antv.* 1568 —Marlorati Thesaurus S. Scripturæ, *Gen.* 1613
258 Ellys (Ric.) Fortuita Sacra, Ejusd. Comment. de Cymbalis ——— *Roterd.* 1727
259 Jackson of the Belief of a Future State, with the Defence ——— ——— 1745
260 Hist. of Ecclesiast. Revenues 1685—Prideaux's Right of Tithes 1710
261 Stillingfleet's Ecclesiast. Cases 1698—Spelman de non temerandis Ecclesiis, *Oxf.* 1676
262 The Clergyman's Vade mecum, 2 vol. 1723
263 Ecton's Liber Valorum ——— 1728
264 Grey's System of English Ecclesiast. Law 1730
265 King of the Primitive Church ——— 1692
266 Bedæ Hist. Eccles. Gentis Anglor. *Lovan.* 1566
267 Jurieu's Critical Hist. of the Doctrines and Worships of the Church, 2 vol. ——— 1705
268 Knight's Life of Erasmus, *no Title*
269 Persons's three Conversions of England, 2 vol. 1603 —Bristow's Motives to the Catholick Faith, *Antv.* 1599
270 Fath. Walsh's Letters 1686—Constitutions and Canons Pastoral Letters, *&c.*

QUARTO.

271 HOmeri Ilias Didimi Gr. et Lat. 1689
272 Pope's Homer's Iliad, vol. 1. 5. 1715
273 Anacreon, Gr. et Lat. a Mattaire *Lond.* 1725
274 Aratus, Gr. et Lat. Grotii, *cum fig.* *L. B.* 1600
275 Lycophron, Gr. & Lat. Canteri, *ap. P. Steph.* 1601

C 276 Sim-

276 Simplicii Comment. in Enchiridion Epicteti Gr. et Lat. Wolfii cum Animadv. Salmasii, *L. B.* 1640
277 Manethonis Apotelesmatica Gr. et Lat. Gronovii, ——— ——— ——— *L. B.* 1698
278 Autores Mythographi Latini cum Notis Varior. curante Van Staveren, *L. B.* 1742
279 Plautus Lambini, ——— *Gen.* 1595
280 Horatius, Virgilius, Terentius, Catullus, Tibullus, et Propertius, 4 tom. *Cant.* 1699-1702
281 Douglas Catalogus Editionum Horatii, *Lond.* 1739
282 Martialis Epigrammata Calderini, *Paris* 1601
283 Tempesta's *Ovid's Metamorphoses*, by De Jode, *Antv.* 1606, 150 plates, *fine Impressions*
284 Jul. Cæsar Davisii, ——— *Cant.* 1706
285 Ciceronis Opera Lambini, 3 tom. *Gen.* 1606
286 Pomp. Mela Hermolai Burbari, 1512
287 Minucius Felix Ouzelii, ——— *L. B.* 1652
288 Minucius Felix et Cæcilius Cyprianus Rigaltii, ——— ——— *Par.* 1643
289 Panegyrici veteres Jac. De la Baune, *in Us. Delph.* 2 tom. ——— ——— *Par.* 1676
290 Higins's Mirour for Magistrates 1610
291 Milton's Poetical Works, 2 vol. *Royal Paper,* 1720
292 *The Phœnix of these Times: or the Life of Mr.* Henry Welby, Esq; *who lived at his House in* Grub Street, 44 *Yeares, and in that Space was never seen by any. aged* 84; *with his Effigies* 1637
293 Pareus in Genesin, ——— *Gen.* 1614
294 Whiston's Chronology of the O. Test. *Cambr.* 1702
295 Cruden's Concordance ——— 1738
296 Le Clerc's Harmony of the Evangelists 1701
297 ——— Suppl. to Hammond on the N. Test. 1691
298 Newton (Sir If.) on Daniel and the Apocalypse 1733
299 Moebii Exercitationes Sacræ *Lips.* 1686
300 Marckii Dissertationes Philologico-Theologicæ, ——— ——— *Rott.* 1721
301 Wise's Confutation of Atheism, 2 vol. 1706
302 Bynæus de Natali Jesu Christi, ——— *Amst.* 1689
303 Walker's (Dr. Obad.) Life of Christ, *Oxf.* 1685
304 Eckhardi Non-Christianorum de Christo Testimonia, ——— ——— *Quedl.* 1725
305 The Lives of the Primitive Fathers, *cuts* 1640
306 Alphonso De Villegas's Lives of the Saints 1615
307 *The Institution of a Christen Man*, B. L. *imprinted by* ——— ——— Berthelet, 1537

308 *The*

308 *The Christian Knight, compiled by* Sir W. Wiseman 1619
309 *Scala Perfectionis, by* Walter Hylton, B. L. *imprinted by* — — Wynkyn De Worde 1533
310 The Ornaments of Churches considered 1761

F O L I O.

311 SChindleri Lexicon Pentaglotton, *Hanov.* 1612
312 Scapulæ Lexicon. Gr. et Lat. *Gen.* 1609
313 Davies *Antiquæ Linguæ Britannicae et Linguae Latinae Dictionarium* — Lond. 1632
314 Somneri *Dictionarium Saxcnico Latino-Anglicum,* — — Oxon. 1659
315 Skinner's Etymologicon Linguæ Anglicanæ — — *Lond.* 1671
316 Calepini Dictionarium Octo Linguarum, *Par.* 1588
317 Minshieu's Dictionary of eleven Languages, 1617
318 Smith Catalogus Librorum Mstorum Bibl. Cottonianæ — — *Oxon.* 1696
319 Lambecii Commentarii de Augustissima Bibliotheca Cæsarea Vindobonensi, *cum. fig.* *Vind.* 1665
320 A Catalogue of the entire Library of the late James St. Amand, Esq; bequeathed to the University of Oxford, 1755 *Ms.*
321 Martinii Lexicon Philologicum, *Francof.* 1655
322 Lloydii Dictionarium Historicum, Geogr. Poeticum, — — *Oxon* 1671
323 Dictionaire de Bayle, 3 tom. *Rott.* 1702
324 Dictionaire de Moreri, 4 tom. en 2. *Amst.* 1702
325 Montaigne's Essays by Florio,—Bacon's (Lord) Hist. of K. Hen. VII. 1622
326 Launoii Epist. — — *Cant.* 1689
327 Diana of George of Montemayor 1593
328 Ingelo's Bentivolio and Urania 1673
329 The Works of K. James I. — 1616
330 Brown's (Sir Tho.) Works — 1686

Impressions of Dr. Stukeley's Works.

331 DR. Stukeley of the Gout, 2 pts, 1736—Dr. Rogers's *Oleum Arthriticum,* or Specific Oil for the Gout, 1735, 8vo
332 Ditto, Ditto

333 Dr.

333 Dr. Stukeley's Tracts, 8vo. *viz.* Of the Gout, 2 parts, 1736—Abstra of ditto, 1740 — Philosophy of Earthquakes, 3 parts, 1750
334 Ditto
335 Ditto
336 Ditto
337 Ditto
338 ———— Abstract of his Treatise of the Gout, 1740, 50 Copies
339 Ditto, Ditto
340 Ditto, Ditto
341 Ditto, Ditto
342 ————Philosophy of Earthquakes, a Bundle of odd Parts
343 ————Tracts in 4to, *viz.* Account of Richard of Cirencester, Monk of Westminster—*Origines Roystonianae* — *Palaeographia Sacra*—*Palaeographia Britannica, &c.*
344 Ditto, Ditto
345 Ditto, Ditto
346 Ditto, Ditto
347 Ditto, Ditto
348 ————Account of Rich. of Cirencester, *with the Map*, 2 Copies
349 Ditto, Ditto
350 Ditto, 4 Copies
351 Ditto, Ditto
352 Ditto, 6 Copies
353 Ditto, Ditto
354 ————Medallic Hist. of the Emp. Carausius, 2 parts, 4to.
355 Ditto, Ditto
356 Ditto, B. 2.
357 Ditto, Ditto
358 Ditto, B. 2. 2 Copies
359 Ditto, Ditto
360 Ditto, B. 2. 4 Copies
361 Ditto, Ditto
362 ————of the Spleen, with Anatomical Observations of the Dissection of an Elephant, with cuts, 1723 fol.
363 Ditto
364 Ditto, 2 Copies
365 Ditto, Ditto
366 Ditto, 4 Copies

367 Dr.

367 Dr. Stukeley of the Spleen, with Anatomical Observations of the Diffection of an Elephant, with cuts, 1723 fol. 4 Copies
368 Ditto, 6 Copies
369 Ditto, ditto
370 ——————*Itinerarium Curiosum* 1723 fol,
371 Ditto
372 Ditto
373 Ditto
374 Ditto
375 ——————*Abury*, fol.
376 Ditto
377 Ditto
378 Ditto
379 Ditto
380 Ditto
381 Ditto
382 Ditto
383 Ditto
384 Ditto
385 —————— Prints and Drawings of various Antiquities
386 Ditto
387 Ditto
388 Ditto
389 Ditto
390 Ditto

Third Evening's Sale, *Wednefday April* 30th

O C T A V O, *et Infra.*

LOT
391 CRufi Medicamentorum Thefaurus, *Lond.* 1701
392 Quincy's Difpenfatory —— 1718
393 Draught for the Reformation of the London Pharmacop. —— —— 1742
394 *Difpenfatorium, Mf.*—Oeuvres charitables de Guybert, —— —— —— *Par.* 1639
395 Pinæus de Virginitatis Notis, *L. B.* 1641
396 Sydenham Proceffus *Lond.* 1705—Sydenham Praxis Medica, *Lipf.* 1695
397 Lewis's

397 Lewis's Abridgment of the Edinburgh Medical Essays 2 vol. —— —— 1746
398 Harlet's State of Physic —— 1729
399 Mead Monita & Præcepta Medica, C. M. *Lond.* 1751
400 Mead Medica Sacra, —— *Lond.* 1749
401 Lawrence Prælectiones Medicæ, *ib.* 1757
402 Mason's Observations in Physic, *Birming.* 1757
403 O Halloran's Treatise on the Glaucoma, or Cataract, —— —— —— *Dubl.* 1750
404 Hutten *of the Wood called* Guaiacum, *that healeth the Frenche Pockes, and also helpeth the Goute in the Feete, the Stoone, the Palsey, Lepree, &c. Translated by* Paynell, B. L. *imprinted by* Berthelet, 1536
405 Colbatch of the Gout —— 1697
406 Wintringham de Podagra —— *Ebor.* 1714
407 Dolæus on the Cure of the Gout by Milk Diet, by Stephens —— — 1732
408 Campbell's Hermippus redivivus — 1749
409 Vigani's *Course of Chemistry at* Cambridge, 1705, *Ms.*
410 Shaw's portable Laboratory —— 1731
411 Tracts *Medical* and *Philosophical*, Stukeley of the Gout, 1734—Ditto, Philosophy of Earthquakes, 1756—Hillary on the Nature and Properties of Fire, 1760
412 Hales's vegetable Statics, vol. I. — 1727
413 Parsons's Analogy of the Propagation of Animals and Vegetables —— —— 1752
414 Raii Methodus Plantarum, *Lond.* 1682—Raii Catalogus Plantarum circa Cantabrigiam, *Cant.* 1660
415 —— Synopsis Animalium, *Lond.* 1693 — Bartholinus de luce Animalium, *L. B.* 1647
416 Goedartius *de Insectis, per* Lister, *cum fig.* *Lond.* 1685
417 Chamberlayne's Manner of making Coffee, Tea and Chocolate —— —— 1685
418 Woodward's Natural Hist. of the Earth 1702
419 De Boot Gemmarum & Lapidum Hist. *L. B.* 1636
420 Lawrence of subterraneal Shells — 1664
421 D'Argenville Fossilia Galliæ — *Paris* 1751
422 Ittigius de Montium Incendiis — *Lips.* 1671
423 Warburton's Enquiry into the Causes of Prodigies and Miracles —— — 1727
424 Gaffarel's unheard-of Curiosities —— 1650
425 Edlyn's Astrological Observations —— 1668
426 Eunapii Vitæ Philosophorum Gr. & Lat. Hadr. Junii, *ap. Plantin.* 1568

—— ——

427 Ray

427 Ray on the Creation — 1704
428 Derham's Physico-Theology — 1714
429 Leibnitz, Essais de Theodicée *Amst.* 1710
430 Welsted's Scheme of Providence — 1736
431 Boyle's Philosophical Works abridged, by Boulton, 4 vol. — — 1700
432 Vallesius de sacra Philosophia — *Lugd.* 1588
433 Toland's posthumous Works, 2 vol. — 1726
434 ———'s Tetradymus, 1720—Tolandi *Adeisidæmon*, — — Hag. C. 1709
435 Hartley's Observations on Man, vol. 2. 1749
436 Bertram's Ethics — *Copenh.* 1751
437 Bevis's Hist. and Philosophy of Earthquakes 1757
438 Whiston's Theory of the Earth, 1708—Whiston's Astronomical Lectures, 1715
439 Whiston's Astronomical Principles of Religion, 1717 —*Cometomania*, a Discourse of Comets, 1674
440 A Collection of Almanacks for several Years past,—A Collection of Almanacks for 1750, *in Turkey*
441 Pluche's Hist. of the Heavens, 2 vol. 8vo. 1740
442 Recorde's Ground of Arts, *B. L.* 1623—De Chales's Euclid, *Oxf.* 1700
443 Walter's Mathematical Dictionary
444 Wells Arithmetica, *Oxon.* 1698—Bernardus de Mensuris et Ponderibus Antiquis, *Ox.* 1688
445 Lawrence and Newton on Leases and Annuities, — — 1722—1730
446 Gardiner's Practical Surveying — 1737
447 Bradley's Improvements of Planting and Gardening, — — — 1726
448 Vitruvius de Architectura, *ap. Juntam*, Flor. 1522 *in Cor. Turc.*
449 Joh. Dauws *Schilderer und Maler* Kopenh. 1755
450 Freart's Idea of Painting by Evelyn 1668

QUARTO.

451 Regia Medicina, *cum multis Notis Mss.* Traj. 1668
452 Orationes Harveianæ— Mead Oratio Harveiana, — — *Lond.* 1724
453 Taylor Miscellanea Medica — *ib.* 1761
454 Battie's Treatise on Madness — 1758
455 Battie Aphorismi — *Lond.* 1760
456 ——— de principiis Animalibus — *ib.* 1751

457 Mal-

457 Malpighii Opuſcula —— *Lond.* 1669
458 Bauhini Pinax Theatri Botanici — *Baſ.* 1623
459 Owen's Natural Hiſt. of Serpents — 1742
460 Short's Hiſtory of Mineral Waters —— 1734
461 Da Coſta's Natural Hiſtory of Foſſils —— 1757
462 Muſæum Hermeticum —— *Francof.* 1625
463 Bottonus de Igne Diſſertatio, *Neap.* 1692—Hierne Acta & Tentamina Chymica, *Holm.* 1712.—Keyſlerus de Dea Nehalennia, *Cell.* 1717
464 Camerarii Themata Aſtrologica, *Amſt.* 1633—Edlyn's *Aſtrological Tables, Mſ. Several Obſervations upon Aſtrological Judgments, by* Dr. Stukeley, *Mſ.*
465 Heydon's Defence of judicial Aſtrology 1603
466 Celſius de Obſervationibus pro Figura Telluris determinanda, *Upſ.* 1736— Hanovii Impoſſibilitas Quadraturæ Circuli a priori adſerta, *Ged.* 1741—Kortholtus de Societate Antiquaria Londinenſi, *Lipſ.* 1735—Severinus de Lapide fungifero, *Guelp.* 1728
467 Argolus de Diebus Criticis —— *Patav.* 1652
468 Tracts. The Viſion of Sir Jo. Perrot, 1682 —Partridge's Nativity of Lewis XIV, 1680—Abp Uſher's Prophecies and Predictions, 1678 — Tryon's Obſervations on the Great Froſt, 1684—Lilly's Monarchy or no Monarchy—Ditto Obſervations on the life and death of King Charles—Knight's Mementos to the World, 1680—Booker's bloody Iriſh Almanac, 1646—Holwel's *Cataſtrophe Mundi*, with the Appendix, 1682—1683
469 Gaſſendus de Vita & Moribus Epicuri, *Hag. C.* 1656
470 Recorde's *Caſtle of Knowledge*, B. L. 1596
471 Ptolemæi Planiſphærium Commandiui, *Ven.* 1558
472 Bayeri Tabulæ Uranometriæ *Ang. Vind.* 1654
473 Bartſchii Planiſphærium Stellatum, *Norimb.*
474 Galilæi Syſtema Coſmicum, *Agu.* 1635
475 Ulugh Beighi Tab. Stellarum Perſ. & Lat. per Hyde —— —— *Oxon.* 1665
476 Wright's *Clavis Cœleſtis* —— 1742
477 Weidleri Hiſt. Aſtronomiæ —— *Vitemb.* 1741
478 Long's Aſtronomy —— *Camb.* 1742
479 Barker's Diſcoveries concerning Comets 1757
480 Des Cartes Principia Philoſophiæ, *Amſt.* 1672
481 Newtoni Principia, *Edit. opt.* *Lond.* 1726
482 ——— de Mundi Syſtemate liber, *ib.* 1728
483 Pemberton's View of Newton's Philoſophy 1728

484 Fontenelle's

484 Fontenelle's Elogium of Sir I. Newton, 1728—and 5 more Tracts philosophical and medical
485 Lowthorp's and Jones's Abridgment of the Philosophical Transactions, 5 vol. — 1705—1721
486 Philosophical Transactions, vol. 45.
487 Philosophical Transactions, 12 vol. 1753 to 1763
488 Philosophical Transactions, 5 vol.
489 Philosophical Transactions several Numbers.
490 Switzer's Hydrostatics and Hydraulics, 2 vol. 1729
491 Vertue's Description of Hollar's Works, *with his Life* — — — — 1745
492 Lady Betty Montague's Etchings — 1759
493 Emblems, small Landscapes, Coats of Arms, &c.
494 The Charter of the Royal Danish Academy of Paintings, Sculpture, and Architecture in Copenhagen, two Copies — — 1758
495 Ditto, two Copies
496 Ditto, two Copies
497 Tomlinson's Art of Dancing, *Cuts* — 1744

F O L I O.

498 Hippocrates Lat. *ap. Cratandrum, Bas.* 1526
492 Lacunæ Epitome Galeni Operum, *Ib.* 1551
500 Mercurii Trismegisti Pymander *Col. Agr.* 1630
501 Gerarde's Herbal, by Johnson — 1636
502 Grew's Anatomy of Plants — 1682
503 James's medicinal Dictionary, vol. 1.—and some Numbers
504 Le Mort Collegium Chymicum, *Mf.*
505 Topsell's Hist. of Serpents — 1608
506 *Confucii Opera Lat.* Studio et Opera Patrum, 4 Societatis Jesu, — *Paris* 1687
507 Platonis Opera Lat. Ficini — *Baf.* 1561
508 Laertius Diogenes Gr. et Lat. Aldobrandini, — — — *Lond.* 1664
509 Thucydides Gr. et Lat. Vallæ *Francof.* 1594
510 Athenæus Gr. et Lat. Casauboni, *ap. Commelin* 1597—Casauboni Animadv. in Athenæum, *Lugd.* 1621
511 Stephanus de Urbibus, Gr. et Lat. Thomæ de Pinedo, *Amst.* 1678—Holstenius in Stephanum Byzantium — *L. B.* 1684
512 Aristophanes Gr. & Lat. Bifeti Aurel. *Allob.* 1607
513 Ovidii Fasti Caroli Neapolis — *Panorm.* 1735

D 514 Ver-

514 Vergilius cum Notis Varior. Lucii *Basil.* 1613

515 Sherburne's Manilius ——— 1675

516 Plinii Hist. ——— *Francof.* 1582

517 Qu. Curtius Raderi ——— *Col. Agr.* 1628

518 Cæsar's Comment. with Edmonds's Observations, 1655

519 Ptolemæi Geographia ——— 1508

520 ——— ——— ——— *Bas.* 1540

521 Strabo Gr. & Lat. Xylandri ——— *ib.* 1571

522 Asiæ antiquissimæ Tabula per Stukeley, *about* 100 *Impressions*

523 Ditto

524 Ditto

525 Speed's Maps, 1631 *bad*

526 Moll's System of Geography ——— 1701

527 Bernardi de Breidenbach *Peregrinatio Hierosolomytana,* ——— ——— *Spir.* 1502

528 Ziegleri Terra Sancta ——— *Arg.* 1536

529 Adrichomii Theatrum Terræ Sanctæ, *Col. Agr.* 1600

530 Amico da Gallipoli, *Trattato delle Piante et Imagini di sacri Edifizi di* Terra Santa, *disegnate in* Jerusalemme, ——— ——— ——— *Fir.* 1620

531 Radzivili (Principis) Ierosolymitana Peregrinatio ——— ——— *Antw.* 1614

532 Scaliger de Emendatione Temporum *Col. All.* 1629

333 Calvisii Opus Chronologicum — *Francof.* 1620

534 Helvicus's Chronology ——— ——— 1687

535 Cary's chronological Account of ancient Time 1677

536 Isaacson's Chronology ——— 1633

537 The Treasure of Auncient and Moderne Times 1613

538 Vossius de Theologia Gentili, 2 tom. *Amst.* 1668

539 Stuckius de Sacrificiis Gentilium *Tig.* 1598

540 A Treatise of the Celtic Religion, *MS.*

541 Klockius de Ærario ——— *Nor.* 1671

542 Suidæ Historica

543 Paulus Orosius, *in Cor. Turc.* *Venet.* 1499

544 Hickesii Thesaurus, Pars 3. ——— *Ox.* 1703

545 Fuller's Holy Warre ——— *Cambr.* 1639

546 Purchas his Pilgrimage ——— 1613

547 Le Brun, *Voyage au Levant,* avec fig. *Delft.* 1700

548 Shaw's Travels ——— — *Oxf.* 1738

549 Perry's View of the Levant ——— — 1743

550 Pocock's Description of the East, 2 vol. 1745

551 Voyage d'Egypte et de Nubie, par Norden, *Cop.* 1755

552 Kæmpfer's Hist. of Japan, 2 vol. in 1, 1727

553 Montfaucon's Antiquities of France, 2 vol. 1750

554 *Plans and Descriptions of the Imperial Chambers,* MS.

Impressions of Dr. Stukeley's Works.

555 DR. Stukeley's *Itinerarium Curiosum*, in Sheets
556 Ditto
557 Ditto
558 Ditto
559 ———— *Abury*, in Sheets
560 Ditto
561 Ditto
562 Ditto
563 Ditto
564 Ditto
565 Ditto
566 Ditto
567 ———— Treatise on the Spleen, 6 Copies, in Sheets
568 Ditto, Ditto
569 Ditto, Ditto
570 Ditto, Ditto
571 ————Medallic Hist. of Marcus Aurel. Valerius Carausius, 2 parts in 1, 1757—59
572 Ditto
573 Ditto
574 Ditto
575 Ditto
576 Ditto
577 Ditto
578 Ditto
579 Ditto
580 Ditto
581 Ditto
582 Ditto
583 ————Account of Rich. of Cirencester, Monk of Westminster, and of his Works — 1757
584 Ditto
585 Ditto
586 Ditto
587 ———— *Origines Roystonianae*. 2 parts, 1743—46
588 Ditto
589 Ditto
590 Ditto
591 Parkin's Answer to Stukeley's *Origines Roystonianae* — — — 1744

592 Stukeley's

592 Stukeley's *Palaeographia Britannica* No. I. II. containing *Origines Roystonianae*, 2 parts and other curious Matters in Antiquity ——— 1743—46

593 ——— *Palaeographia Sacra*, or Discourses on Monuments of Antiquity that relate to sacred History, No. I, 1736—Ditto Sermon before the Coll. of Physicians, 1650—Ditto *Palaeographia Britannica*, No. III. of Oriuna, the Wife of Carausius 1752

594 ——— *Palaeographia Sacra*, or Discourses on sacred Subjects 1763—Ditto Sermon before the Coll. of Physicians 1750—Ditto Letter to Mr. Macpherson, on his Publication of Fingal and Temora 1763

595 ——— *Palaeographia Sacra* 1736—Ditto *Origines Roystonianae*, 2 parts, 1743—46—Ditto Sermon before the College of Physicians 1750—Ditto Discourses on Oriuna 1752—Fontenelle's Panegyric on Sir If. Newton, 1728

596 *The Origin of Astronomy and the History of the Celestial Asterisms Ms. by* Dr. Stukeley 1749—*Palaeographia Sacra* or Discourses on Monuments of Antiquity, that relate to sacred Hist. No. II. containing *Heroologia Sacra Patriarchalis*, or an Attempt to retrieve the Heroical Pictures of the Patriarchs, *Ms. by* Dr. Stukeley.

597 ——— Account of a large Silver Plate of Antique *Basso Relievo*, Roman Workmanship, found in Derbyshire, 1729, *printed* 1736

598 ——— of the Roman Amphitheatre at Dorchester

599 ——— Philosophy of Earthquakes, *in Turkey*, ——— 1756

600 ——— Tracts

601 Ditto

602 Ditto

603 ——— Abstract of his Treatise on the Gout, 1740, 50 Copies

604 Ditto, 50 Copies

605 Periodical Pieces in which some one or other of Dr. Stukeley's Works are reviewed, 2 vol.—Some Numbers of the British Magazine in 1749 & 1750, including some poetical Pieces by Dr. Stukeley —An Account of his Treatise on Earthquakes—Accounts of some of Dr. Stukeley's Works in the Gentleman's and London Magazines, and other periodical Pieces 2 vol.—Accounts of Dr. Stukeley's Works published in the Works of the Learned, the Political State, the Musæum, and other periodical Works, 2 vol.

Fourth Evening's Sale, *Thursday May* 1.

O C T A V O, *et Infra.*

LOT

606 BAxter Glossarium Antiquitatum Britannicarum —— —— *Lond.* 1719

607 Britannicarum Gentium Hist. Antiquæ Scriptores 3 Bertrami —— —— *Hav.* 1757

608 Idem

609 Idem

610 Nennii Historia Britonum —— *ib.* 1758

611 Idem

612 Idem

613 Common Prayer, long-lined, 8vo, *ruled and bound in Morocco* —— —— *Oxf.* 1743

614 Part of an English Com. Prayer, 8vo, *with Ms. Notes by* Dr. Stukeley

615 Common Prayer, *Welsh* —— —— 1709

616 Sparke's Feasts and Fasts of the Church, 1700—Falkner of the Church of England, 1677

617 Abridgment of the London Cases, 1700—Lesslie's Snake in the Grass, 1698

618 Thornley's Examination of Barclay's Apology 1742

619 Life of Bishop Bedell, 1685—Bernard's Life of Archbishop Usher, 1656

620 Whiston's Memoirs, Part 3, 1750—Garner's Primitive Baptism, 1701—and other Tracts

621 Burnet's Pastoral Care, 1692—Norris on the Love of God, 1705

622 Norris's Reason and Religion, 1689—Ditto Theory of Love, 1688—Ditto Reflections on the Conduct of Life, 1691

623 Forms of Private Devotion 1704—Pearsall's Duty of Daily Public Prayer, 1751

624 Opuscules de la Placette, 10 tom. *Amst.* 1701

625 *The Chrisien Rule* B. L. *imprimted by* Nich. Hyll, *no date*

626 *The Sycke Man's Salve*, B. L. *imperfect*

627 Squire's Answer to the Independent Whig 1723

628 Spinckes's Gentleman's Religion 1698—Owen on the Sabbath 1671

629 Wright on the Lord's Day, 1726—Jephson on the Religious Observance of the Lord's Day, 1750

630 Patrick's

630 Patrick's Menſa Myſtica, 1660—Hopkins on the Sacraments 1722
631 Henry on the Lord's Supper, 1708—Hoadly on the Lord's Supper, 8vo 1635
632 Elſtob's Engliſh Saxon Homily — 1709
633 *A moſt Chriſtian and Godly Sermon to the Paſtours of* Antwerp, *tranſlated by* Fenton, B. L. 1569
634 Sundry Sermons and Tracts
635 Adams's Sermons — — 1716
636 Sermons at Berry Street, 2 vol. — 1735
637 Calamy's Sermons on the Trinity — 1722
638 Duke's Sermons, — *Oxf.* 1728
639 Hopkins's Poſth. Sermons — 1708
640 Marſhall's Sermons, vol. 4. — 1750
641 Maurice's Sermons on the Trinity 1720
642 Newton's (Benj.) Sermons, vol. 2. 1736
643 Peck's 4 Sermons — 1742
644 Sherlock's (Tho.) Sermons, vol. 1 1754
645 South's Sermons, 2 vol. — 1692—1704
646 Shower's Sacramental Diſcourſes, vol. 2. 1732
647 Sturmy's Sermons — *Cambr.* 1716
648 Tillotſon's Sermons, 1671—Tillotſon's Sermons on the Incarnation, 1702
649 Wilkins's Sermons, 1701
650 Biſhop Williams's Sermons at Boyle's Lecture, 1708

QUARTO.

651 MOll's Claſſical Geography, *inſcribed to* Dr. Stukeley — — 1721
652 Relandi Paleſtina, 2 tom. — *Traj.* 1714
653 Bocharti Geographia Sacra *Francof.* 1681
654 Borchardi Deſcriptio Terræ Sanctæ *Magd.* 1587
655 Doubdan, Voyage de la Terre Sainte *Par.* 1661
656 Tymme's *Deſcription of Hieruſalem* — 1595
657 Cotovici Itinerarium Hieroſolymitanum et Syriacum, — — *Antv.* 1619
658 Idem
659 Montani Antiquitates Judaicæ — *L. B.* 1593
660 Van Til de Tabernaculo Moſis — *Dort.* 1714
661 Braunius de Veſtitu Sacerdotum Hebræorum, 2 tom. — — *Amſt.* 1680
662 Nicolaus de Sepulchris Hebræorum, *L. B.* 1706
663 Marſhami Canon Chronicus — *Lipſ.* 1676

664 Petiti

664 Petiti Eclogæ Chronologicæ, ——— *Par.* 1632
665 Newton's Chronology, ——— 1728
666 Jackson's Chronological Antiquities, 3 vol. 1752
667 Kennedy's System of Astronomical Chronology 1762
668 Grandamici Chronologia Christiana, *Paris*, 1668
669 Herbert de Religione Gentilium, *Amst.* 1663
670 Cœlum Orientis, & Prisci Mundi Triade, *Ham.* 1657
671 Chiffletii Vesontio ——— *Lugd.* 1618
672 Panelius de Cystophoris, ——— *ib.* 1724
673 Pignorii Mensa Isiaca, *cum fig.* ——— Amst. 1669
674 Godwin's and Rous's Antiquities ——— 1685
675 Aug. Niphus de Auguriis *Marp.* 1614
676 Ferrarius de Veterum Acclamationibus et Plausu, ——— ——— Mediol. 1627
677 Vegetius de Re Militari, *apud Plantinum Antv.* 1585
678 Vegetii aliorumq. aliquot Veterum de Re Militari Libri Scriverii, ——— *L. B.* 1607
679 Walchii Persecutio Neroniana in Hispania, *Jen.* 1753
680 Mosis Chorenensis Historia Armenica, *Arm. & Lat.* per Gul. et Geo. Whiston, *Lond.* 1736
681 *A Turkish Pass*
682 Petri Apologia pro Antiquitate Frisiorum, *Franek.* 1603
683 Cannegieteri Dissertatio de Brittenburgo, &c. ——— ——— *Hag.* 1734

FOLIO.

684 RHodigini Lectiones Antiquæ *Francof.* 1599
685 Reinesii Inscriptiones Antiquæ *Lips.* 1682
686 Gruteri Inscriptiones Romanæ, *ap. Commelin* 1616
687 Icones & Segmenta illustrium e Marmore Tabularum quæ Romæ adhuc extant, a Fr. Perrier *Par.* 1645
688 Pierii Hieroglyphica ——— ——— *Lugd.* 1610
689 Pococke Inscriptiones Antiquæ Gr. & Lat. C. M. ——— ——— ——— *Lond.* 1752
690 Apiani Inscriptiones Romanæ — *Ingolst.* 1534
691 Maittaire Marmora Oxoniensia *Lond.* 1732
692 Hercules Ethnicorum ex variis Antiquitatum Reliquiis Begeri ——— ——— 1705
693 Gyraldus de Deis Gentium — *Lugd.* 1565
694 Noris duplex Dissertatio de duobus Nummis Diocletiani et Licinii ——— *Patav.* 1676
695 Montfaucon's Antiquities *with the Suppl.* 7 vol. 1721

696 Mira

696 Mirabella *Dichiarazioni della Pianta dell' antiche Siracuse,* ——— ——— — *Nap.* 1613
697 *La* Sicilia *di Filippo* Paruta *descritta con Medaglie, per* Agostini ——— ——— *Lione* 1697
698 Kircheri Obeliscus Pamphilius *Rom.* 1650
699 Ciampini de Sacris Ædificiis — *ib.* 1693
700 Porcacchi, *Funerali antichi di diversi Popoli et Nationi con le Figure di* Girol. Porro — *Ven.* 1574
701 Alb. Durerus *de Symmetria Partium humanorum Corporum* impensis *Viduae Durerianae* per *Hier. Formschneyder,* ——— ——— *Norinb.* 1534
702 Les Proportions du Corps Humain, mesurees sur les plus belles Figures de l'Antiquite, *chez* Audran, ——— ——— *Par.* 1683
703 *Vitruvius de Architectura per* De Laet, *ap. Elz. Amst.* 1649
704 *The Origin of Architecture investigated, and carryed down to the Times of the Building of our Churches, by* William Stukeley, 1762—*A collection of Drawings*
705 Wood's Origin of Building ——— 1741
706 Freart's Parallel of Architecture, by Evelyn 1664
707 Pozzo's Perspective, by Sturt — 1707
708 *Liber de Militari Officio,* Nicolao Upton *Sar. & Welliae canonico Authore, Ms.*
709 *Uranologion* Gr. & Lat. Petavii *Par.* 1630
710 Bayeri Uranometria — *Ulm.* 1648
711 Flamsteed's *Atlas cœlestis* ——— 1729
712 Andreas Ornithoparcus his *Micrologus,* or Introduction *containing the Art of Singing, by* John Douland, *Lutenist* ——— ——— 1609
713 Purcell's *Orpheus Britannicus,* 2 Parts — 1706
714 *A Relation of what passed for many Yeers between* Dr. John Dee, *and some Spirits* ——— 1659
715 Porta's Natural Magic ——— 1658

Impressions of Dr. Stukeley's Works.

716 DR. Stukeley's Itinerary, in Sheets
717 Ditto
718 Ditto
719 ——————— *Abury*
720 Ditto
721 Ditto
722 Ditto
723 Ditto

724 Dr.

724 Dr. Stukeley's *Abury*
725 ——————Treatise on the Spleen
726 Ditto
727 Ditto
728 Ditto
729 Ditto
730 —————— *Origines Roystonianae*, Part II. 1746
731 Ditto
732 Ditto
733 Ditto
734 Ditto
735 —————— Account of Richard of Cirencester
736 Ditto
737 Ditto
738 Ditto
739 Ditto
740 Ditto
741 —————— Medallic History of Carausius
742 Ditto
743 Ditto
744 Ditto
745 —————— Tracts
746 Ditto
747 Ditto
748 Ditto
749 Ditto
750 Ditto

Fifth Evening's Sale, *Friday May* 2.

OCTAVO & Infra.

Lot.

751 HOME's Suripture Hist. of the Jews, 2 vol. 1737
752 The Testament of the 12 Patriarchs, *B. L.* 1677
753 Buxtorfii Synagoga Judaica — *Bas.* 1641
754 Relandi Antiquitates Sacræ Veterum Hebæorum *Traj.* 1717

E 755 Re-

755 Relandus de Nummis Veterum Hebræor. *ib.* 1709
756 Relandi Exercitationes de Jehova *ib.* 1707
757 Relandus de Spoliis Templi Hierosolymitani, *ib.* 1716
758 Relandi Dissertationes Miscellanea, Pars I. —— —— *ib.* 1706
759 Hottingeri Cippi-Hebraici *Heidelb.* 1659
760 Marperger de quinto-decimo Mensis A B H. Hebræorum —— —— *Dresd.* 1730
761 Jewish Kalendars for 1693 to 1695—1697 to 1699 *Ox.*
762 Chardin's Agreement of the Customs of the East Indians with those of the Jews —— 1705
763 Saubertus de Sacrificiis Veterum *Jen.* 1659
764 Sykes's Essay on Sacrifices —— 1748
765 Pezron's Antiquities of Nations —— 1706
766 Pelloutier, Hist. des Celtes, 2 tom. *Haye* 1750
767 Smith *Syntagma de Druidum Moribus ac Institutis* —— —— *Lond.* 1664
768 Cumberland's *Origines Gentium antiquissimae* 1724
769 Sanchoniatho's Phænician Hist. by Cumberland 1720
770 Dickinson Delphi Phoenicizantes — *Ox.* 1635
771 Eberi Calendarium Historicum, — *Viteb.* 1556
772 Mahomedis Alfragani Arabis Chronologica & Astronomica Elementa Lat. Christmanni *Francof.* 1590
773 Strauchius's Chronology, by Sault, 1704
774 Bedford's Animadversions on Newton's Chronology, —— —— — 1728
775 Ditto —— —— 1728
776 Kennedy's Chronology of the Greeks and Chinese 1747
777 Anonymi Ravennatis Geographia, *Paris* 1688
778 Munckerus de Intercalatione Variarum Gentium —— —— *L. B.* 1686
779 Olai Magni Epitome, —— *Amst.* 1669
780 Basingstochii Historia, —— *Atreb.* 1593
781 Malalæ Historia Chronica, Gr. & Lat, Chilmeadi —— —— *Ox.* 1691
782 Idem
783 R. P. Philippi Itinerarium, —— *Lugd.* 1687
784 Rutilii Itinerarium, — *Amst.* 1687
785 Kyriaci Anchonitani Itinerarium, *Flor.* 1742
786 Maundeville's (Sir John) Voiage and Travaile, L. P. —— —— —— 1727
787 Voyages de Paul Lucas au Levant, *Haye* 1705
788 Ray's Collection of Travels —— 1693
789 Temple's Observations on the Netherlands 1673

790 Vertot's

790 Vertot's Revolutions of Sweden 1696
791 Campbell's Prefent State of Europe 1757
792 Natalis Comitis Mythologia ——— *Gen.* 1612
793 Aurelius Leffignienfis de Cognominibus Deorum Gentilium, *Franc.* 1696 — Vill Theologia Mythologica ——— ——— *Francof.* 1696
794 Schedius de Diis Germanis, *Amft.* 1648 — Selden de Diis Syris ——— *Lipf.* 1668
795 Needham de Infcriptione Egyptiaca — *Rom.* 1761
796 Chiffletii Difertationes tres ——— *Paris* 1676
797 Murray (Andr.) Commentatio de Kinæis, *Hamb.* 1718
798 Claudius de Salutationibus Veterum — *Ultr.* 1702
799 Mac Gregory's Sepulchres of the Antients — 1712
800 Catalogus Libr. in Thefauris Antiquit. Roman. & Græcar. Grævii & Gronovii ——— *L. B.* 1703
801 Potter's Antiquities of Greece, vol. 1 — *Oxf.* 1697
802 Caftellanus de Feftis Græcor. ——— *Antw.*
803 Kennett's Antiquities of Rome ——— 1699
804 Almeloveen Fafti Confulares ——— *Amft.* 1740
805 Urfatus de Notis Romanor. ——— *Par.* 1723
806 Labbe Notitia Dignitatum Imperii Rom. *Par.* 1651
807 Maffon Jani Templum Chrifto nafcente referatum *Rott.* 1700
808 Leigh's Obfervations on the Roman Emperors, 1657 Johnfon's life of Julian the Apoftate ——— 1682
809 Cuperi Hift. trium Gordianorum ——— *Daventr.* 1697
810 Cuperi Harpocrates ——— *Amft.* 1676
811 Venuti's Defcription of Herculaneum
812 Hotomanus de re Numaria ——— 1585
813 Patini Hiftoria Numifmatum ——— *Amft.* 1683
814 The Knowledge of Medals, tranflated by Roger Gale ——— 1697
815 IndexNumifmatum Romanorum Bernardi *Matur.* 1750
816 Snellius de re Nummaria ——— *L. B.* 1613
817 Gronovius de Seftertiis ——— *Amft.* 1656
818 Hulfii Imp Romanor. Numifmatum Series *Fran.* 1603
819 Patarol Series Anguftorum, &c. ——— *Venet.* 1722

QUARTO.

820 FAbricii Bibliographia antiquaria *Hamb.* 1716
821 Bebelii Ecclefiæ Antidiluvianæ vera & falfa ——— ——— ——— *Arg,* 1675

822 Herbert

822 Herbert de Religione Gentilium *Amst.* 1663
823 Lomeierus de Veterum Gentilium Lustrationibus — — — — *Ultraj.* 1681
824 Frickiii Commentatio de Druidis *Ulm.* 1744
825 *Le Reveil de Chyndonax Prince des Vacies, Druydes Celtiques par* Guenebauld —— *Dijon* 1621
826 Noris Annus & Epochæ Syromacedonum *Lipſ.* 1690
827 Hyde Hiſtoria Religionis Veterum Perſarum *Ox.* 1700
828 Palmerii Græcia Antiqua — *L. B.* 1678
829 Aleandri Antiquæ Tabulæ Marmoreæ *Lutet.* 1617
830 Webb's Account of an antique Copper Table 1760
831 Jamblichus de Myſteriis Ægyptiorum Lat. Scutellii, — — — — *Rom.* 1556
832 Witſii Ægyptiaca —— *Amſt.* 1683
833 Maieri Hieroglyphica Ægyptio Græca —— 1614
834 Cauſſini Symbolica Ægyptiorum Sapientia *Par.* 1647
835 Furerii Itinerarium Ægypti, Arabiæ, Paleſtinæ, Syriæ, &c. —— —— *Norimb.* 1621
836 Mythologie de Noel Le Comte, par Montlyard, *Rouen* 1611
837 Genebrier, Hiſt. de Carauſius prouvée par les Medailles —— *Par.* 1740
838 Stukeley's Medallic Hiſtory of Carauſius
839 Ditto
840 Ditto
841 Auguſtini Gemmæ et Sculpturæ antiquæ a Gronovio, *Franek.* 1694
842 Norden's Drawings of ſome Ruins and coloſſal Statues at Thebes in Egypt —— 1741
843 Lord Pembroke's Statues —— 1731
844 Numiſmata Pembrochiæ, with Ames's Index 1746
845 Landi Numiſmata —— *L. B.* 1695
846 Vaillant ſelectiora Numiſmata e Muſeo, Fr. De Camps —— —— *Par.* 1695
847 Harduini Nummi Antiqui —— *ib.* 1684
848 Seguini ſelecta Numiſmata Antiqua *Par.* 1684
849 Seldeni Liber de Nummis —— *Lond.* 1675
850 Gronovii Pecunia Vetus — *L. B.* 1691
851 Spanhemii Diſſertationes de Uſu Numiſmatum Antiquorum —— *Amſt.* 1671
852 Waſerus de Antiquis Numiſ. Hebræor. Chald. & Syror. —— —— *Tig.* 1605
852 Pagi de Conſulibus Cæſareis *Lugd.* 1682
854 Hulſii Hiſt. 12 priorum Cæſarum *Spir.* 1599

855

855 Smids Romanor. Imperator. Pinacotheca *Amst.* 1699
856 Occonis Numismata Imp. Rom. *Aug. Vind.* 1601
857 Vici (Æn.) Reliquia ad Imperatorum Historiam *Ven.* 1612
858 Vici (Æn.) Augustarum Imagines Du Vallii *Par.* 1618 — *Discorsi di* Enea Vico *sopra le Medaglie de gli Antichi ib.* 1619
859 Fabricii Fragmenta Imp. Cæs. Augusti *Hamb.* 1727
860 Sperlingius de Nummis non cusis *Amst.* 1700
861 Ficoroni de Plumbeis Antiquorum Numismatibus *Rom.* 1650
862 Haym, *Tesoro Britannico, overo il Museo Nummario,* 2 tom. Lond. 1719
863 Arbuthnot's Tables of ancient Coins, Weights, and Measures ——— ——— 1727

F O L I O.

864 VAillant Numismata Ærea Imperatorum, &c. in Coloniis, &c. 2 tom. ——— *Par.* 1688
865 Vaillant Numismata Imperatorum, Græcé Loquentibus *Amst.* 1700
866 Banduri Numismata Imperatorum Romanor. 2 tom. *Par.* 1718
867 Tristan, Commentaires Historiques sur les Empereurs Romains, *avec les Medailles* ——— *Par.* 1635
868 Occonis Imperatorum Romanor. Numismata Biragi *Mediol.* 1683
869 Goltzii Julius Cæsar, ——— *Brug.* 1563
870 Goltzii de Re Nummaria Antiqua Opera, Tom. 2. *Antw.* 1708
871 Consular Annals, *MS.*
872 Patini Familiæ Romanæ ——— *Paris* 1663
873 Begerus de Nummis Cretensium ——— *Col.* 1702
874 Liebe Gotha Numaria ——— *Amst.* 1730
875 Sigonius in Fastos consulares *Ven. ap. P. Manutium* 1556
876 Rosini Romanæ Antiquitates ——— *Bas.* 1583
877 Romanæ Historiæ Scriptores Græci Minores Gr. & Lat. Sylburgii ——— ——— *Francof.* 1590
878 Lauri Antiquæ Urbis Splendor, — *Rom.* 1612
879 *Les Edifices Antiques de* Rome *dessinés & mesurés tres Exactement, par* Ant. Desgodetz ——— Paris 1682

Impressions of Dr. Stukeley's *Works.*

880 DR. Stukeley's Tracts, viz. Tracts on the Gout; Philosophy of Earthquakes; Account of the Roman Amphitheatre at Dorchester; Sermon preached before the College of Physicians
881 Ditto
882 Ditto
883 Ditto
884 ——— Account of Richard of Cirencester 1757
885 Ditto
*885 Ditto
886 Ditto, 2 Copies
887 Ditto, 4 Copies
888 ——— *Palæographia Sacra* ——— 1763
889 ——— *Palæographia Britannica*, 3 parts 1743—1746—1752
890 ——— *Oriuna* ——— ——— 1752
*890 Ditto
891 ——— Carausius, 2 parts —— 1757—59
*891 Ditto
892 ——— Treatise on the Spleen ——— 1723
893 Ditto, 2 Copies
894 Ditto, 4 Copies
895 Ditto, 6 Copies
896 ——— Itinerary 1724
897 Ditto
898 Ditto
899 ——— Stonehenge 1740
*899 ——— Abury
900 Ditto
*900 Ditto, 2 Copies

PRINTS *and* DRAWINGS.

901 SUNDRY Prints of various Antiquities, by Dr. Stukeley
902 Ditto
*902 Ditto
903 Ditto
904 Ditto
*904 Ditto
905 Ditto
*905 Ditto
906 Ditto
*906 Ditto

907 Sundry

907 Sundry Prints and Drawings of Celtic, Britiſh, and other Antiquities, chiefly by Dr. Stukeley
908 Ditto
909 Ditto
910 Ditto
*910 Ditto
911 Ditto
*911 Ditto, publiſhed by the Antiquary Society
912 Sundry Maps, Plans, &c.
913 Ditto
*913 Ditto
914 Prints and Drawings of the O. and N. Teſt. 3 vol.
915 A Portfeuille, containing Prints and Drawings
*915 Ditto
916 Ditto
*916 Ditto
917 Sundry Portraits
918 Ditto
919 Ditto, mezzotinto
920 Ditto, ditto
921 Heads of the Kings of England, *Vander Werf*
922 Monuments in Weſtminſter Abbey, &c.
923 Various Antiquities
*923 Ditto
924 Ditto
*924 Ditto
925 Sundry Prints, various Maſters
*925 Ditto
926 Ditto
*926 Ditto
927 Ditto
*927 Ditto
928 Ditto
*928 Ditto
929 Ditto
*929 Ditto
930 Sundry Portfeuilles
*930 A large Portfeuille, *cover'd with ruſſia*

F 2 Sixth

Sixth Evening's Sale, *Saturday*, *May* 3.

O C T A V O & *Infra.*

LOT

931 MUNDY's Chronicle, *black letter imperf.*

932 Camdeni Britannia *Lond.* 1587 ——Sheringham de Anglorum Gentis Origine *Cant.* 1670

933 Langhornii Antiquitates Albionenses *Lond.* 1673 —— Langhornii Chronicon Regum Anglorum *Lond.* 1679

934 Ricardi Monachi Westmonasteriensis de Situ Britanniæ Bertrami —— —— *Hav.* 1757

935 Idem

936 Historiæ Britan. Scriptores tres, Ric. Corinensis, Gildas, Nennius, per Car. Bertram — *Hav.* 1757

937 Idem

938 Idem

939 Idem

940 Nennii Historia Britonum Bertrami, *in corio turc.* *Hav.* 1758

941 Idem

942 Idem

943 Idem

944 Jeffrey of Monmouth's British History, by Thompson 1718

945 Julii Cæsaris Portus Iccius, per Gibson *Oxon.* 1694

946 Musgrave Antiquitates Britanno-Belgicæ, 3 tom. *Isc.* 1720

947 Owen's Hist. of the ancient Britons — 1743

948 Baxter Glossarium Antiquit. Britannicar. *Lond.* 1733

949 Reliquiæ Baxterianæ ———— *Lond.* 1726

950 Caius de Antiquitate Cantabrigiensis Academiæ *Lond. ap. Bynneman* 1568

951 Butcher's Survey of Stamford, and Tottenham high Cross ———— ——— 1717

952 Cowdry's Curiosities of Wilton House 1751 — Owen's List of the Fairs of England and Wales 1756

953 Kinderley's State of the Navigation of Lyn, Wisbeach, Spalding, &c. ———— 1717

954 Wood's Description of Bath, 2 vol. —— 1749

955 Baylies on the Uses and Abuses of Bath Waters 1757

956 A Miscellany relating to Robin Hood, Earl of Huntington.

ton, *Temp.* Ric. I. *with MS. Notes by Dr.* Stukeley — Robin Hood's Garland

957 Summary of all the religious Houses in England and Wales — — 1717

958 A Kalendar of the Saints of Great Britain and Ireland, 2 vol. *interleaved with MS. Notes by Dr.* Stukeley 1608

959 Les Delices de la Grand Bretagne & de l'Irlande, 6 tom. *Leid.* 1707

960 Wallace's Description of the Isles of Orkney *Edinb.* 1693

961 Elsynge's Manner of holding Parliaments 1660

962 Gadbury's Nativity of King Charles — 1659

963 *A Survey of* England's *Champions, and Truth's faithful Patriots,* with their Heads by Jo. Ley, *a small Crumme of Mortalitie* 1648, *very scarce,* Dr. Stukeley *in a Note says his Name was* Leycester

964 Trial of Dr. Sacheverell — 1710

965 Tracts. Woodward's Account of some Roman Antiquities found in London 1723 — Salmon's Roman Stations in Britain 1726 — Pointer's *Britannia Romana* 1724 — Marsili *Prodromus Operis Danubialis* *Amst.*

966 Fleetwood's Chronicon preciosum, with the Coins 1745

967 Leake's Historical Account of English Money 1745

968 Waræi Antiquitates Hibernicæ — *Lond.* 1654

969 The Irish Historical Library — *Dubl.* 1724

Impressions of Dr. Stukeley's Works.

970 DR. Stukeley's Tracts

971 Ditto

972 Ditto

973 Ditto

974 ——— *Origines Roystonianæ* *Stamf.* 1746

975 Ditto

976 Ditto

977 Ditto

978 Ditto

979 ——— Account of Richard of Cirencester 1757

980 Ditto

981 Ditto

982 Ditto, *the Author's Copy, with MS. Additions*

983 ——— Medallic Hist. of Carausius, 2 Books, 1757

984 Ditto

985 Ditto, Book 2.

986 Ditto

987 ——— Treatise on the Spleen

988 Ditto

989 Ditto, 4 Copies

990 Stuke

990 Stukeley's Treatise on the Spleen, 2 Copies
991 Ditto, 6 Copies

QUARTO.

992 ANTONINI Iter Britanniarum, per Gale *Lond.* 1709
993 Gibson Chronicon Saxonicum — *Oxon.* 1692
994 Lanquette's Chronicle, by Cooper, *b. l. imprinted by Marshe* 1559
995 Stow's Chronicle, *b. l. imperf.*
996 Milton's Hist. of Britain —— 1670
997 Verstegan's Antiquities —— *Antw.* 1605
998 Warner's Albion's England —— 1602
999 Vicars's God in the Mount; or, England's Parliamentary Chronicle —— —— 1644
1000 Peck's Memoirs of Oliver Cromwell —— 1740
1001 Peck's Memoirs of the Life and Works of Milton 1740
1002 Trials of the Regicides —— 1739
1003 Usserii Antiquitates Britannicar. Ecclesiar. *Dubl.* 1639
1004 Willis's Survey of the Cathedrals of Lincoln, Ely, Oxford, Peterborough —— —— 1730
1005 Camdeni Monumenta in Ecclesiam B. Petri Westmonast. *Lond.* 1603
1006 Widmore's Hist. of Westminster Abbey 1751
1007 Ducarel's Repertory of the Endowments of Vicarages in the Diocese of Canterbury —— 1763
1008 Gale's (Sam.) *Hist. and Antiq. of Winchester Cathedral, MS.*
1009 Webb's Tracts
1010 Pettingal's Dissertation upon the Tascia, or Legend on the British Coins —— 1763
1011 Ditto
1012 Masters's Hist. of Corpus Christi College, Cambridge, 2 vol. —— —— *Camb.* 1753
1013 List of Members of Corpus Christi College, *interleaved with MS. Additions*
1014 Wise's Antiquities in Berkshire, 2 parts *Oxf.* 1738—1742
1015 Norden's Description of Middlesex and Hertfordshire 1723
1016 Gardner's Historical Account of Dunwich, Blithburgh, and Southwold —— —— 1754
*1016 Ditto, *in sheets*
1017 Rauthmell's Roman Antiquities of Overborough 1746
1018 Warburton's Vallum Romanum —— 1753
1019 Stukeley's Palæographia Britannica

1020 Stuke-

1020 Stukeley's Palæographia Britannica
1021 ——— Palæographia Sacra
1022 Ditto
1023 *The Historical Part of* Stamford Election, *April* 1734, *drawn up by* Will. Stukeley, *and presented to* Sir Robert Walpole *at* Houghton, 19 May, 1734, *MS.*
1024 Lloid's *Hist. of Wales, by* Powel, b. l. — 1584
1025 Lewis's Antiquities of the Isle of Tenet 1723
1026 Rowland's *Mona Antiqua restaurata*; the Antiquities of the Isle of Anglesey ——— *Dubl.* 1723
1027 Account of a Roman Temple and other Antiquities near Graham's Dike, in Scotland ——— 1720
1028 Usserii Veterum Epistolarum Hibernicarum Sylloge *Dubl.* 1632
1029 *Extracts of Instructions from* K. Edward VI. *and* Qu. Eliz. *to several of their Ministers resident in Foreign Courts, MS.* —Also, *sundry Poems, &c. MS.*
1030 Legh's Accidens of Armory, *imperf.* — 1562
1031 Ferne's Blazon of Gentrie ——— 1586
1032 *Fourteen Plates of British Coins by* Dr. Stukeley, *never published*
1033 Ducarel's Series of Anglo-Gallic, or Norman and Aquitain Coins ——— ——— 1757
1034 Folkes's Tables of English Silver and Gold Coins 1745
1035 Folkes's Tables of English Silver and Gold Coins, with Plates and Explanations, by the Society of Antiquaries 1763
1036 Twelve Plates of English Silver Coins, with Observations ——— ——— 1756
1037 Observations on the Twelve Plates of English Silver Coins ——— ——— 1756
1038 Simon's Medals, Coins, &c. ——— 1753
1039 Perry's English Medals, No. 1. ——— 1762
1040 Stukeley's Carausius
1041 Ditto
1042 Ditto, B. 2. *in morocco*
1043 *The Author's Copy of ditto, with MS. Additions*
1044 Dr. Stukeley's *Drawings of the Medals of* Carausius, *with MS. Notes, Names of the Possessors, &c. preparatory to his Hist. of that Emperor*
1045 Ames's Typographical Antiquities, *in sheets* 1749

FOLIO.

FOLIO.

1046 NIcholson's English Historical Library 1714
1047 Hist. Anglicanæ Scriptores, per Gale, 3 tom. *Oxon.* 1684—1687—1691
1048 Historiæ Anglicanæ Scriptores decem, per Twysden *Lond.* 1652
1049 Bedæ Hist. Eccl. Gentis Anglor. Lat. & Sax. per Smith ——— ——— *Cant.* 1722
1050 Rerum Anglicar. Scriptores post Bedam *Lond.* 1596
1051 Historiæ Anglicanæ Scriptores varii, per Sparke *Lond.* 1723
1052 *The Cronycle of* Englonde, *with the Fruyte of Tymes, b. l. imprynted by* Wynkyn de Worde, *imperfect*
1053 Hollingshed's Chronicle, *imperfect*
1054 Burton's Commentary on Antoninus's Itinerary 1658
1055 Horsley's *Britannia Romana* ——— 1732
1056 *A Transcript of* Leland's *Itinerary, from the Original MS. by* Mr. Burton, *the* Leicestershire *Antiquary*
1057 Stukeley's *Itinerarium Curiosum* ——— 1724
1058 Another Copy
1059 Ditto, *the Author's Copy, interleaved with MS. Additions*
1060 The Cuts to Dr. Stukeley's *Itinerarium Curiosum* 1725
1061 The Proof Prints of ditto
1062 Inigo Jones's Stoneheng ——— 1655
1063 Stukeley's *Stonehenge*, a Temple restored to the British Druids ——— ——— 1740
1064 ——— Abury
1065 Ditto
1066 Ditto
1067 Ditto
1068 Ditto
1069 Drayton's Poly-Olbion, *with the maps*
1070 Slater's *Palæ-Albion*
1071 Camden's Britannia, by Gibson ——— 1695
1072 The Maps and Coins to Camden's Britannia
1073 Samme's *Britannia* ——— 1676
1074 Gordon's Journey thro' Scotland ——— 1726
1075 Speed's Hist. of Great Britain, *imp.*
1076 Moll's Maps of Gr. Britain ——— 1724
1077 Moll's Description of England and Wales 1724
1078 Brady's Introduction to the old English History 1684
1079 Churchill's *Divi Britannici* ——— 1675
1080 Weever's Ancient Funeral Monuments 1631
1081 Lhuyd's Archæologia Britannica *Oxf.* 1707

1082 Foun-

1082 Fountaine (Andr.) Numismata Anglo-Saxonica & Anglo-Danica, *ch. max.* ——— *Oxon.* 1704
1083 Snelling's View of the Silver Coin and Coinage of England from the Conquest ——— 1762
1084 Bedæ Hist. Ecclesiast. Gentis Anglor. per Smith *Cant.* 1722
1085 Harpsfeldii Hist. Anglicana Ecclesiastica *Duac.* 1622
1086 Wharton Anglia Sacra, *ch. max.* 2 tom. *Lond.* 1691
1087 Broughton's Ecclesiastical History of Gr. Britain, *no Title*
1088 Spelman Concilia, Tom. 1. ——— *Lond.* 1639
1089 Tanner's *Notitia Monastica* ——— 1744
1090 Newcourt's *Repertorium*, Vol. 1. ——— 1708
1091 Rocque's Plan of London
1092 A Scheme for founding a Society of Antiquaries in London 1718, *MS.*
1093 Drake's Hist. and Antiquities of York 1736
1094 Thoroton's Antiquities of Nottinghamshire 1677
1095 Wright's Hist. and Antiquities of Rutland, with the Additions, *interleaved, with MS. Additions* 1684
1096 The Church-Warden's Account of the Parish of Holbech, in Lincolnshire, from An. 1453 to 1597, *MS.*
1097 Holbeach Town-Book, written by Mr. John Stukeley 1676, *MS.*
1098 Peck's Antiquarian Annals of Stanford — 1727
1099 Peck's *Desiderata Curiosa*, 2 Vol. *imperf.*
1100 Salmon's Hist. and Antiquities of Essex
1101 Morant's History and Antiquities of Colchester 1748
1102 Loggan's *Cantabrigia illustrata* — Camb. 1704
1103 One Hundred and Forty-one English Views, chiefly by S. and N. Buck, *with a MS. Table and some Notes by* Dr. Stukeley. *bound* — Several ditto, *unbound*
1104 Stafford's *Pacata Hibernia* ——— 1633
1105 Parliamentary Cases and Proceedings, *MS.* *N. B.* Anthony Wingfield, Esq; *wrote several of the Cases from his own Study, and with his own Hand*
1106 Nero Cæsar ——— 1624
1107 A Journal of the Parliament during part of the Reign of K. Charles I. with divers Transactions in the latter Part of King James's Reign, the Spanish Match, the Cales Voyage, &c. *MS.*
1108 Franklyn's Annals of King James and King Charles I. 1693
1109 Nalson's impartial Collection, 2 vol. — 1683
1110 Heath's Chronicle of the Civil War — 1676
1111 The Establishment of his Royal Highness the Duke of York's Houshold at Mich. 1682, *MS.*

G 1112 The

1112 The Entry of Sir Peter Apsley and Sir Benj. Bathurst, Knts Treasurers to his Royal Highness, their Weekly Papers of Receipts and Disbursements for his Royal Highness's Service, beginning Oct. 1, 1684 and ending Sept. 1686, *MS.*

1113 Milles's Catalogue of Honour ——— 1610

1114 A Collection of Arms in Trick, with an Index, *MS.*

1115 A Book of ancient Pedigrees, *MS.*

1116 Registrum Honoris de Richmond, per Rog. Gale *Lond.* 1722

1117 A Treatise of Nobilitie, *MS.*

1118 *A Catalogue of the Nobilitie of* England, *since* Will. the Conqueror, and in what Kings Reigns, with Dates of the Years of their several Creations, *in painfull Manuscript*

1119 *The Nobility of* England *since the Norman Conquest, the Arms coloured, MS.*

1120 *Pedigrees of the English Nobility, with their Arms and Quarterings*, coloured, *MS.* ——— 1617

1121 Dugdale's Baronage of England, 2 vol. 1675—1676

FINIS.

Francis Grose

Francis Grose lumbers obesely and rather raffishly across the late eighteenth-century antiquarian scene: artist and soldier in turn, Richmond Herald, lexicographer of dialect and slang and one of the first journalist-antiquaries who catered for and fostered the growing interest in illustrated serial works on British antiquities.

He was of Swiss origin; his father, a jeweller, by then resident in England, made the coronation crown for George III; and Francis, of independent means, was to remain associated with London and Surrey all his life. Born around 1731, he received a classical education but soon turned his natural ability as a draughtsman to professional use, and was Richmond Herald in the College of Arms from 1755 to 1763. In December 1762 occurred a minor military event which has come down into literary history, when Edward Gibbon's company of Hampshire Militia was disembodied and his three and a half years of service came to an end; within a month, Grose was appointed adjutant and paymaster of the same regiment. So near a meeting — would it have been a success? At least they might, in Gibbon's own phrase, have 'bumperized' together. Grose's military career continued, and he became a Captain in the Surrey Militia.

At first his interests lay in military antiquities and armour, on which he published books between 1786 and 1789, concurrently with his first topographical and antiquarian picture-books, the *Antiquities of England and Wales,* 1773–87. There appeared in 1785 his *Classical Dictionary of the Vulgar Tongue* (which in Pierce Egan's 1811 edition became that of *Buckish Slang, University Wit and Pickpocket Eloquence*), and in 1787, the *Provincial Glossary*. Turning northwards, he entered on the *Antiquities of Scotland*, 1789–91, made friends with Robert Burns, who commemorated him as 'the chiel amang ye takin' notes', and then in May 1791 was about to repeat his triumphal progress through Ireland but dropped dead at a celebratory dinner-party in Dublin. His library was sold a month later in London, and well reflects his varied interests.

There is a large section of the 700 or so lots dealing with military history and practice, even if among the books on fortification one fails to find any of Uncle Toby's favourites. Lexicography is represented by several well-known dictionaries as well as Johnson's, including those of Nathan Bailey (1721) and John Ash (1775) as well as other glossaries, word-lists and grammars. John Ray's *Collection of English Words,* 1695 (lot 14), leads to his *Proverbs,* 1737 (lot 345), and to dialect items such as *The Praise of Yorkshire Ale, with a Dialogue in the Yorkshire Dialect,* 1697, (lot 505), or an undated *View of the Lancashire Dialect,* (lot 339). Brand's *Popular Antiquities,* 1777 (lot 542), and John Aubrey's *Miscellanies,* 1734 (lot 301), take us into a notable group of books on witchcraft and folklore, and to a remarkable series of bound volumes of popular pamphlets, including more tales of witchcraft and ghosts, popular verses and facetiae.

The antiquarian books have a greater topographical than an historical or archaeological bias, as might be expected. Grose had Hearne's Leland, both the *Collectanea,* 1715 (lot 561), and the *Itinerary,* 1768–9 (lot 562); Gough's Camden of 1789 (lot 706), and his *British Topography,* 1780 (lot 654), and a good range of local histories and the tours of Pennant, Wyndham and the others. Stukeley is not represented, and Rowlands's *Mona Antiqua Restaurata,* 1766 (lot 634), and Borlase's *Antiquities of Cornwall,* 1769 (lot 699), are about the only books dealing with prehistoric monuments.

The sale lasted six days, the books taking up only half the time, for the last three days were concerned with 281 lots of prints and original drawings. Many of these were by Grose himself, but they also included drawings by Sandby, Cozens, S. H. Grimm and August Hekel, and have been recently acquired by the Library of the Society of Antiquaries of London.

Of the catalogues in this volume, this one alone has been traced in more than two or three copies. That in the British Museum Print Room is gratefully reproduced. Others have been located in the Department of Printed Books (the British Library), the Bodleian, the Bibliothèque Nationale and the libraries of Harvard and U.C.L.A. Two other sales of Grose's prints and drawings are known: one held by Langford on 12–24 February 1770 (Lugt 1799, copy in Bibliothèque Nationale), and the other held by Hutchins on 22–23 March 1793, of which there is a copy in the British Museum Print Room.

FRANCIS GROSE, ESQ.[R] F.R.S. & A.S.

Author of the Antiquities of England & Wales, &c. &c.

Published by W. Richardson Castle Street Leicester Fields.

The Catalogue of Prints—priced by the late Tho: Kirgate of Strawberry Hill, Lord Orford's Printer.— the Drawings, by the late George Baker, St Paul's Ch: Yard.—

A CATALOGUE,

OF THE GENUINE

LIBRARY,

AND

Valuable Collection of Drawings and Prints,

BELONGING TO THE LATE

FRANCIS GROSE, Esq; F.R.S. & S.A.

DECEASED,

AUTHOR of the ANTIQUITIES of ENGLAND, SCOTLAND, and other valuable Publications;

CONSISTING OF

MANY UNCOMMON and CURIOUS BOOKS,

Particularly in History, Topography, the Military Science, Poetry, Witchcraft, *&c.*

ALSO

A RARE ASSEMBLAGE of DRAWINGS and PRINTS,

Many of the latter from private Plates;

Which will be SOLD by Auction,

By J. EGERTON,

At the ROOM, in SCOTLAND YARD, opposite the ADMIRALTY,

On *MONDAY*, the 20th of *JUNE*, 1791, and the FIVE following Days.

To be viewed on *Friday* the 17th, and to the Sale, which will begin each Day punctually at TWELVE o'Clock.

CATALOGUES may be had of Mr. HOOPER, No. 212, *High Holborn*, Mr. DAVIS, opposite *Gray's-inn*; Mr. DEBRETT, *Piccadilly*; Mr. OWEN, *Temple Bar*; Mr. SEWELL, *Cornhill*; and at the Place of Sale.

CONDITIONS of SALE.

1ſt. THAT the Perſon who bids moſt is the Buyer; but if any Diſpute ariſe, the Lot or Lots to be put up to Sale again.

2d. That no Perſon advance leſs than Three-pence each Bidding; after Five Shillings, Sixpence; and after the Lot ariſes to One Pound, not leſs than One Shilling.

3d. That each Perſon give in his Name, and pay Five Shillings in the Pound (if demanded) for what he buys; and that no Lot be delivered in Time of Selling, unleſs firſt paid for.

4th. The Books are preſumed to be perfect, unleſs otherwiſe expreſſed; but if upon the collating at the Place of Sale, any ſhould prove imperfect, the Purchaſer will be at Liberty to take or reject them.

5th. The Lots muſt be taken away at the Buyer's Expence, and the Money paid at the Place of Sale, within Two Days after the Sale is ended.

J. EGERTON.

CATALOGUE, &c.

FIRST DAY's SALE.

MONDAY, JUNE the 20th, 1791.

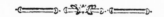

OCTAVO & INFRA.

Lot

1 VARIOUS Monthly and Critical Reviews
2 Bundle of tracts, historical, &c.
3 Ditto, mathematical, &c.
3*A Parcel of odd Volumes, &c. 8vo. and a Bundle of Acts of Parliament, &c. folio
4 Catalogue of the Manuscripts in the Cottonian Library 1777
5 ——— of the library of Topham Beauclerk 1781
6 ——— of Rarities in Litchfield Museum 1782
7 Steele's English Grammar ——— 1782
8 Locke on Education ——— ——— 1687
9 D'Assigny's Poetical History ——— 1685
10 Lowth's English Grammar ——— ——— 1774
11 Echard's Classical Dictionary ——— ——— 1715
12 Dictionary of the Canting Crew
13 The Scoundrel's Dictionary ——— ——— 1754
14 Ray's Collection of English Words ——— 1695

A 2 15 Entick's

15 Entick's Spelling Dictionary ——— 1781
16 Cole's Englifh Dictionary —— —— 1713
17 Dictionary of Hard Words ——— 1707
18 Grofe's Provincial Gloffary ——— 1790
19 Afh's Englifh Dictionary —— ——— 1775
20 Johnfon's Englifh Dictionary ——— 1783
21 Bailey's Englifh Dictionary, 2 vol. —— 1775
22 Sinclair's Obfervations on the Scottifh Dialect 1782
23 Law French Dictionary —— —— 1718
24 Kelham's Norman Dictionary ——— 1779
25 Somneri Vocab. Anglo-Saxonicum, à Benfon 1701
26 La Combe Dictionaire des Vieux Language Francois, 2 tom. ——— ——— 1766
27 Dictionnaire des Proverbes Francois —— 1758
28 Leroux Dictionnaire Comique ——— *Par.* 1752
29 Nouveau Dictionnaire d'Anecdotes, 2 tom. *ib.* 1786
30 Dictionarium Ling. Germ. Gall. Belg. Lat. Hifp. & Ital. 1595
31 Ozell's French and Englifh Dictionary — 1717
32 Phillips's Englifh and Latin Grammar —— 1731
33 Chriftie's Art of making Latin ——— 1760
34 Comenius's Gate to the Latin Tongue —— 1656
35 Bell's Greek and Englifh Grammar —— 1779
36 Schrevelii Lexicon, Gr. & Lat. ——— 1738
37 Backmair's Englifh and German Grammar 1752
38 Gentleman's Dictionary —— —— 1705
39 Dictionary of Hufbandry, Gardening, &c. 1717
40 Sportfman's Dictionary —— —— 1735
41 Owen's Dictionary of Arts and Sciences, 8 vol. 1754
42 Smith's Laboratory, or School of Arts, 2 vol. 1755
43 Evelyn's Chalcography ——— 1662
44 Boffe, Traicte des Manieres de Graver *Par.* 1645
45 —— Traitè de Perfpective —— 1653
46 The Painter's Voyage to Italy ——— 1679
47 Perrault's Abridgement of Vitruvius's Architecture 1692
48 Lamy, Nouveaux Elemens de Geometrie —— 1692
49 Brooke Taylor's Linear Perfpective —— 1719
50 Byrom's Short-Hand —— —— 1767
51 D'Offie's Inftitutes of Chemiftry, 2 vol. — 1759
52 Pegge's Forme of Cury, *portrait* ——— 1780
53 The Englifh and French Cook ——— 1674
54 Twifs on Chefs ——— ——— 1787
55 Burney's Prefent State of Mufic, 3 vol. —— 1773
56 Saunderfon's Algebra —— —— 1771
57 Ward's Mathematician's Guide —— 1752

58 Fergufon's

58 Ferguson's Lectures on Mechanics, &c. —— 1760
59 ——— Tables and Tracts —— 1767
60 Sherwin's Mathematical Tables, by Gardiner 1742
61 Sherwin's Tables —— —— 1771
62 Rowning's Natural Philosophy —— 1738
63 Euclid's Elements, by Cunn —— 1741
64 Maclaurin's Algebra —— —— 1748
65 Fenning's Algebra —— —— 1772
66 Rules for Bad Horsemen —— 1787
67 Dr. Lowers's Receipts in Physic —— 1700
68 Methodus Plantarum Cantabrigiam —— 1728
69 Geoffroy, Histoire des Plantes, *fig.* —— 1619
70 Le Clerc Medicine Aisée —— 1719
71 Charas's Experiments upon Vipers —— 1670
72 Da Costa's Elements of Conchology —— 1776
73 Graham's Medical and Chirurgical State —— 1779
74 Medical Tracts, viz.—Medical Remarks, by Anderson——
Case of Dr. Harwood——Collignon's Enquiry into the Structure of the Human Body, *and other tracts*
75 Anderson on Evacuation —— 1788
76 Dictionnaire Militaire, 2 vol. —— 1751
77 Kane's System of Camp Discipline —— 1757
78 Argar's Young Engineer —— 1777
79 Simes's Military Course —— 1777
80 ——— Military Guide —— —— 1776
81 ——— Regulator —— —— 1780
82 Robins's Treatise on Gunnery —— 1742
83 Robertson on Mathematical Instruments 1757
84 Maizeroy Traité sur l'Art des Sieges —— 1778
85 Muller's Practical Fortification —— 1764
86 ——— Treatise of Artillery —— 1757
87 ——— Field Engineer —— 1773
88 ——— Attack and Defence of Fortified Places 1747
89 Parker's Memoirs —— —— 1747
90 Remarks on the Military Operations in 1747 1760
91 Gray's Treatise on Gunnery —— 1731
92 Bruce's Institutions of Military Law —— 1717
93 Algarotti's Letters, Military and Political 1782
94 Maniere de Fortifier de Vauban —— 1707
95 Instruction que le Roi de France pour Regler l'Exercise d'Infanterie —— —— 1775
96 Exercise for Horse Dragoons and Foot —— 1728
97 Soldier's Pocket Companion —— 1746
98 Exercise of the Foot —— —— 1690
99 Strictures on Military Discipline —— 1774

100 Bruce's

100 Bruce's Institutions of Military Law — 1717
101 Burn's Militia Laws and Militia Acts of Parliament 1779
102 Adye's Treatise on Courts Martial, *with* MS. *Additions by Capt. Grose* — — 1778
103 Patriotic and Military Instructions — 1780
104 Speculative Ideas on an Invasion—Mirror for Courts Martial, *and other tracts*
105 Bland's Military Discipline — 1762
106 Emmerick's Partisan — 1789
107 Williamson's Elements of Military Arrangement, 2 vol.
108 Advice to the Officers of the British Army, *with MS. Additions by Capt. Grose* — 1783
109 Military Instructions for Officers detatched in the Field 1770
110 Military History of Germany, from 1631 to 1648, by Defoe — — 1778
111 Gaya's Art of War, 1678—English Military Discipline, 1780—Military Art of Training, 1622——Fisher's Soldier's Practice
112 Abridgement of Milit. Discipline, 1686—Praissac's Method of resolving any Military Question, 1639—Praissac's Art of Warre, 1639——Fortification and Military Discipline — — 1688
113 Darker's Breviary of Military Discipline, 1692—English Military Discipline, 1680——Burn's Militia Laws 1779
114 Holliday's Practical Gunnery — 1756
115 Abridgement of English Military Discipline, 1686—Rawlins's Compleat Soldier—Breton's Militia Discipline, 1717—New Art of War — 1726
116 Reasons for giving up Gibralter, 1749—Maizeroy on the Use of Defensive Arms, &c.
117 Mars stript of his Armour—Capt. Burrish's Trial, 1745, &c.
118 Moore's (Sir Jonas) Treatise on Artillery, 1683—Answers to the Reasons for Foreign Wars, &c. 1675
119 Railton's Army's Regulator — 1718
120 Dalrymple's (Col.) Tacticks — 1782
121 *Briefe Militarie Directions, with diverse Arithmetical Tables, MS. curiously written*
122 Travaux de Mars, 3 tom. *fig.* — *Par.* 1685
123 Code Militaire, par Briquet, 7 tom. — *ib.* 1761
124 Les Devoirs Militaires des Officiers, par Fontaine *Par.* 1675
125 La Science des Postes Militaires, par Le Comte *ib.* 1759
126 Détails Militaires, par Chennevieres, 4 tom. *ib.* 1750
127 Dictionnaire Portatiff de l'Ingenieur, par Belidor *ib.* 1755

128 Com-

128 Commentaires ſur la Cavalerie, par Bouſſanelle *Par.* 1758
129 ——— ſur les Enſeignes de Guerre, par Beneton *ib.* 1742
130 Hiſtoire de la Guerre contre les Anglois *Gen.* 1759
131 Traité de l'Attaque et de la Defenſe des Places, par Vauban, 2 tom. — *Haye*, 1742
132 Veritable Maniere de Fortifier de Vauban *Amſt.* 1726
133 La Marine des Anciens Peuples expliquée, par Le Roy *Par.* 1777
134 Traité de Mecanique, par Delahire — *ib.* 1695
135 Geographie Abrégé, par Dufreſnoy — *ib.* 1774
136 Hiſtoire de la Santé, par Mackenzie *Haye*, 1761
137 Memoires pour Servir a l'Hiſtoire des Inſectes, par Reaumur, 12 tom. — *Amſt.* 1741

QUARTO.

138 *The Booke of Honour and Armes*, wherein is diſcourſed the Cauſes of Quarrell, with the Nature of Repulſes, *cuts, bl. letter* — — 1590
139 Vincentio Saviola's Two Bookes of the Uſe of the Dagger and Rapier, and of Honor and *Honorable Quarrels* — — 1595
140 The approved Order of Martiall Diſcipline, by Gyles Clayton, *cuts, bl. l.* 1591—Digges's Paradoxes 1604
141 Davies's Art of War — — 1619
142 Markham's Souldier's Accidence and Grammar
143 Digges's *Stratioticos*, a Militare Treatiſe, *cuts, bl. letter* 1579
144 ——— Diſcourſes on Militarie Diſcipline—Inſtructions for Muſters and Armes, 1625—Military Diſcipline, ſhewing the Order for drilling for the Muſket and Pike, *cuts*, 1623—Davies's Art of War, 1619—Markham's Souldier's Grammar — 1626
145 Prynne's Doome of Cowardize and Treachery, 1643—Laws and Ordinances of War *Dub.* 1652
146 Bariffe's Military Diſcipline, *portrait* — 1639
147 Another Copy, *portrait* — 1643
148 Inſtructions for Muſters and Armes — 1631
149 Machiavel's Arte of Warre, by Peter Withorne, *cuts, bl. letter*, 1573—Certaine Wayes for the ordering Souldiours in Battelray, by P. Withorne, *bl. letter*, 1573—Novareſe's Military Tables, *bl. letter*, 1574—De Bellay's Inſtructions for the Warres, *bl. letter*, 1589—Ive's Practiſe of Fortifications, *cuts, bl. letter*, 1589

150 A

150 A Letter on the Regiments called Mariners, 1699—History of Standing Armies, 1698——Lawes and Ordinances of War, 1642, *and other tracts*
151 Ive's Instructions for the Warres, *bl. letter* 1589
152 Kelleie's Arte Militarie, *wants the title*
153 Roberts's Warrefare Epitomized, 1640——Markham's Souldier's Accidence—Digges's Stratioticos——Hexham's History of the Siege of Breda 1641
154 Lawes and Ordinances of Warre —— 1640
155 Achesone's Military Garden —— *Edinb.* 1629
156 Markham's Souldiers Exercise —— 1643
157 Instructions for Musters and Armes, 1623—Arte of Militarie Discipline, *cuts*, 1627—*Lex Talionis*, or the Law of Marque —— —— 1682
158 *A Treatise of Martial Discipline, by Ralphe Smithe*, MS.
159 Journal of the Venetian Campaigne in 1687—The Gentleman's Journal for the War —— 1693
160 Whitehorne's Wayes for ordering Souldiours in Battelray, *bl. letter* —— —— 1573
161 Mendoza's Theorique and Practise of Warre, by Hoby 1597
162 Harwood's Solace for Souldier and Saylour, *bl. letter*, 1592——Mendoza's Theorique of Warre, 1597—Browne's Horsemanship, 1624—Sir B. Gerbier's Military Architecture —— 1650
163 Discourse on the Oath of Allegiance to K. Will. and Q. Mary, *with several Tracts on Standing Armies*
164 Grose's Treatise upon Ancient Armour and Weapons of War —— —— 1785
165 Another Copy —— —— 1785
166 Grose's Military Antiquities, and History of the English Army, 2 vol. —— —— 1786
167 Lloyd's History of the War in Germany, 2 vol. *coloured plates* —— —— 1781
168 Relation of the Battle of Maxen —— 1785
169 Traite des Tournois Joustes & Carrousals *Lyon.* 1669
170 Pieces Authentiques relatives a la presente Guerre 1758
171 St. Remy, Memoires d'Artillerie, 2 tom. *Par.* 1707
172 L'Art Universel des Fortifications, par Bitainvieu *ib.* 1674
173 Pratique de la Guerre, par Malthus *ib.* 1646
174 Histoire, de la Milice Francoise, par Daniel, 2 tom. *ib.* 1721
175 Girard Traité des Armes, *fig.* —— *ib.* 1737
176 Naudæus de Studio Militari —— *Romæ*, 1637
177 Scheffer de Re Vehiculari veterum *Francf.* 1671

178 Vegetius

178 Vegetius de Re Militari, Stewichii *Antv.* 1585
179 Lydius de Militari, *fig.* —— *Dord.* 1698
180 Nomina et Insignia Gentilicia Nobilium Equitumque, sub Edoardo I. rege, Militantium, &c. edidit Edw. Rowe Mores, *wants the preface* *Ox.* 1749
181 Oplomachia, di Bonav. Pistofilo, *fig.* *Scien.* 1621
182 Historia de la Milicia Espanola, par Mendoza *Mad.* 1776
183 Reglement en Generale Ordres voor de Reg. Infanterie van den Staat. —— —— *Grav.*
184 La noble Science des Joueurs d'Espee, *fig.* *Anv.* 1538
185 *Grose's Antiquities of England and Wales, with the Supplement,* 6 vol. *super royal quarto, boards*

F O L I O.

186 Ward's Animadversions of War —— 1639
187 Albemarle's (Duke of) Observations upon Military and Political Affairs —— 1671
188 Lucar's Three Books of Colloquies concerning the Art of Shooting, *bl. letter* —— 1588
189 Crusac's Military Instructions for Cavalrie 1644
190 Guicciardini's Aphorisms, Civill and Militarie 1689
191 Forty-six Drawings of Military Antiquities
192 Barry's Discourse of Military Discipline — 1634
193 Militarie Instructions for the Cavalrie —— 1632
194 Another Copy
195 Hexham's Principles of the Military Art — 1642
196 Turner's Military Essays —— 1683
197 Another Copy
198 List of the Army, 1739—Quarters of the Army in Ireland—Establishment of the Army, MS. 1728
199 Orrery's (Lord) Treatise on the Art of War 1677
200 Another Copy
201 List of the Army, 1739 and 1740
202 Barret's Theorike and Practike of Modern Warres 1598
203 Barry's Military Discipline
204 Venn's Military Observations —— 1672
205 Another Copy 1672
206 Another Copy —— —— 1672
207 Elton's Body of the Art Military —— 1668
208 Norton's Practise of Artillerie
209 Report from the Committee appointed to consider the State of his Majesty's Land forces and Marines 1746

B 210 Barry's

210 Barry's Siege of Breda ——— 1627
211 Watson's Geographical Dictionary, *boards*
212 Sprigge's England's Recovery, *cuts* —— 1647
213 Sandoval's History of the Civil Wars of Spain 1652
214 De Pontis's Memoirs 1694
215 Priorati's History of the Warres of Christendom, by Carey, E. of Monmouth ——— 1648
216 Procopius's Warres of Justinian, by Holcroft 1648
217 Vere's (Sir Fra.) Commentaries ——— 1672
218 Ælian's Tacticks, translated by Bingham
219 Cæsar's Commentaries, by Edmundes —— 1609
220 Monro's Expedition with the worthy Scots Regiment, called Mac Keyes ——— 1637
221 L'Architecture Militaire, par Fritack —— 1640
222 Siege de la Ville de Breda, par Hugo —— 1621
223 *Traité de Fortification*, MS. ——— 1729
224 Les Douze Livres de Rob. Valturin touchant la Discipline Militaire ——— ——— 1555
225 Histoire du Siege de Bolduc, par Heinsius 1631
226 Le Gouvernement de la Cavallerie Legere, par Basta 1627
227 Maniement D'Armes de Nassau, par Van Breen 1618
228 L'Art Militaire pour l'Infanterie, par Walhausen 1615
229 Another Copy
230 L'Etat Militaire de l'Empire Ottoman, Ital. & Fr. par Marsigli ——— ——— 1732
231 Historia di Ferdinando Terzo, Imperatore — 1672
232 Theatro Militare del Capitano Flaminio de la Croce 1617
233 Regole Militari del Cavalier Melzo
234 Ferrettus de Re Disciplina Militari —— 1575
235 Aquini Lexicon Militaris, 2 vol. —— 1734
236 Upton de Studio Militari—Bado Aureo de Armis—— Spelmanni Aspilogia ——— 1654
237 Hugo de Militia Equestri Antiqua & Nova 1630
238 Verbruggen on making Canon, *in Dutch* 1770
239 Crees und Areheley Kunst. *fig.* —— 1620
240 The Manual Exercise on the first Invention of Guns, with the Figures, *in Dutch*

END OF FIRST DAY'S SALE.

SECOND DAY's SALE.

TUESDAY, JUNE the 21ſt, 1791.

OCTAVO & INFRA.

241 BLACKWELL's Military Diſcipline, *cuts, by Hogarth* —— —— 1726
242 Bibliotheque Bleue, 2 tom. — *Par.* 1770
243 Don Quichotte, avec le Suite, 12 tom. *ib.* 1726
244 Contes d'Eutrapel, 3 tom. — *ib.* 1732
245 Memoires ſur l'Ancienne Chevalerie, par St. Palaye, 2 tom. —— —— *ib.* 1759
246 Fabliaux, ou Contes du XII. & du XIII. Siecle, par Le Grand, 4 tom. —— *ib.* 1779
247 Memoires de Gaudence de Luques, 2 tom. *ib.* 1753
248 Nouveaux Contes a Rire, 2 tom. — *Col.* 1722
249 Roger Bontems en belle Humeur — *Amſt.* 1753
250 Le Facecieux Reveillé Matin — *Rouen,* 1656
251 Le Moyen de Parvenir, 2 tom.
252 Le Momus Francois, *Col.* 1781—Vie de Moliere, *Brux.* 1706
253 Apologie pour Herodote, par H. Eſtienne 1566
254 Oeuvres de Regnier —— *Rouen,* 1621
255 La Pucelle d'Orleans, par Voltaire, *fig.* 1764
256 Candide, par Voltaire —— 1759
257 Le Moine Seculariſe — —— *Col.* 1675
258 Hiſtoires prodigieuſes, par Boaſtuau *Anv.* 1594
259 Le Nouveau Recueil de Curioſitez, par Sieur D'Emery, *Par.* 1685
260 Venette, Tableau de l'Amour Conjugal *Col.* 1702
261 Hiſtoire de Rats —— *Ratopolis,* 1738

B 2 262 Les

262 Les Caracteres de M. de la Bruyere, 2 tom. *Par.* 1768
263 Origines des Dignitez & Magistrats de France, par Fauchet — — *ib.* 1606
264 Scaligeriana—Thuana—Perroniana—Pithœana, & Colomesiana, 2 tom. — *Amst.* 1740
265 Le Compere Mattheu ou les Bigarrures de l'Esprit Humain, 3 tom. — *Lond.* 1732
266 Abrégé des Causes celélébres & interessantes, par Besdel, 2 tom. — — *ib.* 1777
267 Essai sur les principes Politiques, par Dignan *ib.* 1776
268 Matinées Senonoises, ou Proverbes François *Par.* 1789
269 La Minorite de St. Louis, avec l'Histoire de Louis XI. & de Henri II. par Varillas — *Haye* 1687
270 Histoire de la Maison de Brandenbourg *ib.* 1751
271 Histoire de la Papesse Jean, 2 tom. — *ib.* 1720
272 Histoire du Seizieme Siecle, par Durand, 4 tom. *ib.* 1734
273 *Coustumier de Bretagnie* — *Rouen,* 1538
274 Memoires de la Reyne Marquesite — *Par.* 1658
275 Balance de la Nature, par Mad. Le Masson Le Golft, *ib.* 1784
276 Les Galanteries Grenadines, par Madame de Villedieu, *ib.* 1763
277 La Giuocatrice di Lotto — *Ven.* 1758
278 Il Mercurio Errante di Rossini — *Rome* 1732
279 Gierusalemme Liberata di Tasso — 1652
280 Bernard's *Bible Battels*; the Sacred Art Military for wageing of Warre according to Holy Writ 1629
281 An Eccho to the Voice from Heaven; a Narration of the Life and special Calling of Arise Evans 1652
282 Clogie's *Vox Corvi*, the Voice of a Raven, that thrice spoke these words distinctly, *Look into Colossians, the 3d and 15th* — — 1694
283 N. Testamentum Lat. Castelionis — 1682
284 Jenyns's Disquisitions on various Subjects 1782
285 Funeral Sermon of Margaret Countess of Richmond and Derby, Mother to Henry VII. — 1708
286 Dodrington's Present State of the Romish Religion 1699
287 Virgilii Opera, à Justice, 3 vol.
288 Idem, vol. 2.
289 Livii Historia, à Ruddimanno, 4 vol. *ch. opt.* *Edinb.* 1772
290 Ovid de Tristibus, Stirling — 1736
291 Horatii Opera, Delphini — 1767
292 Martialis Epigrammata, Delphini — 1701
293 Florus, Delphini — 1744
294 Synopsis Communium Locorum — 1732
295 Nic. Parthenii Giannettasii Poemata *Nap.* 1699

296 J.

296 J. Meurſii Elegantiæ Latini Sermonis
297 Groſſii Compend. Philoſophiæ — *Baſ.* 1620
298 Luſcinus (Ottom.) Grunnius, atque Grunnii Porcelli Teſtam. ——— *Argent.* 1522
299 Urſatus de Notis Romanorum — 1723
300 Trotula Curandarum Ægritudinum Muliebrum, &c. *Lipſ.* 1778—L'Encyclopedie Perruquiere, *Par.* 1762—Bouquet's Poiſſards, par M. Vade *Gren.*
301 Aubrey's Miſcellanies on Dreams, Local Fatalities, &c. 1784
302 Glanville on Witches and Apparitions —— 1726
303 Beaumont's Treatiſe of Spirits, Apparitions, Witches, &c. 1705
304 Syſtem of Magick, or a Hiſtory of the Black Art, by Defoe 1727
305 Hutchinſon's Hiſtorical Eſſay on Witchcraft 1720
306 A Treatiſe on Second Sight, Dreams, and Apparitions 1763
307 A pleaſant Treatiſe of Witches, *their Imps, and Meetings* 1673
308 Satan's inviſible World Diſcovered, by Sinclair 1780
309 Another Copy ——— ——— 1779
310 Wagſtaffe's Queſtion of Witchcraft debated 1671
311 *Pandæmonium*, or the Devil's Cloyſter, by Bovet 1684
312 Glanvil's Blow at Modern Sadduciſm, with an Account of the Drummer ——— 1668
313 The Antiquitie of Magic, by Philalethes 1650
314 L'Hiſtoire des Imaginations de Monſ. Ouſle, *fig.* *Amſt.* 1710
315 The Opinion of Witchcraft Vindicated——Hiſtoire de Notre Dame, *Lille*, 1772——*Almanach du Diable Amſt.*
316 Baxter's World of Spirits ——— 1691
317 Tryon's Treatiſe on Dreams and Viſions
318 Arcandum's Pleaſant Book on Deſtiny, Phiſiognomy, &c. *bl. letter*, 1649—The Knowledge of Things Unknown, *bl. letter* ——— ——— 1617
319 Harvey's Aſtrological Diſcourſes, 1583—The Learned Work of Hermes Triſmegiſtus, *bl. letter*, 1583—Chronological Tables from Will. I. *imp.* 1561
320 Harvey's Aſtrological Diſcourſe on the Conjunction of Saturn and Jupiter ——— 1583
321 *Cataſtrophe Mundi*, or Merlin Revived, *curious cuts* 1683
322 The Knowledge of Things Unknown, *cuts, bl. letter*
323 Indaginii Introd. in Chyromant. Aſtrolog. Natur. &c. *Argent.* 1630

324 A

324 A Treatise on Geomancy and Physiognomy, *in German*
325 Mankind Displayed, or the History of the Little World 1690
326 Barne's *Gerania*, a Discovery of a little People called Pygmies, 1675—Cruelties of the Dutch at Amboyna 1672
327 Digby's Discourse of Sympathy —— 1658
328 The Cry of the Oppressed, shewing the Wickedness of Gaolers, &c. *cuts*
329 Pleasing Reflections on Life and Manners 1787
330 Howell's Familiar Letters —— 1650
331 Waterhouse's Apologie for Learning and Learned Men 1653
332 Portroyal's Art of Thinking —— 1685
333 *Pranceriana*, Fugitive Pieces published in Dublin *Dub.* 1775
334 Repository, or Library of Fugitive Pieces *ib.* 1763
335 Breslaw's Last Legacy, 1784—The Cheats of London Exposed—Love at First Sight, a Collection of Comic Advertisements —— 1751
336 Sir John Fielding's Jests—Garrick's Jests—The Merry Quack Doctor
337 Peter Cunningham's Jests—Tim Grinn's Merry Jester—Food for the Funny—Derrick's Jests—The Merry Miscellany
338 *Bogg Witticisms*, or Dear Joy's Common Places, by Mac O. Bonnyclabbero
339 History of an Old Fringe Petticoat, 1775—Appendix Pranceriana, 1776—View of the Lancashire Dialect—The Oeconomy of a Winter's Day
340 Secret History of the Calve's Head Club 1705
341 Secret History of Clubs —— —— 1709
342 Selden's Table Talk —— —— 1716
343 Apophthegmes, New and Old, *wants the title*
344 A Collection of Proverbs, by N. R. —— 1659
345 Ray's Collection of Proverbs —— 1737
346 Another Copy —— —— 1768
347 Andrews's Anecdotes, Ancient and Modern 1789
348 Another Copy —— —— 1790
349 Grotius on War and Peace —— 1654
350 Montesquieu's Spirit of Laws, 2 vol. —— 1766
351 Toland's Miscellaneous Works, 2 vol. —— 1747
352 Remarks on the Writings and Conduct of Rousseau 1767
353 The Female War, in Letters and Essays 1697
354 Tom Brown's Legacy for the Ladies —— 1705

355 Alexander's

355 Alexander's Hiſtory of Women, 2 vol. — 1782
356 Gentleman's Magazine for 1746
357 Beauties of the Britiſh Senate, 2 vol. —— 1786
358 The Mirror, a Periodical Paper, 3 vol. — 1781
359 Harington's *Nugæ Antiquæ*, a Collection of Original Papers, 3 vol. —— —— 1779
360 Tracts, viz.—Lives of the Thief-Takers—Deſcription of Dr. Graham's Apparatus—Appendix to Pranceriana —The Friſky Jeſter
361 —— Song and Story of Mrs. Draper—Trip to Calais—La Pucelle d'Orleans—The Sixpenny Miſcellany—— Satan's Harveſt Home, &c.
362 —— Ancient Erſe Poems, by Mr. Hill—Free's Hiſtory of the Engliſh Tongue—Farmer on the Learning of Shakſpeare—Blair's Diſſertation on Oſſian's Poems
363 —— Excerpta e Statutis Acad. Cantabrigienſis—— Catalogue of the Rarities at Don Saltero's—— Account of the Expulſion of Seven Devils from G. Lukin, a Taylor—Narrative of the Caſe of Geo. Lukins, who was poſſeſſed of Evil Spirits—*and other tracts*
364 —— Treatiſe on the Cuſtom of Counting Noſes, 1779— Reports, Lies, and Stories, the Forerunners of the Great Revolution, 1732—Deformities of Fox and Burke, 1784—Sir Henry Clinton's Narrative, 1783 An Eſſay to Illuſtrate the Ancient Hiſtory of the Britannic Iſles —— —— 1786
365 —— Thickneſſe's Queries to Ld. Audley—The Swindler Detected—Liſt of the Perſons who ſurrendered to the K. Bench
366 —— Trial of Mrs. Newton for Adultery—The Ænigmatical Repoſitory, with a Key—Lord Mayor's Shew, by Henley—Lives, Adventures, and Eſcapes of J. and G. Weſton
367 —— Hazard of a Death-Bed Repentance—Engliſh Libertine, or Rambling Beau—Marriage between one Man and One Woman only, Aſſerted—The Diſpenſary Tranſverſed, *and other tracts*
368 —— Tracts, viz.—Paſquin, by Fielding, 1736—Count Piper's Packet—*The Merry Thought*, or Glaſs Window and Bog-Houſe, Miſcellany, *Frontiſpiece*
369 Churchill's Annals, *portrait*, 1722—Narrative of Attempt to Murder Edm. Criſp, Eſq.—Gay's Shepherd's Week, *and other tracts*

370 Hiſtory

370 Tracts—History of Sir Bevis of Southampton, 1775—Discourse of the Bookland and Folkland of the Saxons, 1775—*Extracts from the Charters of Hulne Abbey*, MS.—History of the Rebellion in Norfolk, under Kett the Tanner—Davies's Life of Massinger

371 A Collection of Tracts on Various Subjects, 5 vol.

QUARTO.

372 Edinburgh Advertiser, 6 vol.

373 Catalogue of the Portland Museum — 1786

374 *A Catalogue of the Manuscripts belonging to Sir Chr. Yelverton*, MS. — 1648

375 Ascough's Catalogue of the MSS. in the British Museum, 2 vol. — — 1782

376 Strutt's Dictionary of Engravers, 2 vol. — 1786

377 Dictionnaire Francois, par Richelet *Lyon*, 1681

378 Boyer's French and English Dictionary — 1729

379 Ainsworth's Latin and English Dictionary, 2 vol. 1773

380 Cowell's Interpreter — — 1637

381 Hildanus's Experiments in Chyrurgerie — 1643

382 The Secretes of Maister Alexis, *bl. letter* 1558

383 Mountain's Gardener's Labyrinth, 1608—Hill's Arte of Gardening, 1608—Hill on the ordering of Bees, 1608—Mascal on the Government of Cattel 1662

384 The Manœuverer, or Skilfull Seaman — 1788

385 Hodgson's Theory of Navigation — 1706

386 Philosophical Transactions, vol. 71, pl. II. 1781

387 Cowley's Theory of Perspective, 2 vol. — 1766

388 Price's British Carpenter — 1765

389 Analyse des Infiniment Petits, par le M. d'Hospital *Par.* 1716

390 Mathematique Universelle Abregee, a l'Usage et a la porte de tout le Monde — *ib.* 1728

391 Bell's Anatomie of Popish Tyrannie — 1603

392 A Cloud of Witnesses for the Prerogatives of Jesus Christ — — 1714

393 Nieuwentyt's Religious Philosopher — 1724

394 Mercurius Politicus for 1659 and 1660

395 Life of Martin Luther, 1641—Life of Master Henry Welby, who lived Forty-four Years in Grub Street, *and was never seen by any*—Trial of Sir W. Raleigh, 1648

1648—Sir T. Overbury's Obſervations in his Travailes, 1626—Warren's Deſcription of Surinam, 1667—Strange Life of Taſiletta, 1669—Lord Howard's Voyage to Fez, 1670—Diſcourſe touching Tanger, 1680—Mather's Hiſt. of the Wars in New England, 1676—Randolph's State of the Morea, 1686—Count Taaffe's Letters, 1684—The World's Miſtake in O. Cromwell, ſhewing the Decay of Trade, 1668—Plain Engliſh, a Conference concerning the Deadneſs of our Markets, 1673—The Golden Fleece; or Old England reſtored, 1679—Haines's England's Weal and Proſperity propoſed—Haines on Public Working Alms-houſes—Account of the Conſtitution of the General Bank, 1683—*and ſeveral other Tracts*

396 A Collection of Speeches in Parliament in 1641

397 Harris's Deſcription of Loo, 1699—Manwaring's Stichology, 1737—Motives for the Enlargement and Freedom of Trade, 1645—Hiſtory of the Charitable Corporation, 1732—The Cauſes of our Naval Miſcarriages, 1707—Narrative of the Sorceries exerciſed by the *Devil and his Inſtruments* upon Mrs. Chriſtian Shaw, 1698—An exact Relation of the taking of the Saint Eſprit with 54 Pieces of Great Ordinance, 1627

398 Chalmers's Eſtimate of the Comparative Strength of Britain, 1782——Catalogue Raiſonneé d'un Recueil d'Eſtampes, de M. I. Boydell —— 1779

399 A Short Narrative of a Diſcovery of the Jeſuites College, at Come, in Herefordſhire, 1679—Trial of Father Lewis, pretended Biſhop of Landaff, 1679—Narrative of Eliz. Middleton, who was ſtruck Blind, 1679—Tryals of Five Notorious Jeſuites, 1679—Accompt of the Bloody Maſſacre in Ireland, 1642—The Chriſtian Champion, by Col. Walker, *portrait*, 1689

400 Articles for Governing her Majeſties Forces in the Low Countries, 1702—Relation of his Majeſties Succeſſes in Scotland, 1644—Polemo-Middenia à G. Drummondo and Chriſtes Kirk on the Green, publiſhed by Bp. Gibſon ——— *Ox.* 1691

401 A Profitable Booke, declaring approoved remedies to take out Spots and Staines in Silkes, Velvets, &c. 1605—A Proper Treatiſe of the Art of Limning, *bl. letter*, 1605—A Briefe Deſcription of Hieruſalem and its Suburbs, by T. Tymme, 1595—The Arte of Shooting Great Ordnaunce, by W. Bourne, *bl. letter*, 1587—George Silver his Paradoxes of Defence, *wants title*

C 402 Wonderful

402 Wonderful Relations and Views beyond Death, 1787—Parkyns's Cornish Hugg Wrestler, 1713—Eldridge's Book of Rarities, 1743—Ld. Howard's Travels in Germany, &c. by Crowne — 1637

403 *Dæmonologie* by K. James, 1603—Roberts's Treatise of Witchcraft, discovering the *Wickednesse of that Damnable Art*, 1616—Cotta's Trial of Witchcraft 1616

404 *A Declaration of the egregious Popish Impostures to withdraw the Harts of her Majesties Subjects, under Pretence of casting out Devils*, by Bp. Harsnet — 1603

N. B. This is the Book referred to in King Lear; see Warburton's Note to Act IV. Scene I.

405 A Detection of that *sinnful, shameful, and ridiculous Discours of* Samuel Harshnet, entituled, a Discoverie the fraudulent Practise of John Darrell — 1600

406 Last Will and Testament of H. Wickham alias Morrel, being a full Relation of his Cheats and Impostures, 1692—Five Tracts upon Richard Dugdale, the Surrey Demoniack, *with his portrait* — 1698

407 The Wonderfull Discoverie of Eliz. Sawyer, a Witch, late of Edmonton, her Conviction, Condemnation, and Death, *with her portrait* — 1611

408 A True Relation of the Horrid Ghost of a Woman, which hath frequently been seen in various Habits, at the Three Mariners in Deptford, 1673—The Lords call to England, shewing the wonderfull Judgments and Handy Works of God, by Lightening, Whirlwinds, &c. — — 1660

409 Narrative of the Sorceries and Witchcrafts *exercised by the Devil and his Instruments*, upon Mrs. Christian Shaw, of Renfrew, 1698—A Collection of Modern Relations of Witches and Witchcraft, 1693—*Lithobolia* or, the Stone Throwing Devil, 1698——Mather's Trials of the Witches in New England—Mather's Cases of Conscience concerning Witchcrafts 1693

410 *A Manuscript containing Astrological Calculations*

411 *Mirabilis Annus*, the Year of Prodigies and Wonders, *with cuts* — — 1661—2

412 Lilly's *Merlinus Anglicus Junior*, the English Merlin Revived, *with several other tracts by Lilly* 1644

413 The Spanish Mandeville of Myracles, or *a Garden of curious Flowers* — 1618

414 Peacham's Complete Gentleman — 1661

415 Brown's Vulgar Errors — — 1672

416 Ascham's Works, published by Bennet

417 Withall's Detection of Public Frauds and Mismanagements 1717

418 The

418 The Copper Plate Magazine, *fine impressions, boards, uncut* 1778
419 Warton's History of Poetry, vol. 3 —— 1781
420 Berrington's History of Abelard and Heloise 1788
421 The Voyage of the Wandering Knight, by Cartheny, 1670
422 Thomas of Reading, or the Sixe worthie Yeoman of the West, *bl. letter*, 1632—*The Bellman of London*, bringing to light most notorious Villanies, 1608—Theeves falling out, true Men come by their Goods, by R. Greene, 1615—The Academy of Love, 1641—The Arraignment of lewd, idle, froward, and unconstant Women, or the Vanity of them *chuse you whether*, by J. Swetnam, 1682—*Well met Gossip*, or, 'tis merry when Gossips meet, enlarged with *very merry Songs*, pleasant for Maids, Wives and Widows, and delightfull for all to read, *frontispiece* — 1675
423 Histoire de Huon de Bourdeaux —— 1679
424 The Most Famous History of Fryar Bacon
425 The Second Report of Doctor Faustus — 1680
426 The Benefit of F—t—g explained —— 1722
427 Ld. Winchelsea's Relation of the Eruption at Mount Ætna, 1669—The Bellman's Nightwalk, with *cant songs*, by Thomas Dekker, 1638—The Forest, a Collection of Histories by Fenton, *bl. letter*, 1576—The Blazon of Jealousie, 1615—The wonderfull Woorkman of the World, *bl. letter* — 1578
428 Barclay's Argenis, by Sir R. Le Grys —— 1629
429 Warner's Albions England, *imperf.*
430 Kelly's Works, *with portrait* —— 1778
431 The Counter Scuffle and Counter Rat — 1658
432 Sallust, translated by Alex. Barkeley, *bl. letter, wants title*, 1557—The History of Herodium, translated by N. Smyth, *bl. letter, imp.*
433 The Rape of the Infant, 1782—Great Britain's Nosegay, 1768—A Ramble from Newport to Cowes—Trial between Sir R. Worsley and Capt. Bisset, *with other tracts*
434 Peter Pindar's Poems —— 1786, &c.
435 Viator, a Poem, 1782—Wharfdale, a Poem 1782
436 Poems, *viz.* Cloacina—Johnson's Laurel—Netly Abbey—P. Pindar's Lyric Odes and Instructions for a Laureat—Amwell, *and other poems*
437 Fontenoy, by Dr. Strafford—Michel on Earthquakes—Simpson's Laws of Chance—Steele's Conic Sections—Price on Mercury
438 Harding's Shakspeare, 12 numbers, *large paper*
439 Racolti di Poesie, da T. Crudeli —— 1746

C 2 440 Cats's

440 Cats's Emblems —— *Gravenh.* 1632
441 Sir J. Mandeville's Travels —— 1704
442 Ld. Cook's Paſſage by Sea from Wexford to Kinſale, 1650 —The Travailes and Captivitie of William Davies, 1614
443 The Engliſh Spaniſh Pilgrim, a new Diſcovery of Popiſh Stratagems —— —— 1629
444 Voyages de Ferd. Mendez Pinto —— *Par.* 1628
445 Les Croniques et excellentz Faitz des Ducs, Princes, Barons, et Seigneurs de la noble Duche de Normandie, *en lettres gothiques* —— *Par.*
446 Orkneyinga Saga ſive Hiſtoria Orcadenſium *Hafn.* 1780
447 Rymbegla, ſive Rudimentum computi Ecclef. et Annalis Vet. Iſlandorum —— *ib.* 1780
448 Speculum Regale, cum interp. Danica et Latina *Soræ* 1768
449 Le Vite de Pittori, &c. Genoveſi da Soprani *Gen.* 1674
450 Geographia Claſſica —— 1747
451 Middleton, Germanæ quædam Antiq. eruditæ Monumenta *Lond.* 1745
452 Mortimer's Voyage from Teneriffe to Canton 1791
453 Paterſon's Journey to Caffraria, *coloured* — 1789
454 Phillip's Voyage to Botany Bay —— 1789
455 Ireland's Tour through Holland and France, 2 vol. *with plates in aquatinta, large paper* —— 1790

F O L I O.

456 Atlas Nouveau par Sanſon —— *Par.* 1692
457 Philips's New World of Words —— 1706
458 Cotgrave's French and Engliſh Dictionary, by Howell, 1673
459 Howell's Engliſh, French, Italian, and Spaniſh Dictionary,
460 Moreri's Dictionary —— 1694
461 Bayle's Dictionary, by Deſmaizeux, 5 vol. 1733
462 Cartes de Provinces des Pays Bas — *Par.* 1744
463 Les Frontieres de France et des Pays Bas *Par.* 1743
464 *Ceremoniale ad uſum Canonicorum S. Cruſis, Domus Pariſienſis,* MS. on vellum
465 Pet. Victorii Comment. Ariſtot. de Arte dicendi *Florent,* 1579
466 Heywood's Hierarchie of the Bleſſed Angels 1635
467 Camoens's Luſiad, by Fanſhaw —— 1655
468 Bacon's Natural Hiſtory —— 1670
469 Evelyn's Parallel of Antient Architecture — 1723
470 Scot's Diſcovery of Witchcraft —— 1665
471 Malton's Treatiſe on Perſpective —— 1776

472 Hanway's

472 Hanway's Propofal for County Naval Free Schools
473 Gambado's Academy for Grown Horfemen 1787
474 Echard's Ecclefiaftical Hiftory —— 1702
475 La Sainte Bible par Des Marets, 2 tom. *Amft. ap Elz.* 1669
476 Turner's Hiftory of Remarkable Providences 1697
477 Nobilitas Doniæ ex Monumentis Curante T. de Klerenfeld
478 Atlas Portatif par Martiniere —— *Amft.* 1734
479 Croniques de Froiffart, 4 tom. en 1. *Par. Galliot.* 1530
480 Liber Cronicarum Norimbergiæ impreffus, *cum figuris*, 1497
481 Academie des Sciences et des Arts, par Bullart, 2 tom. *avec fig.* —— —— 1682
482 Moryfon's Itinerary —— 1617
483 Jofephus's Works, by Dandilly —— 1701
484 Hiftoire de Saint Louis, par Jehan Sire de Joinville *Par.* 1761
485 Speers's Weft India Pilot —— 1766
486 Barbut's Genera Vermium, part II. *large paper*, *coloured*
487 Hayes's Natural Hiftory of Birds, *part coloured* 1775

END OF SECOND DAY'S SALE.

THIRD

487

THIRD DAY's SALE.

WEDNESDAY, JUNE the 22d, 1791.

OCTAVO & INFRA.

488 SHAKSPEARE's Works, by Rowe, 7 vol. 1709
489 Grey's Notes upon Shakfpeare, 2 vol. 1754
490 Fifher's Poems, *Dumfries*, 1790—Lapraik's Poems, *Kilmarnock*, 1788
491 The Battle of Floddon, *with MS. additions* 1774
492 Blacklock's Poems —— —— 1754
493 Cunningham's Poems —— 1766
494 Wild's *Iter Boreale*, and other Poems —— 1671
495 Le Terrible Vie de Robert le Diable—Foundling Hofpital for Wit —— —— 1769
496 Pecke's *Parnafi Puerperium*, in Six Hundred Epigrams 1659
497 Ramfay's Evergreen, a Collection of Poems, 2 vol. 1761
498 *A Crew of kind London Goffips all met to be merry*, with ingenious Poems of Wit and Drollery — 1663
499 Shirley's (James) Poems —— 1646
500 The Death Song of Ladbroc, by Johnfon 1782
501 Ancient and Modern Scottifh Ballads, 2 vol. *Edinb.* 1776
502 The Frifky Songfter — —— 1770
503 Widow of the Wood —— 1755
504 The Repofitory, a Collection of Poems, 4 vol. 1777
505 The Praife of Yorkfhire Ale, with a Dialogue in the Yorkfhire Dialect — —— 1697
506 *A Collection of ancient Poems, Songs, Epigrams, Effays, and Letters*, MS.
507 Gibfon's Pocket Atlas —— 1758
508 Annual Regifter, 1779 & 1780, 2 vol.

509 New

509 New Annual Regifter — 1780
510 St. John's Letters of an American Farmer 1782
511 Jardine's Travels in Barbary, Spain, &c. 2 vol. 1788
512 Vantroil's Letters on Iceland — 1789
513 Dutens's Travels through Europe — 1782
514 Voyage to the Ifland of Mauritius — 1775
515 Prenties's Narrative of his Shipwreck — 1782
516 Travels of a Gentleman from London to Rome on Foot 1704
517 Hiftory of the Cardinals — 1653
518 The Netherlands Hiftorian — 1675
519 An Excurfion to Normandy, 1774—Tour in Italy, 1769 —Defcription of Eaft Bourne — 1787
520 Greaves's Origin of Weights and Meafures 1745
521 Trufler's Chronology — 1776
522 Linguet's Memoirs of the Baftille — 1783
523 Laffels's Voyage to Italy, 2 vol. — 1670
524 Sentimental Journey through Spain, 2 vol. 1786
525 Life of Hyder Ally, with Anecdotes of Tippoo Saib, by Robfon — — 1786
526 Juftamond's Private Life of Louis XV. 4 vol. 1781
527 Tacitus's Life of Agricola, by Aikin — 1774
528 Kennet's Antiquities of Rome — 1708
529 Parliamentary and Conftitutional Hiftory of England, by Drake, 24 vol. — 1751
530 Granger's Biographical Hiftory of England, 4 vol. 1775
531 Annals of Queen Anne, 7 vol.
532 The True State of England — 1729
533 Memoirs of the Reign of Q. Eliz. and K. James 1658
534 Hiftory of the Rebellion of Wat Tyler in 1381
535 *Mercurius Rufticus*, The Countries Complaint of the Sectaries — — 1685
536 Welwood's Memoirs of Englifh Tranfactions 1718
537 Broughton's Ancient, Holy, and Religious State of Britain — — 1650
538 Staveley's Hiftory of the Churches in England 1773
539 Tanner's Notitia Monaftica — 1695
540 Moore's Lift of the Religious Houfes in England and Wales — — 1786
541 The Britifh Chronologift, 3 vol. — 1775
542 Brand's Popular Antiquities — 1777
543 Nichols's Biographical Anecdotes of Hogarth 1782
544 Lives of Lilly and Afhmole, and K. Charles I. 1774
545 *Manufcripts on Hiftorical and other Subjects*, 2 vol.
546 Gov. Morris's Narrative of his Conduct at St. Vincent's 1787

547 Sheb-

547 Shebbeare's Third Letter to the People of England, 1756 —Case of Adm. Byng—Simpson's Trigonometry, 1748—*and other Tracts*
548 Beatson's Political Index —— 1786
549 Brady's Treatise on Burghs —— 1777
550 Fielding's Penal Law —— 1769
551 Gilbert's Law of Evidence —— 1777
552 Salmon's Peerage of Scotland —— 1759
553 The English Compendium, 3 vol. — 1753
554 Arms of the English Baronets
555 Seventeen Maps of the Counties of England, on Canvas and in Cases
556 Senex's Roads of England——Blome's Maps of the Counties
557 Dury's Universal Atlas
558 Large Map of Europe in a Case
559 Large Map of Normandy in a Case
560 Patterson's Roads and Travelling Dictionary 1781
561 Leland's *Collectanea*, published by Hearne, 6 vol. *large paper* —— —— 1715
562 —— Itinerary, by Hearne, 9 vol. in 3, *l. p.* 1769
563 Symonis Simeonis & W. de Worcestre Itineraria, curâ Nasmith, *ch. max.* —— 1778
564 Verstegan's Antiquities of the English Nation 1673
565 Camden's Remains concerning Britain —— 1674
566 Camdeni Britannia —— *Lond.* 1586
567 England's Gazetteer, by Whatley, 3 vol. 1751
568 A Description of England and Wales, 10 vol. *cuts* 1769
569 Tour through Great Britain, 4 vol. —— 1778
570 Remarks on London by a Company of Parish Clerks 1732
571 Statutes of the Sewers for Westminster —— 1776
572 The Norfolk Tour —— —— 1773
573 History of Guildford—Discourse on the Bookland and Folkland of the Saxons, 1775——Antiquity of Touching for the King's Evil, 1722——Narrative of the Stockwell Ghost——Tour through the Midland Counties —— —— 1775
574 History and Antiquities of Winchester, 2 vol. 1773
575 Antiquities of Tewksbury Church —— 1787
576 Description of East Bourne —— 1787
577 Salisbury Guide—the Antiquities of Old and New Sarum 1782
578 Kirby's Suffolk Traveller —— 1735
579 Another Copy —— —— 1764
580 Description of Bury, St. Edmund's, Suffolk 1782
581 Antiquities of Arundel in Sussex —— 1766

582 Gostling's

582 Goftling's Walk about Canterbury, *cuts* —— 1777
583 Hiftory and Antiquities of Rochefter —— 1772
584 Weft's Guide to the Lakes of Cumberland, &c. 1780
585 Defcription of Winchefter——Hiftory of the Town and Caftle of Knarefborough——Southampton Guide—Defcription of Stonehenge and Abury
586 Tour to the North of England, 1787——Defcription of the Tower of London —— 1782
587 Dawkes's Memoirs of the Willingham Boy——Sketch of a Tour in Derbyfhire and Yorkfhire 1778
588 Sturch's View of the Ifle of Wight —— 1778
589 Parker's View of Manners in England, Ireland, Scotland, Wales, France, &c. 2 vol. —— 1781
590 Powell's Hiftory of Wales, by Wynne —— 1697
591 Another Copy —— —— 1774
592 A Month's Tour in Dublin, North Wales, &c. 1781
593 Taylor and Skinner's Roads of Scotland —— 1776
594 Defoe's Journey through Scotland —— 1723
595 Memoirs concerning the Affairs of Scotland 1714
596 Commentarii de Rebus geftis Caroli I. fub Imperio Jacobi Montrofarum March. *ch. max.* *Par.* 1648
597 Defcription of the Town of Kelfo *Kelfo,* 1789
598 Lindfay's (of Pe:fcotie) Hiftory of Scotland 1778
599 Douglas's Defcription of the Eaft Coaft of Scotland *Paifley,* 1782
600 Sir Tho. Urquhart's Tracts —— *Edinb.* 1774
601 Forbes's Treatife on Church Lands and Tithes *ib.* 1705
602 Bp. Nicolfon's Border Laws —— 1747
603 A Comprehenfive Hiftory of Scotland —— 1790
604 *Scotiæ Indiculum,* the Prefent State of Scotland 1682
605 Kencaid's Hiftory of Edinburgh —— 1787
606 Monnipennie's Abridgment of the Scots Chronicle 1662
607 Scotiæ & Hiberniæ Defcriptio — *L. Bat.* 1627
608 Hiftorical Account of the Blue Blanket, or Craftfman's Banner —— —— 1780
609 Vallancy's Vindic. of the Anc. Hiftory of Ireland 1786
610 Harris's Hiftory of the Irifh Rebellion in 1641 1767
611 Harris's Hiftory of the County of Down 1744
612 Harris's *Hibernica,* Ancient Pieces relating to Ireland 1770
613 Smith's Hift. of Cork, Kerry, and Waterford, 4 vol. 1774
614 Wynne's Hiftory of Ireland, 2 vol. —— 1772
615 *Monafticon Hibernicum,* the Monaft. Hift. of Ireland 1722
616 Waræi Antiquitates Hibernicæ —— *Lond.* 1654
617 Vallancy's Collectanea de Rebus Hibernicis, pt. 4 *Dub.* 1784
618 Ld. Sheffield on the Trade and Pref. State of Ireland 1785

D QUARTO.

QUARTO.

619 Wyndham's Tour in Monmouthshire and Wales, *cuts* 1781
620 Pennant's Tour in Wales, 2 vol. —— 1781
621 A Short Account of the Ancient Britons 1716
622 Pennant's Tour in Scotland, pt. II, *no cuts*
623 Ridpath's Border History of England and Scotland 1776
624 Shaw's History of the Province of Moray 1775
625 Major, de Gestis Scotorum —— *Par.* 1521
626 Cordiner's Antiquities and Scenery in Scotland, *wants title*
627 ——— Remarkable Ruins in Scotland, No. 1, to 15, except No. 3
628 Grose's Antiquities of Scotland, 2 vol. *large paper, proof impressions* —— —— 1789
629 Canons of the Church of Scotland, 1769——Douglas on the Brass Instruments called Celts, 1785——Will of King Henry VII. published by Mr. Astle, 1775—Vallancy's Memoir of the Anglo-Saxon Colony at Wexford——Vallancy's Description of a Monument in the Church of Lusk——Some Account of the Church of St. Neot's, Cornwall 1786
630 Warner's History of the Civil War in Ireland 1767
631 Boate and Molyneaux's History of Ireland 1726
632 *Britannia Sancta*, Lives of the British, English, Scotch, and Irish Saints —— —— 1745
633 Wright's *Louthiana*, Antiquities of the County of Louth 1748
634 Rowland's *Mona Antiqua*, Antiquities of the Isle of Anglesey —— —— 1766
635 Vicars's Parliamentary Chronicle —— 1644
636 Heylin's History of St. George —— 1631
637 Godwin's Catalogue of English Bishops —— 1601
638 *Naunton's Fragmenta Regalia*, MS.
639 Truth brought to Light, History of the First Fourteen Years of K. James —— 1651
640 Strutt's Chronicle of England, 2 vol. —— 1777
641 Annales d'Angleterre sous les Regnes de Henry VIII. Edw. VI. & Marie —— *Par.* 1647
642 Tovey's History of the Jews in England — 1738
643 Sir J. Fenn's Letters of the Paston Family, 2 vol. 1787
644 Life of Ld. Herbert of Cherbury —— 1778
645 Peck's Memoirs of O. Cromwell —— 1740
646 Antiquarian Repertory, 4 vol. —— 1780
647 Liber Quotidianus Contrarotulatoris Garderobæ, Anno Regni Regis Edw. I. vicesimo octavo 1787

648 A

648 A Collection of Ordinances and Regulations for the Government of the Royal Household, from K. Edw. III. to K. Will. III. —— —— 1790
649 Pegge's *Curilia*, Hist. of the Esquires of the King's Body, Gentlemen of the King's Privy-Chamber, and of the Band of Gentlemen Pensioners 1782—4
650 *Archæologia*, Tracts published by the Society of Antiquaries, vol. 5, 6, 7, 8, 9
651 Ducarel's Letter to Watson, on the early Cultivation of Botany in England, 1773——Fitzstephen's Description of London, 1772——Webbe's Account of Domesday Book, 1756——Sir J. Hawkins on the Armorial Ensigns of Middlesex and Westminster, 1780——Williams's Letters from the Highlands, 1777——The Siege of Karlaverok in Scotland
652 Direction for the English Traveller —— 1643
653 Camden's Remains concerning Britain —— 1653
654 Gough's British Topography, 2 vol. in *Russia leather* 1780
655 Pennant's Description of London —— 1790
656 Another Copy, *large paper* —— 1790
657 Wallis's History of Northumberland, 2 vol. in 1 1769
659 Peshall's History of the City of Oxford —— 1773
660 Deering's History of Nottingham —— 1751
661 Boys's Collections for the History of Sandwich 1788
662 Worsley's History of the Isle of Wight — 1781
663 Collections for the History of Bedfordshire 1783
664 Brand's History of Newcastle upon Tyne, 2 vol. 1789
665 Darell's History of Dover Castle, by *Capt. Grose* 1786
666 King's Observations on Ancient Castles —— 1782
667 Magna Britannia, 6 vol. *boards, uncut* —— 1720
668 Grose's Antiquities of England and Wales, 8 vol. 1787
669 Another Copy, 8 vol. *large paper* —— 1787
670 The Antiquarian Repertory, 4 vol. —— 1780
674 Ld. Somers's Tracts, 4 vol. —— 1748
675 Ditto, Third Collection, 1, 2, 4 —— 1751
676 Ditto, First Collection, vol. 1, 3, 4, and Fourth Collection, vol. 1
677 Strutt's View of the Ancient Manners and Customs, vol. 3 —— —— 1776
678 Antiquarian Repertory, Eighteen odd Numbers
679 Molison's Reports of the Commis. of Acc. vol. 1 1783

FOLIO.

F O L I O.

680 Borlase's History of the Irish Rebellion —— 1680
681 Ware's Antiquities and History of Ireland — 1705
682 Ware's History of the Irish Bishops, *large paper* 1739
683 Spotiswoode's History of the Church and State of Scotland 1677
684 Maitland's Antiquities of Scotland, 2 vol. — 1757
685 Keith's History of Scotland —— 1734
686 Fordun Scotichronicon Boweri, 2 vol. —— 1775
687 Howell on the Precedency of Kings, *large paper* 1664
688 Oliverii (Protectoris) nec non Olivæ Paralellum, *cum fig. à G. Faithorne* —— *Lond.* 1656
689 Rymeri Fœdera, vol. 2, 5, 12, 13, 14, 15, 16, 17
690 Churchill's *Divi Britannici*, Remarks on the Lives of the Kings of England —— 1675
691 Collier's Ecclesiastical History of Great Britain, 2 vol. 1708
692 *Arms of the Livery Companies of London, drawn, with a* MS. *account of each*
693 *Arms of the Nobility and Gentry in the Deanaries of Bristol, Hawksbury, Fairford, Cirencester, the Forest, Stonehouse, Whinchcombe,* &c. *emblazoned*
694 Sandford's Genealogical History, *Hollar's cuts* 1677
695 Tanner's Notitia Monastica —— 1744
696 Darell's History of Dover Castle, by Capt. Grose, *large paper* —— —— 1786
697 Burton's Description of Leicestershire —— 1777
698 Morant's Hist. of Colchester, *with large MS. additions,* 1748
699 Borlase's Antiquities of Cornwall, *stained* — 1769
700 Hasted's History of Kent, 4 vol. *interleaved, with additional plates* —— 1782
701 Blomfield's History of Norfolk, vol. 1 —— 1739
702 Cotton's Abridgment of the Records in the Tower 1679
703 An Account of the Manors, Tenements, &c. in England and Wales, held by Lease from the Crown 1787
704 Rolls of Parliament, 6 vol.
705 Journals of the House of Commons, 32 vol.
706 Camden's Britannia, by Gough, 3 vol. —— 1789
707 Gough's Sepulchral Monuments in Great Britain 1788
708 Seventy-four Humorous Prints, *half bound*
709 Sixty ditto ditto
710 Bunbury's Works ditto

END OF THE BOOKS.

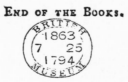

A CATA-

A

CATALOGUE

OF THE

Prints, Drawings, *&c.*

OF THE LATE

F. GROSE, Esq.

A

Catalogue *of* Prints, &c.

FOURTH DAY's SALE.

THURSDAY, JUNE the 23d, 1791.

	Lot	
1-6	1	A PARCEL of maps
2-6	2	Ditto
4-6	3	Ditto of views Fores — 2 of the Castle of Otranto.
15-6	4	Ditto miscellaneous prints Ditto
2-3	5	Sketches and plans Do.
4-0	6	18 Miscellaneous prints
6-0	7	34 Ancient inscriptions, monuments, &c.—prints
10-0	8	54 Ancient buildings—prints
6-0	9	30 Prints of ancient buildings in England and Wales
1-6	10	14 Etchings, characters
4-9	11	16 Prints, characters Fores

A 2 DRAW-

DRAWINGS.

	Lot		
3-3	12	A parcel of miſcellaneous	
4-6	13	Ditto	
7-6	14	Miſcellaneous views, by M. Griffiths, &c.	
14-0	15	50 Sketches in Kent	
6-0	16	40 Views of ancient buildings	
8-0	17	30 Miſcellaneous views in England	
4-9	18	30 Ditto	
7-0	19	20 Views and ancient buildings in Kent	
3-0	20	A Collection of headlands	
16-6	21	12 Views in and near Richmond, Surry, by Hekell×	Sumner
6-0	22	12 Views and ancient buildings in France	
8-0	23	12 Views and ancient buildings in Northampton and Suffolk	Stover
6-0	24	6 Ancient buildings, Northumberland	

PRINTS.

4-0	25	32 Views of ancient buildings, &c.	Thornton
2-0	26	15 Outlines, by Sandby, &c.	
5-0	27	9 Etchings of ruins	
3-0	28	8 By De la Bella	
1-6	29	9 Etchings, by Ferg	
3-0	30	11 Ditto by Weirotter, &c.	
3-9	31	4 Smith's views of the lakes	
4-0	32	23 Etchings of battles, by Baur	Smith
4-6	33	18 Ditto, by Sandby, outlines	
7-0	34	26 Views in Germany, &c. by Holler	
11-6	35	11 Views of London and Iſlington, by Holler	
12-6	36	9 Portraits of F. Groſe, &c.	Sumner

DRAW-

×21. Old Palace at Richmond Green.

DRAWINGS.

	Lot		
4-0	37	12 Views and ancient buildings in Wales	
8-0	38	10 Views and ancient buildings in Kent and Wales	
8-6	39	12 Views of Dover, &c.	Dickenson
6-6	40	10 Ditto, and ancient buildings, Kent and Surry	Storer
4-6	41	10 Ditto, in Surry	
8-0	42	10 Ditto, in Suffolk, &c.	Dickenson
12-6	43	6 Ancient buildings, Scotland	
9-0	44	6 Views, Bath, Briſtol, &c. by Lens	Chapman
W. 6-0	45	10 Views on the Thames, by Hekell	Walpole
4-9	46	12 Views and ancient buildings, Suffolk and Surry	
4-0	47	12 Ditto, Glouceſterſhire, &c.	
3-0	48	10 Ditto, Kent and Northumberland	
6-0	49	8 Ditto, Scotland	Dickenson
16-6	50	6 Ditto, England and Scotland	Ditto
9-6	51	10 Ditto, Ditto	D^o
8-0	52	10 Ditto, Northumberland	Storer
3-0	53	10 Ditto, Scotland	
5-0	54	12 Views and ancient buildings, Wales, Shropſhire and Suffolk	
2-3	55	8 Ditto, Cumberland and Scotland	Clark, Bond Street
6-6	56	6 Ditto and ancient buildings, Kent and Surry	Smith
6-6	57	4 Ditto, Kent and Yorkſhire	
6-0	58	8 Ditto, Northumberland, &c.	
6-0	59	6 Ditto, St. Michael's Mount, Cornwall	
3-6	60	6 Ditto, Cornwall and Kent	
1-5-0	61	6 Ditto, Wales	
9-9	62	8 Ditto in Ireland, &c. after T. Nixon, by T. C.	Dickenson
4-3	63	4 Views and ancient buildings, Suffolk and Surry	
7-6	64	4 Views on the Thames, by Hekell	Storer ×
9-6	65	4 Views and ancient buildings, Hertfordſhire, &c.	Dickenson
4-0	66	6 Ditto, Derbyſhire, &c.	
	67	6 Views	

×64 Two Views of Lord Harrington's at Petersham

Lot

4-3 67 6 Ditto, England and Scotland Hooper

3-6 68 4 Ditto, Market-place at Jersey, &c.

6-6 69 4 Ditto, England and Scotland Dickenson

8-6 70 4 Ditto, Ditto Ditto

3-3 71 6 Ditto, Scotland Do

9-0 72 4 Views in Surry, &c.

4-3 73 3 Ancient buildings, Suffolk, &c. Clark, B. S.

11-6 74 3-6 Views and ancient buildings, ~~Wales and the Isle of Man~~ Hyde Abbey, &c. Hooper

7-6 75 4 Views in Normandy, &c.

6-0 76 2 Arches in the Wall, Canterbury, and Walton Street, Suffolk

4-0 77 2 Views of the Citadel, Plymouth, and Guildford-bridge, Surry

8-0 78 2 The Friary, Canterbury, and St. Germain's church, Peele castle, Isle of Man

10-0 79 3 St. Trinion's church, Isle of Man, Chapel of Notre Dame des Pas, Jersey, and Plashy castle, Essex Hooper

6-6 80 2 Croydon palace, Surry, and Rochester castle, Kent Ditto

8-6 81 2 Croydon church

19-0 82 2 The old church, St. Edmunds Bury, Suffolk, and Catharine-hill, Guildford, Surry Hooper

9-0 83 4 Village of Glenman, Ireland. Tinwall hill and village, Isle of Man. Windmill, near Vaux-hall, and Entrance into Godalmin, Surry Molteno

4-3 84 2 Views near Beddington, Surry, and view near Arwington hall, Suffolk Clark, B. S.

12-0 85 Haling, near Croydon, and inside of the Fox and Hounds, Surry Thane

17-6 86 2 Landguard fort, Suffolk Clark, B. S.

7-6 87 2 Cambridge castle, and keep of Corfe castle, Dorsetsh. Torres

18-0 88 2 St. Botolph's priory, Essex, and Billockby church, Norfolk Sumner

89 4 Gate

Lot

1-2-0 89 4 Gate of Portchester castle, Hants. and 3 views in Surry and Suffolk Clark, B. S.

15-6 90 4 Lanercost priory, Cumberland—Kenelworth priory, Warwickshire—Black Friars, Hereford—and view at St. Asaph

7-0 91 3 Views at Richmond, by Hekell Fores

5-0 92 4 Kenelworth priory, and 3

7-6 93 2 Peele bridge, Isle of Man, and view of the Scowls in Gloucestershire Molteno

7-6 94 4 Little Dunmow church, Essex—Citadel, Plymouth — Tintern, Monmouthshire — and Barfreston church, Kent

11-6 95 2 Views of Framlingham castle, Suffolk Sheldon

8-6 96 2 Chester castle and Warkworth castle, Northumberland Hooper

PRINTS.

8-0 97 Miscellaneous antiquities, published by the Antiquarian Society

12-6 98 Ditto

6-0 99 3 Ditto, viz. the Departure of King Henry VII. from Calais—the Siege of Boulogne—and the Encampment at Marquison Molteno

5-0 100 Vertue's eight sheet map of London

12-6 101 A collection of inscriptions and figures from brass plates Sumner

11-0 102 13 Surveys in the Islands of Jersey and Guernsey, drawn by Mead

9-6 103 2 Portraits of F. Grose and Theophilus Forrest, Esq; Thane

8-0 104 50 Etchings of the Antiquities of Scotland

11-0 105 50 Antiquities of Scotland—proofs Hooper

12-0 106 40 Ditto Ditto

DRAW-

16:6 *99 Procession of Edward 6th

DRAWINGS.

	Lot		
10-6	107		A parcel of miſcellaneous antiquities Simco
6-0	108		Ditto. Ancient Bottle at Strawberry. Ditto
4-6	109	25	of Ancient Armour and Weapons D°
12-0	110	23	Indian Idols, &c. Sumner
11-0	111	3	Books containing miſcellaneous ſketches
7-6	112	2	Eccleſia Militantis Triumphi, and Le Brun's Paſſions—folio
13-0	113	2	Books containing a number of miſcellaneous prints
5-6	114	1 ~~2~~	Book~~s~~ of ditto Molteno
12-6	115	3	Port-folios, interleaved
6-6	116	2	Ditto Blue Paper
	117	1	Ditto
	118	8	Port-folios
	119	5	Ditto
	120	2	Ditto
	121	4	Ditto
	122	6	Ditto
	123	6	Ditto
	124	3	Port-folio's, interleaved
	125	2	Ditto
47:0:0			

END of FOURTH DAY'S SALE.

FIFTH DAY's SALE.

FRIDAY, JUNE the 24th, 1791.

PRINTS.

Lot

1 A PARCEL of miscellaneous views and plans

2 Ditto plans of cities, &c.

3 25 Humorous

4 2 Battles

5 A parcel of miscellaneous views

6 25 Views in Hants

DRAWINGS.

7 92 Perrier's Statues,

8 50 Views in Surry

9 50 Ditto, Kent

10 30 Ditto, Middlesex and Sussex

11 30 Ditto, by F. G. and others

12 30 Miscellaneous views

13 21 Foreign views by Hekell, &c.

14 8 Views and ancient buildings, by Grim, &c.

15 14 Ditto, Cornwall, Essex, and Hampshire

16 18 Views in Surry

B 17 7 Views

Lot

2-6 17 7 Views of churches in Norfolk, by Beck
2-9 18 12 Views and ancient buildings, Kent and Suffex
3-0 19 8 Ditto, Kent
4-6 20 10 Ditto, Surry and Suffex
3-6 21* 25 Of ancient armour and weapens Simco
x 4-6 22* A parcel of mifcellaneous antiquities Ditto

PRINTS.

17-0 23* 50 Antiquities of Scotland, proofs Hooper
18-0 24* 50 Ditto ditto Do
1-4-0 25* 75 Ditto, England and Wales Do
1-5-0 26* 75 Ditto Do
8-6 27* 2 Portraits of F. Grofe and T. Foreft, Efq.

DRAWINGS.

3-9 28* 8 Views and ancient buildings, England and Scotland, by I. B.
2-6 29* 11 Ditto, Scotland
3-0 30* 10 Ditto ditto Hooper
4-6 21 12 Ditto, Shropfhire and Wales, by Grim, &c.
6-0 22 6 Ditto, Suffolk and Surry
4-6 23 8 Ditto, Kent
3-9 24 8 Ditto, mifcellaneous, by Grim, &c. Hooper
6-0 25 10 Ditto, Surry Thane
7-6 26 10 Views in Surry Do
1-9 27 12 Ditto in Cambridgefhire, Dorfetfhire, and Ifle of Wight
W. 7-6 28 6 Views of Richmond, by Hekell, &c. Walpole
3-0 29 17 Views in Surry Thane
3-0 30 12 Views and ancient buildings
11-6 31 7 Ditto, Wales and the Ifle of Man Hooper
18-6 32 6 Ditto ditto

33 8 Views

x22. A Drawing of part of the Armory at Straw.b.
24. Ancient Richmond Castle

	Lot		
2-6	33	8	Views and ancient buildings, England and Scotland Hooper
4-0	34	15	Ditto, Scotland Ditto
2-9	35	12	Ditto, Cornwall and Suffolk Clark, B. S.
5-6	36	10	Views and ancient buildings, Durham, Scotland, &c.
11-0	37	8	Ditto, Surry and Northumberland
1-3	38	10	Ditto, Hampshire, &c.
4-3	39	4	Ditto, London and Middlesex Smith
2-6	40	6	Ditto, Surry and Kent Simes
7-6	40*	5	Ditto, Scotland Hooper
1-6	41	9	Ditto, Middlesex and Northumberland Smith
3-9	42	6	Ditto, Suffolk and Wales
1-9	43	4	Views in Yorkshire
2-0	44	4	Views and ancient buildings in Durham and Northumberland
6-0	45	8	Views in Ireland and Scotland, after Nixon, by T. C. Hooper
4-0	46	4	Ditto in Surry Thane
2-9	47	5	Views and ancient buildings, Northumberland, &c. Smith
3-9	48	6	Foreign views, by Capt. D. G.
2-6	49	7	Views of encampments, &c. Simes
5-6	50	8	Views and ancient buildings, Cumberland, Surry, and Scotland
1-9	51	4	Ditto, Scotland and Ireland
2-6	52	6	Ditto, England and Scotland Simes
4-0	53	4	Ditto, Wales and Scotland Hooper
2-9	54	6	Views and ancient buildings, Scotland and Ireland Majr. Grose
1-5-0	55	5	Views of Landguard fort, Suffolk, and Kingston in Surry
15-0	56	3	Views of Guildford, by F. and D. G. Storer
8-6	57	2	Richmond Park and Kingston bridge
4-0	58	4	Views and ancient buildings, Surry and Kent Simes
10-6	59	6	Views of Richmond, &c. by Hekell Hooper
5-0	60	2	Black Friar's bridge, and Conway castle, Wales
1-3-0	61	2	Hampton Wick Green, Middlesex, and Shotley Ferry, Suffolk Hooper

B 2 62 10 Con-

Lot

62 10 Converſation pieces, by Skelton, &c.

63 4 St. Auguſtine's gate, Canterbury, Bothall caſtle, Northumberland, and two views in Surry

64 4 Views in Surry and Suffolk

65 3 Roquin caſtle, Ruins in the Vale caſtle, and caſtle Cornet, Guernſey

66 2 St. Winifred's well, Wales, and Ely-houſe, London

67 4 Views in Richmond Park

68 3 Caſtle Cornet, Guernſey, Dover Cliff, Kirkſtall abbey, Yorkſhire

69 6 Humorous ſubjects

70 5 Carliſle caſtle, Cumberland, Water Lock Bridge, Canterbury, and three views in Surry

71 3 Abbots barn, Beaulieu, Hants. Keep of Corfe caſtle, Dorſetſhire, St. Briavel's caſtle, Gouceſterſhire

72 2 Holyhead, and keep in Cardiff caſtle, Wales

73 2 Canterbury caſtle, and arches at Bury, St. Edmund's, Suffolk

74 2 Kenilworth priory, Warwickſhire, and Dudley priory, Worceſterſhire

75 4 Views in Richmond park

76 2 Market-place, Kingſton, and farm-houſe, near Croydon, Surry

77 2 Views of Harrow on the Hill

78 2 Eſkdale chapel, and Bolton hall, Yorkſhire

79 2 Cheſter bridge, and Weſt Gate, Canterbury

80 2 Market-place at Aldborough, and view of Walton, Suffolk

81 2 The Vale church, Guernſey, and Whitby abbey, Yorkſhire

82 3 St. Sampſon's church, and Marſh caſtle, Guernſey, Mayfield place, Suſſex

83 3 Farn-

Lot

10-0 83 3 Farnham caſtle, Surry, Cockermouth caſtle, Cumberland, Keep of Corfe caſtle, Dorſetſhire King

6-0 84 2 ~~3~~ View of Holyhead, Wales, and Warkworth caſtle, Northumberland

6-6 85 2 Views in Surry and Kent

8-0 86 3 The deanry, king's ſchool, and ſtrangers hall, Canterbury

1-0-0 87 2 Ham-houſe and Sutton-place, Surry Thane ×

12-6 88 2 Waterfall at Keſwick, Cumberland, and Pont-y-pridd, Wales

18-6 89 St. German's priory, Cornwall, by Payne

9-0 90 3 Shrewſbury caſtle, and 2. Caerphilly caſtle, by P. Sandby Jeffery

11-0 91 Canterbury Cathedral Hooper

16-6 92 2 Landguard fort, Suffolk, and Newark priory, Surry Clark, B. S.

10-6 93 2 Biſhops Palace, Wincheſter, and Tichfield houſe chapel, Hants. Hooper

9-0 94 2 View of Harwich, Eſſex, and Holyhead, N. Wales Ditto

7-0 95 Framlingham caſtle, Suffolk Clark, B. S.

11-0 96 2 Arches in the Wall, Canterbury, and Monnow gate and bridge Hooper

6-0 97 The baptiſty of Chriſt's church, Canterbury Do.

14-0 98 A winter piece

10-6 99 Ely houſe, London Hooper

11-0 100 Durham cathedral Do.

16-6 101 Market Place at Kingſton, &c. Thane

8-0 102 2 Rocheſter caſtle, and Dover caſtle, Kent Fores

7-0 103 Cheſter bridge Hooper

7-6 104 View of the caſtle of Tangier, by Capt. D. Groſe Do.

10-0 105 2 Caerphilly caſtle, Wales, and Rocheſter caſtle, Kent Hooper

6-6 106 2 Rocheſter caſtle, Kent, and Warkworth caſtle, Northumberland

14-0 107 St. Auguſtine's monaſtery, Canterbury, Kent

6-0 108 Conway caſtle, Wales Hooper

109 2 Books

	Lot		
1-12-0	109	2	Books containing a collection of ſtudies and tents, &c. &c. Fores
1-2-0	110		Len's views of Wokey hole, in ten deſigns
14-6	111		Hogarth's Tour, copied from the original of T. Forreſt
1-12-0	112		Genealogie de la Royale Maiſon de France, depuis a Roy Hugh Capet juſqu'au Roy Louis XIII. par La Soyer, Enlumineur ordinaire du Roy, fol. Simco
14-6	113	2	Original deſigns to the ſupplement of the ancient armour, with the letter-preſs, and rules for drawing caricaturas, &c. Hooper

Prints, and Books of Prints.

6-0	113*	3	Numbers of books of prints of ancient buildings Simco
5-6	114	2	Portraits of F. Groſe and T. Foreſt, Eſq. Hooper
1-2-0	115	50	Antiquities of Scotland, proofs Ditto
1-2-0	116	44	Ditto ditto Do
1-11-6	117	75	Antiquities of England
1-12-0	118	57	Ditto, proofs, &c. Hooper
19-0	119		An interleaved folio containing a number of etchings by Fra. Groſe, &c. Chamberlain
11-0	120		Ditto, plates of ancient armour and weapons Chapman
1-2-0	121	20	Views after C. Lorraine, by Earlaom, half bound
4-11-0	122		The Virtuoſi's Muſeum, 30 numbers, firſt impreſſions Hooper
17-6	122*		Cuts to Pennant's Tour in Scotland Chapman
	123	2	Port folios, interleaved
	124	2	Port folios with flaps
	125	3	Port folios
	126	3	Port folios
	127	2	Folio books, ruled
71-4-0			

END OF FIFTH DAY'S SALE.

3-10-0 *119 Grose's Antiq.s of Scotland 8o Hooper

SIXTH DAY's SALE.

SATURDAY, JUNE the 25th, 1791.

PRINTS.

Lot

1 A PARCEL of miscellaneous prints

2 Ditto

3 12 Ditto

4 11 Views—Cathedrals, &c.

5 15 Miscellaneous

6 6 Portraits

7 6 Ditto

8 A parcel of etchings, &c. of ancient buildings

9 50 Views and ditto

10 12 Kirby's churches and monuments

1* 75 Antiquities of England—proofs, &c.

2* 30 Miscellaneous

3* A parcel of etchings of ancient armour

4* 75 Antiquities of England—proofs, &c.

5* 50 Proofs, &c.—Antiquities of Scotland

6* 18 Historical drawings

DRAWINGS.

7* 50 Views and ancient buildings, Kent

8* 30 Ditto

9* A

Lot

9* A parcel of views of ancient buildings, by N. Bailey, &c.

10* 18 Miscellaneous views and ancient buildings

11 12 Views of Richmond, by Hekell

12 A parcel of drawings of natural history, by E. Hicks, &c.

13 23 Miscellaneous, by Planta, &c.

14 15 Views and ancient buildings, Sussex and Wilts

15 6 Views of ancient buildings, by Hekell, &c.

16 15 Miscellaneous antiquities

17 25 Ancient Armour and Weapons

18 15 Views and ancient buildings, Scotland, by M. G. &c.

19 20 Ditto, by M. G. &c.

20 25 Ancient Armour and Weapons

21 12 Views and ancient buildings, Sussex, &c.

22 10 Ditto, Durham, &c.

23 7 Ditto, Bedfordshire, &c.

24 7 Ditto, Kent, &c.

25 10 Ditto, Hants, &c.

26 8 Ditto, Kent and Sussex

27 13 Studies of Trees and 1

28 4 Historical, by Boitard, &c.

29 10 Views in Scotland, by T. C. &c.

30 10 Views and ancient buildings, by Sandby, &c.

31 16 Views in Surry

32 10 Ditto

33 15 Miscellaneous views and ancient buildings

34 20 Views of Belle Isle, by an engineer

35 9 Views and ancient buildings, Hants

36 9 Ditto, Northumberland and Wilts

37 10 Ditto, Kent and Gloucestershire

38 10 Ditto, England and Scotland

39 8 Ditto, ditto

40 10 Ancient buildings, Scotland

41 6 Views

Lot

41 6 Views in Ireland, after Nixon, by T. C:
42 7 Views and ancient buildings, Northumberland and Yorshire
43 10 Ditto, Scotland and Ireland
44 7 Ditto, Durham and Northumberland
45 12 Views and ancient buildings, Cornwall, &c.
46 8 Views of Gibralter and Port Mahon, &c. by D. G.
47 6 Views and ancient buildings, Cornwall and Suffolk
48 7 Ditto ditto and Wales
49 6 Ditto, Hampshire, &c.
50 10 Ditto, Isle of Man and Ireland

PRINTS.

51 11 Miscellaneous prints
52 10 ———— by Hogarth
53 2 Relief of Gibralter, &c.
54 2 Representation of the Mediator, Captain J. Luttrell
55 6 Views of Constantinople
56 5 Portraits of F. Grose and T. Forrest, by Bartolozzi &c.

DRAWINGS.

57 10 Views and ancient buildings, Yorkshire, &c.
58 3 Ditto, Dorsetshire and ditto
59 6 Ditto, Suffolk, &c.
60 6 Ditto, Hampshire, &c.
61 12 Ditto, by Bailey, &c.
62 5 Views in Middlesex
63 4 Views and ancient buildings, Shropshire, &c.
64 11 Humorous subjects
65 15 Ditto

	Lot		
11-0	66	6	Views and ancient buildings, Scotland Dickenson
4-6	67	6	Ditto, England and Scotlond Wilson
5-6	68	14	Landſcapes, by Cozen, &c. Do
17-0	69	13	Figures of market people, after
2-9	70	6	Views and ancient buildings, Scotland and Ireland
13-0	71	6	Ditto, Scotland Dickenson
2-6	72	4	Ditto, Scotland and Ireland Ditto
4-0	73	2	Landguard fort, Suffolk, and Colcheſter caſtle, Eſſex Lenard
6-0	74	4	Views and ancient buildings, Surry, &c. Dickenson
1-2-0	75	8	Ditto, Kent and Suſſex Ditto
17-6	76	5	Ditto, Cornwall and Kent
4-6	77	6	Ditto, ditto, &c.
13-6	78	2	Shotley Ferry, Suffolk, and Beacon Hill
1-1-0	79	2	Waddon court and mill, near Kingſton, Surry
16-0	80	3	Thirlwall caſtle, Northumberland, Canterbury cathedral, and Cheſter caſtle Wilson
13-0	81	3	Abbey bridge, near Douglas, and St. Patrick's church, Iſle of Man Ditto
12-0	82	2	Kirkſtall abbey, and Bolton caſtle, Yorkſhire
16-0	83	2	Weſt gate, Canterbury, great hall, Archbiſhop's palace Ditto
1-2-0	84	3	Arches in the wall, Canterbury, St. George's gate, ditto, Chiding Stone
15-0	85	3	Views in Surry and the Iſle of Man Fernside
1-12-0	86	2	Views of Sturry Mills Thane
14-6	87	2	Canterbury caſtle, Kent, and Shelbred priory, Suſſex Wilson
12-6	88	2	Cathedral, Hereford, and Ayſgarth bridge, Yorkſhire
10-6	89	3	Skirid vaur, Monmouthſhire, Marſh caſtle, Gernſey and Tinwald, Iſle of Man
18-6	90	2	Tower of London, and Orford church, Suffolk

91 2 Town

Lot

91 2 Town hall, Ipſwich, Holy Iſland monaſtery, Northumberland

92 2 Kenilworth caſtle, Warwickſhire, and Dudley priory, Worceſterſhire

93 2 The great hall, Caerphilly caſtle, and Ruſhen abbey, Iſle of Man

94 2 Norwich caſtle, and Bourne ponds, Eſſex

95 3 Hogs mill, Surry, and 2 Standlinch houſe, Wiltſhire

96 2 Views in Derbyſhire, by

97 3 Boyne, Glames, and Campbell caſtles, Scotland, by T. C.

98 2 All Saints church, Dunwich, and Colonel Hall's houſe, Cambridgſhire

99 3 Sturrey court, Kent, Pier at St. Hellier's, Jerſey, and Landguard fort, Suffolk

100 2 St. Peter's port, Guernſey, by Goſſelyn, and Richmond park, by Hekels

101 2 Whitby abbey, Yorkſhire, and Rocheſter caſtle, Kent

101* Original drawings of the Ancient Armour and Military Antiquities, not complete

102 2 Grange bridge, Cumberland, and Ockham mill, Surry

103 2 Cliff, near Bon church, Iſle of Wight, and Red Brook, on the Wye, Monmouthſhire

104 3 St. Patrick's church, Iſle of Man, Landguard fort, Suffolk, and Rocheſter caſtle, Kent

105 2 Chalk pit, at Green Hithe, Kent, and Blithborough priory, Suffolk

106 2 Buſbridge gardens, and Pains hill, Surry

107 2 Lake Blaney, Ireland, and Bon church, Iſle of Wight

Lot

11-6 108 2 Views of the lakes in Cumberland

1-0-6 109 2 Emblematical, by Gravelot Hooper

18-6 110 2 Tintern, Monmouthſhire, and chapter-houſe, Hereford Chamberlain

4-0 111 4 Views by P. Sandby, &c.

19-0 112 2 Upnor caſtle, Kent, and Caſtor caſtle, Norfolk

1-3-0 113 2 Hartford bridge, Northumberland, and Ruſhen abbey, Iſle of Man

18-6 114 2 Mr. Scullard's mill, Pend hill, and Tintern abbey, Monmouthſhire

1-4-0 115 2 Mitford caſtle and Hartford bridge, Northumberland

1-4-0 116 2 Conway church and town, and a view in Surry Eagles

19-0 117 2 Conway caſtle, Carnarvonſhire, and Mount Orgueil caſtle, Jerſey

2-2-0 118 2 Alnwick caſtle, Northumberland, and Landguard fort, Suffolk Forman

1-14-0 119 Guildford caſtle, Surry

18-6 120 Rademaker's Views in Holland, vol. 2 Chapman

1-8-0 121 A Collection of ſtudies, bound Ditto

5-7-6 122 A ditto, ditto Forman

6-0 123 A port folio, interleaved

4-3 124 Ditto

1-4-0 120^x 2 Views Hooper

6-0 121^x 5 Ditto Wilson

122^x 6 Ditto Hooper

F I N I S.

75-4-0 3d Day

71-4-0 2d Day

47-0-0 1st Day

193-8-0 Total

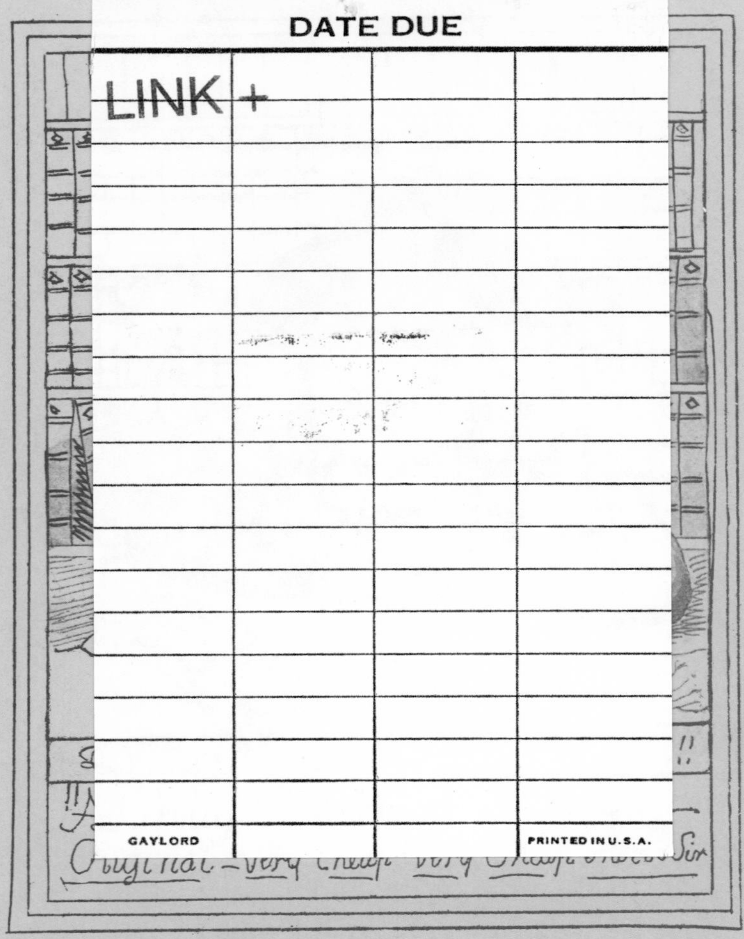

Isaac Gossett, D.D., F.R.S. (1744-1813), was for over thirty years a familiar figure in the London auction rooms, where he took his seat at the auctioneer's right hand, and gave a running commentary, critical and bibliographical, on the lots as they were offered. In the words of an unkind contemporary, 'from his ceaseless comments in favour of lots, one would have imagined that he was pensioned by the Auctioneer; in short, it appeared as if nature had moulded his tongue into the shape of A PRETTY COPY'.

Gossett, in his day, was an influential figure. He could claim Richard Heber as his *protégé,* and his judgment on bibliographical matters was sought after and deferred to by the trade, with whom he appears to have been a general favourite.

When Gossett fell
Leigh rang his knell
and Sotheby 'gan to vapour ...

begins the obituary poem in *The Gentleman's Magazine* for February 1813. Gossett was a 'character' and in 1800, the date of the print illustrated, he still affected the three-cornered hat of an earlier generation. Wounded by the appearance of this caricature he